American Government

Charles V. Hamilton
Wallace S. Sayre Professor of Government
Columbia University

With contributions by:

Larry Stammer
Los Angeles Times

Philip Shabecoff
New York Times

Gerald Finch
Columbia University

Scott, Foresman and Company
Glenview, Illinois   Oakland, New Jersey   Tucker, Georgia
Dallas, Texas   Palo Alto, California   London, England

To Dona

Credit lines for the photos, illustrations, and copyrighted materials appearing in this work appear in
the Acknowledgments section beginning on page
652. This section is to be considered an extension
of the copyright page.

Library of Congress Cataloging in Publication Data
Hamilton, Charles V.
    American government.

    Includes bibliographical references and index.
    1. United States—Politics and government. I. Title.
JK274.H195   320.973   81-16652
ISBN 0-673-15220-0   AACR2

Preface

I wrote this book because I enjoy the study of American government, and I wanted students to share this experience. Learning about the ideas that motivated people to try to "form a more perfect union," the ways they went about it, and the results they achieved are enjoyable tasks for one interested in people, politics, and policies. No small part of the enjoyment in studying this inviting subject comes as a knitted brow of perplexity slowly turns to a quiet smile of understanding.

The government of the United States is a particularly challenging subject. It is replete with seeming contradictions, subtle meanings, and, at times, bold experiments. The goal of the framers was a *more*—not absolutely—perfect union, and they well knew that the founding document could not be written in stone. Yet the political institutions fashioned almost 200 years ago have endured, and the guidelines set forth by the framers have, with some modification, persisted. The American experience remains as one of the more successful efforts in the elusive quest for a stable government.

For a people who have always harbored a healthy skepticism toward government, Americans have managed to put together and sustain a reasonably effective system. It has required the astute balancing of ideas, interests, and institutions. How that system has coped with constancy and change, theory and practice, power and consensus constitutes the central focus of this book. These three themes run throughout the book, and they should be kept in mind as the reader moves from one chapter to another.

If not written in stone, neither were the ideals of the framers written in pencil, easily erasable at the slightest sign of inadequacy and ineptness. Even though times and needs changed, it was clear that many features of American government should be preserved. Yet it was also obvious that the system's reach would inevitably exceed its grasp, and reality would prevail over rhetoric.

There has not been a smooth, straight line in the development of the American political system, and this fact provides much of the dynamism and excitement of the subject matter. The case studies presented at the beginning of each part are intended to help the student analyze American government at work. These cases should be referred to constantly, and students should be encouraged to "second-guess" the participants, unfair as that process of hindsight might seem to be at times. I have found it instructive for students to tease out, given what they have learned about the political system, alternative strategies and to think about possible policy options. This process can build as the student moves from the beginning to the end of the book. It is helpful to think about this material as one continuous story of American government. It is a story students should continue to read and study as thoughtful, active citizens long after the last chapter is finished and the final examination is taken.

There are several common assumptions about American government—that it is controlled by elites or by interest groups, that government is best when it governs least, that official tyranny is best avoided by creating political structures that check and balance each other. These assumptions are presented and examined in various contexts in the book.

The book is organized to introduce the student first to the framework of the political system. Part 1 seeks to explain why American government is structured as it is and to outline the ideas that gave birth to the system. Our governmental framework might be taken for granted now, but definite options were open to the founders. Considerable emphasis is placed on their understanding of human nature

iii

as described in the *Federalist Papers*. The complex, delicate balance they devised was no casual creation. There were, and remain, profound reasons why the government is organized the way it is. One might disagree with the philosophical premises, but it is important to understand what those premises were.

Part 2 describes how individuals and groups participate (and fail to participate) in the system. Here, our concern is with actors and nonactors, the formation of opinion, and the manner and extent of political activity. There is more than a little theory on this subject—how groups affect policy, the role of the citizen, the pluralist ideal, the importance of the vote—yet we also see how practice coincides with theory.

The Student Opinion Survey following chapter 4 is an additional teaching tool. Students should fill out the survey, discuss responses in class, and compare their results with nationwide responses included in the Instructor's Manual. A fruitful exercise would involve a discussion of how students have come to hold certain views, whether their opinions have changed over time, and the extent to which they think their views are similar to those of their parents and peers. These are matters discussed in chapter 4 (Political Socialization, Media, and Public Opinion) and can be usefully related to the material there. Most of the book is concerned with describing the activities of others—politicians, interest groups, and so forth—but here the student can become personally involved.

In part 3 we turn to the formal institutions of government. Here the theme of power and consensus receives special emphasis. From time to time, we hear about an "imperial presidency," or a "reassertive Congress," or "judicial usurpation." The chapters in part 3 show how, in the final analysis, no one branch of government can ever get too far beyond its jurisdictional boundaries without incurring reaction from the other branches and, at times, the public. Consensus is not an idle term in American government.

Part 4 presents individuals, groups, and officials in action as they deal with domestic and foreign policies. Before, through the case studies and textual materials, we identified who they are and how and where they operate. Now we see what has been done and is being done in specific policy areas. In order to provide continuity we return to the topic of the first case study—the energy problem. Thus, the student is constantly urged to recall, to relate, to connect, to put into perspective events and ideas.

The three sets of photoessays in the book highlight the three themes in still another way. These photos show how American government has, over time, pursued the delicate balancing process—of ideas, of interests, and of institutions—that characterizes the system in all its aspects.

Supplementary materials add to the usefulness of the text. Bruce Drury of Lamar University has prepared a *Study Guide* that will help the student organize the material for clearer emphasis and critical analysis. Ron Stidham, also of Lamar University, has constructed an *Instructor's Manual* and a *Test Bank*. These materials are the products of teachers of American government. They know what helps students and colleagues in dealing with this subject, and their materials will be of immense value.

A textbook is written by an author, but it is also produced by countless people who are as vital to the enterprise as any words initially coming out of an author's typewriter. Those people provide the advice, support, technical expertise, and encouragement most authors need every step of the way. I have received that input from people who can only be characterized in the most precise sense as professional experts. From my first discussions with editors Bruce Borland and Bob Johnson at Scott, Foresman, I have been aware that I was involved with people who knew their business and took pride in and cared about their work. Their quiet, persistent, and perceptive comments were as crucial to the enterprise as each paragraph and footnote I ultimately wrote. If lawyers and judges talk about the value of "judicial temperament," I certainly can attest to what is best described as "editorial temperament" on the part of these two. I observed integrity up close. I owe very much to Borland and Johnson, my editors and friends. My copyeditors, Trig Thoreson and Liz Adams, came to know every thought, sentence, and semicolon in this volume. Indeed, they single-handedly kept me alert to the best way to express those thoughts and to write those sentences. They surely used up more than their share of red pencils, and they raised more "queries" (I thought at the time) than the law allows. They must know I am grateful. This project also benefited enormously from the work of Barbara Schneider, who had the responsibility for text design; Jeanne Schwaba, production liaison; Mary Lou Revak, production coordinator; Aileen Maniates, picture editor; and Lisa Gover and Meredith Hellestrae in Marketing. All of these people demonstrated professional talents that leave an author feeling confident and relaxed.

There were also many readers who read all or parts of the manuscript and offered invaluable constructive reviews—noting omissions, suggesting additions, urging modifications. An occasional comment would sting; another would exhilarate. I always found their advice useful and relevant. Specifically, I want to thank Robert Carp, University of Houston; Larry Dodd, University of Texas; Bruce Drury, Lamar University; Larry Elowitz, Georgia College; L. Earl Shaw, University of Minnesota; James R. Soles, University of Delaware; and William Wagner, Foothill College (California).

I was ably assisted by graduate research assistants at Columbia University, Brian Heffernan and Doug MacDonald. I am appreciative of the assistance of Carol Hamilton, who had all the burdens and few of the benefits of working for a father. Sophie Berson patiently typed several first-draft chapters, and she knows that my gratitude for her work and friendship extend far beyond this book.

As always, my wife, Dona, knew all along that even with pressing deadlines and other responsibilities, I would eventually finish, and her balanced judgment and encouragement once again proved invaluable.

Charles V. Hamilton

Contents

The Framework of American Government

"Ten Days at Camp David:
The Energy Crisis, Policies, and Politics"   *12*

2

Political Participation

National Political Institutions

"The Political Struggle for Labor-Law Reform"
by Philip Shabecoff of the New York Times   272

4

Policies and Processes

"After Camp David: Politics, Policymaking, and a New Administration" *476*

Introduction:
The Study of
American Government

Anyone who reads this book ought to be able, when finished, to say that he or she has a basic understanding of the major ways political decisions are made and carried out at the national level of government in the United States.

That is the fundamental purpose of this textbook. It is an *introduction* to American national government. It does presume some elementary knowledge on the part of the reader: that a written Constitution is the basic framework of government (but not precisely how it came about or what it contains in detail or how it has been variously interpreted); that certain officials are selected through periodic elections (but not how the electoral process has changed, who participates and to what extent, or how people become "politicized"); that private groups and the media play important roles (but not to what extent or under what circumstances and with what consequences); that there are basic formal institutions of government such as Congress, the presidency, and the Supreme Court (but not how they interact or how their relations have changed informally over time). This book also presumes that the reader knows there are some basic issues such as energy, inflation, taxes, individual liberties, civil rights, military defense, and social welfare—issues which institutions and individuals grapple with through legislation and other means (but not the intimate details about how or why certain policies are or are not enacted).

If the book is able to supply the "but not" information contained in the parentheses of the previous paragraph, it will have served its purpose.

Our goal is to combine a straightforward description of the process of American government with an ongoing analysis of the relationship between what is *done* and what *results*—that is, between process and product. Therefore, the concern is not only with what, when, and how, but also with why—for example, not only with what the President proposed to Congress regarding the energy crisis and what Congress did or did not do, but why certain proposals were left out and why Congress accepted some and rejected others.

Three Basic Themes

Three major themes recur throughout the chapters. These themes represent particular ways of understanding American government, and they should help focus our study of the American political process over time and in the current context. They are

■ constancy and change;
■ theory and practice;
■ power and consensus.

Where relevant, the material will draw the reader's attention to these three dynamic aspects of American government. There will not be specific sections in the chapters for doing this; rather, the narrative will highlight them for illustrative purposes where appropriate.

Constancy and change. In studying American government, one finds certain things about the institutions and the processes that have remained constant (stable) over time. The Constitution is almost 200 years old (with only twenty-six amendments). It has been a constant in American society. And yet that document has been interpreted in different ways by officials (especially Supreme Court judges), and their interpretations have rendered it a fundamentally "changed" document. We will see this immediately in chapter 1. The constitutional *language* has remained constant; the constitutional *meaning* has changed. Not all societies are able to govern in this manner, and we shall pay particular attention to explanations suggesting why American society has been able to pull it off.

Theory and practice. Things do not always happen in government precisely the way they are supposed to happen. Theoretically, Americans vote every four years for a group of people called "electors," who then proceed to choose a President. The process is set forth in the Constitution, and in principle that is the way it works. But most people believe they are voting *directly* for the President. The perceived practice usually does not conflict with the theory, and therefore there is rarely a problem. But the *theory* of the "electoral college" certainly affects the *practice* of conducting presidential elections. Another example could be found in race relations and in women's rights. *Theoretically,* the American society puts great emphasis on egalitarianism and nondiscrimination. But in *practice,* we know that discrimination based on race and sex has been a prominent part of the American experience. The study of American government shows a long history of attempts to

reconcile theory and practice on these and other issues.

Power and consensus. In the American system of government it is one thing to have the constitutional power and legal authority to do something; it is quite another (and likely just as important) to establish a base of support broad enough to get something done. The President certainly has the *power* to send troops to another country under certain circumstances, but if this is done without a basic *consensus* that such action is sound policy, the act could be undermined. The Vietnam War in the waning years of the early 1970s would be a good example. In a sense, this theme is an extension of the theory versus practice theme, but it is sufficiently different and important to warrant distinct treatment. For example, one party might control Congress and be able to pass whatever laws it properly votes. The dominant party would have the *power* to do so. But under some circumstances, party members might need to get as many members of the other party to go along with them as possible. It might be useful to show "bipartisan" support for certain laws. In other words, the broader the *consensus*, the greater the likelihood that laws will be easier to enforce. Again, this theme takes into account the nature of society and of the American political system.

Three Important Assumptions About American Government

The United States is over 200 years old and has lived under one written Constitution for almost as long. The country has grown from a population of 4 million in 1790 to close to 240 million in 1980, and from thirteen states to fifty (plus Washington, D.C., and the Commonwealth of Puerto Rico). It has developed from an agrarian society to the largest industrial nation in the world. Its population contains a mixture of many different racial, ethnic, and religious groups. Basically, its political system is considered a **democracy** and its economy is characterized as **capitalist**. These are general terms which mean that the government is expected to be chosen by citizens who vote periodically for their leaders in **free elections**, and that the economy is to operate on the principle that private ownership of property is a fundamental basis of economic life. In addition, American society puts considerable emphasis on the freedom of the individual to pursue his or her own life in a manner as unrestricted by government as possible.

One should not be surprised, however, that such a society has been defined and interpreted in many different ways. Sometimes these definitions and interpretations have been diametrically opposed to each other; in some cases they have changed over time. Almost all of them are based on certain assumptions and ideas. We will list three of these here; as we proceed through the book, we will have occasion to return to them and examine them in the context of particular chapter material. These are not stated as absolute truths, but rather as strongly held assumptions and ideas about government and politics; the text will provide evidence to test their validity or invalidity.

"Fragmented government is the best way to guard against tyranny and to protect individual liberty." A major assumption influencing some of the framers of the Constitution was that human beings were naturally contentious and needed to be restrained by government in their relations with each other. But government was also considered a threat to individual freedom and likewise had to be limited and constrained.[1] This led to the creation of particular kinds of political institutions embedded in the Constitution, institutions capable of checking and balancing each other.

"Fragmented government" is government in which power is distributed through many different, and often contending, institutions. This town meeting in Lansing, Michigan, shows citizens performing essentially legislative functions at the level of government closest to the people—the local level.

This 1935 cartoon illustrates the feelings of many Depression-era Americans toward the social programs of the New Deal. Government intervention in the economy was widely perceived as dangerous—holding down the United States by restricting individual freedom and economic growth.

"The best way to assure economic growth and development is to have the government involved as little as possible in the economy." A strong idea in American society is that the government should play a minor role in the nation's economic life. Reliance should be placed on a **free-enterprise**, capitalist system operating with a minimum of governmental regulation. This, it is assumed, is the best way to encourage economic—and social—growth and development. Competition should be the major motivating force.[2]

This idea (creed, some have called it) has been altered somewhat as a result of the Great Depression and the New Deal of the 1930s. During that period, government became much more involved in the economy than ever before and that involvement, while still resisted by some, has become a permanent aspect of American politico-economic life.[3]

"American government is a pluralist system whereby many different groups are involved and no one group is able to dominate and rule exclusively." Many observers believe that American government is best understood by examining the role of various interest groups in the policy-making process. These groups, it is argued, constitute what is referred to as a **pluralist** system; their presence guarantees that no particular group will, for long, be able to control or dominate public affairs. This is considered an important feature of American political democracy.[4]

The pluralist view of American society has been challenged, however, by those who would characterize the system as one that is controlled by an *elite*—a "power elite." They say that the pluralist interpreters of American government are not, in fact, being realistic in what they describe and, indeed, prescribe. A few powerful people, well-placed in government, private industry, and the military, run the society.[5]

Both of these interpretations in turn are resisted by an analysis that suggests still another view of the way political power is exercised in the United States. According to this view, private and narrowly focused groups work in conjunction with specific political agencies to maintain control over *specific parts* of the policymaking process. This is neither a description of an overarching, monolithic "power elite" nor an ideal pluralist description of the way things actually happen.[6]

There are, to be sure, other assumptions and ideas about American government. We could have mentioned the belief that those who govern are and ought to be *accountable* to those they govern, or the notion that the best way to bring about change in the political system is through patient negotiation rather than through violence. These are all important to an understanding of American government. And these ideas, like those listed above, do not go unchallenged, as we shall see. But all such ideas can be dealt with within the context of the three broad points elaborated above.

Approach

It is tempting to write a book on American government that actively engages in ideological debates. The subject matter is fascinating and one is strongly inclined to take sides. A discussion of government—any government—invites debates about the "best" government, about "legitimacy," "efficiency," even about loyalty and patriotism. Authors, teachers, and students are also citizens who have opinions. They have values and desires and goals—the inescapable components of any analysis of government. It is important first, however, to know and understand the basic facts before proceeding to form evaluative judgments. It is important to have a base of knowledge that can be reasonably agreed upon as accurate. Once that base is established, one might wish to engage in more evaluative debates.

This does not mean that the book will only be descriptive; it will, of necessity, contain analyses. One is ever mindful that it is never possible to submerge one's values completely. The choice of issues used as illustrative examples, the decision to emphasize certain aspects of American institutions and processes over others, and the various analyses of government inevitably reflect one's own values. To be conscious of this, as I have tried to be, and to strive for descriptive and analytical balance is as much as one can do.

This, then, is a book that seeks to expose the student to several different interpretations of the American political system. For instance, where a pluralist interpretation is challenged by an elitist or other significant interpretation, this will be made clear. The language sometimes used by social scientists attempts to be "value-free" or "objective." In a book of this kind, it is useful to try to maximize these. But as one seeks to be objective, one need not cease to be concerned.

Organization and Features

There are four case studies, one at the beginning of each of the four parts of the book. The cases are stories—political stories—of specific events in American government. They show public and

The pluralist nature of American government is shown in the variety of existing political pressure groups, representing every conceivable segment of the political spectrum. Below: A member of a senior-citizen lobby demonstrates support for a national health insurance plan. Left: The success of the National Rifle Association in keeping the sale of firearms free and open can be seen in almost any gunshop or sporting goods store.

private individuals and groups in action, influencing policy and making laws. The several chapters in each part refer to the cases immediately preceding, and, in some instances, to cases located elsewhere in the text. Our goal is to weave a thread of continuity throughout the text material, to relate chapter material to case events in order to illustrate points being made. The cases should give the student a sense of how the American system of government works in concrete situations. In addition, the cases should help the student see the material contained in the book as part of the continuing, coherent story of American politics. To emphasize this point, the last case returns to the subject of the first—the energy crisis and politics. We see how a problem was defined and articulated and then we return to see what happened as political institutions and individuals sought to deal with the issues.

The cases were also chosen because they provide information about ongoing issues in American life—energy, taxes, labor-law reform—issues that will be around for some time. Thus, while the Proposition 13 vote in California took place in 1978, and the Camp David energy sessions occurred in 1979, and efforts to reform labor laws belong to 1978, no one believes that these basic issues were *solved* then. As the years go by, the events become less current, but after all this is a textbook, not a daily newspaper or weekly or monthly magazine. Specific events get superseded by subsequent developments, yet those earlier events do provide an opportunity to begin a discussion of government and the political process. Particular officials and parties change—President Ronald Reagan succeeds President Jimmy Carter, the Republican party captures control of the Senate as a result of significant electoral victories in November 1980—but critical issues such as energy and inflation remain. It is our hope that the student will use the basic lessons gleaned from this textbook to analyze these and other issues in the future.

Throughout this book, terms such as *political power* and *democracy* will be used, along with less familiar terms such as *judicial review* and *federalism* and *fiscal policy* and *deterrents*. These terms are part of the intricate operation of American government. Key terms will appear in boldface in the text and will be defined in the glossary; the glossary will also include other useful terms.

The Student Opinion Survey following chapter 4 introduces the student to the substantive and procedural aspects of opinion polling. In addition to seeing the relationship of one's own views to those of the rest of the class or the nation, this survey provides the opportunity to discuss survey sampling, questionnaire construction, as well as the substantive meaning of the data.

Just as each chapter concludes with brief summary statements, each part ends with an overview highlighting and relating the materials in the chapters immediately preceding. Again, the intent is to focus the student's attention on the interrelatedness of the subject matter.

The final part of the textbook does this for the book as a whole—in a sense, rounding out the "story" of American government and taking another look at the three themes and the three assumptions and ideas discussed in this Introduction.

Notes

1. *The Federalist Papers* (No. 51): "Ambition must be made to counteract ambition. The interest of the man must be connected with the constitutional rights of the place. It may be a reflection on human nature that such devices should be necessary to control the abuses of government. But what is government itself but the greatest of all reflections on human nature? If men were angels, no government would be necessary. If angels were to govern men, neither external nor internal controls on government would be necessary. In framing a government which is to be administered by men over men, the great difficulty lies in this: you must first enable the government to control

the governed; and in the next place oblige it to control itself.''

2. William E. Simon, *A Time For Truth* (New York: McGraw-Hill Book Company, 1978), p. 22. "In sum, individual liberty *includes* the individual's economic freedom, and the Founding Fathers knew it. They had good reason to leave the productive activities of men as free as possible. Their calculations, like those of Adam Smith, were correct. When men are left free by the state to engage in productive action, guided by self-interest above all, they do create the most efficient and powerful production system that is possible to their society. And the greatest misfortune in America today is that most people do not understand this. They don't understand our traditional economic system precisely because it is not, in the ordinary sense, a system at all—meaning a conscious organization or detailed plan. Essentially, as always, what they don't understand is how, in the *absence* of conscious planning, millions of men can function efficiently together to produce wealth. But it is precisely that *absence* of conscious planning that accomplishes the miracle! To this very day—obscured by a tragic amount of governmental intervention since the thirties—it is *still* Adam Smith's 'invisible hand' and 'the system of natural liberty' that are producing our goods and services, creating our jobs, paying our salaries, financing our government, and generating American wealth.''

3. David B. Truman, *The Governmental Process* (New York: Alfred A. Knopf, 1971), p. xlvii. "It [the New Deal] was a revolution not only in the sense that certain groups secured a place at the political table from which they had previously been barred but also in the sense that the American people tacitly accepted certain propositions about an industrialized society that ten years earlier would have been rejected by all but an insignificant fraction of the population. Basically they agreed that the misfortunes that may happen to an individual in such a society are not more than partially attributable to his own actions, that it is a public, governmental duty to prevent developments productive of such misfortunes, and that if this duty cannot be fully discharged, it is a public responsibility to provide for those who have been hurt. Ten years earlier the reverse propositions were a part of the creed.''

4. V. O. Key, Jr., *Politics, Parties, & Pressure Groups*, 5th ed. (New York: Thomas Y. Crowell Company, 1964), pp. 6–7: "A closely related characteristic of democratic orders—or at least of the American democratic order—is a wide dispersion of power (in the sense of a substance in a keg). Actual authority tends to be dispersed and exercised not solely by governmental officials but also by private individuals and groups within the society. Moreover, the power structure tends to be segmented: authority over one question rests here and over another, there. All this contrasts with the model of a clear and rigid hierarchial pattern of power. On one matter the President's decision may govern; on another, the wishes of the heads of a half-dozen industrial corporations will prevail; on a third, organized labor or agriculture will win the day; and on still another, a congressionally negotiated compromise completely satisfactory to none of the contenders may settle the matter. Even the journalists may cast the deciding vote on some issues. Thus the locus of power may shift from question to question and even from time to time on the same question.''

5. C. Wright Mills, *The Power Elite* (New York: Oxford University Press, 1957), pp. 3–4: "As the means of information and of power are centralized, some men come to occupy positions in American society from which they can look down upon, so to speak, and by their decisions mightily affect, the everyday worlds of ordinary men and women. . . . The power elite is composed of men whose positions enable them to transcend the ordinary environments of ordinary men and women; they are in positions to make decisions having major consequences. Whether they do or do not make such decisions is less important than the fact that they do occupy such pivotal positions: their failure to act, their failure to make decisions, is itself an act that is often of greater consequence than the decisions they do make. For they are in command of the major hierarchies and organizations of modern society. They rule the big corporations. They run the machinery of the state and claim its prerogatives. They direct the military establishment. They occupy the strategic command posts of the social structure, in which are now centered the effective means of the power and the wealth and the celebrity which they enjoy.''

6. Grant McConnell, *Private Power & American Democracy* (New York: Alfred A. Knopf, 1966), pp. 337, 338, 339: "Neither of these perceptions is adequate. The 'power elite' today rather obviously suffers from internal disarray. It lacks the organization and unity necessary to give it the capacities

which are feared from it. . . . Repeatedly during the past half century, relatively homogeneous groups have been effectively organized and have assumed a strong degree of power over particular areas of public policy through close collaboration with segments of government; and one cannot dismiss as unimportant or insignificant the areas where such power has become a reality. . . . A substantial part of government in the United States has come under the influence or control of narrowly based and largely autonomous elites. These elites do not act cohesively with each other on many issues. They do not 'rule' in the sense of commanding the entire nation. Quite the contrary, they tend to pursue a policy of noninvolvement in the large issues of statesmanship, save where such issues touch their own particular concerns.''

1

The Framework of American Government

Ten Days at Camp David: The Energy Crisis, Policies, and Politics

For a week in June 1979, President Jimmy Carter traveled to two important Asian nations, meeting with the president of South Korea and attending an international economic summit meeting in Tokyo. While he was abroad, he received a memorandum from one of his top domestic affairs advisers, Stuart E. Eizenstat. The memo read, in part:

> Since you left for Japan, the domestic energy problem has continued to worsen. . . . Gas lines are growing throughout the Northeast and are spreading to the mid-East. . . . Sporadic violence over gasoline continues to occur. A recent incident in Pennsylvania injured 40. . . . Gasoline station operators are threatening a nationwide strike unless D.O.E. [Department of Energy] grants an emergency profit margin increase. . . . Congress is growing more nervous by the day over the energy problem. . . . Yesterday, the state of Maryland sued D.O.E. for misallocating gasoline. Other states can be expected to shortly follow that politically popular route. . . . I do not need to detail for you the political damage we are suffering from all this.*

Seventeen months later, in November 1980, Republican presidential candidate Ronald Reagan would defeat President Carter in the latter's quest for reelection. During the campaign, Governor Reagan had been critical of the way the Carter administration had handled the energy problem, especially condemning the Department of Energy. There were many issues in the 1980 election, but certainly the nation's energy problem was a major one.

In the summer of 1979, however, the Carter administration was still in office and still grappling with the energy crisis. In his memo, Eizenstat continued to sound the alarm to his boss. He wrote that nothing that had happened thus far in the two and a half years of the administration had "added so much water to our ship." This, surely, conjured up the image of a sinking presidential administration. And although the President could hardly be expected to shoulder the entire blame for the mounting energy and economic problems facing the country, the memo bluntly stated:

> Nothing else has so frustrated, confused, angered the American people— or so targeted their distress at you personally, as opposed to your advisers, or Congress or outside interests. . . .

*All quoted material in this chapter, unless otherwise noted, is taken from reports printed in the following issues of the *New York Times*: July 3, 4, 6, 8, 10, 1979.

President Carter at the economic summit meeting in Japan, 1979. Shown at right is Japan's Prime Minister Ohira.

The memo minced no words: things were bad and getting worse. The people expected action, "and the Congress seems completely beyond anyone's control," Eizenstat lamented. *The President had to do something*.

The memo also exposed some personal bickering within the President's own White House staff. Jody Powell, the President's press secretary, said that he was sure Eizenstat did not personally write the memo and was probably too preoccupied to pay much attention to it. "The rhetoric itself was a little bit silly," Powell said. The memo was "filled with rhetorical excess."

Eizenstat responded that he, indeed, took full responsibility for the memo, rhetoric and all: "The press secretary is entitled to his own opinion, but my opinion is that the energy problem is a very serious problem."

As soon as he got back to the White House, a weary President huddled for nearly two hours with his top advisers. He decided to present a major television speech to the nation on the following Thursday—July 5, 1979. His advisers were ordered to draft a speech, to come up with something that would begin to put things right. "I want a bold and a forceful program," said Carter, "that, under the scrutiny of the Congress and the public, will be highly acceptable, and we can move without delay."

But, even as the speechwriters worked feverishly on the first draft, the President, who had gone to his Camp David retreat in the Catoctin Mountains of Maryland for the Fourth of July holiday, abruptly canceled the planned television speech—and gave no reasons for doing so.

What had happened? Who had been consulted? What was going on? No one seemed to have answers. Said one senior Energy Department official: "People were working on it [the speech] up to half an hour ago. We just don't know what it means. We had worked all last night to put the thing together."

Speculation ran rampant throughout Washington and, indeed, the country. Some people thought the President was dissatisfied with the proposed solutions his aides had come up with. Others felt he was miffed about apparent internal divisions within his staff. Still others concluded that the President had decided to come forth with a real "blockbuster," a speech that would really grab the public's attention, make the American people *really* believe that an energy crisis existed. It was not even beyond the realm of possibility, some speculated, that he would take himself out of the upcoming 1980 presidential race in order to devote himself full time to the energy problem. But no one really knew. All the speculation was just that. All that was certain was that the President had gone to the mountaintop.

Throughout the next week, the air of mystery prevailed. Political observers were beginning to comment on the economic and political effects of the President's action.

The financial repercussions were immediate. The value of the American dollar overseas dropped sharply. Treasury Secretary W. Michael Blumenthal became so worried that he put in a hurried call to Camp David to speak to the President. He reached a presidential aide, who told him: "He's out walking the dog. Is it urgent?"

Blumenthal was put through to the President and was able to persuade him to issue a brief statement through his press secretary promising "strong measures" in the near future in order to curb the nation's demand for imported oil. The statement promised that something would be done to reduce America's dependence on foreign sources for oil, which sources were raising prices constantly and contributing to the country's growing energy crisis.

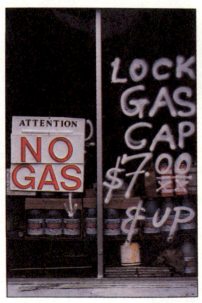

In the summer of 1979, Americans grew accustomed to the sight of long gas lines and closed service stations.

The statement helped. The value of the dollar went back up.

Politically, some observers felt, the abrupt cancellation and the retreat to Camp David reinforced the image of an indecisive, incompetent presidential administration. "The cancellation just adds to the image of confusion," one White House aide said. "We probably shouldn't have scheduled it in the first place. Now, cancellation just adds to the impression that we don't know what we're doing—we're not on top of things."

But the President had his defenders. Some within his administration believed that he still had the opportunity to salvage his image as a leader. To be sure, he had "raised the ante" and as one news reporter said, "It's possible that he has a really big announcement to make and that he has heightened the drama of it."

One cabinet member, Patricia Roberts Harris (then secretary of Housing and Urban Development), argued that the President's willingness to cancel the speech was "an indication of steadiness of nerve and calm." She suggested that "we are not going to have macho decisions made simply to protect appearances."

At any rate, the stage for decision-making was set. The President was ensconced at Camp David, directing one of the most unusual and important scenarios in recent American politics. For the next ten days or so, the actors would come and go as the drama unfolded.

The press poked around for leaks and leads.

Congress bided its time.

And the public waited anxiously.

For those who had been following America's energy problem, it was clear that this was not a recent, late-1970s phenomenon. The United States had not been suddenly thrust into a situation of being dependent on Middle Eastern oil. It was not something that had developed over the last few weeks or months or even the last two or three years.

The warning signs had been there as far back as 1973–74, when Americans first experienced the trauma of long gas lines and rapidly rising fuel oil prices. By that time, the country had become reliant upon oil supplies from an increasingly unstable Middle East. This had not always been the case. America's dependence on foreign sources for oil had been gradually developing throughout the postwar period. In fact, until the late 1940s, the United States exported oil to Western Europe. This began to change in the 1950s. Persian Gulf countries increased oil production and began to export quantities of oil to Western Europe and small amounts to the United States.

Even then some Americans feared that this was an ominous sign. Relying on oil from such relatively unstable places could cause "national security" problems for this country. But as late as the 1960s few people paid attention to this warning largely because the United States imported relatively little oil, and most of it came from Canadian or Caribbean sources.

By 1970, American oil consumption had grown substantially, while American production had peaked at 9.9 million barrels per day. By 1975, domestic crude oil production had fallen to 8.2 million barrels per day. To take up the slack, between 1970 and 1973 United States consumption of foreign oil grew at a 30 percent annual rate (from 3.4 million to 6.2 million barrels per day.) At the same time, the oil-producing nations (which had formed a cartel, OPEC—the Organization of Petroleum Exporting Countries—in 1960) increased their monopoly power as their customers capitulated to repeated demands for higher prices. Libya was one of the first countries, in 1970, to signal what was to happen. First, it ordered production cutbacks totaling approximately 400,000 barrels daily. Then, in September 1970, the Libyan government won a $0.30 increase in the posted price and an increase in the tax rate (the money paid by American oil companies to the foreign governments where the oil was produced) from 50 to between 54 and 58 percent. This was followed in December 1970 by Venezuela's increase of its tax rate from 52 to 60 percent. The round of increases continued. The Persian Gulf countries wanted more; the non-Persian Gulf countries announced that if others got more, they, in turn, should receive an increase. American oil companies wanted to stop this "leapfrogging," and they suggested that a single contractual rate should be negotiated with OPEC. The under secretary of state for economic affairs, John Irwin, went to the Middle East to support the American oil companies. Political scientist Stephen D. Krasner reported the developments:

> On January 16, John Irwin, the under secretary of state for economic affairs, was dispatched to the Middle East supposedly to support the companies' position. He left on one day's notice. In both Saudi Arabia and Iran he found great resistance to global, rather than regional, negotiations. The Shah apparently convinced him that if such negotiations were held, all oil-producing states would be forced to accept the highest common denominator, and this would be established by the most radical states. . . . Irwin accepted the Shah's position. Without consulting the companies he recommended that discussions about Persian Gulf prices be severed from any talks concerning Mediterranean sales. This recommendation was endorsed by Secretary of State Rogers and passed on to the oil companies. By the end of January the oil companies had accepted the Shah's demands.

Oil prices began to rise. With the war in the Middle East in October 1973, there was a cutback in oil production by the Arab countries and an increase in prices. Indeed, prices were *quadrupled*.

This two-fold process had continued, leading to more gas lines, higher fuel prices, a steadily increasing inflation rate—and to Eizenstat's memo to the President.

In his memo, Eizenstat strongly suggested that OPEC be identified as "a clear enemy." He wrote bluntly to the President:

> We have a better opportunity than ever before to assert leadership over an apparently insolvable problem, to shift the cause for inflation and energy problems to OPEC, to gain credibility with the American people, to offer hope of an eventual solution. . . . Use the OPEC price increase to mark the beginning of our new approach to energy. . . . We must turn the increase to our advantage by clearly pointing out its devastating economic impact and as the justification for our efforts against the OPEC cartel and for increased domestic production of all types. . . . A statement which goes light on OPEC or a commitment to synthetics and other domestic initiatives will not convince the public that anything is different, that we are embarking on a new effort, or that there is hope that the energy problem will be solved, or that we will ever stand up to OPEC (which Americans want even more than cheap gasoline). . . . With strong steps we can mobilize the nation around a real crisis and with a clear enemy—OPEC.

At the height of the energy crisis, independent truckers staged a shutdown to protest sharp increases in fuel prices.

So the President came home from Japan to face a troubled nation. Decisions had to be made, problems had to be met. But, having abruptly decided to cancel his speech to the nation, he left an even more frustrated and confused administration and country wondering—and waiting. He went off to Camp David, to the mountains of Maryland, to ponder and to plan. Surely, he must have been remembering his adviser's words in that memo: "In many respects, this would appear to be the worst of times. But I honestly believe we can change this to a time of opportunity."

But how? How could he turn economic and political adversity into advantage? That was the question, that was the challenge, as the scene shifted to Camp David, Maryland.

Shortly after the President arrived at Camp David on Tuesday, July 3, 1979, it became known that he would focus his attention on more than the immediate energy crisis. He wanted to think about a wide range of issues facing the country and his administration: the general "malaise" in the country, the apparent decline in respect for authority, what he perceived as a worsening moral climate, the seemingly uncomfortable relationships among some members of the White House staff and some cabinet officers, his liaison problems with Congress, and an overall deterioration in economic conditions.

It was an extensive agenda, and no one knew exactly how long he would take to consider these matters. What *was* known, however, was that eventually he had to say something to the American public. He had to come before the people in a forceful, confident way. His wife, Rosalynn, was one of those who had advised him to cancel his previously planned television speech. Later, she said she had told him: "People just want to know you're working on the problems and that things are going to be all right, not that you're going to send another program to Congress. And so far what you've said hasn't been enough to rally the people and bring them together."

Almost twenty years earlier, political scientist Richard E. Neustadt in his book, *Presidential Power*, had written about the role of the President as a teacher. He concluded:

> *What kind of teaching job is this? It is no classroom exercise. Presidential teaching is instruction of a very different sort. . . . First, it is instruction aimed at students who, by definition, are habitually inattentive to the teacher: his constituents outside the Washington community. These students only grow attentive when they notice public trouble pressing on their lives. Second, as a consequence, he can expect attention from them only when the things he need interpret to his benefit are on their minds for reasons independent of his telling.*

Clearly, now, the President had an attentive audience.

He conferred long distance with his close adviser, Robert Strauss, who was in Egypt talking with President Anwar el-Sadat. He invited eight state governors to Camp David to talk about a range of matters including inflation, unemployment, energy, and economic projections for the rest of the year. The governors were on their way to Louisville, Kentucky, for the annual meeting of the National Governors' Association. (President Carter had been scheduled to address the meeting, but he canceled his appearance and sent Vice-President Walter Mondale and Mrs. Carter in his place.)

One important energy-related matter that concerned the governors pertained to the gasoline allocation system administered by the federal government's Department of Energy. States and areas were allotted gasoline according to a formula based on the previous year's consumption record. One governor, Hugh Carey of New York, said that he would advise the President to scrap the federal gasoline allocation system. "I would junk it," he said, and require the oil companies to provide full details on their distribution network and pricing. Just a few days before, Energy Secretary James R. Schlesinger had admitted to the President that the allocation system was not working: "What it does is to put the gasoline where the automobiles are not. It puts it in the rural areas where people are no longer going on weekends." He advised the President that the department was trying to come up with a more equitable system which would allow the state governors authority to reallocate gas within their states.

Other guests began to appear at Camp David: public officials and private citizens, an international petroleum consultant, the president of the Audubon Society, labor union leaders, civil rights leaders, educators. The sessions were held informally, morning, afternoon, and evening. Frequently, the President's wife sat in and took copious notes. Always, according to reports that filtered out, the President did more listening than talking. One participant, the president of Wellesley College, Barbara Newell, said: "The President mostly kept his own counsel."

During one of the sessions, the President stated that he was not convinced that the public believed the energy crisis was real.

The President seemed to be holding one continuous "seminar" on the state of the nation. The White House remained officially silent, but the level of expectation increased

Top right: President Carter arrives at Camp David with a contingent of top aides, secret service agents, and military personnel. Above right: A working session at Camp David. Above: The President discusses the energy crisis with private citizens.

when the presidential press secretary promised at one point that actions coming out of the talks "will have a profound effect on the nature of our society" for years to come. Reporters hung on every word and reported virtually every nuance.

Some Congressional leaders went to Camp David and after a four-hour session with the President promised him their support in Congress. The House majority leader, Jim Wright of Texas, said, "I prophesy that when the President comes down off the mountain, he will have a comprehensive, effective, hard-hitting program to offer the American people. I further predict the Congress will be in a mood to approve it." At that particular session, nineteen Democrats and three Republicans from the House and Senate attended.

Several policy issues seemed to be emerging. A powerful energy mobilization board was to be created. There would be a new standby gasoline rationing plan drafted jointly by the White House, the Senate, and the House. This would insure cooperation from and swift passage by Congress. There would be a multi-billion dollar commitment to develop synthetic fuels. There still was no consensus on lifting price controls on gasoline.

In the middle of the ten-day period, the President received good news—both political and economic. Politically, twenty-one governors at their Louisville meeting endorsed the President for reelection in 1980. This helped, coming at a time when his popularity in the opinion polls was declining rapidly. Economically, Saudi Arabia announced that it would "substantially" increase its production of crude oil. This would temporarily help relieve the shortage of oil caused, in part, by decreasing oil supplies from politically unstable Iran. (Just four months earlier, the Shah of Iran had been overthrown and a new Islamic Republic had been established, one not at all friendly toward the United States.)

These were welcome events, but there still was considerable concern about the quality of leadership coming from the White House. Several sessions focused on this problem. The President invited some guests to speak candidly to him about his staff and top cabinet officials. When these discussions were held, the staff people left the room. He heard comments indicating that internal relations in his administration had not been coordinated and that some of his cabinet officials had not been entirely loyal to him, but rather were pursuing their own private, personal ambitions. Others advised him to appoint a chief of staff for the Office of the White House. After each such session, reporters and others speculated about what might happen, who might be fired, shifted, or demoted. It was ten days of rumors and guessing, not an unfamiliar game in government circles, but heightened now by the crisis situation and the quasi-secret Camp David environment.

Clearly, however, the President had come to the conclusion that he had to change his leadership style. He indicated to more than one group that he felt he was spending too much time on managerial matters and not enough time on broad policy issues or on getting out around the nation to meet the people. In addition, he recognized the need to respect the federal system of government by spending more time with state governors. He was quoted as saying he might make a regular practice of "having seven or eight governors in to spend the night with me at the White House and just talk over how we can cooperate and deal with the energy question, because I see the states as kind of fifty experiment stations."

Another theme emerged from the Camp David sessions. The President expressed his concern about the moral climate of the nation, as well as his sense of what he called a "malaise" pervading the society. There seemed to be widespread cynicism about government, about future opportunities for one's children, and so forth. This disillusionment probably had its beginning, he and others concluded, with the assassination of President Kennedy, followed by the societal divisions over the Vietnam War, and the loss of confidence engendered by Watergate. The President sensed also a weakening of family life; at one point, he stated that he and his wife rarely let their daughter, Amy, watch new movies because they were filled with obscene four-letter words.

All these topics came up during the days and evenings of discussions at Camp David. The President felt he should discuss them because they were important matters affecting society. True, Americans were worried and angry about gas lines and rising inflation and crime and unemployment. But perhaps these were symptoms of a deeper problem, and he wanted to understand that problem. Perhaps there was no specific legislation that could be passed that would change the "downspin" mood of the country, but maybe he, as President, could somehow lift the nation's spirit and instill a new sense of confidence. Perhaps that would be the first step toward solving all those other "intractable" problems.

Always, however, he and his advisers knew that after a point—in a few days—he would have to leave Camp David and make a speech. And an important part of that speech would have to deal with what was most immediately on the minds of the American people—the energy crisis. That is what precipitated the entire Camp David episode in the first place. He had to come back with something concrete.

After all the wide-ranging talk, he had to decide on policy options. He had to be clear and forthright. He knew this, and others constantly reminded him of it. One presidential adviser bluntly said to him: "If you don't have something to say in the first five minutes and you don't grab public attention, then you won't have it for the rest of your presidency."

In an editorial published near the end of the ten-day period, the *New York Times* stated: "We hope Mr. Carter comes out swinging." Vernon Jordan of the National Urban League said: "He's going to have to say the right prayer, preach the right sermon, sing the right hymn."

What did all this disparate advice mean? How could it be translated into "bold and forceful" programs that at the same time would be "highly acceptable"? Finding alternative sources of energy from coal, shale, tar sands, and plant waste could cost as much as $40 a barrel. Synthetic fuel production meant increased environmental pollution. And what about cutting back on the consumption of oil? One way, some urged, would be to remove price controls from gasoline and add an additional tax of twenty-five to fifty cents per gallon on refiners. But Hamilton Jordan, the President's close political adviser, had told him that decontrolling gas prices "will kill you politically." Another proposal was to follow Western Europe and raise the price of gasoline above $2 per gallon—up to as high as $2.50. Surely this would cut down on the driving of cars and the use of gas. The option of rationing on a long-term basis also remained open. What about nuclear energy? Following the accident at the nuclear plant at Three Mile Island in Pennsylvania in March 1979, would the President encourage pursuit of nuclear energy as one alternative source? Was solar energy a reasonable item to put on the agenda?

Overall, close to 150 prominent and influential people made the trek to Camp David to counsel with the President. Some were chosen because they represented certain interest groups in various areas of policy; others represented no formal organizations but were prominent and informed on the issues, and the President wanted to hear their advice. Interestingly, most of the thirty-nine members of Congress, twenty governors, and eight mayors who were invited were members of the Democratic party. A few Republicans noticed this and suggested that the list of political invitees could have had a more bipartisan look.

Aside from "overlooking" a few Republicans, the President and his staff probably sought to touch base with as broad a segment of the populace as possible. He needed religious, farm, union, civil rights, corporate, banking, and environmental leaders to support his programs. Thus, the guest lists surely had political as well as substantive policy purposes.

Though virtually all eyes were on the President, it was clearly Congress that was most on the mind of the President. The framers of the Constitution had specifically designed the governmental structure so that policymaking would be a cooperative process among the executive, legislative, and judicial branches. Although some Congressional leaders had promised the President support after their visits, those leaders could not always deliver in the independent-minded, special-interest-dominated Congress. The President knew that he would need strong Congressional support, and he had not had a particularly successful relationship with Congress on the energy issue during the previous thirty months of his administration. Already he had made four major speeches on energy, and he had sent proposed legislation to Capitol Hill. In his first speech, in April 1977, he had stressed conservation and the need to switch from oil to coal. But Congress did little to implement his proposals. He had asked for new taxes on gasoline, on "gas-guzzling" cars, and on domestic oil to encourage conservation; he had asked for tax credits for insulating homes and buildings; and he had proposed plans to increase the production of coal. He had labeled his energy policy the "moral equivalent of war." But Congress had been slow to respond. It had basically given him only the proposed new Department of Energy. In fact, as recently as May 1979, the House had refused to pass legislation giving the President standby authority to ration gasoline.

Most members of Congress seemed less attentive to the entire national constituency than was the President. Congress had recently returned from a week-long Fourth of July holiday, and some members had their own views about the energy crisis gleaned from meetings with their local constituents. Some noted that the energy problem was not as critical for some citizens as for others. A Midwestern Republican senator said: "My big-city constituents are the only ones who are concerned, and they're blaming Jimmy Carter, the oil companies, and OPEC, in that order. I don't feel much of any heat on Congress, at least not yet."

The President—any President—has to be mindful that presidential policies will not necessarily be received uniformly throughout the nation. This diversity of opinion will surely be reflected among locally elected legislators in Congress.

This might have been part of what Eizenstat meant in his memo when he wrote that "the Congress seems completely beyond anyone's control." Correct or not, whether Eizenstat was indulging in "rhetorical excess" or not, the fact was (and is) that Congress is no longer the leadership-controlled, party-dominated body it once was. Leadership is still important, and party affiliation still matters, but newer members and some mid-1970s Congressional reforms brought different people with fewer ties to the political parties into Congress. (It must be remembered that Democratic President Jimmy Carter was working with a predominantly Democratic House and Senate.) And while it is reasonable to conclude that all 535 members of the House and Senate were concerned about energy and economic problems, it is also safe to say that their own interests might have been more particularistic than those of the President.

This is understandable. Some of the framers of the Constitution would have had it otherwise, others clearly believed that it could *not* be otherwise (that all officials chosen to serve local districts would, in fact, speak first for those districts); in any event, the governmental structure they put together—with its federal system, separation of powers, and checks and balances—gave local and personal interests a high degree of importance. The framers deliberately decided against a "parliamentary" form of government (as now exists in most democratic countries) and chose instead a form that separated the executive and legislative branches. The President is not a member of Congress (as a prime minister is of a parliament), and political party discipline is much more difficult to maintain. This is not the case in countries such as Britain and Canada. (These and other structural differences and the political consequences will be discussed throughout the textbook.)

After ten days of meetings at Camp David, there remained the speech the President would make to the country. But first he made surprise visits to two families, one in Carnegie, Pennsylvania, the other in Martinsburg, West Virginia. He had spent ten days listening to the elites, and now he wanted to talk informally with two middle-class families and a few of their neighbors—"ordinary citizens." Both visits were kept secret; until the last hour or so, even the hosts did not know they were going to be chatting with the President and his wife. The discussions covered the same subjects dealt with at Camp David.

The time had come to stop listening and to start leading again. The country had waited and watched the Camp David drama unfold. What had the President learned? What had he decided? How would he project his leadership?

The President seeks support for his newly outlined energy program in Kansas City.

The answers would come over two days, in a nationally televised speech from the White House on Sunday night, July 15, 1979, and in two follow-up speeches the next day in Kansas City, Missouri, to the National Association of Counties Convention and in Detroit, Michigan, before the annual convention of the Communication Workers of America.

An estimated sixty million Americans watched the President on television that Sunday evening. For those thirty-three minutes, at least, he had the attention of a rather large segment of the public. He began with the following words:

This is a special night for me. Exactly three years ago on July 15, 1976, I accepted the nomination of my party to run for President of the United States. I promised to you a President who is not isolated from the people, who feels your pain and shares your dreams and who draws his strength and his wisdom from you.

During the past three years, I've spoken to you on many occasions about national concerns: the energy crisis, reorganizing the government, our nation's economy and issues of war, and especially peace. But over those years the subjects of the speeches, the talks and the press conferences have become increasingly narrow, focused more and more on what the isolated world of Washington thinks is important.

Gradually you have heard more and more about what the government thinks, or what the government should be doing and less and less about our nation's hopes, our dreams and our vision of the future.

Ten days ago I had plans to speak to you again about a very important subject— energy. For the the fifth time I would have described the urgency of the problem and laid out a series of legislative recommendations to the Congress, but as I was preparing to speak I began to ask myself the same question that I now know has been troubling many of you: why have we not been able to get together as a nation to resolve our serious energy problem?

It's clear that the true problems of our nation are much deeper—deeper than gasoline lines or energy shortages. Deeper, even, than inflation or recession. And I realize more than ever that as President I need your help, so I decided to reach out and to listen to the voices of America. I invited to Camp David people from almost every segment of our society: business and labor; teachers and preachers; governors, mayors and private citizens.

And then I left Camp David to listen to other Americans. Men and women like you. It has been an extraordinary ten days. . . .

He recounted some of the advice he had received, quoting verbatim at times from particularly cogent statements made to him. Then the President turned his attention to the matter of the general mood of the country. He was worried about a declining spirit, a malaise, a "crisis of confidence." Clearly, he was attempting to put his finger on what he perceived to be a fundamental and serious phenomenon pervading the land. There were no special laws the government could pass at the moment to deal with this general societal condition, but it had to be recognized before other specific things could be done—before they could be expected to work.

I want to speak to you tonight about a subject even more serious than energy and inflation. I want to talk to you right now about a fundamental threat to American democracy.

. . . The threat is nearly invisible in ordinary ways. It is a crisis of confidence. It is a crisis that strikes at the very heart and soul and spirit of our national will.

. . . The erosion of our confidence in the future is threatening to destroy the social and the political fabric of America. The confidence that we have always had as a people is not simply some romantic dream or a proverb in a dusty book that we read just on the Fourth of July. It is the idea which founded our nation and which has guided our development as a people.

. . . We've always believed in something called progress. We've always had a faith that the days of our children would be better than our own.

Our people are losing that faith. Not only in government itself, but in their ability as citizens to serve as the ultimate rulers and shapers of our democracy.

. . . In a nation that was proud of hard work, strong families, close-knit communities and our faith in God, too many of us now tend to worship self-indulgence and consumption. Human identity is no longer defined by what one does but by what one owns.

But we've discovered that owning things and consuming things does not satisfy our longing for meaning.

. . . For the first time in the history of our country a majority of our people believe that the next five years will be worse than that past five years. Two thirds of our people do not even vote. The productivity of American workers is actually dropping and the willingness of Americans to save for the future has fallen below that of all other people in the Western World.

As you know there is a growing disrespect for government and for churches and for schools, the news media and other institutions. This is not a message of happiness or reassurance but it is the truth. And it is a warning.

. . . We were sure that ours was a nation of the ballot, not of the bullet, until the murders of John Kennedy and Robert Kennedy and Martin Luther King, Jr. We were taught that our causes were always invincible and our causes were always just only to suffer the agony of Vietnam. We respected the Presidency as a place of honor until the shock of Watergate. We remember when the phrase "sound as a dollar" was an expression of absolute dependability until ten years of inflation

began to shrink our dollar and our savings. We believed that our nation's resources were limitless until 1973, when we had to face a growing dependence on foreign oil.

These wounds are still very deep. They have never been healed.

The President then told the public that he felt there were ways to overcome this deep-seated malaise. There was a "path of common purpose" that could lead to restoration. Solving the country's energy problems would be one major step.

We can take the first steps down that path as we begin to solve our energy problem. Energy will be the immediate test of our ability to unite this nation.

And he proceeded to list six basic policy decisions.

POINT 1: *I am tonight setting a clear goal for the energy policy of the United States. Beginning this moment, this nation will never use more foreign oil than we did in 1977. . . .*

POINT 2: *To insure that we meet these targets, I will use my presidential authority to set import quotas. I am announcing tonight that for 1979 and 1980 I will forbid the entry into this country of one drop of foreign oil more than these goals allow. . . .*

POINT 3: *To give us energy security, I am asking for the most massive peacetime commitment of funds and resources in our nation's history to develop America's own alternative sources of fuel from coal, from oil shale, from plant products for gasohol, from unconventional gas, from the sun. I propose the creation of an energy security corporation to lead this effort to replace 2½ million barrels of imported oil per day by 1990. The corporation will issue up to $5 billion in energy bonds, and I especially want them to be in small denominations so that average Americans can invest directly in America's energy security.*

Just as a similar synthetic rubber corporation helped us win World War II, so will we mobilize American determination and ability to win the energy war. Moreover, I will soon submit legislation to Congress calling for the creation of this nation's first solar bank, which will help us achieve the crucial goal of 20 percent of our energy coming from solar power by the year 2000.

These efforts will cost money, a lot of money. And that is why Congress must enact the windfall profits tax without delay. It will be money well spent. Unlike the billions of dollars we shift to foreign countries to pay for foreign oil, these funds will be paid by Americans to Americans. These funds will go to fight, not to increase, inflation and unemployment. . . .

POINT 4: *I'm asking Congress to mandate—to require as a matter of law—that our nation's utility companies cut their massive use of oil by 50 percent within the next decade and switch to other fuels, especially coal, our most abundant energy source. . . .*

POINT 5: *To make absolutely certain that nothing stands in the way of achieving these goals, I'll urge Congress to create an Energy Mobilization Board which, like the War Production Board in World War II, will have the responsibility and authority to cut through the red tape, the delay and the endless roadblocks to completing key energy projects.*

We will protect our environment. But when this nation critically needs a refinery or pipeline, we will build it. . . .

POINT 6: *I am proposing a bold conservation program to involve every state, county and city, and every average American in our energy battle. This effort will permit you to build conservation into your homes and your lives at a cost you can afford. I ask Congress to give me authority for mandatory conservation and for standby gasoline rationing.*

To further conserve energy, I'm proposing tonight an extra $10 billion over the next decade to strengthen our public transportation systems. And I'm asking you, for your good and your nation's security, to take no unnecessary trips, to use car pools or public transportation whenever you can, to park your car one extra day per week, to obey the speed limit and to set your thermostats to save fuel. Every act of energy conservation like this is more than just common sense. I tell you it is an act of patriotism.

Our nation must be fair to the poorest among us so we will increase aid to needy Americans to cope with rising energy prices. . . .

The immediate drama was ended. In the next few days and weeks, the President and his advisers would spell out the proposals in more detail—before interest groups around the country, before Congressional committees, to the press and public. The President had identified what he believed to be some fundamental societal problems. Some were amenable to legislative action, some to executive action, others only to the resolve of the American people themselves. The President's speech was clear in these categories. Where he had the *authority*, the legal right, to do something (as with points 1 and 2), he stated he would act (although a federal court later ruled that the President did not have the authority to impose a particular import fee). Where acts could only be taken through the authority of Congress (as with points 3, 4, 5, and 6), these were specified.

Authority does not guarantee that something will get done, however. Congress might well have the legal right to set up, say, an Energy Mobilization Board, but it may not have the ability or capacity to do so because it cannot get enough members to back the measure. In other words, some legislators might believe that that would not be a *legitimate* (or correct or reasonable) way to deal with the problem. Legitimacy, then, is an important aspect of governance in this society; it relates to perceptions of right and wrong, to values. Indeed, if certain acts or policies are viewed as wrong or incorrect and are thus challenged as not legitimate or even as exceeding authority, there is a duly constituted judicial system to decide such matters. (Recall that Eizenstat's memo told the President that the state of Maryland was going to go to court over gasoline allocation policies.)

None of this, however, speaks directly to the issue of *political power*. Political

power is the capacity to perform certain acts, to achieve certain goals. No one questioned the President's authority to act as he did; and only time would tell if his proposals would be accepted as legitimate. But his power was another matter. Would Congress go along with him? Would the American people support his conservation measures? If the answers were "yes," then one could say that the President had not just authority, but power. In a democracy, political power is believed to be derived from the consent of the governed, and this involves *persuasion*. (Of course, a ruler might gain power from the use of military force, but this would not be considered a legitimate use of power under most circumstances in democratic policymaking.) The basic framework or starting place for dealing with these matters in the American political setting is the written Constitution. (We will examine the creation of that document in the first chapter.) The *politics* of decision-making is conducted within the boundaries set forth in the Constitution.

Thus, after Camp David—after the President came down from the mountaintop and presented his proposed policies—other parts of the political process were set in motion.

This textbook is not an account of that specific policy process—we begin with this issue only to set the stage for our examination of the various institutions, public and private, that make up the governing system of the country. By the end of the last chapter, however, we should have gained an understanding of those institutions and processes that are charged with handling the myriad problems facing our complex, modern, industrial society.

President Ronald Reagan succeeded President Jimmy Carter in January 1981. The decision-makers changed. A new cabinet was chosen; top administrative positions throughout the bureaucracy went to new people; the Republican party captured control

Left: Secretary of Energy James Schlesinger played a key role in the behind-the-scenes development of the Carter administration's energy policies.

Right: President Carter addresses the nation, July 15, 1979.

of the Senate, taking over the committee chairmanships; Democrats lost seats, but retained control, in the House; Republicans gained control of four additional gubernatorial spots. President Reagan said often in his campaign that this country is "energy rich." He indicated a preference for relying more on private industry, rather than on government, to solve the energy problem. He felt that fewer restrictions and government regulations on businesses would be helpful. In a debate with President Carter, Mr. Reagan stated: "I just happen to believe that free enterprise can do a better job of producing the things the people need than government can. The Department of Energy has a multi-billion-dollar budget in excess of $10 billion—it hasn't produced a quart of oil or a lump of coal or anything else in the line of energy." But President Reagan would still have Congress to persuade; he would have to build a consensus for his policies. In the final case study of this textbook, we will return to the energy issue and examine what happened in the fifteen months that intervened between Camp David and the elections. We will also take a look at how the new administration proposed to handle the problems as it took control of the seats of power. The student will have to carry the story from there—as a concerned, attentive citizen aware of the political processes decision-makers inevitably must engage in.

It's worth noting, at this point, that this society functions under the same written Constitution that was drafted almost 200 years ago, when the country was not so massive or modern, and surely not so industrial, as it is today. Is it possible for a 200-year-old Constitution to effectively set the boundaries for political action? How has the nation dealt with this phenomenon? Indeed, one of the crucial questions to be addressed as we proceed through this book is whether, in the 1980s and beyond, American society and its governing system can mobilize the necessary *political* energy, under its Constitution, to deal with its social, economic, and energy problems.

The Constitutional Setting

Chapter

1

When the President traveled to Kansas City, Missouri, in July 1979 to deliver a speech spelling out his energy policies, he concluded by saying: "Today, not only our nation's economy but our very independence is threatened. Our freedom is beyond price. We must not let it be endangered by the energy problem. . . . Let us join together in our struggle to secure our nation's energy independence with all the fullness that we have in our great nation and our will to live in freedom."

Substitute a few words—"British Parliament" for "energy problem," "political independence" for "energy independence"—and the President's words could well have been those of Thomas Jefferson or Thomas Paine, speaking or writing over 200 years earlier.

The thirteen American colonies were part of the British Empire. England, under the rule of King George III, was exercising tight economic and political controls over its subjects across the Atlantic Ocean, and some of the American colonists were growing restive. The issue was becoming one of political liberty in the face of perceived harsh regulations affecting economic property as well as the inability of the colonists to have a voice in making those regulations.

Thus a political crisis was brewing that would, in less than two decades, lead to a declaration of independence from England, a war of independence, an inadequate first step toward nationhood, and finally the establishment of a new federal government.

The Argument with the British Parliament

The thirteen colonies viewed themselves as integral parts of the British Empire. The colonists thought of themselves as full-fledged Englishmen, not as second-class subjects, and therefore they believed they should have the rights and privileges of all those living under the British constitution in England. But it became clear that Parliament in London was not of the same mind. That body saw the colonies as subordinate, existing for the purpose of contributing to the economic well-being of the mother country, even if this meant political and economic hardships and sacrifices for the colonies.

Parliament was not pleased with the colonies' half-hearted response to its requests for troops and money to fight the French and Indian wars. An attempt by Benjamin Franklin to draft a plan for greater colonial unity under British rule—known as the "Albany Plan" of 1754—was rejected by England and the colonies. Parliament issued tighter antismuggling laws and "writs of assistance" which permitted the English to conduct searches in violation, so the colonies felt, of basic private property rights.

One important dispute developed around the issue of the authority to tax. The colonies conced-

The British press often displayed varying opinions concerning the revolutionary conflict. Top: An angry old man (England) attempts to control his unruly American children and therefore is "maimed and forced to go with a staff." Bottom: An idealized figure representing Brittania wields the sword of justice while various enemies (France, Spain, and the Netherlands) seek to join forces with a repentant America (the kneeling Indian).

ed Parliament the authority to tax *for purposes of regulating trade*—they did not particularly like such laws and they frequently sought to circumvent them, but they did not initially contest the right of Parliament in this area. They *did* object to parliamentary taxes *for purposes of raising revenues*. Parliament's disagreement was clear. In the preamble to Parliament's Revenue Act of 1764, it asserted: ". . . It is expedient that new provisions and regulations should be established *for improving the revenue of this Kingdom . . .* and . . . it is just and necessary that a revenue should be raised . . . for defraying the expenses of defending, protecting, and securing the same. . . ."

In 1765, Parliament levied a direct tax—the Stamp Act—on the colonies. Although later repealed, the tax served warning that such a measure was, in Parliament's eyes, lawful.

Colonial opposition mounted. Merchants, lawyers, business people, bankers, journalists, and others raised loud voices in protest. Angry groups resorted to periodic violence. Men formed protest organizations and called themselves "Sons of Liberty."

Taxes on imports were levied by Parliament. One of the most notorious of these was the tax on tea, which ultimately led to the Boston Tea Party in 1773. There, the angry colonists—dressed as Indians—dumped shiploads of English tea in Boston Harbor. Britain responded with harsh measures, including a blockade of the port.

John Dickinson of Pennsylvania, in his *Letters of a Pennsylvania Farmer* (1768), sought to distinguish parliamentary laws for regulating trade from those for raising revenues. He believed that the former were reasonable (legitimate) functions for the administration of government, but not the latter. *Revenue* laws were valid only if the people taxed had—through their duly chosen representatives—consented to them.

But Benjamin Franklin was unconvinced by the distinction, and his position gained ground among his fellow colonists. He wrote:

The more I have thought and read on the subject the more I find myself confirmed in the opinion that no middle ground can well be maintained. I mean not clearly with intelligible arguments. Something might be made of either of the extremes: that Parliament has a power to make all *laws* for us, *or that it has a power to make* no *laws* for us; *and I think the arguments for the latter more numerous and weighty than those for the former.*[1]

When Parliament repealed the Stamp Act, it nonetheless reasserted its view that Parliament was supreme over the colonies by declaring:

that the King's majesty, by and with the advice and consent of the lords spiritual and temporal, and commons of Great Britain, in parliament assembled, had, hath, and of right ought to have, full power and authority to make laws and statutes of sufficient force and validity to bind the colonies and people of America, subjects of the crown of Great Britain, in all cases whatsoever.

Many colonists were willing to accept the legitimacy of the British monarchy, but they were not prepared to accept "taxation without representation." They argued that their constitutional rights (as British subjects) were being violated; they rejected the notion of "virtual representation," in this context meaning that they could be represented in Parliament by people for whom they had not voted. They preferred "real representation," which they enjoyed through their own colonial legislatures.

Military clashes occurred throughout the early years of the 1770s—Paul Revere rode through the night warning that "the British are coming" in Lexington, Massachusetts, in 1775.

The colonists' anger over the Stamp Act is shown by this rather threatening image on a colonial newspaper.

Two colonists, having tarred and feathered one of the king's tax-collectors, are shown offering him tea. The Tea Act of 1773 had strained the already shaky relations between England and the American colonies.

The battle of Lexington, 1775—one of the first armed clashes between American and British soldiers. A little more than a year later, the Declaration of Independence was signed.

In 1774, at the urging of Massachusetts, several colonies sent delegates to Philadelphia, and the First Continental Congress was formed. The following year, the Second Continental Congress selected a representative from Virginia, George Washington, to head the new Continental Army.

The drift toward a separation had clearly begun. But many colonists, known as Loyalists, still believed that it was better *not* to break with England. The problem, they felt, lay with an oppressive Parliament that was overstepping its bounds, creating differences that could eventually be worked out. Some historians have noted:

Moderates persuaded themselves that they were not fighting the King or the mother country, but the "unprincipled hirelings of a venal ministry." They referred to the enemy as the "ministerial," not the British army; they hoped for a political crisis in England that would place their friends in power; as late as January, 1776 the King's health was toasted nightly in the officers' mess presided over by General Washington.[2]

Joseph Galloway of Pennsylvania was one of the leaders of the moderates. He presented a plan to the First Continental Congress in 1774 that proposed to give the colonies control over their internal affairs by combining a legislature chosen from the colonies with a president appointed by the King. The colonial legislature and the British Parliament would have to reach mutual agreement before any measure affecting the colonies could be enforced. This proposal was rejected by the Continental Congress.

On balance, by 1775–76, as Benjamin Franklin concluded, no middle ground appeared to exist. The possibility of a viable political compromise had virtually disappeared.

The Declaration of Independence

In the same month that George Washington's officers were toasting King George III, a pamphlet entitled *Common Sense* began circulating in Philadelphia. Its author was Thomas Paine. Its message was simple and blunt:

. . . I challenge the warmest advocate for reconciliation to shew a single advantage that this continent can reap by being connected with Great Britain. . . .

The injuries and disadvantages we sustain by that connection, are without number; and our duty to mankind at large, as well as to ourselves, instruct us to renounce the alliance: Because, any submission to, or dependence on Great Britain, tends directly to involve this continent in European wars and quarrels; and set us at variance with nations, who would otherwise seek our friendship, and against whom we have neither anger nor complaint. As Europe is our market for trade, we ought to form no partial connection with any part of it. It is the true interest of America to steer clear of European contentions, which she never can do, while by her dependence on Britain, she is made the make-weight in the scale of British politics.

Europe is too thickly planted with Kingdoms to be long at peace, and whenever a war breaks out between England and any foreign power, the trade of America goes to ruin, because of her connection with Britain. . . .

. . . Everything that is right or natural pleads for separation. The blood of the slain, the weeping voice of nature cries, 'Tis time to part. Even the distance at which the Almighty hath placed England and America, is a strong and natural proof, that the authority of the one over the other was never the design of Heaven. . . .

. . . A government of our own is our natural right. . . .[3]

Some colonists might toast the British king, but Paine referred to him as "the Royal Brute of Great Britain."

Events leading to a formal pronouncement of severance followed swiftly. The Continental Congress opened American ports to other nations, excluding England. No more rebellious act of independence was needed. In May 1776, Congress advised all states that had not done so to establish new, independent governments. On June 7, 1776, Richard Henry Lee of Virginia offered a motion in Congress "That these United Colonies are, and of right ought to be, free and independent states." After intense debate, the motion carried on July 2. In anticipation of the outcome, Congress had appointed a committee composed of Thomas Jefferson, John Adams, Benjamin Franklin, Roger Sherman, and Robert Livingston to draft a formal

This engraving shows the intersection of High Street and Second Street in Philadelphia at the time of the Continental Congress. The steeple is that of Christ Church, where Washington and other delegates often worshipped.

New Yorkers pull down a statue
of George III in 1776.

statement declaring independence. That Declaration of Independence was adopted July 4, 1776.

The document turned out to be a ringing statement of charges against King George III, listing the ways he had violated basic human rights and laying the foundation for action by the colonists. Jefferson had included one charge (that the king had encouraged the slave trade) which was deleted from the final document after objection by some delegates. Parliament, against whom much of the previous struggle had been waged, was displaced by the king as the main villain because Parliament was viewed as merely the legislative body of Great Britain.[4] The real power and authority were vested in the monarch, and thus it was he who had to be the target of the declaration.

The Declaration of Independence relied heavily on the political theories of John Locke: the theory of natural rights, and the idea that government is formed by means of a social "compact" (or agreement) among its citizens to protect such rights.[5] When government fails to protect the natural rights of its citizens, it forfeits its legitimacy, and allegiance on the part of the people is no longer expected or due. The memorable opening lines of the document echo many of Locke's ideas:

We hold these truths to be self-evident, that all men are created equal, that they are endowed by their creator with certain unalienable rights, that among these are life, liberty, and the pursuit of happiness. That to secure these rights governments are instituted among men, deriving their just powers from the consent of the governed. That whenever any form of government becomes destructive to these ends, it is the right of the people to alter or abolish it, and to institute new government, laying its foundation on such principles and organizing its powers in such form, as to them shall seem most likely to effect their safety and happiness.

The document lists as inalienable rights life, liberty, and the pursuit of happiness, not property, as is often found in the writings of John Locke. Garry Wills explains this change not as accidental or as a mere casual substitution, but as an indication of Jefferson's belief that *property* was not, in fact, inalienable. Wills writes: "Jefferson's views on property, rights, and the social nature of man fit perfectly the [Francis] Hutchesonian background; and this explains his refusal to put property among the 'inalienable rights' of his Declaration. For him, property is the transferable commerce of those who have pledged moral 'fidelity' to each other and have an equal stake in the public good. To commit one's fortunes and sacred honor to the common effort of society is a duty arising from Hutcheson's belief in property as a form of 'language' meant to promote human intercourse and solidarity.''[6] In other words, property can and ought to be freely exchanged among citizens for the good of society. It is not proper to talk about property as being an inalienable right in the same sense as one would speak of the inalienable right to life and liberty.

At any rate, the colonies declared themselves no longer a part of the British Empire. It took a war of independence to implement that decision.

The American Revolution and Formation of State Governments

The war against Britain lasted until a peace treaty was signed in 1783. The former colonies entered into a treaty of commerce and alliance with France in 1778, which prompted England to declare war on France. Spain aided France, and was later joined by the Netherlands and Russia. Battles raged not only on the American continent; there were also naval engagements involving the European countries on the Atlantic Ocean, the Mediterranean, the Caribbean, the North Sea, and the English Channel. The rebellious American colonies had help in severing their ties from England. Indeed, one might suggest that the American Revolution precipitated, for that time, a "world" war.

While the fighting continued, the former colonies began to form new state governments. In so doing, they had to draft new constitutions and resolve several fundamental issues. Should there be a two-house legislature? What is the best way to

The Declaration of Independence as drafted by Thomas Jefferson. Note the number of revisions that Jefferson made throughout.

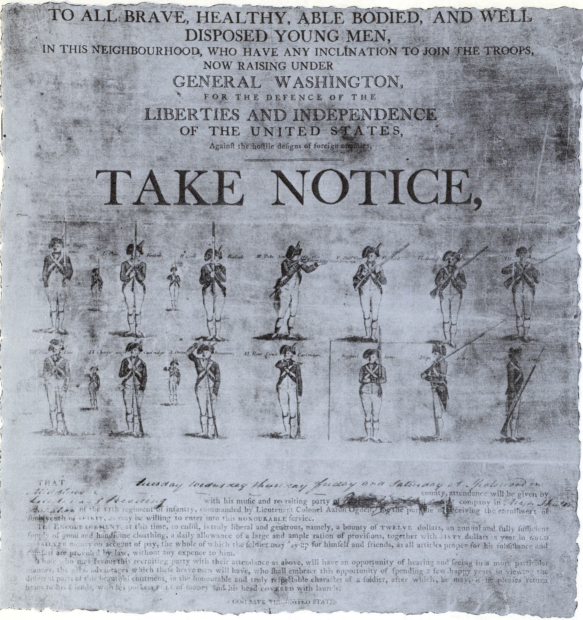

One of many posters calling for volunteers to join Washington's Continental Army.

guard against setting up state governments that could be just as abusive of citizens' rights as the king and Parliament had been? Should there be a separate executive branch? Should the new state constitutions be drafted by the state legislatures or by citizens' conventions and should the constitutions be ratified by the citizens or simply by the state legislatures? These were important questions facing the former colonists, even as they fought a war to solidify their declared break with England.

Most of the state constitutions included bills of rights, which relied heavily on the English Bill of Rights of 1689. They contained such protections as freedom of speech, fair trial by jury, freedom of the press, freedom of religion, and so forth.

Preferences ran in favor of bicameral (two-house) legislatures, frequent elections, separation of the legislative and executive functions, and rotation in office.

Massachusetts pioneered in establishing the "people" as the source of constitutional power. This was achieved by drafting a state constitution by special convention and then submitting it to the citizens for ratification or rejection. In this way, the new state constitution was firmly established as a law "higher" than mere statutory (legislative) measures.

On balance, most of the new state constitutions gave predominant power to the popularly elected "lower" houses of the legislature. In fact, in Virginia, Thomas Jefferson complained about his state's document:

This constitution was formed when we were new and unexperienced in the science of government. It was the first too which was formed in the whole United States. No wonder then that time and trial have discovered very capital defects in it. . . .

. . . All the powers of government, legislative, executive, and judiciary, result to the legislative body. The concentrating these in the same hands is precisely the definition of despotic government. . . . An elective despotism was not the government we fought for. . . .[7]

The new nation was groping its way, searching for viable ways to structure its political system. The men who assumed the task knew that they did not want to repeat the mistakes of the past experienced under British rule; they felt a deep distrust of governmental power. They had suffered under what they perceived as England's autocratic rule, and now they wanted to insure against such rule as much as possible through written constitutions designed to protect individuals from official abuse. This orientation against arbitrary power runs throughout American political history. The American political heritage, grounded in the traumatic experience with England, is steeped in a belief in limited, restricted government. "That government is best which governs least" is a strongly held credo of American society. The result has been a system in constant tension: on the one hand, strong enough to meet the needs of its citizens, while at the same time not so strong as to override the rights of its citizens. The study of American government is a study of the continuous struggle to strike a proper balance between these two contending demands. The task has never been easy, and it is as difficult in the 1980s as it was in the 1780s.

In the 1980s, the government had to have enough power and authority to meet the problems of a growing dependence on foreign energy sources. How much power should the President have? How much power should Congress have? How much power should be given to a federal regulatory agency to oversee the development of new energy sources? Should the states be given more authority to protect and develop energy sources within their own borders? How could rights of individuals, corporations, and interest groups be protected?

The specific policy issues were different, of course, in the 1780s, but the fundamental governmental issue of the authority of particular institutions has not changed.

The Articles of Confederation: America's First "National" Government

The newly declared independent states began to put together a governmental structure that would serve all the states. They knew all the states would be facing problems collectively, and that therefore a central government was needed. At the same time, they did not desire a strong national government to rule over the states as the English government had ruled over the colonies.

As early as June 1776, the Continental Congress appointed a committee composed of one delegate from each state to draft articles of confederation. Led by John Dickinson, the committee set to work and one month later presented its plan, which was finally adopted in November 1777. All the new states had to ratify the plan, and this occurred by 1781.

The plan did not establish a strong national government. In fact, Article II stated that "Each state retains its sovereignty, freedom and independence." Each state retained the authority to tax and regulate commerce; each state, regardless of size, had one vote in the national congress and could veto any proposed amendment. The national congress had the right to enter into treaties and to make war and peace, but it had to rely on the states to support these efforts financially. No national executive or judicial institution was established. In fact, the Articles of Confederation set up what was aptly called "a league of friendship."

The "national" government (and quotes around the term *national* are appropriate) was at best weak and ineffective. The several states carefully guarded their individual prerogatives; they vividly remembered the abuses of a strong English Parliament, and they were determined not to surrender such power to a new national government on this side of the Atlantic Ocean. First Rhode Island and then New York refused to give Congress the power to impose a five percent customs duty.

No less a figure than George Washington, in June 1783 on the occasion of his retirement as head of the army, pleaded for the states to give Congress the necessary power to conduct business for all the states. Otherwise, he feared, the hard-won independence from England would be for naught. The new states, indeed, were, as he put it, in a time of "political probation." He said:

> Unless the States will suffer Congress to exercise those prerogatives they are undoubtedly invested with by the constitution, every thing must very rapidly tend to anarchy and confusion. That it is indispensable to the happiness of the individual States, that there should be lodged somewhere a Supreme power to regulate and govern the general concerns of the confederated republic, without which the Union cannot be of long duration.[8]

There were debts to pay, veterans to care for, a militia to maintain, and Washington was not at all convinced that the "national" government set up under the Articles of Confederation was empowered to meet these tasks.

The road to Philadelphia. Perhaps "anarchy and confusion" did not reign, but the economic and political conditions in the new nation from 1781 through the rest of the decade could hardly have been much worse. If you were in debt and about to lose your farm, things were bad. If you were a creditor trying to avoid being paid in relatively worthless Continental paper money (which was losing value steadily because of inflation), things were bad. If you were John Jay trying to negotiate a commercial treaty with a foreign nation without knowing whether the necessary nine states would ratify it, things were bad. Indeed, many people must have wondered if the fledgling nation had won the war of independence against Great Britain only to lose the peace.

A group of angry, impoverished farmers in western Massachusetts, led by Captain Daniel Shays, staged armed rebellions against the state government. They stormed courthouses in an effort to stop the courts from holding foreclosure proceedings. The rebels also sought to have the legislature issue paper money and to call a state convention to revise the constitution. An economic depression grew worse. Many people feared civil war. Merchants and men of property worried that their property rights could not be protected. The state legislatures appealed to an inept Congress for help, without success. The national government was ineffective.

James Madison convinced the Virginia legislature to take the lead in calling a convention of state representatives to deal with interstate commerce. What was needed, Madison and others felt, was some sort of uniform system of commercial regulation. It was now also clear that there was definite and growing support to devise a more centralized government to overcome the fragmentation and weaknesses of the Confederacy. The convention met in Annapolis, Maryland, in September 1786, but only five states sent delegates. This was not sufficient to conduct the business required. Thus, those in attendance decided to issue a convention call a few months later "to take into consideration the situation of the United States, to devise such

Shays' Rebellion, 1786.

further provisions as shall appear to them necessary to render the constitution of the federal government adequate to the exigencies of the Union, and to report such acts as . . . will effectually provide for the same."

In other words, the move was on to modify the existing political structures so that a more unified government could effectively deal with the nation's economic problems. On February 21, 1787, Congress invited all the states to send delegates to a convention to be held in Philadelphia beginning May 14, 1787, "for the sole and express purpose of revising the Articles of Confederation."

The process of breaking with England and setting up a new government moved now into a new stage. The country's first government was not proving adequate to the task of safeguarding liberty and maintaining order—it was failing just as the English government, in the colonists' eyes, had failed. And now the time had come again, sooner perhaps than some had anticipated, to do something about the form of government under which the people would live. But this time there would be no grand philosophical declaration, no lengthy list of abuses against constitutional rights—only a short, carefully worded statement calling for a meeting to "revise" the Articles of Confederation. No war this time. Sporadic violence, to be sure, but no armed revolution aimed at overthrowing the government by force and involving other foreign nations in international power struggles. No dramatic break with the existing arrangements. Just some modifications that would make things work a little better. Or so it was stated.

By the end of seventeen weeks, they had drafted the blueprint for an entirely new government. Not a shot had been fired. In a sense they had assembled to draft an entirely new "peace treaty," this time among themselves. But all the time, the *official* word was that they simply intended to revise the existing Articles of Confederation.

The Constitutional Convention: "To Form a More Perfect Union"

Some people were suspicious of the motives of the delegates. Patrick Henry of Virginia, who feared a move toward a stronger national government, refused to attend the Philadelphia meeting because, as he put it, "I smelt a rat."

But fifty-five men did come from every state except Rhode Island. They were as young as Jonathan Dayton (New Jersey) at twenty-seven and as old as Benjamin Franklin at eighty-one; the average age was forty-two. They were mostly college-educated: thirty-one in that category. Most of them were lawyers, and most were what could be characterized as "men of property." At least fifteen owned slaves. These were men who owned land, securities, and had economic interests tied up in manufacturing and shipping companies. These facts have led some historians, notably Charles A. Beard, to conclude that the convention participants were concerned mainly about protecting their economic interests. He stated: "It cannot be said . . . that the members of the Convention were 'disinterested.' On the contrary, we are forced to accept the profoundly significant conclusion that they knew through their personal experiences in economic affairs the precise results which the new government that they were setting up was designed to attain. . . . As practical men they were able to build the new government upon the only foundations which could be stable: fundamental economic interests."[9] And that meant the interest of wealth.

Others have thought Beard's position too simplistic. Some historians have argued that the framers wanted to build a nation capable of protecting *varied* interests. Esmond Wright has observed: ". . . the appeals they were making were to interests much wider than Beard seems to have realized: to the public creditor, certainly, but also to the soldier, paid in bounty land that he could not obtain without a strong government, or in paper scrip that was almost worthless; to citizens as well as speculators in the West, who alike wanted protection from Indians and from foreign intrigues; to merchants trading abroad as well as manufacturers and workers seeking economic protection and security."[10]

There were different opinions on the subject of executive authority. Some wanted a monarchy; others, a president elected for life; some, no

Pennsylvania in the 1780s. It was on roads like these that the framers had to travel on their way to the Constitutional Convention.

executive at all. Some wanted a single-house legislature composed on the basis of one state, one vote; others wanted legislative representation on the basis of state population. Some wanted a separate national court system; others, no court system at all.

There were, however, areas of clear agreement. The states would not have control over the currency or over foreign affairs. Likewise, commercial relations between the states would be regulated by a national legislature.

Throughout the debates, virtually all the participants had come to accept the idea that they really were engaged in more than simply revising the old Articles of Confederation. This was the ''rat'' that Patrick Henry smelled way back in Virginia. But

there seemed to have been little dismay about that in Philadelphia. These people would end up doing what they really had no authority to do. Whether they had the *power*, and whether their work would be accepted as *legitimate*, remained to be seen.

The advocates of a strong central government got the jump on their other colleagues by presenting at the outset a plan (known as the Virginia Plan) that provided for a national executive, a national judiciary, and a national legislature of two houses. According to this plan, one house would be elected directly by the people and would in turn select the members of the other house from nominees submitted by the state legislatures. Representation in the lower house would be based on each state's free population or on the value of its property. The legislature would choose the national executive. The national legislature would be empowered to overrule state laws on constitutional grounds, if necessary. This plan was favored by the large, populous states, which stood to gain most by representation based on population or property.

A counterproposal was quickly offered—called the New Jersey Plan—which was championed by the small states. It resembled the existing Articles of Confederation, with a single-house legislature wherein each state had an equal vote, and in which the states would retain their authority. It did, however, contain a phrase that spoke of the national document and treaties and national laws as constituting "the supreme law of the respective States." This was an important concession, indicating that the states should not be able to act contrary to the national law as set down in the Constitution or by statute.

This set the stage for the first major debate at the convention. A committee composed of one member from each delegation came forth with what came to be called the Connecticut Plan or the Great Compromise.

- There would be a two-chamber legislature: one (House of Representatives) based on population in each state; the other (Senate) with each state having two senators.
- All bills relating to taxes would have to originate in the House of Representatives.
- Senators would vote individually and, although selected by the respective state legislatures, would be paid out of the national treasury, not by the states.

The proposal barely passed, five states to four (with one state delegation divided and three states absent, including Rhode Island). The convention moved on—into the hot, contentious, "unairconditioned" summer. The windows were closed to keep the deliberations from the curious ears of those outside; thus there was a lot of fanning and fuming inside. At one point, the venerable Benja-

The drafting of the Constitution did not solve all of the new country's problems. This engraving, entitled "Congressional Pugilists," depicts an altercation on the floor of Philadelphia's Congress Hall in 1798.

min Franklin suggested that each session be opened with a prayer, perhaps, in part, to invoke the Almighty's help in soothing warm tempers!

The Convention's Results: America's Second Government and First Federal Constitution

Finally, after seventeen weeks, a five-man drafting committee, headed by Gouverneur Morris, brought in a finished product, and thirty-nine delegates—after some further debate—affixed their signatures to it.

The document represented "a bundle of compromises," with a complex network of checks and balances built into the structure of government. On the one hand, there was a federal legislature containing two houses independent of each other. But on the other hand, each house could "veto" the acts of the other. On the one hand, only the "lower" house (House of Representatives) could *initiate* appropriation bills, but on the other hand, the Senate could amend these bills.

On the one hand, all members of the House of Representatives were to be elected directly by the voters every two years. On the other, the senators were to be chosen by the state legislatures to serve six-year terms, and only one third were to be up for election at any time (this selection process was later changed by the Seventeenth Amendment in 1913 to one of direct election by the citizens.)

On the one hand, there would be an independent federal court system with the judges serving for life. On the other hand, the President and the Senate had the power to choose the judges. In addition, Congress was given the authority to set up a detailed lower federal court system.

On the one hand, the President could veto bills passed by Congress, but on the other hand, Congress could override that veto by a two-thirds vote of both houses.

On the one hand, the President could negotiate treaties with foreign countries, but those treaties had to be approved by two thirds of the Senate.

The House of Representatives had the power to impeach the President, but the Senate had the power to try the President on the impeachment charges. Judges, incidentally, could also be impeached.

On the one hand, Congress was given powers such as regulation of interstate commerce, establishment of military forces, coining and borrowing money, laying and collecting taxes. But on the other hand, Congress could not tax items exported from any state, suspend the writ of habeas corpus, nor give preference to one state over another in commercial matters.

Congress could admit new states, but if the land of an existing state was involved, that state would have to consent.

On the one hand, the states clearly had protected their existence, but on the other hand, it was made equally clear that the federal Constitution, laws, and treaties were "the supreme law of the land" and the states had to be subordinate to them.

On the one hand, the President would not be elected popularly, but on the other hand, the office would not be subject to the federal Congress. An intriguing, peculiarly American creature called the **electoral college system** was created. Each state would choose "electors," who would then choose a President. The number of electors would be determined by the number of senators and representatives in each state. If no candidate received a majority of electoral votes, the House of Representatives would choose—with each state delegation having one vote. This device was seen as one that

Washington is sworn in as the first President of the United States, 1789.

would really begin to function later—after everyone's assumed first choice, George Washington, had served as the country's first President. Most people also assumed that the choice would most of the time be made in the House, because it was felt that few candidates after Washington would be sufficiently popular to get the required majority of electoral votes.[11]

It was a definitive illustration of the views of many at that time that government had to be made to check government—or better, that those who governed must be able to check those who governed. Governmental power had to be "partitioned" among the "several departments," so that each would provide "the means of keeping each other in their proper places." Why this check and balance approach to structuring a government? The founders' understanding of human nature is an important starting place. James Madison's observations in *The Federalist Paper* No. 51 sum up a widely held view:

> *It may be a reflection on human nature that such devices should be necessary to control the abuses of government. But what is government itself but the greatest of all reflections on human nature? If men were angels, no government would be necessary. If angels were to govern men, neither external nor internal controls on government would be necessary. In framing a government which is to be administered by men over men, the great difficulty lies in this: you must first enable the government to control the governed; and in the next place oblige it to control itself.*[12]

The founding framers had vivid memories of their experiences with England. At the same time, they had no intention of creating a government that was run by "the masses." If they remembered King George III and Parliament, they also did not forget Daniel Shays. They had no notion of creating a "democracy," if by that was meant some form of direct, popular government. Rather, they viewed their product as a "republic," a form of representative government that derived its ultimate *authority* from the people, but one in which the officials who actually served in office would likely be "the best and the brightest" and certainly those "of means."

And so they left Philadelphia and returned to their respective states, confident, for the most part, that they had struck the best balance, reached the best compromises possible—and hopeful that they could get the document ratified by the states and put into operation.

The ratification fight.   One tip-off that the work at Philadelphia was more than simply a process of revising the old Articles of Confederation came with the stipulation that the new document would go into effect when approved by three fourths of the states. Under the Articles, *all* the states had to approve amendments.

But no one was pretending anymore. This was not a set of amendments; this was a wholly new document. At first, things went smoothly and rapidly. Eight states ratified within eight months. But Virginia and New York were crucial, and they held out. The process involved state ratification conventions and in some cases the debates were intense, especially in Virginia. More than a few objections were voiced that the document did not contain an explicit bill of rights. Granted, there were provisions protecting habeas corpus, right of jury trial in criminal cases, prohibiting the impairment of contracts, and requiring no religious test for holding public office. But where were the provisions protecting freedom of speech, press, assembly, religion, and petition? Where were the

provisions guarding against unreasonable searches or seizures, double jeopardy, excessive bail, and cruel and unusual punishment? Where were the provisions specifically stating that people had the right to bear arms and the right not to have troops quartered in their homes?

Most states had bills of rights in their constitutions, but many were not prepared to support the new federal Constitution until a national bill of rights was promised. The promise was given by the Constitution's supporters, and once the new government was in place, Congress immediately submitted twelve new amendments to the states. Ten were ratified and went into effect in 1791, two years after the government was established. These ten amendments are known, unofficially, as the Bill of Rights. The tenth amendment became known as the "state's rights" amendment. It established that the federal government was a government of limited, delegated powers, and that the states and the people had all powers left over—so-called **reserve powers**:

> *The powers not delegated to the United States by the Constitution, nor prohibited by it to the States, are reserved to the States respectively, or to the people.*

This amendment and some other language in the Constitution have been the focus of much legal and political attention over the nearly 200 years of the document's existence. How these provisions have been interpreted through the years has determined in large measure how this country has been governed. Interpretation—by judges, lawyers, politicians, interest groups, ordinary citizens—has been the key.

In any case, by June 1788 nine states had ratified. The new Constitution was in place.

The Constitution:
A Document for All Seasons?

There were two distinct principles embodied in the newly ratified Constitution: *federalism* and *separation of powers*.

Federalism recognized two levels of government: a national governmental structure and subnational structures (the states). As we shall see in the next chapter, this arrangement parceled out power so that each level would respect the existence of the other, but in such a way that—given a conflict—the national structure would prevail. This clearly was a compromise between the Virginia Plan and the New Jersey Plan. Advocates of the former certainly wanted a strong central, national government; those who supported the latter wanted a continuation of the loose "league of friendship." John Roche has concluded that the compromise creating a "federalist" structure was not the result of some grand political theory. The advocates of a central government knew that their views would have a tough time being accepted in some states. Although they had the raw majority votes in the convention, sheer power through a majority was not sufficient. Roche observed:

> *Federalism, as the theory is generally defined, was an improvisation which was later promoted into a political theory. . . . (The advocates of the Virginia Plan) were practical politicians in a democratic society, and no matter what their private dreams might be, they had to take home an acceptable package and defend it—and their own political futures—against predictable attack.*
>
> *. . . Madison had the votes, but this was one of those situations where the enforcement of mechanical majoritarianism could easily have destroyed the objectives of the majority: The Constitutionalists were in quest of a qualitative as well as a quantitative consensus. . . . It was* *a political imperative if they were to attain ratification.*[13]

Here we see an example of the power versus consensus theme. As we have seen, in political affairs it is sometimes not enough merely to have the power and authority to do something; one must also seek legitimacy. This may involve compromise in order to achieve a consensus, which then becomes the basis for legitimacy. In the energy case study discussed earlier, President Carter certainly had the authority to call for deregulation of gas prices, but he was bluntly warned by one of his trusted aides that to do so "would kill you politically." Carter was dealing with the same power/consensus problem that Madison had to grapple with almost 200 years earlier.

The other principle was separation of powers. In this case, the framers deliberately chose not to establish a "parliamentary form of government," one in which the executive is a member of the legislature, and in which there is no independent, coequal judiciary. Surely, the theoretical writings of Montesquieu were influential with the framers, but the precise formulations dividing the three branches of government were devised by individuals intent on constructing a workable, acceptable Constitution. They wanted a government that was well-balanced, yet one that, at the same time, would not lose its balance at the first signs of tension and unrest. Thus, they separated powers so that no particular segment of the population could capture control and dominate the system. Each branch of the federal government would depend upon a different constituency and would remain in office for different (and sometimes overlapping) periods of time.

Some of the precise details drafted in 1787 have changed through constitutional amendment, but the principle of separation of powers has remained intact. For instance, United States senators are no

A somewhat dramatic rendering of the Constitutional Convention as imagined by painter Howard Chandler Christy. Note the image of the rising sun on the back of George Washington's chair. According to notes taken by James Madison, it was to this that Benjamin Franklin referred in the waning hours of the convention. "Whilst the last members were signing [the Constitution], Madison wrote, "Doctr. Franklin looking towards the President's chair, at the back of which a rising sun happened to be painted, observed to a few members near him, that painters had found it difficult to distinguish in their art a rising from a setting sun. 'I have,' said he, 'often and often in the course of this session, and the vicissitudes of my hopes and fears as to its issue, looked at that behind the President, without being able to tell whether it was rising or setting; but now at length I have the happiness to know that it is a rising and not a setting sun.'"

longer selected by the state legislatures; they are elected directly by the voters in the respective states. This is a constitutional change. But what has remained constant is the check-and-balance role the Senate plays in relation to the House and the President.

The framers understood that the Constitution would have to be adapted to new circumstances from time to time. They provided formal means for amending it which involved action by Congress and the states. The following are the ways amendments can be made formally:

- Congress can propose an amendment which then must be ratified by three fourths of the state legislatures or by three fourths of the states in special conventions;
- Two thirds of the state legislatures can petition Congress to call a national convention to propose an amendment, which then must be ratified by three fourths of the state legislatures or by three fourths of the states in special conventions.

To propose an amendment, two thirds of both houses of Congress must pass the proposal. Congress then has the power to determine if the proposed amendment will be ratified by state legislatures or by state conventions. Congress can also set a time limit during which the requisite number of states must accept the proposal. Can that time be extended? Apparently so, as was done when Congress extended the time for passage of the Equal Rights Amendment (ERA) by three years.

The Constitution has been amended twenty-six times (counting the first ten amendments constituting the Bill of Rights) from 1791 to 1971, and in all instances the proposals have been made by Congress. All but one have been ratified by state legislatures, not by special state conventions.[14]

The President is not involved at all in the formal amendment process. Neither is the Supreme Court, unless it is asked to rule on an issue such as the extension of time. Some potential questions are not covered by the clause dealing with the amendment process: can a state rescind its acceptance before the three-fourths goal is reached? Can a state rescind its previous vote during the extended period? If the states petition Congress to call a national convention in order to propose an amendment, must Congress honor the petition? Questions such as these come up from time to time, but the Constitution is silent on answers. Therefore, people turn to the courts to interpret the meaning of the Constitution—even though the Constitution itself does not address such issues.

This leads us to other ways of adapting the Constitution to other times. *Formal* means of constitutional change are not the only ways of changing the impact of the document. Congress passes laws based on the Constitution; the President acts on the basis of Constitutional authority; the courts interpret laws in light of the Constitution. Of course, these acts do not technically amend the Constitution; they are really acts stating what the officials believe the Constitution means and permits. In the process of doing this, however, one might argue that the interpretation in fact changes the previous meaning, thus informally amending the Constitution.

With the constant legislative, judicial, and executive actions taking place in the American government, one could say that the Constitution gets interpreted—possibly changed—in hundreds of ways. This is not surprising. The Constitution is broadly—and sometimes vaguely—worded in some of its passages. The language could have several meanings under different circumstances. If one required or insisted on only the formal means of changing the Constitution, the business of the government would likely not get done. One alternative would be to have a lengthy, detailed, precisely worded, all-encompassing Constitution (which is the case in some countries, where even wages and hours and working conditions of workers are spelled out). This is not preferred in American political culture. The framers surely wanted a written document for protection against potential abuses. But many of the details were to be left to the political process (bargaining, compromising) and were not to be reflected in the Constitution.

In this way, the Constitution maintains a status higher than ordinary statutory laws and executive decrees, and the document has survived with relatively few formal amendments, but certainly with a vast number of interpretations to fit changed societal circumstances.

There are any number of examples to illustrate this point, but two are especially useful to examine: race relations and the energy problem.

The Constitution and black Americans: from slavery to affirmative action. When the framers met in Philadelphia in the summer of 1787, slavery legally existed in the country. There were no great or prolonged debates over the morality or immorality of slavery. There was only compromise. Without ever mentioning the terms *slave* or *slavery*, the Constitution dealt with the subject in three instances. Representation in the House of Representatives would be based on "the whole number of free persons, including those bound to service for a term of years, and excluding Indians not taxed, *three fifths of all other persons*." The latter were slaves—sixty percent of them would be counted for purposes of deciding how much representation a state would have in Congress.

Instead of abolishing slavery, which was never seriously considered by most, the framers gave

Congress the right, if it wished, to prohibit slave trade after 1808.

If a slave escaped to another state, that state had to return the fugitive. Thus, the original Constitution positively recognized the institution of slavery and contained provisions protecting the institution.

But a civil war and two constitutional amendments (the Thirteenth and Fourteenth) ultimately changed that. The slaves were freed and constitutional language was written aimed at guaranteeing their civil rights as citizens. The Fourteenth Amendment (1868) spoke of "privileges and immunities," "due process of law," and stipulated that no state shall "deny to any person within its jurisdiction the equal protection of the laws." Two years later, the Fifteenth Amendment made it unconstitutional to deny any citizens the right to vote "on account of race, color, or previous condition of servitude."

We will examine these issues more fully in chapter 14, but for now it is instructive to look briefly at the way the Constitution, from the Civil War to the present, has changed without being formally amended in regard to black Americans. Much of this was done by judicial interpretation.

At first, the Constitution was interpreted by the United States Supreme Court as permitting legal racial segregation. In 1883, the Court ruled that segregation was legal only if engaged in by private individuals and not by the states. Then, in the 1896 *Plessy* v. *Ferguson* decision, the Court interpreted the Fourteenth Amendment as permitting states to engage in racial segregation, saying:

The object of the amendment was undoubtedly to enforce the absolute equality of the two races before the law, but in the nature of things it could not have been intended to abolish distinctions based upon color, or to enforce social, as

distinguished from political equality, or a commingling of the two races upon terms unsatisfactory to either. Laws permitting, and even requiring, their separation, in places where they are liable to be brought into contact, do not necessarily imply the inferiority of either race to the other, and have been generally, if not universally, recognized as within the competency of the state legislatures in the exercise of their police power. The most common instance of this is connected with the establishment of separate schools for white and colored children, which have been held to be a valid exercise of the legislative power. . . .[15]

Many court battles ensued over the decades and finally in 1954, in *Brown* v. *Board of Education*, the Supreme Court, looking at the same Constitution, ruled that racial segregation in state (public) schools was unconstitutional. The Court said:

In approaching this problem, we cannot turn the clock back to 1868 when the [Fourteenth] *amendment was adopted, or even to 1896 when* Plessy v. Ferguson *was written. . . . We conclude that in the field of public education the doctrine of "separate but equal" has no place. Separate educational facilities are inherently unequal. Therefore, we hold that the plaintiffs . . . are by reason of the segregation complained of, deprived of the equal protection of the laws guaranteed by the Fourteenth Amendment.*[16]

The story has not ended. Other battles involving race are still coming before the Court—and before the President and Congress. Can the federal government give preference to blacks (or any other ethnic group) in an attempt to improve their status? Can a local government require that a certain quota of blacks be hired on the local police force? If so, does this constitute discrimination against white Americans? Chapter 14 will discuss these matters

further, but keep in mind that the specific constitutional language interpreted by the courts and legislators and bureaucrats and university officials and private employers is the same in the 1980s as it was in the 1880s. Only the interpretations have changed.

The Constitution and the energy crisis: from an agrarian society to industrialization.   The Lancaster Turnpike stretched seventy miles from Lancaster, Pennsylvania, to Philadelphia. With good weather and moderate traffic, a traveler in 1791 (the year the turnpike opened) could traverse its entire length in twelve hours. It was gravel-surfaced and free of tree stumps—quite an improvement over the bumpy, muddy roads the framers had to travel on their way to the Philadelphia convention.

In July 1979, President Carter and 150-odd guests were taken from Washington to Camp David by helicopter in less than twenty minutes.

When the Constitution was being drafted, most Americans traveled by horse and buggy, shipped their goods by boats on canals, and made their living by farming the land and by small-scale retailing. Robert Fulton introduced the steamboat on the Hudson River in 1807. Wood was the main source of energy, but "coal as steamboat fuel began to come in on the Hudson and the Great Lakes in the 1840s."[17]

The framers put together a constitutional document during a time when telephones were unknown, when Indians on the frontier constituted the most immediate "national security" threat, and when there were no giant monopolistic corporations. The most pressing economic problems involved stabilizing trade relations among the states, making sure that the country's currency was sound, and seeing that debtors honored their contractual obligations with creditors.

Today, the country has changed. Today, as the Camp David case indicates, Americans use oil, not wood or coal, as their major energy source, oil that is purchased in large quantities from foreign countries. Today, people are urged to form "car pools," to use "public transportation," and to turn their "thermostats" down in the winter. Today, the President asks Congress to order "utility companies" to cut the use of oil, and to impose a "windfall profits tax" on oil companies.

All these things present new language, signifying fundamentally different living conditions. And yet the constitutional document which serves as the basic authority for these acts in the 1980s is the same document drafted in the 1780s.

Article 1, Section 8 (Paragraph 3) of the Constitution reads: "[The Congress shall have power] to regulate commerce with foreign nations, and among the several states, and with the Indian tribes." This language has been interpreted by the courts to allow the federal government to regulate the amount of wheat grown by a farmer on his land and consumed solely on his land. In *Wickard* v. *Filburn* (1942), the Supreme Court held:

> *. . . even if appellant's activity be local and though it may not be regarded as commerce, it may still, whatever its nature, be reached by Congress if it exerts a substantial economic effect on interstate commerce and this irrespective of whether such effect is what at some earlier time has been defined as "direct" or "indirect."* [18]

Thus, although the economic activity of farmer Filburn was entirely confined to his 23-acre Ohio farm, it affected the wider market. This was the way the Supreme Court adapted the Constitution to fit the new times.

Occasionally, protests against federal regulations are raised on the grounds of their exceeding constitutional authority. And these disputes will be weighed not only against the original language of the Constitution but against previous decisions interpreting that document.

It would be difficult to imagine the constitutional framers putting together a document giving the President the authority to impose a fee on imported oil. Yet the Constitution was the basis for a federal judge's 1980 declaration that the President did *not* have such authority. Relying on the Trade Expansion Act of 1962, which allegedly gave the President broad discretionary powers to impose import fees and quotas (should he deem them necessary for the national interest) President Carter sought, in 1980, to levy a ten-cent fee on gasoline. The purpose was to reduce oil imports as well as to raise $10 billion to help balance the federal budget. The federal judge ruled that this presidential action "does not fall within the inherent powers of the President . . . and is contrary to manifest Congressional intent." The court basically upheld the 1962 law, but said that this particular presidential action went beyond regulating foreign oil and affected domestically produced oil as well. [19]

Many observers have suggested that, by structuring the government with an elaborate system of checks and balances, the framers devised a system that made it difficult for the federal government to act expeditiously to meet a crisis such as that posed by energy scarcity. The President must ask Congress for certain authority; Congress is composed of two relatively independent houses. Representatives and senators are elected by their own particular local districts and states, and therefore are answerable only to them. Remember Stuart Eizenstat's memo in the case study: "Congress seems completely beyond anyone's control."

Would it have been better if they had devised a system where the two branches were closer together? The system they built put a premium on consultation, bargaining, and compromise. In today's world, can the various factional interests pull together within the existing governmental framework to work together to meet a crisis? This is not really a question of authority; it is a question of politics and persuasion.

Ultimately, of course, one might suggest that a solution would be to formally change the constitutional structures of government in the direction of less fragmentation and more organizational coherence. That could mean a stronger presidency, or a more unified Congress with greater constitutional powers. But Americans have not yet seriously considered these alternatives, preferring instead to rely on informal means of adapting the Constitution to changing times—to making it, in a sense, a document for all seasons.

Summary

1. Political and economic disputes between the American colonies and Great Britain over taxation and colonists' rights under the British constitution led to the Declaration of Independence and the American Revolutionary War.

2. The Articles of Confederation, established by the new nation, were too ineffective to cope with the internal economic problems following independence. This led to the drafting of a new federal Constitution.

3. The new Constitution sought to create a more centralized, effective federal government, that, at the same time, contained several built-in checks and balances to safeguard against any one segment of the government gaining ascendancy and possibly abusing individual rights.

4. The document the framers created has remained for almost 200 years, but it has been adapted to substantially different social and economic conditions mainly through the informal means of interpretation on the part of courts, Congress, and the presidency.

Notes

1. Quoted in Samuel Eliot Morison and Henry Steele Commager, *The Growth of the American Republic* (New York: Oxford University Press, 1942), p. 156.
2. Ibid., p. 192.
3. Thomas Paine, *Common Sense* (1776).
4. Morison and Commager, *The Growth of the American Republic*, p. 196.
5. One study has suggested that Thomas Jefferson received more influence in his political thinking from the Scottish philosopher, Francis Hutcheson, than from John Locke. See Garry Wills, *Inventing America, Jefferson's Declaration of Independence* (New York: Vintage Books, 1978). Wills claims that "the most vivid and traceable influence Locke had on Jefferson was in the area of religious tolerance" (p. 171).
6. Ibid., p. 237.
7. Thomas Jefferson, *Notes on the State of Virginia* (1801), pp. 171–190.
8. Cited in Jack P. Greene, ed., *Colonies to Nation, 1763–1789, A Documentary History of the American Revolution* (New York: W. W. Norton & Company, Inc., 1975), p. 439.
9. Charles A. Beard, *An Economic Interpretation of the Constitution of the United States* (New York: The Free Press, 1935), p. 151.
10. Esmond Wright, *Fabric of Freedom, 1763–1800* (New York: Hill and Wang, 1978), pp. 189–190.
11. John P. Roche, "The Founding Fathers: A Reform Caucus in Action," *The American Political Science Review* (December 1961), 811.
12. Alexander Hamilton, James Madison, and John Jay, *The Federalist Papers,* No. 51 (New York: Mentor Books, New American Library, 1961), p. 322.
13. Roche, "The Founding Fathers," 804–805.

14. This was the Twenty-first Amendment, which repealed the Eighteenth Amendment, the "prohibition" amendment. Some historians have suggested that Congress did not want to subject the repeal to state legislatures, which were controlled by rural, antirepeal forces. Congress felt urban, prorepeal voters would have more influence in state conventions. Congress was right.

15. *Plessy* v. *Ferguson*, 163 U.S. 537 (1896).
16. *Brown* v. *Board of Education*, 347 U.S. 483 (1954).
17. Morison and Commager, *The Growth of the American Republic*, p. 298.
18. *Wickard* v. *Filburn*, 317 U.S. 111 (1942).
19. "Judge Rules Carter Cannot Impose Fee of 10¢ on Gasoline," *New York Times*, May 14, 1980, p. A1.

The Federal System: Theory and Structure

Chapter

2

As we saw in the Camp David energy story, one of the first groups of visitors to see President Carter consisted of eight state governors. They were, you will recall, on their way to the annual National Governors Conference, and they wanted to counsel the President on the energy crisis from their various vantage points as executive leaders of state governments. The President, ever mindful of the important role of the states, had indicated that he wanted to develop closer relations with governors by having them spend time as overnight guests at the White House. He needed their ideas and cooperation because, as he put it, "I see the states as kind of fifty experiment stations."

The President recognized that while a national energy policy was necessary, it was also important to keep in mind that the various regions of the country, with their different economic conditions, would have different responses to that policy. Thus, in the process of implementing a national energy policy, states in the Northeast (the so-called frostbelt states) might well have needs different from states in the Southwest (the sunbelt states). How one group of states met problems of energy conservation could well differ from the means chosen by other states. In this sense, the states could be "fifty experiment stations."

This is certainly one advantage to be derived from what is called a "federal" system of government. When the national government sets conser-

vation goals to save energy, the individual states can decide on specific ways to meet the goals. Likewise, as was the case after the Camp David talks, while the national government can determine how much gasoline each state is to receive, the Department of Energy can decide to let each state have authority in deciding how that gasoline is to be allocated *within* the state.

This seems to make sense, and few would argue that a single means of energy conservation would be reasonable for all areas. Energy conservation is perhaps a relatively easy issue to demonstrate the apparent merits of federalism. We shall see in this chapter and especially in chapter 3 that matters are not always so easy.

Federal, National, Confederate, Unitary

When we say that the principle of federalism was adopted in the Constitution, we mean that the framers established a government that recognized two distinct levels or units of official authority: a national government and several state governments. Both derive their authority from the United States Constitution. Neither can be destroyed by the other. Neither is beholden to the other for its existence. We sometimes use the words **federal** and **federalism** interchangeably, that is, we say we have a "federal system," meaning two levels of constitutionally based authority. But we some-

FIGURE 1.
Unitary, Confederate, and Federal Forms of Government.

UNITARY
GOVERNMENT

All political power resides in the central government. Regional and local authorities are charged with administering the laws and decrees of the central government.

Regional or local authorities

Citizens

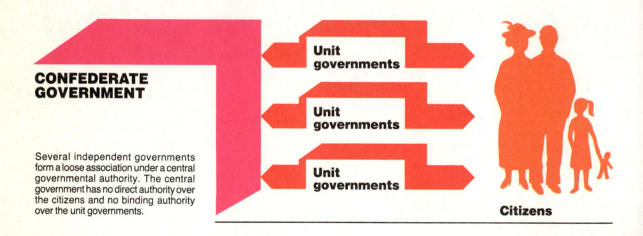

CONFEDERATE
GOVERNMENT

Several independent governments form a loose association under a central governmental authority. The central government has no direct authority over the citizens and no binding authority over the unit governments.

Unit governments

Unit governments

Unit governments

Citizens

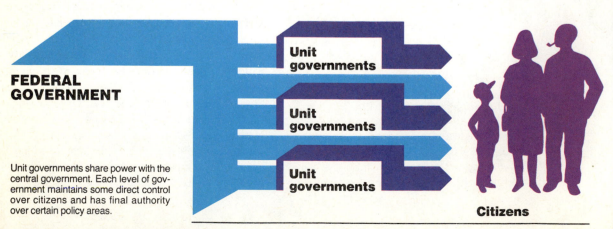

FEDERAL
GOVERNMENT

Unit governments share power with the central government. Each level of government maintains some direct control over citizens and has final authority over certain policy areas.

Unit governments

Unit governments

Unit governments

Citizens

times speak of the *federal* government when we refer to the *national* government. In fact, the federal government really consists of the authorities in both Washington, D.C., and the states. Therefore, state governors and state legislators are officials of America's federal system of government.

More important is the distinction between a federal system and a **confederation**. Whereas the former has "coequal" governmental units, the latter does not. In a confederation, there are two levels, but the several states basically hold more power than the national government. The national government of a confederacy is largely a creature of the states and derives its power from the states. Obviously, this means that the national government in a confederation is weak. The United States had this form of government, of course, under the Articles of Confederation. And, recall, it was precisely that weakness that led to the Philadelphia convention of 1787.

In a federal system, both levels of government have a direct relationship with the citizens. In a confederation, the national government might be able to operate directly, but usually it will reach the citizens through the various states, even on such important matters as levying taxes, recruiting an army, and so forth.

If a confederation leans heavily in the direction of the states, a **unitary** system (also referred to in chapter 1) is structured in the opposite direction. It is a system wherein the national government is supreme. There is no "coequal" status with other levels. The government in the national capital can create and dismantle states or boroughs or districts or any other local subdivisions. Those lesser units are essentially administrative agents of the national government. England and France have unitary systems. Canada and Mexico are other examples of federal systems.

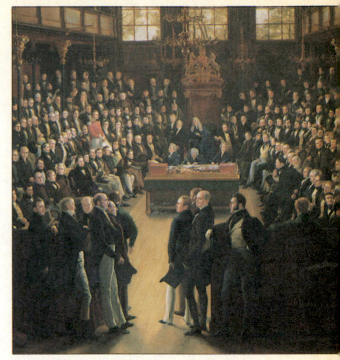

Great Britain is governed by a unitary system, in which Parliament has direct authority over all units of government. This painting shows a session of the British House of Commons in 1833.

In the United States, the concept of a unitary form of government can be best illustrated by examining the relationships of the states to counties, cities, and townships. These governmental divisions sometimes elect their own officials and impose taxes, and they are by no means unimportant governmental entities, but every single one of them is a creature of the state governments. Whatever authority these local governments have —and there is great variation—is granted to them by the states. The state can create them; the state can abolish them; the state can expand or restrict their powers. Only the national government and the fifty states have a constitutional right to exist.

A few paragraphs earlier we used the term "coequal" and we put quotation marks around it when we referred to the relationship between the national government and the states. That was done purposefully to indicate that we should be a bit cautious about the use of the term, We *say* that in America's federal system, the two levels are distinct and coequal. Theoretically, that is correct. But, of course, it is not as simple as that. While the Constitution protects the existence of both levels of government, and while the relationship between the two is reasonably clear and unambiguous in most instances, the fact is that some major disagreements in American history have centered on questions of respective powers, disagreements in which the state governments have not always come out on top. (Nor have not always lost, we hasten to add.) Which level of government has the constitutional authority to perform which functions? The issue of governmental authority has been constantly on the political and legal agenda; the Civil War put it on the battlefield.

To Each Its Own: The Constitution and Governmental Power

To answer questions concerning jurisdiction, we must first turn to the Constitution, the document that spells out the relationship between the two levels of government in our federal system. Even there, the answers are not always too clear.

The Constitution and national government powers. As we noted in the first chapter, the farmers certainly wanted to correct the disadvantages resulting from a woefully weak national government. But they also wanted to create a national government that would not be able to exercise unlimited power. One way to strike this balance was to *delegate* certain powers to the national government. That is, the Constitution would stipulate what powers the national government could exercise. Thus, the very first article sets forth the **express** powers granted to Congress. These are spelled out in various sections, but most notably in Article 1, Section 8, where the Constitution specifically says that "Congress shall have power to":

- lay and collect taxes;
- borrow money;
- regulate commerce with foreign nations and among the several states;
- establish post offices;
- declare war;
- raise and support armies;
- provide and maintain a Navy.

In Article 2, the Constitution tells us what powers the President has. "The *executive* power shall be vested in a President. . . . The President shall be Commander in Chief of the Army and Navy. . . ."

The Constitution created a Supreme Court in Article 3 and stipulated that "judicial power" would be vested in that court and other "inferior" (obviously meaning status, not quality) courts that Congress might subsequently establish. The Article goes on to say that "the judicial power shall extend to all cases in law and equity arising under this Constitution and treaties. . . ."

All this language seems reasonably clear, but without question, some grants of power to the national government are more clearly expressed than others. It would be difficult to misunderstand the express grant of power to Congress "to lay and collect taxes" and "to borrow money." But what else does this express language confer? Is Congress only able to perform specific functions enumerated in the Constitution? And just what does "executive power" mean as it is used in Article 2? Moreover, while Article 3 definitely gives the Supreme Court "judicial power" over cases and controversies ''arising under this Constitution,'' does this mean that the Supreme Court can, in fact, declare a law unconstitutional? If it does mean that, the Constitution does not tell us much, if anything, about the basis on which such a declaration could be made. Therefore, while the Court has ''judicial power,'' and while it exercises this power by interpreting the Constitution, there is really no clear guide to what the Supreme Court can or should consider in reaching its judgments.

Article 1, Section 8 lists seventeen specific things Congress can do. Then comes this paragraph:

> [The Congress shall have power] *to make all laws which shall be necessary and proper for carrying into execution the foregoing powers, and all powers vested by this Constitution in the Government of the United States, or in any Department or Officer thereof.*

This has been referred to as the **residual clause** or the **elastic clause.** Indeed, what constitutes ''necessary and proper'' legislation? And who should make that determination?

For the answers to such questions we must look to the **implied powers** of the Constitution. There are some things the national government can do which are only *implicitly* stated in the Constitution. This is an area that has caused a great deal of constitutional debate in the history of American federalism.

One of the most famous examples of implied powers involved the express grant of power to Congress to lay and collect taxes and to borrow money on the credit of the national government. Did this also mean that Congress had the power to establish a national bank? The Constitution says nothing on that subject. And yet two years after the new Constitution was adopted, a national bank was chartered for twenty years. Alexander Hamilton was the main proponent of the institution. The

The federal government contributes funds to support many state and local programs, including mass transit (top), and education (above).

Constancy and Change

American government has endured in large measure because it has been able to adapt to a changing nation. While the governmental framework and political institutions created by the framers almost 200 years ago remain intact, American society has in the meantime undergone enormous social, economic, and political changes. From a population of 3.9 million in 1790, the country has grown to support a population in excess of 235 million. An agrarian economy has developed into a powerful industrial one. The political system has survived the growth from thirteen states to fifty and a civil war that challenged the very structure of the federal system. Though the centers of power have continually shifted and conflicts have erupted on several fronts, differences have, for the most part, been worked out through the political process and not on the battlefield.

The capital of the national government, Washington, D.C., has grown to accommodate the increasing importance of that level of government. One of the few cities in the world deliberately planned as a national capital, Washington was originally the workplace of 137 federal clerks. Today, its massive government complexes are staffed by more than 2 million employees. Once described by historians Allan Nevins and Henry Steele Commager as "a mere forest village on the north bank of the Potomac," it is now one of the foremost cities of the world.

Though the Constitution has been amended only twenty-six times, it has been a crucial instrument of change throughout the nation's history. The 1868 language of the Fourteenth Amendment ("equal protection of the laws") has remained intact, but interpretations of the amendment by various Supreme Court justices have moved the country from acceptance of racial segregation to a policy of desegregation. In this and in other instances, the Supreme Court has played a major role in the drama of constancy and change.

The executive and legislative branches of government have also accommodated change. While each branch has been "dominant" at one time or another, the delicate political balance established by the constitutional framers has been maintained. No single group or individual has been able to exercise tyrannical power: parties, interests, and people in power change; the institutions they capture and control remain constant.

Washington in 1852 . . .

. . .in 1892 . . .

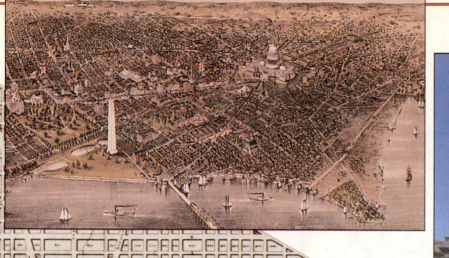

. . . and now.

(When the Constitution was
written,) there was a holy Roman
emperor, Venice was a republic, France was
ruled by a king, Russia by a czar and Great
Britain had only the barest beginnings of a democracy.
All these proud regimes and scores of others have
long since passed into history and among the world's
powers the only government that stands essentially unchanged
is the federal union put together in the 1780s . . .

John Gardner

Some men look at constitutions with sanctimonious reverence and deem them . . . too sacred to be touched . . . But I know also that laws and institutions must go hand in hand with the progress of the human mind . . . Each generation . . . has (the) right to choose for itself the form of government it believes the most promotive of its own happiness.

Thomas Jefferson

Scarcely any political question arises in the United States that is not resolved, sooner or later, into a judicial question.

Alexis de Tocqueville

A desegregated classroom.

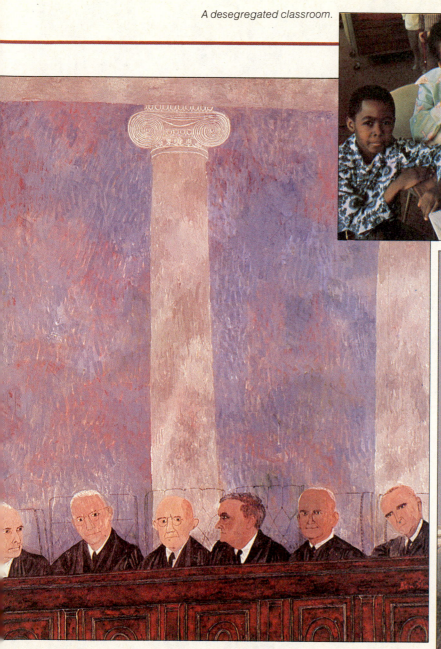

Above: The 1954 Warren Court. Right: Demonstrators seek to overturn the Supreme Court's 1973 decision permitting abortion.

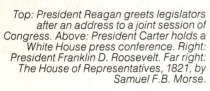

Top: President Reagan greets legislators after an address to a joint session of Congress. Above: President Carter holds a White House press conference. Right: President Franklin D. Roosevelt. Far right: The House of Representatives, 1821, by Samuel F.B. Morse.

The President of the United States was intended by the makers of the Constitution to be a reformed and standardized King, after the Whig model; and Congress was meant to be a reformed and properly regulated parliament. But both President and Congress have broken from the mold and adapted themselves to circumstances, after a thoroughly American fashion. . . .

Woodrow Wilson

bank was a competitor of several large state banks. When its charter came up for renewal in 1811, Congress did not vote for it. Over the years, intense political resistance had gradually built up. As has often been the case in the United States, the resistance arose over political and economic concerns. Professor Carl B. Swisher described such contexts with regard to the first United States Bank:

In spite of the services which it rendered, the bank faced much opposition. A great deal of the stock was owned in England. Although only citizens of the United States could be directors of the bank, substantial profits flowed out to the foreign stockholders. . . . The bank was regarded as an instrument by which the resources of the United States were drained away to foreign creditors. Furthermore, although control of the bank was in the hands of citizens of the United States, those citizens were largely Federalists. In the eyes of many Republicans this fact alone was enough to justify condemnation of the bank.

The Bank of the United States had competitors and influential opponents, furthermore, in the large number of state banks which had been established since 1791. These banks sought the privilege of serving as government depositories, and hoped to see their own bank notes circulate widely in place of those of the national bank.[1]

When the War of 1812 came, there was no national bank to provide financial support, and this put a heavy strain on the state banking system: "... the state banks suspended specie payments, and their notes circulated at depreciated figures, varying in terms of institutions and the distance from the banks of issue at which the notes were offered. . . . Because those notes lost much of their value when moved from the vicinity of the issuing bank, the government was able to transfer money from one section of the country to another

only at the expense of a high depreciation cost.''[2]

Finally, a second national bank was established in 1816. But the states persisted in their opposition. The state of Maryland imposed a tax of $15,000 per year on the branch of the national bank doing business in Maryland. The cashier of the bank, James W. McCulloch, refused to pay the tax, and Maryland sued—*McCulloch* v. *Maryland*.[3]

The state's argument was a simple one: the Constitution did not expressly authorize Congress to establish a national bank, therefore such a bank was unconstitutional.

Of course, in the Supreme Court, arguments are based not on politics and economics, but on the language of the Constitution. The national government defended the bank as a reasonable exercise of Congressional power under the elastic clause. These arguments did not originate in 1819, the year the case was decided. Hamilton and others had made the same points years before. But now the Supreme Court, presided over by Chief Justice John Marshall, a Federalist, would rule on the matter and presumably put the issue to rest. This was a "case and controversy to which the United States" was a party, thus, the "judicial power" of the Supreme Court was applicable.

The Supreme Court decided that the establishment of a national bank was, indeed, an act that came within the "necessary and proper" clause of the Constitution. It was a power that could be *implied* from the other grants of power. Marshall wrote:

Among the enumerated powers, we do not find that of establishing a bank or creating a corporation. But there is no phrase in the instrument which, like the Articles of Confederation, excludes incidental or implied powers; and which requires that everything granted shall be expressly and minutely described. . . . Although, among the enumerated powers of government, we do not find the word "bank" or "corporation," we find the great powers to lay and collect taxes; to borrow money; to regulate commerce; to declare and conduct a war; and to raise and support armies and navies. . . . It may with great reason be contended that a government entrusted with such ample powers . . . must also be entrusted with ample means for their execution.[4]

Therefore, a national bank could be established under the implied powers of the Constitution. (Later in this chapter we will discuss whether the state of Maryland could tax the bank.)

Some powers are neither express nor implied, but nevertheless they may exist. These are called **inherent powers.** That is to say, simply because of the nature of a given office, certain powers are seen to attach to it. This was discussed in a Supreme Court case in 1936, *United States* v. *Curtiss-Wright.*[5]

The first Bank of the United States, Philadelphia, Pennsylvania, 1799.

Congress had given the President the right to prohibit the sale of military weapons to warring countries in South America. One complainant argued that this was an unconstitutional delegation of legislative authority to the executive; perhaps, if this were a domestic matter, the Supreme Court held. But in matters of foreign relations, the national government will have certain *inherent* powers simply because it *is* the national government and must take responsibility for international relations. The Court held that giving the President such authority was understandable because of the special role of the President in dealing with foreign countries. If Congress wanted to make that role easier to perform, the Court would not stand in the way by a narrow reading of the Constitution.

Once again, the political environment figures strongly in a Court decision. The *Curtiss-Wright* case was argued in the 1930s. The country was

thoroughly preoccupied by the economic depression at home; little attention was given to foreign matters. A strong presidency (even in domestic affairs) was becoming an accepted part of American political life. The Court was willing to give Congress considerable leeway in delegating the conduct of foreign affairs to the President. The concept of separation of powers seemed relatively unimportant in the area of foreign policy. But forty years later, with the country in the throes of the Vietnam War, the political atmosphere had changed. Congress passed the War Powers Act of 1973 in an attempt to restrict the exercise of presidential power in international affairs. The legitimacy of the act was based on the same idea as the decision in the *Curtiss-Wright* case, namely, that the national government has *inherent* power to conduct foreign affairs. Whether this power resides primarily in the office of the President or in

Congress depends largely on the political circumstances.

Any discussion of federalism must make mention of the **supremacy clause.** Earlier, we said the two levels of government were ''coequal.'' In the sense that neither can be abolished by the other, this is true. But the Constitution (in Article 6) clearly indicates that if state laws conflict with the Constitution or with national laws, then the states must yield.

The Constitution and state government powers. There have been a few occasions in the history of American federalism when vehement arguments have been made challenging the concept of national supremacy. This challenge began as early as 1798 and continued into the 1950s. It has been associated with the terms *nullification* or *interposition*. Basically, proponents of nullification claim that the states are sovereign entities, that the Constitution was formed by citizens *of the states* and not by citizens acting individually. Therefore, if the national government performs an act that the various states deem contrary to the Constitution, the states can decide whether to disobey that act and declare it null and void.

This position received its most articulate formulation in the writings of John C. Calhoun in the nineteenth century, first in opposition to a protective tariff passed by Congress and then in regard to certain policies relating to slavery. In both instances, Calhoun saw national policies infringing on the sovereign powers of the southern states, especially those of his own state of South Carolina.

One hundred years later, in 1956, ninety-six southern senators and representatives signed a statement called *The Southern Manifesto: Declaration of Constitutional Principles*. The statement specifically objected to the Supreme Court's 1954

John C. Calhoun, leading figure in the pre-Civil War controversy over slavery and advocate of the nullification *doctrine and states' rights.*

decision outlawing racial segregation in the public schools. The southerners stopped short of calling for nullification, but they made it clear that they believed the Supreme Court had gone beyond the legitimate exercise of constitutional authority. The statement read, in part:

We regard the decision of the Supreme Court in the school cases as a clear abuse of judicial power. . . . The original Constitution does not mention education. Neither does the 14th amendment nor any other amendment. . . . We decry the Supreme Court's encroachments on rights reserved to the States and to the people, contrary to established law, and to the Constitution.[6]

Proponents of this constitutional position have always relied on the language in the Tenth Amendment to the Constitution, the "states' rights" amendment. Adopted along with the first nine amendments during the first Congressional session, this amendment reads:

The powers not delegated to the United States by the Constitution, nor prohibited by it to the States, are reserved to the States respectively, or to the people.

Many have interpreted this to mean that the states or the citizens have all powers not granted to the national government. *The Southern Manifesto* contended that since power over education was not mentioned in the Constitution, it must be "reserved" to the states. As with other political questions, however, the matter is not so simple.

In the early part of this century, a dispute arose over migratory birds that flew south from Canada to the southern United States. At first, Congress attempted to regulate by law the times such birds could be killed. This law was declared unconstitutional by two lower federal courts on the grounds that the states, not the national government, had authority over the birds while they flew over state territory. Subsequently, the American government entered into a treaty with Great Britain regulating the shooting of the birds, and Congress then passed another law enforcing that treaty. The state of Missouri objected on Tenth Amendment grounds. The case, *Missouri* v. *Holland* (1920), was decided by the Supreme Court in favor of the national government. Justice Oliver Wendell Holmes, Jr., wrote the Court's opinion. He held that here was "a national interest of very nearly the first magnitude" which could be protected "only by national action in concert with that of another power." It is useful to cite Holmes' language about the Tenth Amendment. He wrote:

The case before us must be considered in the light of our whole experience, and not merely in that of what was said a hundred years ago. The treaty in question does not contravene any

prohibitory words to be found in the Constitution. The only question is whether it is forbidden by some invisible radiation from the general terms of the Tenth Amendment. We must consider what this country has become in deciding what that amendment has reserved.[7]

The Supreme Court felt that conditions at the time required national government action to protect the migratory birds. The Tenth Amendment's "reserve powers" language did not apply. (We will have more to say about the Supreme Court's role in interpreting the Constitution in chapter 12.)

There are many areas of activity that lie within the purview of state control. States run educational systems (or permit their localities to do so); they have considerable power over criminal laws, health services, roads and highways, recreational lands, and, of course, they can impose taxes on

Sorry, but all my power's been turned back to the states.

Drawing by Lorenz © 1981. The New Yorker Magazine, Inc.

The federal government sometimes exercises control over issues directly affecting the states. In recent years, a controversy has developed over use of public lands in Alaska. Many conservationists and environmental groups believe that thousands of acres of federally protected wilderness areas should be closed to developers and commercial interests. Others feel that some limited develoment, especially exploration for new energy sources, should be allowed. Left: McKinley Park, Alaska. Right: A hydraulic mining unit at Dutch Mills, Alaska.

their citizens. States can charter corporations and regulate the insurance industry. They have power over many aspects of the banking industry as well as the industries supplying electricity and other energy resources. Not all of these activities come under the exclusive control of states, but in many instances their leeway to act is great.

A constant concern in a federal system involves the question of **concurrent powers.** These are powers that both levels of government can exercise at the same time over the same subject. For example, both levels can and do impose taxes on gasoline used in motor vehicles; both can and do impose taxes on a person's income.

There are also some areas where the states cannot operate because the national government has already "preempted" the field so that it would not be useful for the states also to act. Likewise, if the national government has not acted in a particular area, perhaps the states will be prohibited simply because of the nature of the problem. To

permit state action in such a situation would conceivably create confusion and conflict. This would be especially true in matters of interstate commerce, where state action might impose an "undue burden" on commerce. Ultimately, any final decision would have to be made by the Supreme Court.

Under no circumstances would state action that conflicts with a lawful action of the national government be permitted. We saw this in *McCulloch* v. *Maryland.* There, the Court said the national government had a right to establish a bank. The state of Maryland was not then permitted to tax that bank. Chief Justice John Marshall, in effect, said that the power to tax is the power to destroy, and to allow such action put the national government at the mercy of the states.

We will have more to say about concurrent powers in the next chapter when we discuss how the two levels of government interact and how they preside over the same areas and subjects. There is

not, as we shall see, a sharp line of demarcation between what the national government can do and what is done at the state and local levels. Even where the national government has the power to act, efforts are often made to defer, to the extent possible, first to state and local action.

We can turn again to our energy case study to illustrate this point. You will recall that after President Carter returned from Camp David to make his Sunday night speech on television, his next stop the following day was in Kansas City, Missouri, to address the convention of the National Association of Counties. This was a meeting of several thousand county and other local officials. One would expect to find some reference to the federal nature of our governmental system, and, indeed, in the President's speech he referred to the concept of concurrent powers:

I urge the Congress to give me power to set mandatory state-by-state conservation goals and to impose mandatory conservation if a state fails to meet its target. I want to give local and state officials authority first and hope that all of you and all governors will carry out this responsibility. If you do not, then I will act from Washington as President.[8]

There is a strong belief today that the national government has clearly won out in its perennial jurisdictional battles with the states. Since the enormous growth of the national government beginning with the New Deal in the 1930s, it seems that, under the federal system, the national government can do almost anything it chooses. There are strong reasons for this view, but let us withhold judgment for now—at least until we look more closely at the matter in the next chapter.

The federal Constitution and interstate relations. Sometimes we refer to relations between the national government and the states as ''vertical federalism,'' implying that the national government in some sense stands *above* the state governments. The relations among the states as defined by the Constitution are referred to under the term "horizontal federalism."

It was important to the framers that the states be on equal footing with each other. They certainly did not want to create a situation whereby the various states had unequal legal or political standing in the body politic. In chapter 1 we saw how this was treated in providing representation in Congress through The Great Compromise.

Article 4 of the Constitution contains three provisions relating directly to "horizontal federalism."

First, each state must give "full faith and credit" to the "public acts, records and Judicial proceedings of every other state." This does not mean that if one state grants a divorce to people living in another state, the latter *must* recognize that divorce decree.[9] If the first state deems that the divorce-granting state did not have legitimate jurisdiction over one of the parties, then the decree does not have to be honored.

Second, each state must extend "all privileges and immunities" to citizens of other states that it extends to its own citizens. But this does not mean that a state cannot, for instance, charge out-of-state residents a higher fee for attending its colleges and universities than it charges its own citizens. Or that a state cannot limit use of its facilities (for example, fishing lakes, beaches) to its own citizens. In other words, a state *can* make such distinctions in the exercise of its "police powers." These are powers used to protect the "health, welfare, and safety" of its own citizens and are considered reasonable exercises of state powers, unlike, for instance, prohibiting out-of-state citizens from moving into the state, doing business there, and so forth.

Third, the Constitution, in Article 4, provides for **extradition.** If a person in one state flees to another state to avoid prosecution for a crime, the original state is entitled "on demand" to have the fugitive returned. The governor of the second state, however, can decide not to honor the demand if it appears the fugitive will not be treated fairly after being returned. Likewise, the Supreme Court has held that the second state should not really be subject to the demand (*request*, perhaps, but not demand) of another state. This would make one state subordinate to another. The language of the Constitution clearly seeks to establish the states as coequal partners. To an extent it succeeds. But in practice, if the language were applied literally, in any given instance one state might not be able to protect its interests in relation to another state. In such cases, we must rely on judicial interpretation. This might cause uncertainty about how particular cases will be decided, but the basic constitutional principles are still there to serve as general guidelines.

There is considerable contact between and cooperation among the states. Most of this results in "interstate compacts" whereby the states agree to work together on particular projects. These formal arrangements must be agreed to by the national government, and most of the time they operate smoothly and to the benefit of all parties. There are also a number of instances (which will be discussed in the next chapter) where the states cooperate on an informal and political basis for their mutual self-interest.

The most serious battles between states today do not occur over their constitutional relations. Rather, disputes usually arise over essentially economic matters. This means that differences are likely to be resolved in the political arenas of the halls of Congress and in the executive branch, rather than in the courts. In these matters as in others, the states can be and are coequal partners in the federal system with each other and with the national government.

The Structure of State Governments

Each state has a governor who is generally well known throughout the state (many of the other state officials—executive and legislative—are frequently less well known), but the powers of the gubernatorial office vary from state to state. Though better known than other officeholders, the governor still must share executive powers with other elected officials, such as the lieutenant governor (a sort of vice-president of the state), attorney general, and secretary of state (who is basically a record-keeper and license-issuer). Today, thirty-nine states provide four-year terms for the governor; the others, two-year terms. In some states, especially in the South, governors cannot succeed themselves; in others they can serve no more than two terms consecutively.

The governor has the responsibility for preparing the state budget, which must be approved by the state legislature. The governor also has the power of veto, an important power in most states. (Only the governor of North Carolina does not have veto power.)[10] In forty-one states, governors have the power of "item veto," which even the President of the United States does not have. This means that the governor can reject only a part of a bill, if he or she wishes, and approve the remainder. Professor Charles R. Adrian has noted:

> The power of the veto and the threat of its use lies in the fact that in most states it is very difficult to override one; the issue must usually be raised in the next political campaign, if it is to be raised at all. Not a single veto was overridden in Minnesota between 1858 and 1935, for example; only one in Pennsylvania in the first half of the twentieth century; only four in Iowa in over a century; and only two in California since 1945.[11]

State legislatures have undergone changes in recent decades. Once, these bodies met only every two years and then for no more than ninety days. But state business has increased, and now the trend is toward annual sessions which can last up to six months (with the possibility of special sessions called by the governor). The pay for such service is generally low, but this has been changing also.

President Carter addresses an audience of northeastern governors.

COALITION OF NORTHEASTERN GOVERNORS *Welcomes* PRESIDENT CARTER

Ella Grasso announces that she will seek the Democratic nomination for governor of Connecticut, 1974.

appeal or superior courts (titles vary) which hear cases brought to them from the lower courts; and the highest state court, the Supreme Court (called the "Court of Appeals" in New York, Kentucky, and Maryland). This top court normally hears only those cases which are appealed to it from below.

Earlier, in the nineteenth century, most state court judges were elected, and their terms varied from two to four years. Today, most state court judges are appointed by the governor. This has been seen as a move to "depoliticize" the judiciary, but it has met with questionable success, since in many places appointments are still based on political partisanship.

Existing alongside these formal state governmental structures is the political party apparatus. (See chapter 6.) Generally, the governor stands at the head of the party in the state and is expected to work closely with the state party chairperson, who in turn should be in close contact with party leaders at the county and city levels. At times, however, squabbles break out among the government officials and the party leaders, often not so much over policies as over patronage. The party people, understandably, want as many appointive jobs as possible to give to the party faithful. The officials have additional interests to keep in mind.

At one time, when state political parties were more influential in nominating presidential candidates (before the days of open primaries and television), governors were very important figures at national party conventions. They frequently came with a bloc of state delegate votes, and they bargained with the candidates. Also, more governors ran as "favorite sons" from their states. This made governors from the large states especially powerful in national party politics. For reasons to be elaborated in chapter 6, that role has diminished. But states as political entities and governors as their chief executives are still important in the federal system.

Although California clearly leads the field, paying its state legislators about $50,000 per year in salaries and benefits, most legislators receive less than half that amount. Most state legislators in the lower chambers serve two-year terms; in the state senates, four-year terms.

State legislatures do their work through committees and, as could be expected, the chairpersons who are able to establish a close relationship with the governor usually exert considerable power. If they are members of the same political party, so much the better.

Each state has a court system with (normally) three levels of jurisdiction: the lower, trial courts in districts throughout the state; the courts of

We must remember that the states have a constitutional basis for their existence. Even if national officials and their counterparts at the local levels want to circumvent the states, in some cases it is constitutionally difficult to do so. In addition, many states do not have large, strong urban entities capable of exerting political pressure on the states. Most state legislatures are still dominated by the rural districts, and the representatives these people send to Congress come from these districts. Thus, for constitutional and political reasons, the states have a reasonably secure position in the federal system.

Local Governments in the Federal System

Earlier in this chapter, we noted that the states had complete control over the subdivisions within their borders. These subdivisions consist of counties, cities, townships, villages, and towns, as well as special-purpose districts. In all, there are approximately 80,000 such subdivisions.

Each state has a legislature (and all but one, Nebraska, have two chambers) made up of representatives from local senatorial and assembly districts, elected locally. These elected officials represent their localities in the state capitols.

Undoubtedly the most visible local officials are the chief executives (mayors) of the large cities. They get the bulk of the media attention; they serve a larger number of constituents; they have larger budgets than other units. (In fact, the annual budget of the city of New York is larger than that of the state of New York.) Yet the officials of the other local units also wield considerable power.

To determine exactly how much formal power the officials have, it is necessary to examine the charter of each subdivision. Some mayors, for instance, have power to choose other executives, veto local bills, appoint minor officials, and pre-

Soldiers escort black students to classes at Central High School in Little Rock, Arkansas, 1957. When local authorities refused to obey a federal court order to integrate the school, President Eisenhower sent federal troops to enforce the order.

pare budgets. Some localities are managed by a local commission and a professional city manager, in which case the role of the mayor is mainly ceremonial. Some cities are granted what is called ''home rule'' by their states, which means that the cities have substantial authority over the day-to-day lives of their citizens. The localities can control certain important matters such as zoning (in which such matters are determined as factory locations, the legal sizes of home lots, the minimum distance of homes from the street), health and fire regulations, and the hiring of local public service employees.

In addition to a state judicial system, virtually every local government has power to operate a court system with jurisdiction over certain criminal and civil cases.

Although most of the money raised by local governments comes from property taxes, some

cities and counties also have the authority to impose sales and income taxes.

With the vast increase of federal and state involvement in social services over the last several decades (as we shall see in chapter 3), many local programs are administered by people employed by the localities.

The local governments are still important focal points for political activity. Certain activists may have never been to Washington, D.C., or seen Congress in operation, but they have served on local school boards, or they have implored their local city council to put a stop sign on a corner or fix a pothole in the street. Whether a local area has a decent library or an efficient garbage collection system or good police protection depends in large measure on the attention paid by local citizens to local government.

Summary

1. As a "federal system," the American government divides power between a national government and several state governments. The two levels are constitutionally independent of each other. In a confederation, a weak national government presides over a loose association of strong states, whereas, in a unitary system, the national government has complete power over all governmental subunits.

2. The national government has delegated powers which can be express or implied, while states have all powers not delegated to the national government or denied to the states. There are instances where the two levels of government can exercise authority at the same time over the same subject, and this is known as exercising concurrent powers. Where there is a dispute or conflict, the national governmental laws are considered supreme, and in instances of disagreement, the Supreme Court makes the final determination, based on its interpretation of the Constitution.

3. The Constitution seeks to make the states equal in their relations with each other by having the states respect certain acts and the rights of citizens of each state. But in order to insure equal footing, sometimes it is necessary for the Supreme Court to interpret the literal language of the Constitution in ways that appear contrary to its meaning. In all instances, however, the sovereignty of each state in relation to the others is the main principle to be observed.

4. State governments remain important in the federal system for both constitutional and political reasons. The powers of governors vary, but all governors exert considerable influence over state budgets and legislation.

5. Local governments, as subdivisions within the states, are completely subordinate to their respective state governments, but some are granted important powers affecting the daily lives of their citizens. Local governments serve as important units of direct contact with local residents in such matters as education, police protection, fire protection, housing, and countless other matters having direct bearing on day-to-day life.

Notes

1. Carl Brent Swisher, *American Constitutional Development* (Cambridge, Mass: Houghton Mifflin Company, 1954), p. 169.
2. Ibid., p. 172.
3. *McCulloch* v. *Maryland*, 4 Wheaton 316 (1819).
4. Ibid.
5. *United States* v. *Curtiss-Wright Export Corporation*, 299 U.S. 304 (1936).
6. Cited in the *New York Times*, March 12, 1956, p. 19.
7. *Missouri* v. *Holland*, 252 U.S. 416 (1920).
8. Quoted in the *New York Times*, July 17, 1979, p. 1.
9. *Williams* v. *North Carolina*, 325 U.S. 226 (1945).
10. Charles R. Adrian, *Governing Our Fifty States and Their Communities* (New York: McGraw-Hill Book Company, 1978), p. 64.
11. Ibid.

The
Federal System:
Development and Operation

Chapter
3

During one eventful, traumatic week in May 1980, three distinct events took place in different parts of the country. These events involved the intense interplay of national, state, and local governments. Each event captured front-page headlines and demonstrated precisely the role of American federalism in contemporary life. Newspaper headlines depicted the developments:

Florida

Guard Reinforced to Curb Miami Riot; 15 Dead Over 3 Days

Civiletti Dispatched to City

Attorney General To Seek To Calm Black Areas—Arrests of 700 Reported By The Police

Miami Declared Disaster Area

New York State

Homeowners At Love Canal Hold 2 Officials Until F.B.I. Intervenes

President Orders Emergency Help For Love Canal

Residents at Love Canal Confused on U.S. Action

State Asked U.S. In '79 For Study On Love Canal, But Plan Was Rejected as Too Limited in Scope

Study Says U.S. Dumped Wastes Into Love Canal

Washington State

At Least 7 Dead as Peak Erupts; Worst Blast Yet

Mt. St. Helens Pours Its Cloud of Ashes Across Northwest

Carter Tours Volcano Area and Promises Federal Aid

Race riots in Miami, Florida; toxic chemicals threatening the health of local residents in upstate New York; a volcanic eruption in Washington state—all elicited immediate federal response in some form. In the first instance, the *national* guard was called in, and the Attorney General of the United States (the country's highest ranking law enforcement officer) went immediately to begin an investigation into the causes of the rioting and looting. In the second case, the federal government announced that aid would be extended to local homeowners and residents anxious to move out of the supposedly contaminated area, at least temporarily. The federal government, operating on the basis of a declared ''emergency,'' offered to pay the costs for families moving temporarily into motels and hotels outside the area. Some homeowners wanted the national government to buy their homes outright, because, as one local citizen put it, ''the state did not have the money and the federal government could afford to do so.'' In the third case, the President of the United States flew over the volcanic mountain and, after declaring the region a ''disaster area,'' promised the state financial assistance in recovering from the devastating eruption. Incidentally, whether the designation is ''emergency'' or ''disaster'' is important in determining the type and amount of assistance the federal government can give.

These events did not provoke extended debates about constitutional powers of the respective governmental entities. They were crises which caused, in each instance, local authorities and citizens to turn to the national government for assistance. The particular roots of the crises were not important. In Miami, the initial catalyst was a local court decision to acquit four white police officers charged with killing a local black citizen. In Love Canal, New York, the toxic chemicals were allegedly buried by both a private chemical company and the national government. And in Washington, the volcano was an act of nature. Initial blame was not in question.

Whatever the constitutional theories of federalism concerning the division of power, in these instances the theories yielded to the realities. State and local people wanted action, not excuses. They wanted the *national* guard to come to Miami and help the local police enforce a curfew to stop the racial violence. They wanted the agencies of the *national* government to purchase the homes of local citizens so they would not end up losing their life's earnings or be forced to live in a community many believed imminently hazardous to their health. They wanted federal money to help rebuild farms, roads, homes, entire towns virtually buried and destroyed by the volcano in the Northwest.

There were laws covering all these instances, and, in effect, laws permitting federal government action cut across the boundaries of theoretical federalism.

As we noted in chapter 2, the Constitution is a convenient starting place for understanding the complex structure called "the federal system." We can examine the language of that document; we can study what the courts have said about the constitutional rights of the distinct levels of government. But we must always keep in mind that politics and practices are not exclusively contained within the boundaries of a written constitution. This can be no more vividly demonstrated than by the history of federalism in the United States.

Indeed, we might paraphrase Mr. Justice Holmes' language on interpreting the Tenth Amendment and say that if we want to get a fuller picture of American federalism, we must attempt to understand the economic and political develop-

The theoretical division of power between local and federal governments often yields to the realities of emergency situations and natural disasters. Above: Mount St. Helens erupts—and an entire region is declared a disaster area, making it eligible for federal relief funds. Right, top: The National Guard is called in to assist the Miami police force in Miami riots, May 1980. Right, bottom: Contamination from toxic wastes dumped in Love Canal forced local residents to leave their homes. The federal government provided aid for their temporary relocation.

ments that have occurred in this country, certainly in the last one hundred years and particularly since the economic depression and the New Deal of the 1930s.

Who in 1787 would have imagined that one day a mayor of a city would say (as Joseph Alioto of San Francisco said in 1972): "No mayor can really do his job unless he spends at least one day per month in Washington."[1] Or who, a century ago, would have understood a 1968 city newspaper editorial that made the following statement: "The mayor lost press support because he spent too much time away from the city on his missions seeking federal aid."[2]

Things have changed. There are no neat lines of demarcation (if, indeed, there ever were) between the national, state, and local governments. Granted, the Constitution is still there to tell us, in some concrete instances, the powers that are delegated to the national government, and, by interpretation, the powers that are reserved to the states. And the Supreme Court occasionally says to the national government that it cannot exercise certain powers because they are reserved to the states. And there is no question that the federal system respects state boundaries in certain matters. For example, presidential candidates are keenly aware of the significance of distinct state electoral laws.

But we also know that policies made at the national level can and do have enormous impact on state and local governments as well as on the people who are citizens of those governments. We also know that social and economic changes over the past several decades have brought about the creation of new cabinet-level departments which attempt to deal with problems that had been earlier handled largely by the state and local governments, departments such as Health, Education, and Welfare (established in 1953 and changed in 1980 to Health and Human Services); Education (1980); and Housing and Urban Development (1965). Likewise, the relatively new Departments of Transportation and Energy reflect a vastly different economic environment and a growing trend toward national government involvement.

Of course, a variety of governmental institutions are involved in this process of policymaking between the national and local governments. A former assistant secretary of Housing and Urban Development, Donna E. Shalala, told a group of political scientists in 1980:

> It doesn't take an astute observer to realize that in Washington the life or death of cities has more to do with decisions made in State, Treasury, Transportation, the Federal Reserve and the Council of Economic Advisors than in HUD and HEW.[3]

Why should this be the case? In later chapters we discuss the various national institutions of government, and in part 4 we deal with policies made by those institutions. It is sufficient at this point to say that the lines of authority in American government run in many directions, crossing, overlapping, sometimes duplicating each other, sometimes contradicting each other. Those lines cross state and local boundaries; they even extend to private interest groups (officially and unofficially). The American system of federalism does not, in practice, resemble a layer cake. More properly, as one political scientist has aptly put it, it resembles a marble cake, with a variety of colors and textures and ingredients interpenetrating and overlapping throughout.[4]

What happened? How did it come to be that what started out as a political formula to divide power and to check potential abuse of government has developed to the point where governors and mayors routinely trek to Washington for help? How did it develop that officials in various national agencies are seen as having the power of "life or death" over cities?

Economic Growth and Political Developments

American federalism has reached its current state because the American economic system and American international involvement have grown so enormously. Industrialization in the nineteenth century brought with it the development of a national economy. Railroads pushed westward; factories shipped products nationally and internationally; the telephone and telegraph made national communication instantaneous. People living and working in big and little cities needed agricultural products grown or raised several states and thousands of miles away on big and little farms.

The depression of the 1930s was a national, not a state or local, economic crisis, and the New Deal measures of social security, unemployment compensation, labor laws, and other social programs enacted by Congress and the President applied to all the states. If remedies were to be effective, they had to be applied nationally, and this required an active national government. Farmers leaving the land in Oklahoma and making their way west with their families to California and north to Illinois and Michigan could not be helped very efficiently by local state laws.

American involvement in World War II and its subsequent permanent involvement in international affairs through treaty alliances and major defense expenditures required national mobilization and action. In addition, the national government had imposed an income tax which gave it far more economic resources than those possessed by any particular state or locality. Never again would the national government be relatively uninvolved in the daily lives of citizens living anywhere in the United States.

Governor Sanford of North Carolina put considerable emphasis on the Depression as a cause of state decline in the face of increasing national governmental involvement:

The Depression of the 1930s forced the nation to reach back for all its historic powers in political, wartime, constitutional, and fiscal experiences, and to convert them to massive action across the nation. As a number of emergencies in the 1780s removed the first layer of retained state sovereignty, so the Depression of the 1930s peeled off all the other layers right down to the core. Out of the ordeal of the Depression came damaging blows to the states. [5]

An even stronger statement concerning ineffectual state action in the face of economic necessity came from political scientist Richard H. Leach. Much of the problem lay with the states themselves, Leach concluded. Most states had long, unnecessarily detailed constitutions, covering too many specific subjects which were better left to state statutes. For example, the California constitution regulated the amount a state legislator should be reimbursed for use of an automobile while conducting official business; the Louisiana constitution had five pages on the powers of a parish (county) in acquiring and financing sewerage improvements.

The California constitution had 82,570 words; Louisiana, 253,830 words. In contrast, the U.S. Constitution had approximately 6000 words. Why was this relevant? A constitutional amendment is much more difficult to pass than a state law; therefore, Leach concluded:

The states contributed to their own eventual ineffectiveness first by the kind of constitutions they drew up. . . . State constitutions . . . work to slow down the rate at which states can meaningfully adjust to altered circumstances. . . . In earlier years, when life moved more slowly and there was less need for governmental involvement at every turn, a cumbersome state constitution made little difference, but today it is one of the prime reasons why the national government has been called on so often when

The involvement of the national government in our lives is often traced to the Great Depression, when the magnitude of the country's economic woes was too great for the state and local governments to handle. Federal grants were provided for such diverse activities as conservation work (left) and theatrical productions (right).

action has been necessary. Rather than supporting and facilitating state action, state constitutions hinder and obstruct it and thereby provide justification for national action.[6]

Given the growth of the American economy, however, even if the states had more flexible constitutions enabling them to adjust rapidly, they still would probably not have the economic capacity to meet the new demands. In a society of small family farms, little red schoolhouses, local markets, horses and buggies, perhaps they would. In a society of multinational corporations, large cities, jet airplanes, satellite communications, they clearly would not. The latter requires federal/national agencies of government, agencies that can cross state lines and fashion political responses commensurate with economic needs.

Federal Grants-in-Aid and Fiscal Federalism

From the beginning of the nation, the national government has given (or sold at a very low price) land to the states, private citizens, and corporations. In the 1780s, land was donated to the states to establish schools, and land was given to settlers. Land was sold cheaply to private enterprises to build canals, roads, and, later, railroads. Objections were sometimes raised on constitutional grounds, and sometimes those objections prevailed, but only for a time.

One notable example occurred in 1854 when President Franklin Pierce vetoed a bill "making a grant of public lands to the several states for the benefit of indigent insane persons." He felt this exceeded the constitutional authority of the nation-

al government. A few years later, in 1857, President James Buchanan vetoed a bill attempting to donate land to the states which would be used for colleges of agriculture and mechanical arts.

Eighteen sixty-two was indeed a very good year for land recipients—states as well as private citizens. Not only did Congress establish a Department of Agriculture that year, it also passed the Homestead Act and the Morrill Act. The Homestead Act made available to settlers up to 160 acres of land after five years of occupancy and the payment of a small fee. Railroads also received generous grants of public land. The Morrill Act accomplished what President Buchanan had vetoed just five years before. It donated land to the states to provide for the establishment of educational programs in agriculture and mechanical arts.

These schools became known as "land grant colleges," and many of them today are designated by the "A and M" in their names. Today, every state has a school or program as a result of this legislation, which was sponsored by Senator Justin S. Morrill of Vermont. There were strings attached, however. No part of the funds received by the states from the sale of federal land could be used for buildings; thus the states had to find other sources for that purpose. In a way, this was a form of "matching," which we shall discuss in a moment.

Throughout the latter nineteenth and early twentieth centuries, federal grants-in-aid, as these programs were called, for the most part covered such needs as highway construction and agricultural and technical training. They were not especially large, but they were quite useful to the states. Because they went for specific purposes, they were labeled **categorical grants**. Beginning with the New Deal, these grants were increased substantially and covered social service programs for various groups, such as the elderly, families with dependent children, and others in need of welfare assistance. The states were not required to take the money, of course, but the offer was so attractive that in most cases it was hard to refuse. And the states were often able to administer the programs subject to relatively minimal controls from the national government. In many instances, the states would be required to *match* the federal grant—usually on a basis such as one dollar for every four dollars received. The matching did not always have to be in dollars. Other forms of resources, called *in-kind* services, could be used. That is, the state or locality might provide the building or office space or a certain number of vehicles or a certain quantity of equipment to be used in administering the program.

Some critics of these programs complained that the grants tied the hands of the state and local governments, and extended the "long arm" of the national government into local domains in violation of the principle of federalism. But the national government did not impose many conditions for receipt of the money, and categorical grants were favored by members of Congress and executive agencies. These programs could be rather easily monitored from Washington, and, as we shall discuss later, it was a prevalent practice to set up an agency at the state and local levels to work with officials at the national level. In addition, the individual national legislators could be more active

Homesteaders, ready to stake their claims on land in Oklahoma parceled out by the federal government, assemble at the starting line (1893).

in getting specific projects for their home districts and in taking credit for doing so—no small consideration come election time.

Another form of federal aid, called the **block grant**, has also come into wide use. This is a broad grant that combines several specific categories under one general subject matter or issue. Block grants are often seen as providing more efficiency in administration and more control at the state and local levels.

While localities have to submit specific project proposals to qualify for categorical grants, block grants are issued normally on the basis of a formula worked out by Congress. Of course, a general plan or proposal stating how the funds are to be used is required, but it need not be as detailed as are proposals for categorical grants. To qualify, for instance, for funds under the Community Development Block Grant (1974), a locality has to fall within certain formula guidelines: so many low-income residents, a certain percentage of its housing of certain age and condition, and so on. The CDBG combined a number of previous categorical grants: urban renewal, model cities, neighborhood facilities, rehabilitation loans, and public facility loans.

The block grant was part of President Nixon's "New Federalism" (also referred to as "special revenue sharing"). President Gerald Ford continued the policy. When Ford signed the Housing and Community Development Act of 1974, he said: "In a very real sense, this bill will help to return power from the banks of the Potomac to people in their own communities. Decisions will be made at the local level. Action will come at the local level. And responsibility for results will be placed squarely where it belongs—at the local level."[7] Thus, block grants were seen as devices for *decentralizing* decision-making power. The national government still retained some authority, as we shall see—far less authority than with categori-

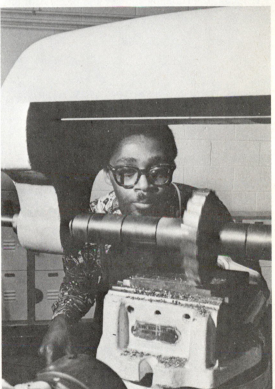

Top: Children at a federally supported Head Start program in San Francisco. Bottom: Federal job-training programs provide employment opportunities for many Americans.

cal grants, to be sure, but certainly more than with still another form of federal aid: **general revenue sharing**.

Also started under the Nixon Administration, general revenue sharing is a means of allocating funds to the states and localities, again on a formula basis emphasizing size of population and amount of taxes collected, with virtually no strings attached. The states receive one third of the funds; the subunits within the states receive two thirds. The local governments can use the money for any purposes whatsoever (unlike money distributed

through block grants, with their broad subject designations). The only restrictions relate to non-discriminatory use based on race, sex, religion, national origin, or physical handicap. And each recipient government must hold public hearings to permit citizens to voice their views on how the money should be spent. Incidentally, no part of the money can be used for purposes of lobbying in relation to revenue sharing. Of course, governors and mayors have generally favored revenue sharing: it gives them additional income to support their frequently strained budgets, and it gives them the widest possible latitude to use that income.

TABLE 1.
Historical Trend of Federal Grant-in-Aid Outlays.
(fiscal years; dollar amounts in millions)

| | Total grants-in-aid | Composition of Grants-in-Aid | | Federal grants as a percent of | | |
		Grants for payments to individuals	Other	Budget outlays		State and local expenditures
				Total	Domestic	
Five-year intervals:						
1950	$ 2,253	$ 1,257	$ 996	5.3%	8.8%	10.4%
1955	3,207	1,623	1,584	4.7	12.1	10.1
1960	7,020	2,479	4,541	7.6	15.9	14.7
1965	10,904	3,931	6,972	9.2	16.5	15.3
1970	24,014	9,023	14,991	12.2	21.1	19.4
1975	49,834	17,441	32,392	15.3	21.3	23.1
Annually:						
1976	59,093	21,023	38,070	16.1	21.7	24.4
1977	68,414	23,860	44,555	17.0	22.7	25.8
1978	77,889	25,981	51,908	17.3	22.9	26.4
1979	82,858	28,765	54,093	16.8	22.4	25.6
1980	91,472	34,174	57,298	15.8	21.1	26.3
1981 estimate	95,343	39,855	55,488	14.4	19.4	NA
1982 estimate	99,829	42,751	57,077	14.0	18.4	NA
1983 estimate	109,961	47,841	62,120	13.5	18.5	NA
1984 estimate	118,599	52,840	65,759	13.3	18.6	NA

NA = not available
Source: *Special Analysis, Budget of the United States Government, Fiscal Year 1982,* Office of Management and Budget, p. 250.

Therefore, if they had to choose between categorical grants and general revenue sharing, their decision would be rather obvious.

In 1980, the Census Bureau issued a report indicating how the states and local governments had spent the general revenue sharing funds they received during 1977–78. Most of the money was spent for education and police protection. In fact, nine states—California, Idaho, Illinois, Montana, Nevada, Oregon, Utah, Virginia, and Wisconsin—used their entire allotments for education during that period. The funds constituted a fairly sizeable percentage of the total expenditures of some cities: 10.8 percent for Baton Rouge, Louisiana; 9.7 percent for Miami; 7.8 percent for New Orleans; 6.4 percent for Pittsburgh; and 6.2 percent for El Paso, Texas. ''Overall, state and local governments spent $6.7 billion in general revenue sharing funds during the 1977–78 fiscal year,'' the Census Bureau reported. (See Figure 1 and Tables 1 and 2 for recent figures on federal grant distribution.)

What we have been describing in this section has been called **fiscal federalism.** This is the use of national tax dollars to aid state and local

TABLE 2.
Distribution of Grants by Region, Selected Fiscal Years.

Federal Region		1980[1] Total grants	Dollars per capita		Average annual percent increase, 1970–80
			1970	1980	
I:	Maine, Vermont, New Hampshire, Massachusetts, Connecticut, Rhode Island	$ 5.7	$119	$467	14.7%
II:	New York, New Jersey, Puerto Rico, Virgin Islands	14.1	120	502	15.0
III:	Virginia, Pennsylvania, Delaware, Maryland, West Virginia, District of Columbia	10.6	127	435	13.3
IV:	Kentucky, Tennessee, North Carolina, South Carolina, Georgia, Alabama, Mississippi, Florida	14.1	117	368	13.8
V:	Illinois, Indiana, Michigan, Ohio, Wisconsin, Minnesota	17.1	85	377	16.0
VI:	Arkansas, Louisiana, Oklahoma, New Mexico, Texas	8.2	127	328	11.9
VII:	Iowa, Kansas, Missouri, Nebraska	4.1	99	346	13.5
VIII:	Colorado, Montana, North Dakota, South Dakota, Utah, Wyoming	3.1	156	451	13.3
IX:	Arizona, California, Nevada, Hawaii, other territories	10.6	150	377	11.5
X:	Idaho, Oregon, Washington, Alaska	3.7	140	464	14.8
Total		91.5	117	400	13.8

[1]Preliminary estimate, in billions of dollars.
Source: *Special Analysis, Budget of The United States Government, Fiscal Year 1982,* Office of Management and Budget, p. 251.

FIGURE 1.
Federal Grants to State and Local Governments.

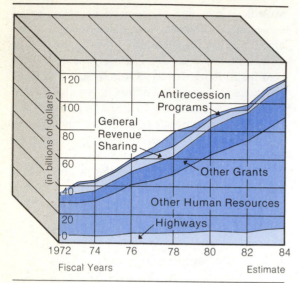

Source: *Special Analysis, Budget of the United States Government, Fiscal Year 1982*, Office of Management and Budget, p. 240.

governments and citizens in their communities. As we can see, economic needs at one level and economic resources at another combine to blur traditionally understood boundaries between state-local and national government. Fiscal federalism is one way of adapting theory to practice, of getting money to those who, presumably, need it most. Even here, however, the practice is not always entirely equitable. Sometimes the formulas do not precisely correspond to social and economic realities. The political problems that result are constantly fought out in the legislative and executive branches of government.

State and Local Governments as Lobbyists

In chapter 5 we discuss the organization and activity of interest groups, and our focus is on private organizations. But governments also have

their **lobbies**, that is, organizations that maintain offices, have full-time staffs in the nation's capital, hold annual conventions, and spend time representing the interests of cities, counties, and states in Congress and before executive bureaus and regulatory agencies.

The first such group to set up offices in Washington, D.C., was the United States Conference of Mayors in 1933, an organization which, interestingly, received the strong backing of newly inaugurated President Franklin D. Roosevelt. Roosevelt was building a strong political base among urban voters, and he and the mayors needed each other to push for national legislation "safeguarding the interests of cities."[8] Donald H. Haider wrote:

> *The Conference's specific goals as developed in the 1930s remain largely intact today: to expand direct federal-city programs, increase federal fiscal support for these programs, gain federal assumption of specific programs like public assistance, establish federal instrumentalities and safeguards for maintaining urban fiscal solvency—like tax-exemption on municipal bonds—and enhance the autonomy of cities as general-purpose units of government.*[9]

This organization later consolidated some of its activities with the National League of Cities, the latter organization (established in 1923) spending much of its time on research and policy analysis.

Another President Roosevelt—Theodore—was instrumental in getting the nation's governors organized as a lobbying group as far back as 1908. The National Governors' Conference (as it later came to be called) began meeting annually in 1910. The two long-standing agenda items consist of "greater federal sharing of national tax sources with the states and also the return to the states of certain ongoing federal-state programs."[10] The organization passes resolutions, and it has a full-time professional staff based in Washington, D.C., to lobby Congress and executive agencies. The staff keeps the governors informed about various pieces of proposed Congressional legislation important to the states.

When the NGC meets, as it did in July 1979, national officials from the President on down know it is important to appear before the group to inform it of proposed policies and to solicit the governors' support for whatever is on the administration's agenda. You will recall that Vice-President Mondale and Mrs. Carter represented President Carter at the 1979 Louisville meeting, and they made a strong pitch for support of the President in his soon-to-be-announced national energy policy. You will also recall that several governors, on their way to their annual meeting, stopped off at Camp David to consult with the President on the country's energy and economic problems. The efforts at influence go both ways.

County governments also have their organization. The National Association of Counties (NACO) was started in the 1930s. Initially concerned mainly with public works, public welfare programs, law enforcement, and tax collections, the organization has expanded its areas of interest as counties have become more involved in other matters. The problems of growing suburbs, housing, revenue sharing, waste disposal, highways, parks and recreation, and environmental and energy issues have come to occupy the attention of county governments. This is due in part to the movement of many Americans from the central cities and farms to outlying towns, creating a nation of millions living beyond crowded city boundaries but within the confines of vast metropolitan areas, with all the attendant problems of those areas. As with cities and states, the counties come in all sizes and have a variety of social problems. This means that NACO has to try to reconcile the many differences among its members as it represents the counties in the policymaking corridors of Washington.

Ronald Reagan, campaigning in the South Bronx, discusses his plans for federal tax-incentive programs aimed at revitalizing the inner city.

Governors from the states of Indiana, Delaware, Arkansas, Alabama, Ohio, Pennsylvania, Louisiana, and Texas meet with President Reagan in the White House, April 1981.

Some of the larger cities and most of the states maintain their own special staffs in Washington for the sole purpose of lobbying for goods and services to benefit their particular locales. Occasionally these staffs might work with the other groups, but that is not their primary function. They are there to serve the particular interest of the state or city which pays their salaries. Basically, they engage in "grantsmanship." That is, they help put together grant proposals to get funds under certain categorical programs. They will also lobby in Congress, but only when the matter is one of particular interest to their state or local employer. These staffs work closely with the senators and representatives from the state.

"Cooperative Feudalism" or "Representational Federalism"?

As we can see, the development of American federalism has left a system not so neatly divided into federal, state, and local units. As problems have crossed city, county, and state lines, so have the evolving governmental structures. Nor can we accurately describe the situation as one of centralization versus decentralization. It is true that the national government has expanded its arena of operation. It is also true that state and local governments have grown—in functions and in the number of people employed in public service. As Figure 2 indicates, employment at the state and local levels not only exceeds federal employment, it has also increased more rapidly than federal employment.

Does this mean that we have more centralized government or more decentralized government? Have block grants caused an increase in decision-making power at the local level? These are not easy questions to answer. Often the answer will depend on one's own ideological orientation. People who favor a strong national government are likely to look with disfavor on efforts to give more authority to the states and local governments. They will see local power groups unjustly dominating less powerful groups. Thus, they will see not enough power exerted at the national level, where, they feel, more coherent national policies can be and ought to be made. Political scientist Grant McConnell is one who distrusts so much emphasis on local, small units of governance. He observes: "In general, the liberty of individuals is more secure in a large constituency than in a small. Moreover, the larger the constituency, the more probable is it that the group is committed to equality; the narrower and more exclusive the group, the more probably will it be a defender of inequality."[11] Thus, McConnell believes that the American federal system and the interests of the American people as a national body are best served by *national* political institutions, namely, the national party system, the presidency, and other agencies of the national government.

Advocates of decreased national authority will not see *enough* decentralization, and they will lament "the long arm of Washington" reaching down to the states and local communities, exercising power in unwarranted (if not unconstitutional) ways. Decisions, they will contend, are best made locally by the people who know the problems best.

In putting together the New Federalism, Presi-

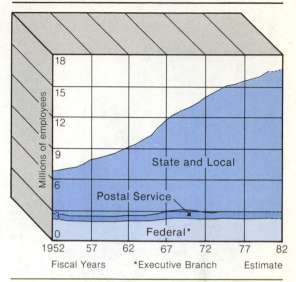

FIGURE 2.
Government Civilian Employment.

Source: *Special Analysis, Budget of the United States Government, Fiscal Year 1982,* Office of Management and Budget, p. 287.

dent Nixon, according to his one-time speech-writer, William Safire, wanted "to come to grips with a paradox, which is a need both for national unity and local diversity; a need to establish equality and fairness at the national level and uniqueness and innovation at the local level."[12] Thus Nixon implemented revenue sharing, which, interestingly, had been first conceived by two liberal Democratic economists in President John Kennedy's administration, Walter Heller and Joseph A. Pechman.

Since President Nixon's introduction of the plan, several studies have attempted to analyze the consequences of revenue sharing. Has it, in reality, returned "power to the people"? Two economists, Richard P. Nathan and Paul R. Dommel, have found that the national government (especial-

The state of Florida received help from the federal government to cope with the large influx of Cuban boat refugees in 1979. Here, a U.S. customs official meets with a refugee family.

ly through the Department of Housing and Urban Development in implementing the CDBG) still wields considerable influence. That influence, according to their study of the first two years of the program, was greater over small cities than large ones; greater over suburban governments than central cities; and greater in procedural matters than in substantive issues. Nathan and Dommel concluded: "Overall, the CDBG program has resulted in the decentralization of decision-making authority from the federal to the local level, compared with the older-style HUD categorical aid

programs. The general view of local officials at the end of two years was that they had more control over community development under the block grant than they did under the categorical programs. At the same time, there was a growing belief at the end of the second year that decentralization was being reduced."[13] Like many outcomes in American politics, the specific results appear to be mixed.

But when one looks at the operation of the categorical federal grants-in-aid, the picture, according to one political scientist, Harold Seidman, might be less than encouraging (depending, once again, on your ideology). The categorical grants are still numerous—approximately 442 administered by twenty-one federal departments and agencies, according to a 1977 report of the Advisory Commission on Intergovernmental Relations (a commission created by Congress in 1959 composed of public and private individuals that studies and issues reports on policies pertaining to relations among the various levels of government).

Seidman describes the situation as "cooperative *feudalism*." This results mainly from the "single-state-agency" requirement. Many federal programs call for administration at the state and local levels by specifically designated agencies. Frequently, these units bypass the chief executives of the states and localities, and operate in direct contact with their counterparts in Washington, D.C. They create vertically structured, vested interests. They are not really politically responsible to either local citizens or to a national constituency. They create highly specialized, professionalized, bureaucratized "guilds," and they operate in and over their own specific domain, excluding any and all others. Seidman concludes:

> *What we have in several important functional areas are largely self-governing professional guilds, or what the Advisory Commission on Intergovernmental Relations calls "vertical functional autocracies. . . ."*
> *. . . According to the Advisory Commission on Intergovernmental Relations, "about a quarter of Federal programs affecting urban development induce or even require special districts for their administration." Federally encouraged special districts include law enforcement districts, community action agencies, comprehensive health and area planning agencies, air quality regions, local development districts within the Appalachian area, and resource conservation development districts.*[14]

What is more, Seidman notes: "In contrast to governors and mayors, the guilds are supported by strong power bases within the federal establishment and have developed a close rapport with functionally oriented Congressional committees. They have the capacity to block or delay reform measures which they suspect contain hidden traps. As a result, progress in obtaining needed reforms has been painfully slow."[15]

Seidman does believe, however, that "block grants have the potential for containing the power of the guilds and eliminating some of the complexities and rigidities of the present system of categorical grants."[16] But he remains pessimistic that very much can or will be done to overcome this system of "cooperative feudalism." He comes close to the position of Grant McConnell in his description and assessment of American federalism.

In his address to the American Political Science Association in 1977, Professor Samuel H. Beer (president of the association) gave yet another analysis of American federalism. What has happened over the years, Beer concluded, is not necessarily greater centralization or greater decentralization. Rather, we have seen the various levels of government interacting more *with each other* and expanding their areas of mutual influence. We have seen the development of what Beer calls "representational federalism." The effects have been greater centralization *and* greater decentralization. The needs, concerns, and expertise of the national government have made contact with the peculiarities, interests, and diversities of the state and local governments. Categorical and other grants, to be sure, have created, as Seidman says, a new group of professionals, or "technocrats." Without question, they have formed influential intergovernmental lobbies. But they have their counterparts, the "topocrats." These people represent and speak for the various states and localities through some of the organizations mentioned earlier in this chapter: the National Governors' Conference, the United States Conference of Mayors, and the National Association of Counties. Technocrats and topocrats meet in the arena of federalism, and while they compete, they also cooperate. Beer sums up his analysis in the following way:

> In brief . . . I am saying that over the past generation and especially since the early sixties the technocratic tendencies of the new professionalism have called forth the topocratic tendencies of the intergovernmental lobby. If one asks whether the process has been centralizing or decentralizing the answer must be a bit complicated. It has been strongly centralizing insofar as the new programs have carried the technocratic perspectives formed at the federal level into the daily thought and action of state and local governments. It has been decentralizing in that these governments, as the administrative agents of the new programs, have often been able to adapt them to their own local purposes, an option that has been deliberately expanded by some loosening of federal strings. The process was centralizing in that it drew state and local office holders into direct contact with the federal government and decentralizing in that it has brought their topocratic perspectives to bear on federal policy making. The trend is not toward a centralized unitary system. Neither is there much sign of significantly greater autonomy for state or local governments.[17]

Beer's analysis provides an illustration of the theme of constancy/change in the American political system. The basic structure of American federalism remains intact, but policies and programs have created circumstances permitting or requiring the different levels of government to alter their relations with each other. They are no longer distinct units, each operating in its own exclusive sphere, uninfluenced by and uninvolved with the other.

Summary

1. The development of a national economy and the country's permanent international involvements have contributed to expanded national government activities, creating new political relationships within the federal system.

2. There are three basic types of federal grants-in-aids: categorical, block grant (special revenue sharing), and general revenue sharing. The latter two were instituted in the early 1970s, and they are based mostly on formulas devised by Congress which determine what communities receive federal assistance and how much. This is referred to as *fiscal federalism.*

3. States, counties, and cities have formal organizations as well as individual lobbyists who represent their interests in Washington and push for policies favorable to the states and localities.

4. Various observers disagree in their analyses of the development of federalism. Some believe American federalism has created exclusive, protective guilds of power to the detriment of less resourceful groups and especially harmful to the development of coherent, national policy. Others believe that American federalism has developed a new form of representation whereby the various levels of government effectively interact and influence each other.

Notes

1. Quoted in Donald H. Haider, *When Governments Come to Washington* (New York: The Free Press, 1974), p. 98.
2. Ibid.
3. Donna E. Shalala, ''Policy and Research: A Tough Combination,'' *P.S.,* Vol. 13, No. 2 (Spring 1980), 207.
4. Morton Grodzins in *The American System: A New View of Government in the United States*, Daniel J. Elazar, ed. (Chicago: Rand-McNally, 1966).
5. Terry Sanford, *Storm Over the States* (New York: McGraw-Hill, 1967), p. 21.

6. Richard H. Leach, *American Federalism* (New York: W.W. Norton & Company, Inc., 1970), p. 120.
7. Quoted in Richard P. Nathan and Paul R. Dommel, "Federal-Local Relations Under Block Grants," *Political Science Quarterly*, Vol. 93, No. 3 (Fall 1978), 422.
8. Haider, p. 2.
9. Ibid., p. 3.
10. Ibid., p. 21.
11. Grant McConnell, *Private Power and American Democracy* (New York: Alfred A. Knopf, 1966), p. 365.
12. William Safire, *Before the Fall, An Inside View of the Pre-Watergate White House* (New York: Doubleday & Company, Inc., 1975), p. 222.
13. Nathan and Dommel, 442.
14. Harold Seidman, *Politics, Position, and Power* (New York: Oxford University Press, 1980), pp. 176, 184.
15. Ibid., p. 193.
16. Ibid., p. 196.
17. Samuel H. Beer, "Federalism, Nationalism, and Democracy in America," *The American Political Science Review* (March 1978), 18–19.

Overview
The Framework of American Government

The Constitution of the United States—now almost 200 years old—was conceived as part of an effort to balance political liberty with socioeconomic order. It was the new nation's second attempt in less than ten years to fashion this kind of evenly balanced system. The framers of the document, mindful of their experiences under British rule and at the same time vexed by the inadequacies of the Articles of Confederation, wanted to construct a government that would be strong enough to govern and yet not so strong as to abuse the rights of its citizens. For the most part, the framers had a healthy distrust of government, believing that abuses of individual liberties would most likely stem from official actions. Therefore, the Constitution they drafted contained an elaborate system of checks and balances. Power was divided among three separate branches of government, though the system has evolved essentially into one of ''shared powers'' separately performed. In addition, a federal system was devised that granted constitutionally protected status to state governments, giving them powers not delegated to the central government. Thus, the framework was not a parliamentary system or a unitary system, as is found in many modern-day democratic states.

Such a system put a premium on the political processes of bargaining and compromise. If things were to get done, several different decision-makers would have to agree on the final results. A politics of consensus would be perceived as necessary, at least among those involved in the political process.

This has made the American political system both complex and slow-moving. The framers consciously sought to create a system wherein political decisions would be made cautiously and deliberately. In some instances, this can be a two-edged sword. In times of crisis, protracted debate and deliberation can hold up action that should be taken quickly and decisively. When the United States has faced a military crisis—war—or a major economic crisis—the Depression of the 1930s—this has not been a particularly serious problem. But for a nation faced with an energy crisis—as is the case with the United States in the 1980s—this can present formidable difficulties.

Though the national government has become increasingly involved in the economic affairs of the nation, the legitimacy of the separate states is still recognized. The states and their subdivisions (Congressional districts) are represented in Congress and cannot be overlooked or bullied—politically or constitutionally. At the same time, the Constitution stipulates that the national government will be supreme in any otherwise unresolvable conflict between the states and the central government.

Increasing economic activity of the national government has led to increased federal involvement with the states and localities. Through the transfer of funds from the federal treasury to assist in specific and general functions, the states and localities receive grants for such activities as education, police and fire protection, highways, recreation, job training, community development, and so forth. This form of ''fiscal federalism'' has substantially altered the theoretical structure of American government.

Duties, rights, and responsibilities have crossed state lines, and the courts have had to step in from time to time to referee jurisdictional disputes. In the process of interpreting the Constitution and deciding constitutional controversies, the courts have been a major source of adapting the Constitution to current circumstances. The decisions themselves have been, at times, very controversial, but the mediating role of the courts has been accepted in the governmental system.

Much has changed in American social and economic life, but the political institutions brought into existence almost 200 years ago in a written Constitution have endured. How the citizens and those institutions and that document function and adapt is the concern and attention of the remainder of this textbook.

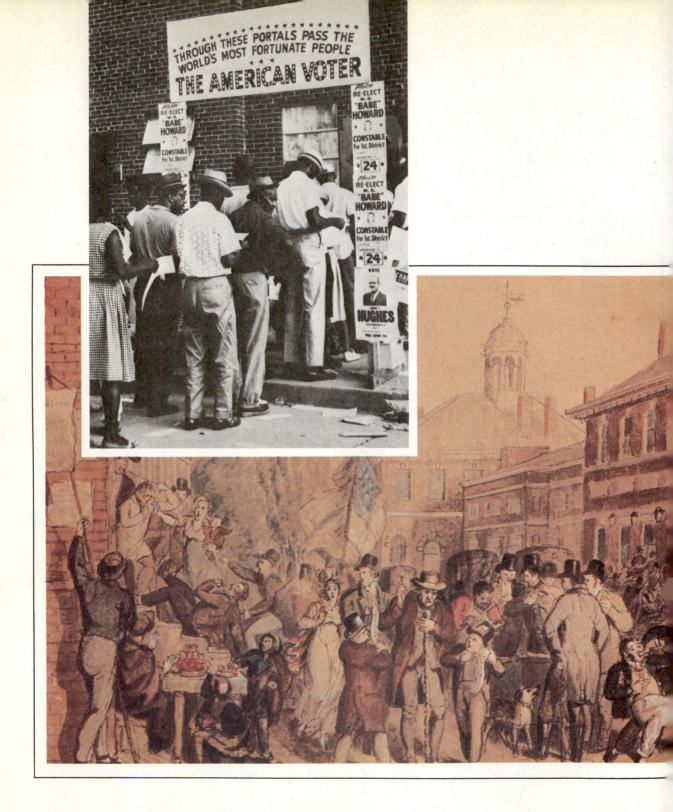

2

Political Participation

Larry Stammer

Protest at the Polls: Proposition 13 in California

June 6, 1978, was a day both widely celebrated and widely deplored. In Howard Jarvis's view, it marked the beginning of "a new American revolution."

That June 6 was a momentous day there is little doubt. But it was neither the beginning nor the end of the revolution proclaimed by Jarvis before an election-night throng of tax protestors who had signed, with their votes, a new manifesto called Proposition 13. Rather, it marked the midpoint of a long-simmering rebellion against what were perceived to be the establishment elites.

Proposition 13 was a protest against politicians and a declaration of distrust; it was a referendum on inflation and high taxes; it was a defense of hearth and home. It was a battle which drew together grocers and bakers, management and labor, Democrats and Republicans, homeowners and renters, social workers and welfare recipients, conservationists and developers, policemen and firemen, students and teachers.

It tested the political will of politicians from city halls throughout California to the state capitol in Sacramento. And because California was a microcosm of the American welfare state, the social and political implications of Proposition 13 would be felt as far as the halls of Congress and the house at 1600 Pennsylvania Avenue.

"We have a new revolution," the 75-year-old Jarvis bellowed before the network television cameras and the crush of supporters. "The message is clear. The government must be limited. We have a new revolution against these arrogant politicians and insensitive bureaucrats, whose philosophy is tax, tax, tax, spend, spend, spend, and elect, elect, elect!"

Finally, it was the culmination of an election campaign and the beginning of a struggle to reshape assumptions which for years had guided public policy in California.

A year earlier, few could have predicted that voters would join ranks behind a measure of the magnitude and political complexity of Proposition 13. There had been protests against high property taxes, to be sure. But these efforts were for the most part unorganized and politically impotent. Property-tax-limitation initiatives on the state ballot in 1968 and 1972 had failed. Governor Ronald Reagan, a conservative Republican, put his political reputation on the line in 1973 and campaigned hard for a

All quoted material in this chapter, unless otherwise noted, is taken from reports printed in the *Los Angeles Times*, January–September, 1978.

Larry Stammer, staff writer for the *Los Angeles Times*, covered California politics for the Sacramento bureau of the *Times* for many years.

A jubilant Howard Jarvis proclaims the "new American revolution."

tax-limit initiative. It was defeated. Ironically, his proposal, mild in comparison to the Jarvis measure, was defeated on grounds that it was too extreme.

So not much attention was paid to Howard Jarvis when, in May 1977, he first announced a campaign for a constitutional amendment that would strip local schools and government of $7 billion in taxes during the first year alone. To many, Jarvis was just an apparition—some said aberration—on the state's political landscape. He had run for office four times (U.S. senator, mayor of Los Angeles, member of the Los Angeles board of education, and member of the state board of education) and lost all four times. He seemed to have been fighting a lonely, quixotic battle against property taxes.

His proposal *was* exotic, but exotic initiatives were not new to California. Jarvis's proposal was, in fact, but the latest example of what author and journalist Lou Cannon of the *Washington Post* describes as the "political exceptionalism" of California, an exceptionalism ushered in after 1910 by the social and political reforms of the legendary governor, Hiram Johnson. Among Johnson's reforms were worker's compensation, child labor regulation, civil service, a direct primary, and the initiative and referendum. In his authoritative book on California politics, *Ronnie and Jesse: A Political Odyssey*, Cannon wrote: "All of the social reforms, though advanced for their day, have long been accepted strands in the fabric of the American welfare state. The political changes, on the other hand, have haunted California's electoral structure ever since the Johnson era and are primarily responsible for the state's political exceptionalism of the last half century."

In recent years, California voters have been faced with ballot initiatives—all unsuccessful—to prohibit blasphemy against the Holy Family; to impede, if not block, construction of nuclear power plants; and to fire school teachers and administrators for "advocating, soliciting, imposing, encouraging, or promoting [homosexuality] in a manner likely to come to the attention of other employees or students."

No one voiced surprise, therefore, when Jarvis's announcement of a new initiative to limit property taxes was relegated to the second sections of many of the state's newspapers. The story in the *Los Angeles Times*, published May 19, 1977, ran only five paragraphs. It was not exactly an auspicious kickoff for the campaign. Nor did it suggest the convulsive economic and political upheaval that would attend the measure's passage a year later.

Jarvis had none of the usual interest groups or traditional actors in the public arena behind him. He was opposed by business, which feared that a reduction in property taxes would force increased business taxes. He was opposed by labor unions and public employee groups, who feared job losses. He was opposed by the PTA and the state's entire educational establishment, which feared cuts in school budgets. Most of the state's leading newspapers opposed him, as did many of the highest elected officials on the local and state levels.

Howard Jarvis had only one thing going for him—public anger over such growing problems as soaring home costs, rising property taxes, inflation, and the ineffectiveness of politicians who seemed to simply take the country from one trauma to another (Vietnam, an economy in distress, racial strife, Watergate).

Governor Edmund G. Brown, Jr., who first led the charge against Proposition 13 and then embraced it with the fervor of a convert after it passed, observed during an interview with the author:

> If we look over the last fifteen years we see a dramatic decline in public confidence about government. We see a decline in the annual rate of productivity increase. We see a decline in the amount of investment that businessmen are willing to make. We see a decline in the amount of savings that people feel able to lay aside. We see the dollar declining by an amount greater than any other time in our history, and we see an inflation rate that is foreign to American history which is now the order of the day.
>
> If we put all those together, we find in Proposition 13 a manifestation of the malaise created by those negative indicators, and to that extent Proposition 13 is probably just another manifestation of a very widespread disenchantment with the governing economic theories of our time. Proposition 13 is probably part of a family of reactions against the last fifteen years. There are other reactions, the rise of Ronald Reagan, the [1976] election of Jimmy Carter, antigovernment rhetoric, some of the statements that I have made. The whole set of people and ideas that have swept across the country all are confronting the same basic problem. Government and its leaders have not yet been able to acquit themselves well in coping with those negative indicators I just described.

But the most immediate cause for the success of Proposition 13 was a pervasive fear among voters that their homes were in jeopardy. Driven by inflation and a hot housing market, the value of homes in Los Angeles County, for example, had skyrocketed. The county's annual price increase on homes was about 3.6 percent a year between 1960 and 1974. The annual inflation rate jumped to 8.4 percent in 1975, rising to an annual price increase of 24.9 percent by 1978. These increases were

reflected in the county assessor's revised assessment rolls. Just a month before the June 1978 election (when Proposition 13 was approved), the Los Angeles County assessor's office projected that the average increase for homes reassessed that year would be 120 percent—or about 40 percent a year. (At that time, only a third of the property in the county was reassessed each year; therefore in most cases any single parcel was reassessed only once every three years.)

Alarmed homeowners feared that a doubling (or more) of the market value of their homes would mean a doubling of their property taxes. In practice, local governments tended to cut the tax rate when the assessment value went up. But in the confusion of a campaign, this detail was obscured.

Clearly, homeowners believed that one of the three fundamental rules of California politics had been broken. "The rules of California politics are simple," said one Brown administration insider. "Don't mess with [the citizens'] homes, tamper with their cars, or violate their wives."

Into this setting came Howard Jarvis, along with his sidekick and Proposition 13 coauthor, Paul Gann, a retired Sacramento area automobile and real estate salesman who had established his own grass-roots tax reduction movement called "People's Advocate." It was time, Jarvis declared, to "cut the property tax and stop the grand felony theft of the present, paranoid, uneconomic, stupid system."

Jarvis and Gann launched their drive to qualify the initiative for the ballot in 1977. Under state law, it was necessary to collect a minimum of 499,846 valid signatures of registered voters to win a place on the ballot. Within six months, the Jarvis campaign collected more than 1.2 million signatures. The success of the petition drive had its genesis in years of unsuccessful campaigning for property-tax relief by both men. Jarvis, for example, had tried and failed in 1966, 1972, and 1976 to qualify property-tax initiatives for the ballot. A similar effort by Gann had also failed.

Both men had worked independently in the past, with Jarvis concentrating most of his efforts in vote-rich southern California and Gann in northern California. Their previous efforts provided important lessons. By 1977, Jarvis and Gann had acquired the political skills necessary to direct the growing public outcry over rising property taxes into a successful initiative drive.

A key element of that success was their use of radio talk shows. California is a big state, and a media campaign is the only practical way to reach the voters. But radio and television advertising was expensive, and Jarvis and Gann had very little money. Their solution was to appear on the talk shows, and both men became regular guests. "It started out," Gann said, "by getting people to write me as I started out across the state on the talk shows. I was on them all the time." The talk shows provided Jarvis and Gann with a growing list of followers, many of whom volunteered to help out in their own neighborhoods. Jarvis and Gann also were able to step up their personal appearances as a result of their radio exposure. At first, they spoke to a handful of people here and there. Later, they filled college football stadiums. "It was just grueling, tough, hard, everyday traveling to all parts of the state, and putting together ten, twenty, or forty people, and establishing a line of communications so when we came out with the petition we had people in every part of the state that were ready and educated somewhat as to what we were doing," Jarvis said. "It was really a basic grass-roots movement. We qualified Proposition 13 with less than $30,000."

Jarvis's army of volunteers was key to the success of the petition drive.

Jarvis and Gann built a network of volunteers in all fifty-eight counties. There were county and city chairpersons. Volunteers armed with initiative petitions fanned out across their communities, wherever voters could be found. They went to shopping centers, offices, and door to door. Meanwhile, Jarvis was careful to avoid any sign of partisanship. He wanted to keep the campaign's appeal as broad as possible. He also sought to minimize charges that his campaign was the product of special interests. In that regard, he specifically asked the powerful California Association of Realtors, whose members strongly backed him, *not* to officially endorse Proposition 13. Jarvis and Gann drew many volunteers, however, from the ranks of real estate agents as well as from apartment-house owners. They also tapped members of small homeowner and taxpayer associations. In all, Jarvis estimated that 10,000 volunteers were involved.

Despite the overwhelming response to the petition drive, the Jarvis election campaign began slowly. Four months before the June 6 primary, the respected California poll conducted by Marvin Field found that while 56 percent of all voting-age residents were aware of the Jarvis initiative, only 30 percent had taken a stand—20 percent in favor and 10 percent opposed. The *Los Angeles Times* poll a month later showed that 35 percent were solidly in favor and 27 percent firmly opposed. The remaining 38 percent, the newspaper found, could be swayed by the side which mounted the best campaign. By May 28, when the *Times* published its last preelection poll, it reported a dramatic rise in support, with 52 percent favoring Proposition 13 and 35 percent opposed. Clearly, the Jarvis forces had waged the best campaign.

"What struck me," Governor Brown would say later, "was there was no great leadership in this [the anti-13] movement. It was not a movement. Thirteen was a movement. The anti-13 [campaign] was a rout, an army in retreat." How was such a rout possible when the state's leading political figures and its most powerful special interests had united to fight Jarvis? Aside from the alarm over inflation, rising property taxes, and the public cynicism described earlier, the anti-Jarvis forces were confronted with a series of events and circumstances which, taken together, proved decisive.

- The legislature failed in late 1977 to enact a controversial property-tax reform program backed by Governor Brown. The proposal died in the state senate after it had been assailed on grounds that it would not help the middle-income homeowner. Its property-tax relief would have been based on the family income of a household and the value of their home. Thus, most of the relief would have gone to low-income homeowners and renters.

- Prodded by the Jarvis initiative, which by then had qualified for the ballot, the legislature was summoned into special session by the governor in January 1978 to approve an alternative to Proposition 13. That alternative became known as Proposition 8. But by the time the legislature had acted, the deadline had passed for inserting an explanation of the complicated proposal in the state voter pamphlet, which is mailed to all voters along with a sample ballot. The pamphlet is widely relied upon to give an objective explanation of each ballot measure, as well as pro and con arguments. The voters received no such explanation because of the missed deadline, and the brief description on the ballot itself was obscure. The sample ballot began, "Constitution Art. XIII, Sec. 9.5 to give

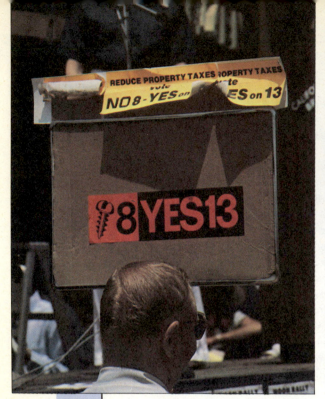

Confusion and bad timing plagued the government's alternative tax-cut plan, Proposition 8, and the plan never gained much ground with voters. Meanwhile, support for Proposition 13 increased.

Legislature power to provide for taxation of owner-occupied dwellings, as defined by Legislature, or any fraction of value thereof, at rate lower than levied on other property." The wording was hardly enlightening, nor could it have been otherwise since, because of printing deadlines, it was written before the legislature approved SB1, the senate bill which would have implemented Proposition 8 had the voters approved it. Meanwhile, Jarvis's explanation of Proposition 13 was easy: he said it would cut property taxes in half, period.

Basically, Proposition 8 would have provided an average homeowner a property-tax cut of about 32 percent the first year, compared to Proposition 13's average of 54 percent. In addition, Proposition 8 tax relief would have been limited to residential property while relief under the Jarvis plan applied to all property. In a move to attract votes from renters who had no guarantee of relief under the Jarvis proposal, the legislature inserted a provision increasing the renter's income tax credit. A similar incentive was offered older voters by increasing the senior citizen's property tax exemption. But the legislature's belated efforts were of no avail.

Charles Winner, a partner in Winner-Wagner & Associates, Inc., the political consulting firm hired to manage the *No on 13* campaign, told the author: "Proposition 8 in itself created problems. It was written by the very people the voters were sending the message to. Furthermore, and probably even more importantly, it was not written in layman terms. Proposition 8 was really difficult to understand if anybody ever saw it, and that problem was compounded by the fact that it didn't appear in the ballot pamphlet as written so that the credibility of our campaign was really damaged."

Intense and costly election campaigns were produced by both sides and both sides admitted to using scare tactics. "I can't honestly deny that I'm using fear," Jarvis said at one point, "but mine is legitimate fear, the fear of losing property." Winner countered, "There's a difference between real fears and imagined fears. Our fears are real fears."

In any case, independent surveys showed that Jarvis's arguments struck a much more responsive chord with the public than did his foe's. "We couldn't win the argument on taxation," Winner said, "because clearly it was in our interest, based on our survey, to say, 'Yes, you're right. Taxes are too high. But Proposition 13 isn't the answer to the problem. This creates more problems.'"

Thus, the leaders of the anti-Jarvis campaign stressed the loss of public services which, according to their polls, the public least wanted cut—police, fire, emergency service, education. In addition, a phalanx of other special interests joined the assault on Proposition 13.

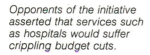

Opponents of the initiative asserted that services such as hospitals would suffer crippling budget cuts.

While Winner-Wagner carried out its strategy in radio and television advertisements, the California Firefighters Coalition issued a public "alert" warning that the state's 600 fire protection districts, which depended almost entirely on property taxes as a revenue source, would face budget cuts of 60 percent. Police chiefs and sheriffs around the state spoke ominously of severe manpower shortages. An official of the California Commission on Aging estimated that local funding for 500 multi-purpose senior centers would be in jeopardy.

The Sierra Club and California Park and Recreation Society expressed deep concern over the future of the public's leisure-time facilities and environmental protection programs, while the California Association for the Retarded and similar groups predicted that the mentally retarded and mentally ill would face "new setbacks" if Proposition 13 were approved.

Proposition 13 was assailed by the Consumer Federation of California as "the largest bait-and-switch swindle ever offered in the political marketplace of California," and the state PTA president said millions of youngsters faced double class sizes, the complete closure of some schools, the elimination of special programs, and the loss of all school security services.

Massive job losses in both the public and private sector were forecast by the California Labor Federation (AFL-CIO) and public employee groups, which cited a UCLA Graduate School of Management study. That study, announced just a month before the election, predicted that Proposition 13 could lead to the loss of 450,000 jobs and push the state's unemployment rate above 10 percent. Governor Brown went so far as to raise the specter of a severe recession.

The Brown administration and opponents of the Jarvis initiative made widespread use of the UCLA study, which was conducted by three economists who admitted that they opposed Proposition 13 and that the university had a stake in the election outcome. Nevertheless, they insisted that the study was free from bias. The economists did, however, lack accurate information on the extent of the state's revenue surplus.

Four days after the election, Governor Brown's director of finance, Roy Bell, suggested that the prediction of 450,000 lost jobs had been significantly overstated. He said job losses would be less than half that figure (and, eventually, there were fewer still).

"A lot of these sort of scare tactics were on the basis that local government didn't trust the state to put any money in at all. Nobody had promised them the state would put in $3 billion or $4 billion," Bell said. Asked by the author if the administration had "soft-peddled" the amount of state financial aid that local governments could expect if Jarvis passed, Bell said, "Right. That's correct. After all, we were supporting Proposition 8."

Opponents of Proposition 13 backed up their words with money. The campaign contribution reports filed by the *No on 13* committee read like a "who's who" of the state's power elites. The 100,000-member California State Employees Association (CSEA) contributed $71,100, and a CSEA chapter in San Jose added another $20,381. Other contributions included the California Fire Service Coalition, $52,100; Teachers Against Proposition 13 (a political committee established by the California Teachers Association), $125,000; the Association for Better Citizenship (another CTA political

The government's preelection disclosure of new property assessments was intended to defuse the Proposition 13 campaign, but instead added fuel to the tax-revolt fire.

action committee), $100,000; Pacific Telephone Company, $15,000; Lockheed California Company, $2500; Kaiser Aluminum and Chemical, $5000; the president, chairman of the board, and a director of Levi Strauss & Company each contributed $500; and tens of thousands were raised by bond brokers.

Meanwhile, many of the state's leading newspapers kept up a steady drumbeat in their editorial columns against the initiative. The initiative campaign came also in the midst of the Democratic and Republican gubernatorial primary elections and injected a new intensity into those contests. While many politicians were running scared, a number openly opposed the Jarvis measure and joined Governor Brown in assailing it as a "ripoff" and a "fraud." The litany of arguments against Proposition 13 moved *San Francisco Chronicle* columnist Abe Mellinkoff to scoff, "Every day, some public official in California dons his own special fright wig."*

Fright wigs or not, by the second week of May the anti-Jarvis strategy appeared to be paying off. *No on 13* campaign manager Winner insisted that his private polls showed the anti-Jarvis campaign had nearly closed a 30 percent gap, a claim questioned by Los Angeles County Assessor Alexander H. Pope. But, Winner said, in what must be regarded as a classic understatement, "other things happened."

Just as the anti-Jarvis campaign appeared to be getting its bearings, developments in Los Angeles County sent a shudder through the anti-Jarvis camp.

*San Francisco Chronicle, May 12, 1978.

Pope, an opponent of Proposition 13, disclosed that for the third of the county's property owners who had been reappraised that year the average increase was 120 percent, or about 40 percent a year for three years. By contrast, new property values had been increasing an average of 20 percent a year for homes reappraised during previous three-year assessment cycles.

Moreover, based on the new values for the 700,000 of the county's two million parcels that had been reappraised, the overall assessment roll for the entire county jumped by 18 percent to $24 billion, the highest increase in thirty years.

Anguished cries of Los Angeles County homeowners echoed across the state and were matched by equally angry headlines on the front pages of newspapers from San Diego to Eureka.

"It just seemed like there was no stopping," Governor Brown said. "One gets the feeling that government is out of control." Winner added, "We believed that once those assessments went out, we were dead."

Pope's decision to release the new assessment figures for the first time *before* the election (a practice followed by some other counties in previous years) was in no small part forced upon him by a Jarvis campaign tactic, as well as by the media. The Jarvis campaign had hit a slump in April and William Butcher, Jarvis's campaign manager, had devised a strategy.

Butcher and his firm, Butcher-Forde Consulting of Newport Beach, had a reputation for hard-hitting campaigns. They were especially skilled in mounting sophisticated direct-mail campaigns which made extensive use of computers. Jarvis needed to raise money for the final campaign push, and Butcher proposed to take the voter lists in each of the state's fifty-eight counties and match them against the property-tax rolls.

By using new assessments as they became available, or by projecting new assessments based on trends, the firm was able to estimate the size of the property-tax increase that individual homeowners could expect if Proposition 13 were to be defeated, or so the Jarvis campaign claimed. These tax predictions were flawed because they assumed higher assessments *plus* maintenance of the current tax rate. In practice, unless there is a spending increase, local governments sometimes cut the tax rate as assessments go up, Pope said.

In any case, after testing seventy-five combinations of voters to determine which group was most responsive, Butcher-Forde settled on eight groups of homeowners—mostly middle-income Republicans and farmers—and dispatched 400,000 "personalized" computer letters. They were mailed in envelopes specially designed to resemble official stationary.

The letter had an immediate impact. California homeowners and businesses had watched their property taxes grow year by year and had been alarmed by reports that property taxes would skyrocket in the coming year. Now, for the first time, they were being told—before the election—what they could personally expect.

Although some of Jarvis's opponents cried foul and charged that the estimates had been exaggerated, many homeowners who had been thinking of voting against the initiative began to wonder where it would all end. If they were not entirely convinced of the accuracy of the Jarvis letter, they were at least disturbed.

"Ferguson claims he's being whipsawed by inflation and taxes. Whoops! There he goes now!"

Drawing by Booth; © 1981. The New Yorker Magazine, Inc.

"It had a great impact," Butcher-Forde associate Harvey Englander said. "What this letter did, aside from creating an aura of public awareness about property taxes, was raise the funds necessary to run our statewide campaign. When people saw the amount of money they would save it was worth it to them to send us $25 or $50. It was unbelievable."

The letter sent to businesses ended with the exhortation, "This is our last chance to permanently reduce property taxes. Your maximum contribution is needed today!" It was signed "sincerely" by Howard Jarvis.

A cry went out from homeowners demanding to know exactly what their new assessments would be—and they wanted to know officially before, not after, the election.

At this point, Alexander Pope, the soft-spoken Los Angeles County assessor who vowed when he was appointed six months earlier that he would not be "leading the parade against any issues," made two clearly political decisions intended to defuse the controversy.

1. Pope announced on April 25 that effective May 15 property owners could personally inspect the new assessments. It was apparent that Pope believed opening the new assessments to public inspection would serve to discredit the allegedly exaggerated projections of the Jarvis letter.
2. Reacting to the outcry and widespread publicity which followed the disclosure of higher-than-anticipated assessment hikes, Pope announced on May 25 a freeze on all assessments. Taxes for 1978–79, he said, would not be based on the new figures, but on the lower 1977 assessments.

Governor Jerry Brown.

Those two decisions were the culmination of intense behind-the-scene debates and consultations, involving not only the political operatives of the *No on 13* committee and members of the Los Angeles County board of supervisors, but also in the case of the freeze, the direct (and until now undisclosed) participation of Governor Brown.

Pope said the decision to make the assessments public was in part an outgrowth of the Jarvis letter. "It became clear we were going to have to take a position on what we were going to do," he said. He added that Winner was "quite concerned about the political implications of the thing."

Although he had been appointed to his job by the board of supervisors to fill the unexpired term of Philip Watson, Pope was now campaigning for election in a hard-fought primary in which one of his opponents was a Jarvis-endorsed rival. Pope had stated publicly that he believed in open government. In part because of that belief, and in part because of the public outcry which followed the Jarvis letter, Pope broke with past practice and for the first time in recent Los Angeles County history made the new assessments available before the election.

There were other considerations as well. Pope did not wish to see his assessments become a central issue in the Proposition 13 campaign. "If we held back, we'd have the press almost universally against us because they almost always are going to come down on the side of freedom of information," Pope said. In addition, Pope's office employed 1500 persons, many of whom had access to the information. News leaks, perhaps based on partial information, could almost certainly be expected and lead to "distorted" news accounts.

Only after the offices had been opened did the first complete review of the figures come out, and it was then that Pope said he first knew of the full impact. Said one of Pope's special assistants, Ms. Jordan Mo, "That's when we recognized the enormity of the increases. It was just staggering." The result, in the words of County Supervisor Kenneth Hahn, was "bedlam."

Hahn, an outspoken and sometimes flamboyant politician who had held elective office for thirty-one years, the last twenty-five on the board of supervisors representing downtown Los Angeles and the black community of Watts, said Pope had made a mistake in disclosing the assessments. He remarked, "I think all of us oldtimers looked at him and said, 'Oh, you just got appointed. You're brand new. You're not skilled in dealing with the public.' It was something not planned properly."

As homeowners marched to their local assessor's office, so, too, did the media, which duly recorded one horror story after another. Those stories were carried prominently throughout the state. "It's time to bring these cotton-picking legislators down to their knees," one irate homeowner declared after learning of an assessment increase of 85 percent. Exclaimed another, "I wasn't going to vote for Jarvis, but there's no way in the world I wouldn't vote for it now. I've sweated blood for that house!"

Winner later observed, "Alex was put in a deeper and deeper box. The assessments were becoming a huge issue. I mean, it was a front-page story almost every day as these people went into their local assessor's offices." Demands for additional information escalated.

The Jarvis campaign called on the county to mail written notices to all persons whose property had been reappraised. Meanwhile, the anti-Jarvis campaign managers were working feverishly to cut their losses. Winner conferred privately with Pope and proposed mailing notices not only to those who had been reappraised, but to *all* property owners so that the two thirds who had not been reappraised would know they had been spared. Winner also proposed including voter information on Proposition 8, the measure which had not been included in the state ballot pamphlet because the legislature had enacted the program after the pamphlet printing deadline.

Within days, the board of supervisors asked Pope to limit the mailing to persons whose property had been reappraised. That vote drew the wrath of state assembly speaker Leo T. McCarthy (D.,San Francisco) who charged that it could only help the Jarvis campaign. McCarthy had become, along with the governor, one of the leading opponents of Jarvis. On the other hand, assembly Republican leader Paul Priolo was delighted with developments in Los Angeles County. Priolo, who had previously endorsed the Jarvis initiative, told the press, "I was getting a little antsy about the possibility of 13 not passing, and every little bit helps."

But other events would soon overshadow and make moot the board's 3–0 vote asking Pope to mail the assessment notices. The notices never were mailed.

Confronted with the public outrage that attended the new assessments, the board voted 4–0 on May 23 to direct Pope to roll back the assessments to the lower levels of the previous year. Actually, the board could not direct Pope to do anything. As assessor, Pope was an independent official. The motion was introduced by Supervisor Hahn, an opponent of Proposition 13.

Ironically, it was a series of trips by Hahn and other public officials to Athens, Greece, to participate (at taxpayers' expense) in negotiations for bringing the 1984 Olympic games to Los Angeles that had itself become an issue in the Jarvis campaign. The *Yes on 13* committee produced television commercials showing a jet taking off as Hawaiian music played in the background and as an announcer talked about politicians on tax-supported junkets.

Hahn had just returned from Greece and promptly announced that he would introduce a motion before the board calling for a freeze. Hahn's plan came as a complete surprise to Pope, even though Pope had placed transatlantic telephone calls to Hahn in Athens to keep him apprised of developments in California.

Later, Pope would say that he believed Hahn and Governor Brown jointly conceived the freeze as a last-ditch effort to minimize the political damage to the *No on 13* campaign resulting from the new assessments. Both Brown and Hahn confirmed they had conferred on the freeze before the motion was offered. And Pope was soon to become the object of Brown's personal lobbying.

Following the board's vote, Pope telephoned Winner that night to say he would stop by the campaign office. Pope wanted to talk about the freeze. "While I was there," Pope related, "they got a call from the governor. The governor, of course, regularly checked in with the *No on 13* campaign." Pope said Brown asked him to meet that evening at the Biltmore Hotel where Howard Jarvis two weeks later would claim victory and proclaim the "new American revolution."

"When the governor asks you about something, that's kind of a command performance and I said, 'Fine, I'll stop by before I go home,' which I did," Pope said. Brown did not hesitate to tell Pope what he thought the assessor should do: freeze the assessments. "He was pretty insistent," said Pope, "not a table pounder or emotional, but just very determined that that's what I ought to do and he felt quite strongly." In Brown's words, "This juggernaut was just rolling down the road absolutely terrorizing people and it had no way to become a reality."

Pope said Brown was unmoved by the probability that such a freeze would be illegal since it would conflict with a state law requiring county assessors to put current market values on the assessment roll. Pope's chief legal adviser, County Counsel John Larson, had raised that issue. But, said Pope, "The governor was not really impressed with the fact that John was still wrestling with the problem. I think the governor didn't really understand the legal problems involved. I think he tended to think that somehow or other . . . if this were the right thing to do that lawyers should be able to figure out a way to do it. I think that he thought it was the right thing to do for reasons of fairness to those people who had been reassessed, and, undoubtedly, he had political considerations in mind."

In the end, Brown was right. Pope's lawyer was able to "figure out a way to do it." Pope could not, however, ignore his own campaign for election against a Jarvis-endorsed candidate. He was not convinced a freeze would be in his own political interests because, first, he might be seen as doing the bidding of county supervisors who urged it on him, and, second, it might be viewed as a cynical attempt to influence the voters to reject Proposition 13.

"I was going to tell the governor to stick it in his ear and tell the board of supervisors to go to hell," Pope said. In the end, however, he relented on grounds of fairness.

Appearing before a battery of television cameras and reporters on May 25, Pope declared, "No homeowner need have any fear of a value increase for his or her 1978 assessment." Under questioning, Pope acknowledged that the freeze would "remove a very emotional issue from the Proposition 13 campaign." The man who promised the previous January that he would not be "leading the parade against any issues" had become the drum major of the hour. Later, Governor Brown, whose efforts to convince

Pope to submit to a freeze were unknown, hailed Pope's decision as "courageous" and urged the state's fifty-seven other county assessors to follow Pope's lead.

Several days later, Brown dropped the idea and withdrew his call for a statewide freeze. The legislature's leadership balked, and Brown claimed he could not get anyone to introduce the bill.

Today, those who played a role in the freeze have admitted to second thoughts about its political wisdom. Some believe that the freeze served either to confuse the voters, heighten their suspicion of politicians, or confirm a belief that the "big spenders" would do anything to defeat Jarvis. The freeze also left the impression among many voters that, if the politicians could so easily order a rollback, maybe Jarvis was right about government waste.

Pope concluded a year afterward, "I think the freeze may have made some people rest in peace. It was at best a wash [in its impact on the anti-13 campaign] if not a negative factor. I don't think there's any question that the timing was very bad politically both for me and the campaign against Proposition 13. It just seemed like a big ploy at the request of the board of supervisors, the majority of whom opposed Proposition 13." The governor agreed. "The whole thing was bad," he said. "It just raised all the level of doubt and questions about everything."

The impact of the assessments and subsequent freeze may have been magnified during the heat of the campaign. Disagreement still lingers over whether the controversy so inflamed the electorate that the passage of Proposition 13 had been assured. In retrospect, both sides believe that the assessments did not in themselves determine the outcome. But there is little doubt that they had a profound influence on the dynamics of the campaign.

It was at that time that Winner privately believed Jarvis had won: "I felt it was bleak when the surveys switched, when we had the overnight turnaround, when the assessments came out. We had pulled even to within a point, and then a week later we were down by twenty points. At that point I knew it was going to take some fantastic action, something out of the blue, to win." Pope observed, "I think Chuck was overly optimistic in April. I somehow just never ran across all those alleged 'no' voters."

There were clear signs of erosion in the anti-13 campaign before the election. Even among interest groups that would presumably be hurt by passage of the proposition there existed a curious dichotomy of public opposition and private support. While public employees and members of the business community through their organizations opposed Jarvis, many of them as individuals supported him.

Pope recalled walking through the underground parking garage in downtown Los Angeles where county employees parked their cars and counting only two *No on 13* bumper stickers on the eve of the election. A month before the polls opened, the California State Employees Association issued a statement warning state workers they would probably receive no pay raise if Jarvis passed (the prediction proved correct). The statement also exhorted CSEA members to campaign against Jarvis. "CSEA cannot overemphasize the urgency of the situation, but members have been slow to see the threat," the statement said. Jarvis would later report that he won the votes of 64 percent of labor union members, and 30 percent of public employees.

Several weeks before the election, Governor Brown told the author that he had privately concluded the battle had been lost. "What struck me," Brown said, "was the seeming complacency of so many forces. Some of their leadership seemed to be fighting it . . . but their own troops were not mobilized." Why? "Because," Brown said, "in addition to being employees, they were concerned about their state and their country, and they're affected by inflation, and they're concerned about the security of their shelter. Down deep, everybody works for government, but they also are affected as the general citizen. That's why this [Jarvis's] movement was so profound. Even people whose own livelihoods were affected still voted for 13, and even if they voted against it they didn't fight that hard because they were upset, and they didn't think [high property taxes] were fair."

A similar dichotomy was evident within the state's business community. One executive told a reporter that many business people were carrying their personal feelings into their boardrooms when corporate policy on Jarvis was under discussion. "They computed how much they would save on their own property taxes on their own homes, and this tended to color their judgment from a higher, overall policy standpoint," he said.

In April, the California Chamber of Commerce reported the results of a poll of its members, the majority of whom ran small businesses. The result: 56.5 percent of those responding favored Proposition 13, 37.4 percent opposed it, and 6.1 percent had no position. After Jarvis finished speaking before the relatively conservative Los Angeles Town Hall business group in May, more than 80 percent of the 400-member audience indicated, by a show of hands, that they backed him.

Describing problems early in the campaign of raising money to fight Jarvis, No on 13 campaign manager Winner said: "The people that were involved truly believed that money was going to be forthcoming and, of course, it wasn't. The money was very slow, very late, and not nearly as much as we anticipated." Actually, Winner's protests notwithstanding, anti-Jarvis forces spent $2,096,723, while Jarvis forces spent $2,158,560.

But raising that much money was always a struggle for the anti-Jarvis campaign. During a late March meeting of fifty of Los Angeles's leading business executives at a posh restaurant, Governor Brown, Winner, and others spoke about the consequences to business if the initiative passed. "The governor spoke quite eloquently about the impact on the state and the problems that would be incurred by the cities," Winner recalled.

Yet afterward, though several sources said the executives had been impressed by Brown personally, their impressions were not immediately translated into campaign pledges. One businessman present made a notable gesture in an effort to prime the pump. Henry Salvatori, a wealthy backer of conservative causes and a member of former Governor Ronald Reagan's so-called "kitchen cabinet," stood up and reportedly said, "I'll pledge $10,000." Turning to another businessman, Salvatori then said, "What about you?" According to one observer, "All eyes turned to this person, and this person appeared to be embarrassed because he was not about to make a pledge, and he hemmed and hawed that this was something he had to discuss with his board and executive committee, etc."

"Salvatori didn't prime the pump," Winner added, "and furthermore, I'm not sure we ever got his $10,000!" Campaign records show no contribution from Salvatori.

Still, major corporations and municipal-bond and banking interests added hundreds of thousands of dollars to those contributed by public employee groups. Unlike federal law, which prohibits corporate contributions, California law allows corporations to contribute to state candidates and ballot campaigns. And the *No on 13* committee made the most of it.

In addition, a group of more than forty investment bankers and securities brokers, apparently alarmed at the possible unfavorable impact of Proposition 13 on certain municipal bonds, contributed a combined total of more than $200,000.

On the other hand, virtually all of the money raised by Jarvis was contributed by real estate interests, homeowners, and apartment owners. "Most of the people who contributed to the campaign had never given a dollar to politics before in their life," Englander said.

In the end, however, the last-minute television blitz financed by all those contributors may have been largely irrelevant. The *Los Angeles Times*-Channel 2 survey of 2482 people as they left the polls on election day found that 44 percent had made up their minds two months earlier, and that two thirds had decided at least a month before the election. Those who voted for Proposition 13 overwhelmingly believed that the initiative would not cripple schools, police, or fire services. They dismissed those warnings as "scare tactics," the poll found. Jarvis observed, "This thing was built solidly for too damn long. There was no stopping it because by that time [the voters] were so disgusted with the politicians they [didn't] give a damn no matter what [they said]."

Election results tended to verify Jarvis's claim. Proposition 13 was approved by 4,280,689 voters—64.8 percent of those voting; 2,326,167 (35.2 percent) voted against it. The initiative carried the votes of 70 percent of the homeowners, 41 percent of the renters (who would receive no direct benefits), 40 percent of the blacks, and 40 percent of the voters whose families included at least one public employee who stood to lose by Proposition 13's passage. Senior citizens voted overwhelmingly for the measure—76 percent. These results indicated that a yes vote for Jarvis was not only an expression of financial interest. Many voted for it who, according to the campaign rhetoric, stood to be hurt financially. These people appeared to want to "send a message" to the politicians. Jacob Citrin, an associate professor of political science and director of the state data program at the University of California at Berkeley, wrote, "Proposition 13 became a convenient vehicle on which to displace accumulated grievances against inefficient and indifferent public employees." He quoted one individual as saying, "Now they'll pay for every silly regulation, long line, rude bus driver, and overpaid garbage collector."

Jarvis's success at the ballot box set the stage for yet another battle in the California legislature. Special interests that had joined forces to fight Jarvis during the election campaign were now competing for their "fair share" of the state's surplus funds.

While Brown, as a campaign tactic, had gone to great lengths during the election to leave the impression that the state would not necessarily bail out local government if the Jarvis measure passed, any doubts concerning the central role the state government was to play vanished as quickly as the surplus seemed to appear in each new postelection estimate.

Perhaps as much out of a sheer sense of political survival as out of acknowledgment of the new fiscal realities, politicians wasted no time in calling the $5 billion surplus "obscene" and pledged their best efforts to help local government.

The state surplus had been fed by what incumbent political leaders described as a "booming economy." California, with its broad industrial base, was better off than most parts of the United States. But the state's surplus resulted as much from inflation as from anything else. Higher prices meant higher sales tax revenues. Cost-of-living raises pushed workers into higher state income tax brackets. The result was that workers were paying a higher percentage of their wages in taxes, even though their disposable income in terms of real dollars had not increased.

The state was wallowing in money. Still, the task of dividing more than $5 billion among local schools and governmental entities that faced the loss of $7 billion in property taxes under the Jarvis amendment was one of the most politically difficult ever confronted by the legislature.

George Skelton, Sacramento bureau chief for the *Los Angeles Times*, wrote at the height of the battle: "Not in the modern history of California government has the legislature been forced to grapple with an issue of this magnitude and complexity, under such deadline pressure and heat from voters, and so torn by competing and powerful political forces."

Proposition 13 not only forced local governments to reexamine spending priorities, it forced the state to look again at its books as well. Governor Brown had proposed a $16.2 billion state budget for fiscal 1978–79 the previous January. After Proposition 13 passed, he trimmed his recommendation by $715 million in order to free more money for local aid. Pet programs in the budget, including the governor's much-derided communications satellite, were abandoned. But the search for places to cut state spending went beyond such easy targets, extended into the domains of powerful special interests, and intruded into the sanctuaries of the disadvantaged.

Cost-of-living grant increases for welfare recipients, pay raises for state and local public employees, abortions for the poor, police and fire services, and demands for constitutional spending limits became inexorably linked as lawmakers struggled to respond to the "new American revolution" proclaimed by Howard Jarvis.

For those politicians who played to the voters, the problem, simply put, was to cut government "fat" while sparing as much "muscle" as possible. But this is not an easy task, as Governor Brown pointed out in his address to United Press International editors in Palo Alto, California, a week after the election:

It is an interesting and difficult problem to find all that "fat." Some of the fat has more political muscle than some of the bone and marrow. And so, as you take out your scalpel, you find you're cutting away at the bone while some of the fat just sits there happily burning on the fire. That's because politics is not necessarily rational. It depends on who and how many there are and what kind of clout they have. As you individually say "no" to this one, "no" to that one, "no" to the other one, the cacophony of negative responses is very great. And that's the problem with cutting out "fat." It's a good metaphor, but it's not a clear guide to what should go.

What should *not* go, however, appeared clear. The *Los Angeles Times*-Channel 2 poll taken election day revealed that most voters agreed that if government spending cuts were necessary (and most voters doubted that they were), then police and fire services should be the last to be trimmed. Voters did not entertain similar sentiments about welfare. No one knew this better than the politicians in Sacramento, regardless of their ideology.

With an eye toward the upcoming November general elections, Republicans took their cue from the opinion polls and devised a strategy intended to meet the public demand while putting Democrats on the spot. The Republicans, of course, had long claimed the mantle of law-and-order leadership, and they were quick to propose that, however else the state might divide its surplus, police and fire services be given full funding.

At the same time, most Democrats were expressing alarm that Proposition 13 would hurt minorities and the disadvantaged, including the elderly and families on welfare. And Democrats were voicing those fears against a backdrop of warnings from law enforcement officials that they could not do their job unless they had the money. The Los Angeles Police Department alone marked 1080 officers for firing because of sharp cutbacks under Proposition 13.

The GOP plan was leaked to the *Los Angeles Times*, and on June 16 ran as the lead story on page one. Democratic Assembly Speaker McCarthy lamely protested, "Not only are the Republicans trying to curry favor with the voters, they're trying to fashion the legislature into a sort of city council. I don't think we, in such an arrogant manner, should tell the local people that the legislature knows best."

The timing of the Republican proposal had two purposes: (1) to tell voters that they were with them on the question of spending priorities, and (2) to serve notice to Democrats that Republicans intended to make the tax controversy an election-year issue and thus pressure the majority Democrats into going along or facing the wrath of voters.

Republicans, once again, had left Democrats at the starting gate on the law-and-order issue, and, McCarthy's protest notwithstanding, the legislature did in fact tell cities and counties that it knew best on issues concerning public safety.

Three days after the Republican coup, Governor Brown emerged from a private meeting with worried law enforcement and fire protection officials and promised "to do everything I can at the state level to minimize and hopefully eliminate police and fire layoffs."

The decision to assure funding for police and fire services was intertwined with policy decisions on welfare and public-employee pay raises—issues which were both controversial and difficult.

Welfare had come for many to symbolize individual failure and seemed to go against the American pioneer ethic of independence and work. For others, welfare was nothing less than a social compact, a secular embodiment of the biblical imperative to be one's brother's keeper. The question was, How could that commitment be upheld and to what extent should it be followed in view of the public mood?

Under law, 2.1 million welfare recipients in the state were due to receive a 7.6 percent cost-of-living increase in their grants, at a total cost of $233 million. When the state's fifty-eight counties (each of which carried some responsibility for welfare costs) were confronted with cuts in property taxes, could those legally required grant increases be afforded? For days, the legislature's Proposition 13 conference committee agonized over the issue, but the discussions only led to further questions.

If welfare recipients received cost-of-living increases, could the state, as a matter of equity (not to mention the political consequences), deny pay raises to the state's 224,000 employees, and the 1.2 million local government workers? Further, it was argued that if those raises were granted, the attendant costs would force financially pressed local governments to lay off up to 65,000 public employees. By not granting pay raises, layoffs could be minimized.

The California State Employees Association (CSEA) would have none of it. The CSEA demanded a pay raise. It had contributed $15,000 to Governor Brown's election campaign four years earlier. When the governor announced he would veto any pay hike, the full wrath of state workers was directed against him. Thousands of state employees held a rally on the state capitol grounds and chanted, "We want Brown." When the governor finally appeared, he was greeted with a chorus of boos and obscenities. One picket sign, in a reference to the governor's oft-heard exhortation that an "era of limits" had arrived, read, "Era of Limits Means One Term."

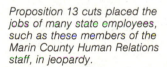

Proposition 13 cuts placed the jobs of many state employees, such as these members of the Marin County Human Relations staff, in jeopardy.

Meanwhile, organized labor was privately pressuring Governor Brown to withhold his threatened pay-raise veto. The plea came just a week before the California state AFL-CIO convention, where Governor Brown had hoped to win an endorsement in his race against Republican Attorney General Younger. The AFL-CIO Executive Council wired Brown that a veto would be "a cruel disservice to 1.5 million public workers."

As a practical matter, despite speculation encouraged by some labor leaders, the AFL-CIO's endorsement of Brown was never seriously in question. First, organized labor had no real alternative in Younger. Second, Brown over the years had proven himself a friend of labor and had appointed John F. Henning, labor's number one Sacramento lobbyist and executive secretary-treasurer of the California Labor Federation, to the University of California Board of Regents.

In the end, the legislature allowed a 2.5 percent pay increase for state employees and welfare recipients. But the hike, small as it was, was vetoed by Governor Brown.

Because of terms of the bailout legislation, Brown's veto automatically meant a freeze on the pay of any local government employee whose employer accepted state bailout aid. A year later, the California Supreme Court would overturn that provision as an unconstitutional impairment of management-labor contracts and local control.

The issue of publicly funded abortions was also affected by Proposition 13. Abortions had always been a volatile subject in the California legislature. Despite the controversy, however, proponents had always managed to appropriate funds without too much difficulty.

But abortion opponents saw in the fiscal restraints imposed by Proposition 13 a new opportunity to strike funding from the budget. Ultimately, the abortion opponents would prevail in the legislature but lose in the courts. After a bruising battle, the appropriation for abortions for the poor was reduced and more restrictive eligibility rules were imposed. As of late 1980, the issue was still tied up in the courts. If abortion opponents were to prevail, it was estimated that up to 90 percent of poor women who previously qualified for publicly funded abortions would no longer be eligible.

In the aftermath of Proposition 13's passage, local and state governments continued to be buffeted by aftershocks. But the jolts were not nearly as catastrophic as opponents had suggested they would be at the height of the campaign. By the end of 1979—two years after the Jarvis amendment's enactment—the total number of government employees, including state, local, special district, and school district workers, had reached 1.46 million, up 2.1 percent from the previous year.

Local governments, due largely to the state's $5 billion bailout in the first year, plus several billion in surplus funds in the second year, managed to weather the storm. But, local governments knew that they could not turn to Sacramento for a helping hand forever, and more cuts in services were forecast.

Government spending still remains an issue in California, but it has been largely defused by Proposition 13's passage. Although voters approved a subsequent initiative placing state constitutional spending limits on state and local governments, they also rejected a later Jarvis initiative which would have cut state personal income taxes by 50 percent. That measure won only 40 percent of the vote. The returns proved that there was no magic in Howard Jarvis's sponsorship. If anything, it showed that Jarvis's campaign for Proposition 13 had happened to come along at an opportune time. The combination of events that led to victory in 1978—inflation, rising assessments on homes, and distrust of government—were not present to the same degree when Jarvis attempted his second initiative.

Additionally, state income taxes—never as onerous as property taxes—were indexed so that cost-of-living wage hikes no longer pushed workers into higher tax brackets.

Moreover, there seemed to be a perception among voters that, for the most part, "the politicians" had finally caught on—that they had become aware of voter dissatisfaction with government waste. Many politicians who had opposed Proposition 13, heartily endorsed a subsequent ballot initiative approved by voters which imposed constitutional spending limits on state and local governments. Known as Proposition 4, the measure was called "the Spirit of 13" by its author, Paul Gann, the man who had coauthored the Jarvis initiative.

Gann, incidentally, capitalized on his fame as a tax-fighter by winning the 1980 Republican nomination for U.S. Senate against five other opponents. However, he lost the November general election to the incumbent Democrat, Alan Cranston, the Senate Democratic minority whip. Cranston was elected to a third term, an unusual circumstance in California.

Meanwhile, certain problems that opponents of Proposition 13 had warned against during the campaign have, in fact, come to pass. The homeowners' share of the total property tax burden has grown in relation to the share paid by commercial and industrial property owners. The reason is simple. Under Proposition 13, all property was assessed at the old 1975 values, plus an added 2 percent for each year thereafter. The hitch: If property changed ownership it would be assessed up to its full market value at the year of the change of ownership. This created two conditions:

1. Property taxes were no longer equal. There are now many cases in which two different homeowners, living in identical houses on the same street and using identical public services, pay widely different property taxes.
2. Because residential property is sold more frequently than commercial or industrial property, the Proposition 13-imposed market value reassessments at change of ownership shifted the largest part of the overall property tax burden to homeowners.

In 1977, before Proposition 13 had passed, single-family homes in Los Angeles County accounted for 42.4 percent of the collected property taxes, while residential income property (such as apartments) accounted for 15.5 percent. Commercial and industrial property accounted for 42.1 percent. By 1980, the percentages had changed dramatically: single-family homes, 47.5 percent; residential income property, 15.2 percent; and commercial and industrial property, 37.3 percent.

A study prepared by Glenn Quinn, director of assessment services for the Los Angeles County assessor's office, indicated that by 1989 single-family homes will be paying 60 percent of the real property taxes. When combined with residential income property, he said the total of the two would be more than 80 percent by that year.

Such a shift in the total property tax burden, many believe, will result in cries for further changes in Proposition 13. In the first few years following Proposition 13, some attempts have been made in the legislature to "refine" it. But a majority of lawmakers, fearful that they would be accused of tampering with the people's hard-won tax relief, have prevailed in urging the legislature to keep its hands off—at least for the moment.

Political Socialization, Media, and Public Opinion

Chapter **4**

We have all heard such terms as *liberal*, *conservative*, and *moderate* used in everyday conversation to describe people, groups, candidates, and political parties. What do you consider yourself to be? Radical, liberal, moderate, conservative, reactionary—or just a plain, uncomplicated American? Some people might honestly not be sure where they stand on a continuum from radical (left) to reactionary (right). It is also true that any particular individual could be liberal on one set of issues and conservative on another. But it is still possible to talk in terms of "general" political orientations. Polls have shown that most Americans identify themselves as being somewhere in the vast middle —from liberal to moderate to conservative. What do these terms mean? They are shorthand labels used to gather a wide variety of attitudes, beliefs, and values under one rather simple roof.

For example, if you believe that private ownership of the major companies (say, steel, auto, oil, coal, utilities) should be abolished in favor of ownership by the national government; if you believe that everyone making over $50,000 should be taxed so as not to be able to keep the excess; if you believe that no one should be allowed to own more than the amount of property absolutely necessary to live and/or make a living on; and if, especially, you believe that in order to bring about these things it is all right or even desirable to use violence—then you would likely be considered a radical in the United States.

If you believe, however, that there should be no government restraints whatsoever on companies; that taxes really amount to an unconstitutional confiscation of private property; that the social security system should be ended and people made to make their own security plans—then you would likely be considered a reactionary in the United States.

Both of these positions are considered extremes in this country, and most people do not fall into either category. When looking at answers to a range of questions, most people want government control, but not too much (you will see this demonstrated in chapter 10 on regulatory agencies). They accept taxes, but not what they consider "unfair" ones; they believe that private initiative and self-help are the main reasons people succeed, but they also understand the necessity for some (though as little as possible) social welfare legislation. They do not want to repeal social security, but they are cautious about extending government care and protection "from the cradle to the grave."

These items deal with economic matters. Others frequently relate to social issues. Thus, one can decide where she or he stands on the radical-to-reactionary spectrum by looking at a number of items: the death penalty; premarital sex; legalized marijuana; homosexuality; legalized abortion.

FIGURE 1.
Social Liberalism by Age.

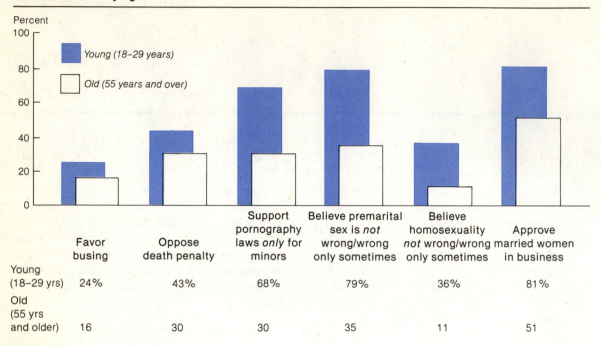

Young (18–29 yrs)	Favor busing	Oppose death penalty	Support pornography laws *only* for minors	Believe premarital sex is *not* wrong/wrong only sometimes	Believe homosexuality *not* wrong/wrong only sometimes	Approve married women in business
Young (18–29 yrs)	24%	43%	68%	79%	36%	81%
Old (55 yrs and older)	16	30	30	35	11	51

FIGURE 2.
Social Liberalism by Race.

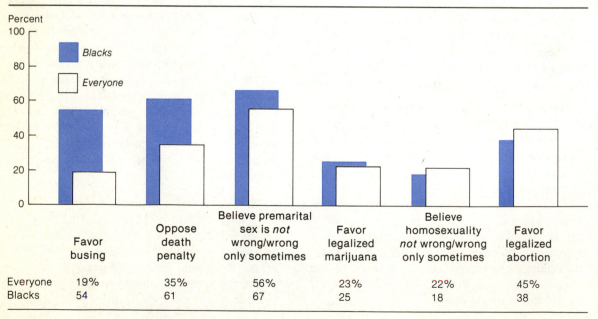

	Favor busing	Oppose death penalty	Believe premarital sex is *not* wrong/wrong only sometimes	Favor legalized marijuana	Believe homosexuality *not* wrong/wrong only sometimes	Favor legalized abortion
Everyone	19%	35%	56%	23%	22%	45%
Blacks	54	61	67	25	18	38

FIGURE 3.
Social Liberalism by Sex.

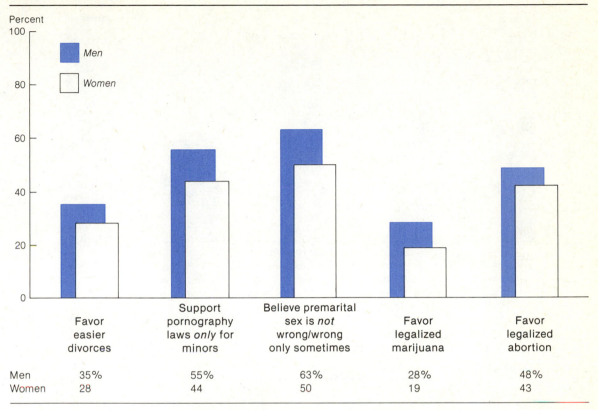

	Favor easier divorces	Support pornography laws *only* for minors	Believe premarital sex is *not* wrong/wrong only sometimes	Favor legalized marijuana	Favor legalized abortion
Men	35%	55%	63%	28%	48%
Women	28	44	50	19	43

Another way to look at the matter is shown by Figures 1–6. These figures show how Americans feel about a number of issues, according to age, sex, race, region, and education. By studying these, you will be able to see where you fit in with your group.

Look, for instance, at Figure 1. Young people are more liberal than older people on all six issues mentioned. In Figure 2, blacks are shown to be more liberal than the country as a whole on several issues (note the two—homosexuality and legalized abortion—where they are less liberal). In Figures 3–5, men are shown to be more liberal than women, Jews more liberal than Catholics and Protestants, and the Northeast and Far West more liberal than the rest of the country.

Remember, these are measures of *social* liberalism. Results may differ on other questions, especially those dealing with economic issues.

How do people with college educations compare with others? Figure 6 indicates that college graduates tend to be considerably more liberal on social issues than persons with less than a high-school education.

In analyzing the data over time, Professor Everett Ladd, Jr., has concluded that we have seen a

FIGURE 4.
Social Liberalism by Religion.

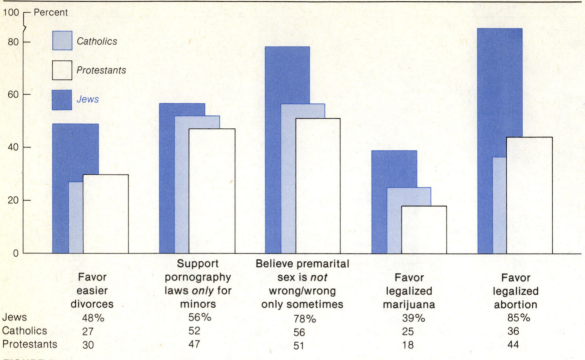

	Favor easier divorces	Support pornography laws *only* for minors	Believe premarital sex is *not* wrong/wrong only sometimes	Favor legalized marijuana	Favor legalized abortion
Jews	48%	56%	78%	39%	85%
Catholics	27	52	56	25	36
Protestants	30	47	51	18	44

FIGURE 5.
Social Liberalism by Region.

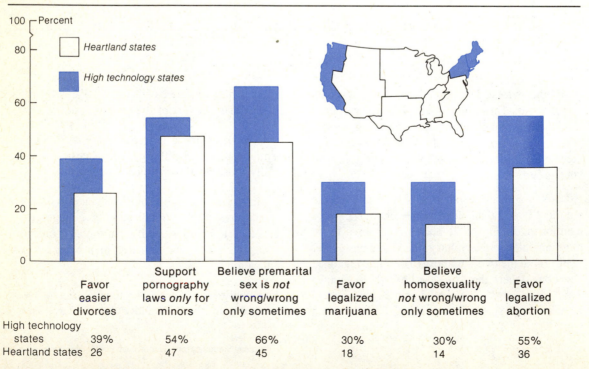

	Favor easier divorces	Support pornography laws *only* for minors	Believe premarital sex is *not* wrong/wrong only sometimes	Favor legalized marijuana	Believe homosexuality *not* wrong/wrong only sometimes	Favor legalized abortion
High technology states	39%	54%	66%	30%	30%	55%
Heartland states	26	47	45	18	14	36

FIGURE 6.
Social Liberalism by Educational Attainment.

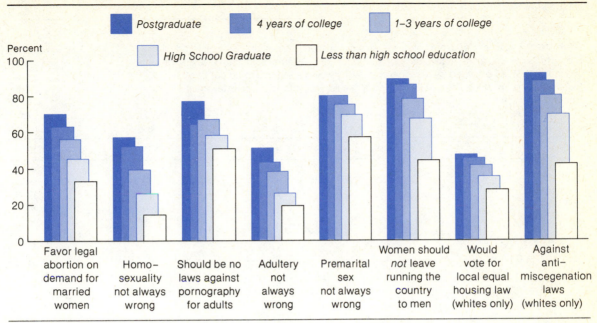

Source: 1972–1977 General Social Surveys, National Opinion Research Center (NORC).

major change in ideological positions of various socio-economic groups. He says:

In general, the college educated and upper-income occupational groups of the New Deal era thus composed a more conservative business class, while the high school and grade school educated and those in blue-collar jobs were a relatively change-oriented working class.

Today, much of this has changed. The primary class conflict is no longer between the lower class and the middle class, but rather pits a lower-middle class against an upper-middle class. . . . The ideological expression of this conflict is now commonly described as between the "new conservatism" and the "new liberalism." And in a reversal of the New Deal relationship, it is the higher status group which is the more "liberal."[1]

What Ladd has found is that "education is the key factor in defining today's class divisions." This means that people with college degrees, whether they are professionals or factory workers, generally share the same political and social views. And the same is true of people who have only a high-school education.

Sometimes, however, an issue will arise that finds most people in the country—whatever their age, education, ideology, etc.—on one side or the other. Let's take a look at the Proposition 13 issue, the subject of our case study at the beginning of this section. You will remember that Larry Stammer, the writer of the case, noted that, "by May 28 when the *Times* published the last in a series of preelection polls [of California voters], it reported a dramatic rise in support, with 52 percent favor-

TABLE 1.
Nationwide Reactions to Proposition 13.

Question: Two weeks ago, the voters in California passed Proposition 13—which reduced property taxes by more than half. Opponents of the measure said that if taxes were reduced, services provided by the local community would also have to be cut back. . . . If there was a proposition like that in your area, would you vote for it, or vote against it, or wouldn't you vote?

	For	Against	Wouldn't Vote	No Opinion
Total	51%	24%	12%	13%
By Race				
White	52	25	11	12
Blacks	43	19	22	16
By Income				
Under $10,000	53	17	15	15
$10–15,000	48	23	12	17
$15–25,000	57	27	9	7
Over $25,000	55	27	8	10
By Age				
18–29 years	47	25	18	10
30–44 years	54	22	13	11
45–64 years	56	23	9	12
65 years and over	48	23	7	22
By Political Ideology				
Liberal	57	22	12	9
Moderate	52	27	11	10
Conservative	54	23	11	12
By Political Party				
Republican	56	29	7	8
Independent	52	20	15	13
Democrat	49	26	11	14
By Homeowner/Renter				
Owner	54	25	8	3
Renter	45	18	22	15

Note: Asked of non-California residents only. Similar questions posed to national samples by other polling organizations have produced comparable results: in June, *Newsweek*/American Institute of Public Opinion (Gallup) found 57% support for such a measure; NBC News/Associated Press, 53% support; and Louis Harris, 63% support.

Source: Survey by CBS News/*New York Times*, June 19–23, 1978.

ing Proposition 13 and 35 percent opposed.'' After the election, he told us:

> *The initiative carried the votes of 70 percent of the homeowners, 41 percent of the renters (who would receive no direct benefits), 40 percent of the blacks, and 40 percent of the voters whose families included at least one public employee who stood to lose by Proposition 13's passage. Senior citizens voted overwhelmingly for the measure—76 percent.*

Two weeks after the vote in California, CBS/ *New York Times* conducted a nationwide survey to find out how other Americans would have voted if a similar measure were put to them in their state. The results are shown in Table 1. For the most part, the results coincide with what happened in California. There are a couple of notable exceptions. For instance, nationwide, only 48 percent of citizens over 65 (senior citizens) said they would vote for Proposition 13, as against the 76 percent reported in California. And 54 percent of the nation's homeowners supported it, while 70 percent of California's homeowners said they voted for the measure. Overall, however, you see a pretty consistent support—cutting across a number of age, income, and ideological boundaries— for tax cut measures resembling Proposition 13. Unfortunately, the survey does not provide information on education.

"Where Did You Get Such Ideas?"

Most Americans—generally or individually—regard themselves as liberal, moderate, or conservative, and some students of political behavior spend a lot of time studying how Americans came to be that way. Their field is called **political socialization**. Basically, students of political socialization seek to know how people acquire their political beliefs and values. Major sources of political socialization are the family, schools, peer groups, socio-economic class, region, religion, and race.

The family. It is generally agreed that probably the most important influence in shaping a person's political values is the family. Certainly, it is the first institution to which one is exposed. In the family setting, the child learns about such things as what is expected of a citizen, what to look on with favor or disfavor and, usually, either a strong sense of patriotism or, sometimes, an intense distrust of the political system. Children, especially before the age of seven, are not likely to acquire from their parents particular orientations toward candidates or specific policies, but they do get a reasonably clear sense of whether the family tends to be for one party or another—even without knowing the differences between the political parties. And this family influence is more frequently than not subtle and informal rather than the result of any intense ''pounding'' of ideas into one's head.

"My grandson, needless to say, is also pro-Reagan."

Left: "Like mother, like daughter." Although children do not necessarily grow up to espouse their parents' views, a parent's political activism—or lack of it—affects a child's awareness of the political system. Below: Mealtime provides a forum for the discussion of issues in the home, where parents' attitudes often shape the political orientation of their children.

If children hear their parents praising or complaining about certain political issues—taxes, inflation, police protection, garbage collection—they come to feel that it is important to be concerned about such matters. On the other hand, if the family environment is one where voting and political issues are never brought up, or if parents consistently profess that they see no value in, say, voting, the likelihood is great that the children will acquire the same attitudes and behave similarly. It is in the family that the child first is introduced to a "style" or attitude toward the political system: the child senses whether the parents are critical or supportive, which later might be translated into firm views on the radical-liberal-moderate-conservative-reactionary spectrum. In other words, *basic values* are often first acquired and shaped in the family setting. The important point is that the family probably best sets a *tone* and provides a framework.

School. The next prominent institution of political socialization is the school—the formal educational system. Here the influence is probably more focused and specific. That is, the influence, especially at the elementary and secondary levels, is generally *aimed* at developing characteristics of support for the political system as a whole. The school inculcates a sense of what is right for a "good" citizen to do—vote, pay taxes, obey laws, attend PTA meetings, contribute to worthwhile charitable causes, defend the country against enemies. The emphasis is not on supporting particular parties or candidates—as is sometimes the case in the family setting—but on upholding certain tenets of the political system.

Sometimes, depending on the locale, this function can be performed quite overtly, with strongly patriotic assembly programs and the like. Or it is simply performed through decisions as to which textbooks to purchase, teachers to hire, courses to offer, speakers to invite to the school, and places to visit on field trips. From time to time, we hear of conflicts arising in some schools as a result of controversial political issues: whether a homosexual teacher should be hired or retained; whether the pledge of allegiance to the flag should be required; whether penalties should be inflicted if one refuses to stand during the playing of the national anthem; whether sex education should be taught in the schools. All these issues are fraught with politics, and when they come up they can turn the school and the community into a political battleground. Very seldom are the debates confined *only* to the school. Parents, interest groups, the press, as well as students, teachers, and administrators, get involved.

In some schools, the teachers and students take the opportunity offered by such incidents to turn the issue into discussions on civil liberties, academic freedom, and so forth. Normally, when this

From the day children are taught to say the pledge of allegience, schools play a significant role in the development of attitudes toward the government.

Congressman William Cohen addresses a high-school class in his home district. Exposing students to various aspects of government is one way schools encourage good citizenship.

is done, it is not really an attempt to persuade the students to think a certain way, but rather to think intelligently about the issues involved. One would expect such an exercise to be a proper function of the school. Unfortunately, there are cases in which some school officials (teachers and administrators) take advantage of the situation by attempting to tell the students *what* to think.

Peer groups. Outside the structured, formal institutions of the family and school are an array of relationships most people have with friends, neighbors, and coworkers. Sometimes these occur in social environments such as bridge clubs or sewing circles or bowling leagues; they might be found in job-related organizations such as labor unions or professional or trade associations. Politics is probably not the top item of constant discussion in these groups, but the subject certainly does come

up, especially around election time or during times of heightened crisis. These peer groups serve as much to strengthen and reinforce one's views as to shape them. Most people tend to associate with others who already think as they do, or at least they are likely to avoid establishing ties with those who do not. Thus, the peer group is a sort of self-fulfilling relationship. It is not likely that one's constant peers would contain people who span the range from strong liberal to strong conservative. Over time most groups of people come to find that they generally agree on most broad issues of politics and policies. It would be strange, indeed, if one's closest social associates included staunch supporters of Ronald Reagan and devoted followers of Teddy Kennedy.

The various peer groups are usually more consensus-oriented than that. Thus, in pursuing such associations—in the beauty parlor, in the union hall, in private dinner parties—people relate to others who end up generally agreeing with them. This serves to confirm their basic values and beliefs, whatever those values and beliefs may be.

Class. Socio-economic status is also an important influence in political socialization. If a person perceives him- or herself as ''working class'' or ''middle class,'' this will have a certain meaning for political orientation. A ''working-class'' person will probably support measures aimed at strengthening labor unions; a ''middle-class'' person might feel that unions have become too powerful and should be restrained. One's perceived class status will also be important, no doubt, in influencing one's general views on the ''welfare state,'' and on the *general* role of government in helping individuals economically and in regulating business.

Two scholars have studied survey data relating class status to attitudes toward business, and they have concluded:

> *It appears . . . that while support for organized labor is very much a function of social and economic status—as status rises, sympathy for unions tends to decline—support for business has a much weaker and less consistent relationship with a person's position in society. Business is most popular among ''managers, officials and proprietors''—in short, businessmen—and least popular among semiskilled workers (who are heavily unionized). Support for business is conspicuously weak, however, among the highest status and best-educated nonmanual workers —professionals, for whom business values show little appeal.*[2]

Region. In a country as geographically large as the United States, it is not surprising that certain interests—and therefore certain values and beliefs—would be associated with particular regions. One sector might be highly industrialized and urban, and people in such areas would develop particular lifestyles and attitudes toward government roles and services. These views would likely differ markedly from those held by people living in the wide-open plains states and essentially agricultural communities. How people live from day to day can be an important factor in determining how they think about political matters.

The history of a region is especially important. For example, the Northeast region has a long history of dense populations composed of different ethnic groups working in large and small factories; this region has experienced the country's most constant contact with emerging industrial unions. The history of slavery in the South was no small factor in that region's racial-political attitudes for decades. The small, pioneering frontier towns of the West gave that region a political orientation different from that of the Northeast. Greater exposure to foreign immigrants (in the latter nineteenth and early twentieth centuries) suggested that the Northeast would be more ''internationalist'' in its political outlook than other regions of the country.

Religion. It is easy to see how one's religious orientation would play a role in political socialization. Although there is no official church in the United States, and even though freedom of religion and separation of church and state are very important tenets of American life, a strong belief in a Supreme Being is held by most Americans. Many American institutions use religious symbols: ''In God we Trust'' is imprinted on our paper money; ''One nation under God'' is part of the pledge of allegiance; the Bible is used in some courts to swear witnesses and in all presidential inaugural ceremonies. Two authors have thus concluded: ''In America the bonds to the nation have potent religious elements that interact and are likely to reinforce each other. The good American is *not* an atheist.''[3]

The Moral Majority, founded by Rev. Jerry Falwell (center), is one religious group that has assumed an active role in politics, by endorsing some political candidates, campaigning against others, and lobbying on Capitol Hill.

Religions, of course, have particular views about human nature and about the duties of individuals toward each other. Some stress that human beings are basically good, others that human nature is essentially evil and must be carefully monitored. Some religions emphasize the obligation to do charitable works as a means of salvation, and views such as these inevitably influence how adherents feel about the role of government. As could be expected, at times religious views are translated into specific positions on policy issues such as abortion, birth control, Sunday Blue Laws (see glossary), and aid to parochial schools. Generally, Americans prefer not to inject explicit religious issues into their politics (and in some instances, this is explicitly prohibited), but it is not possible to exclude the influence of religion altogether.

Race. The one time Mr. Reagan and Mr. Carter debated during the 1980 presidential campaign, one question put to both was:

Blacks and other nonwhites are increasing in numbers in our cities. Many of them feel that they are facing a hostility from whites that prevents them from joining the economic mainstream of our society. There is racial confrontation in the schools, on jobs and in housing as nonwhites seek to reap the benefits of a free society. What do you think is the nation's future as a multiracial society?

Mr. Reagan's response, in part, was:

I believe in it. I am eternally optimistic. And I happen to believe that we've made great progress from the days when I was young and when this country didn't even know it had a racial problem.

His point was that the legal racial segregation and discrimination that had existed since the abolition of slavery had never been particularly troubling to whites. These practices had not affected whites the same way they affected blacks. And he was probably correct.

Racial experiences have been important factors in political socialization. Black Americans have, as a result of their peculiar place in American society, developed attitudes toward the political system quite different from those of mainstream whites. They tend to rely, for instance, much more on federal government actions than on state and local governments (or even on the private sector) to alleviate social and economic conditions. The federal government, on the whole, has been more responsive to complaints of racial discrimination than other levels of government.

Likewise, blacks have a lower sense of political efficacy—that is, of being able to influence decision-making—than whites, because the political process has been less responsive to the needs of blacks. At the same time, blacks have become more liberal in their thinking than they were even as recently as the 1950s. This liberal orientation, as demonstrated by a political science study in the 1970s, embraces issues not only strictly related to civil rights, but also such matters as foreign policy and the role of government in the economy.[4] From the Emancipation Proclamation in 1863 to the present, black Americans have had a particular racial experience that clearly has influenced their political beliefs and attitudes. (This will be discussed further in chapter 14.)

A combination of factors. While we have listed separate items that contribute significantly to the formation of basic political beliefs and values—political socialization—we are aware that a combination of all these things is involved. They interact to reinforce each other. Most people are not ''cross-pressured'' (faced with conflicting influences) to any great degree. The school basically extends the subtle, informal teachings of the family. Frequently, the school one attends is chosen as a result of the family's class status, as is the church one attends. Thus, by the time a person reaches young adulthood, he or she—through a combination of mutually reinforcing influences—has formed a set of more or less permanent beliefs and values about politics and the political system.

This does not overlook the possibility of major events intervening to cause a change. This seldom happens, though, because not that many dramatic, ''disrupting'' experiences normally occur. But let's look at one such possible event: Watergate.

Children and Politics: Did Watergate Make a Difference?

On August 8, 1974, the thirty-seventh President of the United States—Richard M. Nixon—became the first President to resign from office. He did so amidst scandal, corruption, and possible impeachment and conviction, and after several of his closest advisers in the White House had been indicted and were headed for jail terms. This was, indeed, a most traumatic and disturbing period in American political life.

Students who were first- and second-year college students in 1980 and 1981 were just entering high school or finishing elementary school during the two years of intense national focus on the Watergate affair. Daily, on their television sets, on the front pages of their local newspapers, they saw the President fend off attacks from all sides—attacks charging that he had lied, that he had encouraged (if not ordered) his subordinates to break into offices of political opponents, that he had consented to raising and paying bribery money. They saw, as the country saw, one event after another unfold which had the cumulative effect of calling into question the integrity of the man who occupied the highest office in the land.

Americans—through socialization—were not accustomed to such open, blatant charges being leveled against their President. They surely liked and disliked some occupants of that office, but their feelings normally had to do with particular policies which honorable people could argue over. The office itself was supposed to be above reproach, and the individuals holding it were not supposed to be disgraced, charged with criminal acts, and ultimately forced to resign.

Before Watergate, studies had concluded that "an American child's first awareness of the politi-cal system is of the President of the United States, and that the role and occupant are idealized to an overwhelming degree."[5] Young children in elementary school (grades 3, 4, 5) saw the President in very positive terms: as benevolent, wise, strong, protective, infallible. David Easton and Jack Dennis concluded from their work:

Even though the older child may see authority in more critical and less enthusiastic terms, early idealization may create latent feelings that are hard to undo or shake off. This is the major significance of the first bond to the system through the Presidency. The positive feelings generated there can be expected to have lasting consequences.[6]

Richard Nixon, with his wife Pat and daughter Tricia, gives a farewell speech to members of his cabinet and staff on August 9, 1974, after his involvement in the Watergate scandal forced him to resign.

Thus, our beliefs, values, and general orientation toward government rely heavily on early exposure and experiences. And to a remarkable extent many of these feelings are focused on the top job of the presidency. To the young, that office comes to represent much of what government stands for. In fact, some children have understood everyone else in government to be "working under him." The President is the boss, and he is held in high esteem; if he is perceived as worthy of support and respect, this will benefit the entire government. This contributes to a strong sense of legitimacy, and, although obviously views become more sophisticated and differentiated as children mature, the basic values are not easily thrust aside.

Because these ideas have constituted a rather well-established set of premises in the field of political socialization, scholars of the subject were understandably eager to test the theories under rare circumstances. Watergate provided such an opportunity. If early acquired *positive* perceptions of the President (and through him, the political system) would mean continued support, what about the effect of Watergate on the new generation just growing up? F. Christopher Arterton put it this way:

The wholly negative perceptions engendered by Watergate raised the possibility that a generation of citizens might come to political maturity without holding those shared beliefs so necessary to the continued maintenance of our system of government.[7]

Sure enough, studies during and after Watergate by Arterton and others have shown that previously held positive orientations were considerably weakened, if not reversed.[8] Arterton questioned 355 children in an elementary school "in an upper socio-economic-status suburb of Boston, Massachusetts." He compared his results with a nationwide study (using many of the same questions) in

1962, and with a 1973 study (*during* the Watergate crisis).[9] The later findings were not positive. Children in 1975 felt less of an attachment to the President than was the case in 1962; they felt the President was less benevolent. ("Would he want to help you if you needed it?") There was a rather marked change in the question of dependability. ("Does he keep his promises?") Children in 1975 were less confident of the President than those responding in 1962.

But, interestingly, the President was still seen as a powerful figure. "If anything, the President is conceived of as more powerful now than he was thought to be in the early 1960s. Thus, the composite picture of the President which emerged in 1973 was of a powerful, yet negatively valued actor—an image which suggested the label 'malevolent' leader."[10]

Whereas earlier studies seemed to suggest that positive orientations toward the President did not depend on the particular person holding the office, later studies have shown that three different presidents have provided "three very different images."[11] Arterton concluded:

There seems ample documentation for the proposition that the incumbent actor is indeed a variable relevant to the attitudes of children. . . . We must conclude from the evidence supplied by two replications of the 1962 study that politics can enter the world of children and does have an important impact upon their political attitudes.[12]

We still are not able to say precisely what this means for the future. It is clear that Watergate caused negative reactions toward the President and government in the minds of children. It is also clear that children reacted *less* negatively to President Ford than to President Nixon. But the trend away from the earlier rather strong positive attitudes persisted in the 1970s. If this trend is

Despite the trauma of the Watergate era, the country at least had the reassurance that "the system" worked. Here, the Senate Watergate committee, headed by Senator Sam Ervin (arms crossed, center), hears the testimony of Watergate conspirator E. Howard Hunt.

maintained, it could well mean "that we are headed for a profound legitimacy crisis in our political future."[13]

The Watergate story must also be seen in another context. Some people felt that while the events surrounding the break-in at the Democratic headquarters and the later coverup by the White House were to be deplored, nonetheless there were positive aspects to the affair—especially in the roles played by Congress and the federal courts. "The system worked," some said, and they took comfort in the methodical, constitutional manner in which Congress and the courts went about the business of bringing one segment of the executive branch to justice. This aspect seems to have been lost on those who viewed the entire Watergate affair as one huge negative experience. To Ameri-

cans—children especially—who are not socialized to expecting their President to tell lies and engage in underhanded activities, the fact that he was caught and forced from office can be of some comfort.

The Media

The impact of Watergate was made even more dramatic because millions of Americans saw it unfold every evening before their eyes on television. It was not something they merely heard about or read about afterwards. In earlier years they had also seen, in all its stark, unrehearsed reality, a suspected presidential assassin gunned down in a Dallas police station; and—if they could bring themselves to watch—the actual murder of President Kennedy riding in a motorcade, a scene

On November 24, 1963, Jack Ruby shot Lee Harvey Oswald, accused presidential assassin. Oswald's escorts and an entire nation of television viewers looked on in disbelief and horror.

shown more times than one could count. In the 1960s and 1970s, for the first time, a war thousands of miles away was brought daily into their homes showing Americans killing and being killed. And, of course, virtually every major civil rights and anti-Vietnam demonstration was dumped into their laps, sometimes at the very moment they were happening.

Politically attentive citizens could then read about these events daily in a press that wired stories across continents in seconds. The term *attentive* refers to those citizens who take more than a casual interest in civic and political affairs. They are interested in going beyond the daily headlines in an effort to learn more about what happened and why. They are likely to discuss issues with their peers, write letters to Congress, and even join groups seeking to influence public policy.

It is by now a truism to say that "the media" have transformed American politics and in some ways changed what Americans think about politics and the way they act politically. If the media give prominence to people and events and issues, then those things, almost by definition, become important. Media exposure is a kind of stamp of legitimacy: if an item is on the evening television network news or on the front page of a major newspaper, it *must* be important. This does not mean that only the media can set the agenda, as we saw with Proposition 13, but once a person or issue comes to the attention of the media, there is little likelihood of the person or issue being easily dismissed.

Media coverage lends an air of importance to events and issues. Shown here: the sophisticated apparatus involved in bringing events, such as this speech by Henry Kissinger, into American living rooms.

Let's take a look, again, at the evolving role of the media in the Proposition 13 case. We saw that at the beginning, when Howard Jarvis announced he was starting the ballot initiative, the press did not give it much play. His announcement "ran in the second section of many of the state's newspapers. The *Los Angeles Times*, for example, published a short story on May 19, 1977, which ran five paragraphs."

But once the issue began to catch on and people became concerned about what would happen to their property taxes, the media started to take notice. Note the following account in the case study:

As homeowners marched to their local assessor's office, so, too, did the media, which duly recorded one horror story after another. Those stories were carried prominently throughout the state.

The press can help keep some issues alive by continuing to focus on them. In this sense, it is accurate to say that even if the press does not tell people *what* to think, it can strongly suggest what they think *about*. For example, in the summer of 1979, several groups were urging Senator Ted Kennedy to run for the presidency against President Carter. There were many reasons at the time why the senator was reluctant to do so, but one of the most prominent reasons had to do with the tragic event of 1969 at Chappaquiddick Island in Massachusetts, where Kennedy was involved in a car accident in which a young woman died. In 1979, the polls showed Kennedy well ahead of Carter among Democratic voters. But what about Chappaquiddick? Would this be an issue in a Kennedy presidential campaign? As matters developed during the Democratic primaries of early 1980, several polls indicated that Senator Kennedy's "character" was indeed an issue with voters, many of whom refused to support him because of the Chappaquiddick incident. Thus, in some instances, the media can and do determine what people think and talk *about*.

This certainly does not mean that the media have inevitable, predictable influence over viewers and readers. In the Proposition 13 case study, we saw that "many of the state's leading newspapers kept up a steady drumbeat in their editorial columns urging a vote *against* the initiative." Likewise, in presidential campaigns, endorsement by the majority of the media is no guarantee of victory. Studies on this subject have been inconclusive. One report found "some evidence. . . . that explicit endorsements in newspapers are tied to how people vote, although this is true mainly among uncommitted and independent voters."[14] Another study of the 1964 landslide victory of President Johnson indicated that the endorsement of a newspaper (in the North) for the Democratic candidate likely meant about five more percentage points for the winner.[15]

The importance of the media stems, in part, from the amount of time people spend exposing themselves to them. More often than not, in terms of political socialization, the message is one of "soft sell." (Advertisements pushing particular products are another matter.) During the siege of the American Embassy in Iran, one television network noted each day the hostages remained in captivity: "America Held Hostage, Day 12." This was a constant reminder of the ordeal suffered by the prisoners, and it is reasonable to assume that this had some impact on viewers.

One person involved with developing popular TV programs has commented:

Although networks will deny that television has much effect on human behavior, scholars and businessmen and politicians know different. What people see on television is an education for them which runs a close second to real life, and it is not certain that "real life" can effectively compete any longer.[16]

After the takeover of the U.S. embassy in Teheran, Iranian radicals exploited the American media to air their grievances against the United States. Here, an American hostage is paraded before television cameras on November 6, 1979.

FIGURE 7.
Hours Americans Spend Watching Television.

Question: On the average day, about how many hours do you personally watch television?

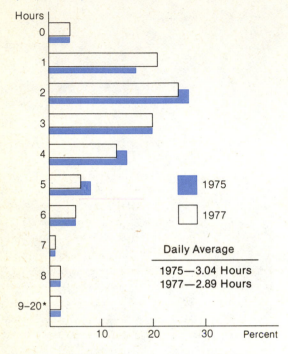

1975

1977

Daily Average

1975—3.04 Hours
1977—2.89 Hours

Question: Thinking about how you spend your non-working time each day, do you think that you spend too much time or too little time watching television? Reading newspapers? Reading magazines?

Total sample	Watching TV	Reading Newspapers	Reading Magazines
Too much time	32%	5%	6%
Too little time	18	48	52
About right	50	46	41

*Note: Nine through twenty hours collapsed due to small percentage of people with those responses.

Sources: Surveys by National Opinion Research Center, General Social Survey, 1975 and 1977. Survey by American Institute of Public Opinion (Gallup), December 9–12, 1977.

This person complained that he was not able to change the thinking of some television producers about the content of various programs being planned for the air. For instance, he was unhappy that virtually all the characterizations for a program called ''All's Fair'' involved casting business executives as cranks and cheats, and all conservatives as ''kooks.'' ''Every time I came up with a suggestion of a crazy liberal, I would be met by blank, incredulous stares . . . . Their [the producers'] stock of characters included wild-eyed conservatives, but no comparable characters on the other side of the political spectrum.''[17] We can imagine that liberals also can find cause to complain that television programming is generally too conservative—from a political point of view.

At any rate, whatever the subtle (and at times not-so-subtle) messages coming from the media, Americans have plenty of opportunity to receive them. Television viewing ranks ahead of other media in exposure, as Figures 7 and 8 indicate. This form of activity seems to have peaked between 1965 and 1975, but it still outranks other forms of leisure-time activity. What straight political information most people get comes from watching the evening news programs on television. At best, these are short, clipped, highly condensed accounts of events. An occasional documentary or a public affairs program of a current news story will be aired, but these are infrequent, and they do not draw consistently large audiences. The Federal Communications Commission (see chapter 10 on regulatory agencies) requires that a certain amount of time be devoted to broadcasts of public affairs.

Another important point about the media—especially the print media (newspapers, magazines)—is that they are increasingly under the control of fewer and fewer owners. The number of daily newspapers is declining (in 1910, there were 2400; in 1978 there were 1,756), and more and more

FIGURE 8.
How Americans Spend Their Leisure Time.

Question: Which is your favorite way of spending an evening?

* = less than 1%	1938	1960	1966	1974	1977
Watching T.V.	N/A%	28%	46%	46%	30%
Reading	21	10	15	14	15
Staying home with family	7	17	5	10	11
Movies/theater	17	6	5	9	6
Listening to radio/records	9	*	2	5	4
Playing cards/games	9	6	5	8	4
Visiting friends	4	10	5	8	4
Dancing	12	3	2	4	*

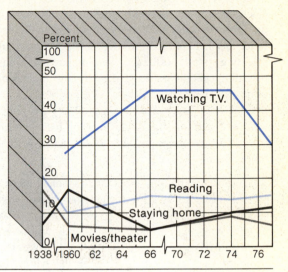

Note: A number of other responses—dining out, resting and relaxing, entertaining friends, participating in sports, sewing, home repair, club and church meetings, crossword puzzles, going to the bar, etc.—are not shown in the table because of the relatively small percentages appearing in each category. In 1977, these responses accounted for 24% of the total.

Source: Surveys by American Institute of Public Opinion (Gallup), latest that of December 9–12, 1977.

local towns and cities are being served by only one newspaper (or by newspapers owned by the same corporation). Some people fear that this can only stifle diversity of opinion. Anyone can start a newspaper (no license is needed, which is not the case with radio or television stations), but what this really means is that anyone who can afford the *cost* can start a newspaper.

As everyone (critics and defenders alike) will acknowledge, the media are businesses. The critic of television programming cited above notes: "All of the people in the television business are *in business*. They are not living off endowed chairs or foundation grants. They are selling a product, door to door, all across the country. They are under no obligation that I know of to do more than make what sells. If they did otherwise, they would not

have their jobs for long."[18] This is sometimes referred to as "the bottom line," and it applies pretty much to all of the media.

We will return to the role of the media in American politics in other sections of this text, particularly in chapter 7 ("Voters and the Electoral Process"), chapter 8 ("The Presidency"), and the chapters on domestic and foreign policies. Clearly, the media pervade every aspect of politics and government.

Public Opinion

In a democratic society, what the citizens think and want done about certain issues are supposed to be important. Granted, citizens can vote for people who will represent them in office, and elections (as will be discussed in chapter 7) can be one mechanism for reflecting the wishes of some citizens. But elections are not the only means for registering opinions. In fact, most national and regional elections are held almost solely for the purpose of selecting public officials. Seldom are elections related to specific issues. The relatively rare exceptions are instances such as Proposition 13 or proposals to legalize casino gambling, where issues are put on the ballot in the form of an initiative, referendum, or state constitutional amendment.

Therefore, ongoing local and national public opinion polls serve to tell what the public feels about specific issues at a given time. Anyone who follows American politics even slightly will often hear politicians and interest groups invoke the name of *the American people* or *the public* to support a particular view. We are constantly being told "what the American people will not stand for," "what the vast majority of the public wants" or does not want, or that "public opinion is running heavily in favor of," or against, something or other.

What is this often-used (and abused) animal, public opinion?

What do the polls tell us? Basically, **public opinion** refers to the statistical results of *scientifically* developed and administered surveys. But it is important to keep in mind that we seldom are able to get a very accurate picture of what approximately 220 million people think at any given time on any given subject. It is best to realize that there are really many publics holding many opinions, and that these opinions are held at different levels of *intensity*.

Usually opinion surveys focus on a specific item or cluster of items. Thus, with the survey of

children's views on the presidency, various matters were covered, such as opinions on assorted government officials and authority figures—teachers, policemen, and others. Sometimes, depending on the purpose of the survey, the results are used to draw conclusions about what policy should be followed or to learn about ways people become politically socialized—the purpose of the studies discussed earlier in this chapter.

Here, we want to discuss three aspects of public opinion: as a means of finding out how and why people feel certain ways, as a guide to what is likely to happen, say, in an election, and in some cases as a cue to what policies government officials should adopt. Our Proposition 13 case study is useful in illustrating all these aspects.

You will recall, for instance, that "independent surveys showed that Jarvis's arguments struck a much more responsive chord with the public than did his foe's." Likewise, when the opponents of Proposition 13 found that they "couldn't win the argument on taxation," they pursued another campaign strategy. Their surveys told them that people wanted taxes cut but also wanted to keep certain governmental services. Given this situation, the anti-Jarvis forces decided to argue that Proposition 13 was the wrong way to go about it:

> *Thus, the anti-Jarvis campaign embarked on a course of stressing the loss of public services which their polls indicated the public least wanted cut—police, fire, emergency service, education.*

Both sides in the struggle over Proposition 13 watched the public opinion polls carefully and constantly. From the case, we find that

■ the anti-Jarvis strategy appeared to have been paying off by the second week of May. *No on 13* campaign manager Winner said that polls indicated the anti-Jarvis campaign had nearly closed a 30 percent gap in the polls.

- at that time Winner privately believed Jarvis had won. "I felt it was bleak when we had the overnight turn around when the assessments came out. We had pulled even within a point and then a week later we were down by twenty points. At that point I knew it was going to take some fantastic action, something out of the blue, to win," he said.
- while polls indicated that police and fire protection were among services that voters did not want cut, voters entertained no similar sentiments for welfare. And no one knew this better than the politicians in Sacramento.

It is safe to say that while some politicians publicly state that they do not pay much attention to polls (especially if the results are unfavorable), few politicians are completely oblivious to them.

Well-conducted polls can tell us how intensely the respondents feel about certain issues. We can know if people feel "strongly," "not so strongly," "mildly," or "indifferently" about an issue. For example, with Proposition 13, we have the following information:

Despite the overwhelming response to the petition drive, the Jarvis election campaign began slowly. Four months before the June 6 primary, the respected California poll conducted by Marvin Field found that while 56 percent of all voting-age residents were aware of the Jarvis initiative, only 30 percent had taken a stand— 20 percent in favor and 10 percent opposed. The Los Angeles Times *poll a month later showed that 35 percent were solidly in favor and 27 percent firmly opposed. The remaining 38 percent, the newspaper found, could be swayed by the side which mounted the best campaign. By May 28 when the* Times *published its last*

"YES. NO. SOMETIMES. NO. NO. YES. DON'T KNOW. SOMETIMES. YES. YES. NO."

pre-election poll, it reported a dramatic rise in support, with 52 percent favoring Proposition 13 and 35 percent opposed.

Public opinion polls can also indicate trends when surveys are conducted over a period of time—that is (as with the data on social liberalism discussed earlier in this chapter), when the same questions are asked for several years or even decades. We then get some *longitudinal* data, which tell us about shifts in views, intensity and persistence of opinions, the "direction" of the country ("becoming more conservative-" or "showing signs of becoming liberal") that commentators like to talk about. Opinion polls are some of the best sources for finding out about these developments. One might not like what one finds, but, after all, it's all a matter of opinion.

How are polls taken?   There are more than 220 million people in the United States. In order to find out whether they prefer Jimmy Carter or Ronald Reagan or Ted Kennedy or Howard Baker for President, some professional pollsters will survey about 1500 of them. Depending on what those 1500 say, the pollsters will seek to determine the preferred candidates for all *220 million.*

Is that reasonable? In fact, it is. It certainly is not feasible to ask all 220 million. Therefore, the pollsters proceed by taking a *sample* of the total population. This has to be done in such a way that that sample will probably reflect the population at large.

First, the pollsters divide the country into units or sections. Then they subdivide those into smaller sections, to the point where they can, through the process of **random sampling**, choose which individuals will be interviewed. The final step in this process requires a method to be chosen that permits all persons to have an equal chance of being

One method of polling—the door-to-door survey. Professional pollsters are able to determine national opinion from a random sampling of only about 1500 individuals.

selected. Thus, the pollster might take every fourth house in the block or every tenth name on a list of apartment dwellers. The process is more refined then this, of course, but this is the basic approach.

By following these steps, the pollster is reasonably assured that the final 1500 will be representative of the proportions of various groups in the population—by age, sex, race, income, and education. This process has proved reliable to the extent that if the sample size were enlarged by, say, a few thousand, the results would not be significantly different. Again, the crucial thing is that the process allow everyone in the population an equal chance of being chosen.

Once the representative sample is established, the pollster must be as careful as possible to ask questions that are simple and understandable. The respondent might not have an answer ("Don't know"), but it should not be because the question is not clear.

Some questions are "leading"—they suggest an answer, or they have rather obvious biases built into them. In such instances, the responses will be of little value. The poll results will show what the pollster wanted, not what the respondents necessarily think.

In public opinion polls taken in many political campaigns, the pollster or the person for whom the poll is taken must file a copy with the local or state or federal election commission. This permits one to examine the legitimacy of the poll—the sampling methods used, the specific questions asked, and the results obtained.

Pollsters should guard against the kind of mistake made by the *Literary Digest*, in 1936. The *Digest* confidently predicted that the Republican candidate, Alf Landon, would defeat President Roosevelt. Roosevelt won in a landslide, carrying forty-six of forty-eight states. The problem with the poll was one of sampling. Only owners of automobiles and telephones were questioned about their choices. Such a "universe" could hardly be considered representative of the total population in 1936, when only the relatively well-to-do could afford cars and phones. Thus, the poll had a built-in economic bias.

Politics and Polls:
Accurate Reflection or Undue Influence?

As we have seen from the Proposition 13 case, polls are used in a variety of ways. They indicate what the public thinks about an issue and if there have been any changes over time. The polls signal to politicians how they might alter their strategies in order to accomplish their goals. Public opinion data can provide some insight into the "mood" of the country. All these things are vitally important to the conduct of democratic government. But it is important to note that some people believe that the use of polls under some circumstances can serve to distort the political process. They assert, for example, that polls showing a candidate or issue either ahead or behind can create a "bandwagon" effect or sometimes a "dampening" effect. That is, some people might be encouraged to support the front-runner, or they might believe that their choice is so far behind (or ahead) that it would not be fruitful (or necessary) to support him or her. It is difficult to assess this charge of undue influence. As long as the polls are sensibly developed and administered, they can be defended as legitimate mechanisms for conveying political information about the populace to citizens and decision-makers. Given the adequacy of the polls, the potential distortion of the political process they might cause is likely a cost a democratic society must bear.

Summary

1. While broad, general labels (radical, liberal, moderate, conservative, reactionary) are rather simplistic ways to characterize people, it is nonetheless possible to determine—based on a set of carefully designed questions—the general orientation a person has toward issues of political concern. From this it is possible to determine whether one is a liberal, conservative, or something else.

2. It is possible to know what demographic characteristics (age, sex, race, religion, region, education) are normally associated with particular opinions. Education appears to be the major variable in determining what people think about political issues.

3. The study of *political socialization* is concerned with how people acquire their basic political beliefs and values. Several institutions (the family, school, peer groups) are primarily responsible, and these (along with influences of class, religion, region, and race) interact to reinforce each other and contribute to the process of inculcating certain basic attitudes and general orientations. Major dramatic events (such as Watergate) can influence the way children, especially, form views toward politics and government. In the case of Watergate, the results were in a negative direction.

4. The media, particularly television, wield considerable influence in American politics. Normally, through the process of focusing (or not focusing) on certain people, events, and issues, the media can determine to a considerable extent what the American public thinks *about*—even if they cannot always influence what Americans actually *think*.

5. Public opinion polls—scientifically devised and administered through a process known as *random sampling*—convey what vast segments of the society think and what responses are *likely* to result from public action. They can also gauge how strongly people feel about certain matters. Frequently, decision-makers gear their policies and actions to the results of public opinion polls.

Notes

1. Everett Ladd, Jr., "The New Lines Are Drawn: Class and Ideology in America," *Public Opinion*, Vol. I, No. 3 (July/August 1978), 49.
2. Seymour Martin Lipset and William Schneider, "How's Business? What the Public Thinks," *Public Opinion*, Vol. I, No. 3 (July/August 1978), 47.
3. Harry Holloway and John George, *Public Opinion: Coalitions, Elites, and Masses* (New York: St. Martin's Press, 1979), p. 74.
4. Norman H. Nie, Sidney Verba, and John R. Petrocik, *The Changing American Voter* (Cambridge, Massachusetts: Harvard University Press, 1979) pp. 253–56.
5. F. Christopher Arterton, "The Impact of Watergate on Children's Attitudes Toward Political Authority," *Political Science Quarterly*, Vol. 89, No. 2 (June 1974), 269–88.
6. David Easton and Jack Dennis, *Children in the Political System: The Origins of Political Legitimacy* (New York: McGraw-Hill, 1969), p. 207.
7. F. Christopher Arterton, "Watergate and Children's Attitudes Toward Political Authority Revisited," *Political Science Quarterly*, Vol. 90, No. 3 (Fall 1975), 478.
8. See also Frederick Hartwig and Charles Tidmark, "Children and Political Reality: Changing Images of the President," unpublished paper presented at the 1974 annual meeting of the Southern Political Science Association, New Orleans, November 7–9, 1974; and Richard A. Joslyn, "Adolescent Attitudes Toward the Political Process: Political Learning in the Midst of Turmoil," unpublished manuscript, Cornell University, Ithaca, N.Y.
9. The 1973 study was conducted in a suburb close to the 1975 study site.
10. Arterton, "Watergate and Children's Attitudes," 485.

11. The three were Kennedy, Nixon, and Ford.
12. Arterton, ''Watergate and Children's Attitudes,'' 493.
13. Ibid., 495.
14. John P. Robinson, ''The Press and the Voter,'' *The Annals*, Vol. 427 (September 1976), 101.
15. Robert S. Erikson, ''The Influence of Newspaper Endorsements in Presidential Elections: The Case of 1964,'' *American Journal of Political Science*, Vol. 20 (May 1976), 207–33.
16. Ben Stein, ''Box Populi: Report from Television Land,'' *Public Opinion*, Vol. 1, No. 3 (July/August 1978), 18–20.
17. Ibid., 18.
18. Ibid., 20.

Gerald Finch

Student Opinion Survey

Most of what we know about the electoral behavior and political beliefs of Americans is based on public-opinion surveys. By interviewing a relatively small number (1000 to 2000) of randomly selected citizens, political scientists can determine with great accuracy the attitudes and partisan preferences of the American public. When combined with computerized methods of research, a public-opinion survey permits us to examine the characteristics of selected groups and the relationships among the opinions that people hold. Although each person is unique, past research has shown that opinions usually follow predictable patterns; on the average, certain types of people tend to hold certain types of beliefs and tend to vote for certain types of candidates.

The chance that you· will be interviewed in a survey of 2000 Americans is approximately one in 100,000. Most Americans will never be interviewed for a survey.

The following questionnaire will give you some idea of the kinds of questions asked on public-opinion surveys. They are typical of those used by social scientists to measure public opinion.

The questions are taken from surveys conducted and made available (in part) by the Inter-University Consortium for Political and Social Research. They are a part of the 1976 American National Election Study (ICPSR Study 7381) conducted by Warren E. Miller and Arthur H. Miller of the Center for Political Studies (CPS) at the University of Michigan under a grant from the National Science Foundation.

This CPS 1976 American National Election Study was the fourteenth in a series of studies of national elections produced by the Political Behavior Program of the Survey Research Center and the Center for Political Studies.

The questions in this survey cover only areas of general political interest such as demographic characteristics, partisan attitudes, policy preferences, and social outlook. There are no references to any particular elections, campaigns, or candidates, all of which were included in the CPS 1976 study. The questionnaire includes an identification of the major problems many people thought to be facing the country, but, again, the list is not all-inclusive.

Once you have finished answering the twenty-seven questions in this questionnaire, you will be able to compare your responses with those of other Americans (the instructor will have such comparative data).* It may be useful to have a class discussion of what the results mean in terms of a general understanding of liberal-conservative ideology (discussed in chapter 4) and the political significance of public-opinion research.

Instructions: Circle the number of the appropriate response.

1. Some people are afraid the government in Washington is getting too powerful for the good of the country and the individual person. Others feel that the government in Washington is not getting too strong. Do you think the government is getting too powerful, or that it is not getting too strong?

   1. Government too powerful
   5. Government not getting too strong
   8. Don't know

2. Some people believe that our armed forces are powerful enough and that we should spend less money for defense. Others feel that military spending should at least continue at the present level. How do you feel—should military spending be cut, or should it continue at least at the present level?

   1. Cut military spending
   5. Continue spending at least at present level
   8. Don't know

*This questionnaire is also printed in the Study Guide for *American Government*.

3. This country would be better off if we just stayed home and did not concern ourselves with problems in other parts of the world.

    1. Agree
    5. Disagree
    8. Don't know

4. The United States should give help to foreign countries even if they don't stand for the same things that we do.

    1. Agree
    5. Disagree
    8. Don't know

5. In recent dealings with the Soviet Union, the United States has given up far more than we have received.

    1. Agree
    5. Disagree
    8. Don't know

6. The government should spend less even if it means cutting back on programs like Health and Education.

    1. Agree
    5. Disagree
    8. Don't know

7. So many other people vote in the national elections that it doesn't matter much to me whether I vote or not.

    1. Agree
    5. Disagree
    8. Don't know

8. Some people feel that the government in Washington should see to it that every person has a job and a good standard of living. Suppose that these people are at one end of a scale—at point number 1. Others think the government should just let each person get ahead on his own. Suppose that these people are at the other end—point number 7—and that others have opinions somewhere in between.

    Where would you place yourself on this scale?

    1. Government should see to providing a job and good standard of living
    2.
    3.
    4.
    5.
    6.
    7. Government should let each person get ahead on his own

9. There is much discussion about the best way to deal with racial problems. Some people think achieving racial integration of schools is so important that it justifies busing children to schools out of their own neighborhoods. Others think letting children go to their neighborhood schools is so important that they oppose busing.

    Where would you place yourself on this scale?

    1. Bus to achieve integration
    2.
    3.
    4.
    5.
    6.
    7. Keep children in neighborhood schools
    8. Don't know

10. Some people are primarily concerned with doing everything possible to protect the legal rights of those accused of committing crimes. Others feel that it is more important to stop criminal activity even at the risk of reducing the rights of the accused.

    Where would you place yourself on this scale?

    1. Protect the right of accused
    2.
    3.
    4.
    5.
    6.
    7. Stop criminal activity
    8. Don't know

11. Recently there has been a lot of talk about women's rights. Some people feel that women should have an equal role with men in running business, industry, and government. Others feel that women's place is in the home.

Where would you place yourself on this scale?

1. Women and men should have an equal role
2.
3.
4.
5.
6.
7. Women's place is in the home
8. Don't know

12. Some people think that the use of marijuana should be made legal. Others think that the penalties for using marijuana should be set higher than they are now.

Where would you place yourself on this scale?

1. Make the use of marijuana legal
2.
3.
4.
5.
6.
7. Set penalties higher than they are now
8. Don't know

13. There are many possible ways for people to show their disapproval or disagreement with government policies and actions. Suppose all other methods have failed and a person decides to try to stop the government from going about its usual business by conducting sit-ins, mass meetings, demonstrations, and similar activities. Would you approve, disapprove, or would it depend on the circumstances?

1. Approve
3. Depends
5. Disapprove
8. Don't know

14. Some people believe a change in our whole form of government is needed to solve the problems facing our country, while others feel no real change is necessary. Do you think a big change is needed in our form of government, or should it be kept pretty much as it is?

1. Need a big change
2. Need some change
3. Keep as is
8. Don't know

Do you agree or disagree with the following statements?

15. Public officials don't care much what people like me think.

1. Agree
5. Disagree
8. Don't know

16. Voting is the only way that people like me can have any say about how the government runs things.

1. Agree
5. Disagree
8. Don't know

17. The poor are poor because the wealthy and powerful keep them poor.

1. Agree a great deal
2. Agree somewhat
4. Disagree somewhat
5. Disagree a great deal
8. Don't know

18. The poor are poor because the American way of life doesn't give all people an equal chance.

    1. Agree a great deal

    2. Agree somewhat

    4. Disagree somewhat

    5. Disagree a great deal

    8. Don't know

    9. Unsure

19. People like me don't have any say about what the government does.

    1. Agree

    5. Disagree

    8. Don't know

20. Generally speaking, do you consider yourself a Democrat, a Republican, an Independent, or do you profess to some other political identification?

    1. Democrat

    2. Republican

    3. Independent

    4. Other (specify) _____

    5. Don't know

21. Below is a seven-point scale on which the political views that people might hold are arranged from extremely liberal to extremely conservative. Which of them best describes your own views?

    1. Extremely liberal

    2. Liberal

    3. Slightly liberal

    4. Moderate, middle-of-the-road

    5. Slightly conservative

    6. Conservative

    7. Extremely conservative

    8. Don't know

Some people say the federal government has to have certain powers to protect the interests of the country as a whole while others say that the rights of the individual always come first. Which of the following do you think the government in Washington should be able to do and which do you think it should not do?

22. Require everyone to carry a national identification card.

    1. Should be able to do

    5. Should not do

    8. Don't know

23. Wiretap phones for national security reasons.

    1. Should be able to do

    5. Should not do

    8. Don't know

(The following questions are for analytic purposes in class.)

24. Which of the following best describes your religious beliefs:

    1. Protestant   4. Buddhist

    2. Catholic   5. Atheist

    3. Jewish   6. Other (specify) _____

25. What is your race?

    1. White   3. Hispanic

    2. Black   4. Asian/Oriental

26. What is your sex?

    1. Male   2. Female

27. What is your estimate of the combined annual income level of your parents?

    1. $7000 or less   4. $25,000–$50,000

    2. $7000–$15,000   5. Over $50,000

    3. $15,000–$25,000

Interest Groups, Protest, and Confrontation

Chapter **5**

On the *best* of mornings—when traffic is moderate—one can expect to be caught in bumper-to-bumper traffic on the Long Island Expressway going into New York City. That is a normal rush-hour experience, and motorists have learned to live with it. One morning in June 1979, however, traffic was especially heavy and moved along at a snail's pace. For thirty miles, cars and trucks poked along—stopping, starting, inching forward. Whether the motorists knew it or not, they were in the midst of a demonstration—an expressway slowdown—by 100 truckers exercising their first-amendment right to protest and to petition the government.

The demonstrators, who represented a group of independent truck owners, were protesting the diesel fuel shortage, burdensome interstate regulations and license requirements, and certain government-imposed restrictions on weight and loads. The slowdown on the expressway was one means of putting their demands before national and state officials. One of the truckers participating in the action said that he did so as a last resort.

> *When you write letters to your Congressman or your Governor, you don't get results. (He was wearing a T-shirt that read "No Crude/No Food.") You do get somewhere with a strike, although we don't like to use that word; we prefer "shutdown."* [1]

These truckers were participating in a political activity with a tradition as old as the political system itself. They were a group of people stating their common interests and "lobbying" to have those interests addressed by the government.

Protest is just one of several tactics employed by pressure groups (we will return to it later in this chapter when we discuss protest and pressure politics). In general, however, most interest-group activities are similar to those described in the political story of Proposition 13; that is, they are based on a more direct relationship with decision-makers in the state and national capitals.

You will recall that interest groups were very actively involved on both sides of the Proposition 13 battle. The California Firefighters Coalition, we were told, "issued a public 'alert' warning that the state's 600 fire protection districts, which depended almost entirely on property taxes as a revenue source, would face budget cuts of 60 percent." The Consumer Federation of California, the state PTA, the California Labor Federation (AFL-CIO), public-employee associations, and business groups were all involved in the Proposition 13 fray. Newly created ad hoc groups, such as the *Yes on 13* committee, took ads in newspapers and produced television commercials. Interest groups constantly polled their members (as did the California Chamber of Commerce) to articulate the group's viewpoint. Both sides of the issue received financial support from corporations and other groups.

Volatile political issues (such as Proposition 13)

at any level of government may call forth a wide range of interest-group activity. **Interest groups** are found throughout the American political process and they represent the entire spectrum of opinion. David B. Truman defines an interest group as "any group that, on the basis of one or more shared attitudes, makes certain claims upon other groups in the society for the establishment, maintenance, or enhancement of forms of behavior that are implied by the shared attitudes."[2] When these groups attempt to make their demands known to the government, they become political interest groups, sometimes referred to as **pressure groups** or as **lobbies**. (The term **lobby** is derived from the practice in which interest-group representatives buttonhole legislators in the corridors and lobbies of the Capitol.)

So pervasive are interest groups that one school of American politics has even suggested that the American political process is based on pressure-group activities. This theory, known as *pluralism*, states that the American political system is made up of competing interest groups, with the government serving as a kind of "broker," balancing demands and reaching compromise decisions. In this view, no one group or even coalition of groups predominates, and ultimately every *organized* interest has some—but not all—of its demands met.

On the other hand, the *elite* theory of American politics maintains that interest groups do exist, but that they are basically controlled by an elite corps of individuals drawn from business, labor, and the military. Members of this elite have the same general orientation and share the same general values; while there is hemming and hawing among them, there is agreement on the general direction (or agenda) of politics. While the labor-union and business leaders may fight over an issue, they ultimately reach an agreement between themselves, relatively independent of the direct influence of the masses, of organized interest groups,

A sampling of interest groups.
Opposite page: Farmers gather
in protest in front of Capitol
building in Washington, D.C.
This page, top: Sandoval Pueblo
Indians at a tribal meeting.
Left: Women's group lobbies
for passage of the Equal Rights
Amendment.

and certainly of those groups with lesser resources. The elite theorists are not as optimistic as the pluralists that all groups can eventually be heard in the political system.

A third interpretation of American politics is based on a mixture of pluralism and elitism. This view holds that interest groups do exist and they are powerful, but there is less trading and compromising than the pluralists believe. Rather, one finds that various groups capture control of specific areas of government activity and maintain hegemony (control) of those areas to the exclusion of other groups. Thus, there is no coherent, intertwined "elite" that presides over the entire governmental structure. Grant McConnell expounds this view in his book, *Private Power and American Democracy*:

> *The first conclusion that emerges from the present analysis and survey is that a substantial part of government in the United States has come under the influence or control of narrowly based and largely autonomous elites. These elites do not "rule" in the sense of commanding the entire nation. Quite the contrary, they tend to pursue a policy of noninvolvement in the large issues of statesmanship, save where such issues touch their own particular concerns.*[4]

McConnell describes how certain powerful farm groups work in conjunction with the Department of Agriculture; labor unions with the Department of Labor; major business organizations with the Department of Commerce, and so forth. In addition, certain professions, such as medicine and law, take on the function of certifying who may practice in that profession. Thus, *private* medical and bar associations exercise control in the *public* process of granting licenses.

It is not necessary to try to resolve these conflicting theories at this point. Rather, it is important to understand just how influential interest groups are—and can be—in the political system.

What Are Interest Groups?

Interest groups provide representation on the basis of issues and functions, rather than, as in the electoral political system, on the basis of geography. That is, the membership of many interest groups is usually not based on where people live, but rather on how they live and what they care about. Sometimes those concerns coincide with geography, but most often not. For example, a person who is a member of a labor union affiliated with the AFL-CIO might live in San Diego, Tacoma, Houston, Iowa City, Bangor, Tallahassee, or any other place. A business person who belongs to the Chamber of Commerce or a conservationist who belongs to the Sierra Club might also live anywhere.

The electoral political system (which we will discuss in the next two chapters) *is* based on geography. Representatives and senators are elected from Congressional districts or states. Senator X represents Mr. and Mrs. Y who live in the state of Z. However, if Mr. and Mrs. Y are also opposed to abortion, they might join an interest group such as the National Right to Life Committee, Inc., which has members from all fifty states. Thus, we may think of interest groups as filling in the "gaps" left by the representational system based on geography.

It is difficult to name an issue or a concern that does not have a corresponding interest group. Although most groups are concerned with economic issues, many groups are socially or politically oriented. To give some sense of the scope of interest group concerns, Table 1 lists just twenty organizations from the thousands that exist (in random order).

TABLE 1.
Twenty National Associations and Interest Groups.

Year Established	Association/Interest Group
1887	American Institute of Certified Public Accountants
1933	American Apparel Manufacturers Association
1892	United States League of Savings Associations
1895	National Association of Manufacturers
1905	National Audubon Society
1941	National Peach Council
1878	American Bar Association
1965	Citizens for Clean Air
1924	Association of Governing Boards of Universities and Colleges
1969	National Abortion Rights Action League
1961	National Council of Senior Citizens
1970	Task Force on Gay Liberation
1961	American Council of the Blind
1847	American Medical Association
1966	Amnesty International
1964	American Conservative Union
1968	Common Cause
1966	National Organization of Women
1966	National Committee for Amish Religious Freedom
1955	National Right-to-Work Committee

Often, one issue spawns several groups, each adopting a different position. This occurs, in part, because of what Professor V. O. Key, Jr., once identified:

Increased specialization almost inevitably means increased governmental intervention to control relations among groups. In turn, governmental intervention, or its threat, stimulates the formation of organized groups by those who sense a shared concern. This chain reaction may be set in motion not so much by government itself as by the formation of one organization to press its claims, through the government, upon other groups which in turn organize in self-defense. Almost every proposed law represents the effort of one group to do something to another. When a law or a proposed law impinges upon a class of individuals, they are likely to be drawn together by their common interest in political offense or defense. Organization begets counterorganization.[5]

Certainly this was the case in the political story of Proposition 13. When Jarvis and Gann launched their drive to adopt Proposition 13, a plethora of other groups for and against the initiative were born.

As Professor Key has noted, pressure groups are often formed initially in response to an immediate concern, but then continue to exist on a permanent basis to address other, new concerns of its membership.[6] Again, this is precisely what happened with the proponents of Proposition 13. One year after the initiative was passed, Jarvis sent a mailing across the nation soliciting funds for continued work. The four-page circular read, in part:

It took me 16 years to get Prop. 13 on the ballot and passed. Now I believe that may have been the easy part! Defending Prop. 13 from Leo McCarthy [remember him from the case study—the assembly speaker] and his gang of tax-money parasites may prove to be much harder.

To carry on the fight I have formed the "Save Prop. 13" Committee as a permanent part of the non-profit California Tax Reduction Movement.

The mailing contained a petition calling on the United States Congress to enact the American Tax Reduction Act of 1979. Among other things, it

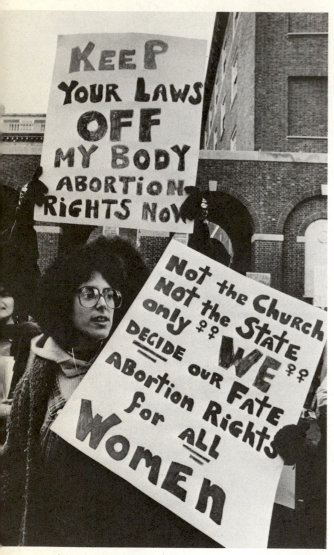
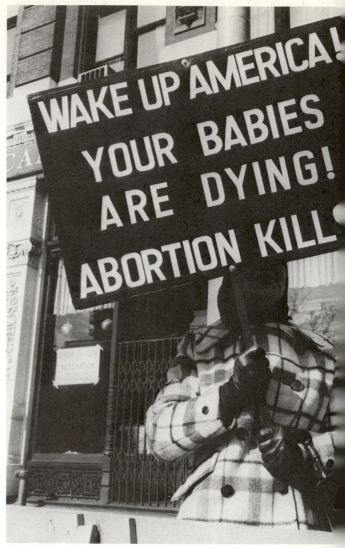

Interest-group activity often breeds counter-interest-group activity. Shown here are demonstrators from both sides of the abortion issue.

called for a twenty-five percent reduction in federal income taxes and a twenty percent reduction in federal spending. The California Proposition 13 interest group had not only become permanent, it had gone national.

About the same time, however, John Kenneth Galbraith, vice-president of Americans for Democratic Action, also mailed a solicitation circular. This two-page mailing read, in part:

> We are having, or are said to be having a great right-wing revival in this country. The privileged, at long last, are coming into their own. We are entering the age of Ronald Reagan, Jesse Helms, Proposition 13, an end to abortion—at least for the poor, federal tax reduction for the large corporations and the deserving rich, and an arms race bigger and better than ever. . . .
>
> Against this tide, as against previous eruptions, there is one organization that is always alert and on guard—Americans for Democratic Action. . . .
>
> It's my own feeling, frankly, that in the longer run the radical conservatives will do themselves in. When the fire engines are needed, it won't be much comfort that people can call Jarvis/Gann or Professor Milton Friedman. . . . But a lot of harm can be done during this reactionary surge. So we must rally and work as never before to limit the damage, roll back this ghastly wave.
>
> So this is it. Whatever you contributed before, I plead with you to double it or treble it for this year. And, if I didn't get through to you before, reflect on what you have saved, reflect also on the current need, and come on really strong this time. I'm writing this from the heart.

Whom does one support? Either? Neither? Some other group? Taken together, these two circulars illustrate one aspect of the political process: the mass appeal of one group, and the counterorganization and mass appeal of another group.

Permanent offices for interest groups and lobbies are as much a part of the Washington landscape as the Capitol and White House.

Obviously, some pressure groups are more influential than others, although they are not always easily identified. Even though commentators and writers make statements such as, "The Business Roundtable is clearly the most powerful group in Washington," or "the health lobby is the most effective group," such conclusions *are* difficult to reach. Nor can one automatically equate the best-known groups with the most powerful ones.

What is certain, however, is the growing trend toward setting up a permanent office in the nation's capital. There are at least 1800 trade associations alone (such as the Aluminum Association,

FIGURE 1.
The Nader Organizations.

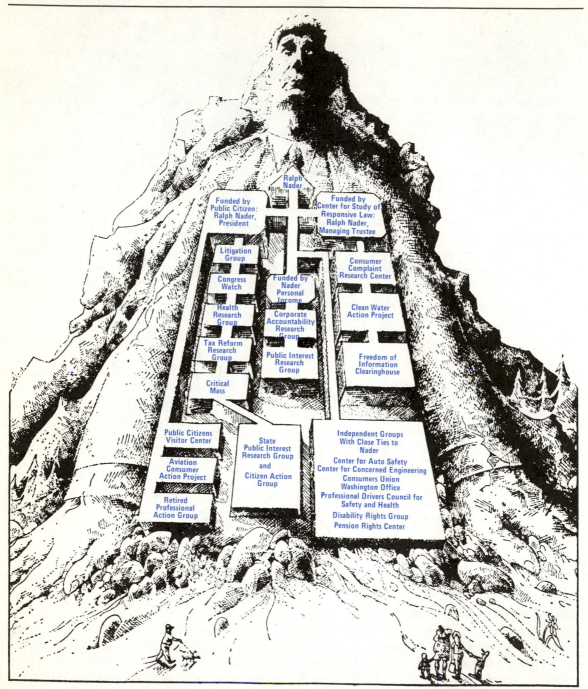

the National Electrical Manufacturers Association, and the Association of Trial Lawyers of America), employing more than 40,000 people, with headquarters in Washington, D.C. The lobbyists simply find it necessary to be conveniently located near Congress and the regulatory agencies.

The growth and influence of the lobbying industry may be demonstrated by two major interest groups—representing rather diverse positions on the ideological spectrum—founded in the last decade. One is the rather extensive complex of *public-interest* groups that began to appear in the 1960s, mainly under the leadership of Ralph Nader. The other is the Business Roundtable, formed in 1974.

Ralph Nader has been in the forefront of a burgeoning consumer protection movement ever since he came to prominence by criticizing the lack of auto safety in his book, *Unsafe at Any Speed*. His main organization is Public Citizen, a tax-exempt group supported largely by contributions (which amounted to approximately $1.1 million in 1977). The complex ''Nader Network'' (also known as Nader's Raiders) is composed of many subsidiary groups, which focus on various issues such as tax reform, health, energy, and Congressional activities (see Figure 1). The various groups essentially see themselves as lobbyists for the consumer interests of ordinary citizens, who do not have well-heeled professional and trade associations to represent them. Nader's Raiders have won many victories in the courts as well as before regulatory agencies. The health group, for instance, succeeded in banning the carcinogenic Red Dye No. 2.

The public-interest groups are, for the most part, liberal in their orientation, supporting such causes as conservation, environmental protection, the Equal Rights Amendment, gun control, and abortion. Generally, they believe that big business is a vital part of the American society, but that it needs to be closely monitored by the government and by public-interest groups. This consumer-advocate lobby helped pass legislation such as the ''truth-in-lending'' and fair credit reporting acts, as well as regulations resulting in the recall of hundreds of thousands of defective automobiles. In addition, the Nader groups have produced more than fifty books exposing defects in corporate and government policy.[7]

In spite of all these accomplishments the consumer-interest groups reached a point in the late 1970s where they needed to reassess their strategies and tactics. They were becoming increasingly removed from the very people they represented. In the words of Mark Green, director of Nader's Public Citizen's Congress Watch: ''Consumer advocacy groups are strong in Washington but weaker in the districts. No matter how brilliant you are in the halls of Congress, if you're weak in the streets, you're weak.''[8]

If the public-interest groups have a ''natural'' adversary on the lobbying scene, it is probably the Business Roundtable. This is an organization of 180 chief executive officers of major American corporations, including General Motors, General Electric, Du Pont, IBM, AT&T, General Foods, Chase Manhattan Bank, U.S. Steel, Citibank, Bristol-Myers, Prudential Insurance, and Coca-Cola. The group has offices in Washington, D.C., and New York City, and a $2 million annual budget contributed by the member corporations. A forty-three-member policy committee meets bimonthly, usually in New York City, to deal with issues of vital concern to the organization. The agenda might include items such as the President's energy policy, tax reform (especially involving capital-formation incentives), various regulatory policies and practices, and any other issues that may affect the business community. Since the entire Roundtable membership convenes only once a year, the policy committee is especially important; in fact, no one below the level of chief

Left: Elliot M. Estes, president of General Motors. Above: David M. Roderick, chairman of United States Steel Corporation. General Motors and United States Steel are both represented on the Business Roundtable.

executive officer may attend the policy meetings. The day after the policy committee meeting the steering committee meets in Washington to give the Washington-based staff of lobbyists its "marching orders."

Undoubtedly, the power of the Business Roundtable stems from its impressive membership roster. An aide to a New York congressman once described the group as men who "are in many ways the senior statesmen of the industrial community. Some even have been advisers to Presidents. They don't dirty their hands with the smaller issues. . . . You can be sure that there would be very few members of Congress who would *not* meet with the president of a Business Roundtable corporation, even if there were no district connection."[9]

The Roundtable members do not apologize for this influence. In fact, they believe it is necessary and useful. In the words of the chief executive

officer of General Electric, Reginald Jones, who headed the Roundtable's task force on taxation:

The main problems of business these days are external to the company and are determined in the arena of public policy. Therefore business managers are obliged to become students of public affairs. They must learn how to hold their own in public debate and know their way around in Washington. . . . When business managers bring their experience to bear in the formation of policy and law, they speak for millions of affected people and deserve a hearing.[10]

We might suspect that very few, if any, interest groups do *not* claim to "speak for millions."

Whose Interests Are Represented?

While it has been estimated that approximately forty percent of adults belong to some kind of

David M. Rockefeller, chairman of the board of Chase Manhattan Bank and spokesman for the business community, and other business and government leaders meet with Chinese officials to discuss trade, December, 1974.

interest group, this does not necessarily mean that millions of people are actively involved in such groups. On the contrary, for most people "belonging" probably means little more than paying annual dues and receiving a membership card or newsletter in return. Most members generally do not participate in political activities. And yet, interest-group leaders are sure to point out the "thousands" (or more) they represent.

Inevitably, we must ask the question: How representative are the mass-based interest groups? Does the National Rifle Association (NRA) speak for all (or even most) of its approximately 1.1 million members? Does the National Association for the Advancement of Colored People (NAACP) "represent" the interests of its approximately 425,000 dues-paying members? Or is it more accurate to say that the preponderant majority of all those members are just that—dues-paying members?

Clearly, such questions are difficult—if not impossible—to answer. Groups can be surveyed as is done from time to time on certain issues, but this is an expensive and time-consuming method. On the other hand, one might assert that if dues keep coming in, the group must agree with its leadership. In this case, however, we must remember that people join interest groups for various reasons, and with different levels of commitment.

Most mass-based groups are run by an elite corps of full-time professional people. They have expertise, knowledge, experience. Sometimes they are elected through annual meetings. Frequently they are able to maintain their leadership positions rather easily: the mass followers normally are preoccupied with other concerns—such as making a living—and have neither the time, talent, nor inclination to devote to the interest group's day-to-day affairs. Thus, in some cases, a kind of self-perpetuating elite runs the group. This has been referred to as "the iron law of oligarchy" by Robert Michels in his classic book, *Political Parties*.[11]

Although such a system potentially allows leaders to ignore the group's members, only an unwise and, indeed, ineffective group leader would completely sever him- or herself from the members. Group strength is an important element in interest-group influence, and a leader who cannot inspire the necessary evidence of group strength—letters, votes, contributions—will fail. Group leaders may thus be assumed to reasonably—but by no means completely—reflect the sentiments of their constituents.

Sometimes it is important to know how accurately the leaders reflect the membership views. For example, in California during the Proposition 13 struggle, we saw that the labor unions and many business organizations went on record opposing Proposition 13, and they contributed thousands of dollars to defeat it. But note the following from the case:

> *Even among interest groups that would presumably be hurt by passage of the proposition there existed a curious dichotomy of public opposition and private support. While public employees and members of the business community* through their organizations *opposed Jarvis, many of them* as individuals *supported him. . . . Jarvis would later report that he won the votes of 64 percent of labor union members, and 30 percent of public employees.*

Clearly, it would have behooved Jarvis to assess this dichotomy before the vote.

Pressure-Group Tactics: Lobbying

Interest groups go about the business of trying to influence policy in several different ways. In all cases, the initial objective is to gain access to be heard.

Some groups, like the Business Roundtable, prefer the one-on-one approach. This is sometimes referred to as the "rifle" approach, where members speak directly with selected sources in the legislative and executive branches. This style is especially suited to an organization that has great prestige and clout. As the Congressional aide pointed out, there are few, if any, members of Congress who would not meet with the president of a major corporation. A simple telephone call could set it up. In this case, mass group meetings or other open displays of strength are not required to attract the legislator's attention. Although success is not guaranteed, the initial contact with a government official is an important first step.

In contrast, the trucker at the beginning of this chapter felt that, for his group of independent truckers, even writing letters to officials was of little value. Therefore, he and his colleagues decided they had to cause "a scene," to slow up traffic during rush-hour, in order to be heard.

A group's tactics are dictated largely by its political and economic resources. These resources include prestige, money, number of members, expertise, organizational stability, and ability to influence voters. Since no single attribute is determinative of success, groups seek to maximize as many of these resources as possible.

Prestige, however, is a vitally important variable. Here we refer to a group's image with the public, the media, and the government. A group viewed as "responsible" (meaning, not too radical—left or right—and willing to negotiate and compromise) is likely to enjoy more access to officials and the media. This is not necessarily a static condition. Some groups may start out as "fringe" or "radical" groups (or may even be called "crackpot" or "irresponsible") but through the force of events become acceptable and influential. The evolution of attitudes toward labor union organizers, civil rights protestors, and Vietnam War demonstrators illustrates this point. These groups were not initially respected and were even repressed. Later, these groups were not only accepted, but many of their policies were adopted: collective bargaining for organized labor, desegregation of public facilities, and the end of American military participation in Vietnam. Such a change in attitudes was also characteristic of the history leading up to Proposition 13, as the case study indicates. Early proposals, "mild compared to the Jarvis measure, were defeated on grounds that they were too extreme," even though they were supported by then-Governor Ronald Reagan. Members of effective interest groups are keenly sensitive to the potential dynamics of their activities. There is no formula or rule of thumb to guide such developments. It is largely a matter of strategy, tactics, and, above all, political sophistication.

In addition, the more controversial the particular issue, the higher the level of interest-group involvement and the greater the number of interest groups involved. This relationship was demonstrated by Proposition 13 in California, and it applies to the national level as well. If an issue does not attract wide attention and can be dealt with in a bureaucrat's office or in a little-noticed Congressional subcommittee hearing, then the interest group will adjust its style and tactics accordingly. Why expend time and resources (and possibly arouse counteractivity) unnecessarily? As one study concluded:

Specifically . . . the legislative activity of lobbyists is most committee oriented in dealing with noncontroversial issues, while it is most floor oriented in dealing with campaign-defined, controversial issues. Lobbyists' techniques reflect this difference in focus of activity.[12]

The widely held image of a lobbyist constantly plying his or her trade on the Washington cocktail-party circuit is fairly accurate. These informal meetings provide an opportunity to "get in a word" for one's cause, and it is one very good reason why it is vitally important to have a permanent staff based in the nation's capital. No opportunity should be missed; a good lobbyist is *always* working—no 9-to-5 jobs for them.

At a reception for freshmen congressmen, a public affairs lobbyist sighted Representative Mickey Leland, a Democrat from Texas. The lobbyist knew that Mr. Leland was interested in drug problems, and he wanted to urge him to seek a seat on the Interstate and Foreign Commerce Committee, which handles many health issues.

But, as he approached Mr. Leland, he found him deep in conversation with another lobbyist of the liberal persuasion. Go on International Relations, the second lobbyist was urging, and push human rights.

Conversations like these are taking place all over Washington as lobbyists try to shape the composition of key committees in the next Congress. Many major decisions on Capitol Hill over the next two years will be strongly influenced by the complexion of these committees, and lobbyists are getting into the battle from the beginning.[13]

Another important tactic is, whenever possible, to form coalitions with other groups, thereby increasing one's ever-important base of support. Ironically, such coalitions are sometimes possible between groups that are usually at odds. For example, labor unions feared (and continue to fear) that the Business Roundtable was established in large part to undermine organized labor. The legislative director of the Laborers' International Union said of the Roundtable: "We saw them emerging as a force to thwart the aims of the labor movement and to turn the clock back to take away the gains that had been won at the collective bargaining table and in legislation, and to create an atmosphere of fear regarding unions."[14] The labor people felt that the Roundtable contributed to the defeat in 1977 of common-situs picketing. (See page 272.)

And yet, in spite of the standing rivalry between the unions and the Business Roundtable, they have joined forces on some issues.

The Roundtable has at times worked with labor unions, notably in the intensive fight this year [1978] over automobile exhaust emissions standards and nondegradation requirements for stationary pollution sources such as smokestacks contained in the Clean Air Act Amendments.

On that hotly lobbied issue, the linkage between production slowdowns and feared job losses had the chief executives of the major auto companies, such as John J. Riccardo of Chrysler, knocking on congressional doors side-by-side with former United Auto Workers head Leonard Woodcock.[15]

This unexpected alliance illustrates Congressman William Clay's (D., Missouri) saying, "There are no permanent enemies, no permanent friends, only permanent interests." And this is precisely what James Madison predicted in *Federalist Paper No. 10.* He knew that factions (interest groups) would exist, and that they would *naturally* push for their own interests. But Madison also realized that the way to control these groups was not by destroying them; instead by allowing many factions to coexist, no one group or several groups could form a permanent majority and thus enjoy unchecked rule. The many factions might form temporary alliances, but they would most likely not be able to predominate for long over the entire nation. Here, Madison was laying the theoretical foundation for the pluralist conception of the political process. And since he believed that such an approach worked better in a large system than in small units of local government, he was an advocate of a stronger national government.

Lobbyists in action: Opposite page: Senator
Dick Clark meets with Russell Hemenway,
chief lobbyist for the National Committee for
an Effective Congress, on a Capitol balcony.
This page, right: George Meany, as president
of the AFL-CIO a leading spokesman for labor
for many years, meets over dinner with
Senator Kennedy. Below: Antinuclear
lobbyists talk to Senator Warren Magnuson in
his Washington, D.C., office.

Another pressure-group tactic is *grass-roots* lobbying. This is when a group attempts to mobilize an avalanche of letters, telegrams, mailgrams, and even telephone calls to government officials. Jarvis's nationwide mail campaign was intended to have this effect. The purpose is to create the impression that there is a ground swell of support for or against a particular issue. Sometimes, this approach is quite sophisticated. Hoping to increase their chances for a favorable response, interest groups with enough resources might hire professional public relations firms who use highly developed techniques for reaching particular segments of the population. Such firms frequently use computers to devise their targeted lists.

Let's look, again, at the political story of Proposition 13 to see how computers can be applied. Recall how the Jarvis forces, working through the Butcher-Forde Consulting firm, used computers to predict new property taxes on 400,000 homes and announced the results to homeowners through ''personalized computer letters.'' The tactic worked. As the case study reported, ''A cry went out from homeowners demanding to know exactly what their new assessments would be—and they wanted to know officially before, not after, the election.''

Usually, the objective of grass-roots lobbying is to generate mass contact with officials. However, *thousands* of pretyped postcards mailed in bulk will probably be less effective than *hundreds* of individually handwritten letters. The latter shows that people were concerned enough to actually take time to express their personal opinions. Still, it is almost impossible to assess precisely the effectiveness of either tactic on decision-makers. As the trucker noted, even personal letters may not work.

Nonetheless, pressure groups continue to employ grass-roots tactics, probably because there is enough evidence to suggest that they work—at least sometimes. For example, in 1978 the Bureau of Alcohol, Tobacco and Firearms (BATF) issued regulations requiring quarterly reports of all gun sales, unique fourteen-character serial numbers on each firearm, and immediate reports of thefts from dealers. The National Rifle Association (NRA), an interest group that follows all government activity involving such matters, went into action. It sent a ''legislative alert,'' charging that the BATF was overstepping its authority, to its members (estimated at 1.1 million) throughout the country. The following ensued:

> *House members are lining up to make statements opposing the new regulations. Critical comments continue to pour in—more than 140,000 letters so far—to the rulemakers. An angry congressional subcommittee already has cut off funding. That's what happens when the National Rifle Association decides a new set of Treasury Department firearms regulations are the first step toward gun registration.*
>
> *The massive lobbying campaign mounted by NRA and its allies has administration officials clearly on the defensive.*
>
> *Meantime, the letters pile up in the office of Jim Hunt of BATF's research and regulations branch. More than 150,000 comments had been received by the end of last week, running about 14 to 1 in opposition to the proposed rules, Hunt said.*[16]

Certainly, one of the main reasons for the potential influence of grass-roots (or indirect) lobbying is that decision-makers link it to *voters*. Pressure groups who use this tactic like to remind government officials that such an outpouring represents the sentiments of their constituents, who will remember how the officials responded when election time rolls around. Exactly how true this is, of course, is hard to say, but most elected officials probably don't want to learn the hard way.

Interest groups know that in the final analysis they must talk in the language that elected officials understand—election and reelection. Thus, one of the major resolutions of the 1979 convention of the National Association for the Advancement of Colored People (NAACP) was "to become more political." The organization resolved to put more pressure on senators and representatives in areas where the black vote was substantial. It also agreed to make its demands known to both the Democratic and Republican party-platform committees in 1980.

Interest-group conventions are the usual places for making such pronouncements. In June 1979, the National Right to Life Committee held its convention in Cincinnati, Ohio. The feeling was strong about the need to stop the proabortion forces. The organization asserted that abortions were legalized murder, and they set a three-year limit for achieving a constitutional amendment that would end legalized abortions, except to save the life of the mother.

"We know we can do it now," the president of the interest group said. "We have matured."[17] The group was beginning to flex—and *feel*—its political muscle around the country. It had already demonstrated electoral successes:

> *Involvement of hundreds of thousands of "right to life" volunteers in the campaigns last summer was a major factor in a number of Senate, House and gubernatorial races, most notably the defeat of Senator Dick Clark, Democrat of Iowa, by a conservative Republican, Roger Jepsen, who supports the "right to life" movement. In New York, the Right to Life Party polled more than 100,000 votes in the gubernatorial election, enough to insure an automatic place on the ballot in future elections.*[18]

In the 1979 convention, the group planned to work for the defeat (at the 1980 polls) of specific senators who had taken proabortion stands. The list included John Glenn of Ohio, Robert Pack-

"Tell us, Master, what is the secret of reelection?"

wood of Oregon, Frank Church of Idaho, John C. Culver of Iowa, Birch Bayh of Indiana, Patrick I. Leahy of Vermont, and George McGovern of South Dakota.

These kinds of tactics are seldom far from the minds of serious interest groups who want to influence policy in Washington or on the state level. When Congress voted in 1978 to reject a proposal to create a Consumer Protection Agency, the executive director of the Consumer Federation of America stated clearly and briefly: "We have to go back to step one—the voting booth."[19]

Another way interest groups keep tabs on legislators is by "rating" their performance for each Congressional session. There are at least eleven groups that do this. The group develops a long list

TABLE 2.
List of Organizations That Rate Congressional Performance.

Americans for Democratic Action (left liberal)
1411 K Street, N.W., Washington, D.C. 20006

Americans for Constitutional Action (conservative)
955 L'Enfant Plaza, Suite 1000, Washington, D.C. 20036

Committee on Political Education (COPE–AFL-CIO: liberal/labor)
815 16th Street, N.W., Washington, D.C. 20006

Consumer Federation of America (consumer issues)
1012 14th Street, N.W., Washington, D.C. 20005

League of Conservation Voters (environmental issues)
317 Pennsylvania Avenue, S.E., Washington, D.C. 20003

National Association of Businessmen, Inc.
1000 Connecticut Avenue, N.W., Washington, D.C. 20036

National Farmers Union (agriculture)
1012 14th Street, N.W., Washington, D.C. 20005

National Security Index of the American Security Council
1101 17th Street, N.W., Washington, D.C. 20036

National Taxpayers Union (tax policy)
325 Pennsylvania Avenue, S.E., Washington, D.C. 20003

Public Citizen (liberal; public interest)
133 C Street, S.E., Washington, D.C. 20003

The Ripon Society (liberal Republican party group)
1609 Connecticut Avenue, N.W., Washington, D.C. 20009

Source: Michael Barone, et al., *The Almanac of American Politics 1978* (New York: E. P. Dutton).

of issues of importance to it, and weighs the official's behavior against the position favored by the interest group. Thus, a senator, say, with a ninety-five percent rating from the Americans for Democratic Action would have agreed with the ADA's liberal views ninety-five percent of the time. This same senator probably would receive a *very* low rating from, say, the Americans for Constitutional Action, a conservative group.

These ratings are used in several ways, depending on the purpose and the occasion. Generally, however, the ratings are of interest to *somebody* for *something*. The groups might mail the results to their members; opposing political candidates might use them in a campaign to advertise their (or their opponents') views; incumbents might send them to their constituents. Although many people do not know their representative's or senator's various ratings, such information is available to politically interested and attentive citizens.

Regulating the Lobbyists

Lobbying has become so pervasive, and there has been such an enormous increase in grass-roots or indirect lobbying, that one New York congressman, Benjamin S. Rosenthal, was moved to observe: "These people are in the process of gaining control of the apparatus of government."[20] This (like more than a few statements coming out of

Washington) is probably a slight exaggeration, but it gives some indication of how pressure-group activity is perceived.

For the last few years, there have been recurring efforts in Congress to tighten controls over interest groups. The federal Regulation of Lobbying Act of 1946 required individuals and groups whose principal business is to influence the passage or defeat of legislation to register with the clerk of the House of Representatives and the secretary of the Senate. In 1954, the U.S. Supreme Court ruled that this did not apply to grass-roots lobbying.[21] The legislation thus did not prove to be very effective: the language was too vague; the definition of a lobbyist was not clear enough; activities aimed at sources outside Congress were not covered.

Thus, recent efforts have aimed to close up the loopholes. But, as might be expected, many lobbyists have turned out in force year after year—in 1976 and again 1978—to defeat the proposed legislation. Traditional adversaries—public interest groups (especially Nader's organizations) and big business—as well as traditional allies—Common Cause and Nader's groups—were all united against Congress. Politics *does* make strange bedfellows! Note the following:

One of the most interesting spectacles of the Capitol Hill season has been the sight of lobbyists lobbying about the practice of their art. Prominent lawyers have emerged from their posh offices downtown and have flocked to the Capitol to work the corridors and anterooms, just as if they were getting their usual $150-an-hour fee. Labor union officials and the staff of the Chamber of Commerce have buttonholed Senators and Representatives with the same vigor they exhibit when the issue is wages and hours. The troops from Ralph Nader's army and the foot soldiers from Common Cause have been

out in force—at times on opposite sides of the question—to advocate the public interest.

The object of this frenetic activity is a bill that would replace the 30-year-old lobby registration law. It has proved ineffective and unenforceable, primarily because its definition of what constitutes a lobbyist is so vague. The proposed legislation would specify precisely who must register and would require those who do so, and their employers, to file detailed public reports about their activities. Lobbyists, for instance, would have to make public whom they meet with, what they discuss at each meeting and how much money they spend.[22]

In addition, the proposed legislation would regulate grass-roots lobbying and lobbying efforts aimed at executive agencies.

The lobbyists argue that such legislation comes very close to violating the First Amendment to the Constitution, which gives lobbyists the right to ply their trade: ''Congress shall make no law respecting . . . the right of the people peaceably to assemble, and to petition the Government for a redress of grievances.'' On the other hand, supporters of the reform insist that the public has a right to know who is influencing the government and, to an extent, how it is being done. Likewise, such legislation would bring more ''sunshine'' into governmental affairs—that is, it would make the political process more visible to the public. However this issue is dealt with legislatively, if a tightened law is passed, it will likely end up in the courts under a test of constitutional rights.

''Sue Me'': When Interest Groups Go to Court

One normally associates interest-group activities with lobbyists talking to elected and appointed officials in the legislative and executive

A lobbyist conferring with a legislator during a break in committee hearings.

branches—and properly so. But interest groups also spend a lot of time in court—suing and being sued.

This is to be expected in a political system characterized by different branches of government, each having power to make decisions, and by the kind of federal system discussed in chapters 2 and 3. There are several avenues for pursuing one's cause, and the courts certainly provide one forum. As long ago as the 1830s, Alexis de Tocqueville observed the proclivity in American politics to resort to the courts. "Scarcely any political question," he said then, and it is no less (and perhaps more) true today, "arises in the United States that is not resolved, sooner or later, into a judicial question."[23]

The struggle for civil rights (discussed fully in chapter 14) is a notable example of a particular interest group, the NAACP, utilizing the legal arena. This occurred, in large part, because the other branches of government were not especially responsive to the needs of black Americans in fighting against racial segregation and discrimination.

The use of the judicial system by interest groups is becoming increasingly more common. One tactic is to "lobby" in the courts by filing **amici curiae** briefs in behalf of one party or the other in a lawsuit. These are arguments presented as "friend of the court" to help (urge) the court to decide a case a particular way.

Since the mid-1960s there has been the enormous development of public-interest law firms, who do the legal work of the political and research-oriented public-interest groups. The major interest groups even maintain legal staffs of their own or retain law firms on an annual basis. These firms file suits against government agencies and private businesses before administrative tribunals as well as in courts of law and equity. Sometimes they file **class-action** suits on behalf of large segments of the society—consumers, nature lovers, etc.—who, singly, do not have the financial or technical resources to pursue legal remedies. Some groups, particularly the NAACP, have been very successful in winning these class actions.

The law on class-action suits is variously applied. For example, federal district-court judge John Sirica ruled in 1979 that Nader's consumer organizations could not sue the Food and Drug Administration on behalf of the general public, partly because the consumer groups did not have democratic structures, dues-paying members, or elected officers. In another instance, the court stated that if a class-action suit is to be filed, notice must be sent to *all* persons in that "class." Of course, this would be a major financial burden for many interest groups. But there have been instances where the public-interest groups have prevailed in their legal efforts.

Frustrated in Congress, these groups [the environmental and consumer movements] *have made an end run to the courts, where they have skillfully exploited and magnified limited legislative gains, especially the National Environmental Policy Act of 1969. Their cases, made possible only through recent changes in the law of standing, have been important in fundamentally transforming the relationship to the public of private interests, in particular corporate business, causing the environmental and consumer damages complained of.*[24]

Public-interest law firms, however, are not all on one side. Even if that were the case at one time, it is not so now. Businesses have started giving financial support to law firms who see themselves as defenders of free enterprise and limited government. One report stated:

Business was obviously disturbed by the successes of these [Nader-type] *law firms. In the spirit of American free enterprise, business has now copied the better idea of its consumer competitors. It has produced its own brand of public-interest law firm. . . . Some of the better-known firms are the Pacific Legal Foundation, the National Chamber Litigation Center, the Washington Legal Foundation, and the National Legal Center for the Public Interest.*[25]

The names of these new groups, you will note, are similar to their counterparts in the consumer and environmental movements. These firms have also had their share of victories. They convinced the Environmental Protection Agency to reverse the ban on the pesticide DDT in the Northwest forests; a Supreme Court ruling in their favor was rendered against the Occupational, Safety, and Health Administration (OSHA), requiring the latter to obtain a search warrant before inspecting a factory.

Thus we have another example of V. O. Key's pronouncement: organization begets counterorganization. In the corridors of the Capitol and the executive bureaus, at the grass roots, and in the courts, the interplay between interest groups goes on.

Protest as Pressure in American Politics

Truckers Choose "Direct Action"

5000 in Colorado Protest a Nuclear Weapons Plant

Nuclear Protest in South Carolina Ends in 3d Day With Arrest of 250

Farmers in Tractors Protest in Capitol

1000 March for Gay Rights

Such headlines are commonplace today, as were the following headlines in the sixties and early seventies:

250,000 Participate in March on Washington For Jobs and Freedom: King Gives Stirring Speech

Students Take Over Campus Building

5000 Demonstrate Against War in Vietnam

One not familiar with American history might erroneously believe that such action began in the 1960s. In reality, it is safe to say that there has not been a decade since the founding of the American republic when there has not been some rather substantial form of political protest—sometimes peaceful, sometimes violent.

An accurate knowledge of American political history reveals protests against the state courts in the 1780s by farmers seeking to block foreclosure on mortgages by banks in New Hampshire, Vermont, and western Massachusetts. One recalls the Sons of Liberty and the protests against British colonial legislation and Tories. Anti- and proslavery mass action leading to the Civil War was common. As Jerome Skolnick has noted: ''WASPS, organized politically as 'native Americans,' tore apart the Irish section of Philadelphia in 1844; similar riots occurred in Baltimore, Boston,

An artist's depiction of the Haymarket Square incident in Chicago, May 4, 1886. Violence erupted when a bomb exploded, killing one policeman. Police opened fire on the crowd, killing many civilians and wounding dozens of others.

and other port cities. On the west coast, Chinese and Japanese immigrants were victims of both riots and discrimination. Italians were lynched in New Orleans and Jews attacked in New York."[26]

Union history is filled with examples of protests and protest groups: the Molly Maguire protests of the 1870s; the Haymarket Square incident in 1886; the Pullman Strike in 1894; and the many walkouts, lockouts, and efforts at strike-breaking that dot the American landscape from the late nineteenth century into the 1930s.

In the first two decades of this century, many Americans were shocked to see hundreds of women march in the streets demanding a constitutional amendment giving women the right to vote, which ultimately came in 1920 with the Nineteenth Amendment. "In 1917 . . . militant women engaged in hunger strikes, picketed the White House, and burned copies of Presidential speeches."[27]

Thus, the young people who burned their draft cards and chanted "Hell no, we won't go" in the sixties and seventies; the women (and men) who held mass rallies for the Equal Rights Amendment in the seventies; and the trucker who slowly moved his diesel truck on the Long Island Expressway on a June morning in 1979—all these people were (as one news account of the last incident said) "fol-

Protestors in San Francisco participate in a "die in" to show their opposition to nuclear power. The 1979 accident at the Three Mile Island plant touched off antinuclear activity throughout the country.

lowing an American tradition that started with the Boston tea party."[28]

Mass political action can be peaceful or violent. We have seen both in American history. Peaceful, nonviolent demonstrations, obviously, are acceptable. They are legal. Usually they only require a permit from the local authorities to use a park or to march along a public thoroughfare. These activities are seen as exercises of the rights of free speech and assembly. They serve to communicate ideas, and they do not disturb the peace. Politicians and decision-makers might pay attention if they consider the group, its size, or the issues to be significant.

Individuals and groups might choose this tactic if they feel that the "quieter," less visible forms of pressure are insufficient or are unavailable to them. Normally, a group with considerable political and economic resources will not resort to mass demonstrations. Like the Business Roundtable, they prefer to operate "one-to-one." Such groups often employ professional lobbyists to pressure legislators behind the scenes. This more private approach to pressure politics is preferred by those who already have access to the centers of decision-making.[29] But weaker groups frequently feel that they must "go public" or "take to the streets" in order to gain attention. This, apparently, is what the trucker meant when he lamented that letters to

Firefighters breaking up civil-rights demonstrations in Birmingham with powerful water hoses. Police chief Connor's violent tactics helped turn public opinion in favor of the civil-rights cause.

legislators did not generate much response. He felt he and his colleagues needed to strike or to engage in public displays of protest.

The purpose, at times, of such action is to win the support of a third party, who in turn will pressure officials on the protesters' behalf. This tactic relates to what Michael Lipsky calls "reference publics."[30] Sometimes this method is effective; other times it might cause a backlash. For instance, A (truckers) inconvenienced B (expressway motorists) in hopes that B would pressure C (federal and state officials) to accede to the demands of A; C is the real target. B might be so infuriated by A's tactics that B turns against A instead of C.

Violence is an illegal form of pressure-group protest, but one that has frequently been used in American politics. Although it *can* be an effective means to communicate grievances, many students of American politics have concluded that violent confrontations serve the political system in a negative way. Such actions, they feel, usually mean that the political process of bargaining, negotiating, and compromising has broken down. Thus, they see political violence as dysfunctional and detrimental.

This is certainly true in many instances, but another factor should be noted. While political violence is not to be encouraged, and while peaceful, nonviolent processes are preferable, in some instances violence has provided opportunities for the political system to function in ways not previously possible. Let's look at one example involving civil-rights demonstrations in the South in the

Mass antiwar demonstrations such as this 1967 protest in Boston not only influenced Johnson's decision not to seek reelection but contributed to the government's decision to withdraw American troops from Vietnam.

early sixties; it took place in Birmingham, Alabama, in the spring of 1963.

About that time, blacks began a series of nonviolent demonstrations against the segregation then prevalent in Birmingham. The demonstrators (many of them children and teen-agers) also demanded nondiscriminatory employment practices, which was not the rule then in the public or private sectors. During the course of the series of demonstrations and mass rallies, tensions between blacks and whites grew to a feverish pitch.

The local law enforcement chief, Eugene "Bull" Connor, often used violent tactics to disperse the black demonstrators. Every day, news pictures and accounts showed police dogs jumping at the demonstrators. Television sets throughout

the country and world (illustrating again, as pointed out in chapter 4, the important impact of the media) showed the police, under Connor's orders, turning powerful water hoses on the demonstrators. In some instances, the force of the water was strong enough to rip bark from trees. More than a few commentators remarked about the sympathy built up around the country for the civil-rights cause simply as a result of these violent episodes. In this instance, of course, the violence came from the local officials, but it was political violence nonetheless.

The federal government and the President, John F. Kennedy, had to act. The civil-rights advocates had been asking for a major civil-rights bill and earlier that year, in February, the President had responded with a rather mild civil-rights program.

But after the violent confrontations in Birmingham and the resultant nationwide support for the civil-rights cause, President Kennedy felt the climate was right to go back to Congress with a much more comprehensive civil-rights package (see chapter 14). Dr. Martin Luther King, Jr., one of the leaders of the Birmingham protests, recalled what Kennedy had said to him.

I am reminded of something President Kennedy said to me at the White House following the signing of the Birmingham agreement.
   "Our judgment of Bull Connor should not be too harsh," he commented. "After all, in his way, he had done a good deal for civil-rights legislation this year."[31]

The President, of all people, was not sanctioning domestic political violence. As an astute politician, he was simply recognizing that under some circumstances violence can provide opportunities for positive political action. It need not *always* have negative consequences. (Of course, if one is of the opinion that the subsequent civil-rights legislation was a bad thing—then that's a different matter.)

It is not easy to assess the role of violence in American politics beyond simply stating that it has played a major role. So much depends on one's values and ideologies. Shays' Rebellion certainly was *one* factor leading to the constitutional convention. John Brown's raid at Harper's Ferry contributed to the growing tension over slavery. The anti-Vietnam War protests certainly influenced President Lyndon Johnson's decision not to seek renomination in 1968. What followed from the protests, violence, and confrontations will be evaluated differently. Let it suffice to say that such forms of interest-group activity were and are important means of influencing the American political system.

Summary

1. Interest groups form when people who share similar beliefs and goals get together in an organized fashion to pursue those beliefs and goals. They make demands on the government and usually, in the process, expect to bargain and compromise with other groups as well as with political officials.

2. There are three major theories of interest-group participation in American politics. The pluralist theory contends that constantly contending, coequal interest groups are the core of the political process. According to this view, the government serves largely as a broker among the groups. The elite theory suggests a "power structure" view of American politics, with business, labor, and military leaders or elites serving as the dominant, yet cooperative ruling class. A third view sees interest groups as very powerful, but in a fragmented way. Various groups capture and control various segments of the government and do not negotiate much with other groups.

3. An increasingly prominent pressure-group tactic is that of "grass-roots" lobbying, whereby groups encourage masses of people throughout the country to contact and to pressure decision-makers. Interest groups like to remind decision-makers that grass-roots concerns can be translated into votes for or against a candidate at the next election.

4. Current efforts to regulate lobbying activities have not been very successful. Opponents of such proposals argue that they infringe on the First-Amendment rights to peaceably assemble and to petition the government. Supporters feel that the public has a right to know about the forces that exert considerable influence on public policy.

5. Interest groups with enough legal and financial resources often resort to the courts, especially when other centers of decision-making (legislative, executive) are not responsive. Class-action suits are often filed by public-interest (both liberal and conservative) law firms. Such suits permit a group to act "on behalf of" large segments of the society, making it unnecessary for individuals to file lawsuits on their own.

6. Protests (both peaceful and violent) are a traditional part of American politics. Normally, groups resort to mass action, which may or may not lead to confrontation and societal disruption, when they feel that they will not be able to satisfy their interests and demands through "quieter," more "private" means of political lobbying. While it is certainly true that political violence has negative consequences much of the time, it is also the case that some instances of violence can provide opportunities for positive governmental action.

Notes

1. *New York Times*, June 27, 1979, p. A19.
2. David B. Truman, *The Governmental Process*, 2nd ed., (New York: Alfred A. Knopf, 1971), p. 33.
3. Some major studies supporting this view are Robert Dahl, *Who Governs?* (New Haven: Yale University Press, 1960); Edward C. Banfield, *Political Influence* (New York: The Free Press, 1961); and Wallace S. Sayre and Herbert Kaufman, *Governing New York City* (New York: W. W. Norton & Company, Inc., 1965).
4. Grant McConnell, *Private Power and American Democracy* (New York: Alfred A. Knopf, 1966), p. 339.
5. V. O. Key, Jr., *Politics, Parties & Pressure Groups* (New York: Thomas Y. Crowell Company, 1964), p. 129.
6. Ibid., p. 43.
7. *New York Times*, February 15, 1978, p. A21.
8. Ibid.
9. "Business Roundtable: New Lobbying Force," *Current American Government CQ Guide* (Spring 1978), 108.
10. Quoted in "Business Roundtable: New Lobbying Force," 111.
11. Robert Michels, *Political Parties: A Sociological Study of the Oligarchical Tendencies of Modern Democracy* (Glencoe, Illinois: The Free Press, 1958).
12. John M. Bacheller, "Lobbyists and the Legislative Process: The Impact of Environmental Constraints," *The American Political Science Review* (March 1977), 262.
13. Steven V. Roberts, "Lobbies Act to Shape Key Panels in Next Congress," *New York Times*, December 7, 1978, p. A18.
14. "Business Roundtable: New Lobbying Force," 109.
15. Ibid.
16. Charles R. Babcock, "Firearms Rule Draws a Fusillade," *Washington Post*, May 17, 1978, p. A13.
17. John Herbers, "Convention Speech Stirs Foes of Abortion," *New York Times*, June 24, 1979, p. A16.
18. Ibid.
19. *New York Times*, February 15, 1978, p. A21.
20. *New York Times*, April 17, 1978, p. A1.
21. *United States* v. *Harriss*, 347 U.S. 612 (1954).
22. David E. Rosenbaum, "Will Lobbying Kill the Proposed Lobbying Bill?" *New York Times*, September 12, 1976, p. E3.
23. Alexis de Tocqueville, *Democracy in America,* Vol. I (New York: Vintage Books, 1957), p. 290.
24. Karen Orren, "Standing to Sue: Interest Group Conflict in the Federal Courts," *The American Political Science Review* (September 1976), 724.
25. "Business Lobbying, Threat to the Consumer Interest," *Consumer Reports*, Vol. 43, No. 9 (September 1978), 530.
26. Jerome Skolnick, *The Politics of Protest* (Washington, D.C.: Government Printing Office, 1969), p. 9.
27. Ibid., p. 11.
28. *New York Times*, July 1, 1979, p. E4.
29. E. E. Schattschneider, *The Semisovereign People* (Hinsdale, Illinois: The Dryden Press, 1975).
30. Michael Lipsky, "Protest as a Political Resource," *The American Political Science Review* (December 1968), 1144–58.
31. Martin Luther King, Jr., *Why We Can't Wait* (New York: Harper & Row, Publishers, 1964), p. 144.

Political Parties

Chapter **6**

In the previous chapter, we noted that several interest groups ''rate'' senators and representatives. This furnishes us with a good place to begin our study of American political parties.

Senator Jesse Helms of North Carolina and Senator Charles Mathias of Maryland are both members of the Republican party. And yet Senator Helms, in the Ninety-sixth Congress, had a rating from the liberal Americans for Democratic Action of 8 percent. He had a rating from the conservative Americans for Constitutional Action of 99 percent. Senator Mathias had an ADA rating of 67 percent and an ACA rating of 11 percent.

Senator Sam Nunn of Georgia and Senator Edward Kennedy of Massachusetts are both members of the Democratic party. And yet Senator Nunn, in the Ninety-sixth Congress, had an ADA rating of 33 percent and an ACA rating of 42 percent. Senator Kennedy had an ADA rating of 81 percent, and an ACA rating of 12 percent.

Someone looking at those ratings might conclude that those four senators had their political party memberships mixed up. A foreign visitor (and even many Americans) might wonder why Helms and Nunn belonged to different parties, or why Mathias and Kennedy belonged to different parties. Based on the issues as exemplified by the two disparate interest groups—ADA and ACA— these would seem to be reasonable questions.

The Functions of American National Parties

There are three major things that the two largest parties do, or are supposed to do, in the American political process:

■ they are said to mobilize or organize the electorate;
■ they aim to bring together or reconcile conflicting interests;
■ they attempt to organize and operate the machinery of government.

Mobilizing the electorate. There is nothing in the Constitution that speaks to the existence and operation of political parties. The Constitution only talks about how people are elected to office, who may run for office, and who can vote. Theoretically, if someone wants to be elected; meets certain age, citizenship, and residency qualifications; and satisfies certain state requirements for getting his or her name on the ballot, that is all that is necessary. The next step simply involves trying to persuade enough people to vote for him or her. In most instances, the candidate will not need a majority (more than 50 percent of the votes cast) to win, but only a plurality (that is, more votes than anyone else). If this happens, the winner becomes a senator, representative, or the President. The Constitution says absolutely noth-

Presidential candidate Edward Kennedy seeks support from local party members, 1980. National candidates depend heavily on the help of local party organizations to get elected.

ing about having to be a Republican or a Democrat or anything else.

Where, then, do political parties enter the picture? They are organizations, formed by private individuals, which seek to present candidates to the voting public. They attempt to serve as a link or bridge between the vast electorate and the government offices. Thus, somewhere between getting on the ballot and being sworn into office, the candidate *usually* utilizes a party in some way.

The party's role is to find potential candidates to run for office, to present the candidates to the voters, and to convince voters to support the candidates. Thus, the candidates become "Republicans" or "Democrats" or representatives of other parties, and the parties urge the voters to vote for the "Republican candidate" or the "Dem-

ocratic candidate," etc. This is intended to help the electorate focus its attention and avoid the confusion that might exist if many candidates were simply running on their own, presenting a myriad of statements and promises. The party frequently provides funds for the candidates of its choice, but the candidates are expected to assist in this regard also.

Over time, as the parties have developed, they have established an "image" in the minds of the electorate. If a candidate is said to be a "Republican" candidate, the voter has *some* notion of what that candidate stands for, even before he or she makes that first pitch.

But we must be careful about this point. What if Nunn and Kennedy were running in the same state on the Democratic ticket—say, one for the Senate and the other for the House? Would the party label really mean very much? In general, "being a Democrat" in one state or region of the country has different implications from "being a Democrat" in some other place. In a sense, that is one of the serious problems faced by American political parties today. That is, some observers have said that precisely because the major parties include proponents with such varying views, the parties "don't stand for anything; they just stand for elections."

Reconciling conflicting interests. This brings us to the second function of political parties. And keep in mind, we are still talking about the two largest, most prominent political parties in the United States—the Republicans and the Democrats (the smaller parties—their nature and operations—will be dealt with later in this chapter). Each of the two parties tries very hard to accommodate as many different views and interests within its structure as possible. Precisely because it is important to get as many votes as possible in order to win, the party attempts to find ways to appeal to a broad range of voters. It knows that some interests are diametrically opposed to others, so it tries to find some common ground between them. Sometimes this is done by finding a candidate who is *most* attractive (or *least* offensive) to the largest audience. And it might seek to state positions in language as broad and general and vague as possible, in order to appeal to as many voters as possible. The more specific the position, the easier it is to disagree with.

Therefore, reconciling conflicting interests on the part of the political party means finding a basis for agreement. This usually involves intense bargaining, negotiating, and compromising.

Sure, the Republicans will say, there are the Mathias people in the party who strongly favor aid to the urban areas and social welfare, and the Helms people who usually oppose such measures. But don't both factions favor "less government control over the economy" and don't both factions "tend to favor a stronger defense posture toward the Russians" than "those Democrats"? The Republican party will try to focus on what the Mathias and Helms people have in common, rather than on where they disagree.

The Democrats do the same thing. This is referred to as *coalition-building*, and the major parties see this as one of their primary roles, along with mobilizing the electorate.

Voters do, in fact, still use the parties as reference guides. Many voters call themselves Democrats or Republicans and view candidates that way. Being a Democrat will likely mean something different to a black voter in Harlem than to a white voter in rural Georgia, but they both see themselves as *Democrats*. Or at least they both register in their home towns that way.

They both go to the party national convention and fuss and argue over whom to nominate as the party's candidate for President. In 1976, they both settled on Georgian Jimmy Carter. They both saw some things in Carter that appealed to them "as Democrats." They reconciled their conflicting interests through the mechanism of the political party. Reconciliation does not always happen, however, and when it fails to occur, that frequently spells defeat for the party. The process of reconciliation can be illustrated by two accounts of how President Carter (and the Democratic party) put together conflicting interests in 1976.

Professor William Lee Miller wrote on "the emergence of Jimmy Carter":

In Atlanta in 1976 I learned how conservative some of Carter's chief supporters were. Many who had backed Carter for governor in 1970 voted for George Wallace for the presidential nomination in Miami in 1972. Many hated and

Above: Democrats Jimmy Carter and Ted Kennedy fought bitterly against each other in the 1980 primaries, but joined forces after Carter won the Democratic presidential nomination. Below: The six contenders for the 1980 Republican nomination. With the exception of John Anderson, all rallied behind the eventual winner, Ronald Reagan.

refused to support McGovern. One Carter campaign worker had been heard to say that he "don't much like niggers." A man in Calhoun (Ga.) said to one of Carter's supporters, "If he turns out to be a blankety-blank liberal, I'm going to get you." A close Carter friend said to me that she didn't like it when Carter took back his "ethnic purity" remark: "That's the way we believe."

Carter courted and willingly accepted the support of George Wallace, and he praised segregationist senators. In the election he received the votes of hundreds of thousands of sometime Wallace voters, Goldwater supporters, white segregationists, and conservative whites.[1]

Another account involved the liberals in the party. Andrew Young, then a liberal Congressman from Atlanta, had been a prominent civil rights activist in the 1960s with Dr. Martin Luther King, Jr. One Washington correspondent wrote:

Carter's liberal supporters realized they were too deeply committed to him now to change (after Carter had won the Florida primary), even if they wanted to. They were, in effect, stuck with a winner. Andy Young suddenly found himself involved in Carter's New York campaign, where he dealt with a flood of phone calls from across the country. "These were people who saw Carter and liked him and just wanted to make sure that he was all right on race," Young later recalled.

"Yeah, he is all right on race," Young told the callers. "There are lots of other questions I may have, but you know . . . ."

For the liberals Young talked to, that reassurance was enough. They did not trouble themselves or him about the "other questions." These liberals, who not long before had been heavily oriented to issues, were now more oriented to winning. In 1968 their opposition to

Hubert Humphrey's nomination had divided their party and contributed to Humphrey's narrow defeat. In 1972 they had seized control of the party with George McGovern, but he had been overwhelmed by Nixon. For the past three years they had looked for another candidate who would speak to the issues that mattered most to them. They had considered Morris Udall, Birch Bayh, Fred Harris, and others, but none seemed to have much prospect of winning the nomination, let alone the election. They decided to settle for success and for Jimmy Carter.[2]

These accounts tell us a lot about the American national parties—their strengths and their possible flaws. The Democratic party wanted "a winner" in 1976, which meant that various conflicting groups would have to reconcile their differences and unite behind a candidate. But you will note that in the second account, the emphasis was on nominating someone who could conceivably "win" against the Republicans. It required submerging issue differences (an example of standing for election, not for issues). What happens *after* the election? Is the winning party then able to organize and operate the government machinery effectively? As a Democratic President, could Carter expect cooperation from a Democratic Congress? (More on this in chapters 8–12.)

Operating the government machinery. Once the various candidates have captured office, under the banner of the party, they proceed to structure the government in a way that usually reflects party affiliation.

We hear, for instance, that "the Republicans are in office now," or "when the Democrats controlled the White House. . . ." This means that most of the people who head the executive bureaus and the White House staff (see chapters 8 and 9) will belong to one party or the other. It means that, in Congress, for example, if the Democrats out-number the Republicans, the leadership positions will be assigned to the Democrats (see chapters 10 and 11).

This sounds rather simple, but our foreign visitor might show some confusion upon learning that the Democrats can be ''in'' at the Congress and the Republicans can be ''in'' at the White House at the same time. And that look of puzzlement will likely turn to downright bewilderment when it is learned that different parties can control the House of Representatives and the Senate at the same time, as was the case in 1981 after the 1980 elections. We can only ask her or him to bear with us. As confusing as all this may seem, the American political system still lives with the theoretical notion that the major political parties serve useful functions in the three categories mentioned.

How the American Party System Developed

Some observers might suggest, given the political system and the process under which the parties must function, that getting *to* office is about as much as parties can pull off. Getting *through* office successfully—that is, performing up to voter expectations and maintaining voter confidence and support—is an entirely different matter. We will look at that system and process, starting with an historical account of party growth.

The first party system, 1790–1824. The party system we know today was by no means contemplated at the founding of the nation. In fact, among the principal founders, it is safe to say that virtually all of them were suspicious of the good that parties could perform. George Washington, Alexander Hamilton, James Madison, Thomas Jefferson—none of these influential public figures cared much for any kind of structured party system. To begin with, they had never seen one in either England or on the European continent.

And yet these very men were intimately involved in governmental policymaking that led to the establishment of the world's first two-party system. This grew out of Hamilton's views on economic policy and the role of the national government. In the first session of Congress, members acted and voted individually, with no discernible attachment to groups or alliances. Indeed, this was the case throughout the country:

In state after state in the American republic until the 1790s, politics remained a gamble of individual endeavor, or of shifting factions; of family cliques in New York, which virtually duplicated the patterns of old-Whig ''connexions'' in England, or of intermittent caucuses in New England; of social elites like the ruling ''Fifty Families'' in Maryland, or of exclusive ''juntos'' in much of the South.[3]

Then, in 1790, Alexander Hamilton developed a set of proposals involving economic growth. He advocated assuming the debts the states had incurred during the Revolutionary War; he also urged the establishment of a national bank and the issuance of interest-bearing bonds in place of the securities of the old Confederacy. Excise taxes would be imposed, as would a protective tariff on manufactured goods. By and large, these proposals appealed to the commercial and manufacturing interests and shipping owners. In addition, Hamilton's foreign policy views leaned heavily toward Great Britain. In a most general way, Hamilton's program could be considered the forerunner of a political party platform.

George Washington slowly, but inevitably, came to side with Hamilton and his followers, comprising a group that came to be referred to as the Federalists.

Hamilton and Jefferson were members of Washington's first cabinet, but the two men began to clash early on. Jefferson disagreed with Hamilton's inclination toward a strong national govern-

Alexander Hamilton, leading figure in the development of the Federalist party and advocate of active government involvement in the nation's economic affairs.

ment. Jefferson favored an agrarian society of small farmers with minimum central government control, and he leaned toward France as this country's main ally.

In the early years of the new republic, the Federalists dominated the government, and they began to reach out into the states—through correspondence, the press, and personal contacts—to enlist people sympathetic to their cause. Washington, by 1795, was appointing only Federalists to office, declaring: "I shall not . . . bring a man into any office of consequence knowingly whose political tenets are adverse to the measures which the general government is pursuing." Thus, a version of **patronage**—appointing people to public office based on partisanship—was established by the first President.

Madison and Jefferson quickly realized that if they were to contend successfully with their politi-

cal adversaries, they, too, would have to pay attention to the necessity of building a political network. And they set out to do that, contacting friends and sympathizers who agreed with their views. Their network came to be known as the Republicans—sometimes called Jeffersonian Republicans or Democratic-Republicans.

With Jefferson's election in 1800, a two-party structure was largely in place. Jefferson saw fit to appoint mostly Republicans to office, following Washington's lead and in an effort to thwart his predecessor's (Adams's) attempt to stack the federal courts with Federalists in 1801, just prior to leaving office. In fact, "Jefferson began the practice of forcing out those who did not agree with him politically."[4]

Thus, although most leaders at that time did not feel that political parties should be encouraged, the nature of the evolving political process was such as to make that development inevitable. Each group wanted to capture and control the presidency and Congress, and the best way to do that was by lining up and organizing adherents who agreed with them.

The Republicans were so successful that by the end of the second decade of the nineteenth century, with the election of James Monroe in 1816, the Federalists had been largely destroyed as a viable political entity. The one-sided Republican victories led to what could almost be called a one-party system. Historians have referred to this period as "the era of good feelings."

The second party system, 1826–1860. One might say that for the Republicans the era of good feelings "was good while it lasted," which was less than a decade. By the 1824 presidential election, the party had broken into quarreling factions. John Quincy Adams led one group, and a frontiersman and military hero, Andrew Jackson, another. The ensuing political struggles took on a

President-elect Andrew Jackson addresses a small-town crowd shortly before proceeding on to his inauguration in Washington, 1829.

decided regional/sectional flavor. Northern interests favored protective tariffs, a U.S. bank, and policies helpful to a growing industrial society. The South was beginning to resent the tariff, which, southerners felt, hurt agricultural production. The newly developing West wanted internal improvements, cheap money, fewer governmental controls.

Clinton Rossiter has observed:

The Era of Good Feelings came to an abrupt end in the elections of 1824 and 1828. . . . The party of Jefferson neither died nor faded away. It grew fat and happy with success, split violently in the manner of many fat and happy parties, was captured by the largest of its components, and emerged from its ordeal as the tough, confident, self-conscious legatee of the political Jefferson.[5]

Two distinct parties emerged: the Democrats and the Whigs. In 1824, a bitter, controversial election was decided in the House of Representatives because no candidate had received a majority of the electoral votes. Henry Clay was the influential Speaker of the House. The loser, Jackson, accused the winner, Adams, of striking a "corrupt bargain" with Clay. Jackson's supporters alleged that Clay supported Adams in return for appointment as secretary of state, a charge Clay denied.

Andrew Jackson subsequently won the presidency in 1828. He was presented as a man for all regions, but he really was identified more as a rugged westerner (Tennessee) with a glorious war record (War of 1812 and the Indian wars). Some historians characterized his political operation in the following way:

Jackson had adroit campaign managers in every section and state. . . . The name of Jackson was cloaked with all the virtues that had sectional appeals. In New England, his followers represented him as a sponsor of commercial expansion; to industrialists he became the advocate of protection, while in the South he was hailed as a slave owner, planter, and foe of the tariff. Everywhere he was the man of the people, the leader of democracy against privilege and political corruption.[6]

Prior to that time, candidates for office were chosen in **caucuses**, closed meetings of party members serving in Congress. There had been opposition to this method as early as 1816, and proposals to nominate candidates in state conventions. This latter method was seen as the more open and democratic. Jackson's ascendancy (after receiving the Tennessee state convention nomination) signaled the death of "King Caucus," and Jackson was heralded as "the man of the people," meaning the common, ordinary citizens. In a sense, many felt that he had beaten the "bosses."

The party Jackson and his colleagues put together is considered the direct forerunner of the present-day Democratic party, making it the oldest political party in U.S. history. It was under Jackson, also, that the **spoils system** became deeply ingrained in the American political system. As noted, Washington and Jefferson had rewarded friends and punished foes through office appointments. But Andrew Jackson brought a distinct view to office that used appointments as clear rewards for party loyalty and service. Jackson said: "I cannot but believe that more is lost by the long continuance of men in office than is generally gained by their experience. . . . No one man has any more intrinsic right to official station than another. It is rotation in office that will perpetuate our liberty." Under Jackson, concerted attention was paid to building an effective, coherent political party.

A Whig parade starts out from party headquarters in one of Philadelphia's northern wards, 1840.

A second party developed in opposition to the Jacksonian Democrats. They even took the name of *Whig* in 1834 to imply that they were opposing "King Andrew," much as the Whigs during the Revolution had opposed King George III. The Whig party was a mixture of slaveowners and abolitionists, industrialists and farmers, who found it difficult to agree on very many issues but were united in their common resentment of Jackson. The leaders were Henry Clay, Daniel Webster, and John Quincy Adams, and they were as interested in reaping the benefits of office patronage as were the Democrats. But the Jacksonian Democrats had built a strong party apparatus, and the Whigs were never able to gain status as the preeminent party.

It was during this second stage in American party development that we began to see the intermittent development and demise of splinter or minor parties: the Know-Nothing party; the Free Soil party; the Liberty party.

The third party system, 1860–present. The two major parties we have today began their rivalry in 1854 with the founding of the Republican party. Not to be confused with the earlier Jeffersonians (who, through the Jacksonians, had become the Democrats), the Republicans of the 1850s were a mixture of antislavery forces, some Whigs, and some Free Soilers. Basically, they were against the extension (not for the abolition) of slavery in the new states. Slavery had become a divisive, politically irreconcilable issue that would eventually lead, of course, to the Civil War. The two major parties were lined up on opposite sides.

The newly formed Republicans represented northern and western industrial interests and became identified as the party to save the Union.

The Democrats, associated with the South and proslavery, had to bear the stigma of being the party of secession. They were supported by the Southern planters and Bourbon class.

This lineup determined American politics for the rest of the nineteenth century until the ''critical election'' of 1896. At that time, the Republicans put together a coalition of business people, industrialists, urban voters, and northern and midwestern farmers against a Democratic party that largely represented the South and some immigrant (mainly Irish) groups in the North.

Franklin D. Roosevelt revitalized the Democratic party by actively seeking the support of working-class people in the midst of the Great Depression.

These two forces vied with each other in presidential elections (with the Democrats winning only twice—1912 and 1916) from the turn of the century until 1932, when the Democrats and Franklin D. Roosevelt, in the midst of the Depression, fashioned a new electoral coalition that captured the presidency for the twenty years from 1932 to 1952. From that point through 1980, the two parties have seesawed back and forth: the Republicans winning five presidential elections, the Democrats, three.

From the Civil War to the Depression, minor parties dotted the scene, with only moderate success.

During that period, the Republicans became identified as the Grand Old Party (GOP), and associated themselves with a rapidly growing industrial America. They also presented themselves as the party of emancipation, with Abraham Lincoln standing as the Great Emancipator. With the crash of 1929 and the ensuing Depression, the Republicans were made to bear another image, that of the party of the Depression. If they were not accused of causing the Depression outright, they certainly had to bear most of the blame for not taking sufficient action to respond to it. They continued to hold on to what some considered outmoded notions of the self-correcting capacity of the free enterprise system. The Democrats, on the other hand, beginning with the New Deal, became identified as the party of "the little man" or at least "the workingman." These images stuck, and have not entirely disappeared in the early 1980s.

At the local level, especially in the northern urban areas, the late nineteenth and early twentieth centuries were periods when the party *machines* were being perfected. These organizations mobilized newly arrived immigrants and gave them help in getting established in a new country in

Richard Daley, mayor of Chicago from 1955 to 1976. Daley was often called one of the last of the big-city political "bosses."

exchange for loyal support—votes. Patronage (political jobs and favors) was the basis for this arrangement. (Southern rural areas had their own version of party machines also, frequently built around the powerful county courthouse.)

Thus, American politics—which began under the control of political activists who, while forming into political groups, professed a dislike of party organizations—ultimately developed into a system with a relatively tight party structure built on patronage and promises. No one started out to build a two-party system, with leaders and followers and platforms, but the country came to that situation less than a hundred years after Alexander Hamilton first presented his program for economic development, a program that appealed to the Federalists and activated the Republicans in opposition. This constituted a major change in the way

Americans conducted their political affairs, but the constitutional framework and governmental structures remained constant. To be sure, the method of selecting the President and vice-president had been changed by the Twelfth Amendment in 1804. Prior to that time, the candidate who received the second largest number of votes became vice-president. The Twelfth Amendment provided for separate elections for each office, and it was, indeed, a reflection of the rise of party organizations—Republicans versus the Federalists. Aside from this, the political parties developed and blended in with the governmental system then in place—a clear example of constancy and change in American government.

Key Features
of the American Party System

If you reflect for a moment on the political story of Proposition 13, you will recall the various positions taken by interest groups and the media and opinion polls. But you will also note that nowhere is there mention of formal, official positions taken by the two major state political parties. The Communist party did make known its "early opposition" to the proposal.[7] But what about the Democrats and the Republicans? It is nice to know where the Communists stand on the issue, but most Californians are registered members of one of the two major parties. Did those two parties take an official position? Did they give their members any "guidance" in deciding how to vote on that initiative?

As you read all of the story you get the impression that more Democratic officials opposed it than did Republican officials, but it is important for our discussion here that there were no definite, clear *party* positions stated. Why this was the case will become clearer as we examine the party system.

Two-party politics. As we have said several times, there are two major political parties in the United States. Except for a very brief period (the "era of good feelings"), this has always been the case. Unlike some European countries, notably France and Italy, the United States cannot be said to be a *multi-party* country. Granted, there are innumerable small, minor parties (often called "third parties"), but most of the time on both the national and state levels, only two parties really matter.

Why is this the case? The most important reason lies in the nature of the electoral system—primarily because of the *single-member district*. That is, Americans elect only one person to serve a district or state or to fill other offices. Thus, the House of Representatives is composed of 435 seats representing 435 separate districts. Only one person can win the district seat, and to do so she or he need only win a *plurality* of votes, not a majority. The same kind of limitation applies to the one hundred Senate seats—two from each state. This means that in order to maximize one's chance of winning, the candidate will try to appeal to as many individuals and groups as possible *before* the election, because all that is needed is a plurality. The winner takes all.

It is therefore wise to go into the election with as broad a base as possible. And this is where the first two functions of the political party mentioned earlier (mobilizing the electorate and reconciling conflicting interests) come in. The process encourages the continued existence just two major parties, because, frankly, that is the best way to have a chance at winning in a single-member electoral system.

If, however, the country had a multi-member system whereby, say, the seats in Congress were awarded on the basis of the *percentage* of the votes a party received, we would undoubtedly see a multi-party system develop. Such systems use the **proportional representation** electoral system. If party *A* receives twenty percent of the votes, that party receives twenty percent of the seats. It is not winner take all; virtually every party has a chance to gain *some* seats. What usually happens is that several different parties must then—*after* the election—attempt to form a coalition in order to gain a majority. In the American system, the two major parties perform this reconciliation and coalitional function under *one* party banner *before* the election.

In addition to this structural reason for a two-party system, some observers have offered other explanations. They suggest that the two-party tradition got its start in the early days of the country when major issues were mostly pro or con, one side or the other: break with England or not, ratify the 1787 Constitution or not, support the Hamiltonian (Federalist) programs or not, support the extension of slavery or not. These sorts of issues, it is argued, contributed to the development of a dual, rather than a multiple, party system.

Further, once such a system was established, along with the single-member district, it was an easy system to perpetuate through habit and tradition. Today, we take it as almost an article of faith that "the two-party system" must be preserved. This sentiment has not quite reached the status of motherhood, but one's patriotism will certainly not be questioned because one champions the two-party system—especially if the two parties being supported are the present major ones.

In 1980, when Congressman John B. Anderson ran for President as an Independent, his supporters had to face the charge that he was a "spoiler," that he could not win, and was therefore siphoning votes away from Carter (and a few from Reagan). Some Anderson supporters surmised that his third-party candidacy might cause the election to be decided in the House of Representatives, where his supporters felt they might be able to exact some political concessions from the ultimate winner. There are many motivations for a third-party

John Anderson of Illinois campaigned for the presidency first as a Republican, then as an Independent. In the general election, he received only about seven percent of the total vote.

candidacy, and, of course, it is difficult to calculate with any degree of precision what strategies will be successful. (The effect of the electoral college on campaign strategies will be discussed in the next chapter.)

Decentralization politics.   As we have seen, political parties try to capture and control government offices. Given the system of federalism and separation of powers discussed in chapters 2 and 3, it follows that the character of the political parties will be affected by the character of the government positions they seek to control. Since those positions are decentralized and fragmented (in the sense that they exist at many different levels and in a variety of political regions), it follows that the two major parties will be also.

If the United States were a unitary system like England, with a parliamentary government (combining the legislative and executive branches), then we would certainly see more "disciplined," centralized political parties. Again, the problem is structural. As we noted earlier, one party can be in the majority in Congress but not control the presidency. Thus, we have Congressional parties and presidential parties.

Likewise, the Republicans can (and do) control some state legislatures and the Democrats others. This fragmentation is increased by the fact that various positions are up for election at various times: representatives serve two years; senators, six years (with only one third up for election every two years); the President, four years. And, of course, different positions serve different constituencies. A senator serves an entire state and is electorally accountable to it. A representative serves a Congressional district. The President runs in all the states. Thus politicians must appeal to different sets of voters, depending on the position sought. This decentralizes the party system.

The foreign visitor we encountered a little earlier might find the following news item somewhat curious:

Paul O'Dwyer [former president of the New York City Council] *said yesterday that President Carter could not carry New York in 1980 and that state Democratic leaders should not let the President intertwine his political future with the party's.*

Democratic aldermen meet informally in Chicago city council chambers. Local party leaders such as these can exercise considerable power within the party, even at the national levels.

He suggested that . . . the state chairman "sue for separation."[8]

Of course, no one is going to go to court in this matter—it is not legally possible or politically necessary!

Also, note the following—remembering that Carter is a Democrat and, as President, was the "titular" head of the Democratic party:

Almost two thirds of the Democrats in the House of Representatives say that, as of now, they would support President Carter for another term, according to a survey. . . .[9]

Two thirds might sound pretty good, except that the news item is talking about Carter's *own party*! The fact is, of course, that the *Congressional* Democrats are not obligated—certainly not legally, and probably not politically—to support the head of their party.

What this means is that in a real sense there are no *national* political parties in the United States, even the two major ones. Rather, what one finds are two major "nationwide" parties, parties that are located in every state under the same banner: Democratic and Republican. It is not even accurate to call the state parties branches of the national party, because they are not. They are autonomous.

Nonideological politics. The two major American "nationwide" parties are frequently characterized as being *nonideological*. Certainly, the seemingly inconsistent party memberships and policy positions described at the beginning of the chapter would tend to confirm this conclusion. This means that they are not as rigidly doctrinaire as some left- or right-wing parties in Europe or in this country. But this should be stated cautiously, because both the Democrats and the Republicans do, in fact, adhere to a set of reasonably broad principles and

In 1973, former Texas Governor John B. Connally renounced his affiliation with the Democratic party and became a Republican. Connally ran for President in 1976 as a Republican.

ideals. For example, both parties are firmly committed to the private enterprise, capitalist system. True, one (perhaps, at times, both) might favor government regulation of and intervention in the economy. One might lean toward a more comprehensive national health insurance program. But neither party advocates, for instance, nationalization of the nation's major industries.

Both parties have a strong commitment to the defense of the country against foreign aggression, although one party might accuse the other of being less than wise in knowing how to do this—or, perhaps, of being "soft on communism." Neither party really believes that the other is out to weaken the nation's military defenses, and neither believes that the other would fail to exert whatever force necessary to protect the security of the country. The political debate would focus on which party knew best how to do this.

Being nonideological also means that there is not much discernible difference between the two major parties—as former Governor George Wallace of Alabama used to say, there is "not a dime's worth of difference" between the parties.

But this view is not entirely accurate. While it is certainly true that on most issues the parties are not at polar ends of the spectrum from each other, it is nonetheless possible to detect clear differences at the national level and in most states. The Democrats tend to support social-welfare spending more than the Republicans. From 1948 through 1976, the Democrats were much more inclined to favor stronger civil-rights laws and enforcement than the Republicans. Since the 1930s and the New Deal, the Democratic party has clearly been the choice of organized labor union leadership. Big business and big farmer organizations have consistently perceived an issue difference between the two parties and, therefore, favored the Republicans.

Looking at the case study of Proposition 13, we can conclude that *on balance* the state Republican party leadership favored Proposition 13, and the state Democratic party leadership opposed it. What we did not see in that political story was any indication that either major party made Proposition 13 a part of its stated platform. Certainly the gubernatorial candidates of the parties took clear positions. Governor Brown, you will recall, called

Proposition 13 a "ripoff" and a "fraud," though he quickly moved to embrace it after the voters overwhelmingly approved the initiative. His opponent, Evelle J. Younger, not only wanted Proposition 13 (and vowed to defend it against court challenges), he also wanted further tax cuts. So if one can infer *party* position from *candidate* position (and sometimes this is possible, sometimes not), then there was a clear difference between the parties.

Therefore, being nonideological really means not adhering to a body of doctrine which is essentially at variance with basic American principles of democracy and free enterprise. Neither party is far to the right or the left. In fact, one might even suggest that both parties are ideologically centrist in the context of American beliefs and values.

The center or the *middle-of-the-road* is also considered the best position from which to appeal to the broadest range of voters in a two-party system. A middle-of-the-roader can reach out to the left and to the right, and that is precisely what the two major parties try to do. This centrist position might be confused at times with being nonideological, when, in fact, it is an ideological position that avoids either of the extremes on the political spectrum.

Minor parties. Precisely because the two major parties carve out rather wide middle-ground positions and, in the process, attempt to bring into the fold many different groups, this leaves some room for the development of "minor" parties. These groups develop for a number of reasons, but the main motivation is that they are not content to find a home within one of the larger parties.

Such parties may originate in any of three ways. One type "bolts" from one of the larger parties. Another type originates on its own and is con-

Teddy Roosevelt's Bull-Moose party was an example of a "bolting" or secessionist party. This cartoon, drawn by John T. McCutcheon for the Chicago Tribune, shows Roosevelt's Bull Moose chasing the Democratic donkey and the Republican elephant into the hills.

cerned mainly with economic issues. The third type is essentially a single-issue group interested as much in educating the public about that issue as it is in winning election to office.

The "bolting" (or secessionist) party breaks away from one of the other parties. The leaders usually have tried to get their programs adopted within the larger party without success. Thus, their faction leaves and establishes its own structure. It hopes, thereby, to accomplish several things, one of which is to demonstrate its value to the parent group. If it can draw votes away from the major party, this might serve later as a bargaining tool for reentering the party on more favorable terms. The Progressive "Bull-Moose" party of 1912, which broke away from the Republicans (effectively permitting the Democrats to win the presidency under Woodrow Wilson) is an example. The

Dixiecrats' break with the Democrats in 1948 is another, as well as the Progressive party's (under Henry Wallace) break with the Democrats the same year. In neither of the 1948 cases, however, did the breaks cause the defeat of the parent party. Democrat Harry S Truman pulled an upset victory.

Usually the bolting minor party represents a small but reasonably significant faction within the parent party. One of the serious problems faced by this type of minor party is that it is not likely to be able to build the extensive nationwide, local vote-getting apparatus that the parent party has. Neither does it have enough of a patronage base to attract and hold party workers. For this reason, it is unlikely that the bolting party will survive very long. In fact, the Progressive "Bull-Moose" party came in second in 1912 (ahead of the Republi-

The final type of minor party is concerned mainly (but not always exclusively) with a single issue. This party usually feels so strongly about one issue that it does not feel comfortable working for it within one of the larger parties. Examples here would be the Right-to-Life (antiabortion) party and the Prohibition party.

An important aspect of the minor-party phenomenon in the United States is that sometimes minor-party programs are adopted by one of the major parties. This can occur over time and, although the minor party might not win elections, it can, at times, influence policy. In this sense, these minor parties serve as "party-pressure groups." They *act* like political parties in running candidates, writing platforms, and so on; they *serve* to pressure the major parties and decision-makers. Sometimes they are able to attract a protest vote, that is, the votes of those for whom the minor party serves as a vehicle to express anger or disgust toward the major parties. This kind of voter will not likely join the minor party and become a regular, consistent supporter, but the minor party has allowed him or her "to send a message" to the public officials.

A minor party can perform several potentially important functions in the political process without ever really having any conceivable chance of winning office. This is especially the case where minor parties operate coherently on a local or state level. There, given the particular relationship between the major parties—for instance, in a highly competitive two-party situation—the relatively small number of votes a minor party might be able to swing could spell the difference between victory and defeat for one of the major parties. Where this is the case, as with the Liberal and Conservative parties in New York, one of the major parties might try to get a minor party to endorse its own candidate.

cans), but the Republicans had the ongoing party machinery to survive the loss and remain in existence. The bolting party did not, and could not.

A second type of minor party starts on its own because it normally takes social and economic positions that cannot be accommodated by either of the major parties. There are several socialist parties and some conservative parties of this type. Their programs are usually stated in doctrinaire terms, and they are not willing to compromise in order to fit under one of the two large umbrella parties. Thus, they run their own candidates, but they are not as "nationwide" as the major parties. They will not likely be on the ballot in many states, and they certainly will not likely have the financial resources to run candidates at each level (local, state, national) of government. The Libertarian party and the Citizens' party are examples of this type.

TABLE 1.
Third Parties and the 1980 Presidential Election.

Party	Presidential Candidate	Votes
Independent	John B. Anderson	5,719,437
Libertarian	Edward Clark	920,859
Citizens	Barry Commoner	230,377
Communist	Gus Hall	43,871
American Independent	John Rarick	41,172
Socialist Workers'	Clifton DeBerry	40,105
Respect for Life	Ellen McCormack	32,319
Peace and Freedom	Margaret Smith	18,117
Workers' World	Deride Griswold	13,211
National Statesman	Benjamin Bubar	7100
Socialist	David McReynolds	6720
American	Percy Greaves	6539
Socialist Workers'	Richard Congress	4029
"Middle Class Candidate"	Kurt Lynen	3694
Down With Lawyers	Bill Gahres	1718
American	Frank Shelton	1555
Independent	Martin Wendelhen	923
National People's League	Harley McLain	296
Write-ins		16,921

Note: Ronald Reagan received 43,899,248 votes; Jimmy Carter received 35,481,435 votes. A total of 86,495,678 votes were cast in 1980.

Source: *New York Times,* January 6, 1981, p. A14.

Party Structure in the United States

Precisely because political parties are decentralized, it is necessary when examining the structure of the party system to separate the national structure from the state structure. Basically, the national structure is composed of four parts: the national convention; the national chairperson; the national committee; and the staff of the national committee.

The national party structures. The national party convention convenes every four years; its twofold purpose is to write a party platform and to nominate candidates for the presidency and vice-presidency. Delegates to the convention (see chapter 7) perform these functions. The presidential nominee becomes the titular head of the party. The delegates have no ongoing function after the convention adjourns. Their task really lasts only for the four days of the convention.

Beginning in 1974, every four years the Democratic party has held midterm ''mini''-conventions. These meetings are used to discuss party policy and to draft resolutions. Delegates are elected, though not necessarily the same ones who attended the previous nominating convention. This experiment in national party activity is too new to assess, but some believe it will be of questionable value, simply because Congress and the President are the main policymakers and therefore the national party structure cannot have much influence as an entity. Others feel that it is potentially a worthwhile mechanism for making the national party more issue-oriented. It permits the national party structure to meet in convention without having to devote the bulk of its time to choosing a candidate, with all the attendant hoopla—such as parading with banners and colorful hats before the television cameras.

The national party committee is composed of one woman and one man from each state, from Washington, D.C., Puerto Rico, the Virgin Islands, and certain territories. Each party has included other persons on the committee as well (state chairpersons, governors, members of Congress). The national committee members are selected in various ways: by election in primaries, by state conventions, or by the state committees. These party people meet approximately once or twice a year, but they do not deal with substantive policy issues. The normal agenda is concerned with party rules and with more effective ways to prepare for the next convention. Certainly one important function of the national committee is to select the city where the next convention will be held. The national committee also chooses the national chairperson.

In reality, the national chairperson is the choice of the President (if the party holds the incumbent's spot). If the party does not control the presidency, then the national committee makes the selection, aware that after the convention the presidential nominee is given the courtesy of designating the person. Mainly, the national chairperson is a party unifier. Her or his job is to take the lead in "reconciling conflicting interests." Therefore, this person should not be too closely identified with one party faction or another. The job calls for superb political skills. There are three national vice-chairpersons, and here the party likes to select representatives from certain prominent segments of the party: labor, business, women, racial groups, and geographical regions.

The day-to-day work of the national party is conducted out of a headquarters in Washington, D.C., by a national committee staff. In 1981, the Democratic staff numbered 40; the Republican, 250. As election time nears, the staffs increase in size. These people are the party faithful. They spend all of their time politicking—keeping in touch with state party members, Congressional party members, national committee members, the media, and the public—especially the financial contributors. Occasionally, they plan fund-raising affairs or simply try to build a positive image for the party. Their jobs are strictly patronage positions. If they *perform* well—and their party wins—they *do* well.

One critical point to keep in mind about the national party structure is that it cannot order anybody to do anything. It is the national party structure, but as we said earlier, it does not have a national party to administer. So it must cajole, coax, persuade, plead—and hope.

State and local party structures. Each state party has a separate apparatus consisting roughly of six parts. At the top is the state party committee with a male and female member from each county or assembly district. They normally meet quarterly, and one of their important functions is to slate candidates for office on the state level or to call a state convention for that purpose, as well as to choose a state chairperson.

In some places the chairperson can be an important figure. Unlike his or her national counterpart, the state chairperson is likely to have greater access to patronage jobs at the state level—if his or her party is in control of the governorship or the state legislature. The chairperson is in constant contact with the county chairpersons throughout the state. This provides him or her with ample opportunity to get to know the political needs of

FIGURE 1.
Party Organization at the National and State Levels.

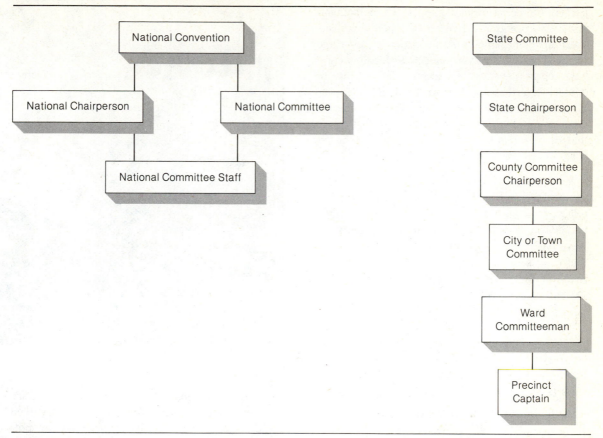

each county and to try to satisfy those needs on a bargaining basis. The state and county chairpersons usually work very closely with each other. Control of a number of important state and local offices is at stake.

Each county has a committee composed of representatives from the towns (or other units) within it. There are various methods for apportioning votes and seats on the county committee. When we get down to the county, city, and ward party levels, we are really at the core of the American political party system. It is at these

levels that the party officials begin to have intimate contact with the voters, if they have it at all. It is here that local, state, and, at times, federal patronage gets funneled. Here strategy is decided in terms of how a candidate (national, state, or local) should be presented to the local voters. If the party is to have vitality in a given area, it must come from this level of party organization.

There remains, however, one last level of party organization: the precinct. The precinct, normally covering no more than 300–500 voters, is *the* last stop between the party and the people. The head of a party's precinct organization is a precinct captain, who preferably lives in the neighborhood, grew up there, knows *everyone* on a first-name basis, is known by everyone, and sees the neighbors, constituents, voters almost daily. This, of course, describes a rather ideal, smoothly operating situation. Such active precinct captains in many communities belong to the past, but where they do exist and function actively, they can be the lifeblood of the local party.

For instance, if a couple up the street is celebrating a fiftieth wedding anniversary and receives a congratulatory letter from the President of the United States (which, incidentally, virtually always happens), it was probably the precinct captain who told the ward leader, who passed the word on to the county chairperson, who suggested to the local member of Congress what a nice thing it would be if the President took time to drop a little note. And some White House staff member would do just that! And, of course, the letter would be promptly and proudly framed and displayed.

The precinct captain and ward leaders do the actual, physical work of getting petitions signed for potential candidates to get on the ballot. They are the ones who "canvass" the community, urging citizens to register and to vote—at least these are the things a "good" precinct captain does. A party organization, as an organization that relies on voters to sustain it, is really only as good as its "foot soldiers" at the very grass roots—namely, the precinct workers. This is especially true in elections at the local level where interest might not be as high as with a presidential or senatorial race.

Party Machines Versus Reform Politics

In the last section we described the kind of party structure that has been called in American politics *the machine.*

Some of the most colorful stories and cartoons in American political folklore have revolved around the "smoke-filled" rooms, and the pot-bellied, cigar-smoking, gruff-talking politicians who sit behind desks in ward headquarters, doling out favors with one hand and taking in votes—and graft—with the other.

Milton Rakove, in his book entitled *Don't Make No Waves . . . Don't Back No Losers,* gives us a classic account of a ward politician practicing his craft:

How does a good precinct captain carry a precinct in cities like Chicago? Not by stressing ideology or party philosophy, not by stuffing mailboxes with party literature, not by debating issues with his constituents, but rather by ascertaining individual needs and by trying to serve

Basic city services, such as street-cleaning (left) and snow removal (below) are often controlled by precinct captains and local ward politicians.

those needs. Good precinct captains know that most elections are won or lost, not on great national, ideological issues, but rather on the basis of small, private, individual interests and concerns. If they don't know this or have forgotten it, their ward committeemen remind them in ward organization meetings. . . .

Four months after the mayoralty election, in which Marzullo carried his ward for the mayor by a heavy majority, Marzullo leaned back in the highback leather chair in his City Hall office and told Sun-Times columnist Tom Fitzpatrick, "I ain't got no axes to grind. You can take all your news media and all the do-gooders in town and move them into my 25th Ward, and do you know what would happen? On election day we'd beat you fifteen to one. The mayor don't run the 25th Ward. Neither does the news media or the do-gooders. Me, Vito Marzullo. That's who runs

the 25th Ward, and on election day everybody does what Vito Marzullo tells them."

What kinds of goods and services do precinct captains in ward organizations provide? According to Marzullo, his captains work 365 days a year providing "service and communication" to his people. This includes free legal service for the destitute, repair of broken street lights, intensified police squad patrol, special antirodent clean-ups in the alleys, new garbage cans for tenants provided for them by their landlords, and talks with the probation officers of youngsters who are in trouble. "Anybody in the 25th needs something, needs help with his garbage, needs his street fixed, needs a lawyer for his kid who's in trouble, he goes first to the precinct captain," says Marzullo. "If the captain can't deliver, that man can come to me. My house is open every day to him."[10]

This is a vivid picture of "machine" politics in action at the grass-roots level. It is based not on issues and discussion; it is based on the exchange of personal favors for votes. This was the mode of political operation that at the turn of the century led to considerable abuses and corruption in many local governments and caused some reformers and "muckrakers" ("do-gooders" in Mr. Marzullo's eyes) to call for reforms.

The reforms involved bringing a more professional form of governance to the cities, with such innovations as city managers and municipal commissions. The reforms included more civil-service workers rather than patronage workers. The direct primary (discussed in chapter 7) was instituted in order to cut down on the influence of the party bosses in choosing candidates.

Despite these reforms, the machines were able to survive to a certain extent. To be sure, they have just about (not entirely) faded away, and the Marzullos of the world are becoming fewer and fewer, but the model of exchange of service for vote is still practiced.

While reforms have helped to weaken the power of machines, other events have also contributed to their decline. Machines work best in low-income communities where the people need the kind of street-level services a ward leader can offer, where a relatively low-paying job is needed and will be appreciated. As people become economically more able to provide for their own needs, or as they develop or join organizations capable of providing for their needs (such as labor unions), they have less need to turn to local party officials.

In addition, the vast array of social welfare programs begun in the New Deal (1930s), wherein many social benefits are provided by law (not by politics), have also supplanted the service function of the machines. People out of work collect unemployment benefits; the destitute can receive welfare payments; the elderly receive medicare and medicaid; many people have social security checks coming in the mail every month.

Another aspect of the machine-versus-reform battle centers on the concept of what politics in a democracy is and ought to be. You will note from the Rakove account that the ward leaders do not spend much time discussing issues. They do not engage in activities aimed at educating the public about candidates and their views. They just provide services and ask (or tell) the people to vote for a particular candidate.

This is precisely what reformers reject. They see this as a detriment to the democratic process. It is not, they feel, the basis for building an informed, intelligent electorate. Reformers seek to concentrate on issues and policies. Among the reforms instituted in the early part of this century were the electoral devices of **initiative**, **referendum**, and **recall**. Proposition 13 is an example of the *initiative* process. The voters themselves, through the means of petitions, can put an issue on the ballot (Proposition 13), and they can, in some states, start the process to *recall* an elected official if they are not satisfied with that official's performance. The *referendum* is a device whereby a piece of legislation, once it is passed, must be "referred" to the voters at an election for their approval, before it becomes a final law.

All these efforts are aimed at undercutting the powers of the politicians, who are seen as having too firm a grip on the electoral process. (In the next chapter we will look at other reforms relating to the political party nominating conventions.)

Whither American Political Parties?

We have seen how political parties got started in the United States. We have seen why we have essentially a two-party system. And yet there is a

FIGURE 2.
The Decline of the Republican Middle-Class Support: Party Identification and Congressional Vote, 1940–1976

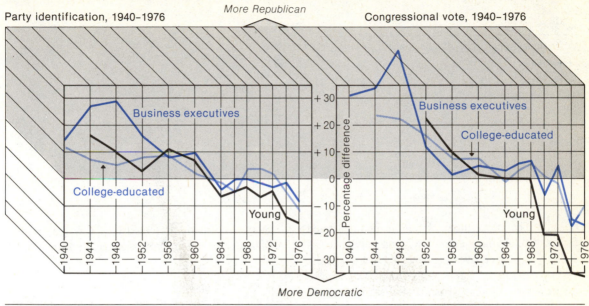

Source: These distributions are based on Gallup survey data, made available by the Gallup Organization through the Roper Center. Reported in Ladd, *Where Have All the Voters Gone?* p. 12.

pervasive view that political parties today are not performing the important functions they are supposed to perform. Very frequently, we hear people proudly announce that they are neither Democrats nor Republicans, but "Independents." We hear people say, "I vote for the person, not the party." We hear people speak disparagingly of party politicians. How often have you heard the term, "party hack"?

Remember, it was not one of the major parties that brought the Proposition 13 issue before the California voters, or even led the fight for or against it. Interest groups, the media, and individual citizens determined the outcome of that battle.

One political scientist, Everett C. Ladd, Jr., has written that "voting for the presidency has come to have less and less to do with the political party. The parties have been weakened organizationally

in recent years, and the American electorate . . . is less strongly attached to the parties and more inclined to vote independently than ever before.[11]

Another student of the American party system, Walter Dean Burnham, has described what he calls *party decomposition*. Political parties, Burnham argues, are less and less important for winning Congressional office (and for being reelected), and there is a definite trend away from relating Congressional party politics to presidential party politics. For both Congressional candidates and presidential candidates, according to Ladd and Burnham, it seems to be more important to rely on one's own resources and organization efforts rather than on the efforts of the political party.

One study, *The Changing American Voter*, concludes: "A substantial proportion of the public has withdrawn support for the major political par-

TABLE 2.
The Ethnic Distribution of Republican and Democratic Identifiers, 1976.

	Republican	Democratic
White Protestants	71%	43%
Northern	56	25
Southern	15	18
White Catholics	20	30
Blacks	3	18
Jews	1	3
Others	5	6

Source: These data are from fifteen national surveys conducted in 1976 by the Gallup Organization. The total number of cases for this combined data set is 23,086. Reported in Ladd, *Where Have All the Voters Gone?* p. 9.

ties:''[12] The percentage of people in the United States who declare themselves Independents has steadily increased over the years. In just ten years, 1964 to 1974, the figure went from 20 percent to 38 percent. Among college students today, 49 percent say they are Independents, while 37 percent say they are Democrats, and 14 percent Republicans.

In a book published in 1978, Professor Ladd suggested that the country is really faced with a situation of having not a two-party system, but a ''one-and-a-half-party system.'' The Republicans (the ''one-half'' portion) have not in recent years exerted much influence as a viable Congressional party or as an entity capable of capturing many state legislatures or gubernatorial seats. The best the Republicans have been able to do, Ladd argued, is to win the presidency every now and then. The GOP has been losing its base of middle-class support, as Figure 2 (page 213) indicates. This has been true even among business executives and the college-educated. ''To a striking extent, the Republicans have become a party of northern white Protestants.''[13] (See Table 2.)

Many have interpreted this inability to attract a significant number of other groups into its permanent fold as a serious weakness of the Republican party. The maps presented by the Social Science Data Center under Professor Ladd's direction tell the story. (See Figure 3.)

In 1980, however, behind the candidacy of Ronald Reagan, the Republicans scored impressive victories in Congress (actually capturing control of the Senate, to the surprise of many observers) and at the state level (see Figure 4). This may or may not indicate a reversal of the apparent Republican decline. Professor Ladd has noted that we must look at how a party does over several elections in order to know its underlying strength. Thus, it is not wise to draw sweeping conclusions about long-term trends from one election. There are many short-term factors that may or may not repeat themselves. A pollster for Republican candidates in 1980 was asked if he thought that a new Republican coalition was forming as a result of the 1980 victories. His response was similar to that of Professor Ladd:

It seems to me that it's a distinct possibility, but the events that are going to determine whether or not that happens haven't happened yet. When you have the people voting for Republican candidates and you have a lot of Republican candidates winning, that provides the opportunity to come back and vote again. And the way you

FIGURE 3.
Decline of Republican Party Strength
in House of Representatives Elections, 1952–1974.

CONGRESSIONAL
VOTE
Percent Republican
by state

| 55 and up |
| 50.0–54.99 |
| 45.0–49.99 |
| 40.0–44.99 |
| 30.0–39.99 |
| 29.99 or less |

ELECTION YEARS
1952–1962
States drawn
proportionate to
1958 population

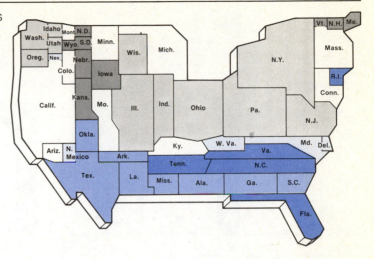

ELECTION YEARS
1964–1974
States drawn
proportionate to
1967 population

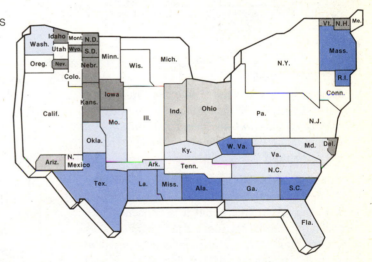

Source: Social Science Data Center, University of Connecticut.

FIGURE 4.
Impact of Republican Victories in 1980: Congress and Governorships.

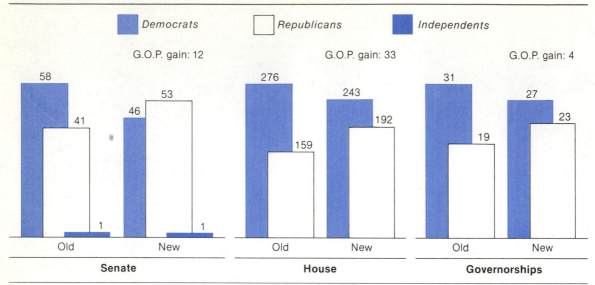

Source: *New York Times*, November 9, 1980. p. 2E.

build a coalition is obviously to get voters to go Republican two or three or four times in a row. I think it goes back to the point that essentially the New Deal coalition, the majority coalition that governed the country for 45 years, now really has broken up.[14]

The problem of the Democratic party, according to Professor Ladd, is a different one. That party has the registered voters, but it is frequently torn asunder by internal factions. Thus, in spite of its majority status, it cannot be confident at any time of its ability to win presidential elections. In regard to presidential politics, the party has within it people whom Ladd calls "new-class Democrats" and those he calls "old-class Democrats." The former are liberal on economic and social issues; they are mainly college-educated, white-collar professionals. They are active in local party councils, usually calling for party reforms in opposition to the regular party functionaries. These people participate actively in party primaries and can exert considerable influence in the selection of party nominees.

The "old-class Democrats," on the other hand, tend to be members of the "bourgeois working class." They have been Democrats, in the New Deal sense, for years, and they enjoy the gains obtained under the party's earlier programs (social security, union recognition, and so forth); but on many social, cultural, and economic matters, they are not nearly as liberal as their new-class counterparts. Table 3 shows how widely divergent the two groups are in their views. These tensions exist *within* the Democratic party, and they surface from time to time, leading to the kind of defeat suffered in 1972, when George McGovern lost the presidential election by a landslide. Many of the old-class Democrats could not bring themselves to support the candidacy of McGovern, whom they perceived to be too liberal.

TABLE 3.
Attitudes of New-Class and Old-Class Democrats on Social and Cultural Issues.

	New-Class Democrats	Old-Class Democrats
Should divorce be easier or more difficult to obtain than it is now? Percentage answering "easier"	59%	21%
Should a pregnant woman be able to obtain a legal abortion if she is married and does not want any more children? Percentage answering "yes"	73	32
What is your opinion of someone having sexual relations with someone other than the marriage partner? Percentage thinking extramarital sex is always wrong	38	80
What is your opinion of sexual relations between two adults of the same sex? Percentage feeling homosexuality is always wrong	27	89
Do you think we are spending the right amount of money to protect the environment? Percentage thinking we are spending too little	85	49
Do you think there should be laws against marriages between blacks and whites? Percentage favoring laws against miscegenation	5	67
Which statement comes closest to your feelings about pornography laws? Percentage thinking "there should be laws against the distribution of pornography *whatever the age*"	13	55
In a community-wide vote on the housing issue, which law would you favor? Percentage choosing law allowing homeowner to decide, even if he or she prefers not to sell to blacks	33	72

Note: New-class Democrats are respondents under forty years of age, college-educated, in professional and managerial jobs. Old-class Democrats are those over age fifty, without college training, in blue-collar occupations. The data are from the combined 1972–1976 NORC surveys. Reported in Ladd, *Where Have All the Voters Gone?* pp. 40–41.

In 1976 these differences were submerged behind the candidacy of Jimmy Carter. But 1980 was another story. Early analyses of the presidential vote in that election indicated that many traditional Democrats either stayed home or switched their votes in support of Ronald Reagan or some other candidate. Figure 5 shows that at least 34 percent of self-identifying Democrats voted for someone other than the Democratic candidate.

Both major parties, therefore, have internal weaknesses that may prevent them from giving coherent, viable leadership to the American public. There have been other changes (or suggested

changes) in such areas as presidential campaign financing which have further lessened the effectiveness of the major parties. These will be examined in the next chapter.

The two parties remain as entities with potential for becoming strong and useful political units. The evidence suggests, however, that the trend is toward the parties acting as little more than labels —not the important mechanisms for fulfilling the three functions discussed at the beginning of the chapter.

Interestingly what has happened to the major parties is close to what the founding framers had

FIGURE 5.
How Democrats Voted, 1980 Presidential Race.

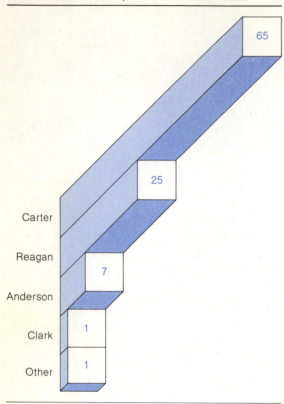

65

25

Carter

Reagan

7

Anderson

Clark

1

Other

1

envisioned and hoped for. Walter Dean Burnham believes that the concept of separation of powers is strengthened by a growing distinction between Congressional party politics and presidential party politics. In addition, Hamilton, Jefferson, and several others wanted an electorate focusing on issues, not on parties. Yet the United States of the 1980s is vastly different from the country of the 1790s. There *is* a need for organizations which can perform the political functions traditionally left to the political parties.

Summary

1. The two major political parties attempt to perform three functions: (1) mobilizing the electorate; (2) reconciling conflicting interests; and (3) organizing the government machinery. In performing these functions (or attempting to do so) the parties frequently bring within their fold a number of diverse groups and individuals who try to submerge their ideological and policy differences in the interest of putting together a winning coalition.

2. There are at least three distinct historical periods in the development of American parties. While not consciously intending to establish parties, the Federalists (under Alexander Hamilton) and the Republicans (under Thomas Jefferson) nonetheless found it necessary to do so. Their differences centered on conflicting views concerning economic policy and the role of the national government. Subsequent party development was also based on economic and regional interests. Modern-day Democrats trace their origins to Jefferson and to the party led by Andrew Jackson. The present-day Republican party was founded in the 1850s, making ours the oldest two-party system in history. The American two-party system owes much to the single-member (winner-take-all) electoral system. Proportional representation, on the other hand, is associated with multi-party systems.

3. The major parties are decentralized and fragmented largely because of the structural characteristics of federalism and separation of powers. Parties are organized to capture and control governmental offices. The varying constituencies (and terms of office) at different levels of government are reflected in the nature of the party system. Thus, instead of national parties, America has nationwide parties, making it difficult to have anything approaching the disciplined parties one finds in unitary governments like that of Great Britain.

4. Three types of minor parties can be identified in American politics: (1) the "bolting" type, which breaks away from one of the two major parties; (2) the economically motivated, doctrinaire type; and (3) the single-issue type. Minor parties virtually never win elections, but they can influence one of the two parties to adopt some of their programs some of the time.

5. The party structure is basically a two-layer structure. There is a national party structure geared mainly toward nominating and electing a President every four years. State and local structures are concerned with capturing offices on those levels. At the ward and precinct levels, the parties supposedly have the most intimate contact with the voters.

6. Party "machines" developed in some local and state areas, built on patronage (and, at times, graft). They were not too concerned with issues, but rather with controlling office and rendering personal services to constituencies as a means of staying in power. Ultimately, reforms were instituted to undercut party machine power. Such reforms, along with the social welfare programs of the New Deal, have largely succeeded in minimizing (if not doing away with) the effectiveness of machines.

7. The two major parties are experiencing increasing problems in performing the three essential functions mentioned in summary item number 1. More and more people are declaring themselves Independents and becoming more issue-oriented. In addition, candidates for office are tending to rely more on their personal organizational efforts while using the parties merely as labels.

Notes

1. William Lee Miller, *Yankee from Georgia, The Emergence of Jimmy Carter* (New York: New York Times Books, 1978), p. 40.
2. Robert Shogan, *Promises to Keep, Carter's First 100 Days* (New York: Thomas Y. Crowell Company, 1977), pp. 44–45.
3. William Nisbet Chambers, *Political Parties in a New Nation, The American Experience, 1776–1809* (New York: Oxford University Press, 1963), p. 5.
4. Oscar Theodore Black, Jr., Walter C. Wakefield, and Hugh Talmage Lefler, *The United States, A Survey of National Development* (New York: The Ronald Press Company, 1952), p. 247.
5. Clinton Rossiter, *Parties and Politics in America* (New York: Signet Books, The New American Library, 1960), pp. 80–81.
6. Black, Wakefield, and Lefler, *The United States, A Survey of National Development*, p. 306.
7. Robert Kuttner, *Revolt of the Haves* (New York: Simon and Schuster, 1980), p. 78.
8. *New York Times*, July 14, 1979, p. 17.
9. *New York Times*, July 15, 1979, p. 14.
10. Milton L. Rakove, *Don't Make No Waves . . . Don't Back No Losers* (Bloomington: Indiana University Press, 1975), pp. 117–118.
11. Everett Ladd, Jr., *Where Have All The Voters Gone?* (New York: W.W. Norton & Company, Inc., 1978), p. 35.
12. Norman H. Nie, Sidney Verba, and John R. Petrocik, *The Changing American Voter* (Cambridge, Mass.: Harvard University Press, 1976), p. 2.
13. Ladd, p. 9.
14. *New York Times*, November 9, 1980, p. E3.

Voters and the
Electoral Process

Chapter

7

When President Lyndon B. Johnson signed the Voting Rights Act of 1965, he said: "The right to vote is the most basic right without which all others are meaningless. It gives people—people as individuals—control over their own destinies. . . . The vote is the most powerful instrument ever devised by man for breaking down injustice and destroying the terrible walls which imprison men because they are different from other men."[1]

It is safe to say that no definition of democracy will stand as meaningful which does not include *voting* by some segment of the citizenry as a part of that political system. *All* citizens in the society need not be eligible to vote, but elections as a means of choosing public officials is an essential aspect of any system that calls itself a democracy. And those persons excluded must not be denied the privilege as a result of unreasonable, arbitrary, and discriminatory criteria.

While this seems self-evident, there is nonetheless disagreement among political theorists over the actual role and usefulness of the franchise. One school of thought maintains that the vote should be exercised only by the most intelligent and qualified citizens in the society and should not be extended on a universal basis to everyone. This "elitist" view assumes that the average citizen does not have enough information to cast an informed ballot, and that, therefore, voting should be restricted. Alexander Hamilton was an advocate of this position. "It is an unquestionable truth,"

wrote Hamilton, "that the body of the people, in every country, desire sincerely its prosperity; but it is equally unquestionable, that they do not possess the discernment and stability necessary for systematic government."[2]

This view sees elections as potentially dangerous since they provide the masses with the means to intervene and lower the standards of government and public policy. John Stuart Mill wrote: "The natural tendency of representative government, as of modern civilization, is toward collective mediocrity; and this tendency is increased by all reductions and extensions of the franchise, their effect being to place the principal power in the hands of classes more and more below the highest level of instruction in the community."[3]

This elitist school of thought seeks to provide for electoral mechanisms minimizing the influence of the electorate and at the same time providing for the selection of more capable people to office. Such mechanisms were incorporated into the original U.S. Constitution through provisions allowing for the electoral college system and the election of U.S. senators by state legislatures (subsequently changed by the Seventeenth Amendment in 1913).

Another school of thought holds that voting is not really a means of exercising direct control over the day-to-day activities of representatives or of policies. Rather, voting provides general, indirect

James Madison, an early advocate of the popular-control theory of voting. According to this theory, elections serve as a popular check on government officials.

influence, and is a means of exerting periodic checks and reminding those elected that they must be held accountable to the voters. Admittedly, this view is distrustful of officeholders and presumes that by making such people subject to periodic elections, they will be less likely to abuse their power. We will call this the *popular-control theory*.

James Madison expressed this position in *Federalist Paper* No. 52 : "As it is essential that the government in general should have a common interest with the people, so it is particularly essential that the [representatives] should have an immediate dependence on, and intimate sympathy with, the people. Frequent elections are unquestionably the only policy by which the dependence and sympathy can be effectually secured."

Thus, elections, according to this view, are expected to serve the purpose of protection rather than to give specific policy guidance. The voters are protected against insensitive actions on the part of representatives. If the latter are aware that they can be removed by the voters, there is greater likelihood that the actions of the officeholders will conform generally to the wishes of those who elect them.

Characteristics of the American Electorate

There have always been restrictions on the right to vote in the United States. Not until the early part of the twentieth century have we seen anything approaching universal suffrage. In the early days of the republic, various states imposed property, sexual, and racial qualifications. Only white males who owned a certain amount of assets or paid a certain amount of taxes could vote. And, of course, there has always been (and remains) an age restriction. Slowly, the states removed property restrictions.

Who can vote. With the passage of the Fifteenth Amendment, racial restrictions were lifted and black males could vote—constitutionally. But, as we discuss in chapter 14, it took several decades and many court battles and subsequent Congressional laws to secure this right for black citizens.

Women were not given the right to vote by the Constitution until the enactment of the Nineteenth Amendment in 1920, after several decades of agitation and struggle on the part of the suffragette movement.

Poll taxes as a requirement for voting were made unconstitutional by the Twenty-fourth Amendment, ratified in 1964.

And, finally, all citizens eighteen years of age and older could vote as a result of passage of the Twenty-sixth Amendment in 1971. (This, incidentally, is the most recent amendment to the Constitution.) There are still varying residence requirements in the states. Each state has the legal authority to determine election laws (voter registration, residency, form of the ballot, primary dates, and so forth) as long as such laws do not impose restrictions that are prohibited by the federal Constitution.

Therefore, from the founding of the nation in 1789, we have seen the slowly evolving concept of *universal suffrage*. There are no restrictions based on education now, although there were such in some states prior to 1965. The country has not adhered to elitist notions of the role of voting, but rather to the popular-control theory.

An important concern is the extent to which registration laws affect voter turnout. There are varying requirements in different states regulating such practices as closing dates, hours for registration, weekend registration, mail registration, absentee registration, location of registrar's offices, and so on. One view is that the easier it is to register, the greater the likelihood of increased voter participation. Two political scientists concluded from their study of voter registration that "registration laws have a substantial effect on the number of people who go to the polls on election

Women campaigning for women's suffrage at a boardwalk stand in Asbury Park, New Jersey, in the summer of 1914. It was not until the passage of the Nineteenth Amendment in 1920 that women were constitutionally guaranteed the right to vote.

FIGURE 1.
Turnout of Eligible Voters in Presidential and Congressional Elections, 1868–1976.

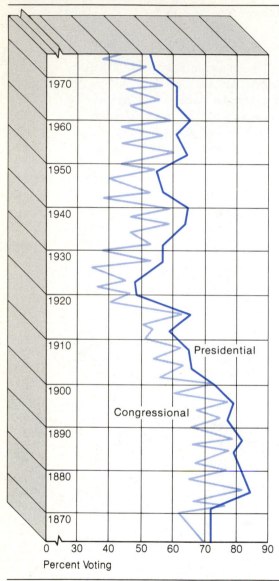

0   30   40   50   60   70   80   90

Percent Voting

day.''[4] They examined data taken from the 1972 presidential election and found that ''state registration laws reduced turnout by about nine percentage points. . . . Early deadlines for registration and limited-registration office hours were the biggest impediments to turnout.'' But Steven J. Rosenstone and Raymond Wolfinger have cautioned that, given a relaxation of registration laws, one should not expect much change in the character of the electorate: ''The electorate would be expanded with virtually no change in its demographic, partisan, or ideological characteristics. It would be bigger, but not different.''[5]

Turnout in American elections. There are a number of factors to consider when studying voter participation in American elections. We should be mindful of regional differences, socio-economic differences, and varying turnout rates in national and local contests and during presidential and nonpresidential (sometimes called ''off-year'') elections. And it is important to understand such factors as registration and voting requirements, the competitiveness of the contests, differences between primary elections and general elections, as well as whether potential voters believe their participation is worth the effort or not.

As Figure 1 shows, the turnout of eligible voters in presidential elections has declined between 1868 and 1976. People in southern states have traditionally turned out at a lower rate than those in other parts of the country, though by 1976 there appeared to be little difference among the regions.

The declining turnout trend continued in the 1980 election. The Federal Election Commission reported that 53.95 percent of eligible voters turned out. This was the lowest percentage since the 1948 election, when only 51.1 percent voted.

Political scientists have offered several explanations for the regional differences over time. From 1900 to 1916, the low southern turnout rates were partly attributed to restrictions imposed on potential black voters in that area. Southern states used various methods—all subsequently declared unconstitutional—to keep black citizens from voting. In addition, the South was then predominantly a one-party (Democratic) region, and that fact tended to lower voter participation.

The overall decline in voter participation since the early years of the twentieth century has been attributed to various causes. Some political scientists, such as Walter Dean Burnham and E. E. Schattschneider, have pointed to the lack of a competitive two-party system and to a general loss of interest in politics on the part of the voting public.[6] Others have looked to the role played by political reforms in contributing to declining turnout rates. In the nineteenth century we experienced relatively high turnouts because party machines actively mobilized and "delivered" a largely uninformed electorate. But after the turn of the century, reforms tended to weaken the party structures. The "Australian," or secret, ballot was introduced; voter registration prior to elections was instituted; civil service began to cut into party patronage. All these reforms made it more difficult for the political party to mobilize and manipulate voters.[7]

Figure 1 indicates that voter turnout in Congressional elections has been consistently below that of presidential elections. People obviously are more attracted to the polls by a presidential contest than by any other political race. We also know that voters turn out less in primary elections than in general elections even though the former may be the decisive contests.

In most instances, we can account for differences in turnouts on the basis of the following factors: media coverage, importance of the office to the

In Miami, citizens cast their votes by punching computer cards at desks shielded from the view of other voters. Secret ballots were not introduced until this century.

Voters in New York City's upper west side sign in on registration books that bear the signatures of all registered voters in that district. Voter registration prior to elections was another twentieth century reform.

voters, importance of issues to the voters, and personal characteristics of the candidates.

The media certainly devote more attention to some elections than to others, with a presidential contest being, of course, the most widely covered. This fact alone helps create public interest and participation. Political scientists often use the terms *high salience* and *low salience* to refer to contests and issues that attract (or fail to attract) public attention. A primary race for a seat on the local town council, for instance, would not have the *saliency* of a general election for President of the United States.

In elections where the outcome is hardly in doubt, there is likely to be a relatively low turnout. If the competition is keen and people feel that either party could win, voter participation is likely to be increased.

Who does and does not vote. It is possible to know quite a lot about who does and does not vote in American elections. For purposes of our discussion here, we can use three categories: the *perennial* voter; the *occasional* voter; and the *nonvoter*.

The perennial voter votes all the time, in all elections. This person is very likely to have at least some college education, will have a middle to upper income, and will probably hold a white-collar job in the urban North and West. Such a voter will often be middle-aged, as Figure 2 indicates. You will also note that as younger people gain more education, they are likely to close the gap between themselves and older voters of comparable education. In other words, in every index, education appears to be a most important predictor of whether a person is likely to vote or not.

The perennial voter usually sees it as his or her civic duty to vote, believing that this is what a responsible, concerned citizen *should* do. Such a person does not necessarily feel that any one vote

FIGURE 2.
Turnout in the 1976 Presidential Election According to Age and Education.

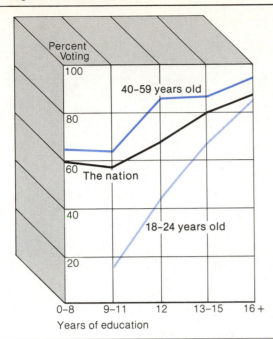

Source: From William H. Flanigan and Nancy H. Zingale, POLITICAL BEHAVIOR OF THE AMERICAN ELECTORATE, 4th Edition, p. 27. Copyright © 1979 by Allyn and Bacon, Inc. Copyright © 1975, 1972, 1968 by Allyn and Bacon, Inc.

will spell the difference between victory and defeat. Rather, he or she sees voting as a way of taking part in the governing process and of holding elected officials accountable.

The perennial voter attempts to keep reasonably well-informed about political issues—especially those that concern her or him specifically—and will no doubt attempt to join together with other voters who share similar views.

This person, in addition to voting, is more likely than others to engage in various forms of political activity: contacting officials, working for a party or candidate, contributing money to campaigns, or simply discussing politics with friends and others. Surely some elections and issues are of greater interest to the perennial voter than others, but this voter considers it important to the *process* and the *system* to participate even in low salience contests.

The occasional voter will register and vote in the high salience elections. This person will be more likely to vote in general elections than in primaries, more likely to stay at home if the weather is bad, and less likely to vote for those offices of low salience which appear at the bottom of the ticket. The occasional voter will probably not be found among those involved in other forms of political activity.

Voting is not necessarily seen as being unimportant, but if there are other distractions the occasional voter will likely not take the time to participate. This person is not likely to be as well-educated as the perennial voter and not likely to be a member of a high socio-economic group. The occasional voter is less influenced by civic duty than is the perennial voter.

This person, however, may be susceptible to particular appeals by the party or candidate and will probably vote if specifically moved or urged to do so. Such a voter might well belong to an interest group—a labor union, for instance—that urges a big turnout on a particular occasion. Political issues are interpreted in personal terms ("What's he done for me?"), and if a rather specific connection can be made between voting and the desired results, this person will probably find his or her way to the polls.

The nonvoter seldom, if ever, bothers to vote. This person might register (in response to concerted voter registration drives, for example), but will probably not turn out on election day.

Invariably, the nonvoter is younger, less well-educated, and of lower socio-economic status than the perennial or occasional voter. As Table 1 shows, there is also a clear correlation between voting and race, sex, and region. You will note that black women in the South constitute the highest percentage of those who have never voted in the four presidential elections surveyed. Notice also the substantial *decrease* in the number of southern

TABLE 1.

The Distribution of Adults Who Have Never Voted According to Race and Sex for the South and Non-South in 1952, 1960, 1968, and 1976.

	1952		1960		1968		1976	
	White	Black	White	Black	White	Black	White	Black
South[1]								
Men	12%	65%	8%	33%	9%	25%	14%	23%
Women	33%	87%	17%	63%	26%	31%	18%	28%
Non-South								
Men	6%	17%	6%	11%	9%	0%[2]	8%	5%
Women	7%	11%	7%	28%	7%	17%	10%	25%

[1]The states included in the South are Alabama, Arkansas, Florida, Georgia, Kentucky, Louisiana, Maryland, Mississippi, North Carolina, Oklahoma, South Carolina, Tennessee, Texas, Virginia, and West Virginia.
[2]This "unrealistic" finding may reflect sampling problems in central cities of the North.

Source: From William H. Flanigan and Nancy H. Zingale, POLITICAL BEHAVIOR OF THE AMERICAN ELECTORATE, 4th Edition. Copyright © 1979 by Allyn and Bacon, Inc. Copyright © 1975, 1972, 1968 by Allyn and Bacon, Inc.

blacks (men and women) who have never voted. Surely this is attributable to the significant civil-rights/voting-rights achievements beginning in the late 1950s. Southern citizens, generally, are less likely to have voted than non-southerners. The major contributing factors appear to be lower educational and income levels.

The changing American voter. In the 1950s, most people voted along party lines, and they tended to vote the way their parents did. Since 1964, however, according to a major study by three political scientists, there has been a definite change toward greater emphasis on issues.[8] Professors Nie, Verba, and Petrocik have stated: "The data suggest that the American public has been entering the electoral arena since 1964 with quite a different mental set than was the case in the late 1950s and early 1960s. They have become more concerned with issues and less tied to their parties."[9]

When citizens were asked, over a period of six presidential elections, the things they liked or disliked about the candidates, *issues* were cited more and more often while references to party were clearly on the decrease. (See Figure 3.)

Along with this development has come the growing tendency of voters to classify themselves as neither Republicans nor Democrats, but as Independents. Figure 4 provides a good picture of this as it relates to new voters over a fifty-year period. Of those people just reaching voting age, the percentage who call themselves Independents has quadrupled between 1920 and 1972. The number of those who identify with one of the two major parties has steadily declined—especially since the early 1960s.

One persuasive explanation for these occurrences is that not only was the electorate faced with new issues in the 1960s (civil rights, Vietnam) and 1970s (Watergate, the environment), but a new political generation came on the scene. "By 1974, 14 percent of the electorate were voters who came of voting age after the 1964 election and had no party affiliation."[10] This new group could not identify with issues of the 1930s, '40s, or '50s—or even 1960s. Thus, what attracted their parents to a particular party was not relevant to them. They would be moved—if at all—by different issues.

The "middle voter" and the 1980 elections. "The electorate that will vote will be a more middle-class electorate than it was in 1976," said Curtis B. Gans, director of the Committee for the Study of the American Electorate, "and that will sink Carter and a lot of Democrats in a lot of places." This prognosis proved correct, and in 1981 Ronald Reagan became the fortieth President of the United States. He outpolled Carter substantially, as Table 2 (page 230) shows, among Independents and moderate Independents, and he made a respectable showing among conservative Democrats. The "middle voter" mentioned above refers to that person most likely to vote.[11] While polls showed Mr. Carter favored by unregistered (nonvoting) Americans, Mr. Reagan's supporters were the ones who would count—because they would vote. One commentator noted:

> *The electorate now is considerably whiter than the nation's population as a whole, and more middle-aged and better educated.*
>
> *This gave Ronald Reagan a head start over President Carter. The polls found that the former California governor's supporters were much more likely to be registered to vote than Mr. Carter's backers. Among unregistered Americans, who were powerless to affect the outcome of* [the 1980] *election, Mr. Carter led Mr. Reagan.*[12]

A relatively high percentage of voters (41 percent) "knew all along" whom they would vote for, and a combined 21 percent had decided during the primaries and the summer political conventions. Thus, 62 percent had made their choice before the general campaigns started, and Mr. Reagan received 55 percent of their votes.

FIGURE 3.
Why People Vote for Particular Candidates, 1952–1972.

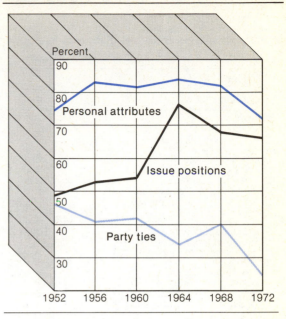

FIGURE 4.
Party Identification of New Voters, 1920–1972.

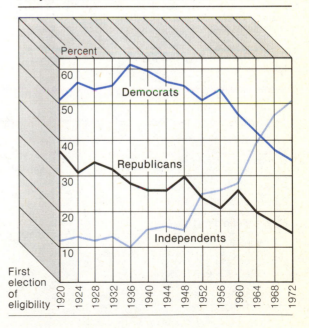

TABLE 2.
How Different Groups Voted for President, 1980 and 1976.

Based on 12,782 interviews with voters at their polling places. Shown is how each group divided its vote for President and, in parentheses, the percentage of the electorate belonging to each group.

	Carter	Reagan	Anderson	Carter-Ford in 1976
Democrats (43%)	66	26	6	77-22
Independents (23%)	30	54	12	43-54
Republicans (28%)	11	84	4	9-90
Liberals (17%)	57	27	11	70-26
Moderates (46%)	42	48	8	51-48
Conservatives (28%)	23	71	4	29-70
Liberal Democrats (9%)	70	14	13	86-12
Moderate Democrats (22%)	66	28	6	77-22
Conservative Democrats (8%)	53	41	4	64-35
Politically active Democrats (3%)	72	19	8	—
Democrats favoring Kennedy in primaries (13%)	66	24	8	—
Liberal Independents (4%)	50	29	15	64-29
Moderate Independents (12%)	31	53	13	45-53
Conservative Independents (7%)	22	69	6	26-72
Liberal Republicans (2%)	25	66	9	17-82
Moderate Republicans (11%)	13	81	5	11-88
Conservative Republicans (12%)	6	91	2	6-93
Politically active Republicans (2%)	5	89	6	—
East (32%)	43	47	8	51-47
South (27%)	44	51	3	54-45
Midwest (20%)	41	51	6	48-50
West (11%)	35	52	10	46-51
Blacks (10%)	82	14	3	82-16
Hispanics (2%)	54	36	7	75-24
Whites (88%)	36	55	8	47-52
Female (49%)	45	46	7	50-48
Male (51%)	37	54	7	50-48
Female, favors equal rights amendment (22%)	54	32	11	—
Female, opposes equal rights amendment (15%)	29	66	4	—
Catholic (25%)	40	51	7	54-44
Jewish (5%)	45	39	14	64-34
Protestant (46%)	37	56	6	44-55
Born-again white Protestant (17%)	34	61	4	—
18–21 years old (6%)	44	43	11	48-50
22–29 years old (17%)	43	43	11	51-46
30–44 years old (31%)	37	54	7	49–49
45–59 years old (23%)	39	55	6	47-52
60 years or older (18%)	40	54	4	47-52
Family income				
Less than $10,000 (13%)	50	41	6	58-40
$10,000–$14,999 (14%)	47	42	8	55–43
$15,000–$24,999 (30%)	38	53	7	48-50
$25,000–$50,000 (24%)	32	58	8	36-62
Over $50,000 (5%)	25	65	8	—

	Carter	Reagan	Anderson	Carter-Ford in 1976
Professional or manager (40%)	33	56	9	41-57
Clerical, sales or other white-collar (11%)	42	48	8	46-53
Blue-collar worker (17%)	46	47	5	57-41
Agriculture (3%)	29	66	3	—
Looking for work (3%)	55	35	7	65-34
Education				
High school or less (39%)	46	48	4	57-43
Some college (28%)	35	55	8	51-49
College graduate (27%)	35	51	11	45-55
When decided about choice				
Knew all along (41%)	47	50	2	44-55
During the primaries (13%)	30	60	8	57-42
During conventions (8%)	36	55	7	51-48
Since Labor Day (8%)	30	54	13	49-49
In week before election (23%)	38	46	13	49-47

Source: 1976 and 1980 election day surveys. © CBS Inc. 1980 All Rights Reserved. Originally published in the New York Times/CBS News (exit poll) November 9, 1980. 1976 election day survey by NBC News.

Voting Patterns in American Elections

From the "era of good feelings" in the 1820s to 1976, Americans have demonstrated a strong tendency to alternate their electoral support between the two major parties in presidential elections. By carefully studying Figure 5 (page 232), you will see only one fairly brief period (during the late nineteenth century, from 1872 to 1896) when presidential elections were reasonably close. Note also the performance of third-party candidates: in general they get between 5 and 20 percent of the vote. Flanigan and Zingale note that "in presidential contests over the years, more than half of the electorate has voted for presidential candidates from different parties."[13]

As we have noted, issues are becoming increasingly important in presidential elections, giving rise to the influence of what are often called *short-term forces*, as opposed to the more stabilizing, continuing influence of political party identification. Of course, voters still rely on parties as "cues" to voting; they simply rely *less* on party identification than in earlier times.

Types of elections. We can speak of four basic types of elections: (1) *deviating*, (2) *realigning*, (3) *maintaining*, or (4) *reinstating*. The first type occurs when a party wins rather substantially in the face of indications (namely, its expected vote based on voter registration) to the contrary. This has happened three times since World War II: with Eisenhower's victories in 1952 and 1956, and with Nixon's reelection in 1972. (Nixon's 1968 victory was not by a substantial margin, and the Democrats gained impressive victories at the state levels.) In each instance, the Republican party had considerably fewer registrants than the Democratic party. Obviously, then, many traditional Democrats "deviated" and voted for the Republican candidate. This is strictly a result of short-term forces—the appeal of a particular candidate, or aversion to the other candidate, or the importance of specific issues.

Of greater significance is the election leading to a *realigning* change—often referred to as a "critical election." Here, we see voters shifting party loyalties (as well as new voters coming into the

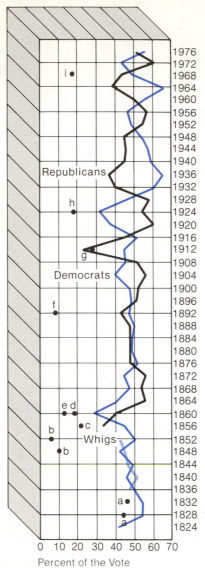

process), causing a long-term alteration in the base
of the parties. This has occurred only three times
in American presidential history. The first was
with the rise of the Republican party during the
time of the Civil War. The second was in 1896
following the depression of 1893, and the third,
which benefited the Democratic party, was in 1932
following the 1929 stock market crash. You will
note that in each instance the realigning election
was associated with a traumatic crisis in American
society. What happens is that voters are shaken
from their traditional political loyalties and find a
home—rather permanently—in another place.

It is during such times that we normally find
clear "choices" in the two major parties. As
Flanigan and Zingale point out:

*The appeals of the parties and the response of
their followings to the realignment crisis provide
an electoral base for governmental policymaking for a number of years. Appeals to voters
on issues during the realignment crisis produce
an exceptionally dramatic division between the
parties. These brief, uncommon crises contrast
with most periods of American electoral history
when parties take less consistent and dramatic
stands.*[14]

Most presidential elections in the twentieth century have been *maintaining* elections. These are
elections in which affiliations dominant in the
preceding period continue, and the majority party
wins the presidency.[15]

Some analysts have defined a fourth category—
the *reinstating* elections. These occur when the
voters return to normal voting habits after a
deviating election. The election of John Kennedy
in 1960 was an example.[16] Democratic voters
resumed their party allegiance after two terms of a
Republican presidency (Eisenhower). If commen-
taries following Reagan's 1980 victory prove to be
accurate (regarding the breakup of the Democratic

New Deal coalition), the result could conceivably be a realignment of party affiliations. Republican national party chairman William Brock has been quoted as saying: "This could be the breakpoint election in bringing about a party realignment. In this election we have brought together the elements of a new coalition. The cementing of that coalition depends on our performance in office." Subsequent elections will tell.

Electoral patterns in Congressional elections are another matter. Voters are much more consistently partisan in Congressional elections than in presidential elections, and this, as Figure 6 indicates, has become especially true in the twentieth century.

Another recurrent pattern is for the party winning the presidential election to do less well in the Congressional elections two years later. This almost invariably happens. "The greater stability of Congressional voting and the apparent return to 'normal' after a presidential victory have led analysts to regard the Congressional vote as more reflective of the underlying strength of the parties."[17]

Elections for the House of Representatives are less salient than presidential elections; therefore, voters are apt to rely more on party identification or, as we noted in chapter 6, on identification with individual incumbents. Incumbency is an exceptionally important factor in House races. It is a rare occurrence for a two- or three-term member of the House to be defeated.

This has been generally true for senators as well, but incumbency in that position seems to be less a guarantee of reelection. In 1976, thirty percent of the senators running for reelection were defeated. Senatorial seats, of course, are of higher saliency than those of the House, and, as with the presidency, voters tend to be influenced by short-term forces. As noted in chapter 6, Republicans

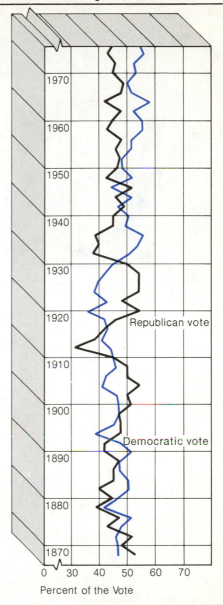

FIGURE 6.
Partisan Division of the Nationwide Vote for Representatives in Congress, 1868–1976.

Percent of the Vote

Source: From William H. Flanigan and Nancy H. Zingale, POLITICAL BEHAVIOR OF THE AMERICAN ELECTORATE, 4th Edition, p. 48. Copyright © 1979 by Allyn and Bacon, Inc. Copyright © 1975, 1972, 1968 by Allyn and Bacon, Inc.

A predecessor of today's national convention: the 1868 Democratic convention held in Tammany Hall, Boston.

won twelve new seats in the Senate and thirty-three in the House in 1980. Eighteen Democratic incumbents sought reelection to the Senate; eight lost. No Republican senator seeking reelection lost to a Democratic challenger.

Nominating Presidential Candidates

The grand prize in American politics is the presidency. With President Reagan, forty men have held the office, and only one, Gerald Ford, was not elected by the voters. In order to be elected, one has to be nominated, which is, as we noted, the major function of the national—or, perhaps we should say, the nationwide—political parties.

The nomination process has undergone major changes since the mid-1960s. Candidates are relying more and more on state primaries to win delegates; television has changed campaign styles; the two major parties (especially the Democrats) have adopted new rules for choosing convention delegates; and federal government financing of campaigns has been instituted.

In the early part of this century, the national convention was a meetingplace for state and local party bosses to gather (with delegates firmly in pocket) and wheel and deal behind the scenes in order to arrive at a compromise candidate. State leaders (frequently governors or big city mayors) therefore figured strongly in presidential selection politics. The delegates were usually selected back home on the basis of their loyalty to the state or local party boss. They would permit their votes to be "delivered" at the appropriate time. These delegates were party workers who spent most of their time at the four-day convention wearing funny hats, attending parties, having a good time, and making sure they showed up on the convention floor to yell and cheer for a particular candidate. They were not asked and they did not expect to be consulted about what the party platform would contain. That was a matter for the "big boys" in the "smoke-filled rooms." Everybody understood. Nobody complained—openly.

In this situation, aspirants to the party nomination would spend preconvention time courting the state and local leaders, not the grass-roots, rank-and-file voters. The national media were not very important in this process.

Until 1936, the Democratic party convention had a two-thirds rule which required the nominee to get two thirds of the delegates' votes. This meant that the southern states, by sticking together, could wield great influence over who would be selected. And they did—that is, stick together and wield influence. Thus, the Democratic nominee would not be likely to take positions that would irritate the South on civil-rights issues.

After 1936, the two-thirds rule was abolished, and a nominee needed only a majority vote. This was a major change in Democratic nomination politics. The South did not become unimportant, but their delegates no longer had awesome convention power. In fact, precisely because they could not effectively influence their party, they walked out of the 1948 convention over a civil-rights plank in the platform and formed their own third party, the Dixiecrats. It was a short-lived effort, but the Southerners had made their displeasure known.

The national party committee determines the site of the convention, and it establishes certain rules to certify which delegates are properly seated. In other matters, the various state parties and state legislatures figure most prominently.

Before we turn to the delegate selection process, let's say a few words about choosing a city to hold the convention. As one reporter noted:

Conventions have become very big business for cities, a "clean" way of stimulating the economy and employing perhaps more unskilled workers—in restaurants and hotels—than heavy industry does. Because of their enormous visibility, political conventions are considered just about the best way of stimulating additional convention activity in subsequent years.[18]

Party conventions receive money from two sources: the federal government, which provides $2 million, and the host city, which provides additional funds. The latter funds come from private contributors (usually local business corporations and chambers of commerce that expect a return in increased business) and from the local government in the form of guarantees of adequate hotel and convention space, and efficient security forces.

Some cities frankly admit, however, that they cannot afford the cost and therefore do not get involved in the bidding. For example, Los Angeles simply decided that it would not try for the 1980 party conventions, in part because of the passage of Proposition 13. Said Los Angeles Councilman Ernani Bernadi, chairperson of a government operations committee that blocked the city's bid: "We'd be pleased to have either the Democratic or Republican convention, but as far as providing any tax dollars, that's out. We have a mandate from the people in the state on Proposition 13 to hold down the cost of government. . . ."[19]

Some symbolic factors play a part in selecting a particular city. In 1980, the Republicans chose a normally Democratic stronghold, Detroit, Michigan, because, it was alleged, the party wanted to make a symbolic point of being associated with an urban area.

Similarly, the Democrats in 1980 could not

Delegates in full convention regalia at the 1976 Republican (below) and Democratic (left) conventions.

choose a city in a state that had not ratified the Equal Rights Amendment. The party did not want to run the risk of offending its contingent of ERA supporters.

In 1976, when the Democrats met in New York City, party officials and others in that city made a point of the fact that New York was coming out of the economic doldrums of the previous few years, when it had teetered on the brink of bankruptcy. Holding the convention there permitted the locals to boast about how they were alive and well enough to host a lively convention where a good time was had by all—except, perhaps, the losing nominees.

Selecting convention delegates. Delegates to the nominating convention may be chosen in any of three ways: in local party caucuses, in state conventions, or in party primaries. Each state determines the method. The national party determines how many delegates will come from each state, based on a formula which takes into account population and whether the state favored the party

the last presidential, gubernatorial, or senatorial race. Delegates chosen specifically because they come from winning states are considered bonus delegates.

There has been an increase in the use of primary elections since 1960, as shown in Table 3. The primary is considered by some as being more democratic, in that it takes control out of the hands of the party bosses—or it *tends* to do so.

Some of the primaries are not for purposes of choosing delegates, but are only popularity contests or ''beauty contests.'' That is, the voters choose one of the candidates, thereby indicating their *preference*. The delegates are actually chosen either by party convention or party caucus and need not be bound by the primary vote. This disturbs some observers, because it permits factions that control the state party to send to the convention delegates who might not be in tune with the rank-and-file party voters. The reaction of an editorial in the *Dallas Morning News* early in the 1980 presidential race is fairly typical of this point of view:

TABLE 3.
Primary Elections, 1960–1980.

The number of presidential primaries from 1960 to 1976 includes two—in Alabama and New York—that were for delegate selection only (no presidential candidates were listed on the ballot). In 1976 Texas also held a delegate selection primary. The total vote excludes these primaries and includes only those in which a presidential preference was permitted.

Year	Number of Primaries	Total Vote	Democratic	Republican
1960	18	11,224,631	5,686,664	5,537,967
1964	19*	12,182,774	6,247,435	5,935,339
1968	17	12,008,620	7,535,069	4,473,551
1972	23	22,217,348	15,993,965	6,223,383
1976	30	26,426,777	16,052,652	10,374,125
1980	37	32,323,622	19,538,438	12,785,184

*Includes presidential preference poll taken by Texas Republican Party. The vote from this primary is not included in the 1964 Republican and total vote columns.

Sources: *CQ Guide to Current American Government* (Spring 1978), p. 126; *CQ Weekly Report,* Vol. 38, No. 27 (July 5, 1980), p. 1869.

Voting in a primary election in Randolph, Massachusetts. In closed and semiclosed primaries, citizens must declare their party affiliation and can vote only for candidates in that party.

Democratic leadership in Texas is pursuing a death wish, the state executive committee has asserted again. As of today, there will be no binding presidential primary on the party's ballot next year. And even if President Carter faces a serious challenge, Texas Democrats will get to participate in only a "beauty contest." Key national convention delegates will be determined at party conventions.

Texas Republicans, on the other hand, have long planned to parade an array of attractive candidates before voters next year. And Republican primary voters will have the satisfaction of knowing their opinions will be proportionally represented at the party's national convention.

Democrats appear willing to sacrifice conservatives and moderates in order to purge the party of dissenters. And that's unfortunate. Without a meaningful presidential primary next year, we may witness the beginning of the end for the state's once proud—and representative—Democratic Party.[20]

The increase in the number of presidential primaries has put considerable strain on potential nominees. They start early (sometimes more than two years before the conventions), criss-crossing the country, making appearances in primary states, trying to get local media coverage, and so forth.

Most primaries are **closed**. That is, only those citizens who have preregistered as members of a particular party may vote in that party's primary. Washington, D.C., and sixteen states fall in this category.[21] Seven states have a **semiclosed** primary system, which requires the voters to declare their party affiliation when they go to vote.[22] Six states have **open** primaries, whereby any voter can vote in any primary without declaring a party membership.[23] This method permits "raiding" of one party by members of another. That is, registered Republicans can take part in the Democratic primary and, possibly, vote for a weaker nominee to run against the Republicans later in the general election, or vice versa. For this reason, some people feel the open primary (while it *sounds* democratic) is a distortion of party responsibility. If Democrats can "invade" the Republican party and influence the latter's candidate choice, this is not an honest way to hold the party system accountable.

Some states frequently revise their nominating rules, especially with the increase in primaries in recent years. Of course, these revisions are of no small concern to potential nominees and would-be presidential aspirants. A number of important considerations come into play. When should the primary or delegate selection process be held? New Hampshire is the lead-off primary state—in February—and jealously guards that role since being first gives that state quadrennial political prominence. All eyes are on New Hampshire to get some hint about who is the "frontrunner," who shows surprising strength, and so forth. After New Hampshire, the "primary season" goes on for over six months—too long, some argue (see Table 4). Thus there have been suggestions for one national primary day (not likely to happen) or for three or four regional primaries on the same date in the different regions (also not likely to happen in the near future). Proponents for reform say it would reduce the cost and, hopefully, the wear and tear on candidates. Opponents are concerned that voters should have the opportunity to consider "unknowns" (or "dark horses"), and that limited primaries may benefit only the best-known (though not necessarily best-qualified) candidates.

Should there be a higher or lower "proportional representation" requirement? Now, with the Democrats, if a candidate receives fifteen percent of the primary vote, that person gets fifteen percent of the state's delegates. If the figure were higher, that would discourage minor or "splinter" candidates

TABLE 4.
1980 Presidential Primary Dates.

Thirty-seven presidential primaries were scheduled for 1980—35 state primaries plus the District of Columbia and Puerto Rico.
The Arkansas primary was for Democrats only, while the Mississippi and South Carolina primaries were only for Republicans.

Primaries by State		Primaries by Date	
Alabama	March 11	Feb. 17	Puerto Rico (R)
Arkansas	May 27 (D)	Feb. 26	New Hampshire
California	June 3	March 4	Massachusetts
Connecticut	March 25		Vermont
District of		March 8	South Carolina (R)
Columbia	May 6	March 11	Alabama
Florida	March 11		Florida
Georgia	March 11		Georgia
Idaho	May 27	March 16	Puerto Rico (D)
Illinois	March 18	March 18	Illinois
Indiana	May 6	March 25	Connecticut
Kansas	April 1		New York
Kentucky	May 27	April 1	Kansas
Louisiana	April 5		Wisconsin
Maryland	May 13	April 5	Louisiana
Massachusetts	March 4	April 22	Pennsylvania
Michigan	May 20	May 3	Texas
Mississippi	June 3 (R)	May 6	District of
Montana	June 3		Columbia
Nebraska	May 13		Indiana
Nevada	May 27		North Carolina
New Hampshire	Feb. 26		Tennessee
New Jersey	June 3	May 13	Maryland
New Mexico	June 3		Nebraska
New York	March 25	May 20	Michigan
North Carolina	May 6		Oregon
Ohio	June 3	May 27	Arkansas (D)
Oregon	May 20		Idaho
Pennsylvania	April 22		Kentucky
Puerto Rico	March 16 (D)		Nevada
	Feb. 17 (R)	June 3	California
Rhode Island	June 3		Mississippi
South Carolina	March 8 (R)		Montana
South Dakota	June 3		New Jersey
Tennessee	May 6		New Mexico
Texas	May 3		Ohio
Vermont	March 4		Rhode Island
West Virginia	June 3		South Dakota
Wisconsin	April 1		West Virginia

Source: *CQ Guide, Current American Government* (Washington, D.C., Congressional Quarterly, Inc., Fall 1980), p. 55.

Antiwar candidate Eugene McCarthy campaigning for the Democratic presidential nomination. McCarthy failed to muster enough support among the relatively conservative convention delegations to win the nomination.

from going to the convention with only a small number of delegates. Such candidates, the argument goes, really do not have a chance to win the convention nomination, and they simply make it more difficult to build party unity. Others believe, however, that it is more democratic to let as many candidates as possible surface, and perhaps bloom.

Should *all* potential candidates be listed on the primary ballot in the state, even if they have not formally declared an intention to enter that particular state primary and therefore likely did no campaigning in that state? As it now stands, candidates can pick and choose which primaries to enter. Obviously, a candidate would not want to enter a state primary where he or she would not be likely to fare well. Some argue, however, that listing *all* candidates would give a better national picture of overall candidate strength and appeal.

Convention reform: delegate selection. One of the major convention reforms has focused on the adequate representation of various groups in the selection of delegates. Following the 1968 Democratic convention, the Democrats appointed a commission to study and recommend changes in rules governing the credentials of delegates. Some groups were deeply disturbed that the state delegations were made up mostly of white, middle-aged males who tended to be moderate to conservative in their political leanings. Women, youth, and racial minorities were underrepresented. The party commission (originally chaired by Senator George McGovern, and then by Representative Donald Fraser) was named the Commission on Party Structure and Delegate Selection, and it consisted of twenty-eight members chosen by the national party chairperson, then-senator Fred Harris of Oklahoma.

The catalyst for this development was the turbulent Democratic convention in Chicago in 1968. Various anti-Vietnam War protest groups conducted demonstrations and were confronted by the local police in violent, bloody clashes. The groups attempted to get the Democratic party to nominate antiwar candidate Eugene McCarthy and to adopt strong antiwar planks in the party platform. Some people interpreted their failure to do this as a direct result of the relatively conservative composition of the convention delegations.

As a result, attention turned to changing the procedures for selecting delegates. The commission issued its report, *Mandate for Reform*, in 1970. Considerable emphasis was placed on the primary as a means of choosing delegates, and several guidelines were articulated which were to be followed in selecting delegates to the 1972 Democratic convention. Proxy voting was forbidden; the *unit rule* (by means of which all the state's votes could be cast for one candidate even if some delegates wanted to vote for another) was outlawed; a ten-dollar fee limit was imposed as a cost of party participation; no more than ten percent of the state delegation was to be selected by the state committee.

The guideline that caused the most trouble was one which mandated the state party organizations to "overcome the effects of past discrimination by affirmative steps to encourage representation on the national convention delegation of minority groups, young people, and women in reasonable relationship to their presence in the population of the state."[24] Some people considered this to be tantamount to the imposition of quotas. If a state were accused of not having enough young people, women, or racial minorities in its delegation, the burden of showing otherwise would be on the state. As a result, the proportion of women, youth, and minorities was substantially increased at the 1972 convention.

A quiet moment at the 1976 Democratic convention, after delegates have adjourned for the day.

Even though the extreme guidelines of the Democrats' 1970 Mandate for Reform have been abolished, women and minority groups are now better represented at the national conventions.

These reforms created considerable tension and debate within and outside the party. One political scientist, Judith A. Center, concluded:

The quotas were meant to prove a point, to lend credence to the rhetoric of the "open party." A number of delegates thus won their seats primarily by virtue of the color of their skin, or their sex, or their age; how representative they were of the candidate preferences of the party members of their district or state was but a secondary consideration. . . . The reformers—waist deep in compliance charts and delegate demographic data—were intensely concerned with the how of delegate selection, and with who the delegates were in terms of biological categories. One wonders why they did not judge worthy of their attention the questions: "By whom are the delegates selected?" and "For whom do they speak?"[25]

The 1972 reforms put a premium on participation in the party primaries and small party caucuses, and normally at these levels few voters take the time to involve themselves. Those who do are usually better-educated, have a higher income, and are more concerned with issues than most other voters.

The Democratic party revised its rules in 1973–74 to do away with the "reasonable representation" guideline. Instead, it put forward an "affirmative action" program aimed at encouraging participation by women, youth, and minority groups "as indicated by their presence in the Democratic electorate." And it was quick to assert that this would not lead to quotas by noting: "This goal shall not be accomplished either directly or indirectly by the party's imposition of mandatory quotas at any level of the delegate selection process or in any other party affairs."[26]

Party platforms. One function the convention delegates perform is to adopt a party **platform**. This is a statement of achievements, goals, and general policies that the party puts before the electorate. It is, above all, a campaign document.

There is a long-standing view that party platforms are rather useless in both the electoral and governing processes. More than a few people share the cynical view of M. Ostrogorski:

The platform, which is supposed to be the party's profession of faith and its program of action is only a farce—the biggest farce of all the acts of this great parliament of the party. The platform represents a long list of statements relating to politics, in which everybody can find something to suit him, but in which nothing is considered as of any consequence by the authors of the document, as well as by the whole convention. . . . The platform has just as little significance and authority for Congress. Its members consider themselves in no way bound to the programs laid down in the convention, for they know perfectly well under what circum-

stances and with what mental reservations it has been promulgated.[27]

On the other hand, the contents of the platform have at times been quite consequential, causing serious intraparty fights. For example, the southern delegates walked out of the 1948 Democratic convention and formed a third party because the platform included an "unacceptable" civil-rights plank. In 1960, the liberal wing of the Republican party refused to support the nominee, Richard Nixon, unless the party's platform reflected some of their views.

Thus, the platform may signal the general direction of the party and identify the party's most influential factions. In this sense, the final platform is hardly unimportant. It is a carefully drafted document, and although it is calculated to appeal to as many elements of the voting public as possible, it will certainly not fail to lean toward those groups making up the party's core support.

While it is likely that most voters do not read the platforms, political candidates sometimes use the platform to highlight how they differ from their opponents. Candidates are also quick to point out when an opponent makes a statement that *seems* to contradict his or her own party platform.

What happens to the platform after the election? One prominent political scientist, David B. Truman, observed:

The platform is generally regarded as a document that says little, binds no one, and is forgotten by politicians as quickly as possible after it is adopted. . . . Considered as a pledge of future action, the party platform is almost meaningless and is properly so regarded by the voters.[28]

Another political scientist, Gerald M. Pomper, is not so pessimistic. He studied the "record of fulfillment" of platform pledges from 1944

Because of their dissatisfaction with the Democratic party platform, Senator Strom Thurmond, shown here, and others led the exodus of southern delegates from the 1948 Democratic convention to form a third party, the Dixiecrats.

through 1964 and found that fulfillment depended mainly on the topic. "Performance is notably poor in three areas: labor, government, and civil rights."[29] But on several other topics, including foreign policy, defense, the economy, agriculture, and welfare, the record was not as dismal:

> *The most important conclusion to be derived from the mass of figures is that pledges are indeed redeemed. Even if we consider only commitments which are met by direct congressional or executive action, we find that slightly over half of the pledges are fulfilled. If we relax our standards and include similar actions or appropriate inaction, nearly three-fourths of all promises are kept. Perhaps most comforting to those who believe in party integrity is that only a tenth of the promises are completely ignored.*[30]

Campaigning for Office

Money and campaign financing. Candidates for public office need votes to win, but they also need money to win votes. Money is needed to pay campaign workers, to buy advertising on radio, television, and in the newspapers, to buy posters, stickers, and buttons, to conduct surveys, and to pay travel expenses. The higher the office, the greater the cost. The less well-known the candidate, the more money must be spent to get the candidate's name (and views) before the public.

Increasingly large sums of money are spent on campaigns. In 1968, campaign expenditures for *all* nomination and election races were around $300 million. In the presidential election that year, the Nixon-Agnew team spent $25 million, and their opponents, the Humphrey-Muskie team, spent $11 million. By comparison, in 1972, expenditures for all races were about $425 million.[31] That year, the Nixon-Agnew team, in their successful reelection bid, spent $56 million; their opponents, the McGovern-Shriver team, spent $49 million.

By 1980, the costs of campaigns had increased substantially. The Federal Election Commission reported that $250 million were spent in the presidential race (including expenditures in the primaries and general election), and more than $300 million were spent to elect members to the Ninety-seventh Congress. Figure 7 gives the breakdown for the three top presidential candidates. You will note that labor unions contributed substantially more to Carter's campaign, and independent committees (usually political action committees of corporations and trade associations) more to Reagan's. The Republicans also spent more through their state and local parties.

There has always been suspicion (sometimes justifiable) that some politicians are "for sale." That is, once elected, they will do the bidding of the highest bidder! Of course, this is illegal. On the other hand, contributing to a candidate's campaign is also recognized as a fundamental right under the First Amendment.

People contribute money to campaigns for several reasons, but usually because they want something in return. That "something" ranges from the legitimate desire to see one's preferred candidate or party elected, to the illegitimate pursuit of an ambassadorship or government contract in exchange for a political contribution. The former is the exercise of responsible citizenship. The latter is a criminal act—bribery.

The law includes a number of safeguards against such abuses, but these laws are not without their loopholes. For example, the law forbids contributions by business corporations and labor unions, but this is circumvented by the establishment of **political action committees**. There are now between 800 and 900 such committees sponsored by corporations and by professional and trade associations. They are limited to giving $5000 in a primary and $5000 in the general election, but there is no restriction on contributing to so-called

FIGURE 7.
Campaign Expenditures for the 1980 Presidential Race.

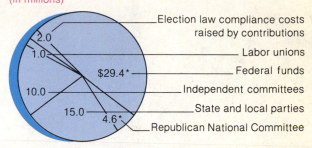

REAGAN:
Total: $62.0
(in millions)

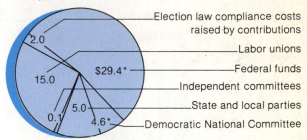

CARTER:
Total: $56.1

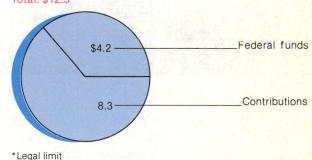

ANDERSON:
Total: $12.5

*Legal limit

Source: *New York Times*, November 23, 1980, p. E3. Based on *projected*, not final, figures.

Elegant dinners with expensive per-plate tickets, such as this 1979 function for the Carter campaign, are one way political hopefuls raise money for their war chests.

independent campaign groups—that is, groups that campaign on behalf of a particular candidate, but independently of the official campaign committee. In 1978, congressional incumbents received almost three times as much money from these committees as did challengers. Labor committees gave mostly to Democrats; corporate committees mostly to Republicans. One source reported: "All told, the committees [in 1978] contributed about $35 million. Among the larger contributors were the American Medical Association with $1.6 mil-

lion, the National Association of Realtors with $1.1 million, the National Automobile Dealers Associations with $975,000, the United Automobile Workers with $965,000, and the AFL-CIO Committee on Political Education with $920,000. The biggest corporate total, $265,000, came from the Standard Oil Company of Indiana."[32] Some observers, however, believe that these contributions will not get out of hand or unduly influence the lawmakers. As Michael J. Malbin concluded:

Committees gave about 25 percent of all of the funds received by general-election candidates for the House of Representatives and about 15 percent of the funds received by Senate general-election candidates in both 1976 and 1978. . . .

The average gift from a single corporate committee was less than $500. If a candidate took more than 5 percent from any one industry, he left himself open to adverse publicity that could easily cost more to counter than the gifts were worth.[33]

In 1971, Congress passed the Federal Election Campaign Act, which required the disclosure of campaign contributions and expenditures. As a result of lawsuits by Common Cause, ''dozens of corporations and corporate officers [were] ultimately . . . found criminally guilty of using company funds for political donations.''[34] Nixon's Committee to Re-elect the President, for example, illegally received $5.4 million from officials of the top hundred defense contractors and almost $5 million from 178 leading oil company officials.

Also in 1971, Congress instituted a **tax subsidy** to encourage *individuals* to contribute to political campaigns. Under this system, taxpayers can list up to $50 ($100 for a joint tax return) in political contributions as income tax deductions. In addition, Congress provided for a $1 *tax check-off* on tax returns. That is, a taxpayer can have $1 of his or her taxes earmarked for political campaigns. Through the tax check-off, the government hoped to raise funds for the public financing of campaigns. In 1971, only 2.5 percent of citizens utilized the tax credit, and only 1.3 percent used the deduction. In 1980, however, approximately 40 million Americans contributed through the $1 check-off on their income tax returns, according to an official of Common Cause.[35]

Watergate and the revelation of widespread abuses of ''political money'' in the 1972 presidential campaign generated serious concern for further reform.

. . . Public attitudes toward reform were changing dramatically. In 1964, opinion polls showed Americans rejected public financing of presidential campaigns by a lopsided 71 percent. By the fall of 1973, the public mood had reversed itself: 65 percent favored tax support for both presidential and congressional campaigns; only 24 percent opposed it. A year later public support had increased to 67 percent.[36]

Thus, Congress passed the Federal Election Campaign Act of 1974. This law limited the amount of money presidential candidates could spend in the primaries and the general election. Independent persons and groups could contribute no more than $1000 to candidates. Public financing of presidential contests was started, allowing for matching funds in the primaries and one lump sum ($20 million) for the general election. Full-disclosure provisions were tightened. The new law also placed limitations on the amount that could be spent by a party whose candidate accepted public financing.

Some people contested the constitutionality of the law, alleging that it violated their First-Amendment rights. In response, the Supreme Court made a distinction between *giving* money and *spending* money.[37] A person could spend any amount he or she wanted in order to support a candidacy or cause. Likewise, there could be no limitation on the amount one could spend on one's *own* campaign, as long as public funds were turned down. A majority of the Supreme Court, however, upheld the limitation on *giving* to a candidate or party by a single individual.

While major parties can receive close to $4 million from the government to hold nominating conventions, most public campaign funds go to individual candidates, not to party organizations.

Theory and Practice

In human institutions there is frequently a difference between the way things are supposed to be in theory and the way they actually are in practice. American government is no exception. This does not mean that theory is necessarily invalid; rather, it may stand as an ideal toward which government may strive. For a political system to be viable, however, significant segments of the society must feel that theory is not too far out of line with practice. Practice consistent with theory should always be the *goal* of the political system, even if that goal can never be perfectly realized.

Political scientist V. O. Key once wrote: "To carve out a place for itself in the politico-social order, a new group may have to fight for reorientation of many of the values of the old order." American politics has certainly witnessed such reorientations—

sometimes violent—in its history. The Civil War erupted when efforts at peaceful resolution of sectional differences gave way to violence, internal strife, and the potential dissolution of the political system. In the course of the last 200 years Native Americans have often resorted to mass action to present their grievances and demands to the government. And at the 1968 Democratic National Convention in Chicago, the theory of peaceful bargaining and compromise lost out once again to violent protest.

Holding elected officials accountable is a crucial aspect of the theory of American democracy. However, this theory assumes that the voters will be able to intelligently cast their ballots. As the country has grown and new means of mass communication have developed, electoral practices have changed.

"Union soldiers at Cold Harbor" by Gilbert Gaul.

Candidates today rely on the mass media to reach and influence voters. Citizens learn about national candidates through carefully planned public-relations campaigns rather than through direct contact with political party leaders.

Perhaps no episode in American life better depicts the tension between theory and practice than the history of immigrants and racial minorities. Most such groups started out economically and politically disadvantaged, and their struggle to enter the mainstream of American life has evolved steadily, if at times slowly. More minority candidates are being elected to public office, thanks to a growing political awareness on the part of their constituencies, yet the present reality of minorities in America still lags far behind the theory of political equality outlined in the Constitution.

Native Americans give a power salute outside the White House, 1978.

Antiwar protestors, Chicago, 1968.

If there is no struggle, there is no progress. Those who profess to favor freedom, and yet [oppose] agitation, are men who want crops without plowing up the ground. They want the rain without thunder and lightning....

Frederick Douglass

That government is strongest of which every man feels himself a part.

Thomas Jefferson

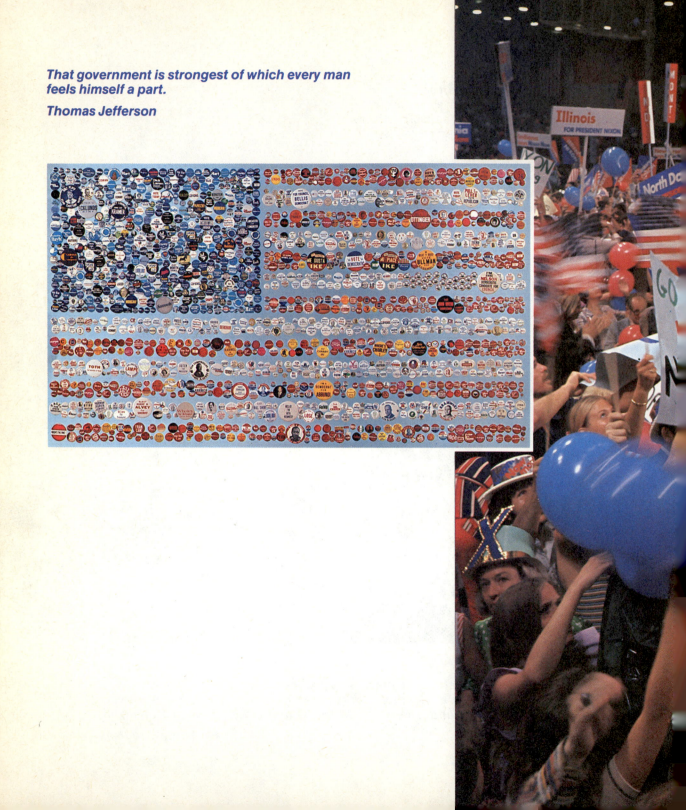

"County Election" by George Caleb Bingham, c. 1851.

The hardest thing about any political campaign is how to win without proving you are unworthy of winning.

Adlai E. Stevenson

Whenever and wherever the constitutional guarantees are violated in the treatment of a minority...the whole fabric of American government is weakened....The test of America is the security of its minority groups.

Ray Lyman Wilbur

The "Trail of Tears": the forced migration of Indian tribes to the western territories (early 1800s).

Man's capacity for justice makes democracy possible, but man's inclination to injustice makes democracy necessary.

Reinhold Niebuhr

Japanese Americans await relocation to detention camps, 1942.

Martin Luther King leads a protest march.

Henry Cisneros, Hispanic mayor of San Antonio, Texas.

Disturbed by the rising costs of running a political campaign, incumbent Millicent Fenwick (R., New Jersey), shown here, and her opponent in the 1978 race for a seat in the House of Representatives, Keirnan Pillion, agreed to spend no more than $22,000 each on their campaigns. Fenwick was reelected by an overwhelming majority.

This has led several observers to conclude that one consequence of public financing is to further weaken political parties as viable entities and to encourage the proliferation of individual candidacies. This gives added impetus, they argue, to the growing trend of candidates not to rely on local, state, and national party structures.

The 1974 law also created a new agency, the Federal Elections Commission, to administer it. As if to underscore its intent to share continuing responsibility in this area, Congress deviated from the usual guidelines for setting up a commission. First, only two of the six commissioners are appointed by the President. Two are appointed by the President Pro Tem of the Senate, and two by the Speaker of the House. Further, and again departing from the usual practice, the commissioners must be confirmed by a majority vote of both chambers of Congress, not just by a Senate majority. In addition, the decisions of the commission are subject to a "legislative veto" (discussed in chapter 8).

Since the passage of the 1974 law, there have been unsuccessful efforts in Congress to extend public campaign financing to Congressional elections. This will likely be a continuing political concern into the 1980s. Table 5 shows the finances for the 1976 Senate contests. They range from a high of $3,004,814 by one winner, H. John Heinz (R., Pennsylvania), to an almost unbelievable low of $697 by another winner, William Proxmire (D., Wisconsin). Note also the "cost per vote" column—ranging from a high of $4.67 in a losing effort by Richard P. Lorber (D., Rhode Island) to a low of $0.00 in a winning effort by Proxmire. Table 6 (page 256) indicates personal outlays by fifteen senatorial candidates in 1976. Except for Mr. Proxmire, one could say that—win or lose—it cost a tidy sum to run.

As noted, there are no restrictions on campaign financing at the state level. In his successful bid for reelection as Governor of West Virginia in 1980, Jay Rockefeller spent an estimated $9 million, mostly his own funds. Fred Wertheimer of Common Cause noted: "That's a classic example of how the political system is not supposed to work."[38]

"The selling of the President."   In recent years —especially since the advent of television—we have been hearing a great deal about the use of "Madison Avenue" techniques in political campaigns. Of paramount importance is the candidate's "image"—how he or she appears and sounds, particularly in the mass media, and especially on television. The "product" (candidate) that results is a combination of sophisticated polling to find out what the public responds to, and of

TABLE 5.
1976 Senate Campaign Receipts and Expenditures.

Candidates	Receipts	Expenditures	Cost Per Vote	Candidates	Receipts	Expenditures	Cost Per Vote
ARIZONA				**NEW JERSEY**			
Dennis DeConcini (D)	$ 598,668	$ 597,405	$1.49	Harrison A. Williams Jr. (D)*	690,781	610,090	0.36
Sam Steiger (R)	722,691	679,384	2.11	David F. Norcross (R)	74,023	73,499	0.07
CALIFORNIA				**NEW MEXICO**			
John V. Tunney (D)*	1,903,527	1,940,988	0.55	Joseph M. Montoya (D)*	461,505	451,111	2.56
S. I. Hayakawa (R)	1,218,485	1,184,624	0.32	Harrison H. Schmitt (R)	473,336	441,309	1.88
CONNECTICUT				**NEW YORK**			
Gloria Schaffer (D)	312,394	306,104	0.55	Daniel Patrick Moynihan (D)	1,219,740	1,210,796	0.35
Lowell P. Weicker Jr. (R)*	500,955	480,709	0.61	James L. Buckley (Cons.-R)*	2,090,126	2,101,424	0.74
DELAWARE				**NORTH DAKOTA**			
Thomas C. Maloney (D)	211,281	211,258	2.15	Quentin N. Burdick (D)*	122,605	117,514	0.67
William V. Roth Jr. (R)*	321,292	322,080	2.57	Robert Stroup (R)	142,774	136,748	1.32
FLORIDA				**OHIO**			
Lawton Chiles (D)*	362,477	362,235	0.20	Howard M. Metzenbaum (D)	1,097,337	1,092,053	0.56
John L. Grady (R)	408,616	394,574	0.37	Robert Taft Jr. (R)*	1,328,283	1,304,207	0.72
HAWAII				**PENNSYLVANIA**			
Spark M. Matsunaga (D)	416,775	435,130	2.68	William J. Green (D)	1,266,375	1,269,409	0.60
William F. Quinn (R)	417,652	415,138	3.38	H. John Heinz III (R)	3,016,731	3,004,814	1.26
INDIANA				**RHODE ISLAND**			
Vance Hartke (D)*	662,389	654,279	0.74	Richard P. Lorber (D)	782,663	782,931	4.67
Richard G. Lugar (R)	742,736	727,720	0.57	John H. Chafee (R)	424,463	415,651	1.80
MAINE				**TENNESSEE**			
Edmund S. Muskie (D)*	322,964	320,427	1.09	James R. Sasser (D)	841,644	839,379	1.18
Robert A. G. Monks (R)	602,851	598,490	3.09	Bill Brock (R)*	1,313,503	1,301,033	1.93
MARYLAND				**TEXAS**			
Paul S. Sarbanes (D)	892,300	891,533	1.15	Lloyd Bentsen (D)*	1,277,364	1,237,910	0.56
J. Glenn Beall (R)*	578,299	572,016	1.08	Alan Steelman (R)	667,214	665,058	0.41
MASSACHUSETTS				**UTAH**			
Edward M. Kennedy (D)*	975,601	896,196	0.52	Frank E. Moss (D)*	365,187	343,598	1.42
Michael Robertson (R)	169,724	168,854	0.23	Orrin G. Hatch (R)	393,278	370,517	1.28
MICHIGAN				**VERMONT**			
Donald W. Riegle Jr. (D)	849,684	795,821	0.43	Thomas P. Salmon (D)	170,156	169,296	1.98
Marvin L. Esch (R)	864,759	809,564	0.50	Robert T. Stafford (R)*	167,469	157,927	1.67
MINNESOTA				**VIRGINIA**			
Hubert H. Humphrey (D)*	664,567	618,878	0.48	Elmo R. Zumwalt Jr. (D)	450,229	443,107	0.74
Gerald W. Br·. (R)	45,775	43,912	0.09	Harry F. Byrd Jr. (Ind.)*	809,346	802,928	0.90
MISSISSIPPI				**WASHINGTON**			
John C. Stennis (D)*	119,852	119,852	0.22	Henry M. Jackson (D)*	223,322	198,375	0.19
MISSOURI				George M. Brown (R)	10,841	10,841	0.03
Warren E. Hearnes (D)	662,737	660,953	0.81	**WEST VIRGINIA**			
John C. Danforth (R)	748,115	741,465	0.68	Robert C. Byrd (D)*	271,124	94,335	0.17
MONTANA				**WISCONSIN**			
John Melcher (D)	321,596	311,101	1.51	William Proxmire (D)*	25	697	0.00
Stanley C. Burcer (R)	578,826	563,543	4.89	Stanley York (R)	66,321	62,210	0.12
NEBRASKA				**WYOMING**			
Edward Zorinsky (D)	240,904	237,613	0.76	Gale W. McGee (D)*	299,908	181,028	2.57
John Y. McCollister (R)	391,289	391,287	1.38	Malcolm Wallop (R)	305,161	301,595	3.56
NEVADA							
Howard W. Cannon (D)*	422,203	405,380	3.18				
David Towell (R)	58,842	58,842	0.86				

Note: Cost per vote compiled by Congressional Quarterly (*1977 Weekly Report*, p. 488). An asterisk (*) indicates an incumbent. The names of winners are italicized.

TABLE 6.
Candidates' Personal Spending, 1976.

Fifteen candidates for the U.S. Senate gave their campaigns at least $50,000 in the form of personal contributions or loans. An asterisk (*) indicates an incumbent. The names of winners appear in red. The chart is based on information compiled by the Federal Election Commission.

	Contributions	Loans	Total
H. John Heinz III (R-Pa.)	$ 1,410	$2,465,500	$2,466,910
Richard P. Lorber (D-R.I.)	111,500	569,737	681,237
Robert A. G. Monks (R-Maine)	530,398	0	530,398
John V. Tunney (D-Calif.)*	0	212,701	212,701
Dennis DeConcini (D-Ariz.)	27,970	165,000	192,970
Sam Steiger (R-Ariz.)	0	125,000	125,000
James R. Sasser (D-Tenn.)	10,525	114,000	124,525
Howard M. Metzenbaum (D-Ohio)	67,000	50,000	117,000
William J. Green III (D-Pa.)	750	100,000	100,750
Lloyd Bentsen (D-Texas)*	13,000	80,000	93,000
Harrison H. Schmitt (R-N.M.)	1,930	85,355	87,285
Warren E. Hearnes (D-Mo.)	28,128	25,000	53,128
Robert Stroup (R-N.D.)	12,364	38,000	50,364
John H. Chafee (R-R.I.)	0	50,000	50,000
Daniel Patrick Moynihan (D-N.Y.)	0	50,000	50,000

Source: Congressional Quarterly Weekly Report (Oct. 29, 1977), p. 2303.

equally sophisticated "packaging" of the candidate to make him or her most appealing to the widest possible market of "consumers" (voters).

Pollsters and media consultants have become prominent figures in political campaigns and are frequently sought out by news reporters and political commentators. Note the following account of Jimmy Carter's pollster, Pat Caddell:

When Patrick Hayward Caddell talks, you can close your eyes and hear James Earl Carter campaigning for re-election.

The President's poll-taker speaks of "courage" and "guts," the "difficult decisions" and the "unpopular issues." He talks about President Carter "doing what's right" and "doing what's best for the country."

These are words and phrases that seem likely to become catchwords of the 1980 campaign.[39]

Joe McGinniss, in *The Selling of the President, 1968*, chronicled the three-month efforts of Richard Nixon's staff to present him on television in the most attractive manner. The following are excerpts from notes prepared by one of Mr. Nixon's advisers at the beginning of the 1968 primary campaign:

So let's decide now that Mr. Nixon will appear in our paid television announcements and start figuring out the best ways to present him.
A few thoughts:
The more informally he is presented the better.

He looks good in motion.

He should be presented in some kind of "situation" rather than cold in a studio. The situation should look unstaged, even if it's not. A newsreel-type on-location interview technique, for example, could be effective. The more visually interesting and local the location the better.

Avoid closeups. A medium waist shot is about as tight as the camera should get. He looks good when he faces the camera head on. . . .

. . . The matter of Mr. Nixon projecting more "warmth" and "humanness" has been discussed at great length. . . . Presenting him informally as suggested above will help. Another suggestion: give him words to say *that will show his emotional involvement in the issues. He is inclined to be too objective, too much the lawyer building a case, too cold and logical. . . . It would also help if his choice of words and phrases was* more colorful. He should be more quotable*, use interesting and unusual labels, dynamic references—occasionally new similes or metaphors.*[40] (emphases added)

Thus, the well-paid "imagemakers" present the American electorate with a packaged "product," for the presidency. We see Nixon in an "unstaged" setting; we see Jimmy Carter walking in his peanut fields, stooping to feel the cool dirt beneath his feet.

This is not confined to presidential campaigns, nor to one party. Most major (and some minor) candidates pay at least some attention to how they present themselves, especially on the television screen. This makes it difficult at times to distinguish the "real" person from the "manufactured" one. If candidates read from scripts written by imagemakers in order to achieve a certain media effect, how is the intelligent voter to know the true views of the candidates on policy issues? What is wrong with a candidate being objective and logi-cal? Why must the candidate use *colorful* language? Why not just plain straight talk?

If the impression is widespread that the presidential contests consist mainly of packaging or "selling" candidates, this can only lead to further cynicism and possible alienation among more of the electorate.

The television debates.   Three times in American presidential elections, voters have had a chance to see the major candidates together on television "debating" issues. This first time was in 1960 between John F. Kennedy and Richard M. Nixon; the second time, in 1976 between Jimmy Carter and Gerald Ford; and the third time, in 1980, once between Ronald Reagan and independent candidate John B. Anderson, and once between Reagan and Jimmy Carter. In each instance,

It's frightening! These hands can change history!

John F. Kennedy and Richard M. Nixon in the first televised debate between presidential candidates, 1960.

the candidates responded to a wide range of questions from panelists, and they were given brief opportunities to respond to each other's answers. Although the format was more like a dual press conference than a debate, the viewers were able to see how each candidate reacted to intense pressure.

Prior to the debates, the candidates were carefully briefed by their staffs, knowing full well that the press and the audience would rate the performances. After each session, there were comments on which candidate "won," which "scored" the most points, which "looked better" (more self-assured, less nervous) on television, and so on.

How much enlightenment on the issues resulted from these sessions is difficult to say. In a way, the debates are another means for staging and "selling" the candidates. However, the public *was* able to make some judgments about the range of knowledge possessed by the respective candidates, and about their ability to articulate short responses to rather complicated subjects.

The Electoral College System

After presidential candidates have campaigned for several months (usually, counting the primaries, for at least ten months) the voters decide. Or do they? The practical answer is *yes*. The technical answer is *no*.

Technically, Americans do not elect their president when they go to the polls on the first Tuesday in November of the election year. It is true that they go to the polls. They cast ballots for, say, Reagan or Carter (or think they do) and are told at some point later that night or early the next morning who the next president will be. The celebration (or mourning) starts. The loser concedes and sends congratulations to the winner. The winner is then referred to as "Mr. President-Elect." He proceeds to assemble a potential cabinet, drafts his inaugural speech, meets with high government officials, and prepares to move to 1600 Pennsylvania Avenue (if he is not already there as the reelected incumbent).

But, technically (that is to say, constitutionally) this is all premature. According to the Constitution, the President is elected by a group of people called **electors**. *These* are the people Americans vote for on the first Tuesday in November. The electors, who represent the presidential candidates' parties, then meet in the state capital a few weeks later and *really* cast votes for their party's candidate. Thus, the voters are actually voting for party electors who then vote for the party candidate. After this "second" presidential election, the ballots are sent to the U.S. Congress, where they are counted, and the official announcement of the winner is made. Since the number of each state's electors is based on its number of members in the House of Representatives plus its two senators, the reapportionment that takes place after each census will be important in determining the size of a state's electoral-college vote.

If no presidential candidate has a majority, then the choice is made by the House of Representatives, choosing from among the top three on the list, with each state delegation having one vote. If no vice-presidential candidate has a majority of electoral votes, the Senate then chooses from among the top two on the list. A majority vote is necessary in both cases.

The Constitution does not specify that the voters in the state must be the ones to choose the electors. The Constitution says simply: "Each State shall appoint, in such manner as the Legislature thereof may direct, a number of electors, equal to the whole number of senators and representatives to which the State may be entitled in the Congress." Therefore, the *state* determines whether the electors are chosen by popular vote. As far as the U.S. Constitution is concerned, the state legislature could choose the electors. And the legislature could decide whether the electors are chosen state-wide by popular vote (as is now the case everywhere but in Maine, where two are chosen statewide and one is chosen from each of Maine's two Congressional districts), or by some other method.

Once the *real* presidential electors are chosen and meet in their respective state capitals, they do not necessarily have to vote for the candidate of their party. Most frequently, however, the electors pledge that they will vote for their party's candidate.

Thus, the electoral college system is an indirect method of electing the President. It was so devised by the framers of the Constitution because, frankly, they did not believe that voters would know enough about the candidates to make a wise choice. In fact, the framers really expected the electors to exercise their own independent judgment when casting their ballots. An elector who did that today would be accused of violating the will of the voters.

"Whew! Can't we find some other route?"

PRESIDENTIAL ELECTION SYSTEM

From *The Herblock Gallery* (Simon and Schuster, 1968).

One problem with the electoral college is that it is a "winner-take-all" system. If a candidate wins fifty-one percent of the popular vote in Texas, for example, he gets *all* the electoral votes from Texas. The other forty-nine percent who voted for someone else will not have their preference counted in any way. Because of this, it is possible for a candidate to win móre national *popular* votes and still lose in the electoral-college vote—and thus not be elected President. This has happened three times: in 1824, with the election of John Quincy

Adams; in 1876, with the election of Rutherford B. Hayes; and in 1888, with the election of Benjamin Harrison. In each case, the winner received fewer popular votes than his opponent. This same situation nearly occurred in 1916, 1948, 1960, and 1976, which has led some observers to call for reform of the electoral college system.

The reformers usually advocate a direct, popular, national vote for the presidency. Opponents are quick to point out that this would favor the large, more populous states. Some minority groups feel, also, that such a reform would dilute their voting influence. Under the present state-by-state, winner-take-all system, such groups can exert significant influence, but they would not be able to do so in a nationwide, popular-vote arena.

Another proposal is to keep the electoral college system, but to abolish the winner-take-all feature. Thus, electoral votes would be awarded on the basis of the candidate's *percentage* of the state vote: fifty-one percent of the popular vote would earn fifty-one percent of the electoral vote.

The biggest concern over the present system is that if a candidate who has, in fact, received fewer popular votes than the opponent is elected, the legitimacy of the electoral process will be undermined, and the President's personal status will be weakened.

During each presidential election, political pundits speculate on the impact of the electoral college system on campaign strategies. For example, larger states, are generally more important to the candidates than smaller states. Therefore, more time and money are spent wooing the voters of the larger states. Likewise, while no candidate will publicly say that certain states are not worth the effort, the fact is that some states are so clearly in one camp or the other that it would not be beneficial to devote much effort to campaigning in them. By paying close attention to the electoral votes, it is possible for a candidate to concentrate campaign resources and win narrowly in a few crucial states, and, while losing the popular vote, win the presidency. Some observers have noted the relevance of such calculations to third-party candidates. In a close presidential race between two major-party candidates, a third-party candidate might be able to win enough of the larger electoral states to cause the election to be decided in the House.

In 1978, a bipartisan task force of private citizens, including both supporters and critics of the present system, issued a report calling for a compromise solution. In order to minimize the possibility of the popular-vote winner losing to the electoral-college winner, the group came up with a "national bonus" plan.[41] The plan would give each state (and the District of Columbia) two additional electoral votes, for a total of 102 additional electoral votes. The winner of the national popular vote would receive all these additional 102 votes, virtually assuring the popular-vote winner the election. Further, the task force suggested eliminating the present system of electors meeting in the state capital to cast a vote. The vote of the people on election day would be the definitive vote. This would overcome the problem of the potential "faithless elector," that is, one who votes contrary to the voters' wishes. In the last twenty years, we have seen electors "defect" only a few times: in 1960, Kennedy won the popular votes of Mississippi, but eight electors voted for Senator Harry F. Byrd of Virginia; Kennedy also won the popular vote of Alabama, but six electors there voted for Senator Byrd; and Nixon won the popular vote in Oklahoma, but one elector cast his vote for Byrd. In 1968, Nixon won the popular vote in North Carolina, but one elector decided to vote instead for George Wallace. In 1972, Nixon won the popular vote in Virginia, but one elector cast his ballot for someone named John Hospers.

In 1976, although Ford won the popular vote in Washington state, one elector exercised his constitutional right and cast his vote for Ronald Reagan.

The compromise national-bonus plan would retain some of the good features of the present system while minimizing some of the bad features. However, a constitutional amendment is required to institute these changes. This issue will continue to be a concern into the 1980s.

Elections and the Democratic Process

The purpose of elections is to serve the goal of representative government. Theoretically, citizens vote for those people whom they wish to have govern the society. Normally, people—not policies—are the specific focus of choice, but presumably the voters' choice is based on some notion of how they want officeholders to perform. Voting is a concept central to democratic theory. Even those scholars who do not believe that elections are a very useful means of conveying specific policy preferences nonetheless believe that it is not possible to have a democratic system without providing for periodic elections. Although all citizens in the United States do not exercise their right to vote (as data in this chapter clearly indicate), there would likely be a major upheaval if the right to vote were denied. After making a rather cautious analysis of the significance of elections as mechanisms for conveying information to decision-makers, one political scientist concluded:

Despite all of these shortcomings, few publics that have experienced competitive elections care to be deprived of them, and in an ultimate sense, at least, these mechanisms do represent a rather powerful source of popular control over government.[42]

Political scientists generally agree that government policy is not determined by voters, especially at the national level. (This is different, of course, with voting for propositions or referenda, as we shall discuss shortly.) The political system is so fragmented and large that no one decision-maker, even the President, has the sole capacity to deliver absolutely on campaign promises and voters' expectations. "Elections probably serve better as instruments for popular decisions on broad and great issues," V. O. Key once wrote; "the details and the trivia may be beyond popular control."[43] And Gerald Pomper has concluded: "In a theoretical sense, elections are significant not as *power* in government, but as an *influence on* government."[44]

This cautious, modest view of elections is not subscribed to by everyone who has studied the subject. Murray Edelman sees elections mainly as rituals, as means of pacifying the public and of exacting loyalty to the system:

> *To quiet resentments and doubts about particular political acts, to reaffirm belief in the fundamental rationality and democratic character of the system, and thus fix conforming habits of future behavior is demonstrably a key function of our persisting political institutions: elections, political discussions, legislatures, courts, and administration.*[45]

At any rate, it is reasonably clear that the *theory* of the role of elections in the American system has to be squared with the *practice*. Theoretically, those who govern are chosen by the governed and are expected to perform in reasonably predictable ways. If the officials do not live up to expectations, they will not be chosen again. This is a core theory of representative democracy. In practice, however, the situation might not be so neat and simple. People can (and do) differ on their evaluations of

performance; or they might not know if an official is performing as they expected—even in societies that are open and democratic.

The Senate confirmation hearings of Secretary of State Alexander Haig present one example of the theory/practice problem. You will recall that we discussed the role of party platforms. Whether these platforms are taken seriously or not, they certainly are a part of the electoral process. People haggle over them at nominating conventions; candidates refer to them; the media dissect them; some textbooks even give charts showing how different platforms compare on specific issues. To the extent that they provide *some* clues to a party's position, party platforms are (theoretically) reasonably important predictors of an official's—or an administration's—policies. But when a senator asked Mr. Haig if he would abide by his party's platform, his response was: "In no way would I anticipate an approach which visualized strict adherence to something that I had no role in drafting." When pressed to clarify his position, Mr. Haig stated that all he meant was that "circumstances do change"; that he did not want to be held to a literal adherence to the document. And then he added: "I do feel that the American people, at the ballot box, clearly registered their support [in the 1980 elections] for the broad outlines of that platform and that any official of the executive branch must feel obligated to give it the greatest weight."[46]

At times, voters will accept this inconsistency between theory and practice. Events develop which make it impossible or unreasonable for officials to deliver on their promises. Or, as noted before, the complexity of the decision-making hierarchy sometimes makes it difficult to locate responsibility or to hold specific officials accountable. Sometimes the electorate is understanding—and forgives; sometimes it is not—and votes the "ins" out.

One means of making voting more directly related to policy is through *initiative*, *referenda*, and *recall elections*. With the first two, the electorate votes directly on policies—not people. Proposition 13 is an example of the initiative. A *referendum* is a law or proposal which must be submitted to the voters for approval before it can take effect. Forty states require referenda for certain types of laws or proposals, and every state except Delaware requires a referendum before adopting a proposed state constitutional amendment. Referenda are fairly common at local levels of government: voting on school bond issues, location of nuclear power plants, noise abatement laws, and a host of other such measures. These issues at times are bitterly fought, generating intense political attention and action on the local level.

The *recall* is an electoral means of unseating an official before his or her term expires. At least sixteen states permit this procedure at the state level, but it is more common at the local levels.

For whatever reasons—frustration with elected representatives, a desire to become more directly involved in policymaking—the initiative appears to be used more and more in the electoral process. Twenty-four states and hundreds of municipalities provide for this method of voting on citizen-sponsored issues, and there is a movement afoot to institute it at the federal government level. Indeed, as the cartoon on page 264 implies, the wave of Proposition 13 appears to be engulfing the entire nation.

Some political scientists, such as Thomas M. Magstadt, are not enthusiastic about the value of this growing phenomenon:

The normal rules of the political game were short-circuited in California: the issue was not voted up or down in a legislative assembly by representatives chosen for precisely such a pur-

Cleveland's mayor Dennis Kucinich narrowly survived a recall election but was later voted out of office in the regular election.

pose, but rather by a plebiscite—that is to say, a direct vote of tax-weary citizens who quite naturally want government to take less out of their paychecks, even if it means taking more out of somebody else's. It is at this point that the question of substance gives way to a question of form: does the direct vote have any rightful place among the interlocking principles underlying the American constitutional system? . . . The answer . . . is demonstrably negative.[47]

The fundamental principle of representative democracy is undercut, Magstadt concluded, by the more immediately satisfying results of "plebiscitary democracy."

Political scientist Thomas E. Cronin sees advantages and disadvantages in the popular initiative. It permits ordinary citizens to become more actively involved in policymaking. "It takes personalities out of politics and focuses on issues."[48] And it provides a means for bringing up controversial issues which elected politicians might wish to avoid, such as Proposition 13, which was initiated by Jarvis, Gann, and their nonelected followers.

On the other hand, there is the argument that the popular initative might attempt to deal with complex economic and social issues beyond the comprehension of the average layperson. Such issues might become the object of emotional appeals and demagogy. This concern was not absent from Proposition 13, as described in the case study:

Intense and costly election campaigns were produced by both sides and both sides admitted to using scare tactics.

"I can't honestly deny that I'm using fear," Jarvis said at one point, "but mine is legitimate fear, the fear of losing property." Winner countered, "There's a difference between real fears and imagined fears. Our fears are real fears."

Of course, neither party would admit to demagogy—it's always the other party.

Cronin concludes that the popular initiative reflects

a tension . . . between those who trust the people will vote with reason and common sense and those who are reluctant to trust the people with complex policymaking. The citizen initiative is a proper safety valve if used sparingly and with due regard for civil liberties and minority rights.

Used too frequently, however, these devices may undercut representative government in several ways.[49]

Summary

1. There are two prominent theories of the franchise: (1) the right to vote as a limited means available only to an elite group in the society; and (2) the franchise as a means of protection for the citizenry and a way to hold officials generally accountable. Subscribing to the second view, this country has evolved away from a restricted franchise with various property, racial, and sexual qualifications, toward "universal suffrage."

2. A number of factors influence voter turnout: regional considerations, socio-economic status, the type or nature of the election, and technical requirements, such as registration and residency. Turnout in both presidential and Congressional elections has declined over the last 100 years. Education appears to be the most important single predictor of voter participation, but it is not the only one.

3. The American voter has become less committed to one of the major parties and more issue-oriented. New voters are increasingly registering as Independents, rather than as Republicans or Democrats. Party affiliation indicates how people will vote in Congressional elections more than it does in presidential elections. Also, the party that wins the presidency invariably tends to do less well in the Congressional elections two years later. For this reason, some observers feel that the vote for Congressional seats is a better indicator of the relative strength of the parties.

4. Choosing delegates to the presidential nominating conventions has undergone changes in the last decade. Primary elections have become more prominent, and the political parties, especially the Democratic party, have been more likely to include women, racial minorities, and young people in the state delegations.

5. Over the last decade, there have been major changes in campaign financing. As a result of rising campaign costs and the revelations of Watergate, new laws regulate campaign contributions and spending. In addition, we now have public financing of presidential campaigns.

6. The electoral college system was instituted by the constitutional framers as a means of removing the election of the President from the direct control of the masses. Recently, there has been considerable interest in reforming the system. A major concern is the current possibility of the winner of the popular national vote losing in the state-oriented electoral-college vote—a situation rendered possible by the present "winner-take-all" system. A substantive change would require a constitutional amendment.

7. When citizens vote for candidates, they affect policy in a very indirect manner. The electoral mechanisms of initiative, referendum, and recall are more direct forms of impact. While these devices actively involve citizens in the policy-making process, they might also potentially undermine the principle of representative democracy. Their utility lies in their judicious use.

Notes

1. *New York Times*, August 7, 1965, p. A8.
2. Quoted in Gerald M. Pomper, *Elections in America* (New York: Dodd, Mead & Company, 1928), p. 19.
3. Quoted in Pomper, p. 20.
4. Steven J. Rosenstone and Raymond E. Wolfinger, "The Effect of Registration Laws on Voter Turnout," *The American Political Science Review*, (March 1978), 41.
5. Ibid.
6. See Walter Dean Burnham, "The Changing Shape of the American Political Universe," *The American Political Science Review* (March 1965), 7–28; and E. E. Schattschneider, *The Semisovereign People* (New York: Holt, Rinehart and Winston, 1960), especially chapter 5.
7. See Philip E. Converse, "Change in the American Electorate," in Angus Campbell and Philip E. Converse, eds., *The Human Meaning of Social Change* (New York: Russell Sage Foundation, 1972), pp. 263–337; and Jerrold D. Rusk, "The Effect of the Australian Ballot Reform on Split Ticket Voting: 1876–1908," *The American Political Science Review* (December 1970), 1220–38.
8. Norman H. Nie, Sidney Verba, and John Petrocik, *The Changing American Voter* (Cambridge, Mass.: Harvard University Press, 1976).
9. Ibid., p. 166.
10. Ibid., p. 352.
11. This type of voter was described in Richard M. Scammon and Ben J. Wattenberg, *The Real Majority* (New York: Coward-McCann, Inc., 1970).
12. *New York Times*, November 5, 1980, p. A23.
13. William H. Flanigan and Nancy H. Zingale, *Political Behavior of the American Electorate* (Boston: Allyn and Bacon, Inc., 1979), p. 31.
14. Ibid., p. 38.
15. Angus Campbell, *et al.*, *Elections and the Political Order* (New York: John Wiley and Sons, Inc., 1966), p. 64.
16. Philip E. Converse, *et al.*, "Stability and Change in 1960: A Reinstating Election," *The American Political Science Review* (June 1961), 280.
17. Flanigan and Zingale, p. 45.
18. Steven R. Weisman, "Party Conventions Mean More Than Just Politics," The *New York Times*, June 24, 1979, p. E4.
19. Ibid.
20. *Dallas Morning News*, July 31, 1979, p. D2.
21. California, Florida, Kentucky, Maryland, Massachusetts, Nebraska, Nevada, New Hampshire, New York, North Carolina, Oregon, Pennsylvania, Ohio, Rhode Island, South Dakota, West Virginia.
22. Alabama, Illinois, Indiana, Michigan, New Jersey, Tennessee, Texas.
23. Arkansas, Georgia, Idaho, Montana, Vermont, Wisconsin.
24. The Commission on Party Structure and Delegate Selection to the Democratic National Committee, *Mandate for Reform* (Washington, D.C., April 1970), p. 34.
25. Judith A. Center, "1972 Democratic Convention Reforms and Party Democracy," *Political Science Quarterly*, Vol. 89, No. 2 (June 1974), 325–49.
26. Report of the Commission on Delegate Selection and Party Structure as Amended and Adopted by the Democratic National Executive Committee, March 1, 1974.
27. M. Ostrogorski, *Democracy and the Organization of Political Parties,* Vol. 11 (Garden City: Doubleday Anchor, 1964), pp. 138–39.
28. David B. Truman, *The Governmental Process* (New York: Alfred A. Knopf, 1951), pp. 282–83.
29. Pomper, p. 189.

30. Ibid., pp. 185–87.
31. David Adamany and George Agree, ''Election Campaign Financing: The 1974 Reforms,'' *Political Science Quarterly*, Vol. 90, No. 2 (Summer 1975), 205.
32. *New York Times*, August 19, 1979, p. E5.
33. Michael J. Malbin, ''Business and Elections,'' *New York Times*, August 19, 1979, p. E23.
34. Adamany and Agree, p. 206.
35. *New York Times*, November 23, 1980, p. E3.
36. Adamany and Agree, 206.
37. *Buckley v. Valeo*, 424 U.S. 1 (1976).
38. *New York Times*, November 23, 1980, p. E3.
39. *New York Times*, August 14, 1979, p. A14.
40. Quoted in Joe McGinniss, *The Selling of the President, 1968* (New York: Trident Press, 1969), pp. 178–80.
41. The Twentieth Century Fund Task Force on Reform of the Presidential Election Process, *Winner Take All* (New York: Holmes & Meier Publishers, Inc., 1978).
42. Philip E. Converse, ''Public Opinion and Voting Behavior,'' in Fred Greenstein and Nelson Polsby, eds., *Handbook of Political Science*, Vol. 4 (Reading, Massachusetts: Addison-Wesley, 1975), p. 77.
43. V. O. Key, Jr., *Public Opinion and American Democracy* (New York: Alfred A. Knopf, 1967), p. 459.
44. Pomper, p. 253.
45. Murray Edelman, *The Symbolic Uses of Politics* (Urbana: University of Illinois Press, 1964), p. 17.
46. *New York Times*, January 13, 1981, p. B6.
47. Thomas M. Magstadt, ''Using Proposition 13 to Introduce Students to Political Science,'' *NEWS, for Teachers of Political Science*, No. 22 (Summer 1979), 6.
48. Thomas E. Cronin, ''The Pros and Cons of Popular Initiatives,'' *Washington Post*, January 22, 1979, p. A21.
49. Ibid.

Overview
Political Participation

In a country of approximately 235 million people, it is understandable that there are various ways citizens can and do participate in government. Whether they participate or not and the attitudes, beliefs, and values they bring to their participation are determined in large part by how citizens are politically socialized. Political ideas and opinions are substantially influenced by factors such as family, education, socio-economic status, and peer groups. And the media play a crucial role in providing information about the political system. Generally, people with more education and higher economic status participate more than their lower-status counterparts.

Citizens often participate by joining interest groups. Such organizations—a growing phenomenon in American society—speak for the concerns of their members in functional—and not necessarily geographical—terms. In this sense, interest groups fill the "gaps" found in a representational system organized around states and their subdivisions. Pressure groups bargain on behalf of their members' interests. They seek to maximize their influence over the facets of the government that are most related to policymaking in the areas of the group's concern. A group's tactics are determined in large measure by its resources (money, size, prestige). Groups with more resources (and thus, with more power) frequently can rely on "quieter" forms of pressure, such as lobbying. Other

groups often find they must resort to more overt forms of pressure and protest, if only to gain the attention of and access to decision-makers and the public. Overt protest, sometimes leading to violence, has been a perennial part of the American political scene.

Side by side with these forms of interest-group participation is the constant process of formal elections, which constitute a central part of any democratic society. Political parties play an integral role in mobilizing the electorate to participate in elections. The United States has two major parties (and several smaller, minor parties that come and go), whose primary goal is to capture and control government offices. Because the two major parties seek to form broad coalitions encompassing rather divergent views, the parties often try to minimize internal differences and conflicts. This makes them appear to be essentially nonideological, and it puts a premium on preelection compromising and building of a consensus in order to be successful at the polls.

As a representative republic, America places heavy emphasis on voting. Over the years, the franchise has gradually been extended to virtually all adults. But at the same time the *rate* of participation in elections has been declining, in part because of the media's focus on presidential politics and in part because of the decreased ability of the political parties to mobilize the electorate. Participation in elections, like participation in other forms of political activities, differs according to various demographic factors.

Various attempts have been made in recent years to "open up the system" and to involve more people in the electoral process. The "smoke-filled rooms" of yesterday have been replaced by primary elections, where delegates to the national conventions are chosen. Convention rules regarding minority representation among convention delegates have been liberalized. New regulations (including public financing of presidential campaigns) now cover campaign financing.

The complexity of policymaking makes it difficult to trace a direct connection between the electoral process and government policies. The "direct democracy" electoral processes of initiative, referendum, and recall have served to substitute for some of the inadequacies of representative democracy. Proposition 13 is an example of a form of participation that permitted citizens to become directly involved in determining policy.

Basically, however, citizen participation aims to influence the actions of elected representatives. These representatives occupy positions of power in formal institutions of government. The next part of this textbook examines those institutions and the processes they use to affect the will and wishes of the body politic.

Part *3*

National Political Institutions

EQUAL·JUSTICE·UNDER·LAW·

Philip Shabecoff

The Political Struggle for Labor-Law Reform

Following the national elections of November 1976, the leaders of organized labor, confident and even a trifle cocky, readied an ambitious legislative program to submit to the new Congress and to the new administration. Over the preceding eight years, most of labor's demands had been unobtainable because of the presence of unsympathetic Republican presidents in the White House. Labor's initiatives on Capitol Hill not only were opposed actively by the executive branch, but, if somehow they were approved, they usually faced a presidential veto.

Now, however, Jimmy Carter, a Democrat, would be taking over, and the union leaders felt they could rely on his gratitude for their political support during the election campaign as well as on his avowed populism. Moreover, a seemingly overwhelming Democratic majority had been installed in Congress. Whatever problems the trade unions had had with the White House, they always had been able to make effective use of their political muscle with the Democrats in the House and Senate.

"It's been a long time since we've had an administration that's sympathetic to working people," said Dick Warden, legislative director in Washington for the United Auto Workers Union, in an interview with *Congressional Quarterly* in December 1976. "It will be practically a new experience for us."*

Labor's extensive legislative goals formed a long shopping list. The list included a *common-situs picketing* bill, which would permit a single union on a construction site to shut down the entire site with a picket line—even though that union was only one of a number of unions representing workers there. Labor also gave high priority to the enactment of the Humphrey-Hawkins *full-employment* bill, which in its original form required the federal government to adopt coordinated policies aimed at reducing the unemployment rate (then running at about seven percent) to three percent by 1980. (Congress later enacted a greatly watered-down version of the bill calling for the reduction of the unemployment rate to four percent by 1983.)

Generally, the union movement pressed hard for greatly expanded government-funded public-service and public-works jobs programs to create new employment opportunities. The unions sought major improvements in the minimum wage law (Fair

*Unless otherwise noted, quoted material in this chapter is taken from the author's notes or from articles prepared by the author for the *New York Times*. The issues of the *Times* consulted are March 3, 1977; June 23, 1977; July 19, 1977; July 21, 1977; April 29, 1978; June 23, 1978.

Philip Shabecoff is a Washington correspondent for the *New York Times*.

Labor's spirits soared when Jimmy Carter, a Democrat, was installed in the White House, only to be disappointed later when labor-law reform met defeat on Capitol Hill.

Labor Standards Act), asking not only for substantial increases in the minimum but also for a new system that would permanently link the minimum to the average industrial wage. Other legislative goals included a reform of the Hatch Act to allow public employees to engage in political activity; a cargo-preference bill requiring a specific amount of freight on American flagships in order to assure jobs for American seamen; tax reform; improved health and safety programs; and a variety of lesser items.

But the centerpiece of labor's legislative program was a long deferred revision of the National Labor Relations Act, or *labor-law reform* as the labor leaders called it.

The labor-relations act, also called the Wagner-Connery or Wagner Act, was passed on July 5, 1935, when President Franklin D. Roosevelt's New Deal was approaching full flower. With the act, the federal government committed itself to the support of trade unionism and made collective bargaining and the right to organize and strike a principle of national policy. The act created the National Labor Relations Board (NLRB) to investigate and to remedy complaints of unfair labor practices, including the coercion of employees engaged in collective bargaining.

Often called the "Magna Carta" of the American labor movement, the Wagner Act promoted the rapid growth of unionism in this country, particularly in the industrial sector where unions had been fiercely resisted by employers. The act has also been credited with helping create an enduring climate of relative stability in labor-management relations.

The labor act has twice undergone major revision, both times with amendments aimed at curbing the power of unions and union leaders. In 1947, Congress passed the Taft-Hartley Act over President Truman's veto. This act authorized the President to obtain injunctions against *national-emergency strikes*, banned closed shops (where only

union members may be employed) and secondary boycotts (in which factories or businesses not directly involved in a dispute are boycotted), permitted states to pass right-to-work laws outlawing union shops, and included a variety of other clauses intended to clip the wings of trade unions. Then in 1959, following hearings on crime and corruption within the union movement, Congress enacted the Landrum-Griffin Act, which provided for federal surveillance of union administrations to monitor corrupt or illegal acts such as misuse of union funds or illegal elections. Also, this act provided business with safeguards against union activities.

For some years, labor leaders had been calling for new amendments to the labor law, aiming at what they said were abuses and flouting of the law by employers to deny workers their right to organize and to bargain collectively. George Meany, president of the American Federation of Labor and Congress of Industrial Organizations (AFL-CIO), said at the February 1977 meeting of the federation's executive council in Bal Harbour, Florida, that the Wagner Act had been passed to put workers on a basis of equality with employers and to encourage collective bargaining. In those days, he said, the employers used "goons, spies, and agents provocateurs" to coerce workers, to break unions, and to prevent collective bargaining. Today, said Meany, they don't have goons but they still flout the law. Instead of hiring goons they hire "high-priced lawyers who use legal technicalities" to find various ways to deny workers the right they have to representation.

Opposite: In 1935, Ford workers, wearing masks to avoid recognition by company spies, protested the Ford Company's noncompliance with the newly created Wagner Act. Right: Laborers protest the Taft-Hartley Act, created in 1947 to curb the power of labor unions.

The most frequently cited example of an employer using these techniques was the J. P. Stevens Company, one of the nation's biggest textile concerns. Stevens, it was charged, routinely dismissed employees engaged in organizing activities, refused to comply with NLRB orders, bugged hotel rooms of union organizers, harassed workers for union activities, and in its successful effort to resist unionization, defied legal orders to obey the National Labor Relations Act.

It is widely believed that Stevens's activities provided much of the original impetus behind the drive to revise the labor law. During the House debate on the amendments, Congressman Clifford Allen (D., Tennessee) declared that if it were not for the Stevens company, the legislation never would have been introduced.

But Stevens was only one of a growing number of companies that found it *less* costly to fight unionization through the NLRB and the courts and, when necessary, to pay court-imposed fines, than to permit the unionization of the plants and to pay the higher wages usually won by workers in collective bargaining.

Moreover, employers were growing increasingly sophisticated in their efforts to keep unions out of their factories and offices. Management consulting firms throughout the country were finding that teaching clients to resist union organizers was becoming a popular and profitable sideline. The National Association of Manufacturers established a "Council on a Union-Free Environment" to help member firms and other enterprises fight organizers with the pooled resources of the association.

But it was far more than the resistance, illegal or otherwise, of a minority of virulently antiunion employers that was troubling the labor leaders. The labor movement as a whole seemed to be in decline, and the leaders were looking for a means to reverse the trend. Labor-law reform seemed to offer an important tool for ending the erosion.

At the labor movement's peak, around 1945, thirty-five percent of all nonfarm workers held union cards. But by 1977, after a prolonged period of decline, only about twenty-five percent of nonfarm workers and twenty-one percent of the total work force belonged to unions, a drop of forty percent in three decades. In 1977, for the first time, unions lost more than fifty percent of *certification elections*—elections held to determine whether or not workers in a given plant or shop want to be represented by a union. Worse than that (from organized labor's point of view), the unions were being subjected to—and losing—a growing number of *decertification* elections, in which workers voted to dismantle already existing union representation.

Union organizers found they were having little success in organizing the industrial areas of the South and Southwest, the so-called **sunbelt,** which was the fastest growing part of the country economically. Social and cultural patterns combined with stiff

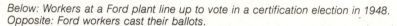

Below: Workers at a Ford plant line up to vote in a certification election in 1948.
Opposite: Ford workers cast their ballots.

employer resistance and an abundant supply of cheap labor made the South infertile ground for the union organizers. Meanwhile, heavy industry in the North and Northeast, the strongest bastion of unionization for two generations, was hiring fewer and fewer workers because of automation and because imports were claiming an increasing share of their domestic markets.

In addition to these external difficulties, there were growing problems within the house of labor itself. One was its image as an increasingly conservative institution led by old men, as exemplified by Mr. Meany, who was now well into his eighties. This conservative image kept the United Auto Workers from rejoining the AFL-CIO. Except for the rapidly growing public-sector unions, there seemed to be a spreading malaise within the labor movement, demonstrated by the dwindling attendance at local union meetings and the drift of rank-and-file members away from the political directions charted by their leaders.

The public image of the trade-union movement also was eroding. Polls showed that labor leaders ranked near the bottom in public trust. A management consultant quoted in *Nation's Business* magazine said that "a growing distaste for union financial scandals, a growing distaste for any connection with organized crime, which has been characteristic of some unions, and a more liberal attitude by many employers toward their employees" was causing many workers to turn their backs on unions and relieve employers of the need to engage in collective bargaining.

Delegates to the AFL-CIO's biennial convention in Los Angeles in December 1977 were informed that the federation's membership had declined by 500,000 since the last convention just two years earlier. In a speech from the floor of the convention, one delegate commented that "most unions are just like mine—we have been running like heck in the last few years just to stand still."

The labor movement quite obviously was in need of a shot in the arm, and its leaders believed that changes in the labor law would supply much of the required medicine. Some of the proposals were simply intended to speed up and to improve administration and enforcement of the law. For example, the unions proposed that the National Labor Relations Board increase its membership from five to seven to help the board cope with the geometrically increasing caseload. But other revisions were intended to expedite union elections and to punish employers who refused to permit legal organizing activities or who declined to bargain with a newly certified union. For example, the union proposals sought to establish a maximum number of days after which an employer petitioned by a requisite number of workers must permit an election to be held. Employees illegally fired for organizing activities would be entitled to double back-pay after mandatory reinstatement. Employers who failed to obey a labor-board order could be debarred from federal contracts. If an employer argued against unionization on company time, union organizers would be granted equal time to present their case. If an employer refused to negotiate with a legally elected collective-bargaining agent, the board would impose an initial contract based on prevailing wages and working conditions.

The union leaders also were seeking, once again, a repeal of the detested Section 14b of the Taft-Hartley Act, the provision that gives states the authority to enact "right-to-work" laws. Additionally, the unions wanted enactment of a new regulation that would permit a union to represent workers if fifty-five percent or more of the workers in a given plant signed *checkoff cards* stating they wanted such representation. In such cases, no certification election would be necessary.

The unions were *not* concerned with the role played by the judiciary in enforcing the Wagner Act. The labor movement has generally not blamed the courts for business's ability to flout the labor laws with relative impunity. Union lawyers say that it is not judicial interpretation but inadequacies of the National Labor Relations Act itself that are to blame. The act, they believe, provides inadequate remedies for victims of unfair labor practices and untimely relief to unions seeking to organize work units.

The courts have been regarded as an obstacle to revised labor law in only one area. The issue was unions' right of access to an employer's plant, shop, or office for organizational purposes. Lawrence Gold, chief counsel of the AFL-CIO, has said that on the issue of union access, the courts have been "very property-minded and very hostile" to organizing efforts on premises of employers. This pattern in the courts was expressed by the Supreme Court of the United States in *Babcock & Wilcox* v. *the NLRB*.

The courts have also played an active role in setting limits to collective-bargaining practices, limiting practices such as secondary boycotts and lockouts, and defining the topics that are subject to negotiation at the bargaining table. But none of these kinds of issues were raised in the labor-law debate. What was at stake in this legislative fight was union organizing, not bargaining, and in that area the courts had played an essentially minor and neutral role.

A United Farm Workers union organizer talks to a grape picker in the fields in the late 1960s.

The AFL-CIO planned its biggest lobbying and public relations campaign in many years, perhaps ever, in support of the labor-law changes. Unions affiliated with the federation were assessed 1¢ a month per member for six months to raise $800,000 for the effort, which eventually would be far larger than originally planned. A special task force, drawn from the diverse experience and talents of the union movement, was organized to direct the campaign.

The labor leaders correctly assumed that the bill would be resisted by business and industry. Harold Coxson, chief labor attorney for the Chamber of Commerce of the United States told an interviewer that there was no question that the Chamber would get involved in the fight to defeat the bill

> because of the magnitude of the issue. It was felt that the legislation, far from being mere corrections, would rewrite the National Labor Relations Act, making it unfair to business. There would no longer be any evenhandedness or balance in the law. It would make things easier for the union organizer and more difficult for the employer to resist. There are existing remedies for abuse. We don't need more. There are some business violators, but to change the law because of a single violator, or a small group of violators, was unfair to all other employers.

The labor-law "reforms," business leaders charged repeatedly, would lead to "pushbutton unionism."

Neither side, in the beginning, realized how bitter and prolonged the battle was to become.

The first real indication that the drive to change the labor law might be in trouble came early in 1977 when the House of Representatives unexpectedly voted down the common-situs picketing bill. Some of labor's strategists had warned that it was a mistake to launch the legislative program with this bill because its passage would benefit only the building- and construction-trades unions, narrow special interests within the labor movement, which itself represented a minority of American workers. But the construction-trades leaders desperately wanted this legislation. With each passing year, nonunion labor had been taking a bigger and bigger bite out of the available construction jobs. The union leaders believed situs-picketing powers would help stem the tide. Moreover, these leaders were convinced that victory in Congress could be achieved easily. The Ninety-fourth Congress had passed an almost identical bill after it had been backed by John T. Dunlop, President Ford's secretary of labor and one of the nation's leading authorities on the building and construction trades. But the bill was unexpectedly vetoed by Ford, which, among other things, led Dunlop to resign from the cabinet. With an even greater Democratic majority in the Ninety-fifth Congress and with assurances from President Carter that he would sign the common-situs bill (although he would not press for its passage), the union leaders were certain they would achieve their goal.

John T. Dunlop, secretary of labor under President Ford, announces at this January 1976 news conference that he is resigning because of the President's veto of a prolabor bill.

In 1981, a strike by members of Local 150 of the International Union of Operating Engineers shut down several construction projects in downtown Chicago. Even though the common-situs picketing bill failed to pass, strikes such as this one have been, and continue to be, effective tools of the labor movement.

They were mistaken. Stunned and ashen-faced after a late-evening vote in the House went against them narrowly, the labor lobbyists could hardly believe the outcome. For a long time thereafter, labor leaders were convinced that the setback had been the result of overconfidence, bad tactics, and poor timing. They vowed they would avoid the same mistakes with the far more critical labor-law bill.

But opponents of the common-situs bill, particularly the major contractor associations, had mounted a sophisticated, well-financed lobbying effort against the bill, recruiting grass-roots support and making extensive use of computerized mailing lists and mass postcard mailings. These techniques, adopted in part from methods designed for the Republican presidential campaign the previous year, would be refined and extended in the subsequent battle over labor law. The coalition of contractor groups, called the National Action Committee, became the foundation of a much broader alliance of employers from a wide spectrum of business and industry united to battle against the labor-law revisions. Business and other foes of organized labor received a major psychological boost from the common-situs vote. Labor's fabled lobbying juggernaut, they found, could be stopped, even with a Democrat in the White House and a heavy Democratic majority in Congress. In fact, they were discovering, this Congress was different: it did not seem to play by all the old rules.

Meanwhile, labor leadership slowly realized that the common-situs defeat was not an aberration, but a signal that the trade-union movement was facing a serious political situation: the old verities with which they had maneuvered for so long in Washington needed reexamination.

Jerry Wurf, president of the American Federation of State, County, and Municipal Employees and long a gadfly within the ruling executive council of the AFL-CIO, told a reporter that

organized labor's mistakes are catching up with it and it is becoming a victim of new perceptions and weaknesses. What happened [in the common-situs vote] *was very simple. Organized labor had displayed cynicism in staying neutral on George McGovern* [in the 1972 Presidential campaign against President Nixon], *in its relationships with Mayor Daley in Chicago and Governor Rockefeller in New York. It displayed blindness on America's role in Vietnam. Suddenly, labor made the discovery that it did not have the real clout it once had in Congress. Its ability to be effective electorally had lessened and so, therefore, did its influence on political leaders. The AFL-CIO treats the situs defeat as a tactical error. But it was more than that. It was the voice of the United States Government it helped elect.*

The labor federation's headquarters conceded that the tried-and-true lobbying methods no longer sufficed. Visits by union legislative officers to Congress, promises of legislative support, and threats of active opposition needed to be supplemented with new tools of persuasion. George Meany selected a young lawyer working in the federation's building-trades department, a former Young Republican named Victor Kamber, to head a special task force that would plan and direct a campaign to enact the labor bill and other legislation. The task force would conduct a grass-roots campaign, Mr. Kamber said, to convince the American people that labor-law reform would benefit not only workers but the entire nation. The labor federation also began to forge a coalition with other groups, including women's, civil-rights, and church organizations with common interests in labor law and other social issues.

Swallowing its pride, the AFL-CIO also sought to enlist the backing of President Carter for the labor-law bill. Previously labor had intended to push the legislation through Congress alone, without seeking the imprimatur of the White House. But union officials were discovering that, to the members of the Ninety-fifth Congress, identification with organized labor was becoming more a liability than an asset.

Despite President Carter's publicly stated support for labor-law reform, it was by no means certain that he would agree to present an administration bill. Key members of his cabinet, including W. Michael Blumenthal, the secretary of the treasury, Charles L. Schultze, head of the Council of Economic Advisers, and Juanita Kreps, the secretary of commerce, warned the President that the bill might not pass, pointing to the situs defeat. Bert Lance, then-director of the Office of Management and Budget, urged the President to "build business confidence" and pointed out that endorsing the labor-law revisions was not the way to do it. President Carter also was warned of the political risks involved in thrusting himself into the middle of a supercharged political issue.

But Secretary of Labor Ray Marshall, with the eventual support of Stuart Eizenstat, President Carter's chief domestic policy adviser, vigorously urged the President to put his name on a draft labor-law bill. According to aides, the President personally believed that reforms were needed to stop law-breaking by employers. Organized labor brought its strongest pressure to bear on the White House through telephone calls to presidential aides as well as through public statements by Mr. Meany and other leaders.

President Carter let it be known that he would not back the repeal of Section 14b nor would he support the checkoff-card certification plan. Without a hint of a *quid pro quo*, the labor leaders quietly dropped their insistence that these provisions be included in the reform legislation. In due course, then, Secretary Marshall held a press conference in the briefing area of the west wing of the White House to announce that President Carter would introduce legislation to make the National Labor Relations Act "fairer, prompter, and more predictable."

Thus, not only the Labor Department but the White House as well was deeply involved in negotiations on the contents of the bill as well as on the strategy and tactics for winning its enactment. This White House involvement started at the beginning of the process and continued through its conclusion.

After that conclusion, labor lobbyists and Congressional staff aides working for the bill criticized the White House legislative-liaison office led by Frank Moore. The White House effort was often described as inadequate and inept. This criticism haunted the administration throughout President Carter's tenure. In fact, his spotty performance in having Congress follow his lead on key issues was regarded as one of the problems that caused many Americans to become disenchanted enough with President Carter's leadership to vote him out of office in 1980.

Armed with a proposed bill that now bore the signature of the President of the United States, and led by George Meany, well into his eighties but still a masterful advocate and a brilliant manipulator of the levers of power in Washington, the labor movement was ready to muster all of its political strength for what was perhaps its most massive legislative campaign ever.

But the campaign was slow in getting under way. First, the labor lobbyists had to fight a number of other pitched battles over the cargo-preference and Hatch Act changes, and, above all, the minimum-wage bill. The fight over the wage legislation was prolonged, involving not only the size of the increase, but also labor's desire to index the minimum as a constant percentage of average manufacturing wages. Some of President Carter's economic advisers wanted to reject the indexing proposal and also to reduce the proposed increases in the wage itself on the grounds that the changes would be the source of unending inflationary pressures. It was some time, therefore, before the AFL-CIO and its ally, Secretary Marshall, obtained the President's blessing for a specific bill. Then, there were protracted fights in both chambers of Congress over the size of the minimum and over the indexing provision, and there was an abortive attempt by business interests to obtain a lower minimum wage for younger workers. Largely because of this minimum-wage debate, the labor-law bill did not take center stage in the House of Representatives until the fall of 1977.

As the first legislative test neared, the rhetoric on both sides grew steadily more intense. Richard L. Lesher, president of the increasingly militant Chamber of Commerce

George Meany, the late AFL-CIO president, addressing a crowd of 2000 persons at a labor rally in downtown Kansas City, May 6, 1977.

of the United States, issued a statement saying: "The so-called labor 'reform' bill, when stripped of its title, is nothing more than an effort to put the power of the federal government behind big labor's organizing efforts. . . . The time has come for our national legislators to stand up to the political threats of big labor and say 'no more.'"

The chairperson of the Senate Human Resources Committee and its labor subcommittee, Senator Harrison A. Williams, Jr. (D., New Jersey), who would later manage the labor-law bill fight in the upper chamber, said at a news conference that "the atmosphere of near hysteria surrounding the Labor Reform Act tends to cloud what to me is a very simple and clear mission—to make the basic law of this country work in the way it was intended. The Wagner Labor Relations Act was passed to guarantee to American workers the right to organize and bargain collectively. It was enacted because there was no national law which guaranteed this right. . . . Tragically, we have found that to an increasing extent over the past decade, the Act intended to open doors is being used to close doors."

After some agonizing, supporters of the bill decided to seek passage of the legislation first in the House, rather than in the Senate. Labor supporters agreed that because the House had killed the common-situs bill, the labor-law reform bill needed to pass a test of strength there before it could gain credibility in the Senate.

Congressman Frank Thompson, Jr. (D., New Jersey), chairperson of the labor subcommittee of the House Education and Labor Committee and longtime friend and ally of the trade-union movement, moved quickly to bring the bill forward. He scheduled a series of hearings concerning J. P. Stevens, including one session in Roanoke Rapids, North Carolina, the site of a number of alleged illegalities. By now the AFL-CIO campaign for the bill was well into gear. In a re-creation of a sixties-style coalition, support had been solicited and won from civil-rights, church, religious, women's, and environmental groups. Individual unions were trying to energize rank-and-file members to contact their local representatives to Congress. One union, the International Association of Machinists and Aerospece Workers, brought 250,000 postcards, signed by workers, to Capitol Hill just before the House vote.

Opponents of the bill also were organizing their operation. A staff was lined up for the National Action Committee, which soon came to include most of the nation's major business organizations, including the Business Roundtable, which had been regarded as a moderate, nonideological group. Supported by the business community, two conservative Republican legislators, Representatives John Ashbrook of Ohio and John Erlenborn of Illinois, prepared their own piece of legislation, the "employee bill of rights," which they intended to put forth as a substitute for the labor-backed bill. The "bill of rights" was in large part designed to help keep workers out of unions and was vehemently rejected by supporters of the labor bill.

In the wake of their experience with the common-situs bill, labor supporters were expecting a tough, close fight—but they were surprised and gratified when the labor-law amendments passed handily by a vote of 257 to 163 on October 6, 1977, after only a few days of debate and a minimum of weakening amendments.

Later, when the bill ran into serious trouble in the Senate, prolabor lobbyists asked themselves why the bill passed so easily in the House. They came up with a variety of answers.

First of all, it was believed, the business opposition had not fully readied its campaign. Its public-relations and grass-roots efforts had not yet gathered momentum. Money was only starting to trickle into the warchests. For weeks, much of the business lobbying effort had concentrated on the minimum-wage fight. Moreover, business had waged what one administration official described as "a battle against the wrong bill." He explained that much of the antilabor-law literature and propaganda was directed at labor's effort to repeal Section 14b of the Taft-Hartley Act and the checkoff card organizing plan. But both of these targets had long since been abandoned by labor and were never even brought to the floor of the House. The opponents simply were not well prepared for the House fight. They would not repeat that mistake in the Senate.

Second, many members of Congress who voted against the common-situs bill supported the labor-law changes. One administration official said they did so out kf feelings of guilt at having voted against labor in spite of labor's political support. Also, some members were probably responding to labor's threats of political reprisal in the upcoming campaign.

A third factor contributing to the bill's easy passage in the House was that labor's enemies tried to change the bill in the direction of the Ashbrook-Erlenborn substitute, rather than concentrating on voting the bill down. An administration official explained

Left: Crystal Lee Sutton, employee of the J. P. Stevens textile plant and the model for Hollywood's "Norma Rae." Below: Labor subcommittee panel hears testimony of union leaders regarding allegations of illegal antiunion activities by the J. P. Stevens Company at hearings held in Roanoke Rapids, North Carolina, August 9, 1977.

that by compromising on a few of the proposals in the substitute, floor managers for the labor bill neutralized sufficient opposition to assure the necessary votes. In addition, the amendments attracted some southern votes because the bill had not yet been branded as a North-South issue.

Another factor was that some of the forces that seemed to affect Congress in 1978, or, at least, that seemed to gain strength in that year, did not play as significant a role in the legislature in 1977. For example, the readiness of individual members of the House to defy the chamber's leadership was not as pronounced in 1977 as it became in 1978 as the election drew close. In 1977, the Democratic party, the President, the Speaker of the House, and other leaders commanded a fairly high degree of loyalty.

Very important, too, was the fact that the so-called Proposition-13 fever, touched off by the successful antitax referendum in California, still lay in the future. Following the vote in California conventional wisdom argued that the referendum generated a wave of antigovernment, as well as antitax, sentiment. True or not, Congress became increasingly affected by the fever.

While assessing the reasons for the victory in the House, labor leaders and their allies gratefully accepted their success and confidently predicted climactic victory in the Senate. At the same time, business groups and conservatives vowed to fight harder to turn back the legislation in the upper chamber, but they glumly conceded that the prospects were not bright following the action of the House.

In retrospect, many of those involved in both sides of the battle believe that the legislation would have been enacted if it had been taken up by the Senate immediately after the House vote. The momentum was clearly with the bill and its supporters. The opposition was still preparing its defenses. Most of the factors that helped produce the relatively easy victory in the House would have carried over to the upper chamber.

But it was six months before the legislation reached the floor of the Senate. Many changes occurred in the interim, and some events shifted the delicate balance of forces that are at play in any struggle over significant, controversial legislation.

The most crucial event was the long and bitter debate over the Panama Canal treaties. The administration exerted all of its influence and called in most of its few political IOUs to win approval of the treaties. Senator Robert Byrd of West Virginia, the Senate majority leader, stood to tarnish his reputation as a masterful parliamentarian if he could not guide the Panama Canal treaties to ratification. Senator Howard Baker of Tennessee, the minority leader, stood to lose even more by supporting the treaties in opposition to the powerful conservative wing of his party. Baker was not only up for reelection in his fairly conservative home state but was also up for reelection to his leadership post in the Senate. Morever, it was no secret that Senator Baker aspired to his party's presidential nomination in 1980. It required courage, therefore, for the Tennessean to support President Carter on Panama.

Most important, a number of senators, including Democrats, who cast pivotal votes to support the treaties were reluctant to incur the wrath of the increasingly powerful political right or to ignore the perceived conservatism of the electorate twice in succession. That, at least, is how many Washington observers assessed the impact of the Canal debate on the labor-law battle.

What caused the delay that enabled the Canal debate to intervene before the labor bill could be acted upon? Some of the bill's supporters took the philosophical view that it was simply another example of how events control the process of government. They said that there was not enough time to prepare the Senate version of the bill between House passage and Congress's year-end recess; and when Congress reconvened, the Senate was girded for the Panama debate and was still preoccupied with the long, irresolute bickering over energy legislation. Thus, the labor-law revisions simply had to wait their turn.

Other disappointed proponents, however, blamed a lack of expedition and will on the part of some senators responsible for shepherding the bill through the Senate. One proponent of the bill commented that while the amendments were quietly expiring at the end of the Ninety-fifth Congress, "we honestly had hopes that Pete Williams [Senator Harrison Williams] would mark up the bill and get it on the floor by the end of the first session." He added that while Senator Williams had been a long and valued ally of the unions, "he never has gotten along with labor leaders that well. Personally, he feels a lot closer to businessmen." He also noted that Senator Williams headed the securities subcommittee of the Senate Banking Committee, and that before the bill was marked up, or drafted, by the committee, he had introduced a number of changes to make the legislation more palatable to business. For example, Williams changed the provision requiring *double* back pay to workers illegally fired for union activities to *one-and-a-half times* back pay; the maximum waiting period before unions would be allowed to demand an organizing election was lengthened. Senator Williams explained that these changes were necessary if the bill was to have any chance in the Senate. But some critics said that the changes only encouraged opponents to resist more strongly and that they indicated Senator Williams's lack of full commitment to sweeping reform.

Senator Harrison Williams of New Jersey. Some blamed the defeat of the bill in the Senate on his lack of full commitment.

Still other observers felt that while Senator Williams did his utmost to bring about passage of strong labor-law reform, his staff was neither committed nor efficient in handling the bill. Before the Carter administration took over the reins of government, the labor subcommittee of the Human Resources Committee had a veteran, highly respected, professional staff. After President Carter assumed office, several members of this staff, including Donald Elisburg, who became assistant secretary of labor, and Nik B. Edes, who became deputy undersecretary of labor, joined the administration. Others returned to private life. The new staff director of the committee, Stephen Paradise, was regarded as an extremely able legislative craftsman. But a number of people on Capitol Hill and in the labor movement believed that he was not interested in labor or in the bill itself. "Steve Paradise didn't have his heart in the legislation," said one disappointed lobbyist when the battle was over, adding, "Steve is an example of the Capitol Hill wheeler dealer. He enjoys the game. But he didn't want to have to deal with the bill by the end of the first session. So it wasn't dealt with." Emphasizing that the actions of a single senator and his staff can frequently decide the success or failure of legislation—even very important legislation—the lobbyist asserted: "We are a government of personalities, not legalities, no matter what anyone says."

While waiting for the bill to appear on the floor, the Senate became the site of what was widely described as one of the most intense lobbying battles in its history. The business community, led by the National Action Committee on Labor Law Reform and including the Chamber of Commerce, the National Association of Manufacturers, the Business Roundtable, construction associations, right-wing organizations, and a number of large corporations, such as Sears, Roebuck and Company, began to pour what eventually added up to many millions of dollars (no one has yet come up with a reliable figure) into the effort to stop the bill. In order to demonstrate a groundswell of opposition to the bill, much of the money was spent on direct-mail and grass-roots campaigns to generate letters, telephone calls, and visits to members of the Senate. Senator Richard Lugar (R., Indiana), who eventually became a floor leader of the fight against the amendments, received some 14,000 pieces of mail for, and 33,000 pieces against, the labor-law revisions. About ninety percent of the mail was postcards, indicating, a staff official in Senator Lugar's office noted, that most of the mail had been generated by the actions of lobbyists. However, "some of the letters were written out of conviction," the official noted. "We had to answer every damn letter and card."

When the labor bill reached the Senate, opponents opened two lines of attack that they had not used in the House. Heretofore the bill had been resisted largely as "a power grab by union bosses." Now it was argued that the bill would have an inflationary impact on the economy because it would open the way for a new wave of unionization and the higher, inflationary wages it caused. This time, inflation was a matter of growing concern in the Congress and in the nation and the focal point of a growing number of policy decisions. "We should have looked at the inflation issue earlier," said Harold Coxson of the Chamber of Commerce. "You never know what arguments appeal to Congressmen. Some of them couldn't care less about being unfair to business but will listen to arguments about inflation or the increase in government bureaucracy."

The second new tack taken by opponents was to claim that the proposed changes in the labor law would have an extremely adverse effect on small business. In fact, the great majority of small businesses are exempt from most provisions of the National Labor Law. But business lobbyists argued that changes in the law would mean that owners of small businesses would be driven to bankruptcy because they would be subject to organizing drives and forced to pay high union wages. The new tactic paid off with waves of small-business representatives flooding Congressional offices to protest the bill. There also was a small-business rally in Washington shortly before the bill came to a vote in the Senate. As it turned out, however, many of the people attending the rally reportedly were employees of the Marriott Corporation and had been bused in at company expense from nearby Maryland. There was no denying the fact, however, that big business and small business had joined forces in a legislative fight.

The business coalition hired at least two public relations firms in Washington to help out with the effort to defeat the bill. Individual corporations took out advertisements in major newspapers and nationally circulated magazines. Companies and their leaders were enlisted to help by exerting their influence. For example, the chairman of Sears, Roebuck sent a "Dear Sears Supplier" letter to all the firms from which the giant retailing concern purchased its products, arguing against the bill and stating, "I am personally concerned it would upset our political and economic system and push our country down the road to a labor- and government-controlled economy." Local chambers of commerce and other groups followed up letters to their members with personal visits, urging the members to contact their senators. A surprisingly large number of businessmen and women actually visited their senators' offices. There was general agreement, at the end, that the effort to turn back the labor-law revisions was the most expensive, intense, and well-coordinated effort ever undertaken by the nation's business community to influence the legislative process. No stone was left unturned in that effort, as this writer discovered personally.

Opposite: The joining of the American Federation of Labor and the Congress of Industrial Organizations in 1955 was a historic moment in the American labor movement. Below: A pro-union billboard in the 1930s criticized the oppressive working conditions of open, or non-union, shops.

Several weeks before the Senate began to debate the bill, I received a telephone call from the executive director of the National Action Committee saying he had a good "exclusive" story for my newspaper. Staff officials in the Small Business Administration, he told me, had prepared a report showing that the legislation would have an inflationary and detrimental effect on small business. The report recommended that the SBA oppose the bill. The lobbyist did not have a copy of the report, he said, but he urged me to try to obtain a copy from the government agency. If they would not comply with my request, the lobbyist suggested I write an article for my newspaper saying that the Administration appeared to be suppressing the report because it would damage the effort to change the labor law.

I asked the agency for a copy of the report and was refused, first by the public-affairs officer and then by a deputy administrator. I was told that it was an internal staff document not intended for release but simply for guidance within the agency. The officials said that the report had been prepared by the SBA's office of advocacy. I was told on "deep background" (that is, not for attribution) by other officials of the agency that the report was a shallow, poorly researched document that had been prepared by several discontented civil servants appointed during the Nixon administration.

Although I threatened to sue under the Freedom of Information Act to try to pry the document loose, I knew that such a suit would have little chance of success. Intraagency reports generally are exempt from the disclosure provisions of the act.

I was then invited to the law offices that were serving as headquarters for the National Action Committee and was introduced to an SBA official who had helped prepare the report. The official described the contents of the report, which he said "documented" the inflationary impact of the proposed amendments on small business. But he said he could not leak a copy of the report to me because he feared it would be traced to him. Two staff members of the National Action Committee urged me to write the story on the basis of the official's description, or, if I would not write the story without having a copy in hand, to call up several conservative senators and ask them to demand that the SBA make the report public. At this point it somewhat belatedly dawned on me that opponents of the bill were seeking to use me and my newspaper for their purposes in a fashion that went beyond the customary symbiosis that exists between reporters and their sources. This suspicion was confirmed some days later when the AFL-CIO public-relations office released the outline of a "battle plan" it had somehow obtained of the National Action Committee's tactics for defeating the bill. One item in the plan indicated I was to be contacted to place the SBA story.

Nevertheless, I continued to press for a copy of the report in case it should offer a legitimate news story. After several weeks, at the urging of Senator Orrin Hatch (R., Utah), a leading opponent of the bill, the agency, noting that the report was an internal document that did not represent the views of the agency, released the report to the public. Upon perusal, the report turned out to be what my sources had indicated: shallow, poorly researched, and designed, it seemed to me, more to create mischief than to advance the state of knowledge about the possible impact of the labor-law revisions. It did not seem to merit an article in my newspaper—and I did not write one.

Labor, of course, was not idle while the avalanche of business lobbying was gathering momentum. Union leaders and their legislative officers, backed by Labor Department and other administration officials and allies in civil-rights, women's, and church organizations, maintained constant pressure on the Senate while diligently courting public opinion. One successful technique was the daily publication of a case history of an individual worker who had been illegally wronged by an employer for union activities but who had been unable to obtain justice.

Secretary Marshall related one such case history at a White House breakfast meeting called to discuss the legislative campaign. He told of a textile worker, Roger Taft, who was "fired for trying to organize a union. This sort of thing isn't supposed to happen in America in the 1970s. It's a throwback to the days before the Wagner Act when the law was one-sidedly in favor of employers. The passage of the Wagner Act in 1935 was supposed to change all that. But because of delays and the weaknesses in the current law, Roger Taft and thousands of people like him are fired each year for union activity. Sure there are remedies under existing laws for cases like Roger Taft's. But the law grinds ever so slowly."

The two sides were like heavyweight boxers standing toe to toe in the center of the ring, throwing punch after punch at each other. The Chamber of Commerce published a public-opinion poll indicating that a majority of the American people were against changes in the labor law. Victor Kamber of the AFL-CIO commented that "obviously the Chamber wanted an antiunion poll and it got what it paid for." Shortly thereafter, a poll commissioned by the labor federation indicated that a majority of Americans were in favor of changes in the law that would provide more justice for workers. The National Action Committee commissioned an economic study of the potential impact of the proposed changes from Pierre Rinfret, a well-known business economist who had advised President Nixon in the 1972 presidential campaign. Mr. Rinfret's study found that the changes would have a substantial inflationary impact. The AFL-CIO then commissioned a study by Robert Nathan, an economist with long and close ties to the labor movement. Mr. Nathan found that the changes would make little contribution to inflation.

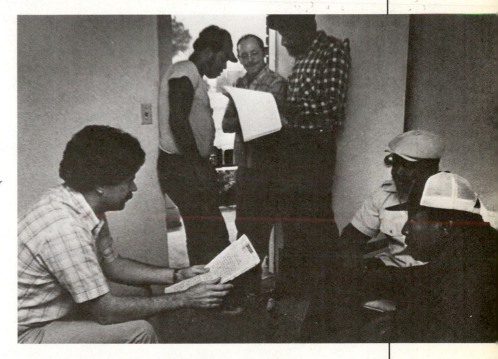

Union leaders from the J. P. Stevens Company reviewing contract with labor organizer before taking it to workers for a vote.

Both sides made serious mistakes. For example, at one point the National Association of Manufacturers announced the formation of its Council on a Union-free Environment. "That almost sunk us," said one business lobbyist later. "We were trying to put across the message that we were trying to protect ourselves from being overwhelmed by the unions. But the reaction to the council was 'Hey, you guys are really out to bust the unions.' It was a poor choice of title." And George Meany made a real blunder when he publicly charged that labor's opponents were really out to take industry away from the unionized North and transfer it to the sunbelt states, where lower wages could be paid to workers. While there was some truth to this contention, Mr. Meany's stating it in public helped polarize the Senate battle along geographic, as well as party, lines.

As the bill moved toward the floor of the Senate, Mr. Meany charged that business's massive drive to stop the labor-law changes constituted a "holy war" against the union movement. However, opponents could claim that labor's efforts to enact the bill were no less fervid. No one, however, disputed Mr. Meany when he said that "this is the toughest legislative fight I have seen since I came to Washington," which was nearly four decades earlier.

Meanwhile, the business community had devised a new strategy for dealing with the bill in the Senate. While the bill's opponents wanted to block completely any change in the national labor law, they realized they probably could not do so. In the House they had tried for what a business lobbyist called "a more balanced bill"—that is, one with at least some provisions favorable to business—by setting up the Ashbrook-Erlenborn substitute, hoping to at least weaken the bill. To their chagrin, the bill passed by the House was, from business's point of view, essentially a disaster.

Now, in the Senate, opponents felt that they should not simply try to weaken or to moderate the bill: they were convinced they had to prevent the legislation from passing at all. They realized that even if they somehow managed to achieve a balanced compromise bill, the Senate version would be subject to a joint House-Senate conference. Since most of the conference members from both chambers would probably be sympathetic to labor, it stood to reason that the final version to emerge from the joint body would be much closer in substance to the strongly prolabor bill adopted by the House.

Opponents also knew that there was little hope that a majority of senators would vote against the labor-backed bill. So they resolved to attempt a *filibuster*, a parliamentary maneuver that uses prolonged debate on the part of a minority of legislators to block passage of a bill. Under Senate rules, a minimum of sixty votes from among the one hundred senators is required to stop a filibuster by invoking *cloture of debate*. Enemies of the labor-law changes thought they might be able to squeeze out enough votes to prevent cloture, thus blocking a vote on the bill itself—a vote they were virtually certain to lose.

In case the filibuster was broken, the opponents drafted well over a thousand amendments to the bill as a second line of defense. This tactic, described as "filibustering by amendment," could prolong the debate endlessly, and, it was hoped, eventually force the Senate to drop the labor-law debate in order to move on to other pressing business before the Ninety-fifth Congress ended.

The filibuster was to be conducted by the core of the right-wing faction of the Senate Republican delegation, including such longtime foes of organized labor as John Tower of Texas, Strom Thurmond of South Carolina, Jesse Helms of North Carolina, Carl Curtis of Nebraska, and Bob Dole of Kansas. The floor leaders for the opposition were

Senator Robert Byrd of West Virginia, a key supporter of the labor-law legislation, and Senator Richard Lugar of Indiana, right, one of the leaders of the opposition.

to be two freshmen Republican senators who had been on Capitol Hill less than two years each—Orrin Hatch of Utah and Richard Lugar of Indiana.

Senator Hatch, a former labor lawyer and former union member, had proclaimed himself an enemy of organized labor from the day he arrived in the Senate, taking a highly visible and vocal stand against all labor-supported issues and generally articulating the positions of the right-wing National Right-to-Work Committee. He staked out a claim as a leader of the opposition to the labor-law revisions almost from the moment the AFL-CIO announced that the legislation was on its agenda. He quickly became a hero of the business community, of conservative organizations, and of other antilabor groups.

Senator Lugar, in contrast, generally "opted for two years of caution on big issues," according to one of his staff aides. A former mayor of Indianapolis and once known as "President Nixon's favorite mayor," Senator Lugar was no liberal by any stretch of the imagination. But because he kept such a low profile, he was considered moderate in contrast to Senator Hatch, who was "perceived as very conservative, even radical," according to the aide. The staff official added that the lobbyists had persuaded Senator Lugar to become a coleader of the filibuster in order to "balance the ticket."

Senator Lugar did not take on the assignment lightly. He knew, the aide said, that the labor-law fight was "big casino," and that if he lost or created too many enemies for himself during the fight, his political future could be compromised. "We were really shocked when he did put his head on the line by agreeing to lead the filibuster," the aide said. But if he could be instrumental in defeating the labor-law revisions, he would almost automatically become a rising star of the Republican right, which was becoming increasingly dominant within the party. He also would command the gratitude and loyalty, and presumably the financial and political support, of the increasingly assertive business community and right-wing activists.

Leading the fight on the floor for the labor bill were Senator Williams of New Jersey and Senator Jacob K. Javits of New York, the veteran minority leader on the labor subcommittee. Senator Williams diligently prepared himself for the debate. He also substantially modified the House bill in order, he said, to enhance its chances of passage in the Senate. Labor leaders complained that he had given away too much before the fight in the Senate even started.

Senator Javits had long been regarded as one of the most able and intelligent members of the upper chamber. But he was now well into his seventies and some of his former drive was absent from his efforts on behalf of the legislation.

The labor-law fight also pitted the two Senate leaders, Senator Robert Byrd of the majority and Senator Howard Baker of the minority, against each other on a key piece of legislation for the first time. The two senators had been allies on the two or three key bills, including Panama and the energy package, that had passed through the Senate in the nearly two years they had shared the leadership. Senator Byrd had aroused the ire of his party's conservatives on these occasions. Now, however, Senator Baker actively maneuvered for the defeat of the labor-law revisions. Among other things, therefore, the prestige of the two leaders was involved in the battle.

In the end, after the million-dollar budgets, the lobbying, the public-relations and advertising campaigns, the emotional oratory, and the long, arduous months of work, the fate of the labor legislation came to hang on the votes of six or eight Senators. The unions knew they could count on a majority to vote for the amendments if the filibuster could be broken. But the votes of sixty of the one hundred senators are required to close debate in the Senate, where the rules traditionally have protected the right of senators to orate to their hearts' content. Not long after the bill was brought to the Senate floor, it became clear that half a dozen or so Democratic senators from the South and West would decide whether or not there would be a revision of the national labor law.

At first, there was considerable optimism among supporters of the legislation. Majority Leader Byrd, who enjoyed a growing reputation for astuteness, had brought the bill to the floor after stating that he would not do so unless he believed that there were sufficient votes for cloture. The labor lobbyists and their administration allies were convinced that they had the votes. A number of the swing senators had told them that they would vote against cloture on the first few ballots to placate constituents, but then would cast their vote to close debate. Although these senators might not vote for the bill itself, the unions felt they still had sufficient votes for the simple majority (greater than fifty percent) needed for enactment. Although the swing senators were conservative Democrats, many of them had the political support of their state labor federations, and often, but not invariably, voted prounion on labor issues.

Proponents of the bill were not expecting an immediate victory and so were not unduly disturbed when the first ballot, taken after eleven days of debate on June 9, 1978, produced only forty-two votes for cloture and forty-seven against. When, on the following day, fifty-one votes could be mustered for shutting off debate, Senator Byrd announced that he and others would sponsor a watered-down substitute bill. They hoped that such a pledge of compromise would end the filibuster and pave the way for passage of the labor bill, and, of great concern to Senator Byrd, that it would clear the Senate floor for the growing crush of other urgent business, particularly the vital energy bill.

But because the filibuster on the original Senate bill had not yet ended, under Senate rules Senator Byrd's substitute could not be introduced. And the promise of a greatly modified bill did not seem to persuade many members—if any—to change their votes on the cloture balloting. A third and then a fourth vote were taken. On the fourth ballot, supporters of the bill were still two votes short of the necessary sixty votes and were getting worried.

Time was clearly running out. Never before had there been more than five cloture votes on a piece of legislation (although there once had been six votes on a procedural issue). Supporters of the bill knew that if they could not close debate with a fifth vote, the momentum was likely to shift in favor of opponents of the legislation. Some senators were not deeply committed to the bill and wanted to move on to other business. An election was coming up in the fall, and those senators standing for reelection were anxious to clear their calendars for campaigning.

The fateful day came on June 22, the nineteenth day of the filibuster. The desperate search for the votes needed to end debate focused increasingly on Senator Russell Long (D., Louisiana), the powerful and influential chairperson of the Senate Finance Committee. Senator Long let it be known that·if the bill were amended to his satisfaction, including removal of the equal-access provision, he would vote to end the filibuster. The bill's proponents also anticipated that Senator Long would bring at least one vote with him—and perhaps more. In any case, they counted on his switch to provide the votes needed to end the filibuster.

The maneuvering on both sides of the floor was as tense, rapid, and subtle as a duel between fencing masters. The first and probably crucial test came when Senator Byrd attempted to send the bill back to the Human Resources Committee with instructions to amend the bill in accordance with Senator Long's and others' objections. Often a motion to recommit a bill to committee is a move intended to effectively kill a piece of Congressional legislation. But Senator Byrd's motion was intended to give the labor-law amendments precedence over all other Senate business when it was returned to the floor.

However, under Senate rules, such a motion requires unanimous consent in order to be adopted, and such consent was not obtainable. Senator Ernest F. Hollings (D., South Carolina), who strongly opposed the labor-law changes, objected to the motion and demanded a sixth cloture vote. He and others fighting the bill believed that a record sixth failure to end a filibuster would persuade enough senators that the cause was futile and that the bill should be buried.

Senator Byrd countered this move by saying that he intended to vote against cloture this time and urged others to join him in order to make the vote meaningless. The record sixth cloture vote ended with fifty-three senators for and forty-five against the motion to end debate. Then the chamber voted unanimously to give the committee the authority to bring a revised bill to the floor after three weeks but did not give specific instructions to do so.

"The bill is still very much alive," Senator Byrd said after the vote to recommit it. "Let it not be said that today's vote was a victory for one side or the other. The issue has not been settled." Senator Williams told the press that the bill would be revised expeditiously by his committee and that the changes would clear the way for passage of the bill.

As it turned out, the foes of the bill knew better. Senator Lugar predicted that the bill would "never reappear on the floor of the Senate," and suggested that the vote to recommit had been "a tactful way to bring it to an end." Said Senator Hatch: "Small business has won the biggest victory in its history."

The labor-law legislation never did reappear during the remainder of the Ninety-fifth Congress. For a while, labor union officials and their administration allies spoke hopefully about a "bare-bones" bill being enacted before the November elections. But it was not to be. No additional support was generated while the bill was in committee. And many senators who had backed the bill initially were in no mood to return to it. Other business and the looming election had a prior claim on the time and interest of most of the Senate. Labor-law reform was dead—at least for 1978.

With the death of the bill began the "might-have-been." What went wrong? What turned the tide? What was done or not done that might have made a difference?

The first postmortems were concerned largely with the slim shortfall of votes in the Senate. Prolabor lobbyists were sure that they had had enough votes to break the filibuster. What happened to those votes?

"We were lied to; it's as simple as that," said one angry labor official.

Another labor lobbyist offered a somewhat fuller explanation. "Several senators told us they would vote for us on the fourth or fifth cloture vote, never expecting there would be that many votes. Sometimes people make promises thinking they never will have to deliver. In this case the bill was on the floor for weeks. There was a record number of [cloture] votes. There came a point where these people just ran out of excuses. If all the commitments we had had been exercised, we would have been all right."

Several lobbyists on both sides of the battle agreed that one southern senator, whose vote was counted on in the crucial vota to permit amendments to the bill but who unexpectedly failed to come through, could have made the difference. The lobbyists believed that the elderly senator had intended to vote with labor but became confused and voted the wrong way.

"There were votes we could and should have gotten but didn't," said a union official. "There was one old man who forgot how he was supposed to vote. There was one crazy senator who voted the wrong way. One senator who should have been with us had to play conservative politics in his state. In one western state a labor union had made a commitment to a senator not to go back to him for his vote for the rest of the year if he voted for the Panama Canal treaties. The union has considerable money and clout in that state, but its leaders had bound themselves not to try for his vote again. They lived up to their bargain and the senator voted against us. That's politics, man."

The North-versus-South issue that Mr. Meany and others had raised was seized upon by opponents of the bill to pressure southern senators, not one of whom voted for cloture. For example, Senator Dale Bumpers (D., Arkansas), a moderate who had enjoyed political support from organized labor, said he voted against cloture for the first time in his career even though obstructionist tactics were "abhorrent" to him. He voted as he did, he said, because of "the suspicion that the bill's supporters believe it may help diminish the attraction of the South for new industry."

A lobbyist said that while President Carter and his staff worked diligently for the bill, the President could have done more. "If Carter had made a deal or two with a dam, as Presidents traditionally have done; if he had been willing to play with a few judgeships . . . .", the lobbyist said, letting the thought trail off.

In fact, the President did attempt some old-fashioned horse trading at the eleventh hour, according to Capitol Hill observers. This included presidential offers to back the sugar-support legislation supported by Senator Long and a number of his colleagues.

At the time of the vote, however, the President's influence and prestige were at a low ebb, despite his victory on the Panama Canal vote. His ratings in the polls were declining, and the perception on Capitol Hill and elsewhere in Washington, which is always finely tuned on questions of political power, was that Mr. Carter's political influence was diminishing. Accordingly, his ability to influence the actions of Congress was less substantial than usual for a sitting President.

This situation reversed itself to a large degree following the dramatic Camp David summit, when Mr. Carter brought President Anwar Sadat of Egypt and Prime Minister Menachem Begin of Israel to the conference table at the presidential retreat in the Catoctin Hills of western Maryland and helped the two leaders forge a tentative (and, as it turned out, tenuous) peace settlement.

"If the sixth cloture vote had been taken after Camp David, the bill would have won," asserted an administration official. "A President with power can make a big difference on a volatile issue on the Hill. But before the summit Carter didn't have that kind of power."

It was clear, however, that forces more significant than tactical error or even presidential power and prestige had produced the defeat of the labor-law bill. The mood of Congress, and indeed of the whole country, was changing. The change influenced the legislative process in a variety of subtle, almost intangible ways that, when added to other factors, were enough to turn back the drive to revise the National Labor Relations Act.

The Proposition 13, antigovernment, antitax, antiregulation syndrome was one part of the changing mood. But as one senior Senate staff official said, "the rest of it just wasn't there for this bill. The Senate is a conservative place these days. The new Republican radicals have no respect for the institution, the conservative Democrats turned against labor even though labor had been an important part of their support. The country itself is like the way it was in the fifties—apathetic. You can't get people interested in causes like labor reform. People are not interested in reforming things like health care or civil rights or the environment either. They are only interested in themselves."

When it was all over, labor officials were unhappy and defensive, particularly over repeated assertions that they had become paper tigers in Washington's political wars. Union lobbyists insisted that although the labor-law bill had died, it had not really been defeated. "The bill passed the House, and we had fifty-eight solid votes in the Senate. If the bill had ever been permitted to come to a vote on the merits we had a clear majority," was the way one such lobbyist characterized the outcome.

In fact, the loss of the labor-law battle was a serious blow to the labor movement because, as a member of Senator Lugar's staff pointed out, "the fight was about more than what was in the bill. It was a test of strength between big labor and big business." And a staff member from a Democratic senator's office said that "this was the conservatives' way of putting labor in its place. Business felt that after all these years, the time was ripe to start taking away the things that labor had been winning."

At a Chicago press conference at the AFL-CIO executive council meeting in August, Mr. Meany said that "corporations . . . still toy with the idea that they might find some way to destroy labor unionism and, of course, they have had that idea for a long time." In his Labor Day speech, Mr. Meany said that "since last Labor Day, the American labor movement has been under concerted attack. Starting with the day President Carter's modest proposals to reform the nation's labor laws were introduced, we have been the target of a vicious, distorted, and unfair barrage of propaganda. Supported and paid for by the business community, this attack was spearheaded by a small band of United States senators with close ties to some of the most extreme right wing organizations in the country."

Meany, Douglas Fraser (president of the United Auto Workers Union), and other labor officials charged that business had reopened "class warfare" against American workers.

After the labor-law defeat, organized labor in the United States clearly was on the defensive. Again in his Labor Day speech, Mr. Meany felt it necessary to declare that "the fourteen million members of unions of the AFL-CIO differ from other Americans in only one way—they carry a union card. They are active in their church, PTA, boys and girls clubs, scouts . . .".

If labor was on the defensive, a newly confident business community was strongly on the offensive. Some goals that had seemed hopelessly out of reach now appeared attainable to business lobbyists and to the leaders of conservative organizations. Before the Ninety-fifth Congress packed up and went home, action was initiated to place restrictions on the Labor Department's Occupational Safety and Health Administration, a perennial whipping boy of employers. Some momentum was gathered for legislation to defer the next minimum-wage increase for youth. Contractor organizations and their allies prepared a fresh drive to repeal or change the Davis-Bacon Act, which requires prevailing (read union) wage levels to be paid on all construction projects funded by the federal government.

Perhaps the most interesting fallout of the labor-law battle was the fact that contributions to corporate political action committees (PACs) soared during the 1978

Students in Boston listen to prolabor appeal from Jibreel Khazan (standing left) and Rev. Ed Rodman (right), a founder of the Student Nonviolent Coordinating Committee. Forming coalitions with sympathetic groups, such as student organizations, is one tactic labor might use to broaden its power base.

election campaign. The business community suddenly was a self-aware giant in the political arena.

The labor leaders, meanwhile, talked about forging new coalitions to redress the political imbalance. Mr. Fraser of the UAW called a conference of civil-rights, women's, church, and other organizations in Detroit to discuss ways to counter what was perceived as the rising conservative tide. But many felt this exercise in coalition-forming was a "sixties" response to a "seventies" problem. And labor was highly uneasy—if not panicky.

There was some tendency on the part of labor leaders to exaggerate the significance of their defeat, and, on the part of the business community, to read too much into their victory. There had been, of course, no absolute reversal of political fortunes. Such fortunes always ebb and flow.

But what could be concluded was that the delicate balance of forces that determine the rewards and penalties meted out by government to various sectors of society had shifted perceptibly—presenting a new set of problems for labor and a new set of possibilities for business.

The Presidency: Office and Occupants

Shortly after his victory in the November 1980 election, President Ronald Reagan's work habits were described by one of his aides in the following way: "He's a homebody." This meant that the President was not likely to spend long hours at his desk in the Oval Office. "He will be inclined to carry a full briefcase back to the White House family quarters at night rather than work late in the Oval Office." In order to "recharge his batteries," President Reagan, one assistant stated, would use Camp David, but he would also plan "regular visits to his beloved ranch in California."

The President's wife, Nancy Reagan, when asked about her husband's reputation as a 9-to-5 administrator, told a television interviewer: "I don't see that it's really necessary to get up at five o'clock in the morning to get things done. I don't think you do yourself or your job any good that way."[1]

Perhaps she was right. At least Jimmy Carter might now agree. Two years before Mrs. Reagan's statement, then-President Carter addressed a group of high-school students in a graduation ceremony in the Rose Garden of the White House. These students had served as Congressional pages, or aides, working in Congress all year while attending a special high school.[2] Their graduation was a festive occasion, and the President good-naturedly provoked laughter when he told the new graduates that he wished he had as much knowledge of Congress as they had gained.

"I should have recruited you a year or so ago to help in my advice and counsel," he said. "I think our achievements would have been even greater than they have been. We have learned a great deal about government, you and I together. We have early morning study hours. I was up at five o'clock this morning getting ready for this week's work."[3]

The Framers' View of the Presidency

A briefcase full of "homework" at night; regular trips across the continent to be refreshed and recharged; early morning study hours. When the framers of the United States Constitution met in Philadelphia in 1787 to "form a more perfect union," it was unlikely that they intended to create an executive office whose occupant would need such work habits. (And a round-trip journey to California at that time would probably have taken an entire four-year term!) The framers' main objective was a strong, independent presidency with limited powers.

Single occupant versus plural executive? Some framers wanted the executive office to be composed of a council or committee, perhaps of three people, making it more difficult for the presidency to assume monarchical, if not dictatorial, powers. Governor George Clinton of New York went so far as to label the one-man executive a potential "generalissimo of the nation." Indeed, what concerned some framers most was that one

President George Washington (shown at far right) with members of his cabinet: (from left to right) Henry Knox, secretary of war; Thomas Jefferson, secretary of state; Edmund Randolph (with back turned), attorney general; and Alexander Hamilton, secretary of the treasury.

person would have sole control over the military. Virginia's Patrick Henry (who refused to go to Philadelphia as a delegate but who was active later in the Virginia ratifying convention) frankly believed that a single, strong President would take the first opportunity to seize absolute power as commander-in-chief of the military forces.[4] Thomas Jefferson, at that time serving in Paris as ambassador to France, voiced similar fears. A President with control of the military, Jefferson wrote to John Adams, "would not easily be dethroned."[5] Roger Sherman supported a plural executive because he considered the presidency as "nothing more than an institution for carrying the will of the Legislature into effect."[6] Some delegates from small states tended to fear a one-man presidency since they felt the large states would always supply the occupants.

These suspicions and preferences did not prevail because a sufficient number of the framers felt there were enough safeguards written into the Constitution to guard against tyranny by a sole executive. James Madison, for example, was always more fearful of potential abuse of power by the legislature than by the executive. Since the government did not provide for a hereditary monarch, there was little likelihood, he argued, of executive abuse of power.

How much power to the President?   The constitutional debates over presidential power did not end with the resolution of the single-versus-plural issue. For example, some framers wanted to give the President sole appointing power, because this would guard against domination over the presidency by Congress. Others, of course, feared vesting so much power in the office. Ultimately, a compromise was reached: the President could fill some positions, such as ambassadors and Supreme Court judges, "with the advice and consent of the Senate."

Another matter of debate was the power of veto over bills passed by Congress. Delegates James Madison, James Wilson, and George Mason (supported by Thomas Jefferson) wanted to give this veto power jointly to the President and the Supreme Court. However, in the minds of most delegates, this would constitute a major violation of the doctrine of separation of powers. The final draft of the Constitution gave veto power to the President alone.

The framers generally planned to allow the President to take the lead in treaties, and they were content to have this power shared with only the Senate. There was only minor support for including the House of Representatives in this process. Most delegates to the Constitutional Convention felt (and probably for good reason at the time) that House members would not have the interest—or talent—for foreign affairs. In addition, the framers probably did not imagine then that foreign relations would become as vitally important as it has.

All in all, the framers used rather broad, imprecise language in outlining the President's powers. The excerpts from Article 2 (see Table 1) illustrate this point. The meaning of "the executive power" or "he shall take care that the laws be faithfully executed" is not spelled out. Political scientist Richard M. Pious has stated that from such language flows what he calls "prerogative powers," which depend on how Presidents interpret the broad constitutional language. So much is *not* explicitly stated in the Constitution about the President's power over departments, in diplomatic relations, and as commander-in-chief during war *and* peace that there is room for wide interpretation.

Pious says that "the key to an understanding of presidential power is to concentrate on the constitutional authority that the President asserts unilaterally through various rules of constitutional construction and interpretation, in order to resolve

---

TABLE 1.
Excerpts from the Constitution, Article 2.

Article 2, Section 1

"The executive power shall be vested in a President of the United States of America. . . ."

Article 2, Section 1 (oath of office)

"Before he enter on the execution of his office he shall take the following oath or affirmation:

I do solemnly swear (or affirm) that I will faithfully execute the office of the President of the United States, and will to the best of my ability preserve, protect, and defend the Constitution of the United States."

Article 2, Section 2

". . . he shall take care that the laws be faithfully executed. . . ."

---

crises or important issues facing the nation."[7] So, before considering the formal constitutional powers of the office, let's briefly turn to this important source for understanding the role of the presidency: the men who have occupied the office. From George Washington to Ronald Reagan, only thirty-nine men have been President. And some have had very specific—and differing—ideas about what their role should be.

Different Presidents View the Office

Even before he was elected, Ronald Reagan told the American public how he viewed the office of the presidency. "I believe the presidency is what Teddy Roosevelt said it was. It's a bully pulpit."[8] The following sampling of views demonstrates how divergent the interpretations of the presidential role can be.

Theodore Roosevelt's "stewardship" theory. For Theodore Roosevelt, the presidency was a place of action. He saw the President's role as a

President Theodore Roosevelt inspects progress in the construction of the Panama Canal, 1906.

vigorous one, not to be hemmed in by a narrow definition of presidential powers and responsibilities. Presumably this is what he meant by the "bully pulpit." He stated his views in his *Autobiography*:

> My view was that . . . every executive officer in high position was a steward of the people bound actively and affirmatively to do all he could for the people, and not to content himself with the negative merit of keeping his talents undamaged in a napkin. I declined to adopt the view that what was imperatively necessary for the nation could not be done by the President unless he could find some specific authorization to do it. My belief was that it was not only his right but his duty to do anything that the needs of the nation demanded unless such action was forbidden by the Constitution or by the laws. . . .[9]

In other words, Theodore Roosevelt believed that he, as President, could and should act—indeed, "broaden the use of executive power"—unless there was a "direct constitutional or legislative prohibition." If he wanted to act, he had to be shown why he should *not* do so.

Taft's "limited powers" theory. Theodore Roosevelt's immediate successor, William Howard Taft, had a different view: if he wanted to act, he had to be shown that he had the right to do so. Taft, like Roger Sherman, saw the role of President essentially as one of carrying out the laws passed by Congress. The President was to execute.

Taft's views on the office, therefore, were the exact opposite of Theodore Roosevelt's views. In Taft's own words:

> The true view of the Executive functions is, as I conceive it, that the President can exercise no power which cannot be fairly and reasonably traced to some specific grant of power or justly implied and included within such express grant as proper and necessary to its exercise. Such specific grant must be either in the Federal Constitution or in an act of Congress passed in pursuance thereof. There is no undefined residuum of power which he can exercise because it seems to him to be in the public interest.[10]

Franklin D. Roosevelt's "prerogative" theory. Probably no President, with the exception of Abraham Lincoln, lived as much with constant crises as Franklin Delano Roosevelt. Certainly none did for as long a period. He assumed office in 1933 in the middle of one of the country's worst economic depressions, and he died, serving his fourth term, in 1945 toward the end of one of the world's biggest wars. For twelve years, FDR was a "crisis" President. As such, it would have been difficult, if not catastrophic, for him to adopt an attitude such as Taft's. FDR loved politics, and his entire presidency was one of executive activism.

When he assumed office, at least 12 million people (out of a labor force of 50 million) were unemployed; the banks and the financial institutions of the country were on the brink of collapse; farmers were not able to get a decent price for their crops; homeowners could not meet their mortgage payments. These crisis situations, in FDR's mind, called for firm, quick presidential action. He believed he would have to seize these "specific events" as opportunities to exercise positive leadership. And it is clear that he was impressed by the presidencies of Theodore Roosevelt and of Woodrow Wilson, who served during another time of crisis, World War I.

Arthur M. Schlesinger, Jr., wrote: "There could be no doubt about the influence Theodore Roosevelt had on him, even if FDR was sometimes irritated when people compared him to TR [Theodore Roosevelt]; nor could there be doubt about Wilson's impact."[11]

FDR himself wrote in a "Memo on Leadership":

Theodore Roosevelt lacked Woodrow Wilson's appeal to the fundamental and failed to stir, as Wilson did, the truly profound moral and social convictions. Wilson, on the other hand, failed where Theodore Roosevelt succeeded in stirring people to enthusiasm over specific events, even though these specific events may have been superficial in comparison with the fundamentals.[12]

There were, indeed, enough "specific events," or crises, to provide the basis for Franklin Roosevelt to pursue his view of the presidency as a place of strong, active leadership. His presidency provides many examples of the use of the prerogative

Franklin Roosevelt confers with British Prime Minister Winston Churchill aboard the H.M.S. Prince of Wales, 1941.

powers described by Richard Pious. He was not always successful in getting what he wanted, as in his "court-packing" plan (discussed in chapter 12) or in his efforts to win voters' support for the candidates he favored for Congress. But at no time could he be accused of not trying.

Richard Nixon's Watergate brief and the "inherent powers" theory. Only one President has ever resigned the office. That was Richard M. Nixon on August 9, 1974, in a simple, one-sentence letter to the secretary of state, Henry Kissinger: "I hereby resign the Office of President of the United States."

While in office, Nixon became involved in a series of events known as "Watergate" and "the coverup." Members of his staff were suspected of planning and participating in the June 1972 break-in at the Democratic National Committee head-

In an address to the nation on August 8, 1974, Richard Nixon announced that he had resigned the presidency of the United States.

quarters and in other illegal activities. The President denied these charges for over two years; and when the special Watergate prosecutor asked him to turn over the tape recordings of his conversations with White House aides, Nixon refused. The matter was then taken to the Supreme Court.

In his argument to the Court,[13] the President (speaking through his lawyers) argued that he did not have to release the tapes because they were protected by ''executive privilege.'' This meant that certain presidential actions and documents could remain secret or beyond the reach of anyone, including Congress and the Supreme Court; otherwise, the theory of separation of powers would be violated. According to the concept of executive privilege, the President has the power to withhold information if he deems disclosure to be contrary to the public interest. ''This follows logically from the President's broad inherent powers under the Constitution,'' Nixon argued. He stated that he, as President, had to use his own discretion, and that he was accountable only to the American people through the electoral process and to Congress through the process of impeachment.

This view of presidential power was the subject of intense debate during the Watergate period. The situation was complicated, of course, because the tapes were suspected of containing evidence of criminal wrongdoing.

The Supreme Court ruled against the President, and he was asked to relinquish the tapes. Material on one of the tapes was thought, by Nixon, to be so damaging that he had no alternative but to resign. But he never admitted that he, personally, was involved in any wrongdoing. In fact, in a television interview with David Frost three years later, he went so far as to say that some presidential actions that normally would be illegal should not be considered illegal under certain circumstances. Needless to say, Nixon's opinion made front-page headlines the next morning.

Frost: *So what in a sense you are saying is that there are certain situations . . . where the President can decide that it's in the best interest of the nation or something and do something illegal.*

Nixon: *Well, when the President does it, that means that it is not illegal. . . . but I do not mean to suggest the President is above the law. What I am suggesting, however, what we have to understand is in wartime particularly, war abroad and virtually revolution in certain concentrated areas at home, that a President does have under the Constitution extraordinary powers and must exert them. And we trust the President will always exert them . . . as little as possible. . . .*[14]

Presidential Character:
A Clue to Presidential Performance

In deciding which candidate to vote for, the attentive citizen listens to the various contenders, tries to differentiate their positions, examines their previous public (and sometimes, private) records and activities, and (as noted in chapter 7) makes a choice based on a number of criteria. Political scientist James David Barber believes that voters should pay more attention than they presently do to psychological attributes of the candidates. A vote is a "prediction" about who would be the "best President," and Barber believes that knowing more about the candidate's character, world view, and style would aid that prediction. As Barber advises: "I am not about to argue that once you know a President's personality you know everything. But . . . the degree and quality of a President's emotional involvement in an issue are powerful influences on how he defines the issue itself, how much attention he pays to it, which facts and persons he sees as relevant to its resolution, and, finally, what principles and purposes he associates with the issue."[15]

Information on a President's personality may be gleaned from an examination of the candidate's childhood, motivations, inner drives, development, as well as emotional attitudes toward politics and the job of President. One might also assess how assertive a candidate is in the political arena.

Barber developed four analytical types of presidential styles: *active-positive*; *active-negative*; *passive-positive*; and *passive-negative*. A President is active or passive depending on the amount of energy invested in the office. A President is positive or negative depending on how he "feels about what he does." An active President spends a lot of time and effort at the job; a positive President is one who enjoys the job. Using a store of biographical and case studies, Barber classified

From Stefan Lorant's *The Glorious Burden* (Author's Edition)

According to Barber's system of presidential classification, William Howard Taft was "passive-positive." Here Taft is shown tallying up his score in a round of golf, 1909.

TABLE 2.
Barber's Classification of Twentieth-Century
Presidents by Personality Type.

Active-Positive	Passive-Positive
Franklin D. Roosevelt	William Taft
Harry S. Truman	Warren Harding
John F. Kennedy	
Gerald Ford	
Jimmy Carter	

Active-Negative	Passive-Negative
Richard Nixon	Dwight Eisenhower
Lyndon B. Johnson	Calvin Coolidge
Herbert Hoover	
Woodrow Wilson	

twentieth-century Presidents as shown in Table 2. In sum, Barber says "Active-positive Presidents want most to achieve results. Active-negatives aim to get and keep power. Passive-positives are after love. Passive-negatives emphasize their civic virtue."[16]

Presidential Roles: Constitutional

It is customary to discuss the constitutional duties of the President by category (chief executive, commander-in-chief, and so forth), and we have used such categories here. It is important to remember, however, that no President is faced with such neat divisions in his workaday life. The duties and responsibilities come all mixed together. He must be aware that performance in one capacity might well have implications in another.

Chief executive. The Constitution says that the President "shall take care that the laws be faithfully executed." In doing so, he must preside over the **executive branch**, which includes a vast bureauc-

racy of approximately 3 million civilian employees, and while he certainly cannot know details of their work, he is responsible for what they do. This is an impossible burden, of course, but it is what Americans have come to expect of their President. In addition, he must participate in countless ceremonies, attend meetings at home and abroad, and read and respond to numerous reports and memos. Some of his acts are strictly symbolic, such as throwing out the baseball to open the major-league season, posing with the newly crowned Miss Red Roses Queen, and participating in the White House Christmas-tree-lighting ceremony. Many Americans have come to associate these functions with the presidency. He is, after all, the chief executive. And although all these functions have little effect on the President's ability to faithfully execute the laws, such functions do add, perhaps, to the stature of his leadership—which is an important consideration. Substance or symbol, these activities nonetheless are a part of the role of chief executive.

The President is paid $200,000 per year plus $50,000 for expenses, and he has to pay taxes on this income. He receives an additional $100,000 (nontaxable) for official entertainment and travel. His living accommodations (the White House) but not his food are free, and when he leaves office, he receives a lifetime pension of $66,000 per year plus a $96,000, nontaxable allowance for an office staff. The federal government provides suitable office space for former Presidents in the place of their choice. For example, although Jimmy Carter resides in Plains, Georgia, his postpresidential office is in Atlanta.

The many facets of a President's work as chief executive may be demonstrated by focusing on one presidential press conference.[17] This situation shows the varied issues facing a President in what has come to be called the "pressure cooker of the modern presidency." President Reagan, who had been in office only nine days, opened his press

The President as chief executive. Above left: President Eisenhower greets the winners of the 1957 Little League World Series. Below left: President Kennedy hosts a gala dinner for Nobel Prize laureates in April 1962. To Mrs. Kennedy's left is poet Robert Frost. Below: President Johnson conducts a press conference in the White House Rose Garden, 1964.

conference with the customary brief statement on a topic of current interest to him and the nation. The statement said, in part:

> *The clear message I received in the election campaign is that we must gain control of this inflationary monster. Let me briefly review for the American people what we've already done. Within moments of taking the oath of office, I placed a freeze on the hiring of civilian employees in the federal government. Two days later I issued an order to cut down on government travel, reduced the number of consultants to the government, stopped the procurement of certain items, and called on my appointees to exercise restraint in their own offices.*
>
> *Yesterday, I announced the elimination of remaining federal controls on U.S. oil production and marketing. . . . I'm taking major steps toward the elimination of the Council on Wage and Price Stability. This Council has been a failure; it has been totally ineffective in controlling inflation and it's imposed unnecessary burdens on labor and business. . . . My second decision today is a directive ordering key federal agencies to freeze pending regulations for sixty days.*

Then many of the several hundred reporters present began raising and waving their hands seeking recognition to ask a question. They asked the President twenty-three questions in all, covering the following topics in this order: policy toward Iran (American hostages had just been released after being held captive for 444 days); extent of budget cuts; retribution for terrorists; strategic arms treaty; Soviet intentions; corporate business in Iran; U.S. prisoners abroad; hiring of minorities; natural-gas decontrol; grain embargo; killings of black children in Atlanta; policy toward Latin America; draft registration; timing of tax cuts; punishment of Iran; abolition of two executive departments; dairy price supports; Iran-Soviet re-

lations; retaliation against Iran; Hispanic appointments; Federal Reserve monetary policy; and attitudes of his conservative supporters toward his administration.

In exercising his duties, the President cannot have complete information or final opinions on *every* subject. Take, for example, the fourteenth question at the press conference:

> *Q. What do you intend to do, Mr. President, about the draft registration law that was passed during President Carter's Administration? And in view of your opposition to it in the campaign, how is that consistent with your avowed intention to strengthen our national defenses?*
>
> *A. Well, to answer the last part first: I just didn't feel that the advance registration, on all the evidence we could get, would materially speed up the process if an emergency required the draft. It did create bureaucracy; it caused, certainly, some unrest and dissatisfaction. And we were told that it would only be a matter of several days if we had to call up in a draft, that we could do that several days earlier with the registration than we would be able to if there was no registration at all.*
>
> *We—this is one that's—something to be looked at further down—I've only been here nine days and most of these nine days have been spent in Cabinet meetings on the economy, getting ready to send our package up to the Hill. And so I just have to tell you that we will be dealing with that—meet with that and make a decision on what to do with it down the road someplace.*

Commander-in-chief. The Constitution explicitly says: "The President shall be commander-in-chief of the army and navy of the United States, and of the militia of the several states when called into the actual service of the United States."

In this role, the President must be constantly informed of sophisticated new weapons, size and deployment of military forces, and he must assess where and when to use those forces to protect the security of the nation. He is also required to be as informed as possible of the military might of other nations. The press conference illustrates this:

Q. Mr. President, you campaigned rather vociferously against the SALT II treaty, saying it was slanted slightly toward the Soviet Union, and yet I noticed your Secretary of State, Mr. Haig, now seems to suggest that for the time being at least the United States will abide by the limits of the SALT II treaty, and he hopes the Soviet Union will too. How long do you intend that the United States should abide by the terms of a SALT agreement which you consider inequitable? And what do you consider its greatest inequities to be?

A. Well, the SALT treaty first of all, I think, permits a continued buildup on both sides of strategic nuclear weapons but for—the main thing authorizes an immediate increase in large numbers of Soviet warheads. There is no verification as to the number of warheads on the missile and no method for us to do this.

I don't think that a treaty—SALT means strategic arms limitation—that actually permits a buildup on both sides of strategic nuclear weapons can properly be called that. And I have said that when we can—and I am willing for our people to go into negotiations, or let me say discussions leading to negotiations, that we should start negotiating on the basis of trying to effect an actual reduction in the numbers of nuclear weapons. That would then be real strategic arms limitation. And I happen to believe, also, that you can't sit down at a table and just negotiate that unless you take into account—in consideration at that table—all the other things that are going on. In other words, I believe in linkage.

As commander-in-chief, the President is the boss of approximately 2 million military personnel, which combined with the approximately 3 million civilian employees is quite a work force to oversee. Ever since the United States' permanent involvement in international affairs following World War II, this function has become increasingly important. In the capacity of commander-in-chief, a President might even commit the country to war, as happened under President Truman with Korea and under Presidents Kennedy, Johnson, and Nixon with Vietnam.

One very important principle in the American governmental system is *civilian supremacy* over the military. In his role as commander-in-chief, the President is a civilian, not a military person. Thus, all generals and admirals take their orders from a *civilian*. However, in his role as civilian leader, the President is heavily dependent on the information given to him from military sources. In order to make sound military judgments, the President must frequently rely on his military advisers, the intelligence networks, and the diplomatic corps for technical knowledge.

Chief diplomat. The President is the central focus of American foreign policy. Congressional leaders, reporters, concerned citizens, and foreign governments all look to him and his office for the policies, signals, and negotiations that pertain to international affairs. Presidents have differed in the way they perform the role of chief diplomat. Some, such as Franklin D. Roosevelt and John F. Kennedy, take a personal role, going to foreign conferences and meeting with heads of states personally. Others, such as Eisenhower and Nixon, rely heavily on their secretaries of state and other emissaries. But at all times, the President is personally responsible for what happens—or fails to happen. The policies that develop are identified with *his* administration. He appoints and receives

The conduct of foreign policy often requires personal and informal contacts among heads of state. Such close contacts were crucial to President Carter's success at the Camp David meetings with Israeli Prime Minister Begin and Egyptian President Sadat in 1978.

ambassadors, and he can take the very important step of recognizing or breaking off relations with another country. Eisenhower, not Congress, broke relations with Cuba in 1961. And it was the dramatic trip by Nixon to China in 1972 that opened direct communication between the United States and that country. These are all presidential initiatives taken in the President's capacity as chief diplomat.

Another means presidents use in their dealings with foreign countries is the **executive agreement**, an arrangement between this country and another that does not require approval by the Senate. This system allows the President to move rapidly in foreign affairs and to bypass the Senate. The use of executive agreements has grown substantially over the years, to the dismay of some senators. During the first fifty years of this country's history, 60 treaties and 27 executive agreements were enacted. During the last forty years, 364 treaties and 6395 executive agreements were made. Initially, executive agreements were used for relatively unimportant subjects, such as mutual recognition of trademarks and international postal agreements. However, some members of Congress have complained that these days executive agreements are being used for matters more properly the subject of treaties, such as agreements to locate American military bases abroad.

The Supreme Court, however, has upheld the legality of executive agreements. Although, strictly speaking, they are not specifically mentioned in the Constitution, most major executive agreements are based on previously passed Congressional statutes or resolutions. An *unwritten* restraint on the use of the executive agreement is that it simply would be politically unwise for a President to conduct foreign policy to the total exclusion of Congress. At some point, the President might need to ask Congress to appropriate funds to implement an executive agreement, and this is more easily achieved if he has not been neglectful in his relationship with Congress.

Thus, politics at home determines in large part how a President conducts politics abroad.

Presidential Roles: Political

The Constitution sets forth some general and specific presidential duties and powers. And as we have seen looking at a few questions at one half-hour press conference, the President has good reason, if he chooses, to rise early to prepare for his work or to take a full briefcase home at night. He was asked about a broad range of issues, from foreign affairs in the Middle East to child killings in Atlanta, from economic matters and budget and tax problems to draft registration. The demands of time and knowledge are such that one cannot perform the duties casually.

These are the formal and day-to-day requirements of the office. There are more. The President of the United States is above all the top *politician* in the country. If he fails in that role, all other roles will probably make little difference.

The President as politician. Every President enters office accompanied by the expectations of those who elected him. Note the observation in the labor-law case study: "Now . . . Jimmy Carter, a Democrat, would be taking over, and the union leaders felt they could rely on his gratitude for their political support during the election cam-paign as well as on his avowed populism." You will also recall from the case study that some labor-union lobbyists became disenchanted with the role of the White House. "The White House effort was often described as inadequate and inept. This criticism haunted the administration through-out President Carter's tenure. In fact, his spotty performance in having Congress follow his lead on key issues was regarded as one of the problems that caused many Americans to become disen-chanted enough with President Carter's leadership to vote him out of office in 1980."

President Ronald Reagan was in office less than a week when some of *his* supporters began to sound notes of alarm and disappointment. Some of them felt that President Reagan was forsaking his essentially conservative base by appointing too many "moderate" Republicans and even some "liberal" Democrats to office. The chairman of the National Conservative Political Action Com-mittee, John T. Dolan, said: "It's mind boggling that conservative, pro-Reagan activists are being bumped off job lists, while people who have no commitment to Ronald Reagan are being given jobs."[18] Thus the President as politician must be sensitive to many political demands, even (per-haps, especially) from within his own party. He must attempt to broaden his base of support without alienating his core supporters. And, in the unlikely event that he forgets, the President will always be reminded—sometimes quite cogently—of his many political obligations. Mr. Dolan is reported as saying at the beginning of the Reagan administration: "To say that Reagan has to employ country-club, silk-stocking, George Bush Repub-licans is garbage. That didn't win him the election. He won by broadening his base to the ethnics, the blue-collar vote, the born-again southern Demo-crats. Reagan has a commitment to these people and he's got to live up to it. He didn't win by being a centrist, he won because he's conservative."[19]

The appointment of Colorado lawyer James Watt to head the Interior Department caused a small furor in the early days of President Reagan's administration. Opposition came largely from liberals and environmentalists; conservative supporters of Reagan were generally happy with Watt, though they disapproved of certain other Reagan appointments.

WATT

INTERIOR

WHAT??

Leader of the party (?) Every President except George Washington was elected on the basis of his leadership of a political party or, in John Adams's case, a political faction. We speak of "Democratic" or "Republican" Presidents, for instance. Precisely what this means, however, is not obvious. If, for example, he is a Republican, does it mean that he can dictate how Republicans in Congress should act and vote? Does it mean that he has the automatic support, say, of a Republican governor or a Republican mayor? Does it mean that he can tell the registered Republicans in a local precinct how to vote in a party primary or even in the general election? In all these circumstances, definitely not. In fact, Franklin D. Roosevelt experienced rather severe defeats in 1938 when he asked local Democrats in Georgia and other places to vote for his preferred candidates in Congressional races.

Then in what sense *is* the President the leader of his party? As we described in chapter 6, the American party system is federalistic. It is not, as in Great Britain, a "disciplined" party structure. The President, as party leader, has most influence over a relatively small segment of his party, namely, the national committee. As we have noted, this committee is responsible mainly for holding a national nominating convention every four years and writing a national party platform. Invariably, the party's presidential candidate appoints the chairperson of the national committee. The presidential candidate has never been denied that privilege, because the committee members recognize that the President and the chairperson must be able to work closely together. Likewise, the presidential nominee influences the party platform considerably. If the candidate is an incumbent seeking reelection, the platform will likely reflect his previous record in office and the positions he has already taken. But it is unlikely that the President's influence as party leader extends beyond the national committee and the national convention.

Obviously, as a Democrat or Republican, the President will have stronger attachments to his own party than to the opposition. He will have, most likely, come up through the political ranks of a particular party (Eisenhower, who came up through the ranks of the army, was an exception). Along the way, he very likely will have done favors for party leaders throughout the country: raising money for them, speaking at their affairs, posing for pictures with them, appointing their choices to the thousands of federal jobs in regional, state, and local areas. In this way, he can possibly strengthen his role as party leader. Still, one cannot assume that the President's mere *titular* leadership makes him the actual or most effective leader of the party. He has to work at it constantly. That is the political reality.

If he is a popular President, with strong support in the opinion polls, local party leaders are more prone to follow him because of the "coattail" effect—the President's influence and possible endorsement may help them in their local races. On the other hand, because of his views, a President could be considered a political liability to some local party officials. In such cases, local politicos try to put as much distance as possible between themselves and the so-called party leader.

Initiator of legislation. The Constitution gives the President certain specific functions and powers in the legislative process. He can, for instance, veto bills passed by Congress. Indeed, his signature is required if the bill is to become law, unless he doesn't sign within ten days. If he chooses this course and Congress is still in session, the bill

As leader of the party, the President must keep in close touch with party leaders in the various states and localities. Here President Reagan visits Illinois to attend a fund-raising dinner for Illinois Governor James Thompson (shown at the top of the stairs).

becomes law without his signature. If Congress adjourns before the ten-day period expires, the bill dies. This is known as a **pocket veto**.

The President's role as the "initiator of legislation" is defined in the constitutional phrase: "He shall from time to time give to the Congress information of the State of the Union, and recommend to their consideration such measures as he shall judge necessary and expedient."

This could be interpreted as a rather perfunctory assignment. The President could simply send a report to Congress every now and then briefly outlining the state of the nation and suggesting improvements in such a manner as, "By the way, I think it might be useful if you. . . ." This, however, is not the normal practice.[20] Presidents use the State of the Union address to set forth what they believe are the nation's major problems, and they list, in *general* terms, the subjects they want Congress to address. This general outline is later followed by a series of specific messages, proposals, and drafts of bills sent to Congress.

These days, Congress and the people *expect* the President to take the legislative initiative. This was certainly the situation described in the case study on the ten days at Camp David. The country was waiting for the President to propose solutions. Likewise, after Ronald Reagan was elected, even though the Republicans had captured the Senate and made strong gains in the House, the new President was the focus of attention. *His* proposals would set the agenda.

Indeed, the President's sponsorship of or support for proposed legislation is very important. Although the President's support is not always decisive, the proponents of a bill generally want his backing, as we saw in the labor-law case study. The president ultimately decided to support the legislation, but only after certain provisions (re-

peal of Section 14b and of the checkoff-card certification plan) were dropped. After that, the secretary of labor announced at a press conference held at the White House that the President would introduce legislation to make the National Labor Relations Act "fairer, prompter, and more predictable."

This active, assertive legislative role of the presidency is essentially a twentieth-century development. Political scientist Stephen J. Wayne observes:

For most of the first 100 years Congress jealously guarded its prerogatives and its autonomy. It was not until the Theodore Roosevelt and Woodrow Wilson era that chief executives became more actively engaged in proposing and influencing the enactment of legislation. A variety of factors contributed to this increased activity: the presidency had become a more visible office thereby enhancing the potential for public support; Roosevelt and Wilson were more personally active and adopted a philosophy inclined toward a more assertive presidential role; the congressional parties were more amenable to strong leadership both from within the congress and by the president; and economic and social conditions created a need for regulatory legislation to which presidents, by virtue of their national perspective and constituency, could more easily respond.[21]

The development of this role was accompanied by a need to increase the size of presidential staffs. Thus we have seen the growth of an array of positions personally attached to the President, leading to what has been called the "institutionalized presidency." The President needed his own people—in addition to the regular cabinet officers—to oversee this important political process of proposing and promoting legislation.

All the President's People: The Loyal Supporters

How is it possible for the President to deal with so many demands? By what mechanism can he be expected to stay on top of what is going on in the Middle East and Atlanta and Congress at the same time? The answer, of course, lies in the vast presidential staff, which began under Franklin D. Roosevelt in 1939 when Congress approved an executive order establishing the Executive Office of the President.

At the beginning of the country's history, the President was assisted by only a handful of people, who were frequently members of his own family. Their function, basically, was to answer his mail, arrange his appointments, and to perform other secretarial functions. They were not policy advisers. For example, President Buchanan's nephew served as his secretary and all-around "boy Friday," as described by political scientist Louis W. Koenig:

> [James B.] *Henry* [the nephew] *attended the President in his office from 8 a.m. until 5 p.m., when Buchanan took a daily walk. Henry kept records of the receipt and disposition of correspondence. "Such letters as the President ought to see," Henry said, explaining his duties, "I folded and briefed and took them to him every morning at eight o'clock and received his instructions as to the answer I should make." Once a day he sent to each department a large envelope containing letters for its attention. In addition, Henry oversaw arrangements for state dinners, managed the library fund, paid the household staff, and kept the President's private accounts.*[22]

Furthermore, until McKinley's administration (1897–1901), the President paid these people out of his own personal funds.

With the increased functions of the office during the New Deal of the 1930s, a specially appointed Committee on Administrative Management concluded clearly and simply, "the President needs help." Congress then appropriated money to hire advisers and a supporting staff. Today, the institutionalized presidency is comprised of two layers: the White House staff, and the Executive Office of the President.

The White House staff. The White House staff employs approximately 550 people on an annual budget close to $17 million. These people range from the President's closest political and administrative advisers to the cooks, butlers, and household servants. This group of advisers includes the press secretary, appointments secretary, counselor to the President, special assistant to the President, legislative liaison officer, and speech writers. All of these have assistants, deputy assistants, and secretarial support staffs of their own. Some have offices in the White House itself—a sign of power and status—but most are housed next door in the huge gray building known as the Old Executive Office Building.

These White House staff advisers are, indeed, the President's loyal supporters. He appoints them personally and does not need Senate approval to do so. Some of the closest advisers have probably been with the President since his early political career. He trusts them entirely. Their sole purpose is to serve him in his multifaceted role as President of the United States. Pierre Salinger, President Kennedy's press secretary, wrote:

> *President John F. Kennedy's personal staff was an unlikely mixture. We were Catholics, Protestants, and Jews. We came from the East, the Midwest, and the Far West, and from backgrounds of poverty and wealth. . . . What we had in common, however, was our salary, which*

President Carter's press secretary, Jody Powell, in a working session with the President.

was $21,000 a year, and our commitment to the President, which was total.[23]

The commitment of the White House staff is indeed total. They may speak to, but not for, outside interest groups. They are the President's spokespersons. Their interests are important, but *his* interests are paramount. Staff members engage in the entire range of activities for the President: gathering information, contacting (lobbying) Congressmembers, meeting the press, and soliciting informal advice from varied sources.

These people are loyal first and foremost to the President, but this does not guarantee smooth internal operation. Common commitment does not always mean agreement. You will recall the squabble between staff members in the energy case study. Likewise, the labor-reform study showed that the President received conflicting advice from his staff. This is to be expected, and in the sense that it allows the exchange of viewpoints, it can be constructive. Such internal bickering is harmful, though, when one camp seeks to discredit another in the eyes of the President[24] or so effectively isolates the President that he is unable to receive any other views. Overly ambitious staffs also present problems. Richard Pious writes:

In recent administrations staff members have become part of the problem rather than part of the solution. They make it more difficult for the president to institute a chain of command working in his interest, and they distort information up and down the executive hierarchy. They issue orders that may not be obeyed, make decisions that may not make sense, and "emit" enough public statements to bury an administration with hostile media coverage.[25]

Recognizing this potential problem, virtually every President promises to give wide latitude to the cabinet secretaries, not to be insulated from a range of views, and not to permit a small White House clique to run the government. Such intentions, however, are difficult to implement. "Unless you are very different from all your post–World War II predecessors," a former State Department official wrote in an open memorandum to newly inaugurated President Ronald Reagan, "your White House staff is going to end up being more important than your Cabinet. And within that staff, it is not likely that the policy group . . . will . . . hold its ground against the . . . decisions being made by [the] operational group. Operations tend to set a lot of policies in concrete."[26]

The Executive Office of the President. The Executive Office of the President (Figure 1, page 323) is more formalized than the White House staff. It is organized into several units developed along specific policy lines: Office of Management and Budget (OMB); Council of Economic Advisers (CEA); National Security Council (NSC); Office of Science and Technology Policy; Council of Environmental Quality; Office of the Special Representative for Trade Negotiations; and Intelligence Oversight Board.

Presidents may use these agencies in various ways; they exist to provide *him* with expert information and analyses. He may also abolish any of them. President Ford established a new unit called the Council on Wage and Price Stability to oversee "guidelines" set forth by the administration in its efforts to control inflation. Although President Carter continued to use it (staffed by his own people, of course), President Reagan (if you recall his first press conference) decided to eliminate the council, calling it "a failure" and "totally ineffective." Since these units are agencies of the presidency, there is no pressure to keep them if a particular President sees no value in them.

Each unit is usually run by a person (or committee) considered expert in the particular field. Although the units are equally important, some are more in the limelight than others. Probably the three most prominent ones are OMB, CEA, and NSC.

Office of Management and Budget. This unit was set up in 1970, succeeding the old Bureau of the Budget established in 1921. The director of the OMB is very influential because this agency actually prepares the final budget the President sends to Congress for enactment. In addition, the OMB must approve all departmental legislative proposals that call for spending money. It monitors the budgets of government programs, always admonishing agencies to try to cut expenditures and to be more efficient. If any division in the Executive Office would be considered the "nay-sayer," this would be it. The Senate must approve the President's appointment for OMB director.

The Council of Economic Advisers. The CEA was established in 1946 and consists of three professional economists who must be confirmed by the Senate. The President designates one as chairperson. It is their job to keep the President

"Refresh my memory. Who was Carter's Director of the Budget?"

Drawing by Lorenz; © 1981. The New Yorker Magazine, Inc.

abreast of economic trends and to interpret potential economic consequences of certain acts. The President's appointments usually signal the direction he wants his administration to take on economic matters. Are his appointments fiscal conservatives? Are they Keynesians, who believe in government spending? Do they tend to favor economic stimulus through job creation? The theories and opinions of these advisers are scrutinized carefully to anticipate the President's economic policies.

The National Security Council. The NSC was a result of the National Security Act of 1947. It is composed of the President, the vice-president, and the secretaries of state and defense. The President may invite others, who have the requisite security clearance, to attend the meetings. The closest person to the President on a day-to-day basis in security matters is the National Security Adviser (who may or may not serve as secretary to the NSC). His job is to advise the President daily on important matters of international and military concern, as well as to help the President with long-term policy questions. He briefs the Presi-

dent on the cables received overnight from American embassies and other sources around the world. He is a member of the Executive Office of the President and must be confirmed by the Senate.

Contrasting Styles of Organization and Operation

Presidents will use the White House staff and the Executive Office according to their own work styles and habits. Franklin D. Roosevelt encouraged his subordinates to disagree among themselves, leaving him the task of reaching a final decision. Dwight Eisenhower was the opposite. He wanted issues "staffed out" and a common consensus reached before the issues came to him for final judgment. According to Pierre Salinger, John F. Kennedy, like Roosevelt, did not mind arguments and disagreements among his staff:

> *The White House Staff* [under Kennedy] . . . *was not one big, happy family. Strong and even angry disagreements among us were common and certain staffers simply didn't like others personally. This didn't concern the President. "The last thing I want around here is a mutual admiration society," he told me one day after a hostile exchange between two staffers in his presence. "When you people stop arguing, I'll start worrying."* [27]

Sometimes, Presidents deliberately seek to appoint people who have varying, if not diametrically opposed points of view. Richard Nixon gave this account of his selection of two particular advisers:

> *Daniel Patrick Moynihan had one of the most innovative minds for domestic policy in the country. Like Kissinger, a Harvard professor, he had served as Assistant Secretary of Labor in the Kennedy and Johnson administrations. I had read several of his articles before the 1968 campaign, and I found his thinking refreshing and stimulating. Unlike so many liberal aca-*

FIGURE 1.
Executive Office of the President.

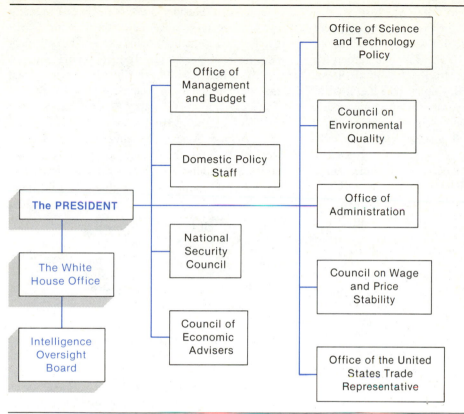

Source: *United States Government Manual, 1980–1981*, Office of the Federal Register, General Services Administration, p. 98.

demics, Moynihan was free of professional jargon and ideological cant. He had helped design the Great Society poverty programs, but he was not afraid to acknowledge that many of them had failed, and he was ready to apply the lessons learned from that failure to devising new programs that might work.

I met with Moynihan to explore his views and to sound him out about coming to the White House. Although he quickly made known his opposition to the Vietnam War, he was clearly interested by the opportunity. . . . I told Moynihan about my intention to establish an Urban

Affairs Council, describing it as the domestic policy equivalent of the National Security Council in foreign affairs. . . . Then I asked him if he would like to head it. He accepted. . . .

I created a new Cabinet-level position, Counselor to the President, for my old friend and adviser Arthur Burns. I thought that his conservatism would be a useful and creative counterweight to Moynihan's liberalism.[28]

Normally, the job of coordinating the vast staff and serving as a final funnel to the President falls to one person, the chief of staff. The title might vary, but the function seldom does. Sherman Adams served in this capacity for Eisenhower; Theodore Sorensen for Kennedy; Bill Moyers for Johnson; H. R. Haldeman for Nixon; Hamilton Jordan for Carter; and James Baker for Reagan. While Presidents might, at times, downplay such hierarchical structure in the White House, the "pecking order" is usually quickly established. Reporters, members of Congress, and interest groups quickly perceive (or think they do) who is "really close" to the President, and they treat this inner circle with respect and deference.

The Vice-Presidency: From Obscurity to Opportunity

Vice-President Hubert H. Humphrey, speaking to an audience about the importance of his job as vice-president, once jokingly remarked, "Oh you surely must remember those great, memorable vice-presidents—Daniel D. Tompkins, George M. Dallas, Hannibal Hamlin." Americans generally do not remember many vice-presidents, since many of the forty-three who have served in that office have not been very memorable.

However, this was not the intent of the constitutional framers. They devised a system whereby the person receiving the second highest number of votes for President would be the vice-president—a system that prevailed until the passage of the Twelfth Amendment in 1804. This amendment established a separate ballot for the vice-presidency. Consequently, the President and the vice-president began running as a team on the same party ticket. Men were nominated for the office of vice-president for political reasons, not because of their qualifications as a potential President. They were slated to balance the ticket geographically and/or ideologically, and sometimes to offset the presidential nominee's age (either too young or too old).

Some vice-presidents *are* remembered in history, but largely because they either became President or had distinguished careers before they became vice-president. The following ten, of which six held the office within the last thirty years may be familiar: John Adams, Thomas Jefferson, Theodore Roosevelt, Harry S. Truman, Richard M. Nixon, Lyndon B. Johnson, Hubert H. Humphrey, Spiro Agnew, Gerald Ford, and Nelson Rockefeller. Of these ten, seven subsequently became President, and the other three (Humphrey, Agnew, Rockefeller) were distinguished for other reasons.

It is difficult to have a distinguished career as a vice-president, even if one works at it! Constitutionally, the vice-president has only three duties other than that of succession: to preside over the Senate, where the vice-president does not engage in debate; to cast a vote there only in the case of a tie; and to participate in deciding, along with the cabinet, if the President is unable to continue to serve. The vice-president serves, by Congressional authority, on the Board of Regents of the Smithsonian Institution and on the National Security Council. Politically, the vice-president is only as active and involved as the President permits. Eisenhower gave Nixon a rather active political role. Ike did not relish hitting the campaign trail or engaging in partisan debates with Democrats, and he gave these assignments to Vice-President Nixon. Nixon also traveled to foreign countries as a goodwill ambassador, a duty that every vice-president since has performed rather frequently. The United States government did not provide an official residence for the vice-president until 1974.

Under Presidents Eisenhower and Carter, the vice-president was an active figure, if not a powerful one. Vice-president Walter Mondale did his share of touring and speaking, but Carter also included him in many foreign- and domestic-policy sessions and decisions.

On December 6, 1973, Congressman Gerald R. Ford was sworn in as the fortieth vice-president of the United States. Less than a year later, Ford succeeded Richard Nixon as President.

Spiro Agnew was the second vice-president to resign the office, and the only one to do so under a cloud of criminal prosecution. He was accused of taking kickbacks from engineers who received state-highway contracts while he was governor of Maryland. This was revealed after he had served one full term as vice-president and had been reelected in 1972. An investigation by federal authorities revealed other possible charges of extortion, bribery, and income-tax evasion. He resigned the office of vice-president in 1973 and was later convicted of income-tax evasion (after entering a *no-contest* plea), fined $10,000, and placed on three years' probation. The only other vice-president to resign was John C. Calhoun, in 1832, to become a United States senator.

The obscurity of the vice-presidency seems to be giving way to political opportunity. Since a President can only serve two terms (according to the Twenty-second Amendment), a vice-president who has served actively during that time and who is not otherwise politically handicapped (by age, for instance) is a strong possibility for the party's next presidential nomination. Although this is by no means automatic, the vice-presidency has more and more been viewed as a grooming place for the number-one slot. Thus, what was once a political dead end has become a position with enormous potential for advancement. In a sense, it is as close as one can come to on-the-job training for the office of President. Obscurity fades, opportunity knocks.

How number two becomes number one: succession. There have been nine vice-presidents since World War II, and four of those have become President: two (Truman and Johnson) assumed office because of the President's death; one (Nixon) was elected eight years after his vice-presidential term; and one (Ford) took over after the President's resignation. Especially since Eisenhower's heart attack while in office in 1955 and Kennedy's assassination in 1963, Americans have given much more consideration to the office of the vice-president, to the quality of the vice-presidential nominee, and to the succession mechanism.

This does not mean that designation of a vice-presidential candidate no longer hinges on "ticket balancing," but simply that the designee is observed by voters for "presidential qualities."

In 1967, the Twenty-fifth Amendment was added to the Constitution. This amendment spells out the circumstances whereby the vice-president can serve as *Acting President*. If the elected President informs Congress that he is "unable to discharge the powers and duties of his office," the vice-president assumes the role of Acting President until the President notifies the Congress otherwise. If the President is unable to or will not take such an initiative, the vice-president and a majority of the cabinet may inform Congress that, in their judgment, the President is disabled. Again, the vice-president becomes Acting President. If the President disagrees, the matter is settled by Congress. Two-thirds of both houses of Congress must agree with the decision of the vice-president and the cabinet before the President is displaced.

If a vacancy occurs in the vice-presidency, the President, under the Twenty-fifth Amendment, can nominate a person who must then be confirmed by a majority vote of both houses of Congress. Two vice-presidents (Gerald Ford, nominated by Richard Nixon, and Nelson Rockefeller, by Gerald Ford) have been chosen by this method. Interestingly, it is not mandatory that the office be filled once a vacancy occurs. In fact, prior to Agnew's resignation, the office had been vacant sixteen times for a total of thirty-seven years.[29]

The Presidency and Operational Realities

If we were to draw a political cartoon of the presidency, we might depict the White House as a pressure cooker with the steam coming out and the lid on the verge of blowing off. Sometimes the lid blows; most times the cooker settles down, only to steam up again a bit later. We suspect President Truman had a similar metaphor in mind when he said about the job: "If you can't stand the heat, get out of the kitchen."

H. R. Haldeman served as President Nixon's chief of staff in the White House from 1969 until 1973, when he was forced to resign. Eventually, his involvement in the Watergate scandal and other criminal events connected with his White House job led him to jail. He describes the pressure-cooker atmosphere thus:

In trying to understand Watergate, it is essential to understand a very basic truth about the White House. By definition almost, only crises come to the White House. Only those things that cannot be handled at a lower level even reach the White House. The President and his staff deal not with both high and low matters, but with high and higher, and sometimes highest.[30]

Expansion of presidential functions. The United States has grown to be a vast, industrial nation with economic, political, and military commitments throughout the world. Government is intricately involved in the daily lives of hundreds of millions of people here and abroad. The kitchen heat is inevitable and intense. With this has come the change and expansion of presidential activities.

As we have discussed, presidents have the constitutional power to **veto** bills passed by Congress. Prior to Andrew Jackson's presidency, this power was used only when the President felt the bill was unconstitutional—that is, when he felt the proposed bill encroached on the constitutional powers assigned to the judicial or executive branches of government. Today, however, presidents veto bills because they disagree with the policies they contain. A President might veto a bill on the grounds that it is "inflationary," that it will lead to more government spending than he feels proper to maintain a sound economy. Of course, Congress can override a veto by a two-thirds vote of each house, but this is seldom done. Eisenhower, for example, vetoed 181 bills, but only 2 were overridden. Nixon vetoed 43, and only 6 were overridden. In his brief two years in office, Ford vetoed 66 bills, and only 12 were overridden.

The President does not have the power of **item veto**, that is, the power to sign into law only certain portions of a bill, leaving out objectionable portions. Instead, he must accept all or nothing.

Although the Constitution says the President "shall take care that the laws be faithfully execut-

ed," some Presidents, most notably in recent years Richard Nixon, have refused to spend money appropriated by Congress for certain projects. This is known as **impoundment**, and, needless to say, it infuriates some members of Congress. In effect, when the President impounds funds, he is telling Congress that he does not feel the project is necessary. Sometimes such an act might be justified, such as if the original reason for appropriating the money no longer exists, or if a better, more efficient way to carry out the project has been found. But Nixon increasingly used impoundment (to the tune of approximately $18 billion) because he had *policy* disagreements with the purpose for which the money was to be used. This is indeed a powerful mechanism. If allowed to stand unchecked in any way, it would give enormous powers to the President. With the addition of this power, the President is involved in the entire lawmaking process, all the way from the beginning (as legislative initiator), through approval (by the possible use of a veto), and if overridden, to the final stage of implementation (by blocking implementation through impoundment). We will see in a few minutes what Congress has tried to do about this.

The President's functions and powers have increased vastly in the realm of foreign affairs in his capacity as commander-in-chief and chief diplomat. As a permanent world power, the United States is continually involved around the globe. The President must lead the nation in hot wars and cold wars. Although Congress is the only body constitutionally authorized to declare war, the President, as commander-in-chief, is empowered to direct the military forces, which can result in actual—albeit undeclared—war. This was the case in Korea and Vietnam. Justification for such military involvement includes the following: the security of the nation requires prompt action; nuclear weaponry means that the country cannot afford to delay one minute; some information calling for military decisions might be based on highly sensitive and classified intelligence that should not be made public. Thus, the power of instant and almost total human destruction rests at the President's fingertips. If any single factor has contributed to this situation, it is the development of the military capability in this country and in a few other major powers to launch instant war and to inflict massive damage and destruction in a matter of minutes. Earlier Presidents were not sitting on top of that pressure cooker!

Constant focus of the media. ''Unlike other politicians, a President's biggest problem is not that of getting into the newspapers, but of staying out of them when he conceives it to be in his interest to do so.''[31]

This is the conclusion of two political scientists who have studied the symbiotic relationship between the President and the media. Professors Michael B. Grossman and Francis E. Rourke state that the media want news and the President wants publicity of a favorable kind. They attempt to satisfy their respective needs through a trading process. The President starts out ahead because of the obviously great interest of the public in the activities of his office. The press follows the President everywhere and reports on virtually everything he does and everything that happens to him. To illustrate, in one of his press conferences, President Kennedy appeared with a bandage over his left eye. At the end of the conference—before the traditional ''Thank you, Mr. President''—one reporter said, ''Mr. President, it would save us a lot of time and badgering of your press secretary, if you would just tell us, sir, about that Bandaid over your eye.'' Everyone laughed, because they knew the reporter was right: they *would* check up on the bandage. The President obliged. He had

banged his head on a desk corner when he reached down to pick up his young son's toy.

The President has great resources for controlling what gets into the press about his activities. He determines when to hold press conferences, how they will be conducted, and which information will be withheld for security purposes. The concept of the press conference began with Woodrow Wilson, but its character has changed over time. They have not always been the wide-ranging, unrehearsed press conferences we know today. In fact, some Presidents (Harding, Coolidge, Hoover) selected their questions from a group that was submitted by the press ahead of time. Eisenhower initiated the filmed press conference, but it was edited before it was released. Kennedy was the first President to hold live television press conferences, and every President since has followed that practice, combining it with other means of addressing the public, such as the highly prized exclusive interview. ''His aides determine how the daily press briefings will be conducted, which reporters get to go on presidential trips, and the rules governing those conferences known as 'backgrounders,' where reporters are not permitted direct quotations or allowed to attribute remarks to their sources.''[32] The President has a large public-relations staff. The office of the White House press secretary, which is part of the White House staff, employs approximately fifty people on a budget of roughly $1.7 million a year.[33]

The press tries to even out the imbalance in its relationship with the President by cultivating official sources beyond the President's immediate office. These executive officials may have their own personal reasons for serving as sources for news stories, although most times they will not permit the reporter to name them publicly. They are the ''high administration'' officials and ''informed'' sources that we hear from so often, and

Jimmy Carter receives members of the press in his home town of Plains, Georgia.

they form an essential part of the President-press relationship. In addition, as the media become more authoritative on particular subjects, they are less easily "manipulated" or, if that is too strong a word, they have greater ability to know what questions to ask and have a greater sense of what sounds like a reasonable answer.

Research has demonstrated that consistently throughout the past century, from 1885 to 1977, the President has received far more press coverage than the Congress in some newspapers.[34] From 1958 to 1977, of all front-page news about the national government reported in two selected newspapers, the portion devoted to the President went from 61.9 percent to 73.1 percent. The portion devoted to Congressional news during the same period declined from 33 percent to 17.8 percent. Thus, although Congress stays in session almost all year, the President dominates the news coming out of Washington, D.C.

The media and the President do need each other. Their relationship at best is one of respectful cooperation. At worst, it could be, and at times has been, one of distrust and confrontation.

Power to insist versus necessity to persuade.
With the constitutional and political powers of the President plus his recognized advantage in press coverage, we nonetheless find the President of the United States not entirely capable of—and in some instances, clearly *incapable* of—having his own way. In spite of the vast machinery of government at his personal disposal and the enormous respect paid to the office and its occupant, we find that what outgoing President Truman said about incoming President Eisenhower and what Richard Neustadt said about presidential power still to be relevant. Almost thirty years ago, Truman said: "He'll sit right here, and he'll say do this, do that. And nothing will happen. Poor Ike—it won't be a bit like the Army. He'll find it very frustrating."[35] And over twenty years ago, Neustadt said:

The essence of a President's persuasive task with congressmen and everybody else, is to induce them to believe that what he wants of them is what their own appraisal of their own responsibilities requires them to do in their interest, not his.[36]

Certainly a President can generally expect his subordinates to obey his orders. (We will see in the next chapter, however, that even this cannot be taken for granted.) But when it comes to dealing with Congress, independent agencies, and interest groups, things are clearly different. To be sure, the President can virtually take the country into war; he can veto bills, impound funds, enter into executive agreements, and issue executive orders. But his leadership ultimately depends on his ability

Ronald Reagan telephones Congressional leaders in an effort to gain support for his economic program in Congress. Calls such as these are often crucial to the success or failure of an administration's legislative proposals.

to work effectively *with* Congress, not over or around it. He has to be able to bargain and compromise; and sometimes the *threat* of the veto is more important and effective than the actual *use* of the veto. In fact, sometimes presidential acts such as the veto or impoundment signal that his political prestige is at a low point; that he has needed to resort to "negatives" of political leadership; that he has failed to persuade.

The Office of Congressional Relations (OCR), part of the White House staff, was first established in 1953 under Eisenhower to help the executive departments establish better relations with Congress. When Kennedy became President, the OCR became a significant office. It became the President's main lobbyist on Capital Hill, keeping track of bills the administration was especially interested in, providing information to legislators and others in an effort to help them argue on the administration's behalf, and above all keeping as accurate a headcount as possible on the probable votes on each amendment and bill at each stage of the complex legislative process. This important work of the OCR has been accurately described by Professor John F. Manley.[37] Its staff of approximately thirty-five must be sensitive to absolutely every detail that could lead to victory or defeat for the President's programs. But even when favors are given (such as a patronage appointment); when the legislative process is watched closely and votes are carefully monitored; when pressure is brought on reluctant legislators by influential interest groups at the urging of the OCR; when the President makes the *right* telephone calls at the *right* times—the President still might not end up with a .500 batting average.

Nonetheless, there is no substitute for the political persuasion process. As Professor Manley has noted:

In [President] *Kennedy's first year alone he held 32 Tuesday morning breakfasts with the* [Congressional] *leadership, 90 private conversations with congressional leaders that lasted an hour or two, coffee hours with 500 legislators, bill-signing ceremonies with a like number, and, in all, had about 2,500 separate contacts with congressmen, exclusive of correspondence.*[38]

We can now understand President Carter's lament to the pages to whom he spoke at the commencement in the Rose Garden. He said he wished he had as much knowledge of Congress as they had gained. He was probably only half kidding!

Imperial Presidency Versus Contentious Congress?

As we noted, the President periodically sends messages to Congress, stating his views on specific matters, and he frequently gets messages in return. Note one such exchange that took place in June 1978, and the differences that can develop between the two branches of the government.

"It is my view, and that of the Attorney General, that these legislative veto provisions are unconstitutional," Mr. Carter said in a message to Congress.

The President discussed the message at a breakfast with Democratic Congressional leaders and received a mixed response.

Representative Jim Wright, Democrat of Texas, the House Majority Leader, said that he "respectfully disagreed."[39]

During the Eisenhower and Kennedy administrations, it was felt that Congress was impeding the President too much. In contrast, during the presidencies of Johnson and Nixon, we heard a great deal about the "imperial presidency"—in the wake of the Vietnam War, the impoundment of funds by Nixon, and the frightening experiences of Watergate. Are we beginning to see the reassertion of Congressional power now? Are we returning to the days when Congress will be more contentious in its relations with the President? The modern history of the relationship between these two branches of government has been one of political struggle for an advantageous position.

Legislative vetoes. We noted earlier that the Constitution gives the President the right to veto bills passed by Congress, and Congress can override these vetos with a two-thirds vote in both houses. Another device used by Congress to check executive and administrative action is the **legislative veto**, which has been used more than a hundred times since its inception in 1932. There are two types of legislative veto. One, the **rescission process**, states that before a rule, regulation, or action can go into effect, it must be specifically approved by one or both houses of Congress within a stipulated period of time (for example, thirty days, two months). The other type is known as the **deferral process**, meaning an action or rule becomes effective unless Congress takes action against it.

Understandably, Presidents have argued with Congress over the scope of this power. Some, such as Mr. Carter, have said that the legislative veto is unconstitutional because it impinges on the President's executive powers. Congress has argued that, in many cases, it is really an extension of the legislative process, allowing Congress simply to oversee the administration of the laws it enacts.

Dr. Louis Fisher has examined this controversy. He writes:

The Senate Foreign Relations Committee conceded in 1976 that the legislative veto could not be used to invade areas of "plenary presidential prerogative, such as the pardon power (article 2, section 2, clause 1) or the recognition power (article 2, section 3). It could not be employed to oversee the finest details of the day-to-day administration of the federal government."[40]

Fisher divides legislative vetoes into three categories: those in which the President or administrative agency is delegated authority; those in which the veto is used in areas "not exclusively legislative in nature"; and those in which there is serious constitutional question over the validity of the legislative veto. Frequently, a President will accept the restraint of a legislative veto because it is politically necessary in order to achieve other goals. "The Nixon Administration readily accepted a one-house veto as part of the price of obtaining new impoundment authority in 1974. Presidents may now report to Congress on 'deferrals' [delays in the spending of funds], subject to disapproval by either house. No constitutional complaint has emerged from the White House. Presidents who want authority delegated to them have to take the conditions that are attached."[41]

In December 1980, a federal appeals court in San Francisco ruled that a provision permitting the House of Representatives to veto decisions of the Immigration and Naturalization Service violated the separation-of-powers doctrine of the Constitution.[42] Although it was not a definitive ruling by the highest court—the U.S. Supreme Court—it was clearly a victory for the executive branch.

The Budget and Impoundment Control Act. In the early 1970s, Congress was sufficiently aroused by President Nixon's impoundment practices to take action. In 1974, the Budget and Impoundment Control Act was passed. For some time, it had been recognized that Congress was at a distinct disadvantage when it came to mastering the complexities of the President's proposed budget. The President has a permanent, professional Office of Management and Budget (OMB) to stay on top of budgetary matters. The 1974 act sought to give Congress greater resources in dealing with the budget. It also restricted the President's ability to impound funds. Under the provisions of the Act, a presidential decision to impound funds permanently is not valid unless both houses of Congress concur within forty-five days. If the President decides not to spend appropriated funds *temporarily*, the action stands unless either house of Congress passes a resolution requiring him to spend the money. Thus, we see the legislative veto being used to counter presidential impoundment—rescission in the first case; deferral in the second.

War Powers Act. In 1973, in the highly charged atmosphere of the widespread displeasure over the Vietnam War, Congress passed the War Powers Act, despite President Nixon's veto. Its purpose was to limit the President's power to commit military forces to combat without Congressional consent. As we have seen, only Congress can officially declare war, but armed forces can be sent into action—fighting and dying—without any official declaration of war. Therefore, to curb this aspect of the "imperial presidency," Congress decided that in times of emergencies, the President may act militarily subject to the following conditions: (1) he must report to Congress within forty-eight hours any commitment of U.S. combat forces abroad; (2) he must terminate the commitment within sixty days *unless* Congress declares war or specifically permits the action to continue; (3) thirty additional days may be allowed if necessary to safely withdraw American forces; and (4) if these conditions are not met, the Congress by concurrent resolution can direct the President to withdraw the troops.

Louis Koenig believes that this will not necessarily curtail the President's powers. It is conceivable, he suggests, that the law has even *increased* the President's powers "to extremes that even the most bellicose Presidents would never dream of. For the War Powers Act can be read as a blank-check empowerment of the chief executive to fight anywhere, for whatever cause, subject only to a sixty-to-ninety-day time limit, indefinitely renewable."[43]

The politics of appointment: checks and balances. The President is constitutionally empowered to fill a number of very important positions "on the advice and consent of the Senate." Perhaps the most important of these are the United States Supreme Court appointments. The President usually—but not always—gets his way here: since 1789, only 26 out of 136 nominees have been rejected by the Senate.[44] The most notable recent examples of rejections occurred within a five-month period in 1969–70, when the Senate turned down two successive Nixon nominees to the Supreme Court—Clement F. Haynsworth and G. Harrold Carswell. Nixon was furious in his defeat. He blamed the Senate rejections on politics and ideological differences—not, as some people felt, on the questionable activities and mediocre qualifications of the nominees. Nixon wrote:

I have reluctantly concluded that—with the Senate as presently constituted—I cannot successfully nominate to the Supreme Court any federal appellate judge from the South who believes as I do in the strict construction of the Constitution. . . . When all the hypocrisy is stripped away, the real issue was their philosophy of strict construction of the Constitution—a philosophy that I share.[45]

Presidential appointments, although not usually rejected, are nonetheless not accepted *pro forma*.

In 1981, Sandra O'Connor, an Arizona appeals court judge, became the first woman to be nominated for a seat on the U.S. Supreme Court.

Usually, the Senate carefully examines the nominee's qualifications (professional and personal) and ideology. President Carter was rebuffed when his first nominee to head the CIA, Theodore Sorensen, was forced to withdraw; although a Senate vote was never taken, the White House was told that there was not enough support for Sorensen in the Senate. Of course, a President can choose to stick it out and fight for his nominees, but he must calculate how much any particular appointment is worth politically and otherwise. If the President loses the Senate endorsement of his nominee, his political prestige suffers.

This confirmation process is one aspect of the check-and-balance system. It is embedded in the Constitution and in custom. One example of the latter is **senatorial courtesy**. When an appoint-

ment for a federal position in a state is to be made, the senator from that state will be given the option either to approve the nominee beforehand or perhaps even to suggest a name. This courtesy may also be extended to presidential appointments, even those that do not require formal Senate approval, and even if the position to be filled is not in the senator's state; a potential nominee who is simply a resident of the senator's state might be cleared with the senator. The political motivation for these arrangements is simple: the White House would naturally prefer to avoid, if possible, naming someone who might be "politically embarrassing" to a senator who might take offense and who later might be unwilling to provide a marginal vote on an important presidential bill. These arrangements are not usually explicit; they are simply understood as part of the politics of the appointive process.

The Presidency in the 1980s: Balancing Action and Accountability

In the coming years, the United States will continue to be a major world power, and the President will be its leader in international affairs: meeting and negotiationg, visiting and receiving heads of state, protecting the security of the nation, and projecting the country's image abroad. In addition, Congress and the nation will continue to look to the President's initiatives in handling economic and social problems at home. The near future calls for an active President. If there are crises—military or otherwise—the presidency will be accorded even wider leeway for action.

It is difficult to ignore the fact that Americans want both a strong, active President as well as one not possessed of too much power. There will continue to be a concern that the President not overstep his bounds, but, as we have seen, those boundaries are not fixed. They shift with political circumstances.

There are always the formal, constitutional, legal means to hold a potentially "imperial President" in check. Under certain circumstances, he can be impeached (see chapter 11); his veto can be overridden; his appointments can be rejected; and legislative vetoes can be used. Above all, the President is limited to two terms. These are all ways to impose some degree of accountability on him, and they can be effective.

Ultimately, the most important form of accountability is political. A first-term President will not necessarily be reelected, which means the opposition will be waiting to seize on his mistakes and weaknesses. Public opinion can be a major factor. We saw this illustrated in the case study on the proposed labor-reform legislation:

> *At the time of the vote . . . the President's influence and prestige were at a low ebb, despite his victory on the Panama Canal vote. His ratings in the polls were declining, and the perception on Capitol Hill and elsewhere in Washington, which is always finely tuned on questions of political power, was that Mr. Carter's political influence was diminishing. Accordingly, his ability to influence the actions of Congress was less substantial than usual for a sitting President.*

And the probing media will always be there to ask questions and to reveal the President's strengths and weaknesses.

American Presidents do, indeed, have substantial constitutional, statutory, and political power. But they cannot rely on that power alone. They must seek to build support—a working consensus —for their programs. The labor-reform case study is a good example of the relationship between power and consensus, and it demonstrates the difficulties, at times, in achieving success.

At least for the next decade, the diverse interests (Congress, opposition party, media, pressure groups) with which a President must contend will probably serve to impose quite sufficient accountability on the office. Sufficient, that is, to guard against executive tyranny. But these groups must be willing to provide sufficient latitude for effective leadership. That balancing process is an important part of the 200-year-old American government story. The political system does not *solve* the matter; it merely provides a framework within which the ongoing process is conducted.

Summary

1. The Constitution uses broad language to define the powers a President can exercise. Thus, depending on the particular President, Congress, the courts, and circumstances, presidential powers may expand or contract.

2. The constitutional functions a President must perform require him to possess a wide range of knowledge and expertise. In addition, as a political figure, the President must lead his political party and initiate and implement legislation.

3. Over the last forty years, presidential staffs have grown from a handful of people to close to 1700 employees.

4. As the central focus of national and international leadership, the President must combine his constitutional powers with his political capacities to persuade others to follow his lead. In so doing, he must constantly strive to achieve a "working consensus" which will permit him the widest possible latitude within which to operate.

5. There are specific constitutional, statutory, and political constraints on the presidency, and these operate at times to check the potential growth of an "imperial presidency" and to hold the President accountable for what he does.

Notes

1. "How Reagan Plans to Govern," *Newsweek* (November 17, 1980), p. 34.
2. "Pages" are high-school students between the ages of fourteen and eighteen who serve as messengers and errand runners for legislators on the floor of Congress. There are approximately fifty-one of them, and each must be sponsored by a member of the House or Senate. Several former pages have gone on to become congressmen, and one—Lyndon B. Johnson—became President.
3. *New York Times*, June 13, 1978. p. D17.
4. Gene W. Boyette, "Developing the Concept of the Republican Presidency, 1787–1788," *Presidential Studies Quarterly*, Vol. 7, No. 4 (Fall 1977), 200.
5. Ibid., 200.
6. Ibid., 204.
7. Richard M. Pious, *The American Presidency* (New York: Basic Books, Inc., 1979), p. 16.
8. *New York Times*, October 29, 1980, p. A27.
9. Theodore Roosevelt, *Theodore Roosevelt: An Autobiography* (New York: Crowell-Collier and Macmillan, Inc., 1913), p. 389.
10. William Howard Taft, *Our Chief Magistrate and His Powers* (New York: Columbia University Press, 1916), p. 139.
11. Arthur M. Schlesinger, Jr., *The Crisis of the Old Order* (Boston: Houghton Mifflin Co., 1957), p. 482.
12. As quoted in Schlesinger, p. 482.
13. *United States* v. *Nixon*, 417 U.S. 683 (1974).
14. David Frost, *"I Gave Them a Sword," Behind the Scenes of the Nixon Interviews* (New York: William Morrow & Co., Inc., 1978), pp. 183–85.
15. James David Barber, *The Presidential Character: Predicting Performance in the White House* (Englewood Cliffs, N.J.: Prentice-Hall, Inc., 1977), p. 7.
16. *Ibid.*, p. 13.
17. This press conference was held January 29, 1981. All quotations are from *New York Times*, January 30, 1981, p. A10.
18. *New York Times*, January 25, 1981, p. 16.
19. *Ibid*.
20. After George Washington and John Adams, most Presidents sent written messages to Congress. Woodrow Wilson reinstituted the personal appearance, and that practice has become established. The President formally addresses both houses of Congress in early January of each year in his State of the Union address.
21. Stephen J. Wayne, *The Legislative Presidency* (New York: Harper & Row, 1978), pp. 22–23.
22. Louis W. Koenig, *The Chief Executive* (New York: Harcourt, Brace & World, Inc., 1975), p. 163.
23. Pierre Salinger, *With Kennedy* (Garden City, New York: Doubleday & Company, Inc., 1966), p. 63. Salaries have more than doubled since the early 1960s. In fact, the salaries of most White House staff members are in the range of the mid-to-high $50,000 bracket.
24. Robert T. Hartmann, *Palace Politics, An Inside Account of the Ford Years* (New York: McGraw–Hill Book Company, 1980), p. 395.
25. Pious, p. 247.
26. Leslie H. Gelb, "Memorandum to the President, Some Counsel for the New Man in the Oval Office from an Old Washington Hand," *The New York Times Magazine*, January 18, 1981.
27. Salinger, p. 64.
28. Richard M. Nixon, *RN, The Memoirs of Richard Nixon* (New York: Grosset & Dunlap, 1978), pp. 341–42.
29. Hartmann, p. 10.
30. H. R. Haldeman, *The Ends of Power* (New York: Times Books, 1978), p. xiv.
31. Michael Baruck Grossman and Francis E. Rourke, "The Media and the Presidency: An Exchange Analysis," *Political Science Quarterly*, Vol. 91, No. 3 (Fall 1976), 458.
32. Ibid., 466.
33. Alan P. Balutis, "The Presidency and the Press: The Expanding Presidential Image," *Presidential Studies Quarterly*, Vol. 7, No. 4 (Fall 1977), 244–50.
34. These findings are based on two newspapers, The *New York Times*, considered a national newspaper, and the *Buffalo Evening News*, a more local or regional paper. Both are in New York State. It would be interesting to know if these findings prevail in other sections of the country.
35. Margaret Truman, *Harry S. Truman* (New York: William R. Morrow & Company, 1973), pp. 551–52.
36. Richard Neustadt, *Presidential Power* (New York: John Wiley & Sons, Inc., 1960), p. 46.

37. John F. Manley, ''Presidential Power and White House Lobbying,'' *Political Science Quarterly*, Vol. 93, No. 2 (Summer 1978), 255–75.
38. Ibid., 270.
39. *New York Times*, June 24, 1978.
40. Louis Fisher, ''A Political Context for Legislative Vetoes,'' *Political Science Quarterly*, Vol. 93, No. 2 (Summer 1978), 245.
41. Ibid.
42. *Chadha* v. *Immigration and Naturalization Service*, No. 77–1702, U.S. Court of Appeals for the Ninth Circuit (1980).
43. Koenig, p. 220.
44. Henry J. Abraham, *Justices and Presidents* (New York: Oxford University Press, 1974), p. 8.
45. Quoted in Abraham, p. 8.

The
Executive
Bureaucracy

Chapter

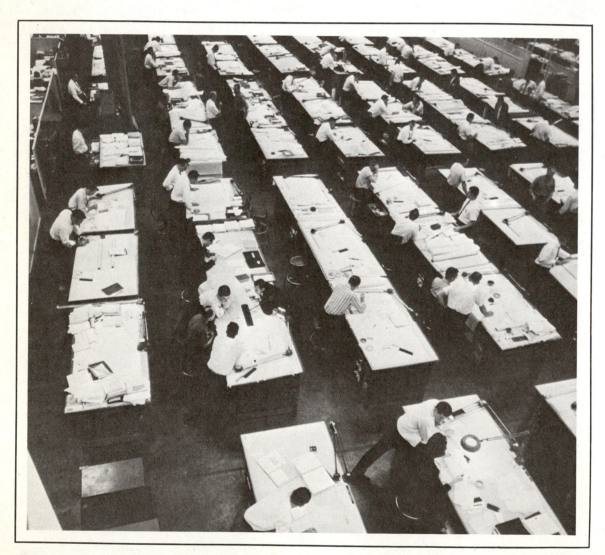

Senator Ernest F. Hollings (D., South Carolina) leaned across his desk during a hearing of the Senate Appropriations Committee a few years ago and said in amazement: "My God, we are over one million." Some of his fellow members on the committee were equally astonished. "You mean, paid out of federal funds?" Senator Thomas F. Eagleton (D., Missouri) asked the witness before the committee. The chairperson stared at the witness rather unbelievingly and pronounced: "This is the best public service job program I have ever heard of."

The witness was then-Secretary of Health, Education, and Welfare (a department that was renamed Health and Human Services when the new Department of Education was created in 1979), Joseph A. Califano. He had just reported to the Senate Committee in July 1978 that not only were there 144,256 regular HEW employees, but the department was paying the salaries of 980,217 others who worked for organizations—public and private—receiving numerous grants and contracts from HEW.[1]

If the one-million figure was a surprise to the senators, then there is no predicting what their reaction would have been had they learned that the total federal payroll at that time had reached between six and seven million people.

Who are all these people? What do they do? How much power do they have?

"Those Bureaucrats in Washington. . . ."

There are close to 2.8 million people employed directly as federal government employees (not including uniformed military personnel). Approximately 300,000 of these work in and around Washington, D.C. The remainder work throughout the country and overseas in regional and branch offices. The vast majority of these people are *civil servants*. They handle the day-to-day business of the federal government: they do the typing, see that social security checks are mailed out, make reports on governmental programs, administer programs authorized by Congress and the President, answer questions from citizens, collect our taxes, deliver our mail, and so on.

The total figure of between six and seven million includes the many people who work for private companies, state and local governments, educational and research organizations, and other institutions which receive federal government money to perform research and produce goods and services for the government. For example, the Department of Defense has 1,000,000 civilian employees directly on the payroll, but an estimated 2,050,000 more receive salaries as a result of DOD research and service contracts. The newspapers constantly report such items as the following:

International Business Machines Corp. received a $119.3 million Navy contract for sonar equipment.[2]

Hess Oil Virgin Islands Corp., a unit of Amerada Hess Oil Co., won a $48.2 million Defense Logistics Agency contract for fuel oil.[3]

AM General Corp., a unit of American Motors Corp., received a $32.7 million Army contract for trucks.[4]

In Norwalk, Conn., the Norden Systems unit of United Technologies Corp., said it won an Air Force contract to modify the radar system for the B52 bomber models G and H. The company said the value of "this program to us is expected to exceed $40 million."[5]

These contracts employ many people in private industry, but those employees are not considered "bureaucrats." When most people use that term, they refer to the employees back in Washington, D. C., who work at government desks and manage the government's business. Those are the ones we hear so many complaints about when we hear references to "red tape," "inefficiency," "impersonality," and so forth.

The complaints are numerous and continuous. "Those bureaucrats in Washington . . ." is a common refrain in American political discussion. It refers to a general view that the bureaucracy is too large, too complex, too insensitive to individual needs, too inflexible—and therefore inefficient. Bureaucrats are fair game for political satirists and cartoonists; you will rarely see a cartoon that depicts a bureaucrat in any but a derogatory or derisive way.

Politicians running for office frequently campaign on the issue of cutting down the size of the bureaucracy or the "red tape" or both. According to the candidates (from either major party), there is always more waste and "fat" in the bureaucracy that can be cut out—and that their opponents obviously did not, cannot, or will not cut. You will recall from the previous chapter's account of President Reagan's press conference the President's statement: "Within moments of taking the oath of office, I placed a freeze on the hiring of civilian employees in the federal government. Two days later I issued an order to cut down on government travel, reduced the number of consultants to the government, stopped the procurement of certain items, and called on my appointees to exercise restraint in their own offices."

There certainly is some truth to the various charges of waste and inefficiency. But it is impor-

tant to keep in mind that bureaucracies have grown over the last several decades because governmental activities have expanded—due in part to international military (defense) growth as well as to citizen demands for new public programs (farm subsidies, veterans' benefits, social services). When governmental activities were on a smaller scale, the size of the government work force was also smaller. A couple hundred employees (mostly clerks) could handle the government's business under Jefferson's administration. Today that would account for less than one half of the White House staff alone.

Of course, there will always be arguments about whether such a large work force is really necessary. Much depends on an assessment of which governmental activities should be cut, and vested interest groups will heartily disagree on this point. Should the cuts come in the Department of Defense or Commerce or Interior or Health and Human Services or Housing and Urban Development or Agriculture or where? Answers will invariably depend more on politics and policies than on an objective assessment of personnel and productivity studies. Cutting out 500 employees from the

Department of Agriculture might mean doing away with a particular farm subsidy program, and the American Farm Bureau might not like that. Instead, the farmers might suggest that cuts could best be made over in the Department of Housing and Urban Development, and of course some big city mayors might resist that.

Likewise, there is some truth to the charge of impersonality and complexity and bureaucratic inflexibility. Almost anyone who has had any dealings with government will be able to relate a story or two of bureaucratic rigidity. The rules and regulations are numerous; the forms to be filled out are unending and always seem to be in triplicate or more.

Even this "red tape" has some rationale behind it. Formal rules and regulations help guard against arbitrary enforcement. They are intended to systematize, to regularize, to make sure that one citizen is not given undue preference over another. In addition, in any very large operation—like the federal government—it is easier to keep tabs on things if procedures are specifically (albeit tediously) set out. This helps guard against administrators making up rules as they go along, which could

The profusion of unnecessary forms, as suggested by this photo of an IRS office, is often cited as one cause of inefficiency in the government bureaucracy.

lead to frustration and chaos in the system, as well as to charges of discriminatory treatment.

The following episode, reported in the *New York Times*, illustrates the kind of thing formal rules and regulations are intended to remedy:

One usually assumes that certain policies leave little or no room for discretion on the part of employees at the lower end of the organizational hierarchy. However, a classmate of mine had an experience which obviously tests this assumption.

She parked her car on Riverside Drive to attend a class at Columbia University which met from 9 to 10:50 a.m. When the class was over, she dashed out to move her car, which was in a spot that was illegal after 11 a.m. To her amazement, she found a city employee with a tow truck preparing to tow her car away.

She yelled: "What are you doing? It's not 11 yet."

The man replied very calmly, "Well, I have to move this whole line of cars today, so I thought I'd better get an early start." [6]

Who said bureaucrats are inefficient and nonproductive!

Bureaucratic waste and inefficiency is sometimes caught and remedied by the bureaucrats themselves, but often not. For example, the Department of Health, Education, and Welfare was once about to launch a study of the government's liability for injuries arising out of the swine flu vaccination program. At the same time, the Department of Interior was getting ready to spend money on a study dealing with the government's liability for injuries received on playground equipment owned by the federal government. A bureaucrat then happened to come across seven volumes of a study on government liability just published by the Department of Commerce. One reporter noted that "at least a dozen such repetitive studies by other agencies and legislative offices on virtually the same subject were not stopped because the people working on them had little or no knowledge that the others existed."[7] One way to try to cure such duplication of effort would be to create an interagency council that would coordinate these activities. Even this could be slow and cumbersome, but many observers suggest that it might be better than the situation whereby one department is totally unaware of what another is doing *in the same area.* One law professor called in by the Department of Commerce to help deal with this problem said: "What we see here are several independent efforts aimed at rebuilding the wheel."[8]

The Managers of Government Business

The Constitution simply says that the President "may require the opinion, in writing, of the principal officer in each of the executive departments, upon any subject relating to the duties of their respective offices." The framers suspected that the President would need a handful of top

people to head the few departments (in the early days there were only three: State, Treasury, and War) and to give advice from time to time. (In addition, an attorney general was appointed to serve as chief legal officer of the government.) The department heads were seen as performing largely managerial functions, although the first secretary of the treasury, Alexander Hamilton, was certainly a policy advocate.

Today, when one speaks of the federal executive bureaucracy, one is referring not only to the thirteen cabinet departments, but to the executive agencies, regulatory commissions, and government corporations that number almost sixty. We will look at the regulatory commissions more closely in chapter 10.

TABLE 1.
Cabinet Secretaries and Assistants to President Reagan.

Position	Name	Age	Background	
State	**Alexander Haig** (Pennsylvania)	56	National Security Council staff Nixon chief of staff NATO commander	
Treasury	**Donald Regan** (Massachusetts)	62	Pres., Chm. Merrill Lynch investment firm	
Defense	**Casper Weinberger** (California)	63	Chm. Calif. GOP State Comm. Calif. Finance Director Chm. Federal Trade Comm.	Nixon Budget Director Sec. Health, Education and Welfare (Nixon)
Attorney General	**William F. Smith** (California)	63	Calif. Board of Regents	
Interior	**James G. Watt** (Wyoming)	43	Staff, U.S. Chamber of Commerce Interior Dept. aide Dir. Bureau Outdoor Recreation	Chm. Fed. Power Commission Dir. Mountain States Legal Foundation
Agriculture	**John R. Block** (Illinois)	45	Member Ill. Farm Bureau Board State Agri. Dir. (Ill.)	
Commerce	**Malcolm Baldrige** (Connecticut)	58	Dir., AMF Dir., IBM Dir., Bendix	Dir., Uniroyal GOP Natl. Finance Comm. Chief Exec., Scovill Inc.
Labor	**Raymond Donovan** (New Jersey)	50	Vice Pres. Schiavone Construction Company N.J. Chm. Reagan-Bush Comm.	
Health and Human Services	**Richard Schweiker** (Pennsylvania)	54	U.S. Rep. Penn. 13th Dist. U.S. Senate	
Housing and Urban Development	**Samuel Pierce** (New York)	58	Asst. D.A. New York County Asst. U.S. Attorney Under Sec. of Labor (Eisenhower) Counsel House Antitrust Comm. N.Y. State judge Counsel, Treasury Department	Dir., Prudential Insurance Dir., General Electric Dir., International Paper Trustee, Rand Corp. Governor, Amer. Stock Exchange
Transportation	**Andrew L. Lewis** (Pennsylvania)	49	GOP National Committee GOP fundraiser	
Energy	**James Edwards** (South Carolina)	53	S. Carolina State Senate S. Carolina Governor	
Education	**Terrel H. Bell** (Idaho)	59	Utah State Superintendent U.S. Commission of Education Utah Higher Education chief	
National Security Advisor	**Richard Allen** (New Jersey)	45		
Budget Director	**David Stockman** (Michigan)	34	Dir. Republican Conference U.S. Rep. Mich. 4th Dist.	
CIA	**William Casey** (New York)	67	Counsel, Senate Small Business Committee Counsel, Marshall Plan Nixon arms control aide	Chm. Securities and Exchange Commission Reagan campaign manager
U.N. Ambassador	**Jeane Kirkpatrick** (Oklahoma)	54		

Source: *Today*, January 30, 1981, pg. 9.

The cabinet. The following departments now make up the executive bureaucracy: State, Treasury (1789), Interior (1849), Justice (1870), Agriculture (1889), Commerce (1913), Labor (1913), Defense (1947, formerly the Department of War), Housing and Urban Development (1965), Transportation (1966), Energy (1977), Health and Human Services (1979), Education (1979).[9] (The Post Office Department was established in 1872 and remained a cabinet department headed by a Postmaster General until 1970, when it was made a government corporation.) The members of President Reagan's cabinet are listed in Table 1.

Presidents handle their relations with their cabinets differently. Some have preferred to hold regular meetings of the whole group, with each member making short reports on the work of his or her specific department. President Eisenhower operated this way, and President Carter liked to assemble his cabinet periodically for such purposes. Other Presidents have preferred to consult with department heads on a less formal basis and to see them individually. This was President Kennedy's style of operation. He felt it was a waste of time to bring the entire group together, and such meetings bored him. He felt that "all these problems cabinet officers deal with are very specialized. I see all the cabinet officers every week, but we don't have a general meeting. There really isn't much use spending a morning talking about the post-office budget and tying up Secretary Freeman, who has agriculture responsibilities. . . . If we have a problem involving labor-management . . . it is much better for me to meet with Secretary Hodges from Commerce and Secretary Goldberg from Labor."[10] President Reagan prefers to meet regularly with his cabinet, pursuing a style of operation more reminiscent of Eisenhower.

Cabinet members certainly do not always agree. You will recall the discussion in the labor-reform case study where President Carter's cabinet members disagreed among themselves over what positions the President should take regarding proposed legislation.

As Table 2 (page 347) indicates, there has *not* been astronomical growth in civilian employment in the cabinet from 1965 to 1980, despite the constant talk about a growing bureaucracy. In fact, the 1980 figures for Defense and State are actually *less* than in 1965.

Through the years, we have seen the number of cabinet departments grow precisely because the country has grown, and because the activities in which the federal government has become involved have increased enormously. Two hundred years ago, for example, it would not have occurred to the framers of the Constitution that cabinet posts of secretary of energy or of housing and urban development were needed, as indeed they were not. But today the activities of those departments are considered by many to be immensely important to the well-being of the nation. (President Reagan has stated, however, that "it was wrong to have created" the Departments of Energy and Education.) The growth in the number of departments has also resulted from the demands of various interest groups to be represented by a cabinet position in the highest executive councils of government. These groups wish to have someone to speak for and "protect" their own particular interests in executive decision-making.

Figure 1 (page 348) shows the organizational chart for the Department of Interior, which has a fairly typical structure for an executive department. Each secretary has subordinates consisting of deputy secretaries, assistant secretaries, and administrators. All of these people are presidential appointees. The further down the organizational chart one looks, the more specialized are the positions and the subunits over which the various officers preside. Some subunits are organized ac-

THE REAGAN TEAM

1. Alexander Haig, Secretary of State
2. Raymond Donovan, Secretary of Labor
3. Donald Regan, Secretary of the Treasury
4. Terrel Bell, Secretary of Education
5. David Stockman, budget director
6. Andrew Lewis, Secretary of Transportation
7. Samuel Pierce, Secretary of HUD
8. William French Smith, Attorney General
9. James Watt, Secretary of the Interior
10. Jeane Kirkpatrick, Ambassador to the U.N.
11. Edwin Meese, counselor to the President
12. James Edwards, Secretary of Energy
13. Malcolm Baldrige, Secretary of Commerce
14. William Brock, U.S. trade representative
15. Richard Schweiker, Secretary of HHS
16. John Block, Secretary of Agriculture
17. William Casey, director of CIA
18. Caspar Weinberger, Secretary of Defense

TABLE 2.
Paid Civilian Employment in Executive Departments, 1965–1980.

Executive Departments	1965	1970	1975	1977	1978	1979	1980
Agriculture	113,017	116,012	120,999	127,497	128,500	127,809	144,124
Commerce	33,668	57,674	36,228	37,761	39,551	54,101	196,544
Defense	1,033,775	1,193,784	1,041,829	981,747	980,313	960,286	987,890
Department of the Army	366,726	443,369	378,937	350,549	353,203	346,694	361,713
Department of the Navy	333,271	376,340	319,719	310,119	309,880	303,472	316,517
Department of the Air Force	291,500	306,323	268,466	243,810	240,182	234,249	239,131
Other Defense Activities	42,278	67,752	74,707	77,269	77,048	75,871	70,529
Education	(x)	(x)	(x)	(x)	(x)	(x)	7,167
Energy	(x)	(x)	(x)	(x)	20,202	20,540	21,680
Health and Human Services	87,316	108,044	147,125	155,886	160,792	160,652	163,921
Housing and Urban Development	13,777	15,190	17,161	17,770	18,177	17,451	17,413
Interior	70,711	73,361	80,198	83,149	78,948	77,647	88,924
Justice	33,222	39,257	51,541	53,081	55,422	55,265	57,041
Labor	9,527	10,991	14,834	16,752	22,501	22,959	24,482
State	39,552	39,753	30,376	29,991	30,310	29,782	23,791
Agency for Int'l Development	15,098	14,974	6,591	6,092	6,073	6,186	
Transportation	45,421	65,985	75,035	75,163	74,795	73,546	74,368
Treasury	88,761	92,521	121,546	123,615	121,876	124,883	131,713

Source: *Statistical Abstract of the United States, 1980*, U.S. Department of Commerce, Bureau of the Census, p. 281.

cording to the functions they perform (such as the Bureau of Mine Safety and Health of the Department of Labor); others according to the clients they serve (such as the Bureau of Indian Affairs of the Department of Interior). Still others are organized on the basis of geographical areas they serve (such as the Saint Lawrence Seaway Development Corporation of the Department of Transportation). These subunits of a department usually are headed by an assistant secretary or a senior executive who reports to the cabinet secretary, who, in turn, reports to the President. Such officials also are called to testify before Congressional committees, an activity which constitutes an important aspect of their participation in the policymaking process. Decision-makers spend a great deal of time determining the structures of departments and deciding on the exact limits of the powers that should be exercised by the various officials.

In 1978, for instance, President Carter proposed an Energy Regulatory Administration within the newly created Department of Energy that would have the power to set prices and regulations for natural gas, oil, and electricity. He wanted a Board of Hearings and Appeals with independent, quasi-judicial authority in the regulatory process. Ultimate price-setting authority would be lodged with the department's secretary. Congress resisted this proposal. Both houses "insisted that sensitive economic decisions on pricing would be shielded better from political pressures if vested wholly in an independent collegial body within the department than if held by a single person serving at the President's pleasure."[11]

After considerable bargaining, a compromise was reached. A five-member, independent Federal Energy Regulatory Commission (FERC) was created within the department with power to set oil,

FIGURE 1.
Organizational Chart, Department of the Interior.

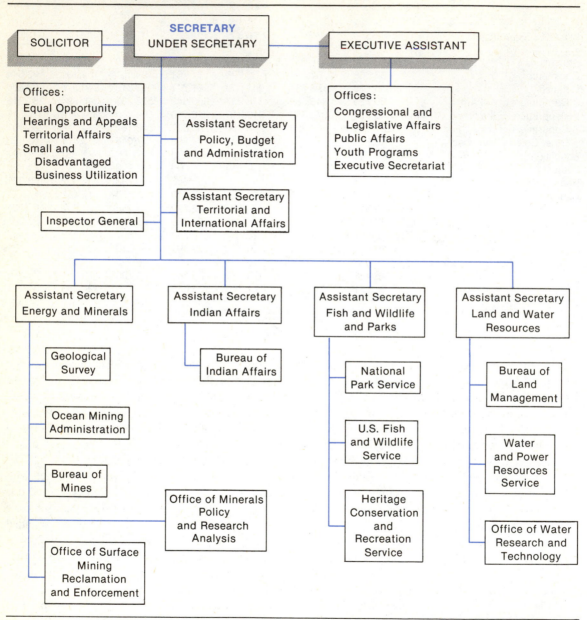

gas, and electricity prices. The secretary could propose commission actions, participate in proceedings, and set reasonable time limits for commission decisions. If the President declared a national emergency, the secretary could circumvent FERC oil-pricing rules. In addition, under emergency conditions either house of Congress would have a legislative veto applicable within fifteen days. Basically, the compromise resulted from a political struggle between the legislative and executive branches.

When President Reagan took office he made it known that he hoped to diminish the power of the new department altogether in favor of action on the part of private corporations rather than government. The energy department simply did not coincide with his overall views about the role of the federal government in energy policy and development. New people and new policies frequently call for different bureaucratic structures.

The executive agencies. Many governmental agencies are not located within any of the thirteen departments. They are separate, independent agencies which report directly to the President and, frequently, to Congress. Table 3 (next page) lists such agencies and their civilian employment from 1965 to 1980; there are additional smaller ones. Since it is not practical for each of these units to report directly to the President, normally the agency head reports to one of the senior officials on the White House staff. In addition, the units are frequently set up outside a department as a means of minimizing presidential (and thereby political or partisan) control over them. The independent regulatory commissions, for example, were intended to be free from presidential influence. They are expected to perform their duties without being subjected to pressure from the White House.

The structure of agencies is important, and there are many different structural formats. Sometimes there is a single head, as with the Veterans Administration or the Office of Personnel Management. Some agencies (such as the Interstate Commerce Commission) have a leadership comprised of several persons. The leaders of these agencies are appointed by the President (with Senate approval) usually for fixed terms.

Some agencies have a single executive with official advisory boards appointed by the President (again, sometimes with Senate approval). These boards or councils usually are filled by people who are not full-time government employees. They are private citizens who devote three or four meetings per year to the work of the agency. They usually serve fixed terms. Two such structures are the National Endowment for the Humanities and the National Endowment for the Arts. (See Figure 2, page 351.) The respective chairpersons are full-time and are appointed for four-year terms. The councils serve staggered six-year terms and advise the chairpersons concerning grants made in the humanities and arts. While the role of the councils is advisory, their existence is mandated by Congress, and they are carefully listened to. Council members serve as a means of Congressional access to the work of the agencies.

The Management of Government Business

Theoretically, the various departments, agencies, and bureaus are supposed to execute and enforce the laws passed by Congress and the President. They are the *administrators*. Their function is not to make laws. But in the process of carrying out laws already passed, bureaucrats sometimes have rather wide latitude concerning *how* to carry out their duties. By deciding how to do something, they can actually end up making policy by decid-

TABLE 3.
Paid Civilian Employment in Independent Agencies, 1965–1980.

Independent Agencies	1965	1970	1975	1977	1978	1979	1980[1]
ACTION[2]	1,104	1,317	1,864	1,921	1,927	1,882	2,008
Amer. Battle Monuments Comm.	439	404	399	386	387	379	387
Arms Control and Disarmament Agency	175	177	190	201	212	226	231
AEC/ERDA[3]	7,329	7,347	8,262	9,536	(x)	(x)	(x)
Board of Governors, Federal Reserve System	667	1,016	1,460	1,483	1,477	1,459	1,495
Canal Zone Government	3,028	3,318	3,299	3,280	3,211	2,924	(x)
Civil Aeronautics Board	846	682	728	784	793	746	822
Commission on Civil Rights	109	153	275	331	314	304	318
Community Services Admin.	(x)	(x)	1,112	1,057	1,052	1,077	1,186
Consumer Prod. Safety Comm.	(x)	(x)	959	952	952	929	1,037
Environmental Protection Agency	(x)	(x)	10,772	11,339	11,693	13,543	15,501
Equal Empl. Opportunity Comm.	19	850	2,183	2,373	2,765	3,630	3,604
Export-Import Bank, U.S.	308	358	444	426	422	398	402
Farm Credit Administration	235	235	223	254	249	267	291
Federal Communications Comm.	1,541	1,537	2,137	2,136	2,165	2,248	2,228
Federal Deposit Insurance Corp.	1,544	2,478	3,103	3,511	3,655	3,512	3,587
Federal Energy Administration	(x)	(x)	3,245	3,807	(x)	(x)	(x)
Federal Home Loan Bank Board	1,300	1,273	1,452	1,450	1,545	1,490	1,518
Federal Maritime Commission	251	233	314	307	338	328	367
Federal Mediation and Conciliation Service	422	450	523	547	557	521	523
Federal Power Commission	1,163	1,132	1,322	1,363	(x)	(x)	(x)
Federal Trade Commission	1,157	1,330	1,661	1,719	1,734	1,860	1,896
General Services Administration	36,524	37,945	39,561	36,625	38,324	37,758	38,620
Int'l. Communications Agency	11,628	10,262	8,809	8,497	8,538	8,245	8,164
International Trade Commission	298	242	427	360	385	372	454
Interstate Commerce Commission	2,427	1,755	2,115	2,145	2,139	2,084	2,067
Nat'l Aero. and Space Admin.	34,049	32,548	26,447	24,435	24,056	23,614	24,547
Nat'l Credit Union Admin.	(x)	419	570	582	621	650	762
Nat'l Endowment for the Arts	(x)	103	503	557	310	300	371
Nat'l Endowment for the Humanities					280	290	313
National Labor Relations Board	2,252	2,144	2,485	2,818	2,938	3,029	3,054
National Mediation Board	135	126	103	101	100	67	70
National Science Foundation	1,116	1,211	1,424	1,420	1,386	1,396	1,605
Nuclear Regulatory Commission	(x)	(x)	2,247	2,822	2,983	3,024	3,426
Office of Personnel Management	3,789	5,508	8,157	8,440	8,630	8,076	8,564
Panama Canal Commission	11,936	12,571	11,689	10,898	11,164	10,040	8,737
Railroad Retirement Board	1,767	1,734	1,961	1,907	1,859	1,820	1,924
Renegotiation Board	184	236	198	178	158	(x)	(x)
Securities and Exchange Commission	1,420	1,454	2,002	1,976	2,072	2,054	2,108
Selective Service System	7,587	8,395	2,257	70	68	73	88
Small Business Administration	3,751	4,269	4,796	5,230	5,764	5,912	5,891
Smithsonian Institution	2,334	2,641	3,746	3,834	4,261	4,621	4,790
Soldiers' and Airmen's Home	1,134	1,126	1,041	1,027	1,040	1,007	972
Tennessee Valley Authority	16,797	22,244	28,423	37,657	47,100	49,941	51,531
U.S. Postal Service	595,512	726,472	699,174	657,832	656,000	661,800	666,228
Veterans Administration	167,059	168,719	213,143	223,398	228,885	226,084	239,625
All other	709	579	2,019	2,728	2,792	3,078	13,402

NA = not available.   X = not applicable.
[1]As of June.
[2]Formerly the Peace Corps.
[3]Atomic Energy Commission/Energy Research and Development Administration. In 1975, the Atomic Energy Commission was divided into Energy Research and Development Administration and Nuclear Regulatory Commission; in 1977, the Department of Energy was established, which comprised ERDA, Federal Energy Administration, Federal Power Commission, and fuel elements of the Department of the Interior.

Source: *Statistical Abstract of the United States, 1980.* U.S. Department of Commerce, Bureau of the Census. pp. 281–282.

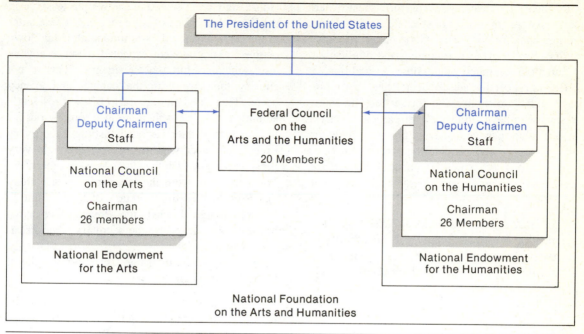

ing *what* to do. Sometimes the language of the law they are administering is stated in broad, vague terms requiring administrative interpretation before the law can be carried out. In other cases, the law will instruct the agency to devise specific rules in order to achieve certain broad policy goals.

The Internal Revenue Service (IRS) is an example of the *rule-making* (interpretive) function of agencies. The tax codes allow taxpayers to deduct certain expenses of doing business from their income taxes. The IRS is the agency that decides whether or not a particular deduction is a "legitimate" business expense. A specific example of the rule-making process occurred in the first days of the Reagan administration. The newly appointed secretary of education, T. H. Bell, revoked a rule requiring public schools to offer bilingual educa-

tion to foreign-speaking students as a condition for receiving federal aid. The secretary ruled that such regulations (issued in the final months of the Carter administration) were "harsh, inflexible, burdensome, unworkable, and incredibly costly."

In the first instance, the IRS performs a quasi-judicial function; it reviews the facts and issues an official decision, which might then be appealed in a tax court. In the second case, the education secretary performed a quasi-legislative function: a judgment was made concerning the soundness of and necessity for a particular policy. This latter type of function is not usually appealable to the courts, unless some violation of procedural due process of law can be shown or unless there is a charge that the secretary did not have the legal authority to make such a decision.

In theory, bureaucracies perform best when they make maximum use of specialization and of a rational chain of command. Good public administrators seek to *avoid* overlapping and duplication of functions as much as possible. In addition, a distinction is often made between "line" positions and "staff" positions. The former refer to those persons who have authority over particular activities and who manage a specific budget. The latter refer to those who provide support and advice. Administrative efficiency is enhanced when these specialized categories are clearly established and respected.

Likewise, a clear hierarchical structure in the organization helps clarify the levels of authority in an agency. One should be able to tell from a good organizational chart what the chain of command is in the bureaucracy—from top to bottom.

The Recruitment Process

Precisely because much of the work of the bureaucrat is so politically involved, great care must be taken in appointing people to the top bureaucratic positions. The higher up the organizational chart (cabinet secretaries, deputy secretaries, assistant secretaries, agency and bureau chiefs), the more politically sensitive is the choice. These people will be involved in making decisions daily affecting the lives and fortunes of millions.

The simple notion that what is needed in politics is a "good administrator" is not realistic. As we noted in the previous chapter, the President must fill one third to one half of approximately 17,000 jobs. While this may seem like a lot of positions (and it is), the number of "plums" is relatively small. The President must be especially aware of political considerations: interest groups must be consulted, members of Congress must be deferred to. The President has much less leeway in appointing bureaucratic leaders than in choosing a White House staff or in selecting the people to serve in the Executive Office of the President. These latter groups are considered more immediately his "own people." They are not expected to serve anyone else's interests but the President's. This is not entirely the case with the cabinet and agency heads. True, the latter are part of "the President's administration," but they are also looking out for the interests of their various constituencies. Every President is faced with this reality, although every President might wish the situation were otherwise. You will recall from the labor-reform case study that President Ford's secretary of labor, John T. Dunlop, resigned when the President vetoed a prolabor bill backed by the secretary. And President Carter's labor secretary, Ray Marshall, strongly supported the same legislation in spite of Carter's opposition to some provisions.

At the same time, political concerns cannot be permitted to completely outweigh considerations of talent and qualifications. A President who puts together a cabinet satisfactory to all significant interest groups but suspect in ability will be courting disaster and embarrassment. Thus, although candidates *X, Y,* and *Z* might be totally acceptable to organized labor as candidates for secretary of labor, the President must decide if any of them have the capacity to handle the job. This means several things. The appointee ought to know when to resist certain demands made by the constituent group. The appointee ought to know enough about the subject area (or at least be able to learn quickly) not to have to rely solely on one side presented by a strong pressure group. The appointee ought to be able to command respect from those within the department or agency, especially from the career bureaucrats who have been around a long time and who invariably have some suspicion about a "political outsider" coming in as their superior. Therefore, the President must do some checking into each candidate's qualifications and background. The administration would be poorly

Unlike the President's personal staff, cabinet and agency heads, although appointed by the President, do not always represent his point of view. Carter's secretary of labor, Ray Marshall, for instance, outspokenly supported a prolabor bill even though the President objected to some provisions.

served if a top appointee turned out to be nothing more than a puppet of outside political interests.

For a new President, the choice of top appointees is the first public demonstration of leadership. The press, the public, Congress and foreign nations scrutinize the *style* of selection as well as the substantive choices to try to gain some initial insight into this newly elected powerful figure. How did the President hold up under pressure from certain sources to appoint a particular person? How widely did he consult? Were his choices bipartisan? How much was he influenced by regional, racial, sexual, and ideological concerns for a "balanced" cabinet? Whom did he consider and later reject? Indeed, who rejected *his* offer of a position—and why?

All candidates for cabinet positions must face the additional hurdle of appearing before one or more Senate committees. If the nomination is reasonably noncontroversial, this appearance can be rather perfunctory. But there have been instances where the President's nominee has received a rough grilling. This serves as another test of the potential administrator's talents—in some cases simply his or her talents for survival. Senators are permitted to pursue any line of inquiry: the nominee's financial status; philosophical ideas; policy orientation; political background; professional experience or lack of it.

Cabinet members receive an annual salary of $66,000, and prior to their appointment they must divulge their entire financial condition. If they hold

Top: General Alexander Haig, Reagan's controversial appointee for secretary of state, being grilled by the Senate Foreign Relations Committee. Bottom: Ernest Lefever, Reagan's appointee for assistant secretary for human affairs, withdrew his name after his 13-4 rejection by the Senate Foreign Relations Committee signaled almost sure defeat on the Senate floor. Among other issues, Lefever's association with the Nestle Company, which has been criticized for marketing infant formula in third-world nations, was cited as a conflict of interest.

stocks or have other interests or organizational positions that might constitute a "conflict of interest" with their new governmental office, they must divest themselves of these in order to receive the appointment. They serve entirely at the pleasure of the President (though their appointments must be confirmed by the Senate). This is not true for some presidential appointees to independent commissions and agencies. Those persons cannot be fired at will, but only through a formal process of charges, hearings, and then dismissal.

Civil service: the career route. Clearly, most of the people who work for the federal government are not political appointees. In fact, something like eighty percent of the 2.8 million federal civilian employees are **civil servants**. This means that they got their jobs usually through an examination administered by the Office of Personnel Management (formerly the Civil Service Commission). The OPM itself has approximately 8500 employees, 3400 in Washington, D.C., and has branch offices in every state of the union.

This system of hiring government workers began in 1883 with the passage of the Pendleton Act (the Civil Service Act). Before then, employees were chosen largely on the basis of party patronage and the *spoils system*.[12] After a new President was elected, there would be—almost literally—a mass rush to the White House by jobseekers trying to get the plums of victory. This had always been case, but it was only with Andrew Jackson's election in 1828 that the spoils system became firmly entrenched. President Jackson believed that government work was uncomplicated enough for the person of average intelligence to perform. He also felt that "rotation in office" would help guard against the feeling that certain persons were *entitled* to a government job.

Be that as it may, this process was often abused. It took the tragedy of a presidential assassination to

Charles J. Guiteau, whose request for an ambassadorial position was turned down by President Garfield, took his revenge by assassinating the President on July 2, 1881. The civil-service system as we know it today was a direct response to this incident.

finally lead to the Pendleton Act. In 1880, James A. Garfield was elected President. He had promised to effect some civil-service reforms. One of his supporters, Charles J. Guiteau, wanted an ambassadorial position and talked to the new President about such an appointment. Garfield turned him down. Shortly afterwards, Guiteau, enraged by his rejection, shot the President in a Washington railroad station. The newly elected President lingered for two and a half months before he died. The country was stunned, and the vice-president, Chester A. Arthur, on becoming President led the fight to pass the Civil Service Act. The law provided for a bipartisan, three-person Civil Service Commission charged with classifying certain federal government jobs by categories, developing competitive examinations for each job, administering the exams, setting personnel policies, and certifying for the various governmental agencies the persons on the "eligi-

ble list" who were available to be hired. At first, about ten percent of federal employees were covered. The number of jobs included under civil service has grown so much that now most bureaucrats enter governmental service through this route. Each job is given a Government Service (GS) classification from 1 to 16, with the higher classifications demanding more in the way of skills and/or experience and receiving higher pay. (See Table 4, page 356.)

Sometimes the OPM has developed and administered examination questions that have become quite controversial. For example, one longtime employee of the Equal Employment Opportunity Commission (EEOC) once devised questions with distinctly political overtones, such as, "If you had been a U.S. senator at the time, how would you have voted on the Panama Canal treaties? Why?" and, "Do you believe that teachers, police offic-

TABLE 4.
U.S. Civil Service Pay Schedule, 1980.

GS Level	Steps									
	1	2	3	4	5	6	7	8	9	10
1	$ 7,960	$ 8,255	$ 8,490	$ 8,755	$ 9,020	$ 9,069	$ 9,189	$ 9,444	$ 9,699	$ 9,654
2	8,951	9,069	9,242	9,531	9,820	10,109	10,398	10,687	10,976	11,265
3	9,766	10,092	10,418	10,744	11,070	11,396	11,722	12,048	12,374	12,700
4	10,963	11,328	11,693	12,058	12,423	12,788	13,153	13,518	13,883	14,248
5	12,266	12,675	13,084	13,493	13,902	14,311	14,720	15,129	15,538	15,947
6	13,672	14,128	14,584	15,040	15,496	15,952	16,408	16,864	17,320	17,776
7	15,193	15,699	16,205	16,711	17,217	17,723	18,229	18,735	19,241	19,747
8	16,826	17,387	17,948	18,509	19,070	19,631	20,192	20,753	21,314	21,875
9	18,585	19,205	19,825	20,445	21,065	21,685	22,305	22,925	23,545	24,165
10	20,467	21,149	21,831	22,513	23,195	23,877	24,559	25,241	25,923	26,605
11	22,486	23,236	23,986	24,736	25,486	26,236	26,986	27,736	28,486	29,236
12	26,951	27,849	28,747	29,645	30,543	31,441	32,339	33,237	34,135	35,033
13	32,048	33,116	34,184	35,252	36,320	37,388	38,456	39,524	40,592	41,660
14	37,871	39,133	40,395	41,657	42,919	44,181	45,443	46,705	47,967	49,229
15	44,547	46,032	47,517	49,002	50,487	51,972	53,457	54,942	56,437	57,912
16	49,198	50,838	52,478	54,118	57,398	58,500	58,500	58,500		
17	53,849	55,644	57,439	58,500	58,500					
18	58,506									

Source: *Firstline*, Vol. 4, No. 1, Office of Personnel Management, Washington, D.C. (October-November 1980), p. 1.

ers, firefighters, and garbage collectors should have the right to strike?" and, "Is the administration of criminal justice in the courts today too permissive, too strict, or about right?"[13]

These kinds of questions struck some people as coming too close to "thought control" and even political intimidation. Both EEOC and civil-service officials ultimately admitted that the questions were "clumsy, insensitive, and inappropriate" and promised that the "staff person who authorized them will be so counseled." In bureaucratic language this meant that *someone* was going to get a severe tongue-lashing. The civil-service employee who designed the questions simply explained: "It never occurred to me that these questions would ever be used for any purpose other than intended, namely, to find out what insights an applicant had, and how aware he was as to what is going on in society. We didn't give a damn what the person's opinions were. I guess I was naive about how this could become controversial."[14]

Naive, indeed! A columnist for the *Washington Post* accepted the examiner's explanation but stated that "in isolation a well-meaning bureaucrat can pull a dumb one and unwittingly give the impression that Big Brother is imposing thought control on poor common souls."[15] He went on to say: "But it is also good to remember that the bureaucracy has such arbitrary and often uncontrolled power, it takes a little whistle-blowing to keep the government on a reasonably even keel."

The people hired from the OPM's lists are "career civil servants." After a probationary period, they can hold their jobs for life, subject to dismissal under quite specific and frequently hard-to-prove circumstances. The civil-service rules set out specific pay increases based on length of service in each job category. Therefore, in some jobs increase in salary as well as promotion are automatic. This has been the basis for some criticism of the system. Some critics charge that the civil service provides a protective haven for those who do not have to compete: their jobs are permanent, their promotions and pay increases are automatic, thus, they have no incentive to improve job performance. This has led to the impression (illustrated by the cartoon on the right, top) that there are thousands of federal employees hanging around doing unnecessary "busy work," all the while drawing their safe and secure government paychecks. This sort of image (accurate or inaccurate) has done a great deal to turn the public against "those bureaucrats in Washington."

Civil service reform. In March 1978, President Carter sent several proposals to Congress calling for reform of the civil-service system. He stated that the system "has become a bureaucratic maze which neglects merit, tolerates poor performance, permits abuse of legitimate employee rights and mires every personnel action in red tape, delay, and confusion." He wanted to provide bonuses for excellent work in place of automatic pay increases, especially at the high managerial levels. He strongly supported what came to be called a "whistle-blower" provision, a section which would protect those employees who disclosed ineptness among their fellow workers. His proposals also called for the abolition of the Civil Service Commission, to be replaced by two separate agencies: an Office of Personnel Management and a Merit Systems Protection Board. The rationale for this change was that the agency that administered personnel affairs should not also be involved in hearing complaints and deciding grievances arising from within that same agency. Carter also wanted to modify the existing "veterans' preference" provision of the civil-service system

"And if Congress ever comes up with an energy program, we have a department with 18,000 employees to put it into action!"

DUNAGIN'S PEOPLE

8-24

1978 Sentinel Star
Field Newspaper Syndicate

". . . But I believe you'll think it an improvement once you get the hang of it!"

FIGURE 3.
Membership (by Agency) of the Senior Executive Service, 1979.

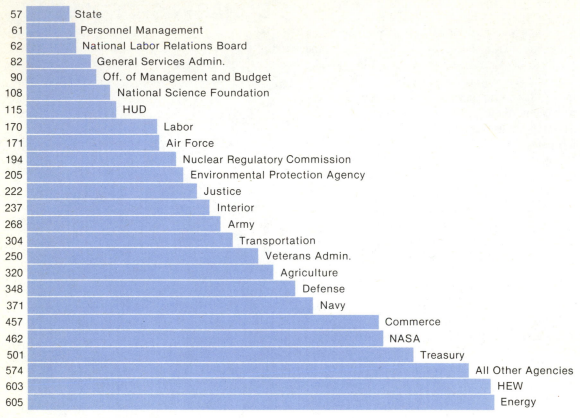

57	State
61	Personnel Management
62	National Labor Relations Board
82	General Services Admin.
90	Off. of Management and Budget
108	National Science Foundation
115	HUD
170	Labor
171	Air Force
194	Nuclear Regulatory Commission
205	Environmental Protection Agency
222	Justice
237	Interior
268	Army
304	Transportation
250	Veterans Admin.
320	Agriculture
348	Defense
371	Navy
457	Commerce
462	NASA
501	Treasury
574	All Other Agencies
603	HEW
605	Energy

Positions Established 7677
*Positions Filled 6950
SES Members 6838

*Due to pending conversions, temporary assignments, and nonconversions, not all of these positions are filled by SES members.

Source: *Civil Service Reform, A Report on the First Year* (Washington, D.C., Office of Personnel Management, January 1980.)

whereby disabled veterans are given ten additional points and all other veterans five points on civil-service examinations. He proposed limiting the preference to veterans of the Vietnam War. After seven months of political bargaining in Congress a new law was enacted. The President was able to get virtually everything he wanted, except the veterans' preference change.

A major change was the establishment of a new Senior Executive Service (see Figure 3). About 8000 top federal managers were made eligible for substantial cash bonuses instead of automatic pay increases if an annual review of their work indicated that they deserved the bonuses and if they chose the bonus program. The new law made it easier to transfer senior executives from one agency to another and to demote them to GS 15 if evaluation of their performance so warranted. Automatic pay raises for some employees in GS 13 through GS 15 would no longer apply, but instead a merit pay system would be instituted. The executives would also be entitled to some cash bonuses. The intent of this provision was to offer incentives for pay raises other than mere longevity on the job.

The new law also established for the first time by statute (rather than by executive order) the right of federal employees to join labor unions and to bargain collectively on such matters as personnel policies/practices and working conditions. The right to strike was not allowed, nor could there be collective bargaining over wages.

The new law was the first major reform in the civil-service system since the Pendleton Act of 1883.

Civil service and the Hatch Act. Career civil servants are not permitted to participate in partisan political activities. They cannot campaign for public office for themselves or for others. This restriction was first imposed by the Civil Service Commission, but it became a law under the Hatch Act of 1939, sponsored by Senator Carl A. Hatch of New Mexico. The law does not apply to top-level political appointees, but only to those who hold their jobs through the civil-service system. The purpose was to remove "administration" as far as possible from "politics," and most states now have such laws on the state level.

Several unsuccessful attempts have been made to modify or repeal this legislation. Some people believe that such prohibitions deny to millions of citizens the privihege of participating in political activity beyond merely voting. President Franklin D. Roosevelt was suspicious of the motivation of the law. He felt that it was aimed at cutting down his patronage powers, not so much at insuring "purity in politics" or developing the "merit system." Supporters of the Hatch Act, then and now, have argued that it protects federal employees from being harrassed by politicians on the threat of losing their jobs if they do not support a particular party or candidate.

President Gerald Ford vetoed a bill passed by Congress that would have repealed the 1939 Hatch Act. President Carter, with strong support from organized labor unions, wished to revise the Hatch Act provision prohibiting federal-employee political participation, but he did not include it as part of his 1978 reform bill, and the law remains in force. Postal workers were especially active in lobbying for repeal, but Hatch Act supporters insisted that they did not want to "politicize the bureaucracy."

Government unions. Federal employees can and do belong to labor unions. There are more than ninety unions in over fifty agencies, and sixty-one percent of all government employees belong to them. The six largest unions are the American Federation of Government Employees (AFL-CIO), National Federation of Federal Employees, National Treasury Employees Union, National Association of Government Employees, Metal Trades Councils (AFL-CIO), and Machinists (AFL-CIO).

The Federal Labor Relations Authority (FLRA) is responsible for administering the government's labor-relations program. It investigates charges of unfair labor practices, decides which issues can be negotiated and which units should do the bargaining, and conducts elections to determine whether a labor organization has been selected as an exclusive representative by a majority of the employees in an agency. In addition to restrictions mentioned earlier, government unions cannot impose "agen-

Right: The Civil Service Commission was established to standardize government hiring practices and to protect government employees, such as those shown here, from the whims of politicians. Below: Although postal workers are unionized, it is illegal for them, or for any other civil servants, to strike.

cy shops'' (that is, the employees do not have to join a union). The government has the right (without having to negotiate with unions) to hire, fire, assign, direct, and lay off employees. The Federal Service Impasses Panel (FSIP), located within the FLRA, provides assistance when problems arise over negotiations.

Are the Managers Manageable?

Bureaucrats as "politicians."   Whenever someone is involved in making choices between several possible alternatives in the public sphere, politics is likely to be involved. The executive bureaucracy should not be seen as some vast array of agencies going about the work of managing government business away from the political whirlpool. To say the least, that would be the utopia many have dreamed about.

Bureaucrats do get drawn into the political arena; it is virtually impossible to separate politics from administration. Obviously this is truer of some agencies than of others, but it is pretty accurate as a general rule.

Though the Hatch Act keeps career civil servants from becoming involved in partisan, electoral politics, bureaucrats *do* participate in the politics of policymaking and implementation. As we have seen, the bureaucracy does much more than merely execute the laws in an objective, efficient, impartial manner. In fact, a full understanding of American government and politics requires an understanding of how politically important the work of top-level bureaucrats and career civil servants really is.

The career civil servants who operate programs and run bureaus stay on the job year after year. They see elected and appointed officials come and go. They are the mainstays of the government, and

this alone gives them some measure of power and influence. They are able to build up a vast knowledge of the work of their agencies, and they develop numerous contacts with outside groups and members of Congress. Most modern-day Presidents have complained of the difficulty of dealing with the bureaucracy. They complain that their orders are either ignored or not carried out fast enough. They complain that bureaucrats sometimes ''leak'' matters to the press, either to pressure the President or to defy him.

One very important source of bureaucratic power is Congress. Some bureaucrats make a point of developing close ties to certain Congressional committee members. After all, Congress is the institution that appropriates the money to keep bureaucratic programs going. If a particularly powerful legislator favors a certain program, the smart bureaucrat cultivates a relationship with that person. Political scientist Harold Seidman notes: ''For many agencies, their natural allies are the legislative committees. . . . A close affinity often exists between a committee chairman and the senior career staff of the departments and agencies under his jurisdiction.''[16]

The relationship is mutually advantageous. The legislator has direct access to day-to-day knowledge about the program, a valuable commodity in the sometimes intricate debates on Capitol Hill. This enables a legislator to become an ''expert'' on that particular subject, and, as we shall see in chapter 11, this can be very important to a legislator's influence and career in Congress. The bureaucrat has direct access to an important friend who can help with appropriations and appointments. Thus, if a President orders some kind of action in regard to a program that the bureaucrat does not like, although the bureaucrat is responsible to the President, he or she can pick up the telephone or (more likely) have lunch with the

friend on Capitol Hill. That friend may then advise the President concerning the matter. Who knows —perhaps the President will need the legislator's vote on another issue. The President might find it wise to reconsider his position on the previous order. Thus, the bureaucrat can celebrate, along with his or her Congressional friend, a victory over the bureaucrat's boss—the President. This does not happen all the time, but it happens.

The same is true with pressure groups. Bureaucrats develop close ties to interest groups with particular interests in the agency's work. Astute career civil servants often pride themselves on their ability to "survive" in Washington by understanding this political game and at times playing it.

In fact, in some cases a *network* exists among bureaucrats, Congressional figures, and interest groups. We should not overlook the episode described in the labor-law case study. You will recall that certain officials in the Small Business Administration (SBA) wanted to defeat the proposed labor legislation. They worked with an interest group and with sympathetic senators to influence unfavorable media coverage of the bill.

A study by political scientist R. Douglas Arnold suggests that "under certain conditions bureaucrats allocate extra benefits to members of those committees with jurisdiction over their programs."[17] He found this to be particularly true with regard to members of the House Armed

Services Committee in their relations with Pentagon officials concerning the allocation of military employment resources.

Presidential recourse.   What can a President do to control the bureaucracy? President Nixon was one (but by no means the only) President who worried about this matter of bureaucratic power. On more than one occasion he complained about the lack of discipline among the bureaucrats. What could be done when a "bureaucrat thumbs his nose" at the elected leadership? Mr. Nixon offered some advice to his director of the Office of Management and Budget, George Schultz:

> *You've got to get us some discipline, George. You've got to get it, and the only way you get it, is when a bureaucrat thumbs his nose, we're going to get him. . . . They've got to know, that if they do it, something's going to happen. I know the civil service pressure. But you can do a lot there. There are many unpleasant places where civil service people can be sent. We just don't have any discipline in government. That's our trouble. Now I'm getting a little around the White House, uh, but we got to get it in these departments. . . . So whatever you—well, maybe he is in the regional office. Fine. Demote him or send him to the Guam regional office. There's a way. Get him the hell out.*[18]

For the most part, however, there is very little a President can do directly unless there is clear evidence of insubordination. Much bureaucratic defiance (if that is what it is) is done in politically subtle and sophisticated ways, so obtaining hard proof is very difficult. Presidents have to recognize this and learn to live with it and hope that it does not become rampant or interfere too often with the administration's "priority" items. The President must settle for less than complete loyalty on the part of the bureaucracy—and hope to win over the most important officials. The vastness and complexities of the governmental apparatus mean that politics will likely pervade virtually every aspect of its operation. And although the President is powerful and at the head of the executive branch, this does not mean that the lower-level bureaucrats are without their own finely developed tools of political leverage.

Legislative oversight.   Notwithstanding the close cooperative relationship between some bureaucrats and legislators, Congress has an interest in maintaining a check on the departments and agencies. This is done at times through what is referred to as **legislative oversight**, that is, the practice of reviewing the work of the bureaucracies. Agencies can be required to submit reports to and testify before committees. The Legislative Reorganization Act of 1946 charged Congressional committees with "continuous watchfulness" of executive agencies, and the government operations committees of the House and Senate were mandated to oversee bureaucratic activities with the goal of ensuring economy and efficiency.

The Legislative Reorganization Act of 1970 required all Congressional committees to report every two years on their oversight activities, and the law assigned oversight authority to the General Accounting Office (GAO) and the Congressional Research Service. In 1974, the House required standing committees with more than twenty members to set up special oversight subcommittees or to require the existing subcommittees to perform the oversight functions.[19]

But as clear and straightforward as these formal requirements seem to be, the fact is that legislative oversight is not very systematic or constant. Political scientist James W. Davis concludes: "Congress can at most spot-check what is going on in

The Pentagon, headquarters for the country's largest bureaucracy, the Department of Defense. Of the department's 3 million employees (2 million uniformed), 25,000 work in the Pentagon. The five-sided building, which stands 5 stories tall and surrounds a 5-acre courtyard; has 17½ miles of corridors, 85,000 light fixtures, and 685 water fountains.

the Executive Branch. It can react to complaints, respond to fires.''[20]

Most scholars who have examined this subject believe that legislative oversight occurs irregularly and with varying consequences. The major motivation will likely be the incentives felt by individual legislators. If it is in their political interest, then they, through their committees, will pursue some degree of oversight. Morris S. Ogul says:

When action is perceived to contribute directly and substantially to political survival, it is likely to move toward the top of any member's priority list. Extra incentives to oversee come from problems of direct concern to one's constituents or from issues that promise political visibility or organizational support. Conversely, problems not seen as closely related to political survival are more difficult to crowd onto the member's schedule. . . . The relationship between policy preferences and the motivation to oversee is intimate. Interviews across several committees revealed that congressmen are seldom eager to monitor those executive activities of which they approve. A member who is indifferent to a program seldom presses for oversight.[21]

Even though legislative oversight has such a spotty record, bureaucrats still must be alert to the actual and potential demands made on them. They must always be attentive to the needs and wishes of the people who vote the money that sustains them and their agencies.

The public, the media, sunshine laws, and the Freedom of Information Act. Bureaucracies in a democratic society cannot be immune from scrutiny by private individuals and groups. There are certain legal steps that can be taken to hold bureaucrats accountable for what they do or fail to do. Appeal from certain administrative rulings is available (see chapter 10). In addition, the media usually keep a watchful eye on bureaucratic activity, especially if the agency deals with a popular issue or program. *Sunshine laws* require many agencies to hold meetings open to the public and press. There are limitations of course (national security, personnel files, fiscal deliberations, and some other matters), but very many sessions are open to those persons who wish to attend and observe, even if they are not always allowed to participate in deliberations. The Freedom of Information Act of 1966 (amended in 1974) makes many records of governmental agencies available to the public. (This does not usually apply to intraagency reports, however, as the labor-law case study noted.) The fact that much of the work of an agency can be examined by others provides some means of scrutiny and a safeguard against arbitrary action.

Interbureaucratic checks. At times, various departments and agencies serve to counter and check each other. This is easily understood in the context of competing for limited budgetary funds, but there is another sense in which it is true. This involves the problem of "turf," or agency juris-

diction. Agencies and bureaus come to regard their work, at times, in very clear terms (from *their* point of view). Each agency believes it should have authority over a certain range of functions. Some intense infighting among the various bureaucratic agencies can result. Morton H. Halperin has described this situation: "One of the central preoccupations of career officials in any organization is the conflict of interests with other organizations over the definition of roles and missions."[22] Indeed, sometimes it is necessary to go so far as to write out formal agreements—"delimiting" agreements—stipulating the functions to be assumed by the various agencies. Halperin explains:

> *This was apparently one of the problems faced by the White House when it tried to get the cooperation of the various intelligence organizations in dealing with what it saw as threats of domestic subversion. The new proposals ran the risk of interfering with the "delimitations agreement" of 1949 between the FBI and the intelligence organizations of the army, air force, and navy. This signed agreement delimited each agency's responsibilities in investigations of espionage, counter-espionage, subversion, and sabotage.*[23]

Therefore, when new programs are started, bureaucratic agencies look very carefully to see that their original "turf" is not impinged upon.

Halperin gives another example of how an agency took on a function even though it really did not want to do so for the sole purpose of keeping another agency from encroaching on its powers. The army had proposed to develop its own capability for transporting its own troops. But the air force and the navy felt they had to assume the function of transporting army forces by air and sea. Otherwise "the air force . . . feared that if the army began to acquire airplanes for transporting troops, this would be another wedge in the army's efforts to gain back control of much of tactical air. Similarly, the navy [was] concerned that if the army were to develop its own troop transport capability, it would quickly turn it into a capability for storming ashore and jeopardize the main mission of the marine corps as an assault organization."[24]

One can imagine the reaction of sophisticated bureaucrats sitting around a table if a naive policymaker were to make the simple suggestion: "Why not let the best qualified agency transport the army troops?" Raised eyebrows and muffled smiles—ship that fellow off to Guam!

Summary

1. The executive bureaucracy of close to 2.8 million employees theoretically is organized in a hierarchical structure calculated to maximize efficiency and specialization of functions. The many rules characteristic of bureaucracies attempt to regularize and systematize government operations.

2. Neither Congress nor the President can tend to all the details of day-to-day operation. This must be done by the bureaucrats, and in the process of administering programs and executing laws, they inevitably make decisions which in effect means they end up "making policy."

3. The highest jobs are held by political appointees, but the vast number of career positions are filled through competitive examinations. Major reforms have changed civil-service employment practices, providing for merit-reward plans where once automatic salary increases and promotion depended only on length of service.

4. Although the Hatch Act prohibits partisan electoral activity on the part of career civil servants, bureaucrats certainly get involved in "politics." They attempt to build alliances with legislators and others in pursuit of common goals.

5. There are formal techniques available to the President, Congress, the media, and private sources to oversee, manage, and monitor the executive bureaucracies. Ultimately, it is in the interests of the various departments and agencies to seek consensual relations with other branches and with each other.

Notes

1. *Washington Post*, July 18, 1978, p. A1.
2. *Wall Street Journal*, September 19, 1978, p. 3.
3. *Wall Street Journal*, August 28, 1978, p. 9.
4. *Wall Street Journal*, August 28, 1978, p. 9.
5. *Wall Street Journal*, August 18, 1978, p. 3.
6. *New York Times*, August 9, 1978, p. C2.
7. *Washington Post*, May 3, 1978, p. C5.
8. Ibid. p. C5.
9. Health, Education and Welfare was established in 1953, but it was changed to Health and Human Services in 1979 when the Department of Education was formed.
10. Theodore Sorensen, *Kennedy* (New York: Harper & Row Publishers, 1965), p. 283.
11. "New Department Given Wide Energy Powers," *CQ Guide, Current American Government* (Spring 1978), p. 49.
12. This term developed from the practice of the winning party turning out the workers of the losing party. A senator from New York in 1832, William Learned Marcy, coined the phrase: "To the victor belong the spoils."
13. *Washington Post*, August 15, 1978, p. A11.
14. Ibid. p. A11.
15. Ibid. p. A11.
16. Harold Seidman, *Politics, Position & Power, The Dynamics of Federal Organization* (New York: Oxford University Press, 1980), p. 53.
17. R. Douglas Arnold, *Congress and the Bureaucracy* (New Haven: Yale University Press, 1979), p. 65.
18. Joel D. Aberbach and Bert A. Rockman, "Clashing Beliefs Within the Executive Branch: The Nixon Administration Bureaucracy," *The American Political Science Review* (June 1976), 457.

19. Randall B. Ripley and Grace A. Franklin, *Congress, The Bureaucracy and Public Policy* (Homewood, Illinois: The Dorsey Press, 1980).
20. James W. Davis, Jr., *The National Executive Branch* (New York: The Free Press, 1970), p. 134.
21. M.S. Ogul, "Congressional Oversight: Structures and Incentives," in Lawrence C. Dodd and Bruce I. Oppenheimer, eds., *Congress Reconsidered* (New York: Praeger Publishers, 1977), pp. 217–18.
22. Morton H. Halperin, "The Presidency and Its Interaction with the Culture of Bureaucracy," in Charles Peters and James Fallows, eds., *The Systei* (New York: Praeger Publishers, 1976), p. 18.
23. Ibid.
24. Ibid.

Regulatory Agencies and the Regulators

Chapter

10

In the spring of 1979, Senator Thomas F. Eagleton (D., Missouri) spoke in Chicago at the annual meeting of the Lead Industry Association. It was time, he said, "to bring a little common sense and coordination back into the regulatory process."[1] He was complaining that a federal agency, the Environmental Protection Agency (EPA), had issued some rules limiting the amount of lead particles in the atmosphere and that these rules were virtually impossible to abide by. The Senator concluded that this regulation "can wipe out an entire industry. It can cost our country millions of jobs and production. . . ." Therefore, the senator told his audience, the President of the United States ought to have the power to overturn those rules and orders of regulatory agencies that "contradicted overall policies."

Some people believe that too much day-to-day living in America is controlled by **regulatory agencies** (those arms of the federal government charged with watching over various sectors of business and government). This has occasioned not only criticism such as Senator Eagleton's, but also a steady spate of political satire and cartoons (such as the one shown on page 370) suggesting that the process has gone too far.

In the same month that Senator Eagleton spoke in Chicago, President Carter addressed the annual convention of the National Association of Broadcasters in Dallas, Texas. He said: "When I came to Washington, I found a regulatory assembly line which churned out new rules, paperwork, regulations and forms without plan, without direction and seemingly without control." He stated that "ninety separate regulatory agencies were issuing 7000 new rules every single year." And, therefore, he too was going to "call for common sense."

Nobody can be against "common sense"; that is not the problem. The question, rather, is, *What kinds of activities require what sorts of regulations and rules?* One month before the President and the senator were speaking on the subject, the head of the Environmental Protection Agency, Douglas M. Costle, gave a talk on regulatory reform in Seattle, Washington. What was really needed, he said, was a "balanced" approach. It was not wise to overlook the good things accomplished by government regulation, and at the same time, it was important to recognize that regulation created some problems and solved others. For example, after safety standards were set for cribs in 1974, the number of small children killed or injured because of design defects in cribs was cut roughly in half; between 1972 and 1977, the number of private-sector workers injured yearly dropped by one million even though the work force grew by a total of 5 million, and this drop could be attributed in large part to the regulations of the Occupational Safety and Health Administration (OSHA).

At the same time, however, administrator Costle admitted that government regulation frequently

SWINGING IN A HAMMOCK ISN'T AS MUCH FUN AS IT USED TO BE.

EVER SINCE THE CLOWNS FROM O.S.H.A. MADE ME IN-STALL A ROLL BAR.

© Jefferson Communications, Distributed by C.T.N.Y.N.S.

created problems: delays and uncertainties for business seeking new plant permits; more red tape; regulations that imposed severe restrictions on free competition and enormously increased the costs of doing business.

Not all business people complain about government regulation. A column in the *Washington Post* noted how companies in the mobile-home building industry actually *welcomed* regulation.

> *Somewhere out there—believe it or not—there is an industry that not only tolerates government regulation, but likes it. . . . Since June 1976, the Department of Housing and Urban Development has regulated the production of mobile and manufactured homes through the creation of uniform building regulations.*
>
> *As the number of complaints about poorly constructed traditional housing mounts, the regulation of the mobile/manufactured home industry begins to look better and better.*
>
> *HUD officials say the number of complaints about the mobile/manufactured home industry have dropped considerably since the outset of regulation.*
>
> *And companies in that industry are thankful that government regulation gave them credibili-*

> *ty at a time when fly-by-night companies had been hurting the reputation of the entire industry.*
>
> *Because of tough government construction standards and a quality inspection process involving state and local officials as well as federal, the bulk of the mobile homes and prefabricated homes sold in the U.S. today are of a consistently high quality.*[2]

But the debate and disagreements continue. You will recall President Reagan's statement in his first press conference: ''My second decision today is a directive ordering key federal agencies to freeze pending regulations for sixty days. This action gives my administration time to start a new regulatory oversight process and also prevents certain last-minute regulatory decisions of the previous administration—the so-called midnight regulations—from taking effect without proper review and approval.''

Regulation in Historical Perspective

Before we go much further into a discussion of the pros and cons and the suggested reforms of the regulatory process, let's take a brief look at how that process developed. In the nineteenth century the federal government spent most of its time aiding private economic growth and expansion. Roads were built, public lands were deeded to homesteaders and railroads, and new industries were helped by protective tariffs. The states performed most of tha functions of regulation, sanctioned constitutionally by a U.S. Supreme Court decision, *Munn* v. *Illinois*,[3] which held that "when private property is devoted to a public use, it is subject to public regulation." But another court decision, *Wabash, St. Louis & Pacific Railway Co.* v. *Illinois*,[4] held that the states could not regulate businesses engaged in interstate commerce. This was a function of Congress under the commerce clause of the Constitution. Thus, Congress established the first federal regulatory agency, the Interstate Commerce Commission (ICC) in 1887. In time, with the enactment of the Hepburn Act of 1906, the ICC gained enforcement powers, subject to review by the courts. Prior to that time, enforcement of government regulations had been a matter of exclusive judicial action. Subsequently, it became a function of administrative agencies exercising quasi-judicial powers.

Beginning in 1913, new agencies were created when it became clear that the ICC could not handle all federal regulation of commerce. The Federal Reserve System was established in 1913; the Federal Trade Commission in 1914; the Federal Power Commission in 1920. The New Deal of the 1930s saw growth in the number and activity of regulatory agencies. Among the agencies established were: the Federal Communications Commission, the Securities and Exchange Commission, the Civil Aeronautics Board, the National Labor Relations Board. The Depression (as we shall discuss further in chapter 15) led many people to believe that the federal government had to play some effective role in monitoring the economy. Efforts had to be made to prevent

Railroad construction in Dakota Territory in the 1880s. Westward expansion of the railroads was made possible in large measure by generous grants of land to the railroad companies by the federal government.

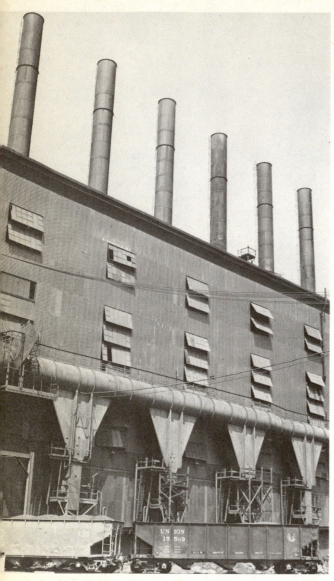

In response to the imposition of federal environmental standards, the Edgar Thomson Works of the United States Steel Corporation installed blast-furnace cleaning equipment to eliminate smoke from the boiler-house stacks. The results can be seen by comparing the stacks before the installation of the equipment (see page 368) to the stacks after the installation (shown above).

economic ups and downs and to achieve some measure of stability and economic equity. The agencies were "to correct or prevent abuses without impeding the effective operation of the industry or imposing unnecessary expense or waste." Independent expertise was to be used in performing such functions. The agencies were to *regulate but also to promote*. There was the general recognition that a totally free-market competitive system, left entirely unregulated, could lead to abuses such as harmful monopolies and unreasonable restraint of trade. When these things happened, the market was no longer "free." Thus, government regulatory functions were to perform a balancing act, and the United States was to pursue a path of government regulation of business rather than one of government ownership of business. The former course was perceived as more consistent with the role of government in a capitalist economy.

The next period of growth of regulatory agencies came in the 1970s with the establishment of such units as the Environmental Protection Agency, the Consumer Product Safety Commission, and the Occupational Safety and Health Administration.

The Regulatory Structure

What comprises these agencies, where do they fit in the overall federal government, and how do they operate?

The cabinet. We can begin by noting that some regulative functions are performed by the departments that make up the cabinet. In the process of carrying out their duties under the overall direction of a cabinet secretary (and ultimately the President), the various bureaus within a department have occasion to issue rules, regulations, and guidelines. These activities are subject to the control of the President. He appoints the top officials, and they serve at his pleasure. For example, OSHA was established in 1971 and is attached to the Department of Labor. This agency has received a great deal of attention (some of it not very favorable) because it is empowered to enforce innumerable rules relating to safety on the job. In 1979, OSHA had 2650 employees and an annual budget of $136.6 million. The Federal Aviation Administration (FAA) in the Department of Transportation regulates air traffic and investigates all aspects of air travel relating to safety. Whenever there is an air accident, the FAA conducts an investigation to determine the cause, and, hopefully, to avoid a recurrence. The FAA has absolute authority to determine whether a new plane is safe to operate, and this involves everything from detailed inspections of the smallest nuts and bolts, to landing distances, to how long it takes to evacuate a fully loaded plane (the requirement is ninety seconds).

The Food and Drug Administration is another powerful regulatory body within one of the cabinet departments—Health and Human Services. The FDA can ban the sale of certain drugs believed to cause cancer. For instance, in June 1979, the FDA, through then-Secretary Joseph A. Califano, recalled from the market most drugs containing a cancer-causing antihistamine that had been used for years in sleeping pills sold over the counter and widely advertised in a number of products available on the market.

These are just three prominent examples of regulative functions performed by the departments. Obviously, every executive cabinet department—in the process of implementing laws passed by Congress—engages in some form of regulation.

The sale and manufacture of prescription drugs is heavily regulated by the Food and Drug Administration (FDA).

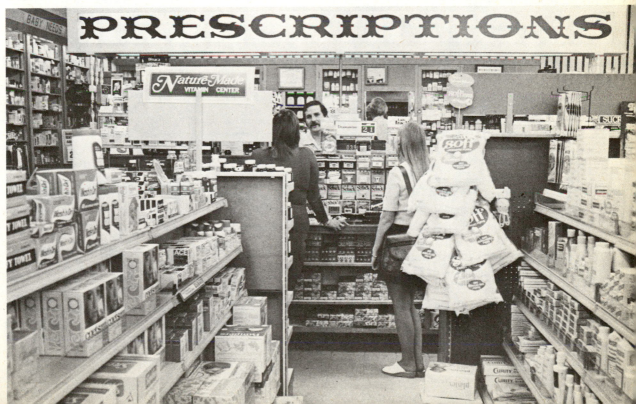

TABLE 1.
Some Independent Regulatory Agencies, Composition and Duties.

Commission	Established	Number of members	Term	Duties
Interstate Commerce Commission (ICC)	1887	11	7	Sets rates and regulates business (railroads, trucks, buses, oil pipelines) engaged in trade across state lines
Federal Trade Commission (FTC)	1914	5	7	Enforces antitrust laws; protects against false advertising and price-fixing
Federal Power Commission (FPC)	1920	5	5	Regulates gas and electric utilities, including setting rates
Federal Communications Commission (FCC)	1934	7	7	Licenses and regulates radio and television stations; sets rates for interstate telephone and telegraph operations
Securities and Exchange Commission (SEC)	1934	5	5	Regulates the stock market industry
Civil Aeronautics Board (CAB) *(to be phased out in 1983)*	1938	5	6	Assigns domestic air routes and grants overseas routes subject to presidential approval
Federal Maritime Commission (FMC)	1961	5	6	Regulates shipping in foreign commerce and domestic offshore trade

The independent agencies. Congress has established several independent regulatory commissions. The purpose of these agencies is to regulate particular industries: to set rates, issue licenses to operate, monitor business practices. These agencies get their mandate from Congress in the form of general guidelines. For example, they are told to perform their work in a way that serves "public convenience," or to set rates that are "just and reasonable." Within these exceptionally broad boundaries, there is considerable room for discretion and interpretation.

Table 1 lists some major independent commissions, their composition, and duties.

The President nominates the members of the commissions, and they must be confirmed by the Senate. Congress has stipulated that commission members must not all be from the same political party. The purpose is to make these commissions as "politically independent" as possible. Thus, they are not supposed to be answerable to either the President or to Congress in the conduct of their duties. Commission members serve overlapping terms, so they are not all up for appointment or reappointment at the same time. They can make rules, hold hearings, subpoena witnesses, and issue regulations that have the force and effect of laws, all of which give them what has been called "quasi" legislative, executive, and judicial powers. Of course, the administrative regulations rendered by these agencies are subject to review by the courts, and Congress can always pass legislation affecting the life and work of the agencies. But until and unless this happens, the agencies are largely on their own. The commissioners are not elected by the voters, and yet they exercise enormous power. They monitor the day-to-day relationship between government and industry in a way not even approached by Congress. The U.S. Constitution does not mention these agencies; ostensibly their powers are delegated to them by Congress under the section in the Constitution that permits Congress "to make all laws . . . necessary and proper for carrying into execution the [foregoing] powers. . . ." (Article 1, Section 8).

In addition to agencies shown in Table 1, there are many other commissions and boards, such as the Equal Employment Opportunity Commission, with authority to oversee various affirmative-action, nondiscriminatory programs throughout the country; the Veterans Administration; the National Labor Relations Board (NLRB); and the Nuclear Regulatory Commission.

How "Independent" Are the Agencies?

Normally, the agencies primarily steeped in the detailed, technical aspects of regulation have continuous contact only with the particular businesses with which they are dealing and, perhaps, a relatively small number of public-interest groups. The general public hears about their work only infrequently—when a drug is banned; when an auto company is ordered to recall defective cars; when a court decision overrules or sustains an agency ruling; or when a dramatic crisis occurs, as happened in late March 1979 when the nuclear power plant at Three Mile Island in Pennsylvania overheated.

For the most part, agencies operate with little public visibility, although the impact of their actions can be great indeed. In the week following the Three Mile Island accident, millions of people were introduced to the Nuclear Regulatory Commission. It is not difficult to gauge the reaction of people to a pronouncement such as that made by the chairman of the commission:

> It seems to me I have got to call the governor. We are operating almost totally in the blind. His information is ambiguous. Mine is nonexistent and—I don't know—it's like a couple of blind men staggering around making decisions.[5]

If the people charged with the legal responsibility for knowing such important things did not know, how could an untutored, lay public know? The *theory* about the way the democratic political system should function did not coincide with this particular example of the *practice*.

In 1975, a new Nuclear Regulatory Commission was established, with five commissioners, a staff of 2788 and an annual budget of $331.4 million (see Figure 1). The NRC was given the task of ensuring that nuclear power plants were safe, but the commission had been accused of the same bias so often leveled at other regulatory agencies—that it so favored the industry it was regulating that it was too lenient in its regulatory task. The General Accounting Office, just two months before the Three Mile Island accident, said in a report that the

FIGURE 1.
Organizational Chart, the Nuclear Regulatory Commission.

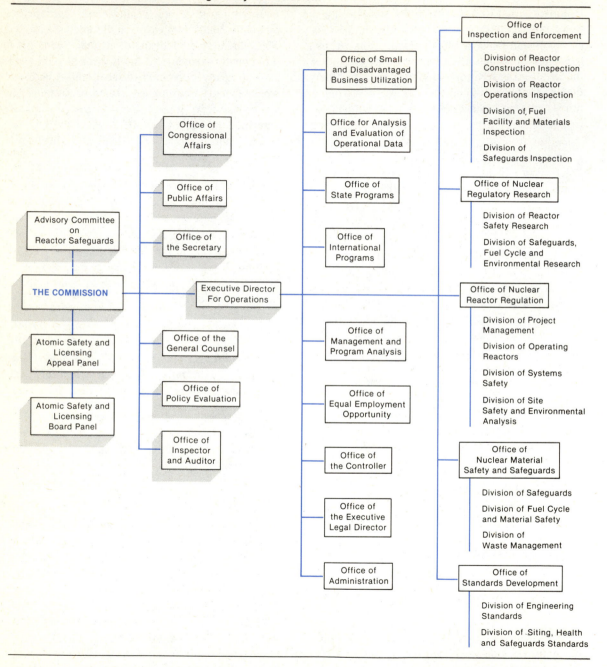

NRC had failed to make "full and effective use" of the power Congress had given it to impose fines on companies that violated its rules. The GAO (an investigative agency of Congress) stated that in a recent year the NRC had discovered 2500 violations in the 6400 inspections it had conducted. But it had imposed civil penalties only thirteen times.

To be sure, there are complaints about too many conflicting, confusing, burdensome, costly regulations on the part of all regulatory agencies. And there are efforts to ease this situation, beginning in the Oval Office itself. But a view has persisted for some time among observers of the regulatory process that, overall, the relationship between the regulatory agencies and the regulated industries is not as contentious as it seems. In theory the regulatory agencies are supposed to monitor and "regulate" the industries. But in practice, some people believe, the industries tend to control the agencies. Independent regulatory agencies may well be "independent" of Congress and the President, but in reality, it is argued, they are not so "independent" of the industries. One political scientist, Grant McConnell, has gone so far as to assert:

> The outstanding political fact about the independent regulatory commissions is that they have in general become promoters and protectors of the industries they have been established to regulate. . . . Originally, independence was conceived quite simply as a matter of independence from partisan politics. . . . The politics of industry and administration remained. In terms of the present analysis, independence substituted a small constituency, that of the industry itself, for a large constituency, that of the whole nation.[6]

For the most part, the agencies deal largely with the regulated industries, and except for required public hearings, the average citizen does not get involved in the process. As a result, the regulators spend a lot of time with representatives of the companies; they come to know each other well, and sometimes form close social as well as business ties. Louis Kohlmeier records the constant interaction in the following way:

> Regulators uniformly and consistently attend the national and regional conventions of the industries they regulate, addressing the sessions and mingling during the social hours. . . . They also see and hear industry representatives in private. A regulator's office door normally is open to industry folks for private chats. . . . Corporate executives who wine and dine the regulators are only doing what's expected of them.[7]

But Kohlmeier is quick to add that bribery is not the goal of these kinds of contacts. What the regulators really seek to accomplish is perfectly legal and understandable, that is, access and influence.

> What regulated businesses expect in return for their considerable hospitality and contributions is an appropriately large opportunity to be heard. . . .
> From the regulators, a lobbyist can hope to purchase, if not a vote for his company, then sympathy for the interests of the industry of which his company is a part.[8]

Even this, however, raises eyebrows among those who feel that there is too much coziness between the regulators and the regulated. This has been criticized by some legislators, as has the matter of regulators later taking jobs with the companies they once regulated. Part of the problem results from the fact that the regulatory agencies are expected to perform two functions: they are expected to *promote* the industries they regulate, on the one hand, and, on the other, they are

Coal-mining has been the subject of intense debate in the regulation/deregulation controversy. Proponents of strict government regulation argue that some coal-mining processes do severe damage to the environment and therefore should be subject to tight controls. The coal industry and allied groups believe that such controls are unnecessary and are, in fact, harmful to the nation's efforts to become energy independent.

expected to monitor and regulate those industries. This is not always easy. For example, some critics of the Nuclear Regulatory Commission have accused the agency of being too lax in regulating safety devices at the nuclear power plants because of its role in promoting the use of nuclear energy. Bank regulation is another problem area. The regulators (especially the Office of the Comptroller of the Currency) frequently must rely on financial support and data supplied by the banks themselves. It is difficult, therefore, for the regulators to adopt a staunch adversary attitude toward the banks. Congressman Benjamin S. Rosenthal (D., New York) "argues that the facts that the agencies are funded directly by banks and that many officials move from government into the banking industry weaken the adversary relationship that he believes should exist."[9]

One obvious area of concern involves regulators who hold financial interests in companies they also are charged with regulating. In 1978, the Oversight and Investigations Subcommittee of the House Commerce Committee reported that a substantial number of regulatory officials in three agencies (FCC, EPA, and FDA) "have financial interests in companies regulated by their agency." These "financial conflicts of interest had been found in 243 of the 630 files investigated at the three agencies."[10]

While it might be possible for a regulator to take an objective attitude toward the regulated company, such close association nonetheless raises understandable questions about the integrity and real "independence" of the regulatory process.

Earlier in the chapter we mentioned the Federal Aviation Administration (FAA) and its duties of inspection and certification of new planes. After the tragic DC-10 crash in Chicago in May 1979 (275 people killed), the FAA regulatory process came under closer scrutiny. The president of the Airline Pilots Association was quoted as saying: "The public would be outraged to know that the FAA does little more than rubber-stamp the self-regulating in which it allows the manufacturers to engage." One wonders, then, how independent an agency really is when the following situation can prevail:

> The FAA is nominally required to certify the safety of every one of the hundreds of thousands of [such] components. It does not, as a practical matter, do so. Rather, it designates employees of the manufacturers to act as surrogate inspectors. On the DC-10, McDonnell Douglas employees performed about three quarters of the required 42,000-plus inspections.[11]

The FAA explained that it relied on the industry employees simply because it did not have enough inspectors (ninety-four in total) of its own. But it defended its procedure by saying that it required detailed and voluminous reports from the regulated companies. In spite of those reports attesting to the safety of the wing pylon and the hydraulic system, the plane crashed and hundreds died.

The case study on labor reform briefly mentions the National Labor Relations Board set up in 1935. As an independent regulatory commission, the NLRB has the job of regulating relations between labor and management, deciding such matters as what constitutes an unfair labor practice, hearing complaints, and determining the appropriate means of organizing—by plant, craft, or some other basis. For most of its life the NLRB has been considered prolabor, but this is not unexpected inasmuch as the National Labor Relations Act itself was basically a prolabor piece of legislation. You will recall from the case study that labor unions considered it the "Magna Carta of the American labor movement," and, indeed, it did serve to spur union organizing and growth. It is not surprising, therefore, that the NLRB would

Almost every aspect of the construction and operation of this aircraft—from the location of exit doors to the ticket prices paid by passengers—is subject to regulation (or deregulation) by the FAA.

tend to lean in the direction of labor, although certainly the unions were not intended to be the "clients" of the NLRB. The case study also told us that the labor movement wanted to increase the size of the board from five to seven to permit it to function more expeditiously. Without question, it is safe to say that organized labor sees this particular regulatory commission as a friend, if not an ally. One can presume, therefore, that some pro-business/management groups would not hold the same view of the agency.

Regulatory Reform

How these various agencies perform their functions has become a matter of growing concern to many people, and this has led in recent years to the call for *regulatory reform*. This concern involves more efficient ways to conduct regulatory activity as well as the issue of **deregulation**. Let's look first at the plans for reform as put forth by the Carter administration in 1979.

New rules for the regulators. In March 1978, President Carter issued an executive order aimed at bringing about some reforms in the regulatory process. These reforms could only apply to agencies within the executive departments, because the President has no power to make changes by executive decree in the independent commissions. Only Congress can do that. Among other things, the President's executive order required that the regulations be determined to be absolutely necessary, that "direct and indirect" effects be "adequately considered," that other approaches be explored and "the least burdensome" alternatives chosen, that a plan be initiated to review the effect of the regulations, and that by all means "the regulation [be] written in plain English and [be] understandable to those who must comply with it."[12]

The analysis of the economic impact of a regulation was a very important aspect of the order. Where a regulation would result in an annual effect on the economy of $100 million or more, or in a major increase in costs or prices, careful analysis would have to be done to justify the new regulation. In addition, the agency would have to show why alternative ways of dealing with the problem were rejected. The executive order also sought to deal with the problem of overlapping or even conflicting regulations, by requiring the agency to show how (if at all) the regulation related to other programs and agencies.

A few months after this executive order, in October 1978, the President established the Regulatory Council. It covered all executive departments and agencies with major regulatory responsibilities; the head of the EPA was appointed as the first chairperson. One of the duties of the council was to publish a unified calendar of all major regulations which would "state the goals and benefits, legal requirements, and expected timetables of the regulations, along with available estimates of economic impacts." President Carter invited the independent regulatory commissions to join the council voluntarily.

It was clear from the start that the council would spend much of its time coordinating numerous regulations and studying the economic impact of regulations. The new head of the council said: "It will help ensure that the regulatory process is balanced and that it meets statutory goals at minimum economic cost and regulatory burden."[13] The calendar would provide a comprehen-

Drawing by Ed Arno; © 1981. The New Yorker Magazine, Inc.

sive list of proposed federal regulations in order to help identify areas of potential duplication, overlap, or inconsistency, and to suggest ways to overcome these. (One such entry in the *Federal Register* is shown in Figure 2 on pages 382–83; it relates to safety at the workplace and was issued by OSHA.)

This was a start. The President was attempting to get a handle on the regulatory maze that seemed to plague so many businesses and create so many headaches. But this was not enough. The independent agencies still were not members of the council. Therefore, in March 1979, the President called on Congress to pass legislation that would cause the independent agencies to deal with regulatory reform. The legislation would require of the independent agencies essentially the same things the earlier executive order required of the executive agencies.

"It is time we take control of federal regulations in America," the President said, "to reduce, to

FIGURE 2.
Excerpt from the Federal Register.

DOL—OSHA

OSHA General Industry Standard for

Walking and Working Surfaces (29 CFR 1910 Subpart D*), and Construction Safety Standards for Ladders and Scaffolding (29 CFR 1926 Subpart L*), Floor and Wall Openings, and Stairways (29 CFR 1926 Subpart M*)

Legal Authority

The Occupational Safety and Health Act of 1970, 29 U.S.C. § 655.

Reason for Including This Entry

The Occupational Safety and Health Administration (OSHA) believes these rules are important because preliminary economic estimates indicate that these revisions may involve compliance costs in excess of $100 million annually because the standards apply to almost all workplaces.

Statement of Problem

The number of occupational injuries resulting from fall accidents associated with unsafe ladders, scaffolding, floors, wall openings, stairways, and walking and working surfaces ranges from 20 to 25 percent of all occupational injuries in general industry and construction. There are approximately 60 million workers in these categories. The National Safety Council estimates that the direct medical cost and lost productivity cost of injuries and fatalities resulting from these hazards may reach $5 billion annually (1977 dollars).

Portions of the current safety and health standards, which were promulgated by OSHA in 1971, are deficient in coverage, ambiguous, or redundant. In addition, industry and construction groups have revised and updated their voluntary standards. Court decisions have held some of the current standards to be invalid, and other standards have been modified by OSHA program directives or variances in an attempt to deal with problems of interpretation. The proposed revision of the standards will allow these deficiencies to be addressed and will incorporate all modifications.

OSHA needs to replace the existing specification-oriented standards with revised performance-oriented standards (where criteria are set but where specific ways of meeting the criteria are not set), and to include specific hazardous items not currently covered, such as catenary scaffolds and roof perimeter guarding. Furthermore, if no Agency action is taken, the existing

more than 5 years of data collection which documents hazards, and on its commitment to prevent hazard-related injuries. OSHA will coordinate the revision of these standards with similar activities of professional and trade organizations and industry and labor representatives.

Alternatives Under Consideration

The first alternative, a comprehensive revision of the existing standards, would incorporate performance-oriented standards, language simplification, and additional coverage for hazards that are not currently regulated, such as those addressing manholes, power utility towers, and the use of body belts and harnesses. The performance-oriented standards would permit and encourage more flexibility in controlling hazards. OSHA believes that greater flexibility would lead to more effective protection at decreased expense. As part of the first alternative, OSHA would include an appendix to the standards document to aid employers and employees in complying with the performance-oriented standards through alternative methods. The appendix would provide specific, non-mandatory ways of complying with the standard. Failure to use any of the alternatives in the appendix would not mean failure to comply with the standard. The purpose of an appendix would be to help employers be aware of acceptable methods of compliance which they may follow if they do not wish to develop their own compliance methods to meet the performance-oriented language of the standard.

The advantage of this alternative is that it would address the most important problems of the existing standards by fully using the research work, support studies, and outside assistance that OSHA has collected to date. A comprehensive revision of the standards would permit more flexible and cost-effective compliance methods, reduce inconsistency among several regulatory standards, and simplify regulatory language. However, this alternative may have a major economic impact because it would cover a greater number of hazards than the present standards. Consequently, this option would involve a greater number of interested parties in the rulemaking procedures.

The second alternative is a phased effort, where a series of rulemaking procedures would be used in an established order of priority to remedy major problems in the existing standards, rather than to

and would not include an appendix listing alternative methods of compliance.

This alternative may cost the affected employers less and may simplify the overall rulemaking process, but it would not address many important hazards that are presently causing working injuries. This alternative would only remove those major problem areas known to exist in the present standards. In addition, it would not advance OSHA's regulatory policy of promulgating performance-oriented rather than specification standards.

The third alternative is to take no action, leaving the present standards as they are. This would greatly hinder OSHA's enforcement and consultation efforts, and certain hazardous areas, such as catenary scaffolding and steep-roof-perimeter protection, would remain unregulated. Many organizations and individuals who have contributed significantly to the development of proposed revisions would be disappointed with OSHA. In addition, there would be no immediate hope of more adequately addressing those hazards that may account for one-fifth of all occupational injuries.

Adoption of any one of the three alternatives would have some effect on most industrial activities. However, under the first and second alternatives, OSHA would stagger the effective dates for implementation to enhance voluntary compliance, to minimize potential economic effects and to provide time to implement an enforcement strategy.

The Agency currently regards the first alternative as the most desirable, since it is the only one that will adequately address all of the injuries associated with falls.

Summary of Benefits

Sectors Affected: All general industries (manufacturing; wholesale and retail trade; transportation, communication, electric, gas, and sanitary services; finance, insurance, and real estate; and service industries); the construction industry; and employees in these industries. Major benefits are expected to be a reduction in work-related injuries and deaths, which now account for approximately 20 percent of all occupational injuries. There would also be a reduction in related personal and family pain and suffering. OSHA expects to see benefits because the proposed standard would cover even marginal improvements in accident rates will be significant when aggregated on a nationwide basis. For example, a 10 percent reduction in work-related falls could save $500 million (1977 dollars) annually in associated medical and lost productivity costs.

In addition to these economic benefits, the revision of the construction standards to include all relevant provisions and the parallel rulemakings for construction and for general industry would encourage compliance by all employers by making it easier for employers to locate the particular regulations covering a specific situation. Further, OSHA will use a new format that will help to eliminate redundancy and ambiguity. Elimination of ambiguity will assist employers and compliance officers alike by reducing confusion as to the exact requirements of the standard. Less ambiguous language will also aid in any judicial review of a citation.

Summary of Costs

Sectors Affected: All general industries; and the construction industry.

The cost of the first alternative, comprehensive revision using performance-oriented standards, may exceed $100 million (1980 dollars) for employers to comply. This cost includes capital costs as well as operation and maintenance costs. These costs primarily affect the private sector and include every employer who is covered by either the OSHA general industry or construction industry standards. We have not yet determined whether there will be differential costs for small businesses. There will be some consideration given to the size of the facility and the frequency of use. OSHA will conduct an economic analysis.

Related Regulations and Actions

Internal: Following this action, OSHA intends to revise its standards for walking and working surfaces in the maritime industries. The agricultural standards do not need revision at this time.

External: Publications by the American Society of Testing and Materials, the American National Standards Institute, and the American Society of Civil Engineers contain or soon will contain related voluntary standards for many of the products and installations that this proposal

Active Government Collaboration

OSHA has worked and is continuing to work with the National Bureau of Standards in the Department of Commerce to develop safety requirements for scaffolding, guardrails, and safety belts. The Consumer Product Safety Commission and OSHA have been working together to establish satisfactory ladder performance standards.

The Coast Guard is also developing standards for maritime vessels and oil drilling platforms on the Outer Continental Shelf where hazards exist that are comparable to those addressed in this rulemaking. OSHA will coordinate this rulemaking with the Coast Guard's action in these areas.

Timetable

NPRM—Summer 1981.
Regulatory Analysis—Accompanying NPRM.
Public Hearings—In at least three cities.
Public Comment Period—90 days after NPRM.
Final Rule—To be determined.
Final Rule Effective—To be determined.

Available Documents

ANPRM–40 FR 17160, April 23, 1976. Comments and transcripts from town meetings which were held on June 8–10, 1976, in San Diego, California; June 15–17, 1976, in Rosemont, Illinois; June 22–24, 1976, in New Orleans, Louisiana; and June 29–July 1, 1976, in New York, New York. These documents are available for review and copying at the OSHA Technical Data Center, Room S–6212, Second and Constitution Avenue, N.W., Washington, DC 20210.

Agency Contacts

General Industry
Thomas H. Seymour
Office of Fire Protection Engineering and Systems Safety Standards
Occupational Safety and Health Administration
200 Constitution Avenue, N.W.
Washington, DC 20210
(202) 523–7216
Construction
Allan E. Martin, Director
Office of Construction and Civil Engineering Safety Standards
Occupational Safety and Health Administration

DOL—OSHA

Regulations for Reducing Safety and Health Hazards in Abrasive Blasting Operations (29 CFR 1910.94(a)*)

Legal Authority

The Occupational Safety and Health Act of 1970, 29 U.S.C. § 655.

Reason for Including This Entry

The Occupational Safety and Health Administration (OSHA) believes this regulation is necessary to protect the 100,000 abrasive blasters and employees who work in and around abrasive blasting operations from respiratory impairment and a variety of occupational safety and health hazards.

Statement of Problem

Abrasive blasting operations expose workers to several occupational hazards which may cause disease and physical injury. Of primary concern are the hazards of (1) dusts of silica (sand) and silica substitutes, (2) excessive noise levels, and (3) safety hazards, such as slippery surfaces and conditions that enhance the development of fires and explosions.

In abrasive blasting operations, streams of silica or sand substitutes are projected by compressed air to prepare a clean surface for subsequent treatment. Large quantities of dust are created which, when inhaled, are responsible for specific types of lung disease.

Silicosis is one of those diseases. It is a tissue-scarring disease of the lung that is irreversible and often fatal. The disease is responsible for a large number of deaths, either directly or by predisposing workers to tuberculosis and other infectious diseases.

The severity of this preventable disease has been repeatedly emphasized by the occupational health community, in which there is general agreement that abrasive blasters usually contract silicosis after about 10 years of occupational exposure. The incidence of silicosis increases progressively with increasing concentrations of dust present in the work environment. Systemic poisoning or cancer may also develop, depending upon the composition of the abrasive. Abraded byproducts (i.e., any materials removed from the surface of the object being blasted) may also contain toxic materials and cancer-causing agents. Furthermore, dust hazards affect not only the abrasive blasters, but also rationalize, and to streamline the regulatory burden throughout American life." The President stated that he would ask Congress to refrain from seeking authority to veto individual regulatory decisions. This would only "increase delay, undermine fair procedures and fragment responsibilities."

The President unveiled his plan before the broadcasters' convention in Dallas, and he answered questions from the audience.

Q. *Can you give us a timetable as to when we are going to be free of some of the paper work that you've discussed?*
A. *We've already made a great deal of progress in the health field. For instance, the HEW has already eliminated more than 300 specific reports that have to be brought in in health. In one day last year OSHA eliminated 1000 regulations as a wonderful gift to the American public and to the President.*

Many of the regulations issued over the years have been seen by some people as "nitpicking." OSHA, for example, regulated the shape of toilet seats companies installed in their places of business. A savings and trust company in Scottdale, Pennsylvania, reported that it once answered some questions on a government report with the word "none." The reports were returned with a request to insert "-0-" instead of "none." These sorts of rules place the regulatory process in a bad light and fan the flames of business discontent. Businesses complain about the precious time and money that are lost by complying with such "nitpicking." "We're spending hundreds of thousands of dollars to keep the Washington bureaucrats happy," the president of one small manufacturing company in Ohio said.[14] He listed fifty-six weekly, monthly, quarterly, and annual forms his company had to file with the Internal Revenue Service, the Federal Trade Commission, the Commerce, Treasury, and Labor departments, the Se-

curities and Exchange Commission, the Federal Reserve Board, and the Occupational Safety and Health Administration.

The changes under President Carter had been aimed at making the regulatory agencies more sensitive to the economic as well as social costs of their rules and regulations. There have been moves in recent years toward "deregulation"—ending controls—altogether in some industries.

The Issue of Deregulation

Certainly those companies being regulated frequently complain that the process imposes unnecessary economic costs which ultimately are passed on to the consumer in higher prices, and which in turn ultimately contribute to inflation. In addition, they complain that some regulations interfere with the free-enterprise system by impeding competition.

Many people—both regulators and the regulated—say they would *prefer* to let the free market determine rates, but this is not always possible. The chairperson of the Federal Communications Commission, Charles D. Ferris, told a telecommunications conference in 1978: "Before we decide to regulate or continue to regulate any service, we must take a hard look at whether market forces can more effectively serve the public interest."[15]

But this is easier said than done. Sometimes regulation is favored by an industry if it feels that that is the best way to protect its interests. Then, later, it might change its mind if circumstances change. Take, for example, the following case:

For many years the Federal Communications Commission imposed rules that protected the television networks and station owners from cable television. Not surprisingly, the cable television industry denounced these rules and called for "deregulation."

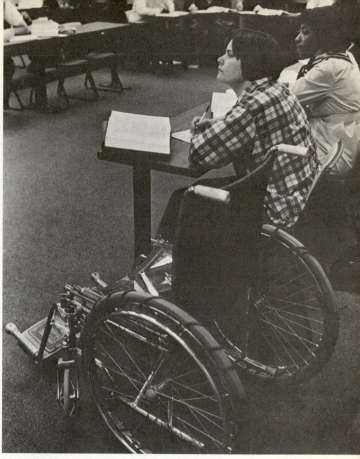

Many public facilities—such as rest rooms, parking lots, and walkways—have special areas set aside for use by the disabled. The sign shown above is used to indicate the location of such an area. Right: A law student, normally confined to a wheelchair, attends class at the University of Notre Dame. Below: Ralph Nader's 1965 book, Unsafe at Any Speed, prompted the government to issue regulations requiring the installation of seat belts in new automobiles sold in the United States.

In the last few months, however, the federal courts have thrown out many of the commission's anticable rules, and industry experts believe that the American Telephone and Telegraph Company is considering entering the market to provide a variety of electronic links between individual homes and the sources of entertainment and news, and banks and other institutions. In that case, the cable television industry would almost certainly abandon its call for deregulation and ask the commission to protect it from the telephone company's "predatory practices." [16]

Likewise, the trucking industry (or at least some companies in that industry) did *not* favor ICC deregulation of their business. They felt that deregulation would mean that new competitors would enter the already crowded field, causing chaos and loss of business.

There have already been substantial moves to deregulate the railroad and airline industries. The theory is that deregulation will increase competition, cause companies to lower prices, and increase the quality of service. And in a free-enterprise, capitalist system, this is considered preferable to a controlled, regulated market. When Congress passed airline-deregulation legislation in 1978, President Carter said: "With this legislation, we achieve two critical national objectives: controlling inflation and, at the same time, cutting unnecessary bureaucratic red tape." [17]

The economic costs of regulatory rules are always major concerns to the policymakers. What would it mean for tuition rates, for example, if colleges had to install ramps throughout the campus for the handicapped? On the other hand, should not the handicapped be provided with adequate means to get to classes? How can one put a dollar sign on some of the social and humane measures required by the regulations?

A good example was the "cotton dust" situation facing the Carter administration. Concerned about the high incidence of brown-lung disease caused by cotton dust in some factories, OSHA ordered the installation of machines to extract the dust from the workplace. The counter-complaint was that such devices would be very expensive and that the companies should be allowed to deal with the problem over a long period of time. The President's economic advisers advocated the latter move, arguing that this would involve less cost and, therefore, be less inflationary. OSHA and the Department of Labor felt this was insufficient.

At the heart of the debate is the fundamental question of how the economic costs and inflationary impact of regulation are to be weighed against the economic and social benefits, such as healthier workers and cleaner air and water. [18]

Some economists have estimated that complying with all government regulations costs as much as $100 billion a year and adds as much as one and a half percentage points to the inflation rate. President Reagan's chairperson of the Council of Economic Advisers, Murray L. Weidenbaum, has been a consistent critic of government regulation on this basis. He believes that regulations impose needless expense, impede innovation because they delay development of new products, and are particularly hard on small businesses because such firms do not have the staff to comply with all the rules and requirements. He favors deregulation wherever it is at all possible. His advice to President Reagan on this matter can be expected to be quite consistent.

But some public-interest groups are skeptical of this emphasis. They argue that there is "no way to measure the value of human life and that the cost-benefit ratio in regulation that deals with health and safety is irrelevant." [19] One OSHA official, Dr. Eula Bingham, argues that inflation, while important, cannot be the main concern of OSHA: "My ignorance of economics is comparable to the ignorance of the Council of Wage and Price Stability and the Council of Economic Advisers of industrial safety and health."[20]

Thus, in these kinds of cases, the President or the courts will have to make the hard decisions. And Congress, through regulatory reform legislation, will have to enter the arena. The measure discussed earlier in this chapter, calling for economic impact statements to accompany regulations, is a move in the direction of attempting to link regulations to overall economic concerns.

As with most aspects of government activity, various groups are only concerned with the particular agencies that directly affect their lives. Thus, although millions ride airplanes and work in factories, and everyone has an immediate interest in clean air, the agencies that deal with rates, safety, and air pollution find themselves usually responding to specific interest groups. Occasionally some groups focus on "national interest" issues. But for the most part, the public does not constitute an organized political force which pushes certain views before the regulatory agencies.

Politicians, decision-makers, and opinion leaders, however, often invoke the name of "the public" in supporting their views and decisions. "The public would be outraged . . ." if such-and-such were allowed to happen. "The public recognizes" the necessity for regulation, the EPA chairperson told his Seattle audience. OSHA's elimination of 1000 regulations was described by President Carter "as a wonderful gift to the American public." So much is stated, claimed, and done in the name of that vast entity called "the public." Let's close this chapter by examining "the public's" position on regulation.

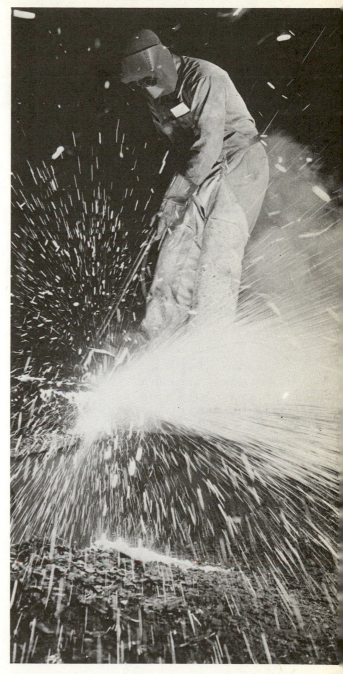

Safety in the workplace is the responsibility of the Occupational Safety and Health Administration (OSHA).

"Granted the public has a right to know what's in a hot dog, but does the public really want to know what's in a hot dog?"

Drawing by Richter; © 1978. The New Yorker Magazine, Inc.

What Does "The Public" Think About Regulation?

For at least four decades, national polling experts have been conducting surveys of Americans' opinions on a variety of issues, one of which is the public's view of government regulation of business. These surveys reveal an interesting, but not entirely unexpected, ambivalence in attitudes toward regulation. Seymour Martin Lipset and William Schneider took a look at the results in an article on the subject.[21] They found that most Americans *oppose* greater regulation, but they do *not* want to decrease regulation. "Basically, most people for over thirty years have continued to state that regulations should be continued at their present level or be made stricter. The message, therefore, is that government regulation of business has become widely accepted, and in many industries, even popular."[22]

The American people, as indicated by these poll data, also appear to understand (or believe) that government regulations involved extra spending for businesses, and that the costs are passed along to consumers.

The main reason for continued support for regulation is the belief that this is the best way to guard against abuses by industry and to protect the free-enterprise system. The public seems to believe that regulation is necessary because business "behaves badly"—and the regulatory agencies need to keep an eye on business. But "keeping an eye on" does not mean telling business "what they can charge, how much they can pay, and so on." That, the public feels, is bad. Lipset and Schneider report the public's ambivalence by concluding:

> *Public ambivalence toward regulation was captured nicely in a 1978 ORC [Opinion Research Center] survey. A majority, 62 percent, said that "many important and positive benefits have resulted from government regulation of business and industry." But a majority of the same respondents, 52 percent, also agreed that "the cost of government regulation outweighs the benefits of such regulation." Thus, the public is clearly aware of both the benefits and the costs of government regulation.*[23]

Some areas of concern are more favored for regulation than others. For instance, a 1976 Harris poll probed to find out the kinds of regulations most people supported:

- product safety and quality standards (85 and 83 percent favored regulation in these areas, respectively);
- pollution controls (82 percent);
- corruption (bribes, payoffs, illegal contributions —75 percent);
- equal employment opportunities for women and minorities (72 and 69 percent, respectively);
- allowable price increases (54 percent).

At the same time, the respondents to the Harris poll did not believe there was a particularly great need for government regulation when it came to such things as "salaries paid top executives," "dividends paid stockholders," and "the amount of profits a business can make."

Two years later, however, a 1978 Harris poll suggested that there appeared to be a growing acceptance on the part of the American public for "wage and price controls" (over "voluntary efforts and government pressures") as a means of controlling inflation.

Ironically, as Lipset and Schneider point out, "politicians and government officials are much more likely than the public to feel that business is overregulated. . . . Politicians and government officials appear to be more in favor of deregulation than the public at large."[24]

Summary

1. Regulatory functions, performed by independent agencies and by executive departments, derive from Congressional and presidential needs to delegate administrative powers. In the process, the agencies frequently exercise quasi-legislative and quasi-judicial functions.

2. Regulatory agencies are expected to promote certain industries as well as to regulate them. In performing the first function, some close ties can and do develop, raising questions about the "independence" of the agencies and the feasibility of their exercising the second function.

3. The move in recent years toward "regulatory reform" involves making the regulatory agencies more sensitive to the economic impact of regulations and moving to deregulate certain industries. In both instances, there are strong social, political, and economic arguments to support regulation *and* deregulation.

4. "The American public" is ambivalent on the issue of government regulation, seeing it as a kind of necessary nuisance—useful and important in some areas, burdensome and pointless in others.

Notes

1. *Chicago Tribune*, April 10, 1979, Section 4, p. 6.
2. *Washington Post*, April 19, 1979, p. D11.
3. *Munn* v. *Illinois*, 94 U.S. 113 (1877).
4. *Wabash, St. Louis & Pacific Railway Co.* v. *Illinois*, 118 U.S. 557 (1886).
5. *New York Times*, April 13, 1979, p. A1.
6. Grant McConnell, *Private Power and American Democracy* (New York: Alfred A. Knopf, 1965), pp. 287, 289.
7. Louis M. Kohlmeier, Jr., *The Regulators, Watchdog Agencies and the Public Interest* (New York: Harper & Row, 1969), pp. 70, 72.
8. Ibid., p. 77.
9. "Ability and Will of Bank Regulators to Monitor Industry Is Questioned," *New York Times*, December 19, 1977, pp. 1, 56.
10. *New York Times*, February 19, 1978, p. 25.
11. *New York Times*, June 10, 1979, p. 4E.
12. Executive Order 12044, March 23, 1978.
13. Statement issued by Douglas M. Costle, administrator, Environmental Protection Agency, and chairperson of the Regulatory Council, November 1, 1978.
14. *New York Times*, March 20, 1978, p. D1.
15. *New York Times*, June 4, 1978, p. E4.
16. Ibid.
17. *Washington Post*, September 22, 1978, p. A1.
18. *New York Times*, June 14, 1978, p. D6.
19. Ibid.
20. Ibid.
21. Seymour Martin Lipset and William Schneider, "The Public View of Regulation," *Public Opinion* (January/February 1979), 6–13.
22. Ibid.
23. Ibid., 10.
24. Ibid., 9.

Congress: Legislators, Staffs, and Constituencies

Chapter
11

Congressman Dan Rostenkowski is a 6'4", 200-pound representative from one of the largest Polish-American communities in the country. Now in his fifties, he was first elected to the House of Representatives in 1958 at the age of thirty, receiving the support of the Cook County (Chicago) Democratic-party machine. As head of the influential House Ways and Means Committee and former whip of the Democratic party, Rostenkowski is both a physically and politically powerful figure. Like Presidents Reagan and Carter, Representative Rostenkowski has been known to work long hours. In his role as chairman of the Ways and Means Committee, which deals with, among other things, tax legislation, he was becoming annoyed at the way the Senate Finance Committee was bullying the House committee in joint conference meetings.

During a 1976 tax bill conference he got mad, and became determined to stop the beating. "I stayed up until 4 a.m. studying and working my head off," Rostenkowski said. Next day, he pounded the table, took on [Sen.] Long [D., Louisiana] and Sen. Lloyd M. Bentsen [D., Texas] and beat them on several major points.[1]

This vignette draws our attention to several important aspects of Congress: political party leadership, powerful legislative committees, the interaction between the House and the Senate, and the role of local party organizations. These matters and others are important to an understanding of the **legislative branch** of our national government, or Congress: what it does, how, and why.

The Framers' Views of Congress: If Men Were Angels . . .

As we pointed out in chapter 1, the structure of the American government is largely the result of the constitutional framers' objective of holding government in check. The **bicameral** (two-chamber) legislature, whereby one house can check the other, is one product of this intent. Let us refer, again, to those important and revealing statements by James Madison in *Federalist Paper* No. 51. Madison pointed out the necessity of

contriving the interior structure of the government as that its several constituent parts may, by their mutual relations, be the means of keeping each other in their proper places.

. . . If men were angels, no government would be necessary. If angels were to govern men, neither external nor internal controls on government would be necessary. In framing a government which is to be administered by men over men, the great difficulty lies in this: you must first enable the government to control the governed; and in the next place oblige it to control itself.[2]

So, when Congressman Rostenkowski stayed up late to prepare his challenge to the Senate committee, he was exercising a check on the Senate in the noblest tradition intended by the framers—even though he may not have had such lofty traditions in mind.

In addition, many framers believed that the "passions of the masses," as represented in the House, ought to be checked by the more "calm and deliberative" body of the Senate. Remember that until the adoption of the Seventeenth Amendment in 1913, senators were chosen by their respective state legislatures. The House of Representatives (sometimes referred to as the "lower chamber," to the chagrin of most representatives), whose members were chosen directly by the people, was to represent the citizens; the Senate was to represent the states.[3]

Some critics of the constitutional convention's work felt that too much power was lodged in Congress at the national level at the expense of the states. But as "Publius" (James Madison's pseudonym) argued in *Federalist Paper* No. 46: "A local spirit will infallibly prevail much more in the members of Congress than a national spirit will prevail in the legislatures of the particular States. . . . Measures will too often be decided according to their probable effect, not on the national prosperity and happiness, but on the prejudices, interests, and pursuits of the governments and people of the individual States."

In other words, Madison felt that the members of Congress would be more inclined to speak for their local districts than to represent the national interest.

From Dominance to Subordination to Reassertion

Virtually all the historical evidence suggests that the constitutional framers and many early political activists and analysts believed that Congress would be an active—even dominant—branch of

President Woodrow Wilson traveled extensively in an effort to gain public support for his concept of a League of Nations. Here he is shown delivering a speech in Los Angeles in 1919.

government. Indeed, through most of the nineteenth century, this was precisely the case. In the 1880s, a young graduate student at Johns Hopkins University, Woodrow Wilson, concluded in his doctoral dissertation that the American national government was basically government by Congress, which meant government by Congressional committee chairpersons.[4] This young man went on to become President, and he saw his last major dream, the League of Nations, rejected by an assertive, powerful, recalcitrant Senate.

However, since the 1930s, with the pressures of a decade-long depression, World War II, the Korean War, the Vietnam War, periodic recessions, and the struggle for equal rights by minority groups and women, we have experienced strong executive leadership. The only exception was President Dwight Eisenhower's tenure, from 1953–1961. But even he was forced to take strong action, such as sending U.S. troops to Little Rock, Arkansas, to enforce court-ordered school integration and using the veto power several times in the last years of his administration. Moreover, since the thirties, the country has been a permanent world power—politically, economically, militarily. This in itself has called for increased presidential activism, as we noted in chapter 8, because Congress, by its nature, at times could not respond rapidly enough to meet fast-developing events.

Although Congress did not enter into a complete eclipse (certainly President Kennedy in his 1000 days in office did not think so), it hardly resembled the Congress of the nineteenth century. But the growing dissatisfaction with presidential conduct during the Vietnam War and the damage wreaked on the White House by the resignations within one year of a President and vice-president in disrepute gave Congress the opportunity—if not the capacity—to reassert itself as an equal partner in policymaking.

Professor Harvey G. Zeidenstein has suggested that Congress has, in fact, moved in the 1970s to reassert itself in relation to the President.[5] In addition to the War Powers Act and the Budget and Impoundment Control Act discussed in chapter 8, Congress has taken steps to curb presidential action in regard to emergencies as well as in connection with intelligence-gathering activities. In 1973, a Senate committee found 470 provisions in federal law relating to wartime and emergency situations. Since some provisions declared years ago by Presidents were still on the books (even though the emergencies no longer existed), the President had exceptional power to act—power which would not be granted under normal circumstances. Thus, on September 14, 1976, Congress passed the National Emergencies Act, stating that

an emergency declared by the President ends in one year unless Congress is advised otherwise by the President. Furthermore, when the President declares an emergency, he must inform Congress of the specific laws under which he intends to act. "Finally, every six months during an emergency or declared war, and within three months after it has ended, the President must inform Congress of the total expenditures directly attributed to the emergency or war."[6]

In addition, in 1974 and 1976 Congress amended the Foreign Military Sales Act to require the President to give Congress thirty days' advance notice of any intention to sell military arms or services involving $7 million or more in defense equipment or $25 million or more in arms or services. Congress, within the thirty days, may pass a resolution disapproving the sale, thus using the "deferral" type of legislative veto described in chapter 8.

Where does all this Congressional reassertiveness lead? Professor Zeidenstein cautions against overexpectation:

> While there will be some retrenchment of the President's influence, there will not be a period of congressional dominance reminiscent of the nineteenth century. The President has too many responsibilities, legal and political, for that. . . . The new restrictions make it easier for Congress to offset the President. Executive actions kept secret in the past now must be reported routinely, giving Congress substantive knowledge on which to act.[7]

This view is probably a realistic one. A representative from New York City, Theodore Weiss, adds that while there is certainly a new posture in Congress today toward the executive leader, the fact remains that "on the really important issues," Congress still waits for the President to initiate policy. This seems to suggest that the chief-initiator role discussed in chapter 8 will not be substantially altered. Nonetheless, it is significant that Congress has increased its activity, in a number of areas—the federal budget, use of the legislative veto, emergency declarations, foreign military sales—to become more involved in the governing process. Reassertiveness of this type will probably continue, unless some catastrophic event upsets the balance.

The Organization of Congress

When we use the term *Congress*, we are referring, of course, to the 435 people in the House of Representatives (plus three additional nonvoting delegates from Washington, D.C., the Virgin Islands, and Guam) and the 100 in the Senate. There are, therefore, 535 ''prima donnas,'' as Hubert Humphrey called them, and immediately we know that some sort of organization must be imposed on this institution or there will be chaos. Basically, organization is achieved through three mechanisms: political parties, formal leadership positions, and committees and subcommittees. Each chamber devises its own formal and informal rules for regulating these mechanisms and maintaining order. Congressional caucuses, based on issues, regions, or ethnicity are a fourth, less formal method of organization.

The role of political parties.   Most members of Congress are affiliated with one of the two major political parties. Occasionally an Independent will be elected to Congress, but not very often. When a new member is sworn in, he or she is assigned a seat on one side of the aisle or the other according to party affiliation. And he or she automatically becomes a member of the overall party *caucus* (for Democrats in the House) or party *conference* (for Republicans in the House and for Democrats and Republicans in the Senate). These broad party groups designate their party's formal leaders and

Legislators are sworn in at the opening session of the 97th Congress.

assign their members to the Congressional committees. In other words, the two major political parties are the first and major means of organizing Congress.

This organizational function is the most binding and important task of the political party in Congress. The political parties, for instance, do not command votes. A Democrat or a Republican does not necessarily follow his or her "party line" when voting—assuming there *is* a party position on a particular issue. Normally, the President represents the party position for *his* party, and the party legislators usually follow his lead. Unlike parliamentary systems such as in England, the President is not a member of the legislature, and his leadership is not automatically followed. On the other hand, Congressional party leaders and members know there are more advantages than disadvantages to supporting their President in the White House, and the record shows that this support is more often given than not. When the presidency is occupied by the "other" party, more emphasis is placed on party-leadership roles in Congress.

We often hear that party discipline is weak in Congress, meaning that most representatives—Democratic or Republican—do not give blind loyalty to their parties. In fact, the political party is only *one* of the reference points used by legislators to determine how to act. The voters back in the state or district are usually the most important consideration. Although each party in each chamber has a campaign committee which donates funds to help elect their candidates, this is not usually a large sum of money. For the most part, the parties in Congress have little effect on electing members. In Mr. Rostenkowski's case, for instance, his bedrock support comes from the *local* Cook County Democratic party. Many other legislators find that they must build and rely on their own local bases of support.

Congressman Rostenkowski confers with a local housing official in his Illinois Congressional district.

Let us now place the Congressional party relationship with members of Congress in perspective. Congressional hopefuls normally run as Republicans or Democrats. They win on one of the two tickets, usually through the efforts of friends and neighbors, with, perhaps, some national party support. They go to Washington and designate themselves as members of one party or the other. They attend that party's organizing caucus or conference meetings. They vote for their party leaders in Congress. They receive committee assignments from the party. They probably associate with similar party types, share the party "cloakroom," attend party strategy meetings, are written up in the newspapers (hopefully, often and favorably) with a *D* or *R* after their names, and sit on a certain side of the aisle in chamber sessions and committee meetings. And, of course, their votes are recorded by the press, the public, and scholars

*Speaker of the House Thomas P. ("Tip")
O'Neill and House Minority Leader
Robert H. Michel.*

as a vote "with" or "against" their party. If there are no other compelling reasons—namely, their own views and interests, and their constituents' wishes—they are expected to go along with the party's leadership on House or Senate votes. The longer they stay in Congress, the "safer" their seat becomes and the greater the likelihood that they will become power wielders, occupying positions of leadership and paying close attention to party unity. Congress becomes their home, and working with the political party leadership makes living there more comfortable.

Formal leadership positions. Although there may be 535 prima donnas, some are more "prima" than others.

House of Representatives. In the House, the top leader is the **Speaker of the House**. This position is designated in the Constitution. Each party nomi-

nates one of its own for the job, and, since the vote on the floor is always along party lines, the majority party wins. The minority party nominee then becomes the House **minority leader**. The Speaker presides over House sessions, appoints members to special temporary committees, recognizes persons who wish to speak, rules on parliamentary questions, refers bills to committees, and chooses the chairperson and most members of the House Rules Committee.

At one time, the Speaker was considered just slightly less powerful than the President of the United States. He made assignments to all committees, chose the chairpersons, and kept tight control over the flow of Congressional business. Speaker Joseph Cannon, who reigned from 1903 to 1910, abused this power and provoked a revolt among House members. In 1910, certain changes were made in order to reduce the power of the Speaker. Thereafter, committee chairpersons and committee memberships were chosen on the basis of seniority. That is, leadership positions went to those with the longest service on the committees. This was a more impartial way of selecting leaders, and while it had its faults, as we shall see later, at least it helped curtail the arbitrary and autocratic use of power by the Speaker. The Speaker remained a powerful figure, however. The position has never been simply an honorary one nor its holder a figurehead.

Both parties have a rather similar House leadership structure. Each has a designated leader, *whips* to assist the leader, and a committee to coordinate broad policy positions or goals. For the Democrats, this is the Steering and Policy Committee, which also gives committee assignments and designates committee leaders (the party caucus can overrule these decisions). The House Republicans have two separate committees to perform these functions: the Committee on Committees, and the Policy Committee.

The **whips** assist the majority and minority leaders. Their job is to corral support from their party members for certain measures. They are assigned certain regions. Knowledgeable whips try to learn as much as possible about what the party members want, need, plan to do and not do, where they are (in Washington or around the country at times of crucial votes), and how they stand on items of importance to the leadership. As their title suggests, they are sometimes, but not often, expected to "whip" members into line (but as we have noted, party loyalty is not the only factor influencing a legislator's actions). More often than not, it is just as important for the whips to inform the leadership what it will take to bring a recalcitrant member or members over to their side.

If the party leaders are not good bargainers, they will not be good Congressional leaders. Although powerful in their positions, leaders like Mr. Ros-

tenkowski must be able to take Congress's pulse, to read its mood. As a *Washington Post* reporter observed:

> *Until recently, reading the House was a throwaway talent. Strong chairmen wrote legislation, politics followed party lines and voting was relatively predictable. But with the decline of parties, the independence of younger members and the uncertainty of the times, the mood often is mercurial, bending with every breeze blowing in the land, and Rostenkowski's mood-reading ability is becoming more important.*[8]

Senate. The vice-president of the United States, by constitutional mandate, is the "president of the Senate." He can, but seldom does, preside over that body, and he votes only to break a tie, which seldom happens. There is also a **president pro tempore** (or pro tem) of the Senate. This is largely an honorific and politically unimportant position, and usually is given to a senior member in recognition of long and faithful service. A visitor to the Senate chamber normally will see a junior senator (one recently elected to the Senate) doing the unexciting, time-consuming work of presiding over the Senate during unimportant "debates" (usually dreary speeches). When a major issue is on the floor and a crucial vote is to be taken, attendance increases.

The real Senate leadership is lodged in the Senate majority leader, assisted by a coterie of whips and committee chairpersons. Since Senate members are fewer in number and serve longer terms than their counterparts in the House (six years), senators, even junior senators, have to be handled a bit more gingerly. They are important back in their home states, and they serve on important committees. It is much tougher "whipping" them into line than it is over in the House of Representatives. Precisely because of the fewer number of votes, each vote is more valuable. In

The United States Senate, 1981.

addition, senators have the added ammunition of the filibuster. It is also likely that senators have their own direct lines to the White House, to the bureaucracy, and to powerful interest groups.

Committees and chairpersons. The business of Congress is conducted mainly in committees, for largely practical reasons. It is here that democratic theory must yield to the realities of the Congressional work load. As one reporter noted about a freshman congressman:

> *Nothing is as he* [the new congressman] *imagined it might be, or substantially corresponds to any textbook or media description, or to his own notion of how Congress ought to address the problems of the country.*[9]

Theoretically, members of Congressional committees carefully and studiously examine the more than 20,000 bills introduced per session; they take their work home every night and stay up until 4:00 A.M. reading and studying legislative proposals; and they give equal time and attention to all subcommittee assignments.

In reality, legislators have little time to reflect on the substance of policy issues. Their days are hectic, as they rush from one meeting to another, from committee hearing to the office, from the voting floor to an interview with a local news reporter, and then back to the office to see a constituent. They seldom have a chance to concentrate on the hundreds of legislative proposals before it is time to vote on them.

Congress is, indeed, a complex place to work, and a conscientious legislator is likely to find constant cause for frustration precisely because the demands on one's time are enormous. But this is exactly why committee work is so very important, and why the wise senators and representatives quickly recognize that they must use the committee system to help them budget their time and focus their attention.

Each chamber has standing committees, 22 in the House and 15 in the Senate; and there are 149 subcommittees in the House and 100 in the Senate. In addition, there are 4 joint committees and 13 special or select committees. The standing committees focus on major areas of concern, such as appropriations, judiciary, international relations, government operations, finance, agriculture, and human resources. Subcommittees deal with more specialized subjects within the broad committee topics, such as the Senate subcommittee on welfare reform within the Senate Finance Committee, and the House subcommittee on Africa of the House International Relations Committee. Members of Congress try to be assigned to committees and subcommittees that deal with subjects that interest them or are of vital concern to their constituents. Sometimes, such assignments can make the difference between an effective representative and an insignificant one.

One example of the committee assignment process involved the first black congresswoman, Shirley Chisholm, and her fight to be assigned to a committee relevant to her background and the district she represented, namely a predominantly black and Puerto Rican, low-income, inner-city district in Brooklyn, New York. This was in 1969, when she first went to Congress. Let Representative Chisholm tell her story.

The first big event in a freshman congressman's career is his assignment to a committee. . . . I

Former New York Congresswoman Shirley Chisholm campaigning among the voters in her district.

sent a letter with a resume of my background to every majority member of Ways and Means [the committee in the House then used by the Democrats to make committee assignments]. . . . I learned by the grapevine that the committee had met and assigned me to the Agriculture Committee. . . . Then I found out what my subcommittee assignments were to be: rural development and forestry. Forestry! That did it.[10]

She immediately went into action, addressing the Speaker: "I don't know if this is protocol, Mr. Speaker, but I wanted to talk to you because I feel my committee and subcommittee assignments do not make much sense." The Speaker was sympathetic, but he told her, "Mrs. Chisholm, this is the way it is. You have to be a good soldier." She argued that she had been a "good soldier," but more importantly that since there were so few (nine at the time) blacks in Congress, they should be in positions to maximize their effectiveness. She then told the Speaker that if he could not help her, she would have to do her "own thing."

"Your what?" the Speaker asked in a surprised and startled voice. Perhaps he imagined that this newly elected black woman from Brooklyn would try to set up her own committee! Party leaders then decided to assign her to a different agriculture subcommittee.

Mrs. Chisholm was not yet satisfied and took her fight to the floor of the Democratic caucus meeting, where it took her a half hour to be recognized. She recalled: "Men were smiling and nudging each other as I stood there trying to get the floor." She was finally recognized and made her argument for a more relevant committee assignment.

"You've committed political suicide," one of her colleagues told her afterwards. "The leadership will have it in for you as long as you're here."

Nonetheless, she was reassigned to the Veterans' Affairs Committee, which she felt was certainly better than the Agriculture Committee. "There are a lot more veterans in my district than there are trees," she wrote later.

Because there are more members in the House than in the Senate, House members serve on fewer committees and subcommittees. This means that they are able to concentrate their attention on a smaller number of issues. A senator, however, must serve on at least two major committees and several subcommittees. Faced with such impossible demands on their time, most senators wisely decide to devote most of their efforts to one substantive issue (or at most, two), becoming as knowledgeable about it as possible. In this way, they are able to master one subject and become something of an expert in that field in relation to their colleagues. In time, their ability to debate and advise on a particular subject may bring respect and possibly power and influence. Senators who attempt to be jacks-of-all-trades frequently end up mastering no subject in depth, and this shortcoming will be evident in debates and committee sessions. Their prestige will suffer, and they might soon become tagged as "lightweights."

Expertise on a single issue is best gained through committee work. Each committee and subcommittee staff is constantly in touch with the concerned bureaucratic agencies and interest groups that feed them data and allow them to keep abreast of new developments in that field. Sometimes executives and lobbyists appear at formal committee hearings and testify about various matters: pending legislation, proposed budgets, the operation of existing programs, proposed personnel appointments, and so forth. As was noted in chapters 5, 9, and 10, a close relationship can develop between the legislators and the administrators and lobbyists in certain areas.

Since most legislation is worked out in committees, those who head the committees, understandably, are very important, despite recent reforms that curtailed some of their power. Although the seniority rule has been modified somewhat, most chairpersons are still chosen on the basis of longevity on the committee: the member of the majority party with the longest tenure on the committee is normally chosen as chairperson. This system has certain consequences for the substance as well as the style of politics. Members of Congress who come from "safe" districts (that is, where there is little or no competition for their seats) are reelected time after time and gradually build up seniority.

The power of the chairperson is magnified when he or she serves on a "key" committee, that is, a committee considered more influential than others.

A meeting of the House Administration Committee in 1978. The committee is responsible for overseeing expenditures and allowances of all House committees and members and for deciding all disputed House elections.

In the House, the Ways and Means Committee (which deals with taxes), the Rules Committee, and the Appropriations Committee are exceptionally important because of the topics they deal with and the scope of their powers. For instance, committees must route their bills through the House Rules Committee, which then schedules a time for each bill to be brought before the full body. The Rules Committee can stipulate how much time will be allowed for debate and whether the bill can be amended or not. In other words, it sets *rules* governing the handling of the bill. Therefore, the leadership of that committee is crucial. A chairperson can sit on a bill, not schedule hearings, not bring it up for discussion, or require changes in the bill before it is put on the calendar. Such a chairperson might work in conjunction with the chairperson of a particular committee and with the Speaker and the majority leader, thus forming a most powerful "inner clique." This is what people refer to when they talk about "the leadership": a handful of people who literally can control what the laws of the country will be in *most* cases.

The *discharge petition* is the only way the House can force a bill out of committee. Since this request must be signed by 218 members, however, it is difficult, but not impossible, to secure.

Later in this chapter, when discussing some reforms that have been adopted in Congress over the last few years, we should keep in mind that we are dealing with a strongly entrenched leadership structure built around the committee system.

Special-issue caucuses. The special-issue caucuses are based on issues, regions, ethnicity, and sex. In terms of their ability to influence their members, these organizations are not as strong as the more formal Congressional committees and leadership, but they can serve a useful role for the legislators. These caucuses have been developing rather rapidly over the last few years, and the newer ones tend to be more single-issue oriented than the older ones. In the early 1960s, the liberal Democrats in the House established the Democratic Study Group (DSG) to balance the older, established, more conservatively oriented Democratic leadership. The DSG, with an executive director and staff, provided its members with position papers and cues to voting, and it formed an identifiable nucleus of between 230 and 280 members at one time. It usually identified with the liberal viewpoint on a range of issues, such as civil rights, social welfare, foreign policy, and the environment.

The caucuses that developed in the 1970s are more specialized: the Congressional Black Caucus (1971); the New England Caucus (1973); the Congressional Rural Caucus (1973); the Metropolitan Area Caucus (1973); the Northeast-Midwest Economic Advancement Coalition (1976); the Western Coalition (1977); the Suburban Caucus (1977); the Congressional Port Caucus (1977); the Congressional Steel Caucus (1978); the Vietnam-Era Veterans of Congress (1978); the Congresswomen's Caucus (1977); the Blue Collar Caucus (1977); the Ad Hoc Committee for Irish Affairs (1978), led, interestingly enough, by an Italian-American congressman from New York, Mario Biaggi; and the High Altitude Coalition (1978).

These groups vary in size from approximately 213 members (from 18 states) in the Northeast-Midwest Economic Advancement Coalition to the small, eight-member High Altitude Coalition. All groups are bipartisan and their membership is sometimes disparate. Most have an executive director and a small staff.

Capitol Hill observers believe that these newly established groups indicate that legislators are becoming more issue-oriented, more specialized, and that they feel the need for an organization beyond the broad committees and even subcommittees to work for their particular goals. One House legislative assistant saw this as an unfortunate trend: "Everyone is becoming single-issue oriented—abortion, the environment, nuclear energy. It's dangerous—a sort of selfishness intruding into our society."[11]

The Work of Congress: Legislation

The Constitution plainly says, "All legislative powers . . . shall be vested in a Congress of the United States. . . ." Thus, the main duty of Congress is to pass laws, and this is how it spends most of its official time. As we shall see, individual representatives and senators perform other functions—such as serving their constituents on an individual basis, intervening on behalf of interest groups, and so forth—but when we think of Congress as a whole, we think of an institution organized mainly to pass the laws that govern the society.

Figure 1 describes the basic steps involved in transforming a piece of legislation from a bill into a law. Although it is an accurate account of the official process, such general outlines obscure the behind-the-scenes details: they do not discuss the politics involved at virtually each step nor the bargains and compromises entered into. This type of information is usually found only in in-depth investigative reports by journalists[12] and in detailed case studies of particular episodes.[13]

On the other hand, *every* piece of legislation passed is *not* the result of a back-room deal struck between the legislators, interest groups, and the President. Some bills pass or die simply on their

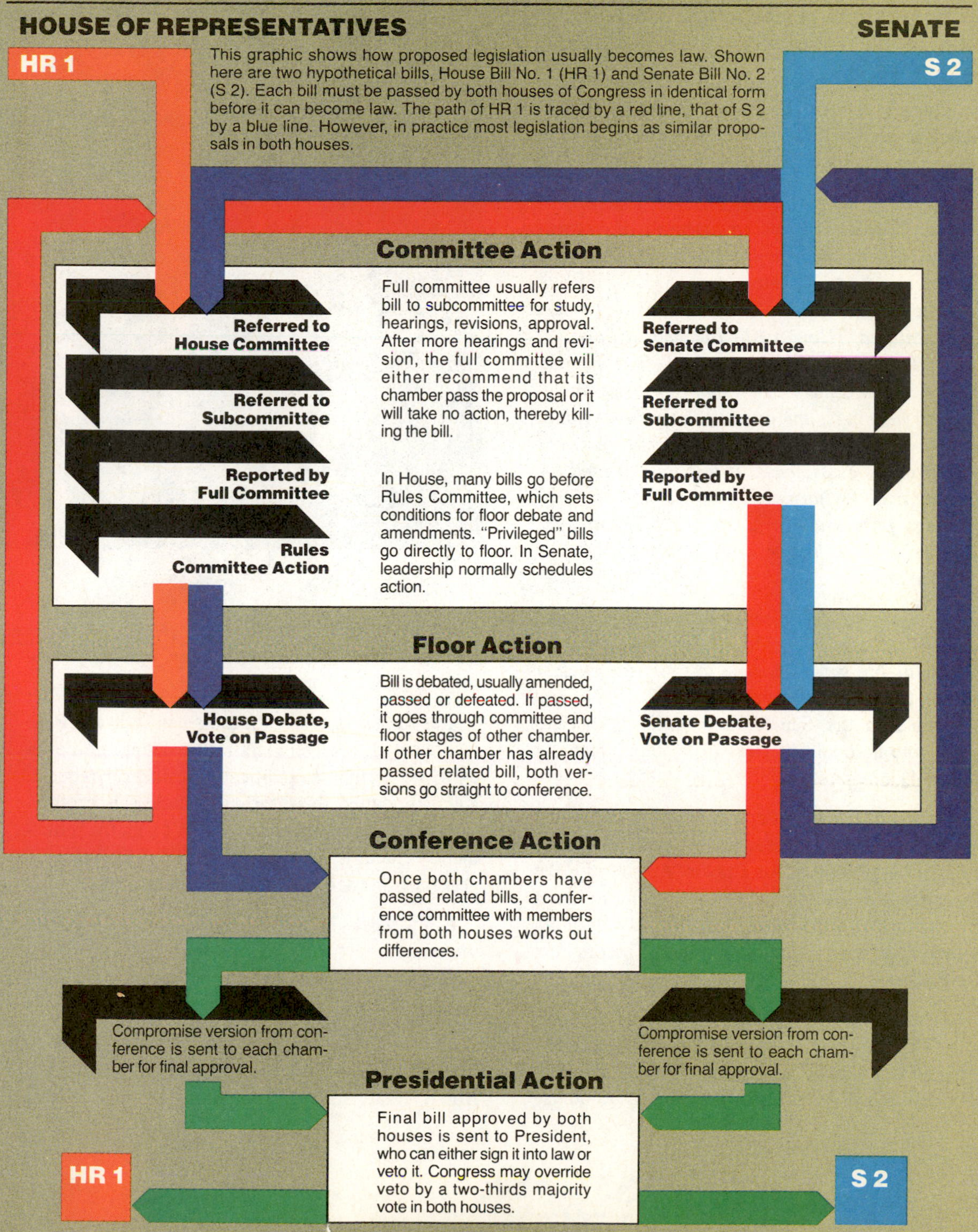

FIGURE 1.
How a Bill Becomes Law.

HOUSE OF REPRESENTATIVES

SENATE

HR 1

S 2

This graphic shows how proposed legislation usually becomes law. Shown here are two hypothetical bills, House Bill No. 1 (HR 1) and Senate Bill No. 2 (S 2). Each bill must be passed by both houses of Congress in identical form before it can become law. The path of HR 1 is traced by a red line, that of S 2 by a blue line. However, in practice most legislation begins as similar proposals in both houses.

Committee Action

Referred to House Committee

Referred to Subcommittee

Reported by Full Committee

Rules Committee Action

Full committee usually refers bill to subcommittee for study, hearings, revisions, approval. After more hearings and revision, the full committee will either recommend that its chamber pass the proposal or it will take no action, thereby killing the bill.

In House, many bills go before Rules Committee, which sets conditions for floor debate and amendments. "Privileged" bills go directly to floor. In Senate, leadership normally schedules action.

Referred to Senate Committee

Referred to Subcommittee

Reported by Full Committee

Floor Action

House Debate, Vote on Passage

Bill is debated, usually amended, passed or defeated. If passed, it goes through committee and floor stages of other chamber. If other chamber has already passed related bill, both versions go straight to conference.

Senate Debate, Vote on Passage

Conference Action

Once both chambers have passed related bills, a conference committee with members from both houses works out differences.

Compromise version from conference is sent to each chamber for final approval.

Compromise version from conference is sent to each chamber for final approval.

Presidential Action

Final bill approved by both houses is sent to President, who can either sign it into law or veto it. Congress may override veto by a two-thirds majority vote in both houses.

HR 1

S 2

merits. But there is a rather widespread impression that all of politics is a series of underhanded deals.

Let's take a look at the situation as described by the former Senate majority secretary, Bobby Baker, in his book, *Wheeling and Dealing: Confessions of a Capitol Hill Operator*:

> *I used to grin, perhaps a bit cynically, when I chanced upon one of the more popular documents congressmen send to their constituents in order to advertise themselves. . . .*
>
> *The booklet which caused me wry amusement was entitled "How a Bill Becomes a Law." It traced the sixteen steps from introduction through assignment to the appropriate committee for hearings, and on until the president signs it into law. Not that it wasn't accurate in the strict civics-class sense: it just failed to tell the whole truth. What is left out was how the winnowing processes work: the trade-offs and the private agreements or understandings between politicians.*[14]

As an example, Mr. Baker describes President Kennedy's efforts—which ultimately proved successful—to get the Senate to ratify the nuclear test ban treaty with Russia in 1963. The treaty was in trouble in the Senate, and Kennedy needed every vote he could muster, from Republicans as well as Democrats.

Earlier, former President Eisenhower had asked the Senate minority leader, Everett McKinley Dirksen (R., Illinois), for a favor. Apparently, the Department of Justice had been planning to indict the husband of a friend of Mrs. Eisenhower and a former Eisenhower aide on charges of income tax evasion.

According to Baker, Eisenhower said to Dirksen: "I'd like you to ask President Kennedy, as a personal favor to me, to put the . . . indictment in the deep freeze. You have the authority to advise

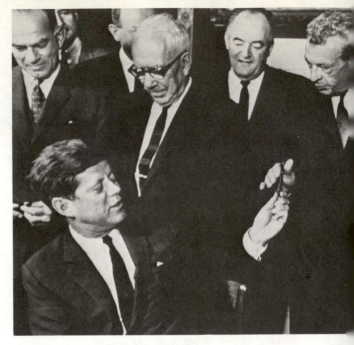

President Kennedy hands one of the pens used in signing the nuclear test ban treaty to Illinois Senator Dirksen, 1963.

him he'll have a blank check in my bank if he will grant me this favor."

The Republican senator took a stroll in the Rose Garden with the Democratic President and delivered the former Republican President's request. Kennedy called the attorney general (his brother, Robert Kennedy) and said, "Don't sign the indictment. Place it in deep freeze." The attorney general protested; the President prevailed.

A few weeks later, back in the Senate, it seemed the nuclear test ban treaty would fall short of the necessary two-thirds vote. Senator Dirksen, among others, had made strong speeches against it.

It was time for the President to go to the bank. Bobby Baker tells the remaining story as it was told to him by Senator Dirksen. Here, then, is one insider telling another insider how politics really works:

> "President Kennedy called me to the White House and said, 'Ev, I must write a check on you and Ike. This atomic treaty is important to me and to the country and, I think, to all mankind. It's imperative that it be approved. Ike said I had coin in his bank, and you say I have coin in yours.' "
>
> "I told the President," Senator Dirksen said, "that yes, we owed him one. He then said, 'Ev, I want you to reverse yourself and come out for the treaty. I also want Ike's public endorsement of the treaty before the Senate votes. We'll call it square on that other matter.' "
>
> Dirksen said, "Mr. President, you're a hell of a horse trader. But I'll honor my commitment, and I'm sure that General Eisenhower will." Both men shortly came out for the bill, and that's how JFK got his nuclear arms limitation treaty.[15]

It is impossible, of course, to verify this story; the four people immediately involved are no longer living. That does not mean that such events do not happen; it means that students of the American political system will have to realize that in this field all is not open for full examination. We can assume these kinds of arrangements are made, and they are important to a full understanding of the process of politics. Still, it would be misleading, indeed cynical, to conclude that all legislation is a result of private arrangements.

Keeping in mind that there may be a few walks in the Rose Garden or talks in the Congressional corridors, let us now describe "how a bill becomes a law." A bill originates when a legislator drops a proposal in a box set aside for this purpose, known as the *hopper*. The clerk of the House or Senate gives it a number: S (Senate) 2 or HR (House of Representatives) 1, for example, and it is referred to a committee (see, again, Figure 1). The committee usually assigns it to a subcommittee, which proceeds to hold hearings on it. The bill is then returned to the full committee where it might be worked on more. If passed, it is sent to the House Rules Committee or to the Senate majority leader where it is placed on the calendar for discussion and vote before the full house. In the House, different types of bills go on different calendars, as determined by the Rules Committee. In the Senate, there is one calendar, which is arranged by the majority leader. However, under the provisions of the *unanimous consent* rule, the Senate may, by unanimous vote, force a bill to be called ahead of others.

When the bill is called, it is debated and passed or rejected. If it is passed, it is sent to the other chamber. If that chamber passes it (or if it has already passed an identical bill), it is sent to the President for his signature. If there is any difference between the bills passed by the two chambers, a **conference committee**, composed usually of members of the major committees or subcommittees of each chamber, meets to iron out the differences. The conference committee reports the results to the two houses, where a vote is taken. If passed (as is usually the case, at this point), it goes to the President, who signs it or vetoes it. If he vetoes the bill, it goes back for a possible override vote (a two-thirds majority in both houses is needed to override the veto). If the veto is overridden, the bill becomes a law.

Procedures and politics. In most cases, committee assignments for specific bills are reasonably clear-cut. Committee jurisdiction is determined by subject matter and by tradition. But occasionally it is possible to help or hurt a bill by assigning it to a friendly or hostile committee. Since only about 2000 of the more than 20,000 bills introduced each session ever get beyond committee, a bill can easily be lost under the crush of other work. Thus, a subcommittee can easily hold a bill "hostage" until some other demands are met, demands which might well have nothing to do with the bill. If persuasion fails, a discharge petition is the only recourse.

When a bill reaches the floor of the Senate, the legislative process can be stalled by a procedure known as the **filibuster**. This procedure, which is unique to the Senate, recognizes unlimited debate and stems from the idea that the Senate ought to be the one place in the political process where deliberation and discussion can continue as long as necessary. However, with the filibuster as we know it today, there is usually no deliberate

Cartoonist Carl Rose's view of a typical Congressional filibuster.

discussion; there is usually only deliberate *delay*— with the intent of deliberate *defeat*. Once a senator gets the floor, he or she may speak indefinitely or yield only to a supporter who will continue the filibuster. The speeches do not have to be relevant at all to the bill before the Senate. One senator once read from the local telephone directory; Senator Huey Long of Louisiana in 1935 filibustered for fifteen hours, covering such subjects as how to fry oysters and make pot liquor! Senator Long's objective was to defeat a bill extending the National Recovery Act. The bill was finally passed, in spite of the senator's efforts.

In 1953, the late Senator Wayne Morse of Oregon spoke for twenty-two hours and twenty-six minutes to block passage of an offshore-oil bill. The record, set in August 1957, is held by Senator Strom Thurmond. He spoke against the pending civil-rights bill for twenty-four hours and eighteen minutes. In both instances, the bills were finally passed. But filibusters have occasionally been quite successful. At times, they succeed in bringing about modification in the bill, and at other times, they cause the bill to be dropped altogether. The labor-law case study provides a good example of a prolonged filibuster that was successful in blocking proposed legislation. During the course of the filibuster, you will recall, efforts were made to modify the bill to make it more acceptable to some legislators. A prolonged filibuster invariably pressures the proponents of a bill to compromise or to withdraw it, because other members want to move on to other business.

The one procedural means to end a filibuster is through **cloture**. Cloture is invoked when sixty senators (that is, three-fifths of the entire Senate)[16] vote to end debate. You will recall that cloture was attempted six times on the labor bill, as it became increasingly clear that there was not sufficient support to close off the filibuster. The bill's supporters had a simple majority—fifty-one—but the rules required more for cloture. The legislative process recognizes different majorities for different purposes, and a bill involving a filibuster is one case where substantial support must be demonstrated.

The case study also referred to another procedural device that can be used to slow up the legislative process—*filibuster-by-amendment*. This is when a senator, sometimes with the help of sympathetic colleagues, introduces hundreds of amendments to a bill and talks at length on each amendment.

Some senators view the filibuster as a means by which a determined minority can block the will of the majority. Others believe it is a good way to protect the rights of minorities. The difference may depend on whose bill is being slowly talked to death.

A piece of proposed legislation is subject to the tug of political forces every step of the way—in subcommittee and committee hearings, at the *mark-up* stage (when the committee puts the bill in final form), in the Rules Committee, on the floor, and in consultation with the other chamber. In this context, it is important to remember that each bill is not isolated from others. That is, one group might agree to support a bill in which it has no real interest in return for support of a bill in which it is especially interested. For example, in 1977, legislators representing tobacco districts needed votes to keep tobacco as part of the Food for Peace Program, a program that lends money to other countries to buy U.S. agricultural products, including, since 1954, tobacco. Congressman James Johnson (R., Colorado) felt that tobacco was a health hazard and the government should not encourage the exportation of health hazards to other countries. (Representative Johnson, incidentally, was a smoker himself.) The tobacco interests needed all the votes they could get to keep Congress from excluding tobacco from the program, so

a *quid pro quo* deal with the Congressional Black Caucus (who needed support for grants to aid inner cities) was struck. Only three black legislators refused to go along with the deal. Thirteen agreed and voted against excluding tobacco from the program. Although the tobacco interests lost the vote in Congress, the next day they kept their end of the bargain and voted two-to-one for the inner-city aid.

Much of Congressional politics is *quid pro quo*: you scratch my back, and I'll scratch yours. Sometimes this works, sometimes not. On some issues it is nearly impossible to piece together a successful coalition of interests. But seeking out the political interests of other groups and making deals is an important part of the legislative process. Some would suggest it is perhaps the only way to get along in such a large political system as the American government.

One method used by members of the House to gain political support is to try to get as many representatives as possible to join in sponsoring a bill. Sometimes the appeal is made through personal, "Dear Colleague" letters. These letters describe the proposed legislation and then invite the addressees to cosponsor the introduction of the bill. A large number of cosponsors, especially from different regions and across party lines, indicates a broad base of political support. Cosponsors are not permitted in the Senate.

It is possible to introduce the same bill in both houses simultaneously, as often happens. Laws involving levying of taxes must originate in the House, however. One advantage of this procedure is that it speeds up the process, since one chamber does not have to wait for the other to send the bill over to it. Our labor-law case study also discusses the timing of introducing a bill and the strategy involved in determining which chamber to introduce it in first. As we saw, these are important political considerations.

A government employee files away yet another issue of the *Congressional Record.*

Everything said on the floor of each house is recorded in an official publication known as the *Congressional Record.* The *Record* also includes speeches, essays, and other items that are not discussed on the floor but that members simply wish to have inserted for posterity. For example, a wonderful essay written by a tenth grader and delivered at the local high school back home might find its way into the *Congressional Record.* (And, of course, the legislator sends copies back to the proud constituent, where the essay will be framed, written up in the local newspaper, discussed in class, and probably be equated with the Declara-

tion of Independence in impact and import!) Also members often have speeches inserted in the *Record* that they never really gave on the floor. This practice was abused so flagrantly that now both chambers require that a dot (called a *bullet*) must appear at the beginning of any item not actually delivered on the floor. The Senate started the practice in 1977, and the House followed in 1978. But members can get around the requirement by reading the first few words of a speech aloud and then inserting the remainder into the *Record.*

Hearings and investigations. Much of a legislator's time is spent attending committee hearings, listening to witnesses, and engaging in discussions over particular aspects of a bill. These activities can be very time-consuming and, occasionally, excruciatingly dull, but there is probably no substitute for them. Here, interest groups and citizens have a chance to ''petition'' the decision-makers directly. Executives in the bureaucracy often ''go up to the hill'' to testify at these sessions, which pertain to budget requests, evaluation of existing programs, and virtually anything else legislators want to pursue. On occasion, a legislator will solicit witnesses (public and private citizens) who will corroborate his or her point of view. The hearings are recorded, transcribed, and printed in volumes that are available to the public free or at a small cost. They constitute a good public record of the positions various groups take on any given piece of legislation.

Not all hearings are held in Washington, D.C. Legislators sometimes take their hearings on the road, frequently heading back to their home district or state. This is a politically useful tactic, since it gives them plenty of exposure in the local press; and these ''field hearings'' sometimes coincide with periods appropriately prior to election time. In April 1977, legislators held twenty-eight

The House Un-American Activities Committee, which investigated alleged communist infiltration in various industries and organizations during the postwar years, has sometimes been cited as an example of the improper use of Congress's investigative powers.

such hearings on the road, fifteen of them in their home districts, and ten in such scenic spots as San Francisco and Honolulu. Five of seven senators were up for reelection in 1978. And never let it be said that they do not know where to hold hearings and when. Note:

Cool Alaska was a favorite locale for field hearings this August. Reps. John Seiberling (D., Ohio) and Morris Udall (D., Arizona) led a seven-member party, with a dozen Interior panel staffers in tow, on a 2-week tour of national park, forest and wildlife refuge sites. Bob Leggett (D., California) took four members on a trek through wildlife refuges around Anchorage, Juneau, and Fairbanks.

Not everybody was in Alaska, though. Before heading home for his field hearings, Ike Andrews decided to drop by Honolulu to see how *various federal programs like ACTION and Head Start were faring beneath the sheltering palms.*[17]

Congressional investigations are similar to hearings, except that investigations usually do not relate to specific programs or even to specific legislation. Investigations tend to be more exploratory, for example, examining a problem that might lead to passage of a law. Sometimes these investigations attract considerable attention (as did the Senate Watergate Investigating Committee headed by Senator Sam Ervin), and sometimes even become sensational, televised events. Witnesses are *subpoenaed* (that is, are compelled by law to appear) and questioned before the glare of nationwide television. If a witness refuses to cooperate or to answer questions, he or she may be subject to prosecution in the federal courts if the committee

Power and Consensus

American government depends upon the exercise of legal powers based on broad consensus among interested participants. A President has the authority to make decisions in foreign and domestic affairs, but his decisions have a greater chance of success if Congress agrees with them and if agreement is solicited beforehand. Exercising legal power can indeed accomplish certain goals in the short run, but obtaining consensus means that what is done will likely have a more lasting effect and be less subject to reversal.

Crises have a way of contributing to consensus. People tend to unite behind governmental action in time of crisis, especially when there are perceived threats to the system from external sources. Even in such situations, it is best to cultivate broad support for policies lest the original consensus be lost. Power can elicit obedience, but in the final analysis consensus, not power, sustains our political system.

The interplay of power and consensus has been evident throughout our history. The founders of the republic, for instance, had to deliberate long and hard before hammering out the Declaration of Independence. At times, of course, consensus has broken down—such as during the Civil War or during periods of labor unrest—and then tumult and often tragedy have been the result.

More recently, the close relationship between power and consensus has been especially prominent. John F. Kennedy enjoyed immense popularity following the 1962 Cuban missile crisis. His successors, Lyndon Johnson and Richard Nixon, both sought consensus with Congress and the people but failed ultimately to achieve it, the former because of foreign-policy failures in Vietnam, the latter because of Watergate. President Carter's boycott of the 1980 Olympics also stirred public disapproval, though on a far smaller scale.

The fabric of American government remains strong, supported by wide public faith in the essential integrity of the system. This faith has been publicly reaffirmed countless times: through Fourth of July parades, through the steady influx of new citizens, through the bicentennial celebrations, and through emotionally charged events such as the spontaneous welcome-home given the American hostages after their long ordeal in Iran.

Above: "Congress Voting Independence," by Robert Edge Pine (1788).

"The Strike," by Robert Koehler (1886)

Abraham Lincoln, a peace-loving man who presided over one of the bloodiest episodes in American history.

The main task of a free society is to civilize the struggle for power.

R.H.S. Crossman

3 CHEERS FOR THE ATHLETES ON TO THE OLYMPICS

U.S. PEACE COUNCIL

The Olympic boycott.

Richard Nixon leaves the White House after resigning the presidency.

*With public sentiment on its side,
everything succeeds;
with public sentiment against it,
nothing succeeds.*

Abraham Lincoln

"Oh, if I could only be President and Congress too for just ten minutes!"

Theodore Roosevelt

Above: President Kennedy meets with his closest adviser, his brother Robert.

Below: President Johnson conducts a meeting with top aides.

Fourth of July parade, San Antonio, Texas.

Swearing in of new citizens.

"The tall ships," New York harbor, 1976.

Welcome-home parade for the Americans held hostage in Iran, 1981.

Americans are still engaged in inventing what it is to be an American. That is at once an exhilarating and a painful occupation.

Thornton Wilder

cites the person for *contempt of Congress*. The witness may have his or her own attorney present. The witness may ask to have the television cameras turned off, but this request may well be denied. Unlike in a court of law, the witness may not object to certain questions; nor may a witness (or the witness's lawyer) cross-examine other witnesses. In other words, a Congressional investigative session is not a court of law: a witness is not on trial. Nonetheless, the damage done to a witness's character and professional life in an investigation can be irreparable.

For these reasons, coupled with the charge that some legislators attempt to use the publicity of these events to further their own political careers, there has been rather intense public debate over the real value of such investigations. Defenders argue that they are useful as means of alerting the public to a particular situation. They also suggest that investigations might lead to necessary legislation. For instance, both the Securities and Exchange Act of 1934 and the Public Utility Holding Company Act of 1935 resulted from the Congressional investigations of the stock-market crash in 1929. The Senate Watergate investigations led to increased legislative concern over campaign financing.

The conference committee. We began this chapter with a short account of Congressman Rostenkowski preparing for a conference-committee meeting. He was determined not to let the Senate members push the House members around. The conference committee, a bipartisan group (the majority party always dominates) with representatives from both chambers, is usually the last substantive stop in the legislative process. At this stage, the differences between the two chambers are ironed out, and the committee's work is normally accepted by the two chambers. Thus, a position on the conference committee is rather prestigious, especially for junior members. Normally, however, the conference committee consists of the senior members of the committee that originally handled the bill.

Congressional Reform: Fact or Fiction?

One of the perennial discussions in Congress centers on reform—meaning, reform of the way Congress organizes itself and conducts its business. Congresswoman Shirley Chisholm, for instance, once called the seniority system the "senility" system. Other members, usually the younger and more liberal ones, have fought to weaken the control of the committee chairpersons. Still others, concerned about the scandals and charges of criminal and unethical conduct that have surrounded Congress over the last few years, have pushed for more financial disclosure rules.

Since the early to mid-1970s, there have been several changes in Congress. Many of the reforms instituted in the House were related to committee and subcommittee appointments and regulations. Most of these reforms resulted from the work of a committee appointed in 1970 and chaired by Congresswoman Julia Butler Hansen (D., Washington). One of the reforms was a subcommittee bill of rights, allowing the Democratic caucus of each standing committee to choose chairpersons of subcommittees. In addition "subcommittee government was given the necessary resources, independence, and incentives for full operation."[18]

Then, in 1975, the veteran chairpersons of three House committees—agriculture, armed services, and banking—were denied reappointment to their positions. Seniority was thus no longer an automatic means of achieving a chairmanship. Professor Leroy N. Rieselbach believes that this is an important reform. He says, "Without the seniority rule's protection, House and Senate chairpersons will most certainly be more open to, and solicitous of, those who may vote to deprive them of their seats of power,"[19] meaning, of course, that since the chairpersons must answer to other members of Congress, it is less likely they will assert any sort of autocratic rule. The reforms also required that committees with twenty or more members have at least four subcommittees. The subcommittees can choose their own chairpersons and hire their own staffs. Furthermore, if a committee chairperson refuses to call a meeting or is absent from a meeting, the committee can still meet with the ranking majority member presiding. Likewise, in order to vote in place of a committee member, the chairperson must have the proxy in writing and it must state the specific matters to which the proxy relates. These rules might seem rather simple and reasonable, but one must understand that they were enacted because some chairpersons ran their committees with an iron fist, leaving no room for expression of opinion, especially from junior members.

The reforms also limit the number of committees and subcommittees on which one member of Congress can serve. This prevents the concentration of power in the hands of a few oligarchs. No House member, for example, can chair more than one subcommittee, and no member of the influential Appropriations, Rules, or Ways and Means Committees can serve on any other committee. Members of the Senate may not chair more than three committees and/or subcommittees.

Since the House reforms, the Steering and Policy Committee and the party caucus have had far more power. Yet because the Speaker plays a major role in selecting this committee, the powers of the Speaker have also increased—an ironic twist to the 1910 revolt against Speaker Cannon. But such is the nature of reform; it sometimes runs in a circle and not in a straight line.

Some reforms resulted from the post-Watergate interest in **sunshine laws**, those laws which call for open hearings and for greater access to information concerning how the government conducts its business. In 1973, the reforms mandated that committee sessions be open to the public unless a majority of the committee votes by roll call to close the meeting. Hearings and mark-up sessions must also be open, though sunshine rules do not apply to matters that might endanger national security. The steady increase in the number of open hearings has been noted by Professors Lawrence C. Dodd and Bruce I. Oppenheimer: "In 1972, prior to the change, 44 percent of committee meetings were closed. In 1973 this dropped to 10 percent, in 1974 to 8 percent, and in 1975 to less than 3 percent."[20] In 1975, there were 3881 meetings.

Under other reforms, the powerful Ways and Means Committee can no longer invoke the *closed rule*, which prohibited amendments to legislation once it reached the floor. Previously, the whole bill had to be voted up or down. Now, as Catherine Rudder observed, "Increasingly, the substance of legislation is determined in the caucus and on the floor."

Clearly, one purpose of the various Congressional reforms was to democratize the Congressional process by spreading the legislative function to a broader segment of the House membership. This objective has been met, but there have been some costs involved. As the legislative process was decentralized it was also slowed down considerably. Also, as Professor Rudder notes, the ones who benefitted the most from the sunshine rules were the special interest groups. At one open committee hearing, a committee member went into the audience, talked with a lobbyist, wrote an amendment, and came back and introduced it! "The public's not there, but the interests are."[21]

Broadening the participatory base has certainly made it more difficult for the Congressional leadership and for the President to push legislative programs through Congress. It is always easier to deal and bargain with one or two people than with fifty or one hundred. According to political scientist Eric L. Davis, the House reforms, in effect, have made the House more like the Senate:

Before the House was "reformed," legislation on the Senate side was written far more on the floor than was the case in the House. In the new House, though, the entire chamber has become more important vis-a-vis the committees. Those in the minority on the committees can bring their positions to the floor, and often defeat their own committees, because the closed rule is only rarely used to protect a committee's product. . . . Thus, a President must exercise influence not only over a relatively small number of committee chairmen and other senior members, but over the entire membership of the House.[22]

Therefore, since the reforms, we have seen much more assertiveness on the part of the rank-and-file members of Congress. Often, they will circulate petitions to call caucus meetings instead of waiting for the leaders to call them. There was some discussion about electing the various whips rather than having them chosen by the Speaker or the minority leader. Another implemented reform was to record votes more often. This would, again, add a bit more sunshine to legislators' activities.

But at the frantic close of the Ninety-fifth Congress in October 1978, some observers expressed doubt about the impact of the reforms.

A *Washington Post* editorial noted the last-minute flurry of business, the late-night sessions, and the uninformed voting on bills that were rushed through at the rate of fifteen to twenty per day. The editorial accounted for this situation as follows:

The volume of business has gotten too great. Past Congresses have created too many programs and agencies for the current Congress to review or at least reauthorize. Moreover, the House's vaunted "democracy"—the advent of lively new members, the spreading out of subcommittee power, the increases in junior members' staff—has generated a constant flood of new projects and proposals, each with energetic sponsors who can tell you in a trice why their measure is vital to the republic.

Streamlining procedures may only increase the glut. House members don't need more time to dream up and promote more projects. What they need is fewer subcommittees, less entrepreneurial staffs and, above all, more self-restraint.[23]

Congressman Frank Annunzio (D., Illinois) responded to the editorial in the following letter:

Your Oct. 12 editorial is an accurate reflection of one of the major problems faced by the House of Representatives and I applaud you for your stand. I only wish that you had taken that position four years ago when the so-called "reform" movement began in the House of Representatives.

As a member of the Hansen Committee, which was appointed four years ago to deal with suggested House reforms, I was extremely concerned that projected reforms would not provide better legislation or a more efficiently operated House of Representatives.

. . . Unfortunately, mine was a minority position and reform flooded the House.

Now, however, we must live with the reform hangover that has brought about 31 committees, 160 subcommittees and a House that spends most of its time answering rollcalls. . . .

It is interesting that many of the members of the House who clamored for reform four years ago now want to abolish those reforms because they do not work.[24]

These organizational questions have faced Congress most of this century, and the debate will probably continue as Congress gropes for better ways to conduct its business. Sometimes, the various goals of reform conflict with each other. Professors Dodd and Oppenheimer have described this tension as a balancing act between the advantages of decentralization and centralization, and the effective coordination of dispersed power.

The late Speaker Sam Rayburn used to advise new, young freshman representatives, "If you want to get along, go along." Although there is doubtless much truth to that maxim today, it is probably less true than when Rayburn said it. By serving on an active subcommittee and doing favors for constituents, newer representatives have to show less deference to the older crowd. The new rules allow them to be less dependent on the wishes and whims of the elders. This is especially the case if the young, ambitious members exert relative united strength in the party caucus. The situation has not been completely reversed, but we are likely to see more cajoling and less coercing on the part of Congressional leaders.

Professor Rieselbach recognizes that the many reforms have tended, as noted earlier, to slow up the legislative process, but on balance he sees positive results. There *is* more airing of points of view from rank-and-file members, and this makes Congress more responsive:

Solutions to pressing policy problems will now require bargaining among a still larger set of legislators than has been customary; responsibility may be even harder to achieve. On the other hand, more lawmakers, speaking for differing sentiments and in contact with broader constituency interests, should bring more points of view into play in the course of legislative decision making. These democratizing reforms have extended congressional responsiveness.[25]

Representative John Brademus (D., Indiana) waits to register a proposed House bill.

Thus, the debate goes on. Congressman Annunzio would heartily disagree with those who view these myriad reforms as beneficial; but Professor Rieselbach believes that the reforms may enhance Congress's reputation. He states that Congress must rise above its image as simply a place for narrowly based local interests: "Congress must enhance its reputation as a body committed to placing national above local interests. . . . Competing for public respect with the unitary executive is not easy for the plural legislature. Yet some of the reforms . . . may help enhance Congress' reputation. More media attention, less internal secrecy, and more forceful imposition of congressional views in policy making may help citizens to realize that the legislature is an important feature of the political landscape."[26]

The People of Congress and Their Aides

According to the Constitution, if you want to be a member of the House of Representatives, you need to be twenty-five years old, a United States citizen for at least seven years, a resident of the state in which the Congressional district is located—and, of course, you need to get elected.

To be a senator, you need to be thirty years old, a United States citizen for at least nine years, a resident of the state you want to represent—and, again, you need to get elected. You will be entitled to be paid for your services, but there is no mention in the Constitution of the help or assistance you will be provided as you join in exercising the "power to lay and collect taxes . . . to borrow money on the credit of the United States . . . to declare war . . . to make all laws which shall be necessary and proper for carrying into execution the foregoing powers." And these are only *some* of the duties you, as an elected member of Congress, will be required to perform.

These are the formal stipulations, and they are the minimum requirements.

Who really gets elected to Congress? Although you need not be a white, Protestant, middle-class, male lawyer or businessman between the ages of forty-nine and fifty-four, the fact is that most members of Congress are. In the Ninety-seventh Congress, beginning in January 1981, ninety-seven percent were white; sixty-five percent were Protestant; ninety-six percent were male; forty-seven percent were lawyers; thirty percent were businessmen; and the average age was forty-nine.

There are a number of reasons for such a heavy preponderance of one racial, sexual, and socio-economic type. Traditionally, persons with these characteristics have dominated the political life of the country. Only in the past two decades have black Americans, for instance, increased their numbers in Congress from two to seventeen, as blacks have begun to run for office at that level and have become more active in local party politics. Black voter-registration drives, spurred by the civil-rights movement of the 1960s, increased political awareness and participation among that group in the South as well as in the North. However, when blacks are elected to Congress, it is from predominantly black districts.

While women constitute approximately fifty-one percent of the total population, their role in politics, particularly as office seekers, has been a recent development. Historically, when women served in Congress, they were usually serving out the terms of their deceased husbands. The executive director of the National Women's Political Caucus, Jane McMichael, stated in 1978: "Women today are seeing politics as a career, and that's a new pattern. In the past, many of them entered politics as an afterthought when they were middle-aged or older."[27] One columnist noted: "In an era when corporate suites and other decision centers are increasingly open to women, Congress remains a bastion of male supremacy. . . . Women have a hard time raising funds because they are not part of the 'old boy network' of

Kansas Senator Nancy Landon Kassebaum, granddaughter of the 1936 Republican presidential nominee Alf Landon, was the first woman elected to the Senate who was not preceded in office by her husband.

business-connected givers."[28] With the addition of three women elected to the House in 1981, there are currently nineteen female representatives. In the Senate, there are two women: Senator Paula Hawkins (R., Florida), and Senator Nancy Kassebaum (R., Kansas).

Many members of Congress are lawyers because the country continues to associate public office with lawmaking, and the lawyer is perceived as particularly knowledgeable at least about the "law," if not about the "making," aspect of government. The work of Congress involves passing statutes, which lawyers presumably know how to draft and to understand. In addition, a law practice promotes participation in politics through contacts with public officials, courts, and other governmental agencies, and it provides the freedom to take time from one's work to campaign for office.

Needless to say, persons with little formal education or who are in the low-income bracket seldom are elected to Congress. Neither their occupations nor their skills foster the public participation or leadership usually required for the establishment of a political career. Although they are not normally chosen to run for office or to speak on behalf of a political group, many such persons work at lower levels in political organizations, sometimes as volunteers. They are the workers rather than the representatives.

The predominance of Protestants largely reflects the fact that most people in this country (and, therefore, most Congressional districts) are Protestant, and religious affiliation still influences voter choice.

Thus, while the formal requirements for being a member of Congress are few (minimum age, citizenship, residence), socio-economic, racial, religious, and sex factors also play a role. In the consideration of these factors, Congress is a far less representative body than some people feel it should be.

Compensation. The Constitution simply says: "The Senators and Representatives shall receive a compensation for their services, to be ascertained by law and paid out of the Treasury of the United States."

In October 1979, Congress voted itself a pay raise from $57,500 to $60,662 a year. Members are given allowances for a staff (approximately $270,000 per year), for official business (at least $41,150 per year), and for office equipment. Senators from more populous states receive more —as much as a total of $1 million per year to run a Senate office. Each office has nine telephone lines—four can be ten-button; the rest are six-button. At one time, the number of reimbursable trips a legislator could take each year to his or her home district was limited. Today there are no

Senator Henry Jackson (D., Washington) in his Senate chambers.

limits, and if a legislator wishes to be reimbursed for using private transportation, it is based on 15¢ a mile for motorcycles, 17¢ for cars, and 36¢ for private planes. Members of Congress can decorate their offices with two art reproductions from the National Gallery of Art, potted palms from the Botanic Gardens, photographs and maps donated from various government agencies and archives, and they receive thirty-seven free subscriptions to the *Congressional Record* and thirty-six free copies of the *Congressional Directory* each year.

It should be pointed out, however, that unless a member has independent wealth—stocks, bonds, real estate, and so forth—serving in Congress can be a financial burden. Most legislators must maintain two places of residence—back home and in Washington, even if the latter is a modest apart-

ment. Recent House reforms restricted the amount of outside income a member could earn to $8743 per year, and members must disclose their assets. The income ceiling does not pertain to unearned income, such as dividends, interest, capital gains, pensions, or spouse's income. House representatives are limited to a $1000 honorarium per speech, but they may accept more if they donate the excess to charity.

The Senate has postponed until 1983 the establishment of an income ceiling, but even now senators are limited to $25,000 annually in honoraria. The limit for any one honorarium is $2000, and any excess amounts must be donated to charity.

Not all legislators have agreed to these restrictions. Congressman Thomas L. Ashley (D., Ohio) said the income ceiling was "the stupidest thing that ever came down the pike," The rule "quarantines certain kinds of income while allowing other kinds," Ashley said. Another legislator said, "I had to take out a loan to pay for my daughter's wedding."[29]

Indeed, some members feel the financial burden is too much to bear. Congressman Joe D. Waggonner (D., Louisiana), retiring after sixteen years in the House, admitted as much when he said that the limit on outside earnings would have hurt him: "It sure would, yes sir. I made more money than that."[30] Another retiree, Otis G. Pike (D., New York) stated that he did not want to give up his lucrative law practice, and he also complained about having to reveal his personal assets, including disclosing and refusing all personal gifts of more than $100.

Having fought and voted for years against people having their phones tapped, their mail opened, their tax returns publicized, their bank accounts examined and for their right of privacy, I am expected to give up all of my own.

Public servants are people, too. I would rather give up my public life and get out of the goldfish bowl.[31]

Members are eligible for a retirement pension according to the following formula: an average of the three highest pay years, multiplied by 2.5 percent and by the number of years of service. Members contribute eight percent of their salary each year to the pension fund, and they become eligible to participate after five years of service. The late Speaker of the House, John W. McCormack, retired in 1971 with a yearly pension of $50,000. By the time he died in 1980, his pension had increased (through cost-of-living increases) to $92,000.[32] There are a number of factors involved in calculating exactly how much a legislator who chooses to participate in the retirement plan is entitled to receive: length of service in Congress; length of service in government, including the military; whether the person was wounded in military service; age at the time of retirement. Even members of Congress convicted and jailed as a result of bribery charges—such as in the Abscam incident—can still be eligible for Congressional pensions.

In addition to these salaries, allowances, and pensions, there are other expenses paid for by the government. The budget for the post office of the House of Representatives exceeds $1 million. There is a 1177-member Congressional police force to protect the employees on Capitol Hill. (In 1969, the number on the force was 681.) Today there are approximately 35,000 people who work on Capitol Hill—so there is one policeman for every thirty employees.

Each chamber has a chaplain who prays before the day's session begins. The following vignette describes one incident which might not appeal to some hard-pressed taxpayers.

During recent testimony in a House subcommittee, George Shipley (D., Illinois) *wanted to make sure the House chaplain was getting as much as the Senate's. The panel finally decided to raise their clergyman's pay to $23,700—$72 more than the Senate's. "More of us to pray for," said Rep. Larry Coughlin* (R., Pennsylvania).[33]

Control over membership. Each chamber has the constitutional authority to determine who was properly elected and should be seated, as well as who has acted improperly once admitted and should be punished.

Deciding who should be seated is a delicate matter inasmuch as it conflicts with the voters' right to choose their representatives. This authority has been exercised less than twenty times since 1789. In 1966, Adam Clayton Powell, Jr., was elected to Congress from Harlem, but the House refused to seat him. He was involved in a libel suit in New York City, and he had refused to obey court orders to appear and pay the libel judgment. Powell won a special election to fill the seat in 1967. The House still refused to seat him. He won again in 1968 but was denied the seat a third time. He took his case to the Supreme Court, where, on July 16, 1969, the Court ruled that the House of Representatives acted unconstitutionally in refusing to seat Powell. The Constitution has only three requirements for membership—age, citizenship, residence—and Powell met those criteria.

Censure involves a rather strong statement of disapproval of the member's conduct; it requires only a majority vote. In the House, the censured member must stand before the rostrum while the Speaker reads the resolution. A censured senator may address the body, but this privilege is not granted to a censured member of the House. (See Tables 1 and 2 on pages 424–25.)

TABLE 1.
Censure Proceedings in the House.

Congress	Session	Year	Member	Grounds	Disposition
5th	2nd	1798	Matthew Lyon, Anti-Fed-Vt.	Assault on representative	Not censured
5th	2nd	1798	Roger Griswold, Fed-Conn.	Assault on representative	Not censured
22nd	1st	1832	William Stanbery, D-Ohio	Insult to Speaker	*Censured*
24th	1st	1836	Sherrod Williams, Whig-Ky.	Insult to Speaker	Not censured
25th	2nd	1838	Henry A. Wise, Tyler Dem.-Va.	Service as second in duel	Not censured
25th	3rd	1839	Alexander Duncan, Whig-Ohio	Offensive publication	Not censured
27th	2nd	1842	John Q. Adams, Whig-Mass.	Treasonable petition	Not censured
27th	2nd	1842	Joshua R. Giddings, Whig-Ohio	Offensive paper	*Censured*
34th	2nd	1856	Henry A. Edmundson, D-Va.	Complicity in assault on senator	Not censured
34th	2nd	1856	Laurence M. Keitt, D-S.C.		*Censured*
36th	1st	1860	George S. Houston, D-Ala.	Insult to representative	Not censured
38th	1st	1864	Alexander Long, D-Ohio	Treasonable utterance	*Censured*
38th	1st	1864	Benjamin G. Harris, D-Md.	Treasonable utterance	*Censured*
39th	1st	1866	John W. Chanler, D-N.Y.	Insult to House	*Censured*
39th	1st	1866	Lovell H. Rousseau, R-Ky.	Assault on representative	*Censured*
40th	1st	1867	John W. Hunter, Ind-N.Y.	Insult to representative	*Censured*
40th	2nd	1868	Fernando Wood, D-N.Y.	Offensive utterance	*Censured*
40th	3rd	1868	E. D. Holbrook, D-Idaho[1]	Offensive utterance	*Censured*
41st	2nd	1870	Benjamin F. Whittemore, R-S.C.	Corruption	*Censured*
41st	2nd	1870	Roderick R. Butler, R-Tenn.	Corruption	*Censured*
41st	2nd	1870	John T. Deweese, D-N.C.	Corruption	*Censured*
42nd	3rd	1873	Oakes Ames, R-Mass.	Corruption	*Censured*
42nd	3rd	1873	James Brooks, D-N.Y.	Corruption	*Censured*
43rd	2nd	1875	John Y. Brown, D-Ky.	Insult to representative	*Censured*[2]
44th	1st	1876	James G. Blaine, R-Maine	Corruption	Not censured
47th	1st	1882	William D. Kelley, R-Pa.	Offensive utterance	Not censured
47th	1st	1882	John D. White, R-Ky.	Offensive utterance	Not censured
47th	2nd	1883	John Van Voorhis, R-N.Y.	Offensive utterance	Not censured
51st	1st	1890	William D. Bynum, D-Ind.	Offensive utterance	*Censured*
67th	1st	1921	Thomas L. Blanton, D-Texas	Abuse of leave to print	*Censured*
96th	1st	1979	Charles C. Diggs, Jr., D-Mich.	Misuse of clerk-hire funds	*Censured*
96th	2nd	1980	Charles H. Wilson, D-Calif.	Financial misconduct	*Censured*

[1]Holbrook was a territorial delegate, not a representative.
[2]The House later rescinded part of the censure resolution against Brown.

Sources: Hinds and Cannon, *Precedents of the House of Representatives of the United States,* 11 vols. (1935–41); Joint Committee on Congressional Operations, *House of Representatives Exclusion, Censure and Expulsion Cases from 1789 to 1973,* committee print, 93rd Cong., 1st sess., 1973. Cited in *Current American Government, Spring 1981 Guide* (Washington, D.C., Congressional Quarterly, Inc., 1980).

In both chambers, expulsion requires a two-thirds majority vote, and as Table 3 (page 426) indicates, this seldom happens. Congress usually prefers to discipline its members with less harsh methods: denial of the right to vote; a fine; stripping of a chairmanship; or a reprimand.

Legislative staffs. You will recall from earlier in this chapter an editorial which complained of too many "entrepreneurial staffs" attached especially to junior legislators. These excessive staffs, it was suggested, contributed to the burdensome increase of unnecessary legislative work. Staffs have grown

TABLE 2.
Censure Proceedings in the Senate.

Congress	Session	Year	Member	Grounds	Disposition
11th	3rd	1811	Timothy Pickering, Fed-Mass.	Breach of confidence	*Censured*
28th	1st	1844	Benjamin Tappan, D-Ohio	Breach of confidence	*Censured*
31st	1st	1850	Thomas H. Benton, D-Mo.	Disorderly conduct	Not censured
31st	1st	1850	Henry S. Foote, Unionist-Miss.	Disorderly conduct	Not censured
57th	1st	1902	John L. McLaurin, D-S.C.	Assault	*Censured*
57th	1st	1902	Benjamin R. Tillman, D-S.C.	Assault	*Censured*
71st	1st	1929	Hiram Bingham, R-Conn.	Bringing Senate into disrepute	*Censured*
83rd	2nd	1954	Joseph R. McCarthy, R-Wis.	Obstruction of legislative process, insult to senators, etc.	*Censured*
90th	1st	1967	Thomas J. Dodd, D-Conn.	Financial misconduct	*Censured*

Source: U.S. Senate, Committee on Rules and Administration, Subcommittee on Privileges and Elections, *Senate Election, Explusion and Censure Cases from 1793 to 1972*, compiled by Richard D. Hupman, S. Doc. 92-7, 92nd Cong., 1st sess., 1972. Cited in *Current American Government, Spring 1981 Guide* (Washington, D.C., Congressional Quarterly, Inc., 1980).

enormously over the years largely in response to the increased work load of committees and the proliferation of subcommittees, and it is not clear whether the staffs have created more work or vice versa. (See Table 4 on page 427.) Certainly, Congress's request over the years for more technical and professional help to cope with the job has been a factor. Today, if a member wants to do his or her job efficiently, it is necessary to master a wide range of complicated and technical matters. Increased staffs have been one response to this need.

Salaries of top staff people go as high as $50,000 a year. The 517 employees on the twenty House committees average $31,840 a year. There is no limit to the number of staff employees for the House Appropriations Committee and the House Budget Committee. They employ, together, about 195 aides who are paid on the average between $28,848 and $30,226. The budget for the staffs of special and select committees in 1978 came to $39 million. Ten years earlier, those committees cost less than $5 million.

Staff members serve individual legislators as well as committees. The distinction between professional and clerical staff is often unclear because there is a lot of juggling and deliberate misnaming of positions. Therefore, there are no clearly identifiable personnel guidelines to determine what positions should be paid how much. A person listed as a clerk or secretary, for instance, could in fact be a legislative assistant and be paid as much as $35,000 a year. This makes it difficult to get a clear picture of the staffing situation on Capitol Hill. The legislators and the committees are given a lump sum of money for staff, and they can allocate the funds as they see fit.

Some legislators try to ride herd on the growing staff budgets, as illustrated by the action of Senator Howard Cannon (D., Nevada).

During his term as Rules Chairman, Cannon . . . became known for imploring Senate committee chairmen to practice thrift. Now he's practicing what he preached. He's asked for a reduction in funds for [the] Commerce [committee], which he took over when former chief Warren Magnuson assumed the reins at Appropriations.

TABLE 3.
Cases of Expulsion in the House.

Congress	Session	Year	Member	Grounds	Disposition
5th	2nd	1798	Matthew Lyon, Anti-Fed-Vt.	Assault on representative	Not expelled
5th	2nd	1798	Roger Griswold, Fed-Conn.	Assault on representative	Not expelled
5th	3rd	1799	Matthew Lyon, Anti-Fed-Vt.	Sedition	Not expelled
25th	2nd	1838	William J. Graves, Whig-Ky.	Killing of representative in duel	Not expelled
25th	3rd	1839	Alexander Duncan, Whig-Ohio	Offensive publication	Not expelled
34th	1st	1856	Preston S. Brooks, State Rights Dem.-S.C.	Assault on senator	Not expelled
34th	3rd	1857	Orsamus B. Matteson, Whig-N.Y.	Corruption	Not expelled
34th	3rd	1857	William A. Gilbert,–N.Y.	Corruption	Not expelled
34th	3rd	1857	William W. Welch, American-Conn.	Corruption	Not expelled
34th	3rd	1857	Francis S. Edwards,–N.Y.	Corruption	Not expelled
35th	1st	1858	Orsamus B. Matteson, Whig-N.Y.	Corruption	Not expelled
37th	1st	1861	John B. Clark, D-Mo.	Support of rebellion	*Expelled*
37th	1st	1861	Henry C. Burnett, D-Ky.	Support of rebellion	*Expelled*
37th	1st	1861	John W. Reid, D-Mo.	Support of rebellion	*Expelled*
38th	1st	1864	Alexander Long, D-Ohio	Treasonable utterance	Not expelled
38th	1st	1864	Benjamin G. Harris, D-Md.	Treasonable utterance	Not expelled
39th	1st	1866	Lovell H. Rousseau, R-Ky.	Assault on representative	Not expelled
41st	2nd	1870	Benjamin F. Whittemore, R-S.C.	Corruption	Not expelled
41st	2nd	1870	Roderick R. Butler, R-Tenn.	Corruption	Not expelled
42nd	3rd	1873	Oakes Ames, R-Mass.	Corruption	Not expelled
42nd	3rd	1873	James Brooks, D-N.Y.	Corruption	Not expelled
43rd	2nd	1875	John Y. Brown, D-Ky.	Insult to representative	Not expelled
44th	1st	1875	William S. King, R-Minn.	Corruption	Not expelled
44th	1st	1875	John G. Schumaker, D-N.Y.	Corruption	Not expelled
48th	1st	1884	William P. Kellogg, R-La.	Corruption	Not expelled
67th	1st	1921	Thomas L. Blanton, D-Texas	Abuse of leave to print	Not expelled
96th	2nd	1980	Michael (Ozzie) Myers, D-Pa.	Corruption	*Expelled*

Source: Hinds and Cannon, *Precedents of the House of Representatives of the United States,* 11 vols. (1935–41); Joint Committee on Congressional Operations, *House of Representatives Exclusion, Censure and Expulsion Cases from 1789 to 1973,* committee print, 93rd Cong., 1st sess., 1973. Cited in *Current American Government, Spring 1981 Guide* (Washington, D.C., Congressional Quarterly, Inc., 1980).

Cannon asked Rules to trim $93,900 off the Commerce budget, which is about $2.8 million. "The chairman has always felt the committee was a little overstaffed," an aide said of the panel's 102-employee panel. But Cannon's 3-percent reduction doesn't come close to the 52-percent cut asked for by the Special Committee on Aging, the 10-percent saving for the Foreign Relations Committee, or the 6-percent asked by Veterans' Affairs. The largest increase ($270,550, or 55 percent) was requested by the Agriculture Committee.[34]

Another problem relating to Congressional staffing has surfaced in recent years. Senator John Glenn (D., Ohio) calls Congress "the last plantation,"[35] meaning that Congress does not have to abide by the fair-employment, affirmative-action rules that it has laid down for other government agencies and private employers. Congress has not obligated itself to take race, sex, and age into account in hiring. It does not have to represent itself as an equal-opportunity employer. Nor does it have to abide by the Equal Pay Act, protecting women against discrimination in salary levels.

TABLE 4.
Size of Committee Staffs, House and Senate, 1947–1978.

HOUSE	1947	1960	1970	1975	1978
House Administration	7	4	25	217	269
Interstate and Foreign Commerce	10	45	42	112	149
Appropriations	29	59	71	98	129
Banking	4	14	50	85	110
Education and Labor	10	25	77	114	103
International Relations	10	14	21	54	101
Ways and Means	12	22	24	63	93
Public Works	6	32	40	88	83
Judiciary	7	27	35	69	82
Government Operations	9	54	60	68	82
Science and Technology	*	17	26	47	80
Merchant Marine and Fisheries	6	9	21	28	79
Budget	*	*	*	67	77
Interior	4	10	14	57	68
Post Office and Civil Service	6	9	46	61	65
Agriculture	9	10	17	48	58
Armed Services	10	15	37	38	45
Small Business	*	*	*	27	40
Standards of Official Conduct	*	*	5	5	37
District of Columbia	7	8	15	43	35
Veterans Affairs	7	18	18	26	34
Rules	4	2	7	18	25
Internal Security	10	46	51	27	*

SENATE	1947	1960	1970	1975	1978
Judiciary	19	137	190	251	200
Governmental Affairs	29	47	55	144	178
Labor and Human Resources	9	28	69	150	123
Commerce, Science and Transportation	8	52	53	111	96
Budget	*	*	*	90	93
Appropriations	23	31	42	72	78
Environment (Public Works)	10	11	34	70	62
Foreign Relations	8	25	31	62	61
Energy and Natural Resources (Interior)	7	26	22	53	49
Banking, Housing and Urban Affairs	9	22	23	55	48
Finance	6	6	16	26	45
Agriculture, Nutrition and Forestry	3	10	7	22	34
Armed Services	10	23	19	30	30
Rules and Administration	41	15	13	29	30
Veterans Affairs	*	*	*	32	24
Aeronautics and Space Science	*	10	12	22	*
District of Columbia	4	7	18	33	*
Post Office and Civil Service	46	20	31	25	*

Source: Schneider, "Congressional Staffing, 1947–1978"; *Report of the Clerk of the House,* July 1, 1979 to September 30, 1979; and *Report of the Secretary of the Senate,* April 1, 1979 to September 30, 1979. Cited in Michael J. Malbin, *Unelected Representatives* (New York: Basic Books, 1980).

And, in fact, it has not followed any of these guidelines. In 1974, the Capitol Hill Women's Political Caucus produced a study that found the median salary of women was $7000 less than that of men doing comparable work on Congressional staffs. In 1978, an updated study found little change. Likewise, one staff aide of then-Senator Birch Bayh (D., Indiana) found only "30 blacks in positions where they can influence policy—administrative assistants, legislative assistants, press secretaries, committee lawyers" in 1976. Two years later, he said, "Nothing has changed." To remedy this situation, a list of 150 potential black appointees was compiled (fifty percent were lawyers; of the rest, twenty-five to thirty percent had master's degrees or doctorates), but in the list's one year of existence, only former Senator Dick Clark (D., Iowa) availed himself of it.

In 1977, as part of the Senate ethics code, the Senate prohibited senators from hiring and firing on the basis of race, sex, and age, and prohibited other discriminatory employment practices. (The House has no similar rule.) The Senate Ethics Committee is charged with enforcing the rule, but no specific procedures have been developed. Senator Patrick J. Leahy (D., Vermont) introduced legislation that would make Congress comply with the Civil Rights Act, Equal Pay Act, and so forth. It would apply to both chambers of Congress. Most observers felt its prospects for passage were slim, and, in fact, it never came up for a vote.

Some staffers can exercise considerable influence in Congress. They are frequently the main sources of information for their employers. They can draft legislation, elicit information from the bureaucracy, help constituents, and can often provide the last-minute advice to an uninformed legislator as to how he or she should vote on a measure pending on the floor or in committee. Some staffers go on to become elected representa-

tives in their own right. But note the observation of Norman D. Dicks, who served for eight years as a staffer to Senator Warren G. Magnuson before himself being elected to Congress in 1977. "People asked me how I felt being elected to Congress, and I told them I never thought I'd give up that much power voluntarily."[36]

Sometimes "that much power" extends to the point of conceiving and implementing plans for a select committee to deal with the President's energy program, as did twenty-four-year-old staff aide to Speaker "Tip" O'Neill in 1977. Sometimes "that much power" means drafting and expediting a Senate reorganization plan. And in an area as complex as military defense, a staff member can become quite influential by developing technical expertise. In time, the legislators come to rely so heavily on the staffer for advice that they simply end up ratifying the staffer's recommendations, as in the following situation.

Although most Congressional committees rely heavily on their staffs, the aides of committees that deal with the nation's defense are regarded as unusually influential. Their influence is due to the complexity of weapons systems and the enormous size, $110 billion, of the defense budget.

For example, Peter J. Murphy, a staff member of the defense subcommittee, made the initial determination to deny additional funds for the E-3A airborne warning and control system. His decision was ratified by the committee. Mr. Murphy also opposed a $35 million appropriation for procurement of the Short Range Attack Missile but recommended $24 million for research and development. He recommended that $20 million in advance procurement be provided for the Air-Launched Cruise Missile. Had the committee and subcommittee voted on these matters? "Some they vote on, some they don't," Mr. Murphy explained.[37]

These kinds of staffers immerse themselves in details. They are able to concentrate on a specific subject in a way not possible for an elected legislator, thereby gaining access to influence and even power. When one realizes that a legislator is inundated from all sides with problems requiring his or her attention, it is understandable how a knowledgeable staffer could become an invaluable and influential resource. One news story reported: "In an eleven-hour day, a Congressional committee reported last year, the average member has only eleven minutes free to think. For more than one third of that day, the Representative is scheduled to be at least two places at once."[38] The staffer, on the other hand, will often concentrate full-time for months on one issue. This aspect of the governing process is not found in the Constitution or the laws of the land. In some ways, it is an unavoidable consequence of the growing workload and complexity of the legislative process.

From time to time, a piece of legislation suffers in the legislative process because of lack of attention or the abilities of a particular staff member, as happened in the labor-reform case study. You will recall that the bill to change certain labor laws did not receive much attention from the staff director of the Senate Human Resources Committee. And it was noted "that the action of a single senator and his staff can frequently decide the success or failure of legislation—even very important legislation."

Some expert staffers are pursued by private interest groups and corporations, since staffers frequently have not only expert knowledge but invaluable contacts on the Hill. If they resign their staff jobs to work as lobbyists or consultants, they might be able to render great service to their clients. For example:

Three major drug firms—Pfizer, American Cyanamid, and Bristol-Myers—may lose tens of millions of dollars under a Supreme Court ruling that they can be sued for triple damages by foreign governments for alleged price-fixing.

Along came legislation last week to undo another, unrelated Supreme Court antitrust decision. No one paid much attention when Senate Judiciary Committee Chairman James O. Eastland (D., Mississippi) attached an amendment that would effectively bar the drug suits. The Pfizer lobbyist who discussed the amendment with Chairman Eastland last March and April was John H. Holloman III, who was Eastland's chief counsel and staff director until 1973.[39]

Congressional agencies. Congress also has several agencies at its disposal for assistance. These are the Congressional Research Service (CRS) of the Library of Congress, the Congressional Budget Office (CBO), the General Accounting Office (GAO), and the Office of Technology Assessment.

The Congressional Research Service was established in 1909 (known then as the Legislative Reference Service) and acquired its present name and increased status in 1970. It has grown from a staff of 250 in 1970 to 850 in 1979. It is available to do quick research on any number of issues raised by legislators and committees. After 1970, it was directed to work more closely with Congressional committees. The CRS responds to as many as 300,000 research inquiries per year, about forty-three percent from committees, forty-eight percent from individual legislators, and nine percent from legislators' constituents (sent through the legislator). The CRS is nonpartisan, and it is not expected to take sides in policy matters, such as whether funds for public service jobs should be increased or decreased. It simply supplies answers to specific fact-related questions.

The Congressional Budget Office, established in 1974, makes assessments and analyses of the budgetary impact of proposed, contemplated, or existing legislation. The CBO keeps Congress abreast of complicated fiscal problems—how much is being spent, how much is being taken in in revenues, what effect certain policies will likely have on inflation and unemployment. The CBO works closely with the Budget committees of the Senate and House.

The General Accounting Office (GAO), while not a direct servant of Congress, monitors the finances of the executive branch, audits the books of the bureaucratic agencies, and provides such information, on request, to interested Congressional committees. The GAO is not supposed to influence policy, but in the process of determining if the executive agencies are spending money in the manner Congress intended, it can and does make suggestions. For example, the GAO suggested that money could be saved by the Defense Department if several facilities supporting military installations in California were consolidated. It also recommended that money could be saved if the government did not follow the policy (set forth in the Davis-Bacon Act) of paying union wages to all employees working on federal projects in a particular locality. The GAO has approximately 5200 employees, with about fifty-five percent located in Washington, D.C. and the rest in fifteen regional and overseas offices. In 1980, its budget was $200.3 million.

The Office of Technology Assessment was established in 1972, but did not start functioning until 1974. It is supposed to provide Congress with analyses of the impact of developing technology on various issues. Several legislators feel that its output does not justify its large budget. They point out that while its budget grew from $2.5 million to $11 million in five years, there was little increase in productive work. This office has a staff of approximately 130 employees.

The Constituents of Congress

Legislative casework. The formal role of the legislator is to participate in the process of passing the laws that govern the country. The Constitution requires Congress to meet at least once a year, but it does not say anything about a member having to report back to constituents or returning calls from them or doing little tasks for them. Yet a considerable amount of a legislator's time is spent doing particular favors and performing special services for constituents. These favors and services include such things as contacting the Social Security Administration to see why a constituent's social-security check has not been received; getting someone's veteran's benefits straightened out, getting an elderly person into a senior citizen's home, helping a constituent's relative receive immigration papers, and innumerable such activities. This activity is called *legislative casework*, and a legislator will usually have a full-time staff member assigned to such functions. In 1978, one newspaper reported:

> *Recent polls taken by the Republican Congressional Campaign Committee showed 50 percent of the voters cited constituent service as the reason they liked or disliked a congressman. In contrast, only 10 percent cited the more controversial national issues a congressman must vote on.*[40]

Most legislators therefore pay close attention to this type of work. They realize that their constituents are normally not very interested in the wide range of issues which require a legislator's vote. "What have you done for me lately?" is the question many legislators must answer when they return to their districts seeking reelection. And "for me" is interpreted, frequently, on a personal level. These are the tangible things a politician can point to. Likewise, many issues and political procedures are so complicated that a legislator often decides not to try to explain in detail the difficulties involved: how the inflation rate or the unemployment rate is supposed to respond to certain government policies, or why one military weapons system is supposed to be superior to another. Thus, a member of Congress opts for the more simple (if time-consuming), manageable things. Most people do not know how their representative voted on most issues (especially on the obscure votes on amendments in committee sessions), but if the legislator smoothed the way to get a constituent's child into one of the military academies, or cut through bureaucratic red tape to get something done for a constituent, these can be pointed to as actual accomplishments. Such services and favors demonstrate attention. They have nothing to do directly with passing laws; they have everything to do with getting elected or, rather, reelected—which will *then* make it possible for a legislator to participate in passing laws.

Keeping in touch back home. Needless to say, it is of utmost importance for most legislators to keep in touch with the home district. This is especially true in a competitive two-party district (not a "safe" district) or where someone in the incumbent's party might be waiting to mount a challenge in a primary election. A legislator, as pressed as he or she is by a heavy work load in Washington, tries to return to the district as often as possible. All members maintain at least one Congressional office (sometimes more) back in the district, largely to do legislative casework between elections. When a member returns home—usually on extended weekends—what does he or she do? There are social and political meetings to attend—though *all* such meetings are at least potentially "political." There are speeches to give, reports to make, constituents to listen to, gripes to hear. These gripes, at times, can become pretty far-fetched. For example, retiring Congressman Otis Pike from Long Island admitted that "people bug

Congressman Jack Kemp meets with constituents in western New York.

me more than they used to." He gave an account of a constituent who called him at his home during a snowstorm to complain that the local hardware store had run out of snow shovels. The constituent wanted to know what Mr. Pike was going to do about it.

Sometimes, critics accuse legislators of not spending enough time in Washington, of going home *too* often (the closer the election, the more frequent the trips). One study concluded that the problem is not the frequency of the trips, but rather the content of the messages the representatives deliver when they return home. More often than not, the legislator will spend time promoting him- or herself and not enough time discussing the institution of Congress. These are frequently *self*-serving, not *Congress*-serving trips. The legislator tells what *he* is doing, how great *she* is, and so forth. One political scientist concluded:

> Instead of criticizing House members for going home so much, we should criticize them for any failure to put their leeway to a constructive purpose—during the explanatory process at home. . . . So long as House members explain themselves but not the institution, they help sustain (wittingly or unwittingly) the gap between a 10 percent approval level for Congress and a 90 percent reelection record for themselves.[41]

Thus while Congress as an institution is not held in high esteem by the electorate, individual legislators see to it that *they* are.

In one sense, this is unavoidable. The legislator must rely on his or her own resources and record to be reelected and must spend time at home doing "self-advertising" or risk defeat in the next election. Those people from safe districts often do not spend much time back home—because they do not have to or they are Congressional leaders and must devote more time to their Washington chores—or

they do not bother to try to explain or defend such a complicated body as Congress. Congress is really a place, as Richard Fenno says, where "performance is collective and accountability is individual." Therefore, the legislator assumes responsibility for accounting for his or her *own* behavior, and not for explaining the sometimes frustrating work of the institution. In attempting to do the latter, the legislator might develop an apologetic or defensive image, and this is not always the best image for a politician.

The impression should not be given that incumbent legislators always live in constant fear of being turned out of office at the next election. In fact, we are now seeing an increase in the percentage of incumbents being reelected. Political scientist Walter Dean Burnham has studied this development and has concluded: "Since about 1956–60, incumbent members of Congress of both political parties have become increasingly invulnerable to defeat in their districts, more or less regardless of the fate of their party's candidates for other offices in the same election."[42] This means that the electoral coalitions that elect Presidents are not necessarily the same coalitions that contribute to Congressional victories or defeats. Therefore, Burnham suggests, what is happening is "reinforcement of the separation of powers . . . which the drafters of the Constitution sought to prescribe two centuries ago." Since members of Congress can be reelected notwithstanding the fate of the candidate running for President, this will likely lead to even more independence of Congress from presidential leadership. And this is largely a result of the decline in the effectiveness of the political party as a mobilizing organization at the local level—a phenomenon Burnham calls *party decomposition* (discussed in chapter 6).

Two other political scientists, Albert D. Cover and David R. Mayhew, agree with Burnham and point out that "elections to Congress have become

TABLE 5.
Reelection Success of Incumbents in the Senate and House, 1946–1980.

	SENATE					HOUSE			
		Defeated					Defeated		
Year	Seeking Reelection	Primary	General	Percent Reelected	Year	Seeking Reelection	Primary	General	Percent Reelected
1946	30	6	7	56.7	1946	398	18	52	82.4
1948	25	2	8	60.0	1948	400	15	68	79.2
1950	32	5	5	68.8	1950	400	6	32	90.5
1952	31[1]	2	9	64.5	1952	389	9	26	91.0
1954	32[2]	2	6	75.0	1954	407	6	22	93.1
1956	29	0	4	86.2	1956	411	6	16	94.6
1958	28	0	10	64.3	1958	396	3	37	89.9
1960	29	0	1	96.6	1960	405	5[3]	25	92.6
1962	35	1	5	82.9	1962	402	12	22	91.5
1964	33	1	4	84.8	1964	397	8	45	86.6
1966	32	3	1	87.5	1966	411	8	41	88.1
1968	28	4	4	71.4	1968	409	4	9	96.8
1970	31	1	6	77.4	1970	401	10	12	94.5
1972	27	2	5	74.1	1972	390	12	13	93.6
1974	27	2	2	85.2	1974	391	8	40	87.7
1976	25	0	9	64.0	1976	384	3	13	95.8
1978	25	3	7	60.0	1978	382	5	19	93.7
1980	29	4	9	55.1	1980	392	6	25	79.0

Note: Number seeking reelection is the total number of seats up for election less those where the incumbent was retiring or running for office or where a vacancy existed.

[1]Includes Sen. William A. Purtell, R-Conn., who challenged incumbent William Benton, D, for a full Senate term rather than seek election to the last four years of the term of a Senate post to which he had been appointed. Purtell defeated Benton, who is considered an incumbent defeated in the general election.
[2]Does not include elections for two-month terms in North Carolina and Nebraska.
[3]Does not include Harold B. McSween, D-La., who was defeated in the primary by Earl K. Long. Long died before the general election, and McSween replaced him on the November ballot and won another term.
Sources: *Current American Government* (Fall 1980 and Spring 1981 Guide).

less competitive."[43] This is especially the case in the House of Representatives. "Before 1966 about three-fifths of the seats (in the House) were safe,"[44] but after the mid-1960s "approximately three-fourths of the seats fell into that category."[45] In the Senate, "the proportion of safe northern seats has risen from one-fifth to two-fifths."

There are several possible explanations for this development. Congressional redistricting has favored incumbents; incumbents have more means at their disposal (franking privilege, reimbursed trips home, added staff) to increase their visibility to constituents; there has been a decline in party allegiance along with a "shift to the incumbency cue." All these are reasonable factors, but Cover and Mayhew conclude with Burnham that the results will bring "Congresses less affected by presidential landslides [and] a clearer separation-of-powers cast to the regime. . . ." And they agree that this trend will likely signal "for better or worse a reversion to the original constitutional design."[46]

As legislators come to rely more on their own resources to get reelected, they tend to become less dependent on the political party for that purpose. The coalitions necessary to elect, say, a President are usually different from the coalitions necessary to elect a person to Congress, and this will mean that the makeup of Congress will not necessarily reflect the desires of party or President. This is what the constitutional framers envisioned in the first place.

At the same time, the conclusion should not be drawn that party affiliation is of no value. As we have noted earlier in this chapter, the political party is one important mechanism for organizing Congress—in making committee assignments, for example. The party might not be too important in getting one *into* Congress, but it can be important in how one operates once there. In addition, political scientist Demetrios Caraley has found that party affiliation is important when looking at urban-support votes of legislators. "Analysis of the 1977 urban votes shows that regardless of the central city, suburban, or rural nature of their constituencies, Democratic members of Congress continued to support urban programs strongly and Republican members continued not to do so."[47]

Looking out for the district: political realities. In *Federalist Paper* No. 46, James Madison wrote that "the members of the federal legislature will be likely to attach themselves too much to local objects. . . . Measures will too often be decided according to their probable effect, not on the national prosperity and happiness, but on the prejudices, interests, and pursuits of the governments and people of the individual States."[48] Madison was warning that Congress might well become a body of people who would be more concerned with what was good for their local districts rather than what was best for the country as a whole. His fears were not entirely misplaced.

When representatives perform services for individuals, that is known as legislative casework.

When they get a bill passed that provides a project for their district, such as a water project or a new road or a bridge or canal, that is called *pork barrel*. The legislator sees to it that his or her district is included in legislation authorizing the expenditure of money for such projects. And, of course, the greater the number of projects that are included in the proposed legislation, the greater the likelihood of gaining enough votes in the House and Senate to pass the bill.

In the Ninety-fifth Congress, Senator Pete Domenici (R., New Mexico) introduced a five-page bill (S.790) calling for the payment of a fee by commercial barge lines using federally maintained waterways. To insure passage, he accepted pork-barrel amendments providing for pet projects in various states, so much so that the bill finally came to 127 pages! The bill went to the House, where various members attached their own special requests for *their* districts. For instance, Representative Joe Rahall (D., West Virginia) asked for a $100 million flood-control project for his district. The chairperson of the subcommittee handling the bill told him: "We appreciate that you've maintained a voting record in support of other projects in other districts. We can probably help you."[49] President Carter did not like the bill, feeling it was too costly, and he promised to veto it.

"I'm not all that worried about a veto," said Rahall after he made the pitch for his flood control project. "I think there's a good chance we'll override it. The committee's got—how many?—three more days of hearings. That's a lot more projects. And that's a lot more votes on our side."[50]

That is the way the legislators dip into the barrel and bring home the bacon ("pork") for their districts. (And, of course, they make a point of announcing the project in the papers back home.) In this instance, President Carter's veto *was* upheld by Congress, so the pork-barrel process did not succeed.

A President is not always successful in guarding against such escalation of local-district requests. A good example is the *impact-aid* program. This is the kind of program in which so many local Congressional districts stand to gain that it is difficult to cut out or even cut back the program. A representative does not like to face a home-district constituency that has been deprived of its federal largesse. In the Ninety-fifth Congress, President Carter was no more successful in curbing this program than previous Presidents had been. The impact-aid program began after World War II, when growing federal agencies were set up in areas which required public education for children (1) whose parents lived and worked on the federal installations free of local taxes, or (2) whose parents worked on the federal installation but lived in the local community. Those areas were considered "impacted" by federal installations; the areas had to spend more money to educate the children of federal employees than otherwise would have been spent. Thus financial aid was provided (and kept increasing) to the local school districts. As one account put it:

Carter faces a losing battle over federal impact aid to school districts. Nor can congressional leaders do much about it. Too many irons are in the fire. . . . Carter told Congress he wanted cuts made in impact aid next year because the program had grown to unreasonable proportions and no longer served its initial purpose. He proposed increasing aid in the first category by $24.1 million and eliminating the $341.5 million in category II altogether.

The leadership went along. House Education Chairman Carl Perkins (D., Kentucky) agrees things have gotten out of hand, but doesn't approach with enthusiasm the task of correcting it. The reason: Carter's cuts would affect two-thirds of all congressional districts, represented by 300 constituent-minded members.[51]

Thus, we find that Madison was reasonably correct, at least in regard to legislators making sure that federal economic resources come into their communities. If anyone is going to "look out" for the overall national interest, this will have to be done by the President and, perhaps, the small number of Congressional leaders. In both the pork-barrel and impact-aid situations, the President felt the cost to the national treasury was too high. But each legislator was more concerned about the impact on his or her career back home. It is easier to go back to the constituents and tell them what the legislator has done for them than to go back empty-handed. One might argue that the legislator could go back and tell the constituents how much of the taxpayers' money was saved by *not* passing the pork-barrel legislation, but few elected officials want to take that risk. The other political reality is that an opponent in the next election might find it convenient to campaign against the incumbent on the grounds that he or she

has been lax in getting projects for the home folks. And while all this political interplay goes on, the federal budget grows and grows. No one wants to be caught taking one's hand out of the political pork barrel.

After President Reagan assumed office in 1981, he introduced a revised budget calling for substantial cuts in many programs (except defense, which received an increase). This set off a round of complaints from many groups within and outside Congress, all of them seeking to protect their interests. Predictably, impact aid was a target for reduction (see Table 6). President Reagan wanted to change the eligibility formula for receiving such aid, thereby substantially reducing the number of school districts (and therefore Congressional districts) coming under the program. (There will be a fuller discussion of the budget, economic policies, and politics in chapters 15, 16, and 17.)

Constituency interest and influence. Much of the material in this chapter would seem to suggest that most legislators do a pretty good job of *representing* their constituents, or at least those constituents who are politically active—the voters and the interest groups. If this is so, then one might conclude that the American legislative process is working pretty much as it was intended to work: candidates run for Congressional office, telling the voters how they feel about issues; the voters choose one candidate, presumably because they prefer that candidate over another; the elected representative does favors for individual constituents; the legislator takes care that Congressional actions will benefit the home district; presumably, if the incumbent is reelected—as most are—the constituents are generally satisfied with the job their representatives are doing in representing them.

TABLE 6.
Proposed Cuts in School Impact Aid, 1981–1986 (in millions of dollars).

Under President Reagan's plan to cut school impact aid, payments would continue to only 330 districts in which children who live on federal property where their parents work make up twenty percent or more of enrollment. This would eliminate 3500 districts. The President contends that most of these parents already pay state and local taxes toward their childrens' education and that more federal aid is unjustified.

	1981	1982	1983	1984	1985	1986
Current base	932	888	968	1,047	1,127	1,196
Proposed Reagan cut	−82	−450	−500	−551	−584	−613
Reagan budget	850	438	468	496	543	583

Source: *New York Times*, February 20, 1981, p. A13.

This ideal picture suggests that the legislator goes to Congress and pretty much votes as the constituents wish. It further suggests that the constituents know how the legislator behaves on the issues. Most of the reliable evidence we have in recent years, however, indicates something a bit different. Warren E. Miller and Donald E. Stokes tell us that Congressional constituents really are not very well informed about the myriad issues facing their representatives. "Far from looking over the shoulder of their Congressmen at the legislative game, most Americans are almost totally uninformed about legislative issues in Washington."[52] Miller and Stokes conclude that "given the limited information the average voter carries to the polls, the public might be thought incompetent to perform any task of appraisal."[53] In the study they conducted, less than twenty percent of the constituents knew how the candidates stood on issues and over fifty percent "conceded they had read or heard nothing about either [candidate]." The constituents' knowledge varied with the issues:

On questions of social and economic welfare there is considerable agreement between Representative and district . . . on the question of foreign involvement there is a good deal less agreement. . . . Apparently it made little difference to the internationalism of the Congressman whether he represented an internationalist or isolationist district. It is in the area of civil rights that the rankings of Congressmen and constituencies most nearly agree.[54]

While this seems to be the case with legislators, we should note the findings of a more recent study about constituency interests and *presidential* elections:

The American public in the mid-seventies differs in fundamental ways from the public of the fifties. In the 1950s the public was only mildly involved in politics, was relatively content with the political process, and had long-term commitments to one or the other of the major parties. Today it is more politically aroused, more detached from political parties than at any time in the past forty years, and deeply dissatisfied with the political process. . . . The increases in issue consistency and in the proportion who used ideological terms to evaluate political stimuli reflected changes in the nature of politics during the 1960s. Similarly, the surge of issue voting in the late 1960s and the early 1970s, while not wholly independent of the greater politicization of the population, clearly reflected a change in the type of candidates presented to the electorate.[55]

One might speculate that this trend toward issue-voting evidenced in presidential elections could, in time, carry over to elections of legislators.

It is also understandable that Congressional districts will differ in their reactions to individual legislators. Perhaps not many legislators would go so far as the former black representative from Atlanta, Andrew Young (later U.S. Ambassador to the United Nations in the Carter administration), who, in explaining his Georgia district's tolerance of his liberal voting record, stated candidly in 1974: "My district is sixty percent white and middle-of-the-road. The reason they tolerate my voting record is that they get outstanding service from my staff. Casework is the reason I get reelected."[56] This is a strong statement illustrating the importance of legislative casework, and it also implies that even if the constituents knew of Young's voting record and perhaps disagreed with it, they would nonetheless support him because of the services we spoke about earlier.

It is important not to get a distorted or unbalanced view of this matter. On the one hand, it may seem that legislators go off to Congress doing pretty much as they please without worrying too much what the voters back home think or know, as long as casework services are performed and pork-barrel projects are delivered. On the other hand, some legislators seem to spend a great deal of time back in the district "selling themselves" and publicizing their virtues, presumably because the people *are* interested and concerned. The true picture lies probably somewhere in the middle, depending on the district and the legislator. Some districts are surely more politically attentive to issues than others. Most legislators probably are freer than they think to act on a wide range of issues, most of which are of little, if any, concern to their constituents.[57]

Of course, constituents have *some* primary interests they expect their representatives to fight for

and protect, and this may give the legislators some latitude to bargain and compromise (as with the tobacco interests and the black representatives mentioned earlier in this chapter) in attempting to get what they want.

Yet the problem of how to gain more constituency interest in and influence over legislators remains. As we have seen, Congress is a complex institution, and the issues coming before it are many and diverse. It is difficult enough for the most politically attentive and sophisticated constituent to keep abreast of the various issues. And yet, if we do not try to deal with this problem and devise ways to make the legislative system more truly representative, the democratic process may be in trouble.

Richard Fenno has stated: "Constituents cannot know whether their views are being represented unless they can know what their representatives are doing."[58] He has suggested a way to keep constituents more informed as well as to help explain the workings of Congress. He would have the local TV news devote a few spots each month to coverage of the local legislator's activities both in Washington and back home. These brief segments would focus on what the legislator is actually saying and doing. It would help explain the complexities of the Congressional process (such as why certain bills were delayed), and it would pinpoint the positions taken by the local representative. Too often, TV news spotlights only the small number of Congressional leaders and the "big" issues, leaving individual local legislators unnoticed and, perhaps, unchallenged. Fenno believes that his suggestion would serve an important educational function, and would keep the local representative on his or her toes.

As with most suggestions for improvement, this one might have unintended and undesirable consequences. The proposal could, for instance, favor the incumbent by giving the incumbent more

Members of Congress use a variety of printed materials to "sell themselves" to their constituents back home.

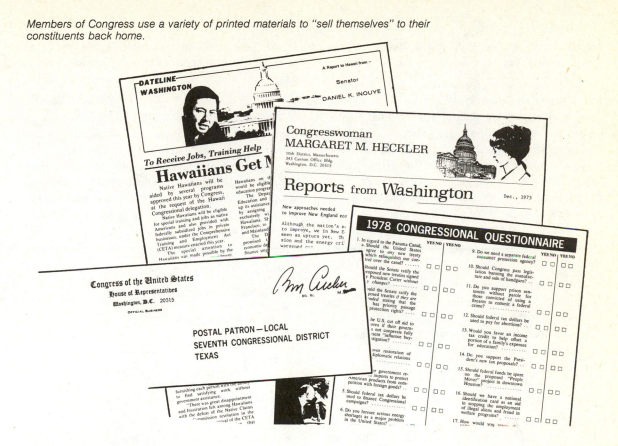

exposure than he or she would normally receive—and at no cost. This could add to the incumbent's electoral advantage (already substantial) at the next election. On the other hand, it can be argued that constituents are entitled to as much information as possible in holding their representatives accountable and in assessing their performances. Without such information, the argument goes, the representative system fails to perform its proper functions.

Summary

1. The two-chamber structure of Congress was deliberately designed to provide a system of checks and balances, both for itself and for the presidency. In recent years (perhaps the last decade) Congress has attempted to reassert itself in relation to the President. We now have nothing like the dominance of Congress during the nineteenth century, but a number of measures have been passed recently that would tend to put Congress on more of a coequal basis with the President in policymaking.

2. Essentially, three mechanisms (political parties, leadership positions, and committees) are used to provide some order and cohesion in Congress. Recent years have seen the development of several special-interest (region, race, sex, issue) caucuses in Congress which cut across party lines. Caucuses are not as cohesive or as demanding of one's time as the regular committees and subcommittees, but they do represent a rather narrow range of interests.

3. Congressional reforms have given rank-and-file members of Congress the chance to participate more actively in legislating, have tended to increase the power of the party caucus/conference, and have strengthened the hand of the speaker, while diminishing somewhat the iron grip of committee chairpersons. At the same time, the reforms have slowed up the legislative process to a substantial extent. The sunshine laws have made the work of the committees more open to the scrutiny of those interested in watching Congressional activities.

4. While it is certainly true that many unrecorded political deals contribute to the legislative process, it is also the case that lawmaking follows certain prescribed, formal steps. At each stage, the participants must be aware of the necessity to bargain and compromise. Frequently this is done openly, and it constitutes a legitimate part of the political process.

5. Staff assistance to committees and individual legislators has grown considerably in the last decade. Because of the unique position of some staff members and their access to information, they are, at times, very influential in policymaking. Some staffs have been known to draft legislation, lobby for and against bills, and even ''suggest'' how committees and individuals should vote on certain measures. These staff people play an important role in government and are not subject to sanction by the voters. In many ways, they operate as the bureaucracy of Congress, exercising as much policy influence in the legislature as the executive bureaucracy does in the executive branch.

6. A considerable part of being a member of Congress involves not only voting on bills and serving on committees, but doing favors for constituents. This *legislative casework* permits a legis-lator to point to specific, tangible benefits provided to the constituents and, in terms of getting reelected, is considered equivalent in importance to the policy positions a legislator takes on issues.

7. Most of the time a legislator spends back in the district is devoted to self-serving (not Congress-serving) activities. The legislator defends and explains his or her record, rather than building up the institution of Congress. Therefore, while most members who run are reelected, the prestige of Congress itself is generally not high among the constituents.

Notes

1. *Washington Post*, June 26, 1978, p. A8.
2. *The Federalist Papers* (No. 51).
3. *The Federalist Papers* (No. 58).
4. Woodrow Wilson, *Congressional Government* (New York: Meridian Books, 1956).
5. Harvey G. Zeidenstein, ''The Reassertion of Congressional Power,'' *Political Science Quarterly*, Vol. 93, No. 3 (Fall 1978).
6. Ibid., p. 397.
7. Ibid., p. 408.
8. *Washington Post*, June 26, 1978, p. A8.
9. Jerome R. Waldie and Michael D. Green, ''Congress and the Realities of Life on Capitol Hill,'' in Charles Peters and James Fallows, eds., *The System* (New York: Praeger Publishers, 1976), p. 58.
10. Shirley Chisholm, *Unbought and Unbossed* (Boston: Houghton Mifflin Company, 1970), pp. 80–86.
11. ''The New Congressional Politics,'' *Empire*, Vol. 4, No. 5 (October-November 1978), 31.
12. A good example is the series of articles over approximately three months (April, May, June, 1978) on S. 790, The Waterways Toll Bill, in the *Washington Post*.
13. See, for example, Stephen Bailey, *Congress Makes a Law: The Story Behind the Employment Act of 1946* (New York: Vintage Books, 1964); Daniel P. Moynihan, *The Politics of a Guaranteed Income* (New York: Random House, 1973); James L. Sundquist, *Politics and Policy* (Washington, D.C.: The Brookings Institution, 1968).
14. Bobby Baker, *Wheeling and Dealing: Confessions of a Capitol Hill Operator* (New York: W. W. Norton and Co., 1978), p. 97.

15. Ibid., pp. 98–99. It is important to note that none of the several major books written thus far about the Kennedy presidency (Sorensen, Schlesinger, Salinger—all insiders) discuss this aspect of the test ban treaty's passage.

16. Until 1975, a two-thirds vote of those present and voting was required.

17. *Congressional Insight*, Vol. 1, No. 45 (Washington, D.C.: Congressional Quarterly, Inc., August 26, 1977).

18. Lawrence C. Dodd and Bruce I. Oppenheimer, "The House in Transition," in Dodd and Oppenheimer, eds., *Congress Reconsidered* (New York: Praeger Publishers, 1977), p. 35.

19. Leroy N. Rieselbach, *Congressional Reform in the Seventies* (Morristown, New Jersey: General Learning Press, 1977), p. 44.

20. Dodd and Oppenheimer, "The House in Transition," p. 40.

21. Catherine E. Rudder, "Committee Reform and the Revenue Process," in *Congress Reconsidered*, p. 124.

22. Eric Davis, "What Can Jimmy Carter Learn About Legislative Liaison from Previous Presidents?" Unpublished paper presented at annual meeting of the American Political Science Association, New York, 1978.

23. *Washington Post*, October 12, 1978, p. A18.

24. *Washington Post*, October 23, 1978, p. A26.

25. Rieselbach, *Congressional Reform in the Seventies*, p. 47.

26. Ibid., pp. 103–104.

27. Dennis Farney, "Women Still Facing Many Hurdles in Drive for Seats in Congress," *Wall Street Journal*, October 11, 1978, p. 1.

28. David S. Broder, "Women in Congress: Still Scarce," *Washington Post*, October 18, 1978, p. A17.

29. "Income Grows Despite New House Ceiling," *Current American Government* (Washington, D.C.: Congressional Quarterly, Inc., Spring 1981), p. 58.

30. *New York Times*, March 27, 1978, p. A15.

31. Ibid.

32. *New York Times*, January 11, 1981, p. 25.

33. *Congressional Insight*, Vol. 11, No. 15 (Washington, D.C.: Congressional Quarterly, Inc., April 14, 1978), p. 4.

34. *Congressional Insight*, Vol. 11, No. 8 (Washington, D.C.: Congressional Quarterly Inc., February 28, 1978).

35. *Wall Street Journal*, July 10, 1978, p. 12.

36. *New York Times*, September 25, 1977, p. E4.

37. Ibid.

38. *New York Times*, March 27, 1978, p. A15.

39. *Congressional Insight*, Vol. 11, No. 32 (Washington, D.C.: Congressional Quarterly, Inc., August 11, 1978).

40. New Rochelle *Standard Star*, October 4, 1978, p. A10.

41. Richard F. Fenno, Jr., "U.S. House Members in Their Constituencies: An Exploration," *The American Political Science Review* (September 1977), 883, 917.

42. Walter Dean Burnham, "Insulation and Responsiveness in Congressional Elections," *Political Science Quarterly*, Vol. 90 (1975), 412.

43. Albert D. Cover and David R. Mayhew, "Congressional Dynamics and the Decline of Competitive Congressional Elections," in *Congress Reconsidered*, p. 54.

44. Cover and Mayhew call a seat "safe" when the incumbent secures at least sixty percent of the vote.

45. Cover and Mayhew, p. 56.

46. Ibid., p. 68.

47. Demetrios Caraley, "Congressional Politics and Urban Aid: A 1978 Postscript," *Political Science Quarterly*, Vol. 93, No. 3 (Fall 1978), 412.

48. *The Federalist Papers* (No. 46).

49. *Washington Post*, June 21, 1978, p. A4.

50. Ibid.

51. *Congressional Insight*, Vol. 1, No. 33 (Washington, D.C.: Congressional Quarterly, Inc., August 12, 1977).

52. Warren E. Miller and Donald E. Stokes, "Constituency Influence in Congress," in Angus Campbell, et al., *Elections and the Political Order* (New York: John Wiley and Sons, Inc., 1966), p. 355.

53. Ibid., p. 366.

54. Ibid., p. 359.

55. Norman H. Nie, Sidney Verba, and John R. Petrocik, *The Changing American Voter* (Cambridge, Mass.: Harvard University Press, 1979), pp. 1, 386.

56. Waldie and Green, "Congress and the Realities of Life on Capitol Hill," pp. 67–68.

57. See David Mayhew, *Congress: The Electoral Connection* (New Haven: Yale University Press, 1974).

58. Richard F. Fenno, Jr., "Strengthening a Congressional Strength," in *Congress Reconsidered*, p. 262.

The
Judicial
System

Chapter
12

When Alexis de Tocqueville visited the United States in the 1830s to begin work on his two-volume *Democracy in America*, he knew his task would be a hard one. In his chapter on judicial power in the United States, he wrote:

I am not aware that any nation of the globe has hitherto organized a judicial power in the same manner as the Americans. The judicial organization of the United States is the institution which a stranger has the greatest difficulty in understanding. He hears the authority of a judge invoked in the political occurrences of every day, and he naturally concludes that in the United States the judges are important political functionaries; nevertheless, when he examines the nature of the tribunals, they offer at the first glance nothing that is contrary to the usual habits and privileges of those bodies; and the magistrates seem to him to interfere in public affairs only by chance, but by chance that recurs every day.[1]

Tocqueville was right, of course, about the complexities of the subject, but in a sense the American judicial system is no more difficult to fathom than the other branches of government we have looked at thus far in this book. Of course, there are special terms and legal language, and much of what the courts do depends on subtle interpretations of phrases in the Constitution and the laws, interpretations that sometimes change without much notice. But the basic outlines can be presented and understood. As we pointed out in chapter 5, Tocqueville felt that sooner or later most political issues in the United States end up as judicial issues. Therefore, he said: ". . . all parties are obliged to borrow, in their daily controversies, the ideas, and even the language, peculiar to judicial proceedings."[2]

This is only a slight exaggeration. Indeed, when President Carter was pondering what particular energy policies to adopt at Camp David in July 1979, he and his advisers were aware that some of his plans would probably be challenged in court. And in fact a federal district court judge ruled that the President did not have the authority to impose a conservation fee on gasoline. (The case did not make it to the Supreme Court, because the fee was rejected by Congress.)

Likewise, after the voters in California adopted Proposition 13, some groups went to the state court to have the new law declared unconstitutional. They were unsuccessful.

In the labor-law case study, on the other hand, we were told that organized labor had little quarrel with the way the courts had dealt with the National Labor Relations Act. Rather, the unions felt the law itself was inadequate in facilitating union organizing. Thus they took their fight to Congress, not to the courts.

Obviously, not every political issue ends up in a court battle, but Tocqueville was not far off the

An early American courtroom in York, Pennsylvania, 1804.

mark—many political disputes *are* ultimately taken to court. This has led Archibald Cox, a prominent law professor and a former special prosecutor in the Watergate episode, to say: "Judge-made law plays a much larger part in the government of the American people than of the British. Our judges are less attentive to the letter of the law or to precedent. . . . Both bench and bar make greater use of statistical and other social studies, and the line between law and policy is often blurred."[3]

Before we examine how the courts play a role in the policymaking process, let us look at the structure and operation of the **judicial branch** of the federal government.

The Supreme Court and "Such Inferior Courts"

Article 3 of the Constitution establishes the existence of the highest court in the land—the United States *Supreme Court*. Congress is given the power to set up other "inferior" (or lower) courts, which it has done from time to time. Basically, there are three levels in the national judiciary (see Figure 1):

1. The Supreme Court is at the top, consisting of nine judges (Congress can determine the exact number, which has changed from time to time) chosen by the President and approved by the Senate. They serve for life.
2. On the next level are the *courts of appeal*. There is one of these in each of eleven judicial *circuits* (including Washington, D.C.) throughout the country. Each circuit has from three to twenty-four judges; as of June 1980, there were 132 authorized judgeships with an additional 45 senior judges. They are also chosen for life by the President and the Senate. A panel of three judges hears each case.
3. Then there is the federal *district court* level—ninety-four districts in the fifty states, Washington, D.C., and Puerto Rico. Some districts have several courts, others only one or two. As of June 1980, there were 516 authorized district-court judgeships, plus 126 senior district-court judges. One judge presides over a case, with or without a jury. Again, judges are selected for life by the President and the Senate.

Other courts authorized by Article 3 are the court of claims, the customs court, and the court of customs and patent appeals. All these, along with the district, appeals, and Supreme Courts, are considered *constitutional* courts.

In addition, there are *legislative* courts. These are also created by Congress but their authority stems from Article 1 of the Constitution. They

FIGURE 1.
The Federal Judicial System.

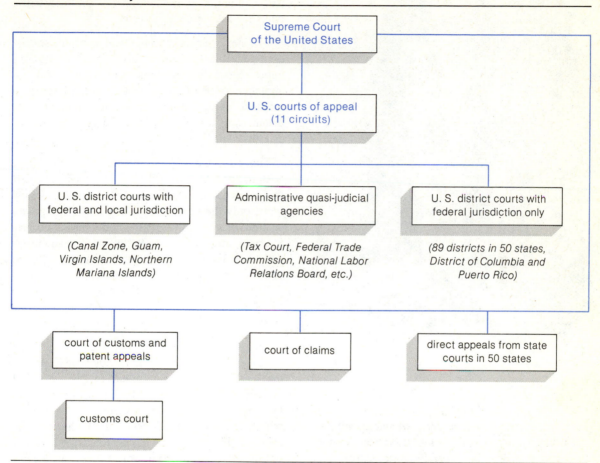

consist of the United States court of military appeals, tax court, and other tribunals Congress might wish to set up to handle matters falling within Congressional purview. The judges of these courts are chosen for fifteen-year terms by the President and the Senate.

We will be concerned in this chapter mainly with the "constitutional" courts, but one example we will refer to later involving the NLRB deals with an administrative-court decision (the NLRB was set up by Congress) as well as the constitutional courts.

Many important rulings in the Watergate case of the early 1970s were handed down in the federal district court of Judge John J. Sirica.

There are two kinds of *jurisdiction* in the American judicial system: **original** and **appellate**. Most cases must first (*originally*) be heard at the trial-court level. The federal district courts are always courts of original jurisdiction. Some cases also originate in administrative tribunals such as the National Labor Relations Board. At this level, parties present their cases, bring their witnesses, present counter-facts, and argue their positions. At this level, the facts of the case are legally established before a **petit jury**. If the matter is a *criminal* case, it will have first gone before a **grand jury**, a panel of from twelve to twenty-three people who hear the evidence presented by the government and who then determine if an indictment should be issued and a trial held. Some cases may and often do originate in the state courts and then are taken to the higher federal courts if a constitutional issue is involved.

The next step is the appellate level. Cases are appealed "from below." Both the U.S. court of appeals and the Supreme Court are primarily appellate courts (although, as we shall see in a moment, it is possible in a limited number of instances to use the Supreme Court as a court of original jurisdiction).

The party that loses in a "lower" court might wish to appeal the decision to a "higher" court. If this happens, the appellate court does not hear new *facts*, only the record of the trial court along with written *briefs* (arguments). Sometimes, lawyers for both sides are permitted to appear personally and state their case in "oral argument." Most appeals stop here, but each year as many as 5000 losing parties try to take their case all the way to the Supreme Court. Needless to say, not all 5000 make it.

There are two ways to move from the court of appeals to the highest level, the Supreme Court: by the method known as **appeal** or by a **writ of certiorari**. The first method technically means that the case falls in a category in which Congress requires the Supreme Court to grant a hearing; for example, if a state court has declared a federal law or treaty unconstitutional, or has upheld a state law whose constitutionality has been challenged, or has declared a state law to be in conflict with a federal law or treaty, then the case can be appealed to the Supreme Court. Even in these instances, the Supreme Court might feel that the matter does not involve a substantial judicial question, in which case the appeal will not be granted.

If the losing party seeks a writ of certiorari, the lower court is directed to send the entire record to the High Court. The Court then reviews the record; if at least four justices agree to hear the case, a writ will be issued.

THE RULES OF THE GAME

Drawing by Richter; © 1981. The New Yorker Magazine, Inc.

Sometimes justices must use their best persuasive powers to get their colleagues to go along with them in granting a writ of certiorari. Some justices might feel a particular case is, indeed, important enough for the Court to hear; others might not. This, of course, could be expected among nine quite influential and in many ways individualistic people. Negotiating, bargaining, and cajoling go on frequently—at least that is what some ''inside'' accounts tell us. One such account, Bob Woodward and Scott Armstrong's *The Brethren*,[4] gives an account of how the justices tried to handle a request for a writ of certiorari when one of the members, William O. Douglas, was very ill and in and out of the hospital, fast becoming mentally incapable of performing his judicial duties:

The Justices . . . decided that they would no longer permit Douglas to be the fourth vote to grant cert. The decision to cut Douglas out was informal, and it was treated as a deep family secret. But [Chief Justice] Burger nevertheless worried; if anyone ever learned about it, he would be remembered as the Chief who had let the conference take away a sick Justice's vote. To avoid the problem, Brennan several times cast his own vote as the fifth (provided he was not already one of the four) when Douglas indicated from the hospital that he wanted the Court to hear a certain case.[5]

There is another means of asking the Supreme Court to hear a case. If one is indigent (without

Justice William O. Douglas, whose illness called forth some delicate behind-the-scenes maneuvering on the part of his fellow justices.

funds), one can file a petition *in forma pauperis*. Many prisoners use this method in an attempt to have their cases heard by the Court. Almost half of the cases on the Court's docket got there by this means.

Various Types of Laws

American society, so the proposition goes, is a "government of laws, not of men." This means that the people who rule must base their actions on rules and regulations, not on their peculiar whims and personal preferences. This is a strong aspect of American political culture, and already in this book we have seen how this maxim has to be modified in practice. But whether it is strictly true or not for most American politicians, American *judges* must adhere to a body of laws available for all to see (if not fully understand).

The oldest form of law applied by the judge is the **common law**. This is the body of law derived from decisions in early England in cases heard over the years by circuit-riding judges. It is based on certain long-established principles of justice; one finds out what the law is by reading and interpreting the opinions of judges in legal cases extending back hundreds of years. Most of the judicial decisions involving contract disputes are based on common law.

Another type of law applied by the courts is **statutory law**, or law based on statutes passed by the legislatures. The courts take the facts in a particular case and decide on the basis of what the relevant statute says. If the statute is broad or vague (as is frequently the case), a court may interpret its meaning in whatever way the facts of the case seem to dictate. But legislative enactment is always the origin of statutory law. An example would be the statute governing "unfair labor practices," the National Labor Relations Act. The statute lays the groundwork for legal action, but it is up to the courts to decide whether the particular facts constitute unfair practices. Criminal law is a form of statutory law.

One might suggest that **constitutional law** is a form of statutory law, except that in the United States the Constitution has a higher status than ordinary legislative statutes. The process is much the same, however. The courts look at the facts in a case and proceed to apply the law as set forth in the Constitution. The courts are also guided by previous rulings concerning the meaning of the law.

Equity, another form of law applied by the courts, also has its roots in early English jurisprudence. Equity developed from the recognition that common law might not be entirely adequate to meet the needs of a complaining party, especially in providing a just (equitable) remedy or solution. For example, if I complain that my neighbor is constantly dumping garbage onto my property and damaging the property, then each time damage is done, I *could* get a court of law to require my neighbor to pay money. But what I really want is to stop him from dumping the garbage. Thus I can go into equity court to get an **injunction** against my neighbor—requiring him to stop. Equity law can require a person to perform or to desist from performing certain acts. It is intended to provide a just remedy that otherwise would not be possible.

Over the last several years, we have seen the development of **administrative law**. This consists of a body of rules and regulations issued by administrative agencies (such as the regulatory commissions). The courts are frequently called upon to review these "laws" to see that they are in accordance with the legislation empowering the agency to act, as well as in accordance with the Constitution. The legal case of *Babcock & Wilcox*, mentioned in the labor-law case study, resulted from a ruling by the NLRB. Each agency has administrative-law judges attached to it. There are, for example, 108 judges at the National Labor Relations Board; 672 at the Social Security Administration; and 51 at the Interstate Commerce Commission. In all, there are approximately 1130 administrative law judges in 29 federal departments and agencies.

An important aspect of law and the courts is the rule of **stare decisis**. Courts will often apply a law in the same manner as it was applied in an earlier case, where the earlier case is similar to the one before the court. This rule of *stare decisis* ("let the decision stand") suggests that the courts look to the past for guidance in deciding present situations. This rule is more strictly followed at the lower-court levels than in the Supreme Court. The highest court certainly feels bound by it, but at times the justices deem it necessary to break with the past and decide a case in light of different prevailing social and economic circumstances. This was demonstrated by the Supreme Court in

the school desegregation case of 1954, *Brown* v. *Board of Education of Topeka, Kansas*. In this case, the Court overturned the 1896 *Plessy* v. *Ferguson* case, stating:

> *In approaching this problem, we cannot turn the clock back to 1868 when the* [Fourteenth] *Amendment was adopted, or even to 1896 when* Plessy v. Ferguson *was written. We must consider public education in the light of its full development and its present place in American life throughout the nation. . . . Whatever may have been the extent of psychological knowledge at the time of* Plessy v. Ferguson, *this finding is amply supported by modern authority.*

We should point out that when a court pursues this approach, it is sometimes accused of deciding cases not on the basis of law but on social-science evidence—psychological, political, and economic. When this is done, the rule of *stare decisis* is not as important as it otherwise would be.

The Selection of Judges

Who sits as federal judges is no small matter to many people in the society. Lawyers care about the choices; politicians try to influence the selection process; interest groups take a keen interest from time to time. Obviously, the President seeks to put people on the bench who share his general philosophical orientation toward the Constitution and his attitudes toward public policy.

In the process of selecting federal district-court judges, the President consults with the U.S. senators from the state in which the district court is located. Frequently, the senators suggest candidates for such positions. A President usually will not nominate someone who has not been approved by the senators, even if the senators are not of the same political party as the President. This practice (discussed also in chapter 8) is known as *senatorial courtesy*.

A huge crowd lines up in the Supreme Court building to hear closing arguments in the 1954 Brown v. Board of Education *court fight. Minorities and civil-rights groups have historically looked to the judiciary as a crucial political instrument in the struggle for equal justice.*

To be sure, there is no explicit political test for selecting judges, but Presidents usually end up appointing people who are of the same political party as the President. In the first place, although Americans do not particularly like to admit it, such appointments are seen as political patronage plums. This does not mean that merit is not important, but simply that all other things being equal, a Republican (or Democratic) administration would prefer to find a meritorious Republican (or Democrat) to appoint to the bench. Once appointed, of course, the judge would not openly engage in partisan political activity. That would be considered improper judicial behavior.

The American Bar Association is keenly interested in who is appointed to the bench. In each state, the association has judicial screening committees that carefully scrutinize potential candidates. (The respective state bar associations also have such committees.) These committees put their stamp of approval ("qualified") or rejection ("unqualified") on a candidate, and if a President proceeds in the face of the latter designation, he can expect the bar association to testify against the nominee before the Senate. This testimony could influence the process of senatorial approval.

Various interest groups can also be expected to voice their opinions. A particular nominee might have voted against racial integration, in which case the National Association for the Advancement of Colored People (NAACP) can be expected to lobby against the appointment. The same is true for other areas of interest: labor, business, civil liberties, environmental protection, right-to-life, and so forth. As we saw in chapter 5, as one group comes forward other, counter-groups will also come forward, either for or against the nominee.

The nominee might have to undergo quite a grilling before the Senate Judiciary Committee, and the testimony need not be confined to the nominee's views about the law or the role of a judge. The hearing can cover personal matters as well, such as a nominee's income tax records or memberships in social clubs.

In recent years, for appointments to the district courts, some U.S. senators have set up their own unofficial, advisory judicial screening committees composed of lawyers and nonlawyers. When a vacancy occurs in a court within the senator's state, applicants are first interviewed by the senator's committee. If approved, the name or names are sent to the senator, who then might forward them to the President through the Attorney General. If an applicant is rejected, he or she can apply directly to the President for the job, but the likelihood of being appointed over a senator's disapproval would be very slim indeed. The organized legal profession follows the work of such committees very closely. (The author of this textbook served for three years on a judicial screening committee appointed by Senator Daniel P. Moynihan of New York.) The screening committees check various aspects of the applicant's career with people who have had contact—professional and otherwise—with the person, and personal interviews are held. The committees ask questions about the applicant's views on such things as sentencing, particular legal decisions, public service activities, academic background, and general intellectual interests.

Senatorial courtesy does not, for the most part, operate for appointments to the U.S. court of appeals, because these courts preside over judicial regions covering more than one state. But President Carter appointed separate appellate-court screening panels to interview and recommend potential candidates for vacancies.

Appointments to the Supreme Court, of course, always attract national attention and are the occasion for considerable lobbying. Observers look to see if the President will nominate a "judicial activist" (one inclined to hear cases and issue opinions over a wide range of issues) or one more inclined toward "judicial self-restraint." They look to see if the President will "send up the name" of a southerner or a woman or a black. Few will admit publicly—at least few, if any, Presidents or judges—that regional, racial, ethnic, or sexual characteristics are considered. But to believe that such factors are not considered is to be out of touch with American political reality. No one really knows, of course, *how* much they matter, nor should it be inferred that care is *not* taken to make qualified appointments.

Though Presidents exercise great care in appointing Supreme Court justices whose opinions reflect their own ideological orientations, more than a few Presidents have come to regret their selections. President Harry S. Truman, for instance, had some choice words to say about one of his appointees. (Truman had some choice words about many subjects!) When asked what he considered the biggest mistake he made as President, Truman made the following remark:

Tom Clark was my biggest mistake. No question about it. . . . That damn fool from Texas that I first made Attorney General and then put on the Supreme Court. I don't know what got into me. He was no damn good as Attorney General, and on the Supreme Court . . . it doesn't seem possible, but he's been even worse. He hasn't made one right decision that I can think of. . . . The main thing is . . . well, it isn't so much that he's a bad man. It's just that he's such a dumb son of a bitch. He's about the dumbest man I think I've ever run across. . . .[6]

Often, a judge, once appointed, will change his or her mind—or views. Political scientist Harold J. Spaeth has suggested that an appointment for life to the federal bench will bring out a judge's "true colors." He contends that Presidents sometimes "misguess":

The liberal Woodrow Wilson certainly did not perceive James McReynolds as anything other than a dutiful trust-busting Democrat when he nominated him to the Court in 1914. Wilson's two other nominees, Brandeis and John Clarke, fully mirrored Wilson's views. But McReynolds turned out to be another story. Not only was he conservative, he was the Court's all-time leading reactionary. He had difficulty coming to terms with the nineteenth century, much less the twentieth. Did the leopard, then, change his spots? Not likely. It is more probable that a lifetime appointment brings out a justice's true colors. Hence, the need to assay the real *politics of a nominee rather than his nominal affiliations.*[7]

The President also has the authority to appoint, with Senate approval, the United States attorney for each federal district court along with several assistant U.S. attorneys. These officers serve four-year terms, and their duties are to serve as the government's lawyers by prosecuting and defending cases. The same screening and selection process applicable to district-court judges applies to these positions, with senators being able in most instances to exercise senatorial courtesy. In some instances, service in these positions has been a good route to later appointments to the federal bench.

The attorney general, a member of the President's cabinet, is the highest law enforcement officer in the country and head of the Justice

Judge G. Harrold Carswell, one of two Nixon nominees to the Supreme Court to be rejected by the Senate. Here Judge Carswell makes an appearance before the Senate Judiciary Committee.

Department. Perhaps the most important function of the office of the attorney general is to decide which cases to prosecute when there is evidence of a violation of federal law. The deputy attorney general is the top assistant in the Justice Department.

The solicitor general in Washington, D.C., is another important position in the federal judicial system. This officer, appointed by the President with Senate approval, functions as the national government's top lawyer, deciding what cases to argue on behalf of the United States before the Supreme Court. This is the third highest job in the Department of Justice behind the attorney general and the deputy attorney general.

It is not absolutely essential that a Supreme Court justice have prior judicial experience, but most do. On occasion, a very successful lawyer or a prominent law professor will be appointed directly to the Court. Most often, however, a kind of apprenticeship has been served either at the district or appellate levels. And at times there have been appointments of basically political people— governors, cabinet officers—whose careers have been mostly outside the courtroom and not especially involved in the daily practice or teaching of the law. As of 1981, 101 men and one woman have served on the Supreme Court, and of these, 40 had no previous judicial experience.[8]

It can be a source of political embarrassment to a President to have his nominee rejected by the Senate. (This happened twice in succession in 1969–70 when the Senate rejected two of President Nixon's nominees, Clement Haynsworth and G. Harrold Carswell. Both had blemishes—personal and professional—on their records that were either overlooked or ignored by the Nixon administration.) Such action brings into question a President's judgment about quality and judicial standards, though invariably the President will explain the rebuff as an exercise of senatorial politics. In all, twenty-seven Supreme Court nominees have failed to receive senatorial confirmation.

The Work and Work Load of the Federal Courts

Each year the director of the Administrative Office of the United States Courts makes a report to the chief justice of the United States, giving a detailed account of the business of the federal courts at all levels below the Supreme Court. It tells how many cases were filed in the district courts, how many were tried, the average length of time for disposal of cases, how many were appealed, how many terminated, and the types of cases handled. By consulting the tables, one can see the general growth of judicial activity over the last several decades, especially in civil cases and appeals courts (see Tables 1 and 2 on page 454).

One of the functions of the administrative office is to certify federal court interpreters. Candidates must be proficient in both English and the designated foreign language, passing both a written and an oral test. In 1980, 2000 persons applied to take the tests, 1336 actually took the examinations, and 412 passed the written part. The oral test was then administered, with the assistance of three bilingual federal judges and professional linguists using actual trial transcripts.

Table 3 on page 455 indicates the length of trials in the district courts. Note that trials have been getting longer over the eight-year period from 1972 to 1980, especially trials with juries.

District court judges may appoint United States magistrates to assist them in processing cases. The magistrates conduct pretrial hearings and probation hearings, issue arrest warrants, set bail, and often dispose of many cases falling in the misdemeanor category. In October 1979, there were 196 full-time and 400 part-time magistrate positions authorized. Their appointments are for eight years.

How the Supreme Court Operates

By all standards, the United States Supreme Court is an imposing place. The black-robed justices sit behind a long, elevated bench and fire menacing questions at lawyers. A wall of secrecy (sometimes breached) surrounds the conferences held by the justices once a week. The highly visible give-and-take of everyday politics is notably absent, and deliberate efforts are made to keep it that way.

Various interest groups, for instance, are not supposed to lobby judges the way they are expected to do with legislators and administrators, but

TABLE 1.
Work Load of U.S. District Courts—Civil and Criminal Cases, 1940–1980.

Year Ending June 30	Authorized Judgeships	Criminal Cases Commenced Number	Criminal Cases Commenced Cases Per Judgeship	Criminal Cases Terminated	Criminal Cases Pending (as of June 30)	Civil Cases Commenced Number	Civil Cases Commenced Cases Per Judgeship	Civil Cases Terminated	Civil Cases Pending (as of June 30)
1940	190	33,401	176	33,861	9553	34,734	183	37,367	29,478
1950	215	37,720	175	37,414	8181	54,662	254	53,259	55,603
1960	245	29,828	122	29,864	7691	59,284	242	61,829	61,251
1970	401	39,959	100	36,819	20,910	87,321	218	80,435	93,207
1975	400	43,282	108	43,515	22,411	117,320	293	104,783	119,767
1976	399	41,020	103	43,675	19,756	130,597	327	110,175	140,189
1977	398	41,589	104	44,233	17,150	130,567	328	117,150	153,606
1978	399	35,983	90	37,286	15,847	138,770	348	125,914	166,462
1979	516	32,688	63	33,442	15,124	154,666	300	143,323	177,805
1980	516	28,921	56	29,297	14,759	168,789	327	160,481	186,113

Source: *Annual Report of the Director of the Administrative Office of the United States Courts,* 1980, pp. 3, 5.

TABLE 2.
Work Load of United States Courts of Appeals, 1940–1980.

Year Ending June 30	Authorized Judgeships	Appeals Commenced Number	Appeals Commenced Cases Per Panel	Appeals Terminated	Appeals Pending (as of June 30)
1940	57	3446	184	3434	1678
1950	65	2830	131	3064	1675
1960	68	3899	172	3713	2220
1970	97	11,662	361	10,699	8812
1975	97	16,658	515	16,000	12,128
1976	97	18,408	569	16,426	14,110
1977	97	19,118	591	17,784	15,444
1978	97	18,918	585	17,714	16,648
1979	132	20,219	460	18,928	17,939
1980	132	23,200	527	20,887	20,252

Source: *Annual Report of the Director of the Administrative Office of the United States Courts,* 1980, p. 1.

TABLE 3.
Length of Trials in U.S. District Courts (Twelve-Month Periods Ending on June 30, 1972–1980).

	1972	1975	1978*	1979*	1980*
Total Number of Trials	18,780	19,236	18,725	18,454	19,585
Length of Trial					
1 day	10,014	9718	9358	8863	9329
2 days	4204	4140	3831	3879	3905
3 days	1968	2183	2218	2245	2381
4 to 9 days	2262	2758	2860	2972	3261
10 to 19 days	273	355	344	384	528
20 days and over	59	82	114	111	181
Percent 4 days and over	13.8	16.6	17.7	18.8	20.3
Number of Jury Trials	8527	8607	7180	7082	7353
Percent of total	45.4	44.7	38.3	38.4	37.5
Length of Trial					
1 day	2385	2086	1208	1066	1057
2 days	2724	2543	2009	1958	1859
3 days	1475	1558	1531	1516	1539
4 to 9 days	1698	2094	2089	2194	2385
10 to 19 days	205	270	263	264	390
20 days and over	40	56	80	84	123
Percent 4 days and over	22.8	28.1	33.9	35.9	39.4

*Excludes trials of miscellaneous cases.

Source: *Annual Report of the Director of the Administrative Office of the United States Courts,* 1980, p. 110.

groups and individuals may offer **amicus curiae** ("friend of the court") briefs in cases before the Court. These are presented by people who are not directly involved in a particular case, but who are granted permission by the Court to present written arguments on one side or the other. Frequently, these briefs stress the viewpoint of a special-interest group. The contending parties like to solicit as many of these briefs as possible. They might not be decisive in winning a case, but they are likely not harmful. The *amicus* process thus is one means interest groups have of lobbying the Court. The briefs are careful to cite not only previous cases to support their argument but also law-journal articles by prestigious legal scholars and jurists. Supreme Court justices may understandably be impressed by reference to such authorities. They want to know what the most respected minds in the field think about a subject.

Since it would be quite improper for a justice to discuss a case with outsiders, this process is the only acceptable means of attempting to influence judicial decisions. In cases where the U.S. government is one of the contending parties, consent to file an *amicus* brief must be given by the solicitor general. The number of such briefs can be controlled by the Court. In one case, *Gideon* v. *Wainwright*, involving the right of indigents to

Clarence Gideon, right, signs copies of Gideon's Trumpet, *the Anthony Lewis bestseller that brought wide publicity to the plight of indigent defendants. In 1963, responding to* amicus curiae *briefs filed on Gideon's behalf, the Court ruled that every state must provide counsel to destitute prisoners charged with a felony.*

have a lawyer in noncapital as well as capital offenses, twenty-four *amicus* briefs were filed on behalf of the prisoner, Clarence E. Gideon. Two were filed on the other side. In the 1979–80 term of the Supreme Court, a case involving the right of Congress to deny funds for abortions was decided (*Harris* v. *McRae*). The Court held that such denial was constitutional, but more than 200 members of Congress, including the House majority and minority leaders, joined in an *amicus curiae* brief urging the Supreme Court, on the basis of separation of powers, to stay out of the matter of how Congress appropriates money.

No news briefings or press conferences are ever held concerning business before the Court. There is, indeed, an aura about the Court that differs from that of the presidency and that certainly does not exist with Congress. Many Americans expect and believe that the nine Supreme Court judges are really *above* politics—although politics was probably involved in their appointments, and the decisions they render inevitably affect American policy and are, therefore, political.

The Supreme Court starts its term in October and stays in session, with a few holiday breaks, until late June. The chief justice of the United States (*not* chief justice of the Supreme Court; the correct title is meant to convey leadership of *all* the judiciary) is the leader of the nine very independent individuals on the Supreme Court. The chief's functions include administering the Court's business, presiding over the weekly conferences (attended *only* by the justices to discuss cases), and assigning everything from office space to the task of writing opinions.

The chief justice and the eight associate justices each have at least three law clerks to assist them in their work of research and writing opinions. These clerkships are the prizes of the law-school graduation season. Normally, only the top graduates of the better-known law schools are considered for and offered clerkships. They serve for one term. The clerks gain invaluable experience and sometimes can be influential in helping a justice reach a decision in a case. Obviously, law clerks are not supposed to disclose court matters to the outside world—about cases or about the quirks of the justices they work for—but "leaks" do sometimes occur (as the Woodward and Armstrong book has made abundantly clear).[9]

The chief justice schedules cases to be heard, and during the weekly private conference (usually on Fridays) presents his views first. Then the justices, in order of seniority on the court, proceed to discuss the case. Afterward, they vote in reverse order, with the most recent appointee casting the first ballot. If the chief is a member of the majority, he assigns the writing of the opinion to himself or to an associate justice. If not, the most senior justice in the majority makes the assignment. Likewise, the chief justice or the most senior justice in the minority makes the assignment to write the *dissenting* opinion. There may be more than one dissenting opinion if the minority cannot agree on *why* they disagree.

Likewise, justices who agree with the final decision but disagree with the reasons for it may write a *concurring* opinion. At times, such opinions create more than a bit of confusion for lawyers and others trying to figure out precisely where the Court stands on a particular point of law. For this reason, considerable effort is expended to reach unanimous opinions, especially on cases of wide importance and of great policy significance. The quest for unanimity can be the occasion for bargaining and compromising. Justices know that it is useful to present a united front at times—as with

"Packed and hushed. Ready, Your Honor."

the school desegregation cases—in order to make the Court's rulings as broad and firm as possible. If the justices are unanimous in their ruling and in the reasons that lie behind it, this signals that the final outcome is strongly felt and should not be misinterpreted, nor should attempts be made to circumvent it. Thus, at times, justices will fight just to change a particular sentence or a particular point stressed in the majority opinion. If they succeed, they might then join the majority without writing either a concurring or dissenting opinion.

"All the Way to the Supreme Court"—Maybe

While Tocqueville might have been correct about most political issues ultimately becoming judicial matters, few attempts to "fight a case all the way to the Supreme Court" are successful. The Supreme Court receives approximately 5000 requests each year to hear cases. Only about 150 end up being argued before the Court, however. This is understandable. The Court could hardly be expected to cope with thousands of cases.

Even if a case presents an important issue, it might be turned down. The Supreme Court has developed several rules to help decide whether or not to take a case.

First, the petitioner must have "standing to sue," that is, he or she (or the organization) must be able to show that the case involves a real dispute between the parties. The case cannot be "moot." By this it is meant that the case cannot involve a situation which has otherwise already been resolved. Thus, a white law student who sued a university because he believed the university's affirmative-action admission policy discriminated against him was unable to take his case all the way to the Supreme Court, because by the time the Court was ready to hear the case, the student had been admitted and was about to graduate.[10]

Likewise, "standing to sue" will not exist if the case is simply a hypothetical one or if the parties are not *real* adversaries. If the parties concocted the case simply to see how the Court would rule, they will not have their case heard.

Another stipulation is that the complainant must be able to show a "legal injury" and be able to show that he or she has been injured directly. Thus, a medical doctor in Connecticut could not sue on the grounds that the state's laws against contraception prevented his giving advice to his female patients whose lives would be endangered if they bore children. The patients, not the doctor, presumably would have standing to sue.[11]

Sometimes the Court will rule that a case is not *justiciable*. This means that it is not a matter best handled by a court, but should more properly be resolved by another part of the political process. Questions concerning whether a constitutional amendment was properly ratified, or whether an enemy alien was properly deported on orders of the attorney general—questions such as these are considered political and not within the realm of the judiciary.

The Court has been known to change its mind, however. For a long time, the Court did not get involved in state reapportionment of legislative districts. As Justice Felix Frankfurter once said, this would involve the Court in a "political thicket," and it is "hostile to a democratic system to involve the judiciary in the politics of the people."[12] Yet sixteen years later, the Supreme Court held in *Baker* v. *Carr* that it could and ought to rule on the matter. It declared that certain districts which had not been reapportioned denied the citizens proper political representation. Justice Frankfurter, still on the bench, remained true to his previously stated position; he dissented.

Judicial Review—Judicial Supremacy?

Once a complainant convinces the Court to hear a case, one of the remedies available (if it is relevant) is to have the Court declare an act of Congress or of a state legislature, or a policy of the executive branch, unconstitutional. Obviously this gives the Court major power in the American governmental system, but it is a power that is not explicitly stated in the Constitution. Article 3 states: "The judicial power shall extend to all cases in law and equity arising under this Constitution, the laws of the United States, and treaties made . . . under their authority. . . ." Article 6 states: "This Constitution and the laws of the United States which shall be made in pursuance thereof and all treaties made . . . under the authority of the United States, shall be the supreme law of the land; and the judges in every state shall be bound thereby. . . ."

From this language, the Court has interpreted its right to exercise **judicial review**. That is, in the process of deciding a case or controversy, the Court can (indeed, must) declare a law unconstitutional if the Court believes the law to be at variance with the Constitution. This gives the Court, seemingly, an upper hand over the other two branches of government. While this might seem to be an unwarranted usurpation of power, Americans have come to accept that power residing in the courts.

Some observers would argue that although the Constitution does not explicitly provide for judicial review, the practice was not unknown in early American colonial preindependence experience. The British Privy Council had invalidated laws of the colonial legislatures at least 469 times.[13] During the period of the Confederacy, state courts were known to exercise judicial review, and for the first fourteen years after 1789, the courts in ten states had declared state laws null and void under state constitutions.[14]

More than a handful of delegates to the constitutional convention in Philadelphia (between twenty-five and thirty-two) "are generally considered to have called for [judicial review]."[15] Alexander Hamilton, writing in *Federalist Paper* No. 78, addressed the issue directly. He was aware that the exercise of judicial review might indicate that the courts were superior to the other branches. But this was less a concern to him than the alternative of permitting the legislature to be the judge of its own acts. Congress passed laws; the people established a Constitution, and "no legislative act . . . contrary to the Constitution, can be valid." Hamilton therefore concluded:

It is not otherwise to be supposed that the Constitution could intend to enable the representatives of the people to substitute their will *to that of their constituents. It is far more rational to suppose that the courts were designed to be an intermediate body between the people and the legislature in order, among other things, to keep the latter within the limits assigned to their authority. The interpretation of the laws is the proper and peculiar province of the courts.*[16]

Virtually everyone cites Hamilton on this subject, as political scientist Alan Dionosopoulos notes.[17] But James Madison was just as, if not more, explicit. When Congress was debating the meaning and effectiveness of the proposed bill of rights, the argument was made that the rights guaranteed there probably could not be enforced by any governmental agency. Madison, however, disagreed. The courts would be the protector. He argued:

Independent tribunals of justice will consider themselves in a peculiar manner the guardians of these rights; they will be an impenetrable bulwark against every assumption of power in the legislative or executive; they will be naturally led to resist every encroachment upon rights expressly stipulated for in the Constitution by the declaration of rights.[18]

The matter of judicial review received its most forceful affirmation, however, from Chief Justice John Marshall in 1803 in *Marbury* v. *Madison*. This was, aside from being the first of many landmark cases, the first time in the country's history that the Supreme Court declared a provision of a *Congressional* act unconstitutional.

The ironies of *Marbury* v. *Madison* are many. The case can only be understood in the context of the political environment of that time. An institution of the government—the Supreme Court—which many Americans prefer to think of as being above politics, seemed to be moving into the mainstream of America intimately embedded in politics. The *theory* of separation of powers appeared to be yielding to the *reality* of judicial interference.

The Federalists, led by John Adams, had been defeated by Thomas Jefferson and the Republicans in the election of 1800. The Republicans were taking control of the presidency and Congress. Political parties were just beginning to take shape, and this was the first time in the brief history of the new nation that there would be a change of political regimes. What would happen? Would the new group be vengeful against the former rulers? Would there be peaceful change of political power? Old questions now in the 1980s, but not so obvious then. To ensure Federalist control of the courts, the outgoing Congress created several new judgeships, and Adams, almost up to the last minute before he left office, appointed Federalists to these positions, including one William Marbury as a justice of the peace. His commission was signed and sealed, and needed only to be delivered

by the outgoing Federalist secretary of state—John Marshall. And Mr. Marshall had been named by Adams to be the new chief justice of the United States!

Thomas Jefferson became President and appointed James Madison his secretary of state. When Jefferson found out about the last-minute (''midnight'') judicial appointments, he directed Madison not to deliver the commissions. Marbury, anxious to receive his commission and to start his duties as justice of the peace, brought a lawsuit against Madison—*Marbury* v. *Madison*.

Marbury brought his case originally (initially) to the Supreme Court, seeking a **writ of mandamus**. This is an order from a court to an official ordering that official to perform a certain act. Marbury based his suit on Section 13 of the Judiciary Act of 1789, which stated:

The Supreme Court . . . shall have power to issue . . . writs of mandamus, in cases warranted by the principles and usages of law, to any courts appointed, or persons holding office, under the authority of the United States.

So Marbury did not go first to a federal district court, but directly to the highest court in the land. He sought to invoke the *original* jurisdiction of that court.

Just to indicate further how political this entire affair was, the newly elected, Jeffersonian-controlled Republican Congress delayed voting any money for the Supreme Court to operate. Therefore, the case was not heard for two years! And when Marbury finally got into court, who should be sitting in the middle of the then six-man bench but John Marshall, a Federalist and the one who failed (through negligence) to deliver the commission in the first place.

What would happen? What if the Court ordered Madison to deliver the commission, and Madison refused? How could the Court enforce its order? What if the Court ruled in favor of Madison; would not this be a blow against the Federalists in favor of their political opponents?

John Marshall's decision was based on an opinion that has been variously praised and condemned. It has been called brilliant, masterful, skillful, preposterous, weak, contrived—but it is cited to this day as the authority establishing once and for all the power of judicial review.

Was Marbury entitled to his commission? Of course he was, Marshall ruled. Was there a legal remedy, a way for him to get his commission? Of course there was, Marshall held: through the lower courts.

Could the Supreme Court grant a *writ of mandamus* to Madison ordering delivery of the commission? No, Marshall concluded. Why not? Because Section 13 of the Judiciary Act of 1789, which Marbury relied on to bring his case, was read by Marshall as giving the Supreme Court *original* jurisdiction to issue the writ. Yet Article 3 of the Constitution specifically states that the Supreme Court can have original jurisdiction *only* if a state or ambassadors or other foreign consuls are involved. Therefore (Marshall surely must have smiled a bit sheepishly at this point) Section 13 is an unconstitutional grant of *additional* original jurisdiction to the Supreme Court by Congress. And the Court must refuse the additional power offered by Congress.

Marshall and the Federalists had succeeded. Marbury was told that he could get his commission. The Supreme Court had told the Jeffersonians that the Federalist-dominated Court had the power to check the Republican-dominated Congress by judicial review if the latter got out of line.

Marshall really presented no new arguments for judicial review, stating pretty much the same position as Hamilton's in *Federalist Paper* No. 78:

William Marbury, central figure in the celebrated case that firmly established the power of judicial review.

It was the duty of the Court to decide cases and controversies under the Constitution. If a law conflicted with the Constitution, a judge was clearly empowered to declare the law unconstitutional.

The Jeffersonians were furious, but they could do nothing since Marshall had ordered them to do nothing.

To this day, constitutional authorities debate Marshall's ruling. He did not have to interpret Section 13 in that manner. He could have held that when a case was properly before the Court, a *writ* could be issued. In addition, if the Court did not have jurisdiction over the case, why even consider Marbury's entitlement to the commission? Why not simply dismiss it? The reason is that Marshall wanted to lecture the Republicans.

There is some irony in Marshall's role in all this. Judges usually disqualify themselves from a case if they had any previous connection with it. Here was Marshall deciding a case that developed precisely because of *his* negligence in not delivering the commission. Political scientist C. Herman Pritchett contends that Marshall's interpretation of Section 13 was "preposterous, and Marshall knew it." Pritchett proceeds to say:

Section 13 had been drawn by Oliver Ellsworth, later the third Chief Justice of the United States; it had been passed by the First Congress, which contained many ex-members of the Convention; and it had been actually enforced in 1794 by a Court which contained three ex-members of the Convention.[19]

The debate goes on. But it is really academic, because judicial review is as firmly established in the American political system as any power could be.

It is important to point out, however, that the Supreme Court has not run amuck in declaring laws unconstitutional. From 1789 to 1980, only 115 provisions of federal laws have been declared unconstitutional. "Out of a total of over 75,000 public and private laws passed, some 900 state laws and provisions of state constitutions have run wholly or partly afoul of that judicial checkmate . . . some 800 of these coming after 1870."[20]

The Supreme Court has developed four important rules in exercising judicial review. It attempts, at times—most times—to exercise *judicial self-restraint*. These rules were cogently stated in 1936 in a concurring opinion by Associate Justice Louis D. Brandeis.[21]

First, the Supreme Court will not anticipate a question of the constitutionality of a law; the question must be absolutely necessary to decide the case.

Second, the constitutional ruling will be stated as narrowly as possible, confining itself to the precise facts of the case before the court.

Third, if the case can be decided on grounds other than by ruling on the constitutionality of a law, those other grounds will be used.

Fourth, the Court will take almost extra pains to construe a law in such a way as to avoid ruling it unconstitutional.

Thus, if these rules had been in force in 1803, presumably Section 13 of the Judiciary Act of 1789 would not have been declared unconstitutional. But we must bear in mind the basic political motivation behind John Marshall's decision. One has to believe that Marshall was not entirely interested in exercising judicial self-restraint—to say the least. We have already noted how he *could* have read Section 13 differently. As Pritchett noted, "such an interpretation would not have suited Marshall's purposes."[22]

The opposite of judicial self-restraint is known as *judicial activism*. Some judges do not hesitate to use their positions to involve the Court in a range of issues others might feel are beyond the purview of the judiciary. A judicially active court frequently will find itself involved in making decisions that border on policymaking.

The Supreme Court as Policymaker

Once the courts gained the power to exercise judicial review, it was clear that they would be drawn into the policymaking process. The laws they review are policies. As they *review* policies to see if they are constitutional, they therefore *make* policies by the decisions they render. This is inevitable. It might not look or sound that way in theory, but it is that way in practice.

The Supreme Court has always played an impor-

Dred Scott, 1857.

tant role in policymaking, at least since 1803. It is possible to distinguish at least three periods of Supreme Court activity in this area.

In the first period, from 1803 to about the end of the Civil War, the Court was instrumental in issues of federalism. We saw in chapters 2 and 3 that the Court decided such matters as the right of the national government to establish a bank and the inability of the states to tax that bank. In the *Dred Scott* decision of 1857, the Court held that slavery could be protected by state laws. But, for the most part, the Court usually came down on the side of strengthening the powers of the national government, especially in areas involving the regulation of interstate commerce.

In the second period, from the end of the Civil War to the late 1930s and the New Deal, the Supreme Court was important in establishing a strong constitutional base for the protection of private-property rights and the development of modern-day American capitalism. Injunctions against striking labor unions were issued,[23] the antitrust laws were weakened,[24] and laws attempting to regulate child labor and maximum work hours were disallowed.[25] Without question, the Court was involved in policymaking. This was the same period that saw the Supreme Court severely restrict the constitutional rights of recently emancipated slaves. Racial segregation was constitutionally sanctioned by the Court.[26] At the same time, however, during this second period the Supreme Court permitted states to regulate businesses "affected with a public interest,"[27] supported some state legislation aimed at employee safety,[28] and even rendered an important decision in favor of the right of black Americans to vote under the Fifteenth Amendment.[29]

In the 1930s, when President Franklin D. Roosevelt was instituting his New Deal measures, the Supreme Court stood as a major obstacle, declaring several of the laws unconstitutional. For example, the Court struck down the National Industrial Recovery Act (NIRA)[30] on the grounds that Congress was delegating too much power to the executive branch and that the law was an infringement on *intrastate* commerce. Roosevelt was furious. He believed that the concept of "interstate commerce" needed a more modern (and broader) definition. The Court, in Roosevelt's view, was holding to a narrow definition of the Constitution, one that placed too many transactions under the heading of "intrastate commerce." In a press conference, he asserted that the nation had been "relegated to the horse-and-buggy definition of interstate commerce."[31] Historian William E. Leuchtenburg wrote: "Not only had the Court

THAT COMPASS
DOESN'T POINT THE WAY
I WANT TO GO.
CHANGE IT.
NOW!

This 1937 cartoon illustrates the negative feelings many Americans held toward Franklin Roosevelt's "court-packing" plan.

destroyed Roosevelt's industrial recovery program but, by its narrow interpretation of the commerce clause, it threatened the remainder of the New Deal."[32] Other reform provisions of the New Deal were also declared unconstitutional.

President Roosevelt decided to take on the Court. Since several of the Court decisions against him were based on 5-to-4 votes, he hit on the idea of trying to get Congress to pass a law permitting an increase in the size of the Court. The proposed law held that if a justice had served for ten years and had reached seventy years of age without retiring a new member could be appointed up to an overall Supreme Court membership of fifteen. Roosevelt based his rationale on crowded court dockets and suggested that some of the judges were getting too old to perform efficiently. Thus he claimed his plan would "vitalize the courts." Many disagreed, but the President was out to get "the nine old men" by "packing the Court" with people more sympathetic to his policies.

Although Roosevelt had just won reelection in 1936 by an overwhelming landslide (he carried forty-six out of forty-eight states—all but Maine and Vermont), he was not able to persuade the country or Congress to go along with him on his Court "reform" plan. Reaction was swift and clear, even from people who did not like the rulings of the Supreme Court. They simply did not like the idea of a President attempting to take control of the Court in such a blatant, political manner. The Supreme Court as an institution still possessed an enormous amount of societal respect and support. It survived the court-packing plan.

But all was not lost for Roosevelt. Even during the 168 days of Congressional battling over the proposed plan, the Court began to change—both in composition (one justice retired) and in its rulings (one justice switched to the liberal side). The Supreme Court began to rule in favor of New

Deal measures, and within two and a half years after the defeat of the court-packing plan, Roosevelt was able to name five people to the Court—men more in tune with his views about social and economic policies and the role of government. This is another example of the theme of constancy and change. The Court remained intact as an important institution in the political system, while its composition and decisions changed and adapted to new times.

In the third period, from the 1940s to the end of the 1960s, the Supreme Court was noted for its role in civil rights and civil liberties. This was the period when the Court took the lead in dismantling legal racial segregation in the country; it substantially extended the protection of the Bill of Rights to persons accused of crimes; it interpreted freedom of speech and press rights liberally. (These matters are examined in chapters 13 and 14.) Of course, there were many who strongly condemned the Court for going beyond its strict judicial role and, in fact, legislating new policy. This was especially true of those who disagreed with the Court's school desegregation rulings under Chief Justice Earl Warren. "Impeach Earl Warren" signs began to dot the highways in the South. No serious move was made to impeach the chief justice, but the signs did give an indication of the feeling of more than a few citizens toward the "policies" issued by the Supreme Court.

Six justices have joined the Supreme Court since 1969, four appointed by President Nixon and one each by Presidents Ford and Reagan. As a conservative Republican President, Nixon generally selected justices who would not be as liberal as those on the Court during Warren's time. Nixon wrote:

During the 1950s and 1960s, under the leadership of Chief Justice Earl Warren, the Court had become unprecedentedly politically active. Like

Angry reactions to the liberalism of the Warren Court reached beyond the South. This sign was erected near a highway just outside of Decatur, Illinois.

many legal and political moderate conservatives, I felt that some Supreme Court justices were too often using their interpretation of the law to remake American society according to their own social, political, and ideological precepts. . . .[33]

In discussing his reasons for nominating Warren Burger as chief justice, Nixon wrote: "I knew Warren Burger to be philosophically a moderate conservative and personally an impressive man."[34] And when he was seeking to fill another vacancy with a woman, Nixon candidly admitted: ". . . we found that in general the women judges and lawyers qualified to be nominated for the Supreme Court were too liberal to meet the strict constructionist criterion I had established."[35] Nixon concluded: "It is true that the men I appointed shared my conservative judicial philosophy and significantly affected the balances of power that had developed in the Warren Court."[36]

Although judicial methods and procedures keep changing, the power and influence of the courts remain constant. Left: Ohio Common Pleas Court Judge James McCrystal reviews testimony on a videotape machine. Below: Copies of a Supreme Court decision are distributed to reporters in the Court pressroom. From here, news of the decision will be flashed to the public by means of radio, newspaper, and television.

The United States Supreme Court, 1981. From left to right: Harry Blackmun, Thurgood
Marshall, William Brennan, Chief Justice Warren Burger, Sandra Day O'Connor, Byron
White, Lewis Powell, William Rehnquist, John Paul Stevens.

The Supreme Court since the early 1970s has not been as liberal as it was during Warren's time, but neither has it returned to the days before the New Deal. The Court has ruled on some cases in a way that would put it in the liberal camp: it has upheld the voluntary adoption of affirmative-action programs to improve employment opportunities for blacks and other minorities;[37] it has held that a teen-ager has a right to an abortion without her parent's consent.[38] At the same time, the Court has issued decisions which many consider conservative: it has upheld Congressional and state restrictions on federal funding of most abortions,[39] it has approved the government's use of a "drug-courier profile" in deciding who to stop and question as suspected drug carriers;[40] and it upheld an at-large (that is, city- or county-wide) electoral system for electing city officials on grounds that intent to discriminate on a racial basis must be shown before such a system can be disallowed.[41]

In the early 1980s, the Court was in transition, given the age of the justices and the arrival of a new administration and a Republican-controlled Senate. In 1981, five of the justices were in their early to mid-seventies, and two of these, William Brennan and Thurgood Marshall, were the most liberal of the justices. Future appointments from a new conservative President and Senate promised to alter court decisions perceptibly. Certainly, the make-up of the Court itself was radically altered when, in 1981, President Reagan appointed Sandra Day O'Connor to the seat vacated by retiring Justice Potter Stewart.

Proposals to Restrict the Court

The struggle to limit the Court's influence has had a long history in American government. Efforts have centered on three basic approaches: (1) attempts to restrict the number, salaries, operation, and tenure of judges; (2) Congressional efforts to pass constitutional amendments specifically overruling Supreme Court decisions; and (3) Congressional attempts to revise laws previously interpreted by the Court as contrary to Congressional intent.

With *Marbury* v. *Madison*, Congress refused to vote money for the courts to operate for fourteen months. From time to time, there have been Congressional proposals to amend the Constitution in order to do away with life tenure for federal judges or to permit removal of judges by a two-thirds vote of the House and Senate. In 1923, Senator William E. Borah (R., Idaho) introduced a bill to require concurrence by seven judges before a Congressional act could be invalidated. He was not successful. We have already discussed President Franklin D. Roosevelt's court-packing plan. In 1953, the American Bar Association wanted a constitutional amendment to make retirement mandatory for all federal judges at age seventy-five. The Senate passed this proposal in 1954, but it was stopped in the House. There have also been attempts to pass legislation restricting the Court's jurisdiction over certain specific issues. This was tried in the late 1950s in an effort to deny the Supreme Court authority to review cases involving contempt of Congress, the federal loyalty security program, state antisubversive laws, and admission to the practice of law in any state. All were unsuccessful. In 1964, the House passed a bill to deny federal courts jurisdiction over matters relating to apportionment of state legislatures. The measure failed in the Senate. In 1964, the salaries of Supreme Court justices were raised by only $4500 per year while those of other federal judges were raised by $7500. Some observers felt this was motivated by a desire on the part of legislators to punish the Court for some of its rulings. (Today, the chief justice makes $84,675 per year and the associate justices, $81,288.)

There have been twenty-six amendments to the Constitution. Four have been in direct response to Supreme Court decisions and have been intended to reverse or offset those decisions. These amendments have dealt with the ability of citizens of one state to bring suit against another state (the Eleventh Amendment, ratified in 1795, prohibits such suits); the application of the Bill of Rights to the states (the Fourteenth Amendment, ratified in 1868, extended to all persons in all states the protection of certain individual rights); the income tax (the Sixteenth Amendment, ratified in 1913); and the eighteen-year-old vote (the Twenty-Sixth Amendment, ratified in 1971). Several other attempts have been made to pass constitutional amendments to counter Supreme Court decisions.

After the Supreme Court ruled a compulsory twenty-two-word prayer in New York State public schools unconstitutional,[42] an amendment to legalize voluntary student participation in prayers in public schools was proposed, and failed to pass the Senate by nine votes in 1966. Constitutional amendments have been proposed in response to court rulings allowing abortions, and in response to court-ordered school busing to achieve racial integration.

The quickest, and sometimes easiest, way to counter court decisions is to change a law that the Court has interpreted in a manner contrary to Congressional intent. Congress can simply modify the law to make it more specific. This has happened a few times, notably in 1978 when Congress passed a law requiring employers to include bene-

FIGURE 2.
The Judicial Dollar.
(Fiscal Year 1980)

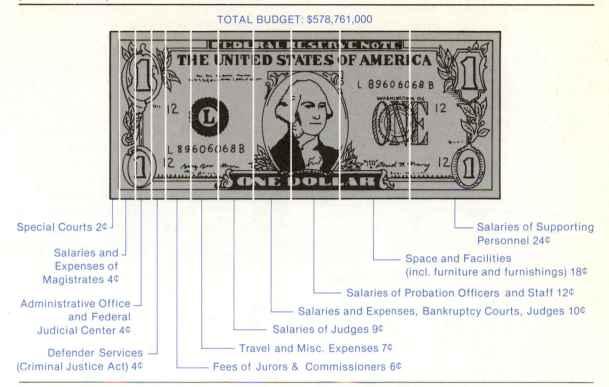

TOTAL BUDGET: $578,761,000

Special Courts 2¢

Salaries and
Expenses of
Magistrates 4¢

Administrative Office
and Federal
Judicial Center 4¢

Defender Services
(Criminal Justice Act) 4¢

Fees of Jurors & Commissioners 6¢

Travel and Misc. Expenses 7¢

Salaries of Judges 9¢

Salaries and Expenses, Bankruptcy Courts, Judges 10¢

Salaries of Probation Officers and Staff 12¢

Space and Facilities
(incl. furniture and furnishings) 18¢

Salaries of Supporting
Personnel 24¢

Source: *Annual Report of the Director of the Administrative Office of the United States Courts,* 1980, p. 29.

fits for pregnancy, childbirth, and other medical conditions in health insurance plans. Earlier the Court had held that pregnancy did not have to be included.

The Judicial System in American Society

Ultimately, the Court can only deliver opinions. It does not have its own mechanisms for enforcing decisions. For this, it must rely on the executive branch. In addition, the Court does not have the capacity to raise its own funds to operate. For this, it must rely on Congress. Like the President, justices can be impeached (which has occurred only once, in 1804 with Samuel Chase and even then the Senate failed to convict by a margin of four votes). Therefore, the Supreme Court and the entire judicial system must derive support from the other branches and from the general public. The justices are not elected, but they must be accountable to the public. Accountability must be based on an acceptance of the Court as an institution deserving respect and obedience. If it ran roughshod over the other two electorally chosen branches, we might indeed see successful political moves to curb its power of judicial review or to limit the kinds of cases it can hear. While the Court does not "follow the election returns," it must be sensitive to basic values and beliefs as embedded in the Constitution, laws, and customs of the society. Clearly, maintaining and nurturing respect and at the same time rendering judicial decisions grounded in the law and adaptable to current needs is no easy assignment, but it is one the Court must seek to perform.

Summary

1. Many issues are ultimately brought to the judicial system of the United States for final resolution. The federal courts have a three-layer system. The United States Supreme Court, the highest court in the land, has developed several criteria to determine if it will hear a case. Most cases are dealt with in the lower courts.

2. Frequently, the rule of *stare decisis,* or legal precedent, is followed, but at times the courts (especially the Supreme Court) will see fit to ignore previous rulings and decide a case on the basis of social and economic conditions.

3. Political as well as professional factors are considered in making judicial appointments. Senatorial courtesy is usually observed at the lower-court level, and various professional and other interest groups take a keen interest in who gets selected as judges. Presidents normally seek to nominate Supreme Court judges whose general views and judicial attitudes are compatible with their own.

4. The Supreme Court's work is adminstered by the chief justice who, among other duties, schedules cases and assigns opinions to be written. Justices may write concurring and dissenting opinions, but the Court prefers to render unanimous decisions whenever possible. Such agreement tends to strengthen the decision and bolster accept-

ance, as well as provide clearer guidance to the meaning of the ruling.

5. Judicial review is the most important power held by the Court. This right to declare acts of other branches of government unconstitutional, which can be understood as a form of judicial policymaking, is balanced by the Court's own rules of judicial self-restraint, as well as by efforts from time to time (some successful, some not) on the part of Congress to restrict the influence of the Court. Ultimately, the Court must rely on public support and the public's sense of the legitimacy of the Court's role inasmuch as it holds neither the power of the purse nor the power of the sword to enforce its decisions.

Notes

1. Alexis de Tocqueville, *Democracy in America*, Vol. 1 (New York: Vintage Books, 1957), p. 102.
2. Ibid., p. 290.
3. Archibald Cox, *The Role of the Supreme Court in American Government* (New York: Oxford University Press, 1976), p. 1.
4. Bob Woodward and Scott Armstrong, *The Brethren* (New York: Simon and Schuster, 1979).
5. Ibid., p. 368.
6. Merle Miller, *Plain Speaking* (New York: Berkley, 1973), pp. 225–26.
7. Harold J. Spaeth, *Supreme Court Policy Making* (San Francisco: W. H. Freeman and Company, 1979), p. 102.
8. Ibid., p. 100.
9. See, for instance, the anecdote concerning Justice Stewart and Chief Justice Burger in Woodward and Armstrong, p. 105.
10. *DeFunis* v. *Odegaard*, 416 U.S. 312 (1974).
11. Spaeth, pp. 32–33.
12. *Colegrove* v. *Green*, 328 U.S. 549 (1946).
13. P. Allan Dionosopoulos, "Judicial Review in the Textbooks, 1979," *NEWS* for Teachers of Political Science, American Political Science Association, No. 25 (Spring 1980).
14. Henry J. Abraham, *The Judicial Process*, 3rd ed. (New York: Oxford University Press, 1975), p. 306.

15. Ibid., p. 304.
16. Alexander Hamilton, *The Federalist Papers* (No. 78).
17. Dionosopoulos, ''Judicial Review in the Textbooks, 1979.''
18. Quoted in Dionosopoulos, p. 3.
19. C. Herman Pritchett, *The American Constitution* (New York: McGraw-Hill Book Company, 1959), pp. 139–40.
20. Abraham, *The Judicial Process*, p. 280.
21. *Ashwander* v. *Tennessee Valley Authority*, 297 U.S. 288 (1936).
22. Pritchett, p. 140.
23. *In re Debs*, 158 U.S. 564 (1895).
24. *United States* v. *Knight*, 156 U.S. 1 (1895).
25. *Hammer* v. *Dagenhart*, 247 U.S. 251 (1918); *Lochner* v. *New York* 198 U.S. 45 (1905).
26. *Plessy* v. *Ferguson*, 163 U.S. 537 (1896).
27. *Munn* v. *Illinois*, 94 U.S. 113 (1877).
28. *St. Louis Consolidated Coal Co.,* v. *Illinois*, 185 U.S. 203 (1902).

29. *Guinn* v. *United States*, 238 U.S. 347 (1915).
30. *A.L.A. Schechter Poultry Corporation* v. *U.S.*, 295 U.S. 553 (1935).
31. Quoted in William E. Leuchtenburg, *Franklin D. Roosevelt and The New Deal* (New York: Harper Torchbooks, 1963), p. 145.
32. Ibid.
33. Richard M. Nixon, *The Memoirs of Richard Nixon* (New York: Grosset & Dunlap, 1978), p. 418.
34. Ibid., p. 420.
35. Ibid., p. 423.
36. Ibid., p. 424.
37. *United Steelworkers* v. *Weber*, 443 U.S. 193 (1979).
38. *Planned Parenthood of Central Missouri* v. *Danforth*, 428 U.S. 52 (1976).
39. *Harris* v. *McRae*, 65 L. Ed. 2d. 784 (1980).
40. *U.S.* v. *Mendenhall*, 64 L. Ed. 497 (1980).
41. *Mobile* v. *Bolden*, 64 L. Ed. 2d. 47 (1980).
42. *Engel* v. *Vitale*, 370 U.S. 421 (1962).

Overview
National Political Institutions

Each of America's national political institutions has power to act on its own in the governing process, but considerable emphasis is placed on action based on consensus. This means that agreement must be reached at several different points in the system. Those given official responsibility are required to consult with and at times accede to the wishes of their counterparts in other branches of government.

The presidency has evolved into a major institution that is expected to initiate policies and to take the lead in implementing decisions. The growth of governmental activity, especially in international affairs and in economic matters, has enhanced this role. A vast executive bureaucracy has developed under the President, possessing at times powers not envisioned by the framers of the Constitution. These agencies and individuals are not elected, but the administrative and regulatory functions they perform are critical to the operation of government.

Congress remains the central focus for the enactment of legislation. Despite executive ascendancy in recent decades, Congress has taken steps to reassert its policymaking role. Several mechanisms have been devised to achieve this goal and to make Congress a more viable partner in the policymaking process. Achieving consensus between the executive and legislative branches is

complicated because the executive is becoming increasingly centralized while Congress is subject to inevitable pressures toward fragmentation. Special, single, and local interests find almost a natural home in an institution like Congress. Therefore, a President whose primary concern is the "national interest" must contend with legislators who are initially and largely concerned with what they can obtain for their particular local interests and constituents. This puts a premium on bargaining, negotiating, and compromising, that is, on *consensus*.

The courts represent a formidable force in American life. Judges are not popularly chosen, and they can declare acts of the other branches unconstitutional. But even the judiciary is subject to checks and balances of various kinds. And the legitimacy of judicial decisions is dependent as much on the respect and general public support of the courts as on the theoretical powers granted to them under the Constitution.

Thus the themes of theory vs. practice and power vs. consensus clearly apply to our description of the formal institutions of American government. Likewise, while those institutions have undergone rather substantial changes—in size, composition, orientation, roles—they have remained as constant forces in the American constitutional system.

Given the enormous size of the political system and the complexities of the governing process, the dynamic interplay of these three themes is inevitable. Human beings govern in America, but they do so on the basis of definable laws. Each political institution has power to act, but most of the time that action is made contingent on agreement of some sort from some other sources of power in the government. And as social and economic needs change, the political institutions likewise must adapt—without neglecting or abusing the traditional roles and responsibilities constitutionally defined for them.

In part 4 we shall see more precisely how these institutions have met these challenges in their efforts to grapple with specific domestic and foreign problems. We will see the significant contribution of the three branches of government in formulating policy in such areas as civil liberties, civil rights, the economy, social welfare, and foreign policy. And we will note as well the critical policymaking role played by those unofficial actors on the political stage: the media, interest groups, political parties, and, of course, the voters.

4

Policies and Processes

After Camp David: Politics, Policymaking, and a New Administration

We now return to the story of the first case study, the energy problems faced by President Jimmy Carter during ten days of meetings at Camp David in July 1979. You will recall the ominous memorandum sent to him by his domestic policy adviser, Stuart Eisenstat, the cancelled television speech, the retreat to Camp David, and the dramatic sessions with officials and leaders of various interest groups. The country waited anxiously as the President pondered how to deal with the growing gas lines, the growing United States dependence on foreign oil, and the growing frustration of the country.

You will also recall the rather optimistic pronouncement of the House majority leader, Jim Wright (D., Texas) after he left the President's four-hour meeting with Congressional leaders: "I prophesy that when the President comes down off the mountain, he will have a comprehensive, effective, hard-hitting program to offer the American people. I further predict the Congress will be in a mood to approve it."

There was a pervasive atmosphere that something had to be done. The President had to offer programs, and Congress had to respond. The political process would be called upon to deal with a series of specific proposals.

But, based on what we've learned thus far about American government and politics, it should not be too surprising to learn that Congressman Wright's prediction was a bit off. For one thing, Camp David participants were aware that the country was just a few months away from the beginning of the 1980 presidential election campaign. President Carter's standing in public opinion polls had reached an all-time low. He was faced with a potential challenge within his party from Senator Ted Kennedy (D., Massachusetts) in the upcoming primaries. There were more than a few potential Republican candidates—one of whom was former California Governor Ronald Reagan—waiting to announce their candidacies and to begin the trek toward the Republican nomination. It is safe to say that many Republicans and Democrats believed that Mr. Carter was vulnerable to defeat in November 1980. The energy crisis was only one of his problems, but it was a major one.

Other political realities had to be faced. If Mr. Carter's energy proposals were to receive support in Congress, they would have to contend with an institution that was, at best, highly fragmented. Eisenstat's memo, you will recall, stated that "Congress seems completely out of control." Table 1 on page 478 shows the House and Senate committees and subcommittees that had jurisdiction over various aspects of energy policy. This fragmented structure normally would mean that the legislative process would be slow and tedious. In early 1980, a proposal was made to remedy this situation in the House of Representatives by creating a House energy committee. This plan was rejected by the chairpersons of the various committees, who feared an erosion of their power over important energy issues. Self-interest also motivated some private groups to oppose the plan. As has been pointed out in earlier chapters, the fragmented nature of the policymaking process enables various groups to wield influence over different parts of the system, thus making it unnecessary to capture control over the entire process. With energy policymaking spread out among many sources, interest groups have access at several different points. Other concerns in Congress reflected regional interests. California Democrat Phillip Burton explained his objection to a consolidated House energy committee: "My fear is that, over the long term, members of the producing states are likely to get on the energy committee, as members of the agriculture districts get on the agriculture committees." Political scientist Walter A. Rosenbaum concluded: "In the end, self-interest was the winner." Rosenbaum quoted one member of Congress as saying: "A majority of members of existing energy committees were more concerned with protecting their jurisdictional turf than in improving the way the House deals with energy legislation."*

In the meantime, the White House took steps to act in areas that would not require Congressional action. It was important, Carter's advisers felt, to recognize that the legislative process was long and complicated and would not be understood by many Americans. Therefore, early in the fall of 1979 a twenty-page memo prepared by a presidential assistant set forth several suggestions. These included such things as insulating five hundred to one thousand "showcase" homes around the country, selling federal vans for use as commuter carpool vehicles, and announcing the installation of wood-burning stoves in the White House and at Camp David. There would be weekly meetings with local community leaders and weekly energy phone calls to local officials. In addition, the White House would mail out periodic "progress reports" on energy to people who had written the President on energy matters. Admittedly, many of these acts were symbolic, but they were conceived as means of demonstrating "the effectiveness of [the President's] personal leadership and vision." The memo stated: "Many of the actions suggested . . . will provide 'good news' items on which we can build support for our legislative program."

This was all well and good, but most people knew that the real battle would be in Congress.

Earlier in 1979, prior to the Camp David energy speech, the President announced that he would gradually end price controls on domestic oil to encourage energy conservation. It was known that this would probably result in higher prices in the short run—and bring "windfall" profits to the oil companies. The oil companies argued that such profits were necessary to permit further exploration for new sources of energy.

*Unless otherwise noted, quoted material in this chapter is taken from the following sources: Walter A. Rosenbaum, *Energy, Politics, and Public Policy* (Washington, D.C.: Congressional Quarterly Press, 1981); *Wall Street Journal*, September 18, 1979, p. 8; *Energy Policy*, 2nd ed. (Washington, D.C.: Congressional Quarterly, Inc., March 1981), p. 233; *New York Times*, October 29, 1980, p. A28; November 26, 1980; and December 28, 1980.

TABLE 1.
Congressional Committees with Energy Policy Jurisdiction, 1979–1980.

HOUSE OF REPRESENTATIVES

Committees with Energy Jurisdiction	Energy Subcommittees
Agriculture	Conservation and Credit; Forests.
Appropriations	Energy and Water Development; Interior; Transportation.
Banking, Finance and Urban Affairs	Housing and Community Development.
Budget	
Education and Labor	Health and Safety.
Government Operations	Environment, Energy and Natural Resources.
Interior and Insular Affairs	Energy and the Environment; Mines and Mining; National Parks and Insular Affairs; Water and Power Resources.
Interstate and Foreign Commerce	Energy and Power; Health and the Environment; Transportation and Commerce.
Merchant Marine and Fisheries	Coast Guard and Navigation; Oceanography.
Public Works and Transportation	Surface Transportation; Water Resources.
Science and Technology	Energy Development and Applications; Energy Research and Production; Science, Research and Technology; Transportation, Aviation and Communications.
Select Committee on Outer Continental Shelf	
Small Business	Energy, Environment, Safety and Research.
Ways and Means	

SENATE

Agriculture, Nutrition and Forestry	Agricultural Credit and Rural Electrification; Environment, Soil Conservation and Forestry.
Appropriations	Energy and Water Development; HUD-Independent Agencies; Interior and Related Agencies.
Banking, Housing and Urban Affairs	Housing and Urban Affairs.
Budget	
Commerce, Science and Transportation	Consumer; Science, Technology and Space; Surface Transportation.
Energy and Natural Resources	Energy Conservation and Supply; Energy R&D; Energy Regulation; Energy Resources and Materials Production; Parks, Recreation, and Renewable Resources.
Environment and Public Works	Environmental Pollution; Nuclear Regulation; Resource Protection; Transportation; Water Resources.
Finance	Energy and Foundations; International Trade.
Governmental Affairs	Energy, Nuclear Proliferation and Federal Service.
Labor and Human Resources	

The administration, however, proposed a *windfall profits tax*, and Congress struggled with the matter for several months. The amount of the tax, how long it should remain in effect, what type of oil production it should cover, what tax incentives it should provide to businesses to encourage conservation of oil and natural gas, how much aid it should provide to low-income families who would be hit hard by rising energy costs—these were all issues that had to be negotiated first in the committees, then on the floor, and then between the two chambers in conference committee. As a tax measure, the proposal had to be considered first in the House of Representatives (originating in the House Ways and Means Committee) before it could be taken up by the Senate. Compromise was the order of the day. The task was finally accomplished, and President Carter signed the bill on April 2, 1980. One leg of the national energy policy was in place.

The President also proposed the creation of a Synthetic Fuels Corporation. You will recall that in his speech of July 15, 1979, the President asked Congress to create such an entity to lead the way in discovering alternative sources of energy from coal, oil shale, plant products, and the sun. He likened it to the synthetic rubber corporation during World War II. The windfall profits tax as well as special low-denomination energy bonds would be used to finance the new fuels corporation, an $88 billion, ten-year effort. The proposal met with opposition from various interest groups. Environmentalists feared that the new corporation would use its powers to ruin the environment. Free-market advocates saw the corporation as another powerful government-owned enterprise that would rival private companies. Western agricultural interests feared that the corporation would threaten fast-dwindling water supplies in western states. Again, more compromises were in order—Congress finally approved $20 billion instead of $88 billion for the first phase, with the remaining $68 billion to be granted if Congress did not object, and no tie-in with the windfall profits tax. The President signed the bill on June 20, 1980, and another leg of the national energy policy was in place.

A third proposal involved the establishment of an Energy Mobilization Board, which was intended to cut through bureaucratic red tape and speed up high-priority energy projects. There were several objections from various sources to such a potentially powerful agency. Some people feared the board would override state's rights and prerogatives; others felt the board might circumvent environmental laws. Thus, there were political objections from both conservatives (states' rights advocates) and liberals (environmentalists). Although both chambers of Congress passed the general proposal and a conference committee resolved the differences, the House of Representatives, in an unusual development (since each chamber usually supports the work of the conference committees), voted against the compromise bill. The House sent the bill back to the conference committee, which was an effective way of killing the measure. One account of the action noted the effect of the impending presidential election campaign:

Although some objected to the bill because of its potential impact on states' rights and the environment, many of the 125 Republican votes against the conference version reportedly were cast to embarrass Carter and boost the presidential campaign of Ronald Reagan, who had announced his opposition to the Board.

The Energy Mobilization Board was defeated, but the President had won on two of his three main proposals. He was not able, however, to get standby gas-rationing authority, and he was denied authority to impose a fee of ten cents per gallon on imported oil. In these areas, Congress was not the only institution the President had to contend with. While the courts had not been too involved in energy policy, they still, as always, were called upon from time to time to decide whether particular presidential and Congressional actions were permissible. Such was the case in May 1980, when a federal district-court judge in Washington, D.C., ruled that the President did not have legal authority to impose the ten-cent per gallon fee on imported oil. The President had sought to add such a fee as a means of reducing oil consumption. He cited as authority a provision in the Trade Expansion Act of 1962 giving him broad discretionary powers to impose import fees and quotas, should he deem them necessary for the national interest. The federal judge stated that the President had misread the intent of the statute. The ten-cent fee, the judge said, would only have indirect effect on foreign imports, plus it would also apply to gas produced domestically. The court held that Congress had not intended the law to permit this.

Before the Department of Justice (acting in behalf of the President) could appeal the decision to the Supreme Court, Congress amended the Trade Expansion Act of 1962 to limit the President's unilateral authority to impose oil-import fees. The amendment permitted the two houses of Congress to block presidential action in such matters by means of a joint resolution. Therefore, in this instance, both the court system and Congress checked presidential action.

By the summer of 1980, one year after Camp David, the presidential score card stood as follows:

- *no more oil imported than in 1977*   *yes*   (presidential action)
- *import quotas*   *yes*   (presidential action)
- *Synthetic Fuels Corporation and Solar Bank*   *yes*   (Congressional compromise)
- *windfall profits tax*   *yes*   (Congressional compromise)
- *cut in use of oil by legally required shift to coal*   *no*
- *Energy Mobilization Board*   *no*
- *ten-cent per gallon fee on imported oil*   *no*
- *standby gas rationing*   *no*

The first two policies were achieved by executive action alone. Congressional action was necessary to accomplish the other policies.

In attempting to understand the policymaking process as it applied to energy, we must take into account confused public perceptions and the "data dispute" issue. Although the gas lines were real enough, many Americans remained unconvinced that the country was actually facing an energy crisis. As Professor Rosenbaum reported:

In 1979 . . . 22 percent of a national sample spontaneously listed energy as one of the nation's most important problems; in a similar poll taken seven years earlier, no one had mentioned energy. But most citizens apparently are not convinced that a genuine, chronic energy shortage exists. And the number fluctuates widely. One poll reported in May 1977 that 40 percent of the public believed the crisis was "real," but only 29 percent did by early 1979. By November 1979, more than half the respondents in another national poll asserted that the energy crisis was "fabricated."

There was some justification for this uncertainty. The various official statements coming from Washington were conflicting. For example, when the Shah of Iran was overthrown in early 1979, the American public was presented with widely divergent figures concerning the effect of this on United States oil imports. The Department of Energy said it would result in a shortage of from 500,000 to perhaps 800,000 barrels of crude oil daily. The Congressional Research Service set the figure at no more than 80,000 barrels daily. The General Accounting Office estimated the new Iranian government was reducing American oil by ten to fifteen percent, but the figure (according to Rosenbaum) was closer to four percent.

Such conflicting information puzzled legislators as well as private citizens. "I don't know the answers," Congressman Romano L. Mazzoli (D., Kentucky) said. "I don't know if we're being conned."

Certainly, this would make it that much more difficult to enact effective policies. To be sure, there was general distress over gas lines and rising prices, but what were the causes of these problems? If there was no consensus over the causes, there could hardly be consensus over the cures.

By June 1980, the political environment was considerably different from what it had been a year before. For the previous eight months, fifty-two Americans had been held hostage in the American embassy in Iran by a group of Iranian political militants. Americans were becoming increasingly angry and frustrated over the seeming inability of anyone in or out of the administration in Washington to do anything (politically or militarily) to resolve that situation. President Carter seemed assured (having defeated Senator Kennedy in most of the Democratic primaries) of gaining renomination of his party. Governor Ronald Reagan was virtually assured (having defeated several opponents in his party primaries) of receiving the Republican nomination. By the end of the summer, the presidential campaign was on; the gas lines had disappeared, though fuel prices were still rising and a politically unstable Middle East was becoming even more unstable. The intense atmosphere of crisis and doom that had characterized the ten days of the previous July had subsided. But no one believed that the country did not continue to have critical energy problems.

The two major candidates in the 1980 presidential race held quite different views on what energy policies to pursue. Mr. Reagan placed heavy emphasis on private-industry initiatives to develop energy alternatives. He criticized Carter's emphasis on windfall profits taxes, conservation, and the Synthetic Fuels Corporation. He also showed no enthusiasm for the relatively new Department of Energy or for government regulations that impeded private energy exploration on public lands. In a televised debate with President Carter during the campaign, Ronald Reagan said:

> This nation has been portrayed for too long a time to the people as being energy poor when it is energy rich. . . . One-eighth of our total coal resources is not being utilized at all right now. The mines are closed down; there are 22,000 miners out of work. Most of this is due to regulations which either interfere with the mining of it or prevent the burning of it. . . . I . . . happen to believe that free enterprise can do a better job of producing the things the people need than government can. The Department of Energy has a multibillion dollar budget in excess of $10 billion—it hasn't produced a quart of oil or a lump of coal or anything else in the line of energy.

The day after the election, President-elect Reagan was presented with a forty-page report prepared by his Energy Policy Task Force. The report called for "unleashing the oil companies" and relying more on a market economy to solve energy problems. Taxes, controls, licensing, and other such "onerous constraints" should be removed. In addition, the report recommended "opening up public lands for exploration and development, placing environmental policy on a cost-benefit basis. . . . Much has been done, but what has been done is to impede production and curtail consumption. Energy in this nation is not rare or scarce. The United States has the potential to produce as much oil and gas in the future as we have produced in our entire history."

The newly elected President responded to the report by saying:

> There may be a few points here and there where I might put something in a second priority rather than a first, but basically those recommendations substantiate the very things that I've been favoring and saying.

The new administration that took office in January 1981 had quite different ideas, therefore, about how the country should deal with its energy problems. The days of worry and wonder at Camp David were over. New laws and agencies were established; newly elected and appointed officials were in Congress and the executive agencies. The new administration promised policies that would have the government less involved as an active participant. In fact, the newly appointed secretary of the Department of Energy, Dr. James B. Edwards, clearly stated: "I'd like to go to Washington and close down the Energy Department and work myself out of a job." While this was a sentiment shared by many people, some expressed concern that the federal government could not extricate itself altogether from energy issues. An editorial in the New York Times raised several points in response to Secretary Edwards:

> The notion that everything would magically get better if government went away is simply wishful. . . . Someone must oversee the development of energy reserves against the threat of foreign oil cutoffs. . . . When cutoffs do come . . . someone must be prepared to allocate scarce supplies in the least disruptive ways.
> . . . Some member of the President's inner circle must speak for America on international energy issues. . . . The invisible hand of capitalism could not effectively induce Western Europe and Japan to share temporary reductions in oil supplies. . . . The United States is the largest importer of energy, and the only

importer with any military capacity to protect the oil lifeline from the Middle East. Its leadership is critical to any effective alliance of energy consumers. . . . Rational choices about the relative merits of nuclear and coal power cannot be left solely to private interests.

Whatever policies the new administration developed, they would be debated and decided by the same political process that dealt with the previous administration's proposals. The same political institutions that Mr. Carter faced would now have to be faced by Mr. Reagan. To be sure, there were new voting alignments in the Senate and the House. On the strength of the 1980 election, it would seem that President Reagan had a Congress much more sympathetic to his views than the previous Congress had been to President Carter's. But the legislators were still distinct public officials with their own particular concerns, and private interest groups would still be fiercely protective of their own specific interests. Some things had been changed by the election, but there were still very many constants.

Thus, the case study which began with a memorandum to one President ends with another memorandum to a new President. Both outlined proposed policies, both issued calls to action. It remained for the political process to respond. And the story of America's quest for energy self-sufficiency continued.

The purpose of government is to conduct the public's business. Throughout this book, we have described the political processes by which this takes place. In the following chapters we focus on the particular areas of government which constitute the substance of public business: civil liberties, civil rights, economics, welfare, foreign affairs, and defense. Each of these areas generates an array of ideas about what should be done in order to achieve certain results, ideas which are usually based on ideological preferences, considerations of self-interest, and assumptions about what is likely to happen if certain actions are taken. This collection of ideas and assumptions form the basis of **public policy**: the general goals and actions outlined by government officials in their efforts to resolve problems of public concern. In 1979, the President went to Camp David to reformulate energy policy by thinking and talking about what should be done, how, by whom, and when. Many people visited him there to help him in that *policymaking* process.

It is important to keep in mind the distinction between *policy* and *practice*. It might be the policy of an administration to end racial discrimination or to lower the inflation rate or to contain communism, but these are ideals (goals, objectives) and they may not be achieved in practice. Many factors determine the extent to which policy can be translated into practice, and these factors will be discussed in the following chapters.

Here, we turn our attention to the various aspects that contribute to policymaking.

Individuals, groups, and governments have *agendas*, that is, lists of goals they want to accomplish. These agendas contain items to be achieved at varying times—immediately, in the near future, over a longer term. Often the items are ranked in order of priority. Some goals are more important than others, and some are therefore considered more expendable (subject to trade-off and compromise) than others. In the American political system, there is never simply one agenda. An important aspect of the political process is the reconciliation of many different policy agendas.

You will recall in the labor-law case, the AFL-CIO had a set of ideals and ideas it wanted to accomplish. On its agenda were such things as the common-situs picketing bill as well as general reforms in labor-management relations. The business community had an agenda that substantially conflicted with labor's goals. At the same time, the administration and Congress had policy agendas of their own. Even within Congress, different legislative groups had agendas, as did, indeed, different bureaucratic agencies in the executive branch. Likewise, in California, we saw the development of private groups with Proposition 13 as their major agenda item, and others with Proposition 8 as theirs. These represented different policy positions about how to deal with the problem of rising property taxes in that state.

The more heterogeneous and pluralistic a society, the more we see many policy agendas emanating from many different sources—private and public, unofficial and official.

Agenda-building stems from a variety of causes. The oil crisis of 1979 was the immediate crisis that led to Camp David. Long simmering discontent with high property taxes was the catalyst for the petition drive to put Proposition 13 on the California ballot.

Some agendas tend to call forth counter-agendas. The fifty-five men who met in Philadelphia in 1787 to amend the Articles of Confederation and then proceeded to draft a new Constitution were moved, as we recall, by the inability of the existing government to deal with the growing economic and social problems of the new nation. In other words, they decided to discard the old agenda and substitute a new one.

Once established, policy agendas are subject to change, modification, and reformulation. Events can change agendas. Likewise, agendas can change through accomplishment. Having achieved the passage of Proposition 13, the Jarvis forces (see chapter 5) turned their attention (they developed a new agenda) to the national arena and worked for a Congressional law limiting federal spending and reducing federal income taxes. Virtually everything you have read thus far in this book can be related to the process of agenda-building and agenda-changing. This is the dynamic aspect of the governing process.

Political scientists sometimes say that some matters never get fully or fairly considered in the political process (we will discuss this further in the epilog). They believe that powerful private and public elites can block items from coming up for official decision-making. Some issues never are put on the agenda for official determination. This does not mean, however, that the matters are of no concern to various groups and individuals, or that they can't become a part of the public agenda. What we find is that occasionally low-salient issues burst on the scene and literally force their way onto the official agendas, as in the case of the truckers (chapter 5) who conducted their traffic-stall protest. Therefore, it is not quite accurate to call some matters "non-agenda" items. Rather, they are not on those agendas where, for the time being at least, they are likely to get official attention.

In another sense, however, one *can* talk about "non-agenda" items. As we saw in chapter 12, the Supreme Court will refuse to hear some cases because those cases

At this December 1978 meeting in Abu Dhabi, OPEC delegates voted to end a two-year price freeze on oil and to raise prices. Independence from foreign oil is a basic goal of American energy policy.

involve "political questions." That is, they may be best handled by other branches of government. An issue can therefore be determined to belong to one agenda rather than to another. In this instance, constitutional interpretation determines the matter. But constitutional interpretation can and does change. Thus, what the Supreme Court does not put on its agenda at one time (for example, reapportionment of legislative districts within states), it may put on its agenda at another.

Policymaking is **policy formulation**, which involves a systematic process of answering three questions. First, *what* is the problem? Second, *how* should the problem be handled? Third, *who* should handle the problem? It is important to be as clear and precise as possible at each stage. It is not sufficient to know that there are general problems of oil imports and rising fuel costs. To be sure, these are important, but they are symptoms, not causes. The real problems are lack of energy independence and reliance on politically unstable sources for oil. Policymakers must carefully examine the fundamental causes of such situations. Frequently, there is disagreement at this point, and this makes the process very difficult. Is OPEC the basic cause of the energy crisis, or American oil companies, or the failure to develop domestic energy sources? You will recall Reagan's disagreement with Carter on this point in the energy case.

Having identified the problem, the next step is to decide how it should be handled. This involves looking at a range of policy options, choices, or alternatives, since it is likely that there will be a number of possible approaches. These options should contain analyses of costs and benefits, calculated on the basis of what one hopes to achieve and a determination of how important (a question of values) it is to achieve the goals. Options or choices may also be ranked. That is, under certain circumstances, it may be more desirable to pursue policy option *A* rather than *B*. Perhaps *B* is not inconsistent with *A*, and then both should be pursued simultaneously. There should also be "fall-back" options or contingency choices: if *A* is tried but does not work, then perhaps it would be best to proceed to *B* or *C*. Having tried *A* and failed, it might be best *not* to proceed to what was originally the second choice. The potentially altered situation might call for *D* or *E*. In any case, this aspect of policymaking contains the element of calculation. Based on the goals one wants to achieve, given what one knows from past experience and the accumulated empirical data (facts, rather than hunches or impressions), and projecting as accurately as possible, the decision is made concerning which courses of action are likely to lead to the desired results.

A related aspect of the policy-formulation process involves deciding lines of responsibility. This is also a matter of presenting options, and the same process of calculation is involved. In the energy case, for example, decisions had to be made concerning the specific powers to be assigned the new Synthetic Fuels Corporation.

Of course, political considerations are always present. Deciding between options and choices can be (and frequently is) heavily influenced by what is politically feasible. You will recall what one of Carter's advisers told him would happen if he decontrolled gas prices: "[That] will kill you politically." In the labor law reform case, we saw how one senior Senate staff official, explaining the defeat of the labor reform legislation, bluntly stated: "The Senate is a conservative place these days. . . . You can't get people interested in causes like labor reform." These political observations may not have pinpoint accuracy, but politicians who make policy must take them into account.

Deciding policy and getting it enacted must be followed by the process of **implementation**—carrying it out. Frequently, there are as many layers to penetrate in this process as there are in policy formulation. A growing body of policy literature focuses on this process.* At times, several sources must "sign off" on a project before it can be implemented. This means that different agencies must agree that the project satisfies certain requirements before the project can proceed to the next step. Has an acceptable environmental impact study been conducted? Have equal-employment hiring procedures been followed? Have the contract bidders used the cheapest and yet most efficient materials? Have local agencies agreed to various aspects of the project? These various checkpoints represent the successful efforts of various interests over time to be included in the policymaking process. As the base of participation in that process expands, the implementation process becomes more complicated and slower. Efforts are sometimes made to circumvent these checkpoints, but this is difficult to do. Note what happened to the proposal to establish an Energy Mobilization Board aimed at cutting through bureaucratic red tape. It was defeated.

The policymaking process includes **policy evaluation**, or assessment of the policies' effectiveness. In order to do this properly, it is important to have a clear set of criteria by which to measure results. The more precise and specific those criteria, the more useful the analysis. Therefore, policies should contain clearly stated goals and a statement of expected results. This is not always possible, because sometimes the

*See, for example, Jeffrey Pressman and Aaron Wildavsky, *Implementation* (Berkeley: University of California Press, 1973); George C. Edwards III, *Implementing Public Policy* (Washington, D.C.: Congressional Quarterly Press, 1980); and Robert T. Nakumura and Frank Smallwood, *The Politics of Policy Implementation* (New York: St. Martin's Press, 1980).

President Carter signs the bill creating the Synthetic Fuels Corporation as members of Congress and administration officials look on. The third proposal in Carter's program, the Energy Mobilization Board, was defeated in the House.

policies are stated in broad, vague, general language in order to accommodate varying political interests. Where this occurs, it should be a warning that subsequent evaluation of the policy will be difficult. In addition, policy evaluators must take care to use the correct methods in their evaluation. If certain variables are not considered, this might lead to an inaccurate evaluation of the impact of a policy. For example, in deciding how effective certain welfare policies have been (food stamps, Head Start programs), one would need to consider a range of factors: the number of people for whom the program was intended and the number actually reached; the administrative methods used to publicize the programs; the reasons some people not originally eligible were able to receive benefits; a comparison of those served with those not served (referred to as a control group). It is often advisable to provide resources for evaluation of the policy at the beginning of the program. That way, evaluation can proceed along with implementation.

Once a policy has been decided, enacted, implemented, and evaluated, there is usually reaction to it. People intended to benefit from it might complain that it is not doing the job and should be revised—as in the labor-law case. Some people might want it repealed, because it is imposing an excessive burden on them—see the discussion of regulatory agencies in chapter 10. New policy agendas develop, and the process starts all over again. The public's business and the policymaking process never end.

The Bill of Rights
and Individual
Liberties

Chapter

13

The First Political Demand: A Bill of Rights

One of the first political demands facing the newly formed United States government in 1789 was for a more explicit set of statements in the Constitution protecting individual rights. As was pointed out in chapter 1, more than a few citizens in the ratifying states were not content with the document as originally drafted in Philadelphia. They wanted specific provisions that would prohibit the government from violating those inalienable rights they had accused King George III of violating, and they agreed to ratify the Constitution only if such provisions were promised as part of the first order of business of the new government. Thomas Jefferson was a particularly prominent advocate of these provisions.

Initially, almost eighty amendments were submitted to Congress. The states ultimately approved ten. There was nothing very complicated about these provisions, and yet they were vitally important. To be sure, the provisions would be interpreted and reinterpreted as the years went by, but at least the essential ingredients were permanently embedded in the Constitution: the national government was not to infringe on the right of individuals to speak freely, publish freely, assemble peaceably, practice the religion of their choice, bear arms, and be free from having to testify against themselves. In addition, individuals could not be forced to house soldiers, nor could one's home or other possessions be searched and seized under "unreasonable" circumstances. Persons accused of crimes had to be treated in certain stipulated ways that guaranteed just and fair treatment. Even more, the list of rights was not limited to those rights that were specifically mentioned, but included "others" that resided with "the people." Finally, to set limitations on the national government, the Tenth Amendment was added (see chapter 2), stating that the people or the states retained all rights not delegated to the national government.

Majority Rule Versus Individual Rights

The rights were thus defined, and they were seemingly clear: "Congress shall make no law . . ."; "The right of the people . . . shall not be infringed . . ."; "No soldier shall . . ."; "Excessive bail shall not be required . . ."; "No person shall . . . be deprived . . . without due process of law . . ."

This language was sufficient to satisfy the original demands. We shall see, however, that these provisions did not resolve the problems definitively. There were still other values to protect, other rights to pursue. For example, one of the values of a democratic system that deserved constitutional protection was rule by the majority, operating through properly conducted elections. In order to rule effectively and maintain order, the majority might need to impose *some* rules over individual actions—even, in some cases, in the areas of

The conflict between the rights of the individual versus the rights of the majority came to a head in March 1965, when John J. Thomson insisted on his right to use and display a four-letter word in the cafeteria at the University of California, Berkeley. University officials condemned Thomson's action and ultimately the president and chancellor resigned over the controversy.

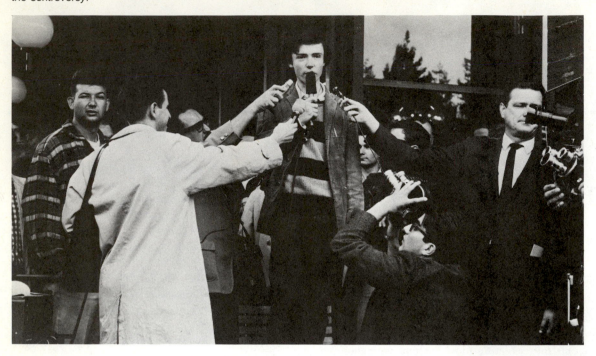

speech, press, religion, assembly, and so forth. Otherwise, some believed, the constitutionally guaranteed individual freedoms could conceivably lead to anarchy and the breakdown of the system. Individual liberties made sense only in the context of an existing, functioning political society.

This has been the focus of an ongoing constitutional debate. On the one hand, individual rights—frequently referred to as **civil liberties**—should be protected. The concept of civil liberties is strongly valued in this political system. On the other hand, it needs to be balanced against the requirement of majority rule—another important political value. The problem is that these values often clash, and it is difficult to implement them simultaneously.

For instance, if the rights of the majority are overemphasized, *tyranny* of the majority could result. Suppose a majority intent on guarding against potential sabotage and subversion—a reasonable goal—decided that no individual should be allowed to publicly call for the overthrow of the government by violent means? Some have argued that the government—following the majority's wishes— should be able to take such action. But at what point does an effort in this direction go too far and become an unreasonable and unconstitutional restriction on free speech? Doesn't this ultimately amount to tyrannical government? Under such circumstances, would Thomas Paine's speeches and writings have been allowed? On the other hand, how far does one go in granting individual rights? Should anyone be allowed to say absolutely anything at any time in any place? Should an individual, for instance, be allowed—under the guise of freedom of speech—to shout "fire" in a crowded theater as a practical joke? Couldn't such "speech" create such desperation and panic that as the crowd rushes for the exits, innocent people would be trampled to death? Shouldn't people be protected from such unbounded and unfounded exercise of free speech?

These same kinds of questions have been raised regarding several areas of civil liberties. For example, certainly freedom of religious choice should be guaranteed. But what if one's religion permits polygamy (marriage to more than one spouse)? And what if the majority of the society decided that polygamy was against society's values and morals?

How far can the majority go? How much freedom can the individual or minority group demand? These are the basic questions, and they are really questions of degree. The question is not whether there should be constitutionally protected civil liberties. The answer to that question is a definitive *yes*; but even this answer is too simplistic.

This chapter will examine the complexities involved in trying to strike a proper balance between individual freedoms and majority rule in various circumstances. We shall see that the nation has changed its stance on this matter from time to time in various situations. Most of the time these decisions have been made by the courts; the issues have been resolved (for the time being) on the basis of judges' interpretations of the constitutional language *as applied to specific circumstances*. You should be sure to refer again to chapter 12 in studying this material.

Although the courts have been major actors in this arena of balancing and making policy, they have not been the only ones faced with such tasks. A police officer on the street stops a suspicious-looking driver of a car. The driver looks like a criminal suspect described over the police radio or on a poster in the post office. To what extent and on what grounds can that officer at that moment search the driver's car? At what point can the individual driver claim violation of his or her Fourth Amendment right ''to be secure . . . against unreasonable searches and seizures . . .''? Should the officer dash to the judge and get a search warrant? Would the driver wait around? The decision has to be made on the spot by the officer: whether to search or not; and, by the driver: whether to resist or not. Countless incidents of this kind occur daily, and the Constitution is constantly being interpreted right on the street. This is *one* way to strike a balance. Indeed, the courts might have already made a decision on this kind of situation, but at that exact moment, courts and judges and constitutions are not around to arbitrate. And it is likely that any given encounter will never go to court, and the police officer's final decision will never be reviewed by the courts—certainly not the United States Supreme Court.

The important point is to understand the basic issues that arise in the area of individual rights and to recognize that virtually every situation can be interpreted in innumerable, diverse ways and on various grounds. Although we may not be certain how far a particular official (representing the majority) can go in a particular circumstance, we ought to be familiar with the general factors that should be taken into account in reaching the decision.

The issue is not one of weighing one desirable value against a clearly undesirable value. That would be easy; the former should prevail. Rather, the question is how to strike a proper balance, under the circumstances, between two equally important, desirable goals.

First Amendment Freedoms

Some of the toughest ''balancing'' problems have developed around the freedoms covered in the First Amendment: religion, speech, press, assembly, and petition.

TABLE 1.
The Bill of Rights.

1 Religion, Speech, Assembly, and Politics

Congress shall make no law respecting an establishment of religion, or prohibiting the free exercise thereof; or abridging the freedom of speech, or of the press; or the right of people peaceably to assemble, and to petition the Government for a redress of grievances.

2 The Right to Bear Arms

A well regulated Militia, being necessary to the security of a free State, the right of people to keep and bear Arms, shall not be infringed.

3 Quartering of Soldiers

No Soldier shall, in time of peace be quartered in any house, without the consent of the Owner, nor in time of war, but in a manner to be prescribed by law.

4 Searches and Seizures

The right of people to be secure in their persons, houses, papers, and effects, against unreasonable searches and seizures, shall not be violated, and no Warrants shall issue, but upon probable cause, supported by Oath or affirmation, and particularly describing the place to be searched and the persons or things to be seized.

5 Grand Juries, Self-incrimination, Double Jeopardy, Due Process, Eminent Domain

No person shall be held to answer for a capital, or otherwise infamous crime, unless on a presentment or indictment of a Grand Jury, except in cases arising in the land or naval forces, or in the Militia, when in actual service in time of War or public danger, nor shall any person be subject for the same offence to be twice put in jeopardy of life or limb; nor shall be compelled in any criminal case to be a witness against himself, nor be deprived of life, liberty, or property, without due process of law; nor shall private property be taken for public use, without just compensation.

6 Criminal Court Procedures

In all criminal prosecutions, the accused shall enjoy the right to a speedy and public trial by an impartial jury of the State and district wherein the crime shall have been committed, which district shall have been previously ascertained by law, and to be informed of the nature and cause of the accusation; to be confronted with the witnesses against him; to have compulsory process for obtaining witnesses in his favor, and to have the Assistance of Counsel for his defence.

7 Trial by Jury in Common-Law Cases

In Suits at common law, where the value in controversy shall exceed twenty dollars, the right of trial by jury shall be preserved, and no fact tried by a jury, shall be otherwise reexamined in any Court of the United States, than according to the rules of the common law.

8 Bail, Cruel and Unusual Punishment

Excessive bail shall not be required, nor excessive fines imposed, nor cruel and unusual punishments inflicted.

9 Rights Retained by the People

The enumeration in the Constitution, of certain rights, shall not be construed to deny or disparage others retained by the people.

10 Reserved Powers of the States

The powers not delegated to the United States by the Constitution, nor prohibited by it to the States, are reserved to the States respectively, or to the people.

Freedom of and from religion. The First Amendment prohibits government involvement in religion in two ways: the government may not establish any particular religion as the official religion of the United States, and it may not interfere with the way a person practices his or her chosen religion. The Constitution also prohibits religion from being used as a requirement for holding office.

Sometimes this is referred to as the "wall of separation between church and state." But religious symbols *are* sometimes connected with the government. For instance, the official currency has imprinted on it, "In God We Trust"; most courts still swear in witnesses; and the President takes his oath of office with his hand on a Bible. People are free to practice the religion of their choice *as long as* such practice does not constitute "acts inimical to the peace, good order, and morals of society."[1]

Exactly how high that "wall" is between church and state, then, has been the subject of considerable controversy over the years. In 1962, the Supreme Court ruled in *Engel* v. *Vitale* that New York State could not ask students to recite a prayer at the beginning of each school day.[2] The twenty-two-word prayer read: "Almighty God, we acknowledge our dependence upon Thee, and we beg Thy blessings upon us, our parents, our teachers and our country." Although students could remain silent or leave the room during the recitation, the Court still felt the prayer was unconstitutional: "There can be no doubt that New York's state prayer program officially establishes the religious beliefs embodied in the . . . prayer."[3] The Court maintained that the First Amendment clause prohibiting the establishment of a state religion "rested on the belief that a union of government and religion tends to destroy government and to degrade religion," and that this **establishment clause** "rested upon our awareness of the historical fact that governmentally estab-

Freedom of religion allows many different religions to coexist in the United States. Top: A child dressed in traditional Amish attire in the Pennsylvania Dutch countryside. Bottom: A member of the Hare Krishna sect distributes literature.

A parochial school classroom in Washington, D.C. Whether the government should aid parochial schools is an ongoing debate in American politics.

lished religions and religious persecutions go hand in hand."[4] Many angered legislators subsequently sought a constitutional amendment to overrule the Court, but they were unsuccessful.

The extent to which the government should provide aid to religious schools has been a long-standing controversy. An absolutely insurmountable wall of separation could conceivably mean that government could not grant tax exemptions to churches or church-affiliated schools, or provide textbooks, other instructional materials, or transportation for their pupils. Some aspects of religious education have received government support, others have not. Public funds for lunches, standardized tests, and remedial instruction not connected with the religious segments of the curriculum have been permitted. But government funds for teachers' salaries or tuition grants have not been allowed. The Supreme Court has devel-

oped a three-part set of criteria to decide these issues. First, governmental support must have a clear, secular justification. Next, it must not primarily affect the advancement or prohibition of religion. Thirdly, it must avoid "excessive governmental entanglement with religion."[5] These guidelines, like other Court rulings, must be applied to the particular facts of specific cases, and they are, of course, subject to varying interpretations by the judges.

Where state support has been allowed, the basic argument is that it is for the legitimate public purpose of general education and not for the support of religion; the sectarian components of the school program must be financed by nonpublic funds. The counterargument is that even such limited support ultimately affects all the school's activities in that it leaves more private funds for nonsecular uses. Proponents of government support for parochial-school tuition argue that parents of parochial-school students are required to pay taxes that support the public schools, and also that the church-affiliated schools ease the financial burden on the public schools by reducing the size of the latter's student body. They do not see such aid as a fundamental breach of the wall of separation. Opponents argue that parents exercise free choice in sending their children to the parochial schools, and they should be willing to shoulder that additional burden. This is a continuing debate in American politics.

The First Amendment says "Congress shall make no law . . . prohibiting the free exercise [of religion] . . . ." And yet Congress does make such laws. As noted, Mormons cannot exercise polygamy; Christian Scientists can be required to have their school children vaccinated; certain religious groups cannot use snakes in their religious rituals. On the other hand, the Jehovah's Witnesses do have the right to refuse to participate in school ceremonies pledging allegiance to the American flag. The group was not unpatriotic; rather, its religious beliefs prohibited it from paying homage to any secular institution or symbol in such a manner. Congress also recognizes the right of conscientious objection to serving in the military service or going to war. Where such objection pertains to any and all wars, it will be upheld. In fact, the objection need not be based on membership in any organized religious group.[6] But the objection cannot be selective, that is, directed only against serving in a particular war, such as the Vietnam War.

In the area of freedom of religion, the Courts lean very far in the direction of individual rights. Ruling in 1972, the Supreme Court said: "Only those interests of the highest order and those not otherwise served can overbalance legitimate claims to the free exercise of religion."[7]

Freedom of speech. The temptation is great to say that this is the most important freedom, but that would be a distortion. All the freedoms in the Bill of Rights are important, some may be more so than others to particular individuals or groups at particular times. But certainly freedom of speech is always of major importance. We can analyze it along a continuum and distinguish the following types: freedom of what one believes, freedom of what one says, and freedom of what one does. Beliefs in and of themselves are inviolate and are not prohibited. At the other end of the continuum, where attempts are made to translate those beliefs into action, we frequently find attempts at regulation. In both cases, the extent of freedom is fairly easily defined. However, there is a broad area in between; to what extent can one's *statements* connect belief with action? For example, one might privately *believe* that the government should be overthrown by violence, and this does not present any problem. However, there are clearly problems if one places sticks of dynamite at the entrance to the White House and lights the fuse. Yet, is one allowed to believe in such action (without actually performing the act), or give a speech to that effect in Lafayette Park across the street from the White House to an assembled group of two sympathetic listeners, and say precisely how and when the violent acts of revolution ought to proceed? (Would it make a difference to the government if the assembled group numbered 22 or 2000?)

Essentially, there have been three doctrines or tests or "rules of thumb" regarding free speech. Each test recognizes that when the Constitution says, "Congress shall make no law . . . abridging the freedom of speech," it really means that under certain circumstances Congress *may* pass laws prohibiting speech.

One test, referred to as the **dangerous tendency test**, holds that legislatures may pass laws prohibiting speech that would, in the opinion of the lawmakers, lead to substantive evil. The judgment is based on the legislators' assessment that "utterances advocating the overthrow of organized government by force, violence and unlawful means, are so inimical to the general welfare and involve such danger of substantive evil that they may be penalized in the exercise of its police power. . . . Such utterances, by their very nature, involve danger to the public peace and to the security of the State. . . . And the immediate danger is none the less real and substantial, because the effect of a given utterance cannot be accurately foreseen. The State cannot reasonably be required to measure the danger from every such utterance in the nice balance of a jeweler's scale."[8] Therefore, if the local government passed an ordinance declaring that public speeches attacking a racial group were not allowed because of the likelihood of inciting violence, such an ordinance would be upheld under the dangerous tendency doctrine. The Court might not agree with the law, but it would defer to the judgment of the body that passed the law. This test is the most lenient in permitting the government to regulate speech.

A second test or doctrine is known as the **clear and present danger test**. Justice Oliver Wendell Holmes, Jr., first enunciated this standard in 1919: "The character of every act depends upon the circumstances in which it is done. . . . The question in every case is whether the words used are used in such circumstances and are of such a nature as to create a *clear and present danger* that they will bring about the substantive evils that Congress has a right to prevent. It is a question of proximity and degree."[9] Thus, using this test, one makes a judgment on the basis of the particular circumstances; reasonable people could and do disagree, but this doctrine does not hold that it is possible or valid to offer firmer guidelines. Many constitutional and legal interpretations depend on what "rea-

sonable" people would conclude, given all the facts. Unlike the dangerous tendency test, the clear and present danger test permits the courts more latitude in reviewing the particular facts in the case. In essence, the dangerous tendency test allows *legislatures* to pass *general* laws restricting freedom of speech; the clear and present danger test allows the *courts* to make judgments concerning the use of free speech in *specific* situations.

A third test, one that is more strict in constraining governmental action, is the **preferred position test**. Whereas the dangerous tendency test leans in the direction of presuming (but, of course, not concluding) that governmental restriction of speech is valid, the preferred position test leans in the opposite direction. It says that the First Amendment freedoms are so vital to a democracy that they may be restricted only under extraordinary circumstances: "Whatever occasion would restrain orderly discussion and persuasion, at appropriate time and place, must have clear support in public danger, actual or impending. Only the gravest abuses, endangering paramount interests, give occasion for permissible limitation."[10] This test presumes that a restriction is invalid unless very strong evidence is presented that proves otherwise.

No single test has been relied on exclusively, and there may be times when a Supreme Court opinion will combine some elements of at least two doctrines in reaching a decision. Admittedly, the judicial orientation of the judges is important. What particular approaches, doctrines, or tests they apply will depend often on their own social, philosophical, and political orientation. They are, after all, human beings applying law to human conditions. They might have more time to reflect and weigh and ponder and discuss with each other than a police officer on the street stopping a motorist, but in the final analysis, decisions have to be made.

Freedom of the press. The critical issues here involve two types of efforts at restriction: **prior restraint** and **subsequent punishment**. Under what circumstances may the authorities refuse to permit something to be published (censorship), and to what extent and in what situations is one liable for having published something?

Prior restraint: censorship. There is a very strong inclination in the courts to limit the extent to which censorship can be imposed, whether in newspapers, television broadcasting, books, magazines, movies, or any other form of "publication." Again, we see the clash of competing values. On the one hand, there is the clear value of having a press free to criticize; comment; gather and dispense news, information, and opinion; and reach as many people as possible in doing so. The belief that a democracy cannot really exist without such an institution is strongly held. On the other hand, there is the need to guard against the dissemination of news and information that would threaten national security; and many believe that pornographic or other obscene "literature" should not be permitted because it demeans the morals and offends the sensibilities of society.

As with freedom of speech, there is no absolute right of freedom of the press. The balancing process always operates. For example, a person accused of a crime has a constitutional right to a fair trial, and press coverage is often considered an important means of ensuring that correct and proper legal procedures will be followed. But what if a judge believes that extensive and sensationalist media coverage would prejudice the jury and make it impossible to hold such a trial? Should the media be barred from the courtroom? The Supreme Court normally has not permitted such a restriction of the press, sometimes referred to as a "gag order." In a 1976 Nebraska case, Chief Justice Warren Burger ruled that a local judge could not bar the press from reporting a pretrial hearing. He stated that "prior restraints on speech and publication are the most serious and the least tolerable infringement on First Amendment rights."

However, this right does not necessarily extend to television filming of courtroom proceedings. A defendant's objection to the presence of TV cameras is usually sufficient to keep the cameras out. A judge might bar television from a trial if he feels the presence of television cameras will be distracting and disruptive of a fair trial.

Several criminal convictions have been set aside by appellate courts on grounds that sensational publicity has created an environment prejudicial to the defendant. In one case, the Supreme Court held that a defendant accused of murdering his wife was tried and convicted in the "atmosphere of a 'Roman Holiday' for the news media."[12] Cases such as this have led some observers to conclude that there is a growing tension between the free-press right of the First Amendment and the fair-trial guarantee of the Sixth Amendment. These two liberties, it has been suggested, are on a "collision course." The Court has usually held that the defendant, not the press, is entitled to an "open" trial, and it is the defendant whose interests must be protected when deciding whether to open or close the courtroom. The press is not to be unduly restricted, but, in the weighing and balancing process, the defendant's rights must be given paramount consideration.

This issue surfaced recently in a case involving the right of reporters to protect the confidentiality of their sources. A *New York Times* reporter had written a series of articles about a doctor subsequently accused of murder. The doctor, through the court, sought to get the reporter's notes. The newspaper and the reporter refused and were cited for criminal and civil contempt. The reporter ended up going to jail for forty days and the newspaper had to pay a stiff fine.[13]

New York Times *reporter Myron Farber went to jail after refusing to disclose his sources for a series of articles on a Doctor X, who at the time was on trial for medical malpractice.*

In other instances, the Court has even said that the telephone company may divulge records of calls made by reporters. Understandably, this has infuriated the press and many civil libertarians, who argue that it is impossible to maintain a free press and therefore protect against First Amendment violations if reporters cannot claim a privileged relationship between themselves and their sources. Again, we see a clash of competing values.

The Supreme Court, in 1972, ruled that Congress and the state legislatures can pass **shield laws** stipulating how much protection should be accorded the media in protecting (shielding) its sources. According to the Court, this protection could be "as narrow or broad as deemed necessary" by the individual states. Thus far, more than twenty states have passed such laws, providing varying degrees of protection. But even this has

not completely settled the matter. For example, in the case of the *New York Times* reporter, the state of New Jersey *had* passed a shield law giving journalists the right "to refuse to disclose, in any legal . . . proceeding" or to "any court" the "source . . . from or through whom any information was procured . . . and . . . any news or information obtained in the course of pursuing his professional activities, whether or not it is disseminated."[14] Citing this clear definition, the *Times* reporter refused to divulge his sources or his notes. He was ordered to produce his notes nonetheless by the New Jersey Supreme Court on the grounds that the state's shield law conflicted with the U.S. Constitution's Sixth Amendment right of an accused person "to have compulsory process for obtaining witnesses in his favor."

Subsequent punishment. Subsequent punishment involves libel laws. It refers to punishment for violations of freedom of the press that have already occurred, that is, for false information that has already been published or broadcast or otherwise disseminated. If something is published which damages a person's character or reputation and is based on incorrect information, the person may sue for damages. But even here, the Supreme Court has not been entirely consistent in its rulings. A private citizen in Kentucky was arrested for shoplifting but was never tried for the charge. Charges against him were dismissed. A year and a half later, his picture appeared on a notice sent to merchants by the local police listing him as an "active shoplifter." He sued for damages under a federal law prohibiting actions done under "color of law" (having the appearance or semblance, without the substance, of legal right). Such actions are normally considered violations of one's liberty and property rights. Yet in 1976, the Supreme Court ruled against the Kentucky man in a five-man majority opinion written by Justice William H. Rehnquist. "We hold that the interest in reputa-

tion asserted . . . is neither 'liberty' nor 'property' guaranteed against state deprivation.''[15]

The law rather clearly states that public officials and other people in the public eye (celebrities, for example) do not have the same protection that private persons have. The former, precisely because of their public status, are vulnerable to ''fair comment and criticism.'' Only if they can show malice and a reckless disregard for the truth will they be able to win a libel suit. In a 1979 case, a scientist won a libel suit against Senator William Proxmire. The senator had ''awarded'' the plaintiff-scientist the ''Golden Fleece Award,'' indicating that, according to Proxmire, the scientist's government-supported research measuring aggression in certain animals was a waste of taxpayers' money. The Supreme Court held that such an award damaged the character and reputation of the scientist, and furthermore, that since

the scientist was not a public figure (inasmuch as he had not thrust himself into the public eye and did not have the same access to the media that public figures have for responding to libelous remarks), he did not have to show ''actual malice.''

Obscenity and pornography. By what definition are materials so offensive to society's morals that they should be banned or censored? Certainly these definitions are subject to change over time; today certain words and pictures appear in print, in the movies, and on television that even a few years ago would not have been allowed. Not only nudity, but depictions and descriptions of people engaged in sexual intercourse are allowed. ''Rough'' language is commonplace even in ''PG'' movies, and some television programs now warn that ''viewer discretion is advised'' or ''this

Comedian George Carlin, shown shortly after his arrest for using "the seven words you can't say on TV" in his act at Milwaukee's Summerfest, July 1972.

program is for mature audiences" if the producers feel that the material might be too violent or might be morally offensive to some people.

The Supreme Court has struggled with this problem, recognizing that the definitions are elusive and that standards vary from community to community, even from person to person. Although he could not define hardcore pornography, Justice Potter Stewart once said, "I know it when I see it."[17]

In a recent obscenity case, the Federal Commu-nications Commission penalized a radio station for airing a twelve-minute radio broadcast entitled "Filthy Words," which included seven "ob-scene" words. In a 1978 decision, the Supreme Court upheld the FCC. The Court compared the unacceptable argument that people can always turn off the radio to saying that "the remedy for an assault is to run away after the first blow." The Court felt that with a radio broadcast, unlike with bookstores or movies that are restricted to adults, children were especially vulnerable. But essential-ly the Court said that "the Commission's decision rested entirely on a nuisance rationale under which context is all-important." In other words, the same language under other circumstances might be per-missible, but in this situation, given the time of the broadcast and the medium, it was not.[18]

Absolutists feel that *under no circumstances* should censorship be imposed, but the Supreme Court and Congress have interpreted the phrase, "Congress shall make no law," to mean "except in some cases." In struggling to come up with a set of rules, the Court has devised the following, admittedly less-than-perfect, guidelines for ob-scenity cases:

- "applying contemporary community standards," the material should not be allowed if it "appeals to prurient interest";
- it should not be permitted if it shows "in a patently offensive way" sexual conduct prohibit-ed by state law;
- the material will not be allowed if it "lacks serious literary, artistic, political, or scientific value."[19]

Certainly each of these phrases or words con-tains problems of interpretation, and the guidelines seem to rely heavily on the judgment of local authorities. Thus we begin to appreciate Justice Stewart's dilemma. Cases have been decided vari-ously, as would be expected in such a vague area.

Demonstrators in downtown Chicago protest a planned march by the American Nazi party in Skokie, Illinois, 1978.

In a sense, you publish your material, make your arguments, and take your chances.

The right to assemble.   The First Amendment permits people to hold peaceful political meetings, but the definition of "peaceful" is not always clear. Can local officials refuse to permit a pro-Nazi group to march and hold a rally in the heavily Jewish town of Skokie, Illinois? In this incident, the officials argued that such an act would be inflammatory and could possibly lead to violence. On the other hand, the pro-Nazi group argued that their actions were peaceful and that they should be protected from any violence their march might cause rather than have their First Amendment right

denied. The Supreme Court instructed the lower federal court to consider the First Amendment. The group was permitted to march but at the last minute decided to do so in another community in Illinois.[20] The issue died down for the time being, but threatened to resurface at some time in the future.

The Supreme Court is cognizant of the competing values involved in this type of issue. It seeks to limit government regulation of assembly under reasonable circumstances, protecting both the right to assemble and the right of the public at large not to be unduly disturbed. To this end, laws may require a permit to assemble in a public place. The

A 1980 Ku Klux Klan/American Nazi rally held in South Carolina to commemorate Adolf Hitler's birthday. The Constitution recognizes the right of all people, regardless of their views, to express those views publicly.

permit might limit the size of the group as well as the length of the meeting. These rules were intended to satisfy both protection of civil liberties and to maintain public order. If in the judgment of the officials, violence could occur, then they may assign police officers to maintain order. The Supreme Court does not permit government authorities to deny any and all forms of public assembly before specific application is made. That is, peremptory denial violates the First Amendment. Again, circumstances will play an important part in the determination. A mass meeting on the steps of the public library or a meeting in a park adjacent to the library might both be noisy and disturb reading and study inside, but the former would probably impede access to the building. Thus denying a meeting on the steps and permitting one in the park might be a reasonable decision.

The Fourth Amendment: Searches and Seizures

The Constitution does not specifically mention what is often referred to as the ''right of privacy,'' but the Fourth Amendment does come close:

The right of the people to be secure in their persons, houses, papers, and effects, against unreasonable searches and seizures, shall not be violated, and no warrants shall issue, but upon probable cause, supported by oath or affirmation, and particularly describing the place to be searched, and the persons or things to be seized.

Since 1914, illegally obtained evidence has not been allowable in federal courts under the **exclusionary rule**. In 1961, the Supreme Court extended this ruling to the state courts.[21] But again, the problem is one of definition: what constitutes an "unreasonable" search and seizure? If a person is stopped and questioned for one reason, can the police officer make an arrest for another reason? The Supreme Court decided an officer can, stating: "The Fourth Amendment does not require a policeman who lacks the precise level of information necessary for probable cause to arrest to simply shrug his shoulders and allow a crime to occur or a criminal to escape."[22]

For all searches, a warrant must first be secured if there is sufficient time to get one, unless "consent" to search is given. But what if *A* is in *B*'s car as an invited passenger, and *A* gives consent to search the car where narcotics are found belonging to *B?* This has been held to be a valid search based on consent. When the police ask the court for a search warrant, they must give **probable cause**—facts that indicate that a search will lead to evidence of the commission of a crime. Probable cause requires that the warrant specify the premises to be searched and the items sought. There must be some basis for suggesting that those items will be found on those premises.

In recent years, the Court has gone quite far in permitting authorities to obtain information about people without their knowledge or consent. Now, one's bank account records and credit records may be obtained, and the telephone company's records of one's calls must be turned over to the authorities if requested. In both these instances, the Court has said that citizens voluntarily convey such information to "third parties" (banks, telephone companies) and therefore cannot expect the information to remain private. This was farfetched reasoning according to one dissenting justice, Thurgood Marshall, who held that one has to question just

how "voluntary" such disclosure is in today's society. "The fact that one has disclosed private papers to the bank, for a limited purpose, within the context of a confidential customer-bank relationship, does not mean that one has waived all right to privacy of the papers."[23]

With the development of highly sophisticated wiretapping devices, it is possible for the authorities to overhear almost any conversation they want. Evidence seized in this manner with a properly issued warrant may be used in court. In addition, the law allows wiretapping without a warrant for forty-eight hours in "an emergency situation relating to conspiratorial activities threatening the national security."[24] This forty-eight-hour provision also applies to organized-crime activities.

The Fifth Amendment and the Right to Remain Silent

The responsibility to prove a person's guilt lies with the state, and the Constitution states that a suspect does not have to do anything to contribute to that effort. This means that in a trial a person does not have to testify against his or her own interests, and he or she does not have to answer the questions of investigating authorities.

In all instances, the person is entitled to a lawyer.

The rights of arrested persons were firmly established in the famous case of *Miranda* v. *Arizona*. In 1966, the Supreme Court ruled that the police had to inform a suspect that he or she had the right to remain silent; that anything the suspect said could be used in court; that he or she had the right to a lawyer; and that if the suspect could not afford a lawyer, one would be provided before any questions were asked. The last item on this list of "Interrogation Warnings to Persons in

The "Miranda card," carried by San Francisco police to inform arrested persons of their constitutional rights.

DEFENDANT	LOCATION

SPECIFIC WARNING REGARDING INTERROGATIONS

1. You have the right to remain silent.

2. Anything you say can and will be used against you in a court of law.

3. You have the right to talk to a lawyer and have him present with you while you are being questioned.

4. If you cannot afford to hire a lawyer one will be appointed to represent you before any questioning, if you wish one.

SIGNATURE OF DEFENDANT	DATE
WITNESS	TIME

☐ REFUSED SIGNATURE   SAN FRANCISCO POLICE DEPARTMENT   PR.9.1.4

Police Custody'' reads: "Now that I have advised you of your rights, are you willing to answer questions without an attorney present?" In other words, a suspect can waive his or her rights. But above all, the authorities must not use coercion or third-degree tactics to extract a statement or confession.

Although these so-called **Miranda rights** form an integral part of the justice system, in the 1970s the Supreme Court began to chip away at them. In a 1971 case, the Court held that if the state extracts a confession in violation of the *Miranda* rules, this statement can still be used in court, not as a confession, but in order to "impeach the credibility" of the defendant if he or she testifies differently on the stand.[25] Such a ruling certainly undermines the intent of the *Miranda* decision. In another case, in 1980, two police officers arrested a suspect for a shotgun murder. They read him his *Miranda* rights and proceeded to drive him to the police station. On the way, as they passed a school for handicapped children, one policeman said to the other: "God forbid one of the children might find [the missing shotgun] and hurt themselves." The defendant overheard this remark and led the police to the shotgun. On trial, the weapon was offered as evidence; the defendant was convicted. The Supreme Court upheld the conviction, deciding that the conversation of the police officers leading to disclosure of the weapon by the defendant did not constitute a violation of the *Miranda* ruling.[26]

The Rights of the Criminally Accused

A basic tenet of American justice is that a person is innocent until proven guilty. This is the theory, but the practice at times is quite different. Some defendants, especially lower-class citizens and habitual lawbreakers, clearly come into court with a cloud of guilt hanging over their heads. In addition, if a suspect refuses to take the stand, some people feel he or she must have something to hide. Most people never have been involved in a serious violation of the law. For many, the most serious encounter is a traffic ticket for parking illegally or running a red light. Therefore, it is not too surprising that many people believe that when the police arrest someone for a major offense, the suspect is probably guilty. Such an attitude reverses the presumption of innocence theory.

It is, therefore, very important that the Bill of Rights provisions pertaining to the rights of the accused be enforced most diligently. The provisions in the Sixth Amendment include the defendant's right to: (1) have a speedy and public trial by an impartial jury; (2) cross-examine witnesses; (3) call witnesses on his or her behalf; and (4) have a defense lawyer. The right to a jury trial is granted in the Seventh Amendment, and protection against "excessive bail," "excessive fines," and "cruel and unusual punishment" is granted in the Eighth Amendment.

As with the other Bill of Rights provisions, these provisions are interpreted from time to time in view of the particular facts in a given case. It is not always clear when a fine is "excessive" or a jury "impartial," or what constitutes "unusual" punishment. Sometimes previous rulings seem clear and the law on the subject seems established, but then new situations arise and the Supreme Court comes up with a different interpretation of the language or with a point that distinguishes a case from previous ones. On the issue of right to counsel, the Supreme Court overruled in 1963 a decision that had been standing for twenty-one years. In 1942, in *Betts* v. *Brady*, the Court held that, at the state level, an indigent defendant who was unable to hire a lawyer was not constitutionally entitled to have one appointed by the court.[27] The Court argued that the Sixth Amendment gave such a right in federal cases only, but the defendant, Betts, argued that he was entitled to a lawyer under the due-process clause of the Fourteenth

Capital punishment has been banned in many states on the grounds that it constitutes cruel and unusual punishment, though the Supreme Court has ruled that capital punishment is constitutional. Shown here: the electric chair.

A cell block at the New Mexico State Penitentiary after thirty-six hours of rioting. The inmates were protesting overcrowding and substandard conditions in the prison.

Amendment. (This issue of "incorporation" will be discussed in the next section.) Twenty years later, in *Gideon* v. *Wainwright*, the Supreme Court overruled *Betts* v. *Brady*:

> *That government hires lawyers to prosecute and defendants who have the money hire lawyers to defend are the strongest indications of the widespread belief that lawyers in criminal courts are necessities, not luxuries. The right of one charged with crime to counsel may not be deemed fundamental and essential to fair trials in some countries, but it is in ours.*[28]

The treatment of prisoners is receiving more attention in the press and the courts, especially with the development in recent years of public-interest law firms. In 1980, the Supreme Court held that a woman whose son died allegedly from medical malpractice while in a federal prison could sue prison officials for damages under the Eighth Amendment prohibition of cruel and unusual punishment.[29] The decision relied on and extended a ruling by the Court in 1971 in *Bivens* v. *Six Unknown Named Agents*.[30] In that case, the Court held that where an individual's constitutional rights under the "search and seizure" provision of the Fourth Amendment were violated, the person could sue the federal agents who had conducted the search. In the 1980 case, the Court extended this right to sue. Associate Justice William H. Rehnquist, however, dissented. He felt that the Court was wrong in the *Bivens* case and was repeating its error in 1980. He accused his colleagues on the Court of "fashioning for itself a legislative role resembling that once thought to be the domain of Congress."

With such disagreement at the highest court, it is no surprise that consensus among members of the general public on these issues is rare. The *process* of balancing individual rights and societal values remains constant, but what one chooses to put on the scale varies considerably at times.

The Theory of Incorporation

The Bill of Rights applies to the national government. It does not speak directly to the states. But through the **theory of incorporation**, all of the provisions except four are now applicable in the state courts. It is interesting to note how the American government evolves—case by case, step by step, and ad hoc, and sometimes in contradictory ways.

In 1833, the Supreme Court specifically stated that the Bill of Rights did not apply to the states.[31] This decision prevailed for the next ninety-two years, until in 1925 in *Gitlow* v. *New York* (mentioned earlier in connection with freedom of speech) the Court said that the First Amendment provisions for freedom of speech and press *did* apply to the states. This decision, however, would have been impossible without the passage of the Fourteenth Amendment in 1868. That amendment reads, in part: [No] state shall deprive any person of life, liberty, or property without due process of law.'' In *Gitlow*, the Court stated that freedom of speech and of the press were ''fundamental personal rights'' and thus could not be denied by the states to anyone who had been guaranteed such rights under the Fourteenth Amendment.

Then, slowly, one provision in the Bill of Rights after another was incorporated into the language of the Fourteenth Amendment. The standard for incorporation was provided by Justice Benjamin Cardozo in a 1937 case. The case involved **double jeopardy**, or trying a person twice for the same offense, which is prohibited under the Fifth Amendment. Frank Palko was sentenced to life in prison for killing two policemen in Connecticut. The state, however, was not satisfied with the sentence; it appealed, tried Palko again, won, and sentenced him to death. The defendant argued in the U.S. Supreme Court that this violated the double-jeopardy provision of the Fifth Amendment, which, he hoped, would be incorporated

Pro-gun demonstrators protest a Morton Grove, Illinois, ordinance outlawing handguns. The right to bear arms is a provision of the Bill of Rights that is unincorporated—meaning that it does not have to be guaranteed by the individual states.

into the Fourteenth Amendment and applied to the states. Cardozo, speaking for the majority of the Court, held that *some* rights were so fundamental that "neither liberty nor justice would exist if they were sacrificed." Thus, some rights listed in the Bill of Rights could and should be incorporated into the Fourteenth Amendment. Although Cardozo did not feel double jeopardy measured up to his standard for incorporation, his standard was later used to incorporate most of the protections in the Bill of Rights into the due-process clause of the Fourteenth Amendment. This standard has changed only slightly over time. The Court is concerned now with whether the protection is basic to American values of liberty and justice, not necessarily to "civilized society," which was the language used in the *Palko* case.

The process has been one of *selective incorporation*, whereby the provisions have been "absorbed" case by case. The *Gideon* decision on the right to counsel is an example of selective incorporation. In that case there was no one ruling that covered all the provisions. Today, the following provisions of the Bills of Rights remain unincorporated or unabsorbed:

- the right to keep and bear arms (Second Amendment);
- the prohibition against housing of soldiers without homeowner's consent (Third Amendment);
- the right to indictment by a grand jury for major crimes (part of Fifth Amendment);
- the right of jury trial in certain civil cases (Seventh Amendment).

The Tenth Amendment, because of its focus on the national government is not applicable to incorporation. Double jeopardy, incidentally, was finally incorporated in 1969 when the Court saw fit to overrule the *Palko* decision in the case of *Benton* v. *Maryland*.[32]

Due Process—Procedural and Substantive

The protection of individual liberties in a democratic society depends in large measure on the *process* as well as on the final result—the product. If the process is thought to be fair and just, if one gets an honest hearing, if all the facts are presented without distortion, and so forth—all this helps build acceptance for whatever decision is finally rendered or policy enacted. This is an aspect of "procedural due process" as distinguished from "substantive due process." **Due process** is mentioned in the Constitution in two amendments. It is applied to the national government in the Fifth Amendment: ". . . nor be deprived of life, liberty, or property, without due process of law," and it serves as a restraint on state action in the Fourteenth Amendment: ". . . nor shall any state deprive any person of life, liberty, or property without due process of law."

Procedural due process pertains to *how* laws are enacted and carried out. If a policeman is dismissed from his duties without a hearing, the Supreme Court must decide not whether he should be dismissed, but whether the lack of a hearing constituted a violation of *procedural* due process of law. In a 1976 case, the Court held that inasmuch as no one has a constitutional right to a public job, the dismissal without a hearing was not unconstitutional.[33] The same reasoning applied to an untenured college professor who was not retained.[34]

As might be expected, precisely what procedures will be required to validate acts cannot be decided by one specific rule or formula. Each case is judged on the basis of what seems just and fair, leaving considerable room for disagreement. Some practices, however, would certainly seem to be obvious violations of procedural due process, such as appointing a lawyer for a defendant charged with murder and then scheduling the trial before the counsel has reasonable time to prepare the defense; or terminating one's parole without a hearing.[35]

Procedural due process can also be violated simply because the statute being enforced is too vague to give proper guidance to those attempting to enforce it or abide by it. In such case, it is not fair to hold one liable for violating the law.

Substantive due process involves deciding whether a law itself constitutes an unreasonable restraint on life, liberty, or property. Prior to the latter part of the New Deal (before 1937), the Supreme Court did not allow many legislative enactments aimed at regulating certain business practices. Under the theory of *liberty of contract*, laws regulating workers' wages and hours, child labor, and prices were not allowed. A conservative Supreme Court felt such laws would deny substantive due process to members of the business community. With a change in Supreme Court judges came different interpretations, and more latitude was given to legislative enactment of laws involving the government in the economy. More restraints on business were allowed. But at the same time, we also saw greater limitations on the government in matters concerning individual civil liberties. This resulted in the decisions we examined earlier in this chapter extending the freedoms of speech, press, religion, and assembly, and offering greater protection to individuals accused of criminal acts.

It is important to remember that the interpretation of both procedural and substantive due process depends in large measure on the philosophical views of the judges and policymakers. Conservative officials tend to lean toward greater restriction of governmental action in economic matters, toward what has been called a free-market approach (more on this in chapter 15). In social matters, conservatives tend toward protecting what they perceive to be the interest of the majority—such as, for example, enacting tougher laws on suspected criminals who pose a threat to law and order. Liberal officials tend to lean in the other direction on both economic and social issues.

Civil Liberties in a Democratic Society

In the spring of 1980, the press and a Senate investigating committee devoted considerable attention to the business relationship between Billy Carter, brother of then-President Jimmy Carter, and the Libyan government. The investigations sought, among other things, to determine if Billy Carter had attempted to use his influence with his brother to gain favors for that foreign (and not so friendly) government. On one occasion, the First Lady, Rosalynn Carter, stated in a television interview that she had called Billy Carter's wife at one point during the investigations simply to express her sympathy for the family. Mrs. Carter remarked that the conversation was rather short and that her sister-in-law gave only short, nonconversational responses. The First Lady then stated: "I got the impression—and I told Jimmy this—that she felt her telephone might be tapped. And she didn't want to say too much. She just said 'Thank you.'"

Some Americans might find such an episode disturbing. But it indicates the extent to which even the possibility of having one's private conversations overheard has come to be feared. It is almost as if official eavesdropping has become a fact of life, and the First Lady could somewhat casually comment on it on nationwide television. In a sense, one might suggest the damage has been done: it is probably as significant when one *suspects* that individual privacy is being invaded as when such invasion actually occurs. Once the suspicion sets in, a democratic society has already begun to transform itself in a direction inconsistent with the basic principles of civil liberties and democracy.

The American democratic society, properly understood, must put a high priority on the individual liberties stipulated in the Bill of Rights. It cannot afford to be casual about those freedoms and expect to remain for long a viable political democracy. This does not mean that one must adopt the absolutist view that "Congress shall make *no* law . . . ." But in the process of deciding precisely when Congress *should* make laws, it is important that the act of balancing be respected and desired.

It takes a particular kind of society—and there are not that many in existence today—to permit the luxuries of political dissent, free and open discussion, and maximum protection of individual liberties. Civil liberties thrive best—given the balancing process—where the body politic is stable and where there is a reasonably equitable economic order. A politically unstable society is threatened by the freedom to criticize public officials and the freedom to assemble and form contentious political associations. A stable political system is better able to withstand and tolerate a gathering such as the one in Lafayette Park advocating the violent overthrow of the government.

A society with a rising crime rate might call for "law and order" and move against "coddling criminals." Thus, the protections afforded accused criminals will tend to be weakened. The public will become impatient with arguments protecting the accused's rights. "What about the rights of the victims?" they will ask. This is a proper question, but when it is discussed in an emotional atmosphere, the balancing process may be upset.

Corruption and scandals in high office may lead to public cynicism and mistrust, resulting in the belief that respect for law is honored more in the breach than in the observance. If public mistrust is aroused, then no laws are immune to disobedience,

especially those pertaining to protection of individual rights.

A society in which sizeable segments are uneducated and economically deprived finds in its midst vast numbers of people vulnerable to political demagoguery. In such circumstances, it makes little sense to talk about free speech as a means of letting ideas compete in a marketplace of open discussion and rational judgment. A democratic society requires a certain degree of socio-economic equity and political consciousness before the kind of environment necessary for the legitimate exercise and protection of civil liberties can exist.

It is difficult, even under the best of circumstances, to build a society where unpopular ideas and opinions are tolerated. The United States has written such tolerance into its governing documents and has, thereby, made certain assumptions about itself and its people. Throughout this chapter we have talked about the necessary balance that has to be struck between competing values: free press versus fair trial; national security versus free speech; freedom of religion versus societal norms; majority rights versus individual rights, and so forth. These are delicate issues to be weighed, and this is best done in the context of what kind of society we *want* to be. We must, of course, take into account the kind of society we *are* in fact. If people already believe that their telephones are tapped, that police officers and judges will do whatever they can to circumvent the *Miranda* guidelines, that those who "take the Fifth" are *really* guilty, it is doubtful that the prerequisite environment for a careful balancing of competing civil libertarian values exists. Already, the scales have been tipped too far in one direction.

The thoughtful balancing of civil libertarian values presumes an environment where the conflicting values of individual rights and societal

The balancing of individual versus societal rights remains a sensitive political issue. At times, people may feel that the scale has been tipped too far in a given direction.

norms are mutually respected. And this respect cannot exist only when it is convenient. The true test of a free society is to be able to accord each individually accused rapist full constitutional rights even in the face of rising crime rates; to accord political orators maximum freedom to advocate unpopular anti-American ideas even while American embassies overseas are being attacked by anti-American terrorists. A democratic society wishing to extend maximum individual liberties proves its strength and viability by doing so in the most difficult, not the most comfortable, times.

This does not mean that a society (democratic or otherwise) should passively permit its own destruction. But a society that is internally healthy— politically and economically—will be less apt than one that is not to interpret various threats, acts, or movements as a ''clear and present danger'' to its well-being. In this sense, one would, for example,

expect civil liberties to be far more protected in the United States than in the Republic of South Africa.

It is one thing to adopt a set of rules outlining individual liberties; it is quite another to pursue and implement those rules judiciously. It is important, also, to note that this process is most meaningful in the context of a politically and economically stable society. Where stability does not exist, it is likely that true civil liberties will not exist.

Summary

1. The protection of individual liberties always involves balancing competing values, deciding to what extent the state or the individual may pursue its goals at the expense of the other. National security versus freedom to advocate revolution is an example.

2. In deciding such matters in the various areas of speech, press, assembly, and so forth, the Supreme Court tries to adopt reasonably clear guidelines which are flexible enough to allow application to specific circumstances. Sometimes, this flexibility causes uncertainty and ambiguity.

3. Civil liberties thrive best in politically stable and economically equitable societies. Without such conditions, it makes little sense to consider seriously extending individual liberties.

Notes

1. *Reynolds* v. *United States*, 98 U.S. 145 (1879). In upholding a federal law making polygamy illegal, the Supreme Court said: "Congress was deprived of all legislative power over mere opinion, but was left free to reach actions which were in violation of social duties or subversive of good order."
2. 370 U.S. 421 (1962).
3. Ibid.
4. Ibid.
5. *Walz* v. *Tax Commission*, 397 U.S. 664 (1970).
6. *Gillette* v. *United States*, 401 U.S. 437 (1971).
7. *Wisconsin* v. *Yoder*, 406 U.S. 205 (1972). The Supreme Court permitted parents of the Amish religion to withdraw their children from school after the eighth grade in violation of a state's compulsory education law. The religious beliefs of the group held such further education to be against their faith.
8. *Gitlow* v. *New York*, 268 U.S. 652 (1925).
9. *Schenck* v. *United States*, 249 U.S. 47 (1919).
10. *Thomas* v. *Collins*, 323 U.S. 516 (1945).
11. *Nebraska Press Association* v. *Stuart*, 427 U.S. 539 (1976).
12. *Sheppard* v. *Maxwell*, 384 U.S. 333 (1966). In describing the kind of atmosphere it found unacceptable, the Supreme Court recounted the following circumstances: "Apparently prodded by newspaper editorials, the coroner subpoenaed Sheppard and staged a three-day inquest in a school gymnasium. The proceedings were broadcast live. In the presence of a swarm of reporters and photographers, Sheppard was questioned for 5½ hours about his actions on the night of the murder, his married life and a love affair with his nurse. . . . The movement of reporters in and out of the courtroom often caused so much confusion that, despite the installation of a loud speaker system, it was difficult for the witnesses and counsel to be heard. Sheppard and his counsel frequently had to leave the courtroom to talk confidentially. . . . Much of the material printed or broadcast during the trial was never heard from the witness stand, such as the charges that Sheppard had purposely impeded the murder investigation and must be guilty because he had hired a prominent criminal lawyer . . . and broadcaster Walter Winchell's report that a woman convict had stated that, as the defendant's mistress, she had borne him a child. This deluge of publicity during the trial reached at least some of the jury. On the only occasion the jury was queried about these reports, two jurors admitted that they had heard the Winchell broadcast."
13. *The State of New Jersey and Dr. Mario Jascaleovich* v. *Myron Farber and The New York Times Company*, 439 U.S. 1317 (1978).
14. Sidney Zion, "High Court vs. The Press," *The New York Times Magazine*, November 18, 1979.
15. Ibid., p. 138.
16. *Hutchinson* v. *Proxmire*, 443 U.S. 111 (1979).
17. *Jacobellis* v. *Ohio*, 378 U.S. 184 (1964).
18. *Federal Communications Commission* v. *Pacifica Foundation*, 438 U.S. 726 (1978).
19. *Miller* v. *California*, 413 U.S. 15 (1973).
20. *Village of Skokie* v. *National Socialist Party*, 373 N.E. 2d. 21 (1978).
21. *Mapp* v. *Ohio*, 367 U.S. 643 (1961).
22. *Adams* v. *Williams*, 407 U.S. 143 (1972).
23. *California Bankers Association* v. *Shultz*, 416 U.S. 21 (1974).
24. U.S.C., Section 2510 (1968).
25. *Harris* v. *New York*, 401 U.S. 222 (1971).
26. *Rhode Island* v. *Innis*, 100 S. Ct. 1682 (1980).
27. 316 U.S. 455 (1942).
28. 372 U.S. 335 (1963).
29. *Carlson* v. *Green*, 446 U.S. 14 (1980).
30. 403 U.S. 388 (1971).
31. *Barron* v. *Mayor and City Council of Baltimore*, 32 U.S. 243 (1833).
32. *Benton* v. *Maryland*, 395 U.S. 784 (1969). Associate Justice Thurgood Marshall wrote: "Our recent cases have thoroughly rejected the *Palko* notion that

basic constitutional rights can be denied by the States as long as the totality of the circumstances does not disclose a denial of 'fundamental fairness.' Once it is decided that a particular Bill of Rights guarantee is 'fundamental to the American scheme of justice,' the same constitutional standards apply against both the State and Federal Governments.

. . . Like the right to trial by jury, [the guarantee against double jeopardy] is clearly 'fundamental to the American scheme of justice.' "

33. *Bishop* v. *Wood*, 426 U.S. 341 (1976).
34. *Board of Regents* v. *Roth*, 408 U.S. 564 (1972).
35. *Greenholtz* v. *Nebraska Penal Inmates*, 442 U.S. 1 (1979).

Civil Rights
and
Group Conflicts

On Friday, June 20, 1980, the *Birmingham News* ran two front-page news stories which are significant to anyone who is aware of the history of race relations in the United States, and especially in Birmingham, Alabama. One story headlined a pending federal district-court appointment in that city; the other dealt with the mayor and the city police.

The first headline read:

Clemon approval seems assured; "will serve with distinction," Heflin says.

Attorney W. W. Clemon is a Birmingham lawyer; he is black. Senator Howell Heflin is a U.S. Senator; he is white. The Alabama senator was supporting the Birmingham lawyer's nomination by President Carter to a position on the federal district court. (You will recall from chapter 12 our discussion of senatorial courtesy and judicial appointments.)

The other headline read:

Shooting review unit asks changes; mayor wants further study.

The mayor of Birmingham, responding to citizens' complaints about certain police actions, had appointed a committee to look into various aspects of law enforcement in that city. The committee, composed of white and black citizens, recommended some changes in police practices. Some black citizens were particularly upset with what they considered to be acts of "police brutality." The mayor, Richard Arrington, is a former college professor; he is also black.

Less than twenty years before, Birmingham had been a rigidly segregated city (it was called by civil-rights supporters the "Johannesburg of the United States"). There were no black elected or appointed officials, and relatively few black citizens were permitted to register and to vote. In 1963, the city's top police official, Eugene "Bull" Connor, gained national attention when he ordered police dogs and water hoses turned on full-force against civil-rights demonstrators. (His action, as we noted in chapter 5, was an important factor in convincing President Kennedy to introduce a stronger civil-rights bill.)

Birmingham is not alone in the story of the struggle for racial justice. It is a story with many plots, characters, and settings. It has involved many sectors of the country and various political and private institutions. In this chapter our focus will be on the role of the political institutions and on the part played by interest groups, not only in the struggle of blacks for equal rights but in the struggles of other minority groups and women. We want to know not only what happened, but also how the country got "from there to here," and what the various issues will be in the coming years.

The Battle Against Legal Segregation and Discrimination

Slavery was abolished by the Thirteenth Amendment (1865). The Fourteenth Amendment (1868) stipulated that persons in each state were entitled to "privileges and immunities" and "due process of law" provided by each state and to "equal protection of the laws." The Fifteenth Amendment (1870) made it unconstitutional to deny anyone the right to vote on the basis of race.

In spite of these constitutional provisions, a series of state laws relegated black Americans to a political and economic "second-class" status. Legal racial segregation and discrimination (**de jure** segregation) existed in many places in this country. **De facto** ("according to reality") segregation existed, and continues to exist, in those places where certain practices, although not sanctioned by law, nonetheless result in the denial of rights and opportunities. Private discriminatory real-estate practices and the refusal to hire people because of race or sex are examples of *de facto* segregation and discrimination.

In the last two decades of the nineteenth century the Supreme Court upheld southern state laws segregating the races. In the *Civil Rights Cases* (1883)[1] the Court held that the Fourteenth Amendment applied only to states and not to individuals; thus, private owners of public accommodations (such as restaurants, theaters, hotels) could legally exclude blacks and other racial groups. In *Plessy v. Ferguson* (1896)[2] the Supreme Court held that separate facilities for members of different races were constitutional. Some southern states began to revise their state constitutions to disfranchise black citizens, who had been granted the right to vote following the Civil War.

Some efforts on the part of blacks and whites to protect rights presumably guaranteed in the Constitution were directed toward the President and Congress. But the main attack was in the courts, especially after the founding of the National Association for the Advancement of Colored People (NAACP) in 1909. This organization began to file lawsuits challenging the segregated system and the discriminatory voter laws that had for so long been a part of the political structure.

The legal battle to implement the Fifteenth Amendment was a protracted one. As soon as blacks were able to overcome one obstacle, another one was set up. In 1915, the Supreme Court disallowed the so-called **grandfather clause**, which stated that if an applicant for voting could not pass a stiff literacy test, he could nonetheless become a registered voter if he were a "lineal descendant" of a person who had voted prior to say, 1870 or 1860, when, obviously, most blacks were slaves and could not vote. The Supreme Court said this was a clear subterfuge whose purpose was to circumvent the Fifteenth Amendment.[3]

The South during the first half of this century was dominated by the Democratic party. The only elections that really meant anything were the primary elections. Several states therefore proceeded to restrict participation in primaries to white voters. The Democratic party of South Carolina, for example, had adopted rules under which control of the primaries in that state was vested in clubs that excluded blacks, and taking an oath professing belief in the social and educational separation of the races was prerequisite to voting in the primaries. A federal district-court judge ruled that a state or political party could not do indirectly what the Constitution had prohibited them from doing directly. In other words, even though the election laws did not mention race specifically, the laws could not be administered in such a way as to discriminate against blacks. In this case, the Democratic party of South Carolina was in fact taking over and performing

Racial violence and racial conflict have a long history in the United States. Here black Americans stage a 1917 march in New York City to protest lynching in the U.S.

a vital part of its [the State's] electoral machinery. . . . Courts of equity are neither blind nor impotent. They exercise their injunctive power to strike directly at the source of evil which they are seeking to prevent. The evil here is racial discrimination which bars Negro voters from any effective participation in the government of their state; and when it appears that this discrimination is practiced through rules of a party which controls the primary elections, these must be enjoined just as any other practice which threatens to corrupt elections or direct them from their constitutional purpose.[4]

The Supreme Court, after a series of cases spanning at least two decades, finally ruled that turning the primary-election process over to private clubs (thereby making such elections the affairs of *private*—not state—groups) could not be used to keep blacks from voting in those elections.

By the late 1940s and 1950s, it was clear that the federal courts were not going to be easily misled by state legislatures or by private organizations performing state functions. But it was also clear that the forces resisting change were not easily deterred. Local boards of registrars retained considerable leeway in administering voter-registration tests. They could be, ostensibly, color-blind, but in fact they could perform their duties in such ways as to effectively preclude the registration of significant numbers of black applicants. Literacy tests and other means were used to slow the registration process. Political scientist V. O. Key, Jr. wrote in 1949:

No matter from what direction one looks at it, the southern literacy test is a fraud and nothing more. The simple fact seems to be that the constitutionally prescribed test of ability to read and write a section of the constitution is rarely administered to whites. It is applied chiefly to Negroes and not always to them. When Negroes are tested on their ability to read and write, only in exceptional instances is the test administered fairly. Insofar as is known, no southern registration official has utilized an objective test of literacy.[5]

With the enactment of the civil-rights laws of 1957, 1960, 1964, and 1965, these obstacles were substantially overcome.

Separate facilities for whites and blacks were common in many parts of the South through the 1950s and 1960s. Left: Separate public drinking fountains clearly indicate the inferior social status assigned to blacks. Right: Rosa Parks, whose arrest in 1955 for sitting in front of white passengers on a Montgomery, Alabama, bus touched off a citywide boycott. The Montgomery bus boycott is frequently pointed to as a crucial early step in the struggle for civil rights.

Other significant victories for civil-rights advocates that were achieved in the courts included bringing the salaries of black teachers up to parity with those of white teachers. In 1948, racially restrictive covenants in real-estate transactions were forbidden. That year, too, segregation of interstate passengers was declared unconstitutional (though this ruling was not enforced until 1961), and discriminatory selection of jurors was outlawed.

The NAACP's court battle to end segregation in education had begun as early as the 1930s. As a result of these early battles, colleges, universities, and professional schools were prohibited from refusing admission to black students. The attack then centered on elementary and secondary schools, and finally, in 1954, the Supreme Court held that "separate educational facilities are inherently unequal."[6] At the time that decision was handed down, seventeen states still *required* racially segregated schools and four other states permitted legal segregation.

By the late 1950s, momentum was building for greater enforcement of civil rights and for the dismantling of *de jure* segregation in all aspects of American life. Mass direct action in the form of boycotts, sit-ins, marches, voter-registration drives, "freedom rides" (to desegregate interstate travel), and mass rallies was occurring almost weekly in some part of the country, especially in the South. In the early 1960s, the scene broadened to include many northern cities as well. A full-blown civil-rights movement swept the country. Blacks and whites combined persistent action with strong moral appeals and were able to gain significant allies in Congress and the executive branch.

The courtroom victories had provided a foundation, but in several areas new laws were needed. Racial discrimination in housing and employment, for example, was still pervasive. The Civil Rights Act of 1964 established a mechanism, the Equal Employment Opportunity Commission (EEOC), for guarding against employment discrimination. The work of the commission was not always successful; complaints of discrimination piled up, and settlement of claims sometimes took years. The Civil Rights Act of 1968 prohibited discrimination in the sale or rental of housing by real-estate brokers and mortgage lenders, but private owners selling their own homes were not subject to the law. In any case, enactment of the laws was one thing; enforcing them was another. At times, technical procedures and bureaucratic requirements made enforcement a tedious and often unrewarding process. It is sometimes difficult, if not impossible, to legally *prove* intent to discriminate on the basis of race. Some practices of employers and real-estate agents are not as blatant as earlier practices of the voter registrars of the South. And yet such proof is necessary if protection is to be obtained under the statutes.

The federal government is charged with enforcing the approximately 130 statutes and executive orders prohibiting discrimination based on race, color, sex, national origin, handicap, and social or economic status. Efforts have been made in recent years to make civil-rights enforcement more efficient. In 1978, the EEOC was given primary responsibility in the field of employment discrimination. Before 1978, responsibility had been divided among seventeen departments and agencies (see Table 1 on page 520). In 1980, the Director of the Office of Management and Budget (OMB)

FIGURE 1.
Agencies Reporting Civil-Rights Activities.

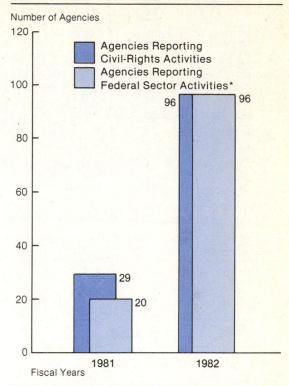

*Includes Agency Affirmative Action and Complaint Processing
Source: *Special Analyses, Budget of the United States Government, Fiscal Year 1982*, Office of Management and Budget, p. 292.

established a unit within his office to oversee the federal civil-rights effort. Agencies had to prepare budget estimates that included detailed performance and expenditure information on civil-rights activities. As shown in Figure 1, more agencies than before are now required to report expenditure activities in the civil-rights field, both externally (in relation to private companies and individuals doing business with the government) and internally (in federal-sector activities). Presumably, such reorganization will facilitate the enforcement of prohibitions against civil-rights violations.

TABLE 1.
Reorganization of Equal-Employment Authorities, 1978.

Equal-Employment Authorities		Agency	
Program	Employees covered	Before	After
Title VII	Private and public nonfederal employers and unions.	EEOC	EEOC
Equal Pay Act, Age Discrimination in Employment Act.	Private and public nonfederal employers and unions.	Labor (Wage and Hour)	
Title VII, Executive Order 11478, Equal Pay Act, Age Discrimination in Employment Act, Rehabilitation Act.	Federal government	Civil Service Commission	
Coordination of all federal equal employment programs.		EEOC	
Vietnam Veterans Readjustment Act, Rehabilitation Act.	Federal contractors	Labor (OFCCP)	
Executive Orders 11246, 11375	Federal contractors	Commerce, Defense, Energy, EPA, GSA, HHS, ED, HUD, Interior, SBA, DOT, Treasury.	Labor (OFCCP)
Title VII, Executive Order 11246, Selected federal grant programs.	Public nonfederal employers. Federal contractors and grantees.	Justice	Justice

Source: *Special Analyses, Budget of the United States Government,* Fiscal Year 1982, Office of Management and Budget. p. 294.

Voting Rights: Developments in Court and Congress

The Voting Rights Act of 1965 was passed on August 6, 1965, five months after President Lyndon B. Johnson presented it to Congress. It has been extended twice, in 1970 and 1975. It is scheduled to go out of existence in 1982, unless Congress extends it again.

One important provision of the act is Section 5, which requires certain states and counties to get permission from the Justice Department or the federal district court in Washington, D.C., before making changes in election laws or procedures. The purpose of this provision is to give the vote to minorities in those areas where minority registration historically has been particularly low. In the past, many have felt that low registration automatically reflected discriminatory election laws.

However, in 1980, the Supreme Court held in *City of Mobile* v. *Bolden*[7] that *intent* to discriminate racially must be shown before the Court would require Mobile, Alabama, to hold district elections (rather than "at-large," or citywide, elections) for the three-member city commission. Blacks had maintained that at-large elections served to dilute the effectiveness of black votes because black candidates would not be likely to be successful in those elections where they had to appeal to a majority of white voters. The *effects*, they argued, of at-large elections were racially discriminatory. The Supreme Court required proof of clear intent.

Civil-rights advocates recognized that this standard would be tough to meet. They also feared that proposed election-law changes that worked to the detriment of blacks (and in some cases Hispanics) would be more likely to be upheld because of this ruling. Such changes could include (1) altering election districts, (2) rearranging hours and places for registration, (3) changing elective offices to appointive, (4) eliminating assistance to illiterate voters, and (5) increasing the number of signatures required on a petition of candidacy.

Since 1965, there has been a steady increase in the number of proposed election-law changes submitted to the Justice Department. In that time, with 34,798 proposals submitted, objections have been raised only 815 times. With the election of President Reagan in 1980, many observers felt that the requirement to "preclear" proposed changes might disappear altogether. Noted one commentator: "The seeming retreat by the Supreme Court occurred almost simultaneously with the election of a new president [Reagan] who in 1964 had opposed the Civil Rights Act passed that year and who had expressed reservations about extending the Voting Rights Act when it comes up for renewal in 1982. At a minimum, failure to renew the Act would cut out the protection of the pre-clearance feature and allow for imposition once again of literacy tests.''[8]

Some opponents of renewal of the 1965 law argued that it should be extended throughout the country or to no part of the country. Senator Sam Nunn (D., Georgia), who voted for extension in 1975, called for modification: "I don't think there should be a presumption that states don't treat all citizens alike. Perhaps that was justified years ago. It's not justified today.''[9] The attorney general of Texas complained about a provision requiring

The issue of voting rights was given special emphasis in the march to Selma, Alabama, 1965.

bilingual ballots for every election even if there were no Hispanics in the counties. "But that doesn't matter [to federal authorities]. We still have to submit [law changes] no matter how minute they might be.''[10]

It was up to the Ninety-seventh Congress to decide the issue; as of 1981, many supporters and opponents of extension believed that a compromise of some sort would likely result.

Political Developments

The intense mass direct-action of the 1960s subsided somewhat in the 1970s, but there were substantial changes in the political arena. As a result of the

TABLE 2.
Changes in Numbers of Black Elected Officials, 1970–1980.

Year	Total Black Elected Officials		Federal		State		Regional		County	
	Number	Percent Change	Number	Percent Change	Number	Percent Change	Number	Percent Change	Number	Percent Change
1970	1469	—	10	—	169	—	-	—	92	—
1971	1860	26.6	14	40.0	202	19.5	-	—	120	30.4
1972	2264	21.7	14	0.0	210	3.9	-	—	176	46.6
1973	2621	15.7	16	14.3	240	14.3	-	—	211	19.8
1974	2991	14.2	17	6.3	239	−0.4	-	—	242	14.7
1975	3503	17.1	18	5.9	281	17.6	-	—	305	20.6
1976	3979	13.6	18	0.0	281	0.0	30	—	355	16.4
1977	4311	8.3	17	−5.6	299	6.4	33	9.1	381	7.3
1978	4503	4.5	17	0.0	299	0.0	26	−21.2	410	7.6
1979	4607	2.3	17	0.0	313	4.7	25	−3.8	398	−3.0
1980	4912	6.6	17	0.0	323	3.1	25	0.0	451	13.3

Source: Joint Center for Political Studies, Washington, D.C., 1981.

1965 Voting Rights Act, southern black voter-registration increased dramatically. Blacks were elected to school boards, city councils, mayoralties, and Congress. Elected positions at the state level increased also. Indeed, in 1973, the newly elected black mayor of Atlanta, Georgia—Maynard Jackson—stated: "Anyone looking for the civil rights movement in the streets is fooling himself. Politics is the civil rights movement of the seventies. Politics is the last nonviolent hurrah." From 1970 to 1980, the total number of black elected officials increased from 1469 to 4912. These people came to constitute a new leadership class in many black communities. Whereas leadership had earlier come mainly from ministers, civil-rights activists, and a small core of lawyers and independent business leaders, now these individuals were joined by people elected to public office. (See Table 2.)

On the national level, during the peak of the civil-rights movement in the early 1960s, the major leaders headed organizations such as the NAACP, National Urban League, Southern Chris-tian Leadership Conference, Congress of Racial Equality, National Council of Negro Women, and the Student Nonviolent Coordinating Committee. In fact, the heads of these organizations constituted a "Big Six" of black leadership that frequently met with Presidents, Congressional members, the press, and other power brokers. Now there is a Congressional black caucus composed of seventeen (one is a nonvoting delegate from Washington, D.C.) black members of Congress who hold meetings, issue reports, meet the press, consult with the President, and bargain for legislation on Capitol Hill. There are other organizations as well: Local Black Elected Officials; National Association of Black State Elected Officials; National Association of Black School Superintendents. In recent years, a number of newer black organizations have come into the spotlight: Operation PUSH, National Association of Black United Front, and an array of other black professional and locally active (and frequently more militant) groups.

Understandably, as blacks have made gains in

Municipal		Judicial/Law Enforcement		Education	
Number	Percent Change	Number	Percent Change	Number	Percent Change
623	—	213	—	362	—
785	26.0	274	28.6	465	28.5
932	18.3	263	−4.0	669	43.9
1053	12.9	334	27.0	767	14.7
1360	29.2	340	1.8	793	3.4
1573	15.7	387	13.8	939	18.4
1889	20.1	412	6.5	994	5.9
2083	10.3	447	8.5	1051	5.7
2159	3.6	454	1.6	1138	8.3
2224	3.0	486	7.0	1144	0.5
2356	5.9	526	8.2	1214	6.1

the political arena, there has been a proliferation of leadership. The base of black support for the most part is heavily embedded in the respective black communities, but public officials must represent all of their constituents—white as well as black—especially where they serve in mayoral posts and legislative districts that include more than black communities. This does not mean that they can afford to be less concerned about black constituent interests, but that such interests cannot be their exclusive concern. They are, in a word, leaders in the electoral political sphere, not ones heading up pressure groups, in which the membership is more selective and the interests more particularistic.

The new crop of black elected officials has probably been most visible at the mayoral level. Whenever a black mayor is elected, the occasion receives notice in the national media, especially when the election takes place in a rather large urban area such as New Orleans, Birmingham, Detroit, Los Angeles, Atlanta, Gary, or Newark.

Wherever black mayoral candidates have run

and been elected, the black vote has been relatively high and has gone overwhelmingly for the black candidate. This has led some observers to speculate that the election of blacks might create unreasonably high expectations on the part of black constituents—expectations of performance which could not easily be fulfilled. Political scientist William E. Nelson, Jr., has written: "The gravity of these [urban economic] problems [is] accentuated for black mayors by the expectation held by many of their black constituents that they will be miracle workers, able magically to 'make a way out of no way.'"[11] In many cases, black mayors are no more able to deliver expected benefits than white mayors. Several factors must be considered. Many cities are financially weak, with decreasing tax bases and rising service costs. Manufacturing industries are moving out of many cities where many low-skilled minorities live, taking jobs with them and leaving behind deteriorating housing conditions as well as poor schools. Mack H. Jones has suggested some additional reasons for lack of black political power in places such as Atlanta, Georgia. In spite of the existence of a black mayor and other black officials in that city, Jones believes that basic economic and political changes will be minimal because the black leadership remains tied to white economic interests. "The elected black political leadership . . . even though propelled into office by black votes, has no organizationally based support. There are no regular structures for political debate and deliberations between black officials and black rank and file. Political discussion of consequence continues to be monopolized by the white commercial and business elite and the elected officials."[12]

Some studies have shown, however, that black elected officials are able to achieve some positive results for their constituents. Edmond J. Keller has made the following observation about Gary, Indiana, where a black, Richard Hatcher, is mayor:

Maryland Congressman Parren Mitchell, head of the Congressional black caucus, talks to the press after he and other black legislators met with President-elect Jimmy Carter in Plains, Georgia, 1976. Groups such as these have gained considerable power in recent years in high political circles.

Immediately upon assuming office, Hatcher accorded the highest priority to improving the housing situation in Gary. The amount of the city's expenditure on housing skyrocketed from 4.9 percent of total expenditures in 1967 to 20.9 percent in 1968, a higher proportion than any other budgetary item. When Hatcher came to office, no public housing had been built in 10 years, and what low-rent housing there was was deteriorating due to the fact that Gary's building department had virtually ignored the city's building code. Since 1968, Gary has constructed more than 1075 units of public housing, and leased an additional 976 units for similar purposes.[13]

A study of developments in Alabama found similar results:

When they were excluded from political participation, southern blacks experienced group-targeted, legally sanctioned exclusion from equal educational and employment opportunities and were denied adequate housing, health, welfare and other benefits by local officials. Once enfranchised, the new voters sought to use their political influence to expand the supply of these goods and met considerable success in their efforts. Paired comparisons among counties with substantial black electorates support a causal relationship between growth in black political participation and policy change: the greater the change in political mobilization, the greater the change in social welfare policy. . . . The presence in the county of black elected officials increased the likelihood of program expansion, particularly in public housing and AFDC [Aid to Families of Dependent Children] *coverage.*[14]

To be sure, the election of blacks to office has been by no means a panacea. In many instances, the economic positions of black constituents and the fiscal situations of the towns and cities they inhabit have not improved; in some cases the problems have worsened. So much depends, as could be expected, on factors external to the electoral process. Change inevitably is slow and incremental. And the very slowness of the process will often clash with the desires of many who have been systematically deprived for so long and who seek—in a hurry—to achieve political and economic justice.

This is part of the tension built into America's socio-political system. Occasionally it boils up into acts of expressive violence, as happened in the 1960s and has occurred periodically since then. Pointing to progress already made does not allay such discontent, because it is felt that such injustice should not have been allowed in the first place.

This built-in tension places a stress on the political system and creates volatile, unpredictable situations, which can become aggravated when certain groups become politicized and make demands even as the economic system is finding it increasingly difficult to equitably distribute goods and services to those already politically established. It is relatively easy for the political system to accommodate new, demanding groups when the economy is expanding and healthy. But in times of economic scarcity and recession, political accommodation is very difficult.

At an earlier time—in the nineteenth century and in the early part of the twentieth century—immigrant groups coming to this country were absorbed into a growing industrial economy needing their labor (frequently unskilled) although often paying them pauper's wages. The urban political machines corralled many of these recent arrivals and helped turn them into full-fledged citizens. Though they were crowded into ghettos and their labor was frequently exploited, their children and grandchildren eventually made it up and out into a relatively comfortable working and middle-class America. Today, black Americans

and some other minority groups discussed in the next section face a much different economic situation.

America: "One Nation Indivisible"?

The United States is a heterogeneous society. It contains many different ethnic, religious, and racial groups. This has always been the case, and this fact has been an important aspect of this country's unique political experiment. American "Indians" or Native Americans were here when the European explorers and English settlers came in the fifteenth century. Indentured servants came from Europe, and black slaves from Africa. Immigrants came from Ireland and the European continent—Italy, eastern Europe, northern Europe. Various Hispanic groups from Latin America migrated northward over the years. Oriental groups came from China and Japan beginning in the nineteenth century. All these groups came for varying reasons and settled in different parts of the country. They came to seek economic opportunity and in some cases to escape political oppression or religious persecution. Most came voluntarily—except, of course, the slaves.

As these groups came into the country in ever increasing numbers, several questions arose. Would the new society be able to accommodate all these groups into one "melting pot?" Or would they come and exist side by side but basically maintain their separate neighborhoods, identities, languages, customs, and values? Would they constitute one body politic, with one common political citizenship, building one strong economic system? They were of different religions. Would they worship together, have one officially recognized church, rear their children and generally conduct their social lives in similar fashions? What distinctions, if any, would the political system make between these various groups? What distinctions, if any, should be *politically* relevant? Some groups

Top: Navajos register for tribal elections on the reservation in Arizona. Below: In 1973, members of the American Indian Movement occupied the trading post and church at Wounded Knee, South Dakota, site of a 1890 massacre of Sioux Indians by the U.S. cavalry, in an effort to draw attention to the plight of Native Americans. Here a sentry shields his face from the cold prairie winds.

heavily outnumbered others. For a time, there were quotas on the numbers of immigrants admitted from certain places. Were these quotas discriminatory on ethnic and racial grounds?

In many ways, these questions have always been paramount in American politics. They are not easy questions to answer. They involve delicate issues of race, religion, and nationality—issues charged with emotion and not easily subject to political compromise. And they relate to another area—the role of women in American society—that is very much on today's political agenda. Women, of course, do not constitute a "minority group" in numerical terms, but they comprise a group that has experienced perennial discrimination.

The first part of this chapter dealt with the status and struggle of blacks, but that group is not the only one that has felt the need to turn to government for a redress of grievances. In some ways the black struggle has been more prominent than the struggles of other groups. When one speaks of the "civil-rights movement," one normally thinks of the struggle of black Americans. But clearly the rights achieved through the courts and other institutions would normally apply to all other people "similarly situated," that is, discriminated against.

Native Americans. There are approximately one million "American Indians" in the United States. (The term *Indians* is a misnomer. When European explorers first arrived in North America, thinking they had reached India by sailing west, they referred to the inhabitants as Indians. We shall refer to them as Native Americans.) The arrival of the Europeans eventually led to a series of wars, the intermittent signing of a number of treaties, and a final agreement. Reservations were set aside for those Native Americans who preferred (or in some instances were forced) to live apart from the more recent European arrivals. They were granted

American citizenship in 1924. The Bureau of Indian Affairs in the Department of Interior (formerly in the Department of War) is the governmental agency that deals with Native Americans.

The socio-economic conditions of members of this group are by almost all criteria low, and in recent years many Native Americans have begun to exert pressure in efforts to improve their status. Some Native Americans have gone to court to reclaim or to receive compensation for lands taken from them by broken treaties or by outright fraud. In 1980, the Supreme Court ruled that the federal government had to pay $105 million to eight tribes of Sioux Indians in South Dakota. The government admitted that land had been illegally taken in the 1870s, but it argued that only $17.5 million (the value of the land in 1877 when the land was seized) was owed. The Court held that the additional amount was for interest at five percent annually for 103 years. This, according to the Court, would be "just compensation" under the language of the Fifth Amendment.[15] At times, Native American groups organize mass protests or even seize property, such as government buildings and land, in their efforts to dramatize their plight. As with blacks, there are several different leadership groups, some more oriented to conventional interest-group tactics than others.

Chicanos. The United States has had an uneven relationship with its neighbors to the South, especially Mexico. Through war and treaty, large portions of what is now central and western United States were acquired from Mexico. Mexican-Americans ("Chicanos" is the name preferred by many) constitute a sizeable portion of the population in the states of Texas, California, New Mexico, Arizona, and Colorado. There are approximately seven million Chicanos in this country.

Chicanos have always suffered from discrimination and poor living conditions, and they, too,

TABLE 3.
Persons Below Poverty Level, by Age, Region, Race, and Spanish Origin, 1978.

Age and Region	Number Below Poverty Level (in thousands)				Percent Below Poverty Level			
	All races	White	Black	Spanish origin	All races	White	Black	Spanish origin
Total	**24,497**	**16,259**	**7,625**	**2,607**	**11.4**	**8.7**	**30.6**	**21.6**
Under 14 years	7,583	4,468	2,898	1,115	16.5	11.7	42.0	27.7
14 to 21 years	4,384	2,710	1,563	480	13.4	9.8	35.4	23.9
22 to 44 years	5,794	4,004	1,596	674	8.2	6.6	20.9	17.0
45 to 64 years	3,502	2,547	905	213	8.1	6.6	22.3	13.9
65 years and over	3,233	2,530	662	125	13.9	12.1	33.9	23.1
Northeast	5,050	3,547	1,377	730	10.4	8.2	29.1	32.3
North Central	5,192	3,826	1,256	195	9.1	7.4	24.8	17.4
South	10,255	5,737	4,429	847	14.7	10.2	34.1	21.9
West	4,000	3,148	560	834	10.0	8.9	26.1	17.3

Source: *Statistical Abstract of the United States 1980*, United States Department of Commerce, Bureau of the Census, p. 466.

have evidenced a growing political militancy ("Brown Power") over the last two decades. Hampered by a high proportion of unskilled workers and by the language barrier, they have been vulnerable to those who would exploit them as a source of cheap labor, especially as migrant farm workers. The migrant workers account for a large number of "undocumented aliens," or people who cross the border without proper immigration credentials in order to work farms during the agricultural season.

For years Cesar Chavez, a Chicano, has been a prominent figure in union organizing, especially in the vegetable-growing fields of California.

In some southwestern states, a fairly successful political movement has developed among Chicanos. *La Raza Unida*—the United People—has run successful local, county, and statewide political campaigns, electing their own candidates to office and promoting the election of people favorable to Mexican-American constituency.

Hispanics. American citizens with a Spanish cultural background other than Mexican also have been in the United States for many decades. Most of these, approximately two million, come from the island of Puerto Rico, which has been an American "commonwealth" since 1952. "Commonwealth" status is midway between colony status and outright statehood. From the Spanish-American War in 1898 to 1952, Puerto Rico was, in fact, an American colony.

Most Puerto Ricans live in northeastern cities, especially New York City, with some in midwestern cities. Like Chicanos, Puerto Ricans generally suffer from poverty, language barriers, and discrimination. And like blacks, they are struggling to build political influence, hampered by relatively low levels of voter participation even in places such as New York, where they constitute more than ten percent of that city's population.

For many years, United States officials dealt with mainland Puerto Ricans through the Office of the Commonwealth, but that relationship has been changing as various local Puerto Rican communities have begun developing indigenous political leadership to represent their interests.[16]

Likewise, Puerto Ricans have taken note of the tactics of blacks in the civil-rights movement and have attempted, in some instances, to emulate the tactics of that group. The demands have not been very different from those made by other subordinated groups: better schools, decent housing, more employment opportunities, better health care.

The Struggle for Women's Liberation

In 1976 Americans all over the country celebrated the two hundredth anniversary of their country's declaration of independence. Exhibitions were held. There were parades, plays, conferences on the meaning of liberty, sailboat regattas, and of course speeches. One of the bicentennial speakers, a woman who was then a federal appeals-court judge, said: ''We have tended to forget that in 1776 liberty and equality were inalienable rights for white men only. . . . The Revolution freed white American men from white English men. . . . A bicentennial celebration of women's equality in law and in fact cannot be scheduled because the inaugural date has not arrived.''[17]

From the earliest years of nationhood, women occupied a low social position. They were not permitted to attend college; they could not vote; they were not allowed to perform most jobs. Their legal rights to own property, enter professions, sue in court, and engage in economic activities were severely restricted. There was a pervasive view that woman's place was in the home, rearing children and caring for the family. Women were themselves to be cared for by their menfolk. One Supreme Court Justice, Joseph P. Bradley, writing in 1873, held that ''the natural and proper timidity and delicacy which belongs to the female sex

Cesar Chavez, head of the United Farm Workers.

evidently unfits it for many of the occupations of civil life. . . . The paramount destiny and mission of a woman are to fulfill the noble and benign offices of wife and mother. This is the law of the Creator.''[18]

To say the least, some women, before and since, did not agree. As members of the Quaker Society of Friends, Sara and Angeline Grimke in the 1830s shocked and angered many people by publicly speaking out against slavery and the subordination of women.

In 1848 at a convention in Seneca Falls, New York, Lucretia Mott and Elizabeth Stanton took the lead in issuing a Declaration of Sentiments, which began by paraphrasing the Declaration of Independence: ''We hold these truths to be self-evident: that all men and women are created equal.''

When the country went to war in the 1860s and women were needed in the labor force, they left their homes and went to work. But only for the

Two pioneers in the struggle for women's rights, Susan B. Anthony (standing) and Elizabeth Cady Stanton, in a photograph taken circa 1900.

duration. With the passage of the Fourteenth and Fifteenth Amendments following the Civil War, Susan B. Anthony and others struggled unsuccessfully to get women included under the constitutionally guaranteed protections. Finally, after decades of protests, the Nineteenth Amendment was ratified (1920) extending the right to vote to women.

In many ways the struggles of the women's liberation movement in the 1960s, '70s, and '80s have been similar to the struggles of earlier women's movements, especially in their battles to overcome economic deprivation. In recent years women have gone to court to protest against gender discrimination in hiring, credit transactions, marital relations, and a host of other matters. In 1961 President Kennedy appointed a Commission on the Status of Women, chaired by Eleanor Roosevelt. The commission's report in 1963 presented documented evidence of economic and political discrimination against women. Influenced in part by the report Congress passed the Equal Pay Act in 1963. The Civil Rights Act of 1964 extended protection against employment discrimination to women.

In several specific areas, discriminatory economic practices worked strongly against women. Many banks and credit agencies would not lend money to wives, even though employed, without the cosignatures of their husbands. Many employers preferred not to hire married women for fear that they would be more attentive to their families than to their jobs or that they would disrupt their employment for reasons of pregnancy. Whether these attitudes were justified or not, the fact is that many potential women employees never got a chance to enter the labor force and prove otherwise.

While there are now laws on the books prohibiting gender discrimination, many people feel that a

TABLE 4.
Weekly Earnings of Male and Female Salaried Workers, 1970—1978.

	Median Earnings (1978 dollars)*					
	1970	1973	1975	1976	1977	1978
All Workers	**$130**	**$159**	**$185**	**$197**	**$212**	**$227**
Male	151	188	221	234	253	272
16–24 years old	112	136	149	159	168	185
25 years and over	160	203	235	251	273	294
White	157	193	225	239	259	279
Black and other	113	149	173	187	201	218
Female	94	116	137	145	156	166
16–24 years old	88	103	117	125	133	142
25 years and over	96	121	146	154	165	175
White	95	117	138	147	157	167
Black and other	81	107	130	138	147	158

*Figures are for May and represent medians of usual weekly earnings.
Source: *Statistical Abstract of the United States 1979*, Department of Commerce, Bureau of the Census, p. 420.

constitutional amendment is needed to provide a stronger base of support for equality for women. The country is undoubtedly undergoing major changes in its perceptions of sex roles. More and more women are working outside the home. Many women are working full-time *and* caring for families. A Carnegie Corporation report stated: "What is new in the twentieth century . . . is the increasing proportion of women working away from their homes. In 1920, 20 percent of all women 16 years and over were in the work force. Their labor force participation has risen steadily since then, accelerating during the 1960s and reaching 43 percent in 1970. By the end of 1976, nearly half of all women were working or looking for work, making up approximately 41 percent of the labor force."[17] In 1972, Congress passed the Equal Rights Amendment (ERA) and submitted it to the states for ratification. Thirty-eight states must approve it before it can become the Twenty-seventh Amendment to the Constitution. Within ninety days, nineteen states ratified it, but in 1981 the amendment was still three short of the necessary thirty-eight for ratification.

Opponents of the amendment base their opposition on several grounds. They argue that it is not needed, because women are already protected under several pieces of civil-rights legislation. They feel that the position of women would, in fact, be threatened because of possible setbacks in such matters as alimony, child custody, and so forth. Some opponents fear that the ERA would damage the institutions of marriage and the family. And some envision an avalanche of court suits challenging the constitutionality of such things as "Father's Night" at Little League baseball games, or even the separate existences of the Boy Scouts and Girl Scouts.

Others agree with Shirley Hufstedler, the speaker quoted at the beginning of this section, who holds that

Equality within the meaning of the equal protection clause of the Fourteenth Amendment, or

within the meaning of the Twenty-Seventh Amendment [the proposed ERA], does not [imply] equal treatment of unequals. At the minimum, it means that the law shall not treat differently persons who are similarly situated. In the context of the Equal Rights Amendment, equality means that women cannot be treated more or less advantageously than men solely because of their sex. . . .

After 200 years of sound and fury, of accommodation and acrimony about the place of women in our society, only one reason emerges requiring the adoption of the Equal Rights Amendment: The reason is that it is just.[20]

Reverse Discrimination or Reversal of Discrimination?

On June 4, 1965, President Lyndon B. Johnson delivered the commencement address at Howard University in Washington, D.C. He said:

You do not take a person who, for years, has been hobbled by chains and liberate him, bring him up to the starting line of a race and then say, "You are free to compete with all the others," and still justly believe that you have been completely fair.

Thus it is not enough just to open the gates of opportunity. All our citizens must have the ability to walk through those gates.

This is the next and the more profound stage of the battle for civil rights. We seek not just legal equity but human ability, not just equality as a right and a theory but equality as a fact and equality as a result.[21]

Some observers at the time recognized that President Johnson was moving the racial struggle from its traditional base of concern with ending de jure segregation and discrimination toward other areas of concern—areas requiring the introduction of special, nonjudicial remedies. One writer noted that "what the President was saying . . . was that society must pay indemnity for the damage it had done to one of its minorities."[22]

President Kennedy had first used the term **affirmative action** in an executive order (10925) in 1961. In the early to mid-1960s, the terms normally used to refer to this policy of active recruitment of women and minorities were "preferential treatment," "compensatory programs," "special efforts," and "indemnification." Whatever the terms used, however, it was clear that many people were opposed to their explicit and implicit meanings. The consensus that had developed for traditional civil-rights goals (namely, ending *de jure* segregation) did not exist for the goals of this "next and more profound stage," or at least for the affirmative-action methods likely to be used in achieving them.

As Doris Kearns has observed:

In the middle sixties the civil rights movement shifted from the rural South to the Northern slums, from lunch counters and laws to employment, broken homes, and disease. With this shift, the earlier consensus on ends and means split apart; in 1964 only 34 percent of the American people believed that Negroes were trying to move too fast; by 1966 the percentage had increased to 85. Nearly one-third of the whites interviewed said they thought differently about Negroes now than before—they felt less regard and respect; the Negroes were demanding too much, going too far. This was not, the media said, a temporary downturn. It was, instead, "the end of the civil rights era."[23]

An increasing number of traditional civil-rights supporters were beginning to reject the demand for "special consideration." The managing editor of *Christian Century* argued that

Compensation for Negroes is a subtle but pernicious form of racism. It requires that men be dealt with by society on the basis of race and color rather than on the basis of their humanity. It would therefore as a public policy legalize, deepen, and perpetuate the abominable racial cleavage which has ostracized and crippled the American Negro.[24]

Many felt that favoring minorities over whites would unfairly penalize whites for the sins of their forefathers. It would end up discriminating against whites, causing **reverse discrimination**. As Kyle Haselden put it: "It leaves with the descendants of the exploiters a guilt they cannot cancel and the descendants of the exploited a debt they cannot collect."[25]

These arguments, pro and con, form the basis of much of the discussion concerning the statutes, executive orders, guidelines, and court decisions that have laid the foundation for today's affirmative-action programs. Should *special* effort be made to hire women, blacks, Chicanos, Hispanics? If so, should a fixed minimum number be hired? If a specific number of seats in an entering medical school class is set aside for designated minorities, does this constitute reverse discrimination against white student applicants (*Regents of the University of California* v. *Bakke*, 1978)?[26] Can private companies in conjunction with labor unions voluntarily set up special employment and promotion programs with quotas designed to favor particular minority groups (*Kaiser Aluminum Co.* v. *Weber*, 1979)?[27]

In the *Bakke* case, the Supreme Court ruled that a state university could take race into account as one of several factors (along with academic qualifications, region, outside interests, age, etc.) in determining admission policies for its medical school. But the university could not set aside a specific number of positions (sixteen out of a hundred in the *Bakke* case) for a designated group. This constituted a quota and was disallowed as a violation of the Civil Rights Act of 1964. In the

The Supreme Court's Bakke decision stirred strong feelings on both sides of the issue. Here people opposed to Bakke's claim of "reverse discrimination" demonstrate outside the Supreme Court building.

Weber case, the Supreme Court permitted a voluntary-employment quota system entered into between the company and the union.

In the absence of any final, definitive ruling on the affirmative-action/quotas issue,[28] a number of executive orders, agency guidelines, court decisions, and some voluntarily established programs have moved increasingly toward defining "overt" (specific) criteria for measuring achievement of goals. In his book, *Affirmative Discrimination*, social scientist Nathan Glazer laments this development and suggests that it has created a catch-22 situation for employers.[29] Federal agencies insist that they are not requiring quotas and proportional hiring, while all the time such solutions are really the only way employers and others can reasonably satisfy the demands of the Equal Employment Opportunity Commission (EEOC) and the Office of Contract Compliance (in the Department of Labor). Glazer concludes:

"Affirmative action" originally meant that one should not only not discriminate, but inform people one did not discriminate; not only treat those who applied for jobs without discrimination, but seek out those who might not apply. This is what it apparently meant when first used in executive orders. In the Civil Rights Act of 1964, it was used to mean something else—the remedies a court could impose when some employer was found guilty of discrimination, and they could be severe. The new concept of "affirmative action" that has since emerged and has been enforced with ever greater vigor combines both elements: It assumes that everyone is guilty of discrimination; it then imposes on every employer the remedies which in the Civil Rights Act of 1964 could only be imposed on those guilty of discrimination.[30]

In 1968 the Department of Labor required "written affirmative-action compliance" statements from every major contractor and subcontractor with more than fifty employees and a contract of $50,000 or more with the department. These statements had to specify the steps to be taken, and in some circumstances establish a timetable, to guarantee equal-employment opportunity for members of minority groups. Other agency guidelines talked in terms of "increasing materially the utilization of minorities and women."

Court decisions have held that more is required than simply *not* consciously pursuing discriminatory practices. In *Griggs* v. *Duke Power Company*, the Supreme Court ruled that "good intent . . . does not redeem employment procedures or testing mechanisms that operate as 'built-in headwinds' for minority groups and are unrelated to measuring job capability."[31] In another case, *Albermarle Paper Company* v. *Moody*, the Court held that even if tests are job-related, if alternative nondiscriminatory means can be used to accomplish the employer's goal of a good work force, then those other means should be used.[32]

Many advocates of affirmative action go to great lengths to avoid calling for quotas, but do support (in line with certain court rulings) interim, fixed numbers to guide policy achievement. The U.S. Civil Rights Commission concluded:

Typically, a court may require that a specified percentage of all new hires be members of the minority group discriminated against until a specific goal of minority participation in the work force is reached. . . . Once the goal of minority participation is achieved, past discrimination may be deemed to have been remedied and the employer or union is no longer subject to fixed hiring requirements.[33]

In an editorial in 1979 discussing the *Weber* case, the *Wall Street Journal* stated:

It is no mystery why this system has developed its tough, punitive, numbers-oriented character. Before the civil rights legislation of the 1960s, normal processes of group accommodations were manifestly not working for black Americans. That is why the civil rights movement was forced to rely so heavily on the courts, the law, national opinion and federal action.[34]

Thus, we find pressure for more specific, *quota-like* remedies (and, in some instances, quotas *per se*). Anything less, some civil-rights advocates argue, will not achieve the desired results. The courts and the executive agencies, they feel, are the sources to turn to. Others, opposed to quotas, look to Congress. Nathan Glazer writes:

Those of us who oppose rigid goals and quotas as a travesty of what America is supposed to be and wishes to be have nothing to hope for from the Carter administration and its bureaucratic appointees. But there is still the Congress, still responsive to public opinion, and capable of being troubled by the use of racial and ethnic categories to govern state action.

It is there in the Congress, that we should seek for a sharper and clearer statement, spelled out so that administrators and courts will have no alternative but to follow it, that no American may be discriminated against on grounds of race and ethnicity.[35]

These views highlight not only different positions on what policy should be, but differences concerning which institution should take the lead in making that policy. The Glazer view sees some affirmative-action policies as reverse discrimination, with white American males as the chief victims. Others see these policies as necessary efforts to reverse the discrimination practiced over so many years. They take the view expressed in President Johnson's Howard University speech. Each group will turn to the political institution most receptive to its own view.

This has always been the case in American governance and policymaking. A group will work through the institution that seems most likely to produce the desired results. Thus, for years, blacks turned to the courts because the other branches were not receptive to their needs. Later, of course, the other two branches became more amenable to civil-rights demands.

In all cases, of course, no definite results are guaranteed, and few results are ever ultimately final. Such is the nature of the American political system; it is always unpredictable. We noted that Nathan Glazer felt Congress would be likely to deny the use of quotas, yet in 1977 that body did pass a law (Public Works Employment Act) allowing ten percent of government-contract funds to be "set aside" for minority-owned businesses. In July 1980, the Supreme Court upheld the law as constitutional.[36] Whether subsequent Congresses will be inclined to so legislate and future courts to so rule remains to be seen.

Summary

1. During the first half of the twentieth century, the Supreme Court was instrumental in dismantling the legal system of racial segregation and in overcoming various forms of voter discrimination in the South. The Fourteenth and Fifteenth Amendments were the constitutional sources for the rulings.

2. Unquestionably, the most dramatic achievements of black Americans have been in increasing the numbers of new voters and black elected officials. Literally millions of blacks have been added to the electorate since the 1960s, and there has been a twenty-fold increase in the number of blacks holding public office, mostly in the South. These changes have stemmed largely from the civil-rights legislation of the 1960s, and they have brought a new leadership class into existence. Some evidence suggests that such changes have, in fact, made a difference in the kinds of benefits received by the newly politicized group.

3. The civil-rights movement has served as a catalyst for political activism among other subordinated groups in the society (especially Native Americans, Chicanos, Hispanics, and women). These groups have mobilized and have begun to make demands for improvement of their economic and political status. The struggle for ratification of the Equal Rights Amendment is a major goal of women's liberation groups.

4. Affirmative-action programs and quotas have stirred debate in America over efforts to ensure "equality of results" rather than simply "equality of opportunities." Some argue that these approaches constitute discrimination in reverse; others believe they are legitimate means of overcoming the effects of deliberate past discrimination. The earlier goals of the civil-rights movement (against *legal* segregation) having been achieved, the ultimate result of this new struggle will depend in large measure on the economic resources available in the society.

Notes

1. *Civil Rights Cases*, 109 U.S. 3 (1883).
2. *Plessy* v. *Ferguson*, 163 U.S. 537 (1896).
3. *Guinn* v. *U.S.* 347 (1915).
4. 174 Fed. 2d. at 394.
5. V. O. Key, Jr., *Southern Politics* (New York: Knopf, 1949), p. 576.
6. *Brown* v. *Board of Education*, 347 U.S. 483 (1954).
7. 446 U.S. 55 (1980).
8. Jack Bass, "Election Laws and Their Manipulation to Exclude Minority Voters," unpublished paper presented at Rockefeller Foundation Conference on Voting Rights, New York, April 23, 1981, p. 32.
9. *Congressional Quarterly Weekly Report*, Vol. 39, No. 15 (April 11, 1981), p. 636.
10. Ibid.

11. William E. Nelson, Jr., "Black Mayors as Urban Managers," *The Annals of the American Academy of Political and Social Science*, Vol. 439 (September 1978), 57. See also Lenneal J. Henderson, "Administrative Advocacy and Black Urban Administrators," *Annals*, Vol. 439 (September 1978), 68–79; Michael Preston, "Limitations of Black Urban Power: The Case of Black Mayors," in Louis H. Massoti and Robert L. Lineberry, eds., *The New Urban Politics* (Cambridge, Mass.: Ballinger, 1976).

12. Mack H. Jones, "Black Political Empowerment in Atlanta," *The Annals of the American Academy of Political and Social Science*, Vol. 439 (September 1978), 117.

13. Edmond J. Keller, "The Impact of Black Mayors on Urban Policy," *Annals*, Vol. 439 (September 1978), 48.

14. M. Elizabeth Sanders, "New Voters and New Policy Priorities in the Deep South: A Decade of Political Change in Alabama," unpublished paper presented at the annual meeting of the American Political Science Association, Washington, D.C., August 1979.

15. *United States* v. *Sioux Nation of Indians*, 65 L. Ed. 2d. 844 (1980).

16. James Jennings, *Puerto Rican Politics in New York City* (Washington, D.C.: University Press of America, 1977).

17. Shirley M. Hufstedler, *Women and the Law* (New York: Aspen Institute for Humanistic Studies, 1977), p. 1.

18. *Bradwell* v. *Illinois*, 83 U.S. 130 (1873).

19. Alan Pifer, *Women Working: Toward a New Society* (New York: Carnegie Corporation of New York, 1976), pp. 3–4.

20. Hufstedler, *Women and the Law*, p. 14.

21. Lyndon B. Johnson, commencement address delivered at Howard University, Washington, D.C., June 4, 1965.

22. John Herbers, *The Lost Priority: What Happened to the Civil Rights Movement?* (New York: Funk & Wagnalls, 1970), p. 43.

23. Doris Kearns, *Lyndon Johnson and the American Dream* (New York: Harper & Row, 1976), p. 304.

24. Kyle Haselden, "Should There Be Compensation for Negroes? No," *New York Times Magazine*, October 6, 1963, p. 43.

25. Ibid.

26. 438 U.S. 265 (1978).

27. 443 U.S. 193 (1979).

28. See *Bakke, Weber, and Affirmative Action* (Working Papers, The Rockefeller Foundation, December 1979).

29. Nathan Glazer, *Affirmative Discrimination* (New York: Basic Books, 1975).

30. Ibid., p. 58.

31. 401 U.S. 424 (1971).

32. 422 U.S. 405 (1973).

33. *Statement on Affirmative Action*, The United States Commission on Civil Rights, Clearinghouse Publication 54 (Washington, D.C.: Government Printing Office, October 1977), p. 7.

34. *Wall Street Journal*, April 6, 1979, p. 10.

35. Nathan Glazer, "Why Bakke Won't End Reverse Discrimination," *Commentary*, Vol. 66, No. 3 (September 1978), p. 41.

36. *Fullilove* v. *Klutznick*, 65 L. Ed. 2d. 902 (1980).

Economic
Policies and
Political Processes

Chapter

15

The Chrysler Corporation, headquartered in Detroit, Michigan, is the third largest producer of automobiles in the country. In 1979, Mr. Lee Iacocca became the head of that company and stated: "I came to run an auto show. I don't want to do it in Washington. I'd rather do it in Detroit."[1] Although this seemed to be a reasonable expectation, matters were not that simple. The Chrysler Corporation was in serious financial trouble and had to ask the federal government for help.

"Lee isn't a government handout type," one company source said. "He is more inclined to want Chrysler to do it on its own." Iacocca himself stated that going to the government for money "gets you in a bureaucratic and political tangle, and I don't like it. That should be stronger. I detest it." But, detest it or not, he believed that the private auto company had no choice. He said that Chrysler's troubles "are more than we're able to bear. . . . Hell, I don't care what form [the aid] takes now. I'm very innovative."[2] Thus, Iacocca and the Chrysler Corporation did indeed become involved in a "political tangle"—one that involved both the executive and Congressional branches. The President and the secretary of treasury were asked to support some form of government aid to the private company. The Senate Banking Committee (then chaired by Senator William Proxmire of Wisconsin) was intimately involved.

The financial plight of the Chrysler Corporation illustrates the complexity of the free-enterprise versus government-intervention debate. Should the federal government step in and help a major private industry? If so, would such help ultimately harm the free-enterprise system? Should a private company be left to pull itself out of the financial doldrums by its own efforts? What would be the economic consequences—in the Chrysler case, in terms of thousands of jobs and the price of automobiles—if such private efforts were not enough? What about the argument that government intervention (such as regulations that incur greater production costs) was part of the problem in the first place?

Free Enterprise Versus Government Intervention

Basically, Americans have always preferred a capitalist economy, with prices and profits determined by competition and the free market, and with a minimum amount of control and involvement from the public sector. Private ownership of the major means of production is preferred. Although a capitalist orientation has strongly persisted, it has been modified in several areas of the country's economic life, as we shall see later in this chapter and in the following chapter on social welfare. This development has generated a major debate within the private business community itself.

Japanese cars await shipment to the United States. Government-imposed import quotas and taxes on foreign cars protect the American auto industry from the stiff competition presented by these popular foreign imports.

A private interest group, the Council for a Competitive Economy, took a full-page ad in *The Wall Street Journal* raising the question: "Are America's businessmen cutting their own throats?"[3] The ad cited, by name, business leaders and corporations who had asked for specific government regulations, protective tariffs, and restrictions on their competitors. "They *think* they're gaining special advantages for their firms by approving and encouraging government intervention in the economy. But they're deluding themselves. They are selling out their futures for a few short-term benefits. . . . Today, America's free, competitive economy is in jeopardy. And a major cause of the problem is that many businessmen actually prefer not to operate in a free market. They may pay lip service to free enterprise. But at the same time, they demand tariffs, subsidies, licensing or some other form of political protection from the rigors of competition."[4]

Other free-enterprise advocates see the problem differently. A vice-president of the Chrysler Corporation hastened to remind his business colleagues that a greater danger lay in not helping a company like Chrysler. He argued that "government has taxed the lower income earner [Chrysler in relation to the larger auto makers] a higher per unit rate than the higher income earner. . . . Government product regulation [emissions, fuel-economy, and auto-safety requirements] of the automobile industry has placed a greater proportional burden on Chrysler than on its larger competitors." In other words, although all auto makers were required to meet the same standards, Chrysler argued that the smaller companies were less able to absorb the increased costs than the larger companies. The Chrysler official then added: "I find no ethical base to a position that admits to unequal treatment by government of its citizens, but then condemns any steps by government to compensate for that unequal treatment. If this is the position of the defenders of free enterprise, then the battle will surely be lost to those who would regulate our lives and leave us completely dependent on government for its favors. It places no check on them, because it relieves them of all economic responsibility for their actions."[5]

Senator Proxmire, another free-enterprise advocate, was not impressed by this argument placing blame on government regulation. He wrote: "No one has seriously suggested that the government should resolve the inequality among American companies by paying the difference in cost to outfits bearing a higher relative burden. It would require billions upon billions of dollars a year."[6] Thus, the advocates of the free-enterprise system differ in their interpretation of the impact of government involvement, but they agree on limiting such involvement.

A different view stresses a much more forceful, systematic role for the government in the economy of the nation. This role generally is described as one of *planning*. The government should constitute a public planning authority; it should coordinate the activities of major industries: setting wage, price, and profit levels; determining amounts of production; and guaranteeing its citizens an annual income. John Kenneth Galbraith is a prominent exponent of this view.[7] He advocates turning certain industries—such as the major defense contractors—into public corporations, since, in his view, they already have ceased to be private. He says:

I . . . argue that we would reduce and make much more visible the power of some parts of the planning system by taking firms into full public ownership. A particular case here is the big weapons firms. Working capital is supplied by the government; a large fraction of their fixed capital is supplied by the government; their business comes from the government. Yet the fiction is maintained that they are private firms. This fiction allows them to lobby, encourage lobbying by unions, promote political contributions and candidates and otherwise engage in activities that would be forbidden to full public firms. . . . I suppose the day will come when the really mature corporation will be recognized for what it is—a public corporation.[8]

Professor Galbraith's views are socialist, but he recognizes that such a term is not very respected in American politics. He feels, however, that socialism in fact, even if not in name, is probably inevitable.

The action may be disguised by the semantics. It will be some time before we get around to talking about planning. It will be longer, no doubt, before we get around to using so obscene a word as socialism. I sometimes use the phrase "social action," which is more benign.[9]

Professor Robert Lekachman is another economist who believes in some form of national public-planning system. He advocates a full-employment economy, saying that it is "necessarily egalitarian."[10]

If conservatives and radicals both fear that their enemies will control the planning decisions, it is tempting to conclude that both groups are wrong and that the community at large will have rather more influence on political choices than they do on the decisions taken by General Motors and its few peers. Democratic planning holds the promise of increased public participation in the making of allocative choices and clarification of the values which ought to shape these choices.[11]

Proponents of free enterprise, such as those mentioned above in connection with the Chrysler crisis, feel that the advocates of a planned, "socialist" economy call for far too much government intervention, which could lead to the destruction of the free-enterprise system. Such intervention, some observers argue, should not be permitted even to prevent an economic depression (in the 1930s the government intervened for that very reason). One political scientist, Roger D. Masters, warns that the cost of intervention outweighs the benefits. He argues that government intervention tends to make the country falsely secure. "To avoid depression, our politicians increasingly resort to centralized administrative rules. Could the cost (the loss of freedom) be worth the benefit (material comfort)? Continuous prosperity and economic security has the same drawback as spoiling a child: It becomes harder and harder to say no without facing a tantrum."[12] Professor Masters adds:

A depression can be healthy because it forces businessmen to compete. Although our country is supposedly based on free enterprise, the advantages of weeding out inefficiency are hardly mentioned anymore. Both labor and manage-

Wall Street, October 27, 1929, the day the stock market crashed, as throngs of stunned investors filled the streets. The New York Stock Exchange Building is on the right.

ment seem to prefer the cozy comforts of governmental intervention.[13]

The Depression and the New Deal of the 1930s was the turning point in American politics on the subject of government intervention. Prior to then, few expected (or wanted) the federal government to play a role in the nation's economy. But with the Crash of 1929, followed by soaring unemployment rates, business failures, mortgage foreclosures, and deflation, demands from all sectors were made for government action. Leonard Silk summed up the situation when he wrote: "What the country was demanding was no less than a new role for the government that would safeguard the economic well-being of the American people."[14] Little was known about how to do that and still keep within the boundaries of a market-oriented, capitalist system. Should taxes be cut or increased? Should the budget be balanced or should there be deficit spending? Should the government spend more of its own resources? Should the government regulate the stock market, insure home mortgages, lend money to businesses on the brink of bankruptcy, provide assistance for the elderly and for dependent children? All these issues posed new prob-

lems for the American people and politicians. And President Herbert Hoover frankly admitted: "We had to pioneer a new field. There was little economic knowledge to guide us."[15]

Fiscal Policy: The Budget and Taxes

The most concrete (and probably the most tedious and difficult) way to learn about the economic stance of a particular administration and Congress is to look at the annual budget: how it was first presented by the President, and how it was finally passed by Congress.

The annual budget sets forth the President's proposals for spending by the government and for taxing the people. It also estimates how much all proposals will cost. It is furthermore a statement of the President's economic and political views. It tells how involved the President wants the government to be in every facet of American life: whether more or less money should be spent on military defense; whether more or less should be provided for urban development, and so forth. The budget will indicate whether taxes should or should not be increased; it will suggest the President's general approach to problems such as inflation, unemployment, and other serious economic problems.

The President's budget becomes, then, the **fiscal policy** of the administration. It is submitted to Congress, and when it is passed, it becomes, for that year, the fiscal policy of the country.

As we have seen, there are different theories about what role the government should play in the economy and what the budget should do. One view, *fiscal orthodoxy* (a term used by James Sundquist in his book, *Politics and Policy*),[16] holds that inflation is more serious to the long-term health of the economy than anything else— including unemployment and recession. One way to curb inflation, it is argued, is to reduce government spending and to avoid deficit spending. **Deficit spending** occurs when the government (or anyone, really) spends more than it takes in or has to spend. This means that the government runs a deficit and must borrow money, thus increasing its debt. The fiscal-orthodox position favors balanced budgets and believes that taxes should not be decreased if deficit spending would result. In addition, this view holds that government fiscal policy should not be a means of managing, regulating, or influencing the economy. That is, taxes should be levied only for raising the funds needed to pay the government's bills. Taxes should not be increased or decreased in order to stimulate or slow down the economy.

The onetime powerful chairperson of the House Ways and Means Committee, Wilbur Mills, once stated: "People think of me as a conservative and I guess I am. In the first place I believe that the function of taxation is to raise revenues. That may sound obvious; but I say it to make clear that I don't go along with economists who think of taxation as an instrument for stimulating, braking, or otherwise manipulating the economy."[17] President Ronald Reagan voiced similar sentiments in a speech to Congress early in his administration: "The taxing power . . . must not be used to regulate the economy or bring about social change."[18]

"The Economists"

This position differs from that held by those economists who follow the theories of a British economist, John Maynard Keynes. Keynes advocated a more active role by the government in economic matters through fiscal policies. He believed it was proper for the government to use its budgetary authority to stimulate the economy, if necessary. Thus, in times of high unemployment, the government should spend more money to create jobs; to combat inflation, the government should take steps through its taxing power to reduce consumer spending. The more people have to pay in taxes, the less they have to spend for consumer goods. To the *fiscal activist,* or *Keynesian*, deficit spending and unbalanced budgets were not necessarily evils to be avoided at all costs. Instead, it is the government's proper duty, under certain circumstances, to impose controls on wages and prices.

In our lifetime, we have seen federal spending increase enormously. In 1964, when many present college students were born, the federal government spent $118.6 billion (see Table 1). The budget for 1982 approached $695.3 billion. Thus, in eighteen years, the budget increased by almost $577 billion. This figure does not account for inflation during that time, which has been considerable and has lessened the value of the dollar. In other words, $695 billion in 1982 is not the same as $695 billion in 1964. But even when inflation is taken into account, as Figure 1 shows, federal-budget expenditures (outlays) have increased substantially. This figure also shows that the upward trend began long before the 1960s, with a dramatic increase in the years just after World War II. The American people clearly wanted their government to be more economically active. Fiscal activism was not something forced on a reluctant society. As Professor Donald Ogilvie noted about the postwar era: "For the first time, Americans delegated economic management to the federal government."[19]

TABLE 1.
Federal Budget Outlays, 1956–1977.
(in billions of dollars)

Fiscal Year	Total Outlays	Fiscal Year	Total Outlays
1956	70.5	1968	178.8
1957	76.7	1969	184.5
1958	82.6	1970	196.6
1959	92.1	1971	211.4
1960	92.2	1972	232.0
1961	97.8	1973	247.1
1962	106.8	1974	269.6
1963	111.3	1975	326.1
1964	118.6	1976	366.5
1965	118.4	TQ[a]	94.7
1966	134.7	1977	401.9
1967	158.3		

[a]This was the three-month transition period from July 1, 1976, through September 30, 1976, which resulted from changing the beginning of the fiscal year from July 1 to October 1.
Source: *The Budget of the United States Government, Fiscal Year 1978* (Washington, D.C.: Government Printing Office, 1977), p. 436; *The Budget of the United States Government, Fiscal Year 1979* (Washington, D.C.: Government Printing Office, 1978). Cited in Dennis S. Ippolito, *The Budget and National Politics* (San Francisco: W. H. Freeman and Company, 1978), p. 24.

With the election of President Reagan, however, this trend began to be reexamined, as we shall see in the next section. The new administration, together with a sympathetic Ninety-seventh Congress, sought to reduce government spending in many areas. While the proposed federal budgets will continue to increase in the coming years, they will grow at a much slower rate than before.

The budget-making process. Though the President starts the annual budgetary process, it is not completed until Congress passes the budget. Once the budget is approved, laws actually appropriating the money must be passed.

Each bureau, agency, and department in the executive branch prepares a budget for its unit. This is sent to the Office of Management and

Budget (OMB) which goes over each item line by line. These individual budgets tell the President what each unit proposes to do with its funds in the coming fiscal year. Much of the budget has already been committed from previous years, but according to **zero-based budgeting**, each agency is supposed to take a fresh look each year—starting from zero—to see if old allocations are still necessary. The OMB has the task of putting the entire budget together. It frequently calls in the heads of the various units to explain, justify, or defend particular items. The President, likewise, becomes intimately involved in the final stages, working with the director of the OMB. In January, the President sends the proposed budget, along with his budget message, to Congress. The fiscal year starts the following October 1; thus, Congress has nine months to review and pass (usually with some major modifications) the budget.

With the passage of the Budget and Impoundment Act of 1974, Congress substantially changed its procedures for dealing with the budget. Now, unlike before, Congress does not simply react to the President's proposed budget; Congress initiates and conducts its own budget-making process in tandem with the executive branch. Around December 31, two Congressional budget committees (one in each chamber), with staff assistance from the Congressional Budget Office, receive estimates of specific expenditures and taxes from appropriate Congressional committees, as well as recommendations from the Joint Economic Committee (a committee composed of members from both chambers). This process results in the first **concurrent resolution**, completed in each house by May 15 of each year. This concurrent resolution sets tentative spending and revenue targets for the coming fiscal year. At this point it is clear how Congress's budget compares with proposals from the President, particularly on such broad matters as the size of a deficit, if one is projected, and where policy priorities lie.

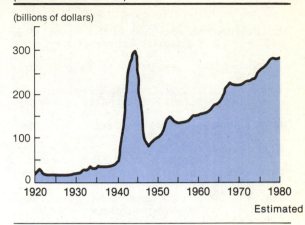

FIGURE 1.
Federal Budget Outlays.
(based on 1967 dollar)

(billions of dollars)

Estimated

Sources: 1920–1939, Donald Ogilvie, Yale; 1940–1980, O.M.B. Cited in *Wall Street Journal*, October 10, 1979, p. 1.

In the meantime, the President is allowed to send Congress amendments to his initial proposal, along with supplementary messages explaining the modifications. During this period, cabinet officials and other top executives, as well as interest groups, testify before the various Congressional budgetary and appropriations committees.

The next deadline in the process is September 15, when a second concurrent resolution is passed. This resolution takes into account changes in the economy and other factors that might have developed in the intervening months. The first resolution basically deals with general, broad targets; the second, with compromises between committees and the President. The second resolution is a firmer statement of goals and budget priorities. The final step is for Congress to pass a budget—including authorization and appropriation—in time for it to take effect by October 1.

These are the formal steps. In addition, various groups lobby for their pet projects throughout the process. Legislators closely guard against any cuts

TABLE 2.
Congressional Budget Deadlines.

October-December: Congressional Budget Office submits five-year projection of current spending as soon as possible after October 1.

November 10: President submits current services budget.

December 31: Joint Economic Committee reports analysis of current services budget to budget committees.

Late January: President submits budget (fifteen days after Congress convenes).

Late January-March: Budget committees hold hearings and begin work on first budget resolution.

March 15: All legislative committees submit estimates and views to budget committees.

April 15: Budget committees report first resolution.

May 15: Committees must report authorization bills by this date.

May 15: Congress completes action on first resolution. Before adoption of the first resolution, neither house may consider new budget authority or spending authority bills, revenue changes, or debt limit changes.

May 15 through the 7th day after Labor Day:

Congress completes action on all budget and spending authority bills.

- Before reporting first regular appropriations bill, the House Appropriations Committee, "to extent practicable," marks up all regular appropriations bills and submits a summary report to House, comparing proposed outlays and budget authority levels with first resolution targets.
- CBO issues periodic scorekeeping reports comparing Congressional action with first resolution.
- Reports on new budget authority and tax expenditure bills must contain comparisons with first resolution, and five-year projections.
- "As possible," a CBO cost analysis and five-year projection will accompany all reported public bills, except appropriation bills.

August: Budget committees prepare second budget resolution and report.

September 15: Congress completes action on second resolution. Thereafter, neither house may consider any bill or amendment, or conference report, that results in an increase over outlay or budget authority figures, or a reduction in revenues, beyond the amounts in the second resolution.

September 25: Congress completes action on reconciliation bill or another resolution. Congress may not adjourn until it completes action on the second resolution and reconciliation measure, if any.

October 1: Fiscal year begins.

Source: *Congressional Quarterly Almanac,* Vol. 31, 1975 (Washington, D.C.: Congressional Quarterly, Inc., 1976), p. 918. Cited in Dennis Ippolito, *The Budget and National Politics* (San Francisco: W. H. Freeman and Company, 1978), p. 104.

in the budget that would hurt their home constituents. Senator Russell B. Long (D., Louisiana), of the powerful Senate Finance Committee, once jokingly observed: "I could muster the statesmanship to vote for almost anything that saves money as long as it didn't affect my state."[20]

Budget deadlines are not always, in fact are seldom, met. One observer suggested that the new budget process had become too cumbersome.

> *Why such a foul-up in fiscal legislation this year? Congress blew its budget deadline long ago and still has no budget plan [Oct. 12, 1979]. . . . Appropriations for the current fiscal year began Oct. 1. . . . The House and Senate couldn't even agree on a spending measure that was necessary to cover government expenses in the interim.*
>
> *Some say it's a sign of the times . . . life is complex and so are the issues Congress must address. Some more practical reasons for the logjam:*
>
> *Deadlines. Once Congress misses one, as it has done repeatedly this year, it stops pushing so hard. Attitude is, why bother to hurry now?*
>
> *Budget Process. While meant to force Congress to deal more effectively with the federal budget, it has also added another layer of Hill bureaucracy. Also, administration recommendations for spending receive more attention in committees than ever before; and once on the floor, they are often used as vehicles for substantive legislation. Example: Fighting abortions through appropriations. That makes conference action much trickier.*[21]

The budget of the federal government is above all a political document. It reflects not so much abstract theories about the role of government in the lives of people, but political interests. Nor is it an administrator's or accountant's opinion of how to deliver services most efficiently and effectively.

One Washington reporter summed up this situation as follows:

> *Last spring, as the gospel of Proposition 13 swept eastward out of California, "fiscal restraint" and "balanced budget" became Capitol Hill's most popular cliches. Last week, the lawmakers were faced with the reality, and were discovering that it is one thing to promote austerity in the abstract and quite another to make decisions that hurt their own constituencies.*[22]

Thus, as we have seen in many issues discussed in this book, efforts aimed at reform may be motivated by sincere attempts to make the government more efficient, rational, and responsible; they may be supported by well-reasoned theories of government and human affairs; but they must always pass by the altar of politics. This interplay between theory and reality is a persistent theme and is nowhere more evident than in the budget-making process.

On January 15, 1981, a few days before he left office, Jimmy Carter submitted a proposed budget to Congress for the fiscal year 1982. On March 10, 1981, a few weeks after he came into office, Ronald Reagan submitted revisions to that proposal. The differences between these budgets show how Carter and Reagan disagree on policy (see Table 3, page 548). For example, the receipts of the Reagan budget were based on a tax cut (resulting in less revenue), which was an important element of Reagan's economic policy. Also, consistent with his view that one way to fight inflation is to cut the growth of government spending, the President proposed approximately 283 major cuts and reductions in government programs. You will recall from the energy case study that President Reagan was not very enthusiastic about the Department of Energy; in this area, Carter and Reagan clearly disagreed. For example, for just one section of the department, the Energy Information Administration, Carter proposed $127 million in 1982, with steady increases projected to $161 million in 1986. Reagan proposed a thirty-seven percent reduction for 1982 ($80 million) with a projected fifty percent decrease by 1986. The Reagan budget allowed for increases, but it was still substantially less than the Carter budget. In his statement explaining the proposed revisions, President Reagan told Congress:

> *In times such as these, requiring fiscal austerity, the benefits of ever more data and statistical precision fall short of the costs, which include significant costs inflicted on the private sector in*

TABLE 3.
Carter vs. Reagan Proposed Budgets, 1980–1982.
(billions of dollars)

	Actual	Estimate	
	1980	1981	1982
Budget Authority			
Carter's January budget	658.8	726.5	809.8
Change	*	−16.3	−37.5
Reagan's revised budget	658.8	710.1	772.4
Outlays			
Carter's January budget	579.6	662.7	739.3
Change	*	−7.6	−44.0
Reagan's revised budget	579.6	655.2	695.3
Receipts			
Carter's January budget	520.0	607.5	711.8
Change	*	−7.2	−61.4
Reagan's revised budget	520.0	600.3	650.3
Deficit			
Carter's January budget	−59.6	−55.2	−27.5
Change	*	0.3	−17.4
Reagan's revised budget	−59.6	−54.9	−45.0

Source: *Budget Revisions Fiscal Year 1982* (Office of Management and Budget: March 1981), p. 6.

burdensome reporting requirements. Therefore, EIA will go back to basics and try not to satisfy each and every demand for energy data and analysis. There will be less need for such services as energy consumers' and producers' decisions are guided more by the free play of market prices than by federal planning and regulation.[23]

Another area of significant difference was the student loan program. President Reagan stated that "benefits to the highest income students will be eliminated. In the Guaranteed Student Loans program, student loan amounts will be limited to remaining need, ending the in-school interest subsidy on loans to students, and eliminating the federal special allowance to lenders on loans to parents."[24] The rationale for such proposals was:

Without these reforms, the GSL program would be recklessly expanded in a few years. Under the GSL program, students can borrow regardless of their educational need, with the Federal Government paying all interest on the loan until the student is out of school. The result is that the Federal Government pays high rates on interest, on free *money that students spend as they see fit.*[25]

Taxes and politics. When he was campaigning for the presidency the first time, Jimmy Carter called the tax system in the country a "national disgrace." He voiced a complaint often heard about the inequities of the system: too many "loopholes," permitting the rich to pay much less than they "should"; too great a tax burden on the middle-income wage earner who cannot take advantage of tax shelters; and so forth. And in his March 1981 budget message to Congress, President Reagan stated, "We must cut tax rates so that once again work will be rewarded and savings encouraged."

Since 1913, with the passage of the Sixteenth Amendment to the Constitution, we have had a federal income tax. It has become more complex (and, to some, more burdensome) over the years. The individual income tax is based on the theory that the more one earns, the higher the *rate* of one's taxes. This is known as the **progressive tax system**. Thus, an income of $20,000 is charged a tax rate of eighteen percent; while one earning $102,000 pays fifty-two percent. In practice, however, people with substantial assets are able to take advantage of a number of tax provisions that permit them to pay substantially less in taxes than their wealth would indicate. In fact, some millionaires are known to pay *no* income taxes. They can take advantage of various *tax shelters* such as business or investment losses, tax-free municipal bonds, and so forth.

The federal government also levies taxes on corporations at a forty-eight percent rate, but, again, there are various ways to circumvent this and to lower the amount actually paid into the federal treasury. Social insurance taxes and contributions from employers and employees constitute another tax source. These funds are used to pay social security benefits. There is also a federal sales (excise) tax on such items as tobacco, gasoline, and alcoholic liquors.

The Internal Revenue Service (IRS), in the Treasury Department, has the responsibility of administering and enforcing the country's tax laws. Headed by a commissioner appointed by the President and confirmed by the Senate, the IRS receives the tax returns filed by the taxpayers (as many as 123 million) and reviews a selected number of returns to see if they are accurate. A return that appears to have irregularities may be *audited*, meaning the IRS can require the taxpayer to come in and bring *all* records justifying the information contained in the tax return. Each year, the IRS audits upwards of 2.2 million taxpayers. Sometimes these people are selected at random; other times, they might be ones who have a history of filing questionable returns. The IRS employs approximately 80,000 full-time workers.

The tax laws are written by Congress, with the major responsibility vested in the House Ways and Means Committee and the Senate Finance Committee. These committees, as one could imagine, are the constant focus of interest groups seeking to protect their particular interests from what *they* perceive to be unduly burdensome taxes. Consumer advocate Ralph Nader has observed: "The average taxpayer works three months out of the year for the government. That is how long it takes to pay the taxes for federal, state, and local budgets. . . . The average taxpayer is not a participant in tax politics; the wealthy and special-interest taxpayers play tax politics—and are missing from the tax rolls."[26]

Monetary Policy: The Federal Reserve System

At his first press conference in January 1981, President Reagan was asked the following question:

Mr. President, Paul Volcker, the Chairman of Federal Reserve Board, has been implementing policies that are exactly opposite in basic thrust from what you recommend. . . . Are you concerned that there might be a sabotage . . . of your policies by programs that the Federal Reserve might be putting forward?

The President answered:

No. . . . I've met with Mr. Volcker and not with the intention of trying to dictate; because it is an independent agency and I respect that. . . . We do want from the Fed and would ask for a moderate policy of money supply increasing relative to legitimate growth.[27]

If the President and Congress, as publicly elected officials, have direct responsibility over fiscal (budgetary) policies, the Federal Reserve Board, which is appointed—not elected—has direct responsibility for **monetary policy** (control of the nation's money supply).

Congress established the Federal Reserve System in 1913 after a series of bank failures and a major shortage of money. The purpose of "the Fed," as it is called, is to determine how much money will be available to conduct business in the country. Basically, it does this in two ways: by adjusting the interest rates it charges banks that borrow money from the Fed, and by buying and selling government securities, or stocks and bonds.

The Federal Reserve Board, headquartered in Washington, D.C., consists of seven "governors" appointed by the President with the advice and consent of the Senate. They serve fourteen years and their terms are staggered. The President chooses the chairperson, who serves for four years.

All federally chartered banks and many state banks are members of the Federal Reserve System: the former by necessity, the latter, voluntarily. There is one district, or reserve, bank in each of twelve regions in the country. In each region the member banks elect the district bank's president and a majority of the directors. The member banks also pay the salaries of the district bank's officers. Thus, these officers are beholden to those private banks that select them and pay their salaries. In

addition, there is considerable overlap between district-bank leadership and private-industry leadership. Therefore, every President of the United States must always be mindful of having "the confidence of the business community," since it is quite influential (some would say, autonomous) in determining monetary policy. If a President pursues certain *fiscal* policies, these can be undermined by a set of counter *monetary* policies. And we must remember that the business and banking leaders who have considerable control over the Fed are not publicly elected officials. They are leaders in the private sector.

The Fed influences interest rates directly by raising or lowering the rate it charges its member banks to borrow money from it. Thus, if the Fed wants to pursue a "tight" money policy, it will raise the interest rate. Member banks will then borrow less money, and in turn they will raise the

Left: Paul Volcker, chairman of the Federal Reserve Board, meeting with members of the press. Right: Federal Reserve headquarters in Washington, D.C.

interest rate they charge their customers, such as corporations. The corporations will then borrow less and invest less. A "loose" money policy means just the opposite.

The money supply may also be influenced by the Federal Open Market Committee (FOMC), which buys and sells government securities. It consists of the seven "governors," the president of the district bank in New York, and four district-bank presidents who serve on a rotating basis. If this group decides to sell government securities, this has the effect of reducing the money supply because the Fed takes in money. If it buys securities, the money supply is increased because the Fed pays out money.

The Fed does not receive its operating funds from Congress. Rather the board makes semiannual assessments upon the reserve banks in propor-

tion to their capital stock and surplus. The original intent was to make the Fed reasonably independent of the political whirlwinds coming from the executive branch and Capitol Hill, but some observers have complained that the Fed should be more accountable to the government. In addition, the Fed's meetings are closed, in order to avoid leaking information that might lead to money-market abuses. Several unsuccessful efforts have been made to subject the Fed to an audit by the Government Accounting Office. When Congress passed the Budget and Impoundment Act of 1974, it required the chairperson of the Federal Reserve Board to make quarterly reports to Congress on the board's plans for dealing with the money supply. This requirement has not been an especially effective tool of accountability since the reports have tended to be very general and ideological, not policy-focused.

The Government and the Economy: An Overview

As we have seen, three areas of government, each operating relatively isolated from the other, can have a direct influence on the economy. The Fed can pursue one set of monetary policies; the President, a contradictory set of fiscal policies; and both not in conjunction with Congress as it grapples with the budget. During the Carter administration, an editorial in the *New York Times* referred to this situation as "schizophrenia," saying: "The President and Congress are moving in opposite direction, talking about vast tax cuts or increases in federal spending to offset the effects of recession, to reduce the burden of Social Security payments and to buy new weapons. No one seems to know the right strategy, but surely such schizophrenia has to be wrong. To enlarge budget deficits only to have the Fed respond with even tighter credit controls is a recipe for economic disaster. . . . While the Fed is fighting inflation, Congress is preparing to fight recession, and the President keeps a leg in both camps."[28] With the beginning of President Reagan's administration, however, there was relatively high expectation that the Federal Reserve Board would pursue the kinds of monetary policies that were consistent with the administration's fiscal policies. Whatever the case, the fact remains that economic policies are a function of three distinct, official entities, a situation that requires maximum cooperation and coordination if the entire system is to be effective. This situation is further complicated by the different interests of each group and the different ways each gains its power and is held accountable.

Three major economic issues Certainly for the next decade and possibly for the remainder of this century, the American government will be faced with three overriding economic issues: inflation, energy, and unemployment. These problems will occupy the center of attention of the national decision-making apparatus—however fragmented. Americans will expect their President to give solutions, even though it will not be within the sole purview of that office to present and implement such solutions. Different opinions on the best course to take will abound. There will be many policy agendas.

FIGURE 2.
Consumer Price Index, 1967–1980.

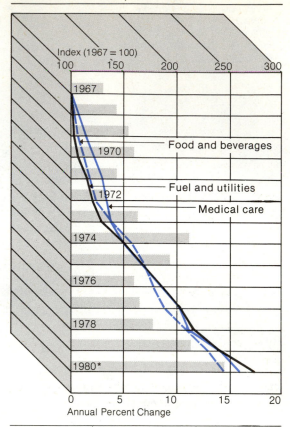

*Annual rate for five months ending May. For 1980, percent change May 1979–1980.
Source: *Statistical Abstract of the United States 1980,*
U.S. Department of Commerce, Bureau of the Census, p. 477.

TABLE 4.
Annual Percent Change in Wage Rates, 1970–1980 (Private Nonfarm).

Year	1970	1971	1972	1973	1974	1975	1976	1977	1978	1979	1980
Percent change	6.3%	6.8%	7.2%	6.5%	7.6%	6.8%	7.3%	8.0%	8.4%	8.3%	7.9%[1]

[1]From May 1979 to May 1980.
Source: *Statistical Abstract of the United States 1980,* U.S. Department of Commerce, Bureau of the Census, p. 474.

Inflation. When there is an undue increase in wholesale prices and the cost of living, along with an increase in the paper-money supply and the expansion of credit, **inflation** is said to exist. This makes the value of money decrease. Thus, one hears that a dollar buys much less in 1980 than it did, say, in 1960. A person making $15,000 in 1960 was probably able to buy a very comfortable suburban home for $20,000. That same house twenty years later might cost $80,000, and a buyer would need a substantially higher income to afford it. Such increases in the cost of living are measured by the **consumer price index (CPI).** (See Figures 2 and 3 and Table 4 for data on the cost of living and inflation.)

Economists suggest that inflation is caused by two types of situations, and possibly a third. The first is called *demand-pull inflation.* When the demand for goods and services exceeds supply, prices go up. (This is sometimes described as too much money chasing too few goods.) Producers are able to raise their prices and maximize their profits. Likewise, when there is a demand for labor, workers make demands for higher wages. When this situation occurs and inflation sets in, the economy is said to be "heated up." The economy is growing too fast.

The second situation is called *cost-push inflation*, or the wage-price spiral. This occurs when business and labor alternately bid up prices and wage rates as each side comes to "expect" inflation and raises its rates in anticipation. Neither side wants to be caught bearing the burden of the increases. Thus, the results of the spiral are ulti-

mately passed on to the consumer in inflated costs for goods and services.

In 1957, a New Deal economist, Gardiner C. Means, introduced still another explanation for inflation: *administered prices.* In testimony before a Senate subcommittee, he argued that the increase in wholesale prices had occurred mainly in those industries dominated by a few firms. Such firms were able to raise prices even when not justified by demand because they controlled the supply of goods and services on the market in their particular industry.

We have seen an inflationary trend in this country for several years. "From 1952 to 1967 the annual inflation rate never exceeded four percent. Since that period the inflation rate dropped below four percent only in one year [1972]."[29] Sometimes we hear the term "double-digit inflation." This means that the rate has reached ten percent or more, and most people see that as a serious danger sign for the economy.

It is generally conceded that inflation destabilizes the economy. Businesses are reluctant to invest and expand. Over time, workers' paychecks purchase fewer and fewer goods and services. Those persons living on fixed or low incomes suffer especially. No one can make long-term economic plans.

One anti-inflation policy is to slow the rate of economic growth by reducing government spending and by adopting monetary policies that make it more difficult for businesses to borrow money—a

FIGURE 3.
Purchasing Power of the Dollar, 1940–1980.
(in 1967 dollars)

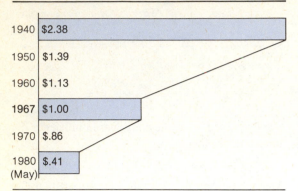

1940	$2.38
1950	$1.39
1960	$1.13
1967	$1.00
1970	$.86
1980 (May)	$.41

Note: All figures represent consumer prices. Data obtained by dividing the average price index for the 1967 base period (100.00) by the price index for a given period and expressing the result in dollars and cents. Annual figures are monthly average.

Source: Chart based on data in *Statistical Abstract of the United States 1980,* U.S. Department of Commerce, Bureau of the Census, p. 476.

tight-money strategy. (Some economists firmly believe that government spending is the basic cause of inflation.) If this strategy is pursued, it will probably result in higher unemployment— possibly leading to a recession or a depression. Some people argue that this is a short-term cost that must be borne in order to curb inflation. Others contend that such a strategy places the immediate burden on the poor and unskilled, those least able to fend for themselves on an open labor market.

Energy. Since the mid-1970s, millions of Americans have experienced waiting for as long as two hours in line to buy gasoline for their cars; they have seen the speed limit on highways set at a top limit of fifty-five miles per hour; they have seen the price of gas for their cars and heating fuel for their homes more than triple; they have heard more and more about a group of countries called OPEC;

and they have seen the federal government order that thermostats in public buildings be set no lower than 78 degrees in the summer and no higher than 65 degrees in the winter. All these things have come to be associated with "the energy crisis."

Today, the United States imports almost half the oil it consumes. Most of this supply comes from countries in the Middle East that have both cut back production and steadily raised prices. This has made this country seriously dependent on others for critical sources of energy. One side effect of this situation has been increased inflation. When there is a change of political systems in one of those countries (as in Iran in 1979) from a government friendly to the United States to one that is decidedly less friendly, the problem is aggravated even more. For instance, President Carter stated:

With the government shakeup in distant Iran last winter, we lost, in imports, about 100 million barrels of oil. The gasoline lines are directly related to this particular vulnerability. So are the diesel fuel shortages among our farmers and among our truckers, and so are the present low home heating oil stocks that we face next winter. We simply must remove this threat to our people.[30]

As with the problem of inflation, there are several (sometimes differing) proposed solutions to the energy problem. Many people recognize the necessity of pursuing them simultaneously. The common goal is to make the country more "energy-secure," that is, less dependent on others for the vital energy sources. President Carter told a meeting of the National Association of Counties in Kansas City, Missouri in July 1979:

The first thing we've got to do is to face facts. There is simply not enough oil available in the world to meet all the demands of all the people in all the nations on earth.

Americans are just now beginning to realize, with simple common sense, that there are only two ways to guarantee supply. One is obviously to control our demand—to cut back on the waste of energy. And the other is to develop our own sources of energy to replace foreign imports so that we can have control over our own destiny.[31]

Specific proposals include developing solar energy as an alternative source, developing nuclear power plants as another source, producing synthetic fuels as a substitute, possibly rationing gas, building a pipeline to bring natural gas from Alaska, shifting more to coal from oil, weatherizing homes so less heating fuel will be needed, driving cars less and using carpools more, relying more on public mass-transit systems, regulating highway speed, building more fuel-efficient cars, and so forth.

Economically and socially, the energy problem has caused and will continue to require a drastic change in American lifestyles. The full implications are not yet known. But it is certain that the federal government will have to assume a major, continuing role. In some ways, the energy problem is similar to the economic crisis of the Great Depression, which led to more government involvement in the economy. This is exactly what some observers fear. They believe the energy problem will expand the role of "big government," especially the federal government. The dilemma seems unavoidable. Any crisis that affects the society so pervasively will tend to demand national government action.

Unemployment. Inflation and energy scarcity affect everyone in the society, albeit in different degrees. But the unemployment issue essentially is one felt only by those who do not have jobs. However, when the unemployment rate reaches a certain level, it can be a major national problem. For example, the Depression, when as many as twelve million people were out of work and had no means of supporting their families, was indeed serious enough to spur the government to act to alleviate the situation and to enact measures that would guard against any such situations in the future. (See chapter 16.)

Today, many people who are unemployed are only temporarily so. They have left one job and will find another one soon. Thus, there is no great urgency on the part of the government to take special action on their behalf. As the economy begins to expand, such people eventually find a place in the work force.

This is not true for a vast number of *structurally* (sometimes referred to as *chronically*) *unemployed* people. This is the group of people that cannot enter the labor market even in the best of times due to lack of skills to fit the available jobs, poor education, and discrimination, among other things. The people who make up this group are mainly poor, young, unskilled, female, inexperienced, and, increasingly, from minority groups. The unemployment rate among such people usually is triple that of the national average at any given time. Even when the economy "picks up," the likelihood of such people finding jobs is slim.

How much effort the government should make to help such people is a serious policy issue. Some people believe a government program that involves the expenditure of large sums of money, such as government work programs, is inflationary. Others believe that a certain level of unemployment is healthy for the economy. Note the following comment in *Business Week* as long ago as 1952—a view some people still hold:

Unemployment remains too low for the work force to have flexibility. Anytime the jobless total is less than 2 million, even common labor is scarce. Many employers must tend to hoard skills. And certainly, the labor unions are in the driver's seat in wage negotiations. More workers can be had, to be sure. But only at considerable cost. And they probably wouldn't be of the skills most desired. There's no assurance against inflation like a pool of genuine unemployment. That is a blunt, hard-headed statement, but a fact.[32]

Thus, some people do not necessarily believe in full employment: a job and a decent salary for everyone able and willing to work. They might view an economic recession as one viable means of combating inflation. In a recession, businesses do not invest in expansion and even cut back on production, which, of course, results in higher unemployment. According to the demand-pull theory, if fewer people are working and earning incomes, there is less money to spend—thus curbing an inflationary trend.

Proponents of a full-employment policy, however, see this as a cruel way to manage the economy; it puts an enormous economic burden on those unable to find jobs. Such advocates are more likely to support other measures for dealing with unemployment and inflation, such as government job programs and wage-price controls. In addition, they point out that we now have a situation where inflation is high at the same time unemployment is increasing, especially among the "hard-core unemployed" (another synonym for structurally unemployed). This situation is known as **stagflation**, and it defies traditional explanations of the relationship between inflation and employment.

A Matter of Politics

In response to the question "What lessons were learned from the 1929 stock market crash?" the Nobel laureate in economics Frederick von Hayek responded: "The paradox is that we are much too afraid of another depression to really fight infla-

tion. I think you could stop it completely by just keeping the money supply and money wages where they are. It would cause a short, severe depression, but it might be over in six months. In any event, you cannot stop inflation without causing depression. . . . The only thing the Depression gave us was the curse of Keynesian economics."[33] Another economist, Arthur Okun, former head of the Council of Economic Advisers under President Lyndon B. Johnson, responded to the question by saying: "The Depression did two things. It left us so preoccupied with the downside risk that we ignored the risk of inflation, which we didn't take terribly seriously until the 1970s. The danger today is that we could become so concerned about inflation that we could bring on another depression."[34]

There is no dearth of suggested remedies for the economic problems facing the country. But one economist, Professor Lester Thurow, believes that the answer lies not with the economists, but with the political system. The government, Thurow points out, could pursue at least three strategies to ease inflation. One approach involves imposing controls on wages, prices, and even profits. Another calls for tight monetary and fiscal policies. Still another would have the government remove various protective tariffs and other measures that now exist and that serve to keep prices up. But any of these solutions, Thurow says, will mean some groups will have to suffer, and the serious political issue concerns choosing which groups should bear the brunt of the policy decisions.

For example, President Carter, recognizing the need to grapple with both the energy and inflation issues, suggested developing a synthetic-fuels program as one means of finding alternative energy sources to oil. Such a program would require vast amounts of water reserves, which might adversely affect the northern-plains states, where water is a necessary and scarce resource.

Environmental officials say at least a dozen local groups, some with as many as 1,000 members, have begun organizing opposition against any federal demands for water for synfuel development.

"Water has always been the key out here," said James Posewitz, an official of Montana's Fish, Wildlife and Parks Department. "I can assure you that any attempt by the Feds to take away the states' prerogative to allocate its water is certainly going to be resisted."[35]

As another example, Lester Thurow says: "Take the third solution [for fighting inflation], which is go through the economy and knock prices down wherever you can do it. Well, whoever's price you knock down, that's somebody's income. If you get rid of protection for the steel industry, incomes fall in the steel industry. If you get rid of protection for the textile industry, they fall for those people who work in the textile industries. So in all of these solutions there are enormous costs, and the people who have to suffer those costs object to the solutions politically."[36]

Even with the pervasive, post-Proposition 13 concern for budget-balancing, there is still the political problem of deciding what to cut from the budget. We are reminded of Senator Long's statement about how he must look out for his state's interests.

The major budget reductions proposed by President Reagan would indeed slow the rate of growth of federal government spending. But this would not mean that specific interests would cease to contend for what was left. Rather there would simply be a smaller pie to fight over, and this could make the political struggle that much more intense. We have examined this interest-group aspect of American politics in earlier chapters. It is made manifest when we examine specific economic problems and the budget-making process. It is not

difficult to agree on the broad economic goals of reducing inflation, balancing the budget, and making the country energy-secure. How to allocate the burdens of achieving such goals is yet another—political—matter.

To illustrate the point further, we might appropriately end this chapter by returning to our discussion of the Chrysler Corporation. While the ideological debate over free enterprise versus government intervention continued, the Carter administration made a decision to support government aid for the ailing private company. The following account appeared in the press:

The Carter Administration, weighing the political dangers of massive unemployment in the wake of a bankrupt Chrysler Corporation, decided last week to support a $1.5 billion federal loan guarantee for the nation's third-largest auto producer.

Clearly, . . . as an Administration official acknowledged, "it's hard to argue with the fact that this is a fundamental political decision."

Mr. Fraser [president of the United Auto Workers union] had said earlier that his union—whose 1.5 million members are a political force of major proportions—was "neutral for Kennedy," possibly leaning toward the endorsement of Senator Edward M. Kennedy of Massachusetts, should he decide to challenge President Carter.

Although Administration leaders forcefully reject any idea of a deal between Mr. Fraser and the Administration, in exchange for the rescue plan, union leaders said that Presidential aides had asked the U.A.W. to remain neutral in the campaign as long as possible.[37]

The title of the news article was: "Politics and Jobs: Chrysler Corporation's $1.5 Billion Bailout."

It is difficult to draw definite conclusions about

the motivations behind particular policy decisions. But students of American government should be aware of the possible political considerations. It is not cynical to suggest that many policies have little to do with philosophical or abstract ideological arguments, but rather with the ability of various organized interest groups to bargain and prevail in important decision-making places in the government. Ideological debate is not superfluous, but it must be kept in perspective.

Summary

1. While there remains a strong preference in the American society for the private enterprise system, there is continuing debate about the role of government in the economy. Since the New Deal of the 1930s, there has been a widespread belief that the government must perform some economic functions to guard against inflation and to deal with unemployment, involving the government in a range of activities impinging directly and indirectly on the lives of individuals and private businesses. A balance between absolute free enterprise and total government involvement is sought.

2. The budget is a political document reflecting, first, the President's policy agenda, and, finally, after Congress has passed it, a compromise agreement on what programs should be pursued with how much money. The budget also indicates how much money the government expects to receive in taxes and other revenues and from what sources.

3. The Federal Reserve System, authorized by Congress in 1913, has authority to regulate the nation's supply of money. It does this in two ways: by setting interest rates at which member banks can borrow money from the Federal Reserve System, and by buying and selling government securities.

4. The federal government derives its revenues mainly from taxes on incomes, sales, and borrowing. Theoretically, income-tax policy is progressive, that is, those earning more pay at a higher rate, but there are several "loopholes," or tax shelters, which permit one to circumvent this. There is a constant call for "tax reform," but political considerations make this difficult to achieve.

5. Issues of inflation, energy, and unemployment will be critical problems facing the country at least through the 1980s. Experts disagree on the causes of and solutions to inflation and unemployment; other experts differ on how best to solve the problem of American dependence on foreign sources for energy. Ideological views and political self-interests are very important in determining which economic policies are adopted.

Notes

1. *Wall Street Journal*, September 20, 1979, p. 15.
2. Ibid.
3. *Wall Street Journal*, September 18, 1979, p. 18.
4. Ibid.
5. *Wall Street Journal*, September 27, 1979, p. 22.
6. William Proxmire, "The Case Against Bailing Out Chrysler," *The New York Times Magazine*, October 21, 1979, p. 98.
7. John Kenneth Galbraith, *Economics and the Public Purpose* (Boston: Houghton Mifflin Company, 1973).
8. Quoted in Myron E. Sharpe, *John Kenneth Galbraith and the Lower Economics* (New York: International Arts and Sciences Press, 1974), p. 113.
9. Quoted in Sharpe, p. 118.
10. Robert Lekachman, *Economists at Bay* (New York: McGraw-Hill Book Company, 1976), p. 287.
11. Ibid., pp. 289–90.
12. *New York Times*, August 31, 1979, p. A23.
13. Ibid.
14. *New York Times*, October 28, 1979, p. 1.
15. Ibid.

16. James L. Sundquist, *Politics and Policy* (Washington, D.C.: The Brookings Institution, 1968).
17. Ibid., p. 42.
18. *New York Times*, February 22, 1981, p. E1.
19. *Wall Street Journal*, October 10, 1979, p. 32.
20. *New York Times*, September 10, 1979, p. E2.
21. Quoted in *Congressional Insight*, Vol. 3, No. 41 (October 12, 1979).
22. *New York Times*, September 16, 1979, p. E2.
23. Office of Management and Budget, *Budget Revisions Fiscal Year 1982, Additional Details on Budget Savings* (April 1981), p. 115.
24. Ibid., p. 103.
25. Ibid.
26. Robert Brandon, Jonathan Rowe, and Thomas H. Stanton, *Tax Politics* (New York: Pantheon Books, 1976), p. vii.
27. *New York Times*, January 30, 1981, p. A10.
28. *New York Times*, November 2, 1979, p. A30.
29. Joseph A. Pechman, ed., *Setting National Priorities, The 1980 Budget* (Washington, D.C.: The Brookings Institution, 1979), p. 58.
30. *New York Times*, July 17, 1979, p. A14.
31. Ibid.
32. "Business Outlook," *Business Week*, May 17, 1952, p. 17.
33. *New York Times*, November 1, 1979. p. D1.
34. Ibid.
35. *International Herald Tribune*, September 6, 1979, p. 9.
36. *The McNeil/Leherer Report* (Washington, D.C.: Corporation for Public Broadcasting, June 26, 1979); Professor Thurow developed his thesis further in his *Zero-Sum Society* (New York: Basic Books, Inc., Publishers, 1980).
37. *New York Times*, November 4, 1979, p. F19.

Social Welfare
and
Politics

"They make money the old-fashioned way," the TV spokesman for an investment brokerage company said. "They *earn* it." In that statement is contained a great deal of information about the basic feelings of many Americans toward work, self-reliance, and individualism. In more subtle terms, it also says something about American attitudes toward government and social welfare.

The Ethic of Individualism and Self-Reliance

There is a strong, long-standing ethic in American society which holds that one can succeed if one works hard and competes fairly, and that if one fails, it is likely a result of some personal defect or fault. Reliance on the government, if not frowned upon, is certainly seen as a result of personal weakness and inefficiency. Any such "dependency," it is believed, should be ended as soon as possible.

Professor William Lee Miller has traced this ethic to the very religious, political, and economic foundations of American society:

The United States was settled in the age of spreading protestantism. . . . Calvinism and the "free churches" . . . were transported to this promising new environment. . . . They represented the most individualistic development out of the most individualistic wing of the most individualisitc part of the Judeo-Christian heritage. . . .

This religious foundation—by no means dead —was reinforced by and itself reinforced liberal democratic ideas. . . . The individual existed before and beyond the society, creating it (in the myth) by a contract for his own purposes. The purposes were limited, the society was limited, the state was limited; the solitary human person ultimately transcended all of it, and it was made for and by him. . . .

The United States was open territory to the individualist ideas of classic liberal economics —individual entrepreneurs, individual decisions, communicating to each other by means of the market. . . .

Almost all the forces shaping this culture tend in the individualistic direction. . . .

The frontier, continuing economic growth, a stable constitutional system, and victory in the nation's wars . . . made it possible for enough of the promissory notes of individualistic democracy to be fulfilled to help the ideology retain persuasive power.

Collective measures, undertaken by government for the general good, for distributive justice, or for generosity have had an uphill road in American culture.[1]

Americans are still attracted to the Horatio Alger stories of rags to riches, and to the notion that one can and ought to "pull oneself up by the bootstraps" rather than seek "hand-outs" or "charity" from anyone else (especially the government). Whenever we see government move toward providing benefits and support for individuals and groups, we hear warnings against the effects of "creeping socialism," and we are told that government action is destructive of the ethic of individualism, self-reliance, and the free-enterprise system.

Although it is not particularly embarrassing or demeaning to be *poor* in America, there is a stigma attached to being *dependent*. Not dependent as a child is on parents, or even as some elderly or disabled persons are on their relatives or the state. These conditions are understandable; other kinds of dependency are not.

The policies developed in this country to help various categories of people reflect the political realities of the distinction. In the early 1970s, before he became a U.S. senator, Daniel Patrick Moynihan made the observation:

To be poor is an objective condition; to be dependent, a subjective one as well. . . . Being poor is often associated with considerable personal qualities; being dependent rarely so. . . . Concern for the poor . . . does not necessarily or even commonly extend to those who are dependent, that is to say those who own nothing and earn nothing and depend on society for their livelihood. When such persons are very young or very old, allowances are made. But when they are of the age when other persons work to earn their way and, further, if they are dependent during periods when work is to be had, dependency becomes a stigma. . . . This is the heart of it. The issue of welfare involves a stigmatized class of persons.[2]

This has led some people to make a distinction between what is called the "deserving" poor and the "undeserving" poor. The latter are seen as lazy, shiftless—drags on society. They are seen as people who do not want to work and who are perfectly content to let others (through government hand-outs) take care of them. It is difficult to develop political support for such a group. Why, the argument goes, should hard-working taxpayers have to support people who do not want to exert themselves enough—the ethic, again—or who do not have enough "get up and go" to take care of themselves or their families?

Counter-arguments are based on concepts of humanitarianism and social justice. It is considered humane to help those who need help, who, for various reasons, cannot help themselves—even when the reason is related to their own personal faults. Such people, it is argued, can be "salvaged," and they should be helped to "get on their feet," notwithstanding their dependency. Another counter-argument stresses social injustice. Many people are thought to be victims of a system that has deliberately discriminated against them and their foreparents and has thereby rendered them less able to compete on an equal footing. These people have been victims of racial injustice, sex discrimination, economic injustice, and so forth. To apply a harsh, theoretical ethic to such people is unfair, argue the proponents of social-welfare policies, and invariably involves a distortion of reality.

This is a basic, perennial debate in American politics. In a sense, it is similar to the debate we examined in the previous chapter over free enterprise and government intervention. As we proceed in this chapter, the student should keep in mind the tenets of each position and note the ways the government has attempted, under varying circumstances, to accommodate the two basic views. It is also important to refer back to the items on the questionnaire earlier in the text relating to this subject.

TABLE 1.
Estimates of U.S. Labor Force and Unemployment, 1929–1940.
(in thousands)

Year	Total Labor Force	Armed Forces	Civilian Labor Force	Unemployment	Unemployment as a Percentage of the Civilian Labor Force
1929	48,065	262	47,803	1,499	3.1
1930	48,683	263	48,420	4,248	8.8
1931	49,270	260	49,010	7,911	16.1
1932	49,830	254	49,576	11,901	24.0
1933	50,403	252	50,151	12,634	25.2
1934	51,032	258	50,774	10,968	21.6
1935	51,663	269	51,394	10,208	19.9
1936	52,273	301	51,972	8,598	16.5
1937	52,849	322	52,527	7,273	13.8
1938	53,465	335	53,130	9,910	18.7
1939	54,095	369	53,726	8,842	16.5
1940	54,479	535	53,944	7,476	13.9

Source: U.S. Department of Labor, Bureau of Labor Statistics, Employment and Occupational Outlook Branch, Occupational Outlook Division, June 29, 1945. *Technical Memorandum* No. 20, July 4, 1945.

New Deal Responses to the Depression

The Depression of the 1930s was one of the worst economic and social disasters in the history of this country. During the thirties, the percentage of unemployed leaped from 3.1 percent in 1929 to a record high of 25.2 percent in 1933, and throughout the decade the percentage never got below 13 percent (see Table 1). One writer noted the constant stories of personal tragedy:

The economic depression which began with the Wall Street panic of October, 1929, was the most important event of the years from 1929 to 1932. News of it seldom appeared on the front pages of the newspapers unless a story reduced the disaster of society to personal terms. But such stories abounded: suicides of speculators, flights from justice of utilities magnates and bank presidents, a farmer's use of wheat instead of coal to heat his house, the murder of his starving family by an unemployed workman—in endless variation.[3]

As Professor William E. Leuchtenburg put it: "Many Americans came to despair of the whole political process, a contempt for Congress, for parties, for democratic institutions. . . ."[4] To many, the country no longer seemed to be "the land of opportunity." Leuchtenburg records:

The longer the depression persisted, the more people began to conjecture whether they were not witnessing the death of an era. No longer did America seem a land bright with promise. In the spring of 1931, West African natives in the Cameroons sent New York $3.77 for relief for the "starving"; that fall Amtorg's New York office received 100,000 applications for jobs in Soviet Russia. On a single weekend in April, 1932, the Ile de France and other transatlantic liners carried nearly 4,000 workingmen back to Europe; in June, 500 Rhode Island aliens departed for Mediterranean ports.[5]

Something had to be done. In March 1933 (following his election the previous November),

Franklin D. Roosevelt was inaugurated as President, and he vowed to restore confidence in the government and the economic system through his program of economic recovery. Banks were ordered closed to prevent people from wildly withdrawing their savings and thereby causing further bank failures; Congress established the Tennessee Valley Authority (TVA) to provide cheap hydroelectric power to a vast region and to engage in various government-sponsored economic ventures. Measures were adopted to help homeowners and farmers keep their property; large sums of money were voted to undertake public-works programs. The American government was now in the business—fully and permanently—of using its powers to help restore the economy.

The Federal Emergency Relief Administration (FERA), established in 1933 under Harry Hopkins, made grants to local public agencies. Direct assistance was given to those people who could show they needed help through a "means test," a demonstration that one did not have the *means* to properly care for oneself. This lack of means could be shown through low (or no) income, physical or mental disability, or youth or old age. In some instances "work relief" was instituted. Hopkins felt it was better for people to work for an income whenever possible rather than simply receive assistance. Professor Arthur M. Schlesinger, Jr., has noted:

Instead of putting the unemployed on the dole, why not offer the weekly government check in exchange for labor performed for the public welfare? Work relief, Hopkins said, "preserves a man's morale. It saves his skill. It gives him a chance to do something socially useful. . . ." Although FERA, thrown so suddenly into the breach, could not escape direct relief as its main instrument, a wide variety of work relief projects were devised under Hopkins's relentless prodding. Thus teachers on relief rolls were *assigned to country schools which would otherwise have had to close their doors; by December, 1933, about 13,000 teachers, paid from relief funds, were holding classes in rural areas. FERA too had a special program to take care of transients—the thousands of jobless men roaming the country in search of work and hope.*[6]

One of the most important pieces of social legislation coming out of the New Deal was the Social Security Act of 1935. Basically, the law provided protection of two types: for the wage earner through old-age insurance and unemployment compensation; and for those persons who could not work through public-assistance programs.

The old-age insurance program provided income for persons after they retired. While employed, workers would contribute a certain percentage of their wage to be set aside and controlled by a Social Security Administration. Employers would also be required to contribute a certain sum. Some of Roosevelt's advisers did not like the provision requiring "payroll deductions." These, they argued, were unfair to the worker, because the employer could pass his or her added expenses on to the consumer. Thus, the worker—as consumer—would be paying twice. This would act as kind of double taxation on the worker. But President Roosevelt wanted a "contributory" aspect in the insurance portion of the social-security program for quite *political* reasons. He explained: "I guess you're right on the economics, but those taxes were never a problem of economics. They are politics all the way through. We put those payroll contributions there so as to give the contributors a legal, moral, and political right to collect their pensions and their unemployment benefits. With those taxes in there, no damn politician can ever scrap my social security program."[7]

Thus, Roosevelt understood that by having the worker contribute a part of the proceeds, the

A poster promoting FDR's 1935 Social Security Act.

program would be seen as an *entitlement*, as a *right*. It would not have the stigma of dependency or of being a hand-out. People receiving social-security checks after retirement and even those receiving unemployment compensation while out of a job would not feel they were being given something for nothing. Indeed, they would feel "entitled" precisely because they had given something through their labors. This is no small consideration in view of the ethic discussed in the first section of this chapter.

Politics was, of course, of central concern in Roosevelt's efforts to pass the old-age insurance

law. Certain groups were not covered under its original provisions. In addition, agricultural and domestic workers were dropped from both the insurance and unemployment-compensation programs, as were workers in charitable, educational, and religious institutions. In most instances, there were lobbyists urging, for various reasons, that such categories of workers be excluded.

The Social Security Act also initiated public-assistance programs for those persons not able to work. Four categories ultimately were established: old-age assistance, blind assistance, aid to dependent children (abbreviated ADC and changed later to AFDC—aid to *families* of dependent children), and (added in 1950) disability assistance.

These were not contributory programs, of course; they were *welfare* programs. Costs were to be borne by both the states and the federal government on a matching basis. To understand these programs it is important to look to the thinking of policymakers at the time. Aid to the elderly was considered a temporary matter. It was for those who had no job or other means of support. In the future, it was thought, the elderly would be covered by the social-insurance provision. Public assistance for dependent children was considered quite worthy because it was viewed as providing help for the unfortunate families who had lost the "breadwinner" in the family. The image of the typical ADC recipient was the white, West Virginia widow and her several children left penniless by the death of the husband/father in a coal-mining accident. Most people believed the government could and should help such a family.[8]

Both sets of recipients were poor and dependent, but neither was considered in that stigmatized category later to be characterized as the "undeserving poor." Later, the AFDC program (especially in the 1960s) became controversial as generation after generation of fatherless families joined the welfare rolls, and as the race of the

TABLE 2.
Distribution of Aid to Families with Dependent Children, 1973–1977.

Families Receiving Aid

	1973	1975	1977
Total (in thousands)	2,990	3,420	3,523
Metropolitan areas	77.9%	78.5%	77.1%
Nonmetropolitan areas	22.1	21.5	22.9
White	46.9%	50.2%	52.6%
Black	45.8	44.3	43.0
American Indian and other	7.3	5.5	4.4
Families with 1 child	33.8%	37.9%	40.3%
Families with 2 children	25.5	26.0	27.3
Families with 3 children	16.3	16.1	16.1
Families with 4 or 5 children	17.2	15.0	12.7
Families with 6 or more children	7.2	5.0	3.6

Children Receiving Aid

	1973	1975	1977
Total (in thousands)	7,725	8,121	7,836
Basis for eligibility:			
Father is			
Deceased	4.0%	3.7%	2.6%
Incapacitated	10.2	7.7	5.9
Unemployed	4.1	3.7	5.0
Absent from home:			
Divorced	17.7%	19.4%	21.4%
Separated	28.8	28.6	25.5
Not married to mother	31.5	31.0	33.8
Other	2.4	4.3	4.1
Mother is absent, not father	1.2	1.6	1.6

Source: *Statistical Abstract of the United States 1980*, U.S. Department of Commerce, Bureau of the Census, p. 358.

recipients began to change—from almost entirely white to disproportionately black and Puerto Rican. In addition, the dependent children increasingly were identified not as ones who had lost their fathers through accidental deaths, but rather those children who had been born out-of-wedlock. (See Table 2 for recent data on AFDC recipients.)

Thus the public-assistance programs were designed to serve a particular kind of "deserving" constituency for, it was hoped, a limited period of time. A few decades later, much of this had changed, and the earlier political support had also diminished. State legislatures, which had major responsibility for setting welfare (public-assistance) standards of eligibility and benefit levels, found themselves increasingly under pressure from taxpayers to "get tough" with the "welfare chiselers" who took advantage of the public dole by any means available, including, so it was believed, bearing children out-of-wedlock. There could be no greater affront to the ethic of individualism and self-reliance.

The Social Security Act of 1935 did not contain a provision on health care. When Secretary of Labor Frances Perkins made a speech suggesting that health should be included, the American Medical Association and other powerful health-care lobbyists mobilized opposition against such a move. President Roosevelt was deluged with telegrams from doctors; the *Journal of the American Medical Association* editorialized against it. The idea was dropped.

If the New Deal was to do anything to alleviate *immediate* conditions for millions, it had to respond to the vast unemployment rate. The point was not to wipe out unemployment totally, but to adopt practical measures that would quickly and drastically put as many able-bodied, employable people back to work as possible. The FERA was one response, but the major program came in 1935 with the introduction of the Works Progress (later changed to "Projects") Administration (WPA). The federal government paid money directly to people working in projects created by local authorities. The activities included such things as working on roads, repairing and constructing buildings, streets, and parks, maintaining parks and recreational facilities, painting murals in public buildings, writing and researching historical research projects. "About $10.5 billion was spent on WPA projects from 1935 to 1940. Seventy-five percent of this went into the wages of WPA workers, who reached a peak of 3.3 million in November, 1938."[9]

Through the National Youth Administration and the Civilian Conservation Corps, hundreds of thousands of young people were given jobs planting trees and working in various building and maintenance projects.

The New Dealers also recognized the need to do something about the housing problems of poor people. The Public Works Administration (PWA), established in 1933 and led by Harold Ickes, had been very active in building public projects, but its record in residential housing had not been good:

From 1933 to 1939, PWA helped construct some 70 percent of the country's new school buildings; 65 percent of its courthouses, city halls, and sewage plants; 35 percent of its hospitals and public health facilities. PWA made possible the electrification of the Pennsylvania Railroad from New York to Washington and the completion of Philadelphia's 30th Street Station. In New York, it helped build the Triborough Bridge, the Lincoln Tunnel, and a new psychiatric ward at Bellevue Hospital. It gave Texas the port of Brownsville, linked Key West to the Florida mainland, erected the superbly designed library of the University of New Mexico, and spanned rivers for Oregon's Coastal Highway. . . . The PWA's work in slum clearance and low-cost housing proved disappointing.[10]

The main support for a serious governmental housing program came from Senator Robert Wagner (D., New York), aided by Congressman Henry Steagall (D., Alabama). The Wagner-Steagall Housing Act of 1937 created the United States Housing Authority (USHA). The USHA provided funds to cities to build low-cost public housing projects. "By the end of 1940, almost 350 USHA projects had been completed or were under construction."[11]

The 1930s saw millions of farmers, sharecroppers, and tenant farmers leaving the farms and moving westward. Movies and novels such as John Steinbeck's *The Grapes of Wrath* and Erskine Caldwell's *Tobacco Road* captured the tragic plight of many people—victims of foreclosures, dust storms, and economic failure. The Bankhead-Jones Farm Tenancy Act of 1937 set up the Farm Security Administration (FSA) to provide loans to farmers to enable them to hang on to their properties. Again, politics was an important factor. Professor Leuchtenburg notes:

The FSA had no political constituency—croppers and migrants were often voteless or inarticulate—while its enemies, especially large farm corporations that wanted cheap labor and southern landlords who objected to FSA aid to tenants, had powerful representation in Congress. The FSA's opponents kept its appropriations so low that it was never able to accomplish anything on a massive scale.[12]

To many, the New Deal represented a very significant innovation in American life. It firmly established the principle that the national government had a responsibility to act to protect individuals from economic ruin. The ethic of individualism and self-reliance had by no means been destroyed, but it had been put in a new perspective. Before the New Deal, people in dire economic straits (for whatever reason) who could not help themselves had to rely on private charity or on the meager assistance provided by local or county authorities. After the Depression, all this changed. It could well have been what political scientist David B. Truman has called "the unacknowledged revolution":

It was a revolution . . . in the sense that the American people tacitly accepted certain propositions about an industrialized society that ten

Many Depression-era farms, such as this one, had to be abandoned when dust storms hit the West and Midwest.

years earlier would have been rejected by all but an insignificant fraction of the population. Basically they agreed that the misfortunes that may happen to an individual in such a society are not more than partially attributable to his own actions, that it is a public, governmental duty to prevent developments productive of such misfortunes, and that if this duty cannot be fully discharged, it is a public responsibility to provide for those who have been hurt. Ten years earlier the reverse propositions were a part of the creed.[13]

The Employment Act of 1946

Immediately after World War II, Congress passed a law calling for the federal government "to use all practicable means . . . to coordinate and utilize all its plans, functions, and resources for the purpose of creating and maintaining, in a manner calculated to foster and promote free competitive enterprise and the general welfare, conditions under which there will be afforded useful employment, for those able, willing, and seeking to work, and to promote maximum employment, production, and purchasing power." This was the Employment Act of 1946. It created the Council of Economic Advisers (described in chapter 8) and the Congressional Joint Economic Committee.

This law was a compromise version of an earlier bill (S. 380) calling for "full employment" and stating that all Americans able to work and seeking work had a *right* to a job. Basically, the 1946 law did not require the creation of new jobs—only reports by the President to Congress. The President was to submit to Congress an annual economic report and "a program for carrying out the policy" of *maximizing* employment.

Stephen K. Bailey's book, *Congress Makes a Law*, is a very good account of the political struggle that defeated the stronger bill (S. 380) and led to the passage of the weaker law. He summarized the conservative opposition's main arguments under five headings:

- full employment cannot be guaranteed in a free society since it would invite government into areas that are rightly controlled by the private sector: price controls, investment, plant location;
- initiative would be killed by the adoption of S. 380;
- government spending undermines business confidence;
- economic forecasting for overall employment planning is impossible;
- S. 380 would lead to inflation.[14]

Some of these arguments have appeared consistently throughout the history of the discussion concerning the role of the government in the economy. Bailey concludes: "Through educational campaigns, testimony, and direct and indirect pressures on Congress, the conservative lobby made its weight felt. . . . The conservative pressures helped to shape the prepossessions which a majority of our national legislators brought with them to the 79th Congress. This educational campaign pays enormous dividends."[15]

Thus, while the New Deal had instituted many government programs that signaled a new role for the federal government, there remained (and remains) a constant concern over just how far the public sector ought to go in establishing social-welfare programs. It is important to remember that not only were economic conditions of poverty and devastation widespread in the Depression—touching millions directly—but most of the emergency measures adopted were seen as for the emergency situation only. Government action was understood to be an effort to get over the immediate crisis; it was perceived as strictly temporary. Once the private economy reestablished itself, it could resume its proper role in society.

But even with the "unacknowledged revolution" of the 1930s, the issue of government responsibility was faced again on a major scale in the 1960s with what came to be called the *Great Society* programs.

The Great Society and the War on Poverty: The 1960s

Fifteen years after the end of World War II, with the inauguration of a new President, John F. Kennedy, it was clear that America had come a long, successful way toward establishing a "good life" for most of its citizens. The 1950s had seen the development of sprawling, comfortable suburbs; the creation of a vast interstate highway network that facilitated cross-country auto travel; a tremendous boom in the automobile industry; the location of new manufacturing plants in outlying communities; a highly successful G.I. education bill that permitted hundreds of thousands of veterans to obtain college educations, and the development of a new communications medium—television—that was fast creating a new national culture.

During this same period, however, Michael Harrington wrote a book entitled *The Other America*, wherein he described a large segment of the society which was almost permanently mired in poverty.[16] This group had not benefited from the steady economic boom of the postwar years. President Kennedy got a glimpse of this stark reality while campaigning in West Virginia among unemployed coal miners in 1960. In fact, the first executive order he issued as President doubled the

President Kennedy's efforts to aid the poor gave rise to the Great Society programs of Lyndon Johnson.

rations of surplus food provided free by the government to poor people. Arthur M. Schlesinger, Jr., wrote that "this was a response to his memories of West Virginia and the pitiful food rations doled out to the unemployed miners and their families."[17]

But Kennedy's assassination prevented him from pursuing his goals, and responsibility for the Kennedy program passed to President Lyndon B. Johnson. Johnson knew of Kennedy's concerns, and was aware that a program to fight poverty was being put together. He instructed his assistants: "Go ahead. Give it the highest priority. Push ahead full tilt."[18] In Johnson's words:

We have the opportunity to move not only toward the rich society and the powerful socie-

ty, but upward to the Great Society. The Great Society rests on abundance and liberty for all. It demands an end to poverty and racial injustice.[19]

What followed was a host of measures—legislative proposals aimed at aiding elementary and secondary education, services to poor people to help them out of poverty, health-care programs, and other antipoverty efforts.

Economic Opportunity Act of 1964. The War on Poverty legislation consisted of several laws, but the law passed in August 1964 was perhaps the most important. It created work-study programs for college students, a Job Corps program, and a new policy idea called Urban and Rural Community Action Programs. The latter became the main focus of attention and controversy. Local groups were to be given funds to develop and run programs dealing with a wide range of poverty conditions. There was to be "maximum feasible participation" by the people in the local communities to be served. Just what this language meant was subject to varying interpretations, and it caused rather considerable political struggles at the local and national levels.

The law permitted programs in job training, services to the elderly, drug and alcohol rehabilitation programs, family counseling, child-care programs, and so forth. One prominent provision allowed for the creation of the Head Start program, which provided concentrated preschool training for children from poor educational and economic backgrounds.

This law was mainly the work of the executive branch. There was no mass demand for it from the poor, although poverty was widespread and visible. To be sure (as discussed in chapter 14) there were mass civil-rights demonstrations, but these

The Economic Opportunity Act of 1964 was initially intended to aid destitute families such as the one pictured here.

were aimed largely at racial segregation and discrimination. One observer noted:

The Economic Opportunity Act is a prime example of executive legislation: it was written in the executive branch and subsequently endorsed by the Congress. It is part of a twentieth-century development in which the president's role as "chief legislator" has been "institutionalized" not only in the sense of establishing the congressional agenda, but also for proposing the specific content of bills.[20]

Medicare. If a person is sixty-five years old or older and is receiving or is entitled to social-security or railroad-retirement benefits, or is disabled and eligible for such benefits, that person may receive *medicare*. There is no means test—that is, one need not show economic need to receive the benefits. It is not necessary to be poor or destitute. Hospital and posthospital care are covered by the insurance. Payments are made to providers of inpatient hospital services, health maintenance organizations, posthospital extended care units in licensed nursing homes or in the recipient's home, and these payments cover the reasonable costs of such services. Medicare hospital insurance is financed by a payroll tax paid by the employee and the employer. The Social Security Administration runs the program with the assistance of federal, state, and health agencies.

This program was started in 1965. Prior to that time, federal health-care support was largely available only for the construction of hospital facilities and for medical research.

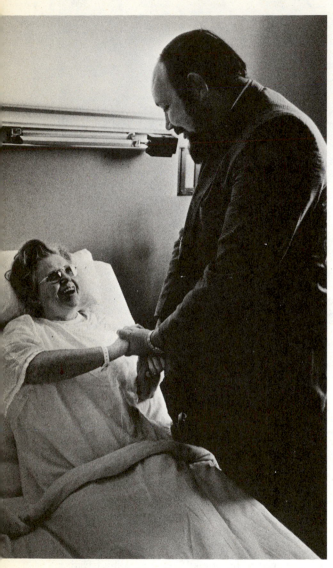

Health care for older citizens has been a problem for years, due to increasing medical costs and the diminished ability of senior citizens to pay. Medicaid has helped offset—though has not solved—this problem.

Medicaid. Also established in 1965, *medicaid* was designed to provide health care for persons receiving public assistance and for those with low incomes. Thus, it is means-tested, and pays virtually all the health costs of one in need—hospital, doctor, prescriptions, and so on. The money for medicaid is provided by federal, state, and local taxes.

Even with these two programs in operation, many Americans are not covered by any form of governmental health insurance. Each session of Congress has seen some measures proposed to extend coverage to all persons. The proposals range from complete assumption of the costs to some form of beneficiary-contribution plan tied in with private insurance companies and agencies such as Blue Cross and Blue Shield.

Food stamps. The federal government has sponsored programs involving the use of stamps in exchange for food since 1939, but no permanent program was in existence until 1964. The government now makes it possible for poor people to buy coupons, or ''stamps,'' which can be used at stores to purchase food at costs lower than retail. It is a form of welfare/public assistance. The federal government then reimburses the retail grocer for the difference. Politically, it is important that such a program not work to the disadvantage of the private retail market. If private retailers were to suffer, there would not be sufficient Congressional support to sustain the program. ''Economically,'' one person has noted, ''the stamps were designed to increase the aggregate effective demand for foods purchased through ordinary retail channels, on which the retailer made his normal margin of profit.''[21] Even before a permanent food-stamp program was established, there was the necessity for political bargaining and trading. Congressional supporters of food stamps had to make various deals to make sure their program would receive favorable treatment. Of course, one way was to find a bill another group wanted and "make a trade"; at times this involved more than one committee.

In 1964, food-stamp legislation was tied to legislation for tobacco research as well as to legislation dealing with wheat and cotton. The House Committee on Agriculture handled all three —food stamps, wheat, and cotton. One food-stamp supporter on the House Rules Committee (Congressman B. F. Sisk, D., Texas) blocked action on a tobacco bill because he was not happy with the way the Agriculture Committee was treating food stamps. A tobacco supporter (Congressman Watkins M. Abbit, D., Virginia) was opposed to food stamps and voted against the program in the committee. One political scientist who studied the process wrote:

> *The Rules Committee voted 6 to 5 not to grant a rule on the tobacco bill.* [Chairman of Agriculture] *Cooley reportedly expressed himself to Abbit: "See, Wat, I told you that you shouldn't have voted against food stamps." Sisk reserved a motion to reconsider the tobacco bill, implying that it could be saved given favorable Agriculture Committee Action on the food stamp bill.*[22]

The legislative battle continued. The following account illustrates, again, the political bargaining that is characteristic of the entire governing process. Note also the various actors involved:

> *During the last few weeks before Easter vacation it became evident that the wheat-cotton bill was in much more danger of defeat than the food stamp program. The House leadership took a poll on both bills through the Democratic whip organization. This poll showed that 212 Democrats should vote for the food stamp bill— enough to win even if no Republicans voted for it (if there were the usual number of absentees). On the other hand, the poll on the wheat-cotton*

TABLE 3.
Average Yearly Outlays of Welfare and Food-Stamp Benefits for Families of Four, 1979.

Hawaii	$7884	Oklahoma	$5124
Alaska	7296	Colorado	5112
Vermont	6540	Kansas	5100
New York	6528	Wyoming	5088
Michigan	6480	Ohio	4980
Wisconsin	6384	Delaware	4944
Washington	6216	Virginia	4920
Oregon	6120	Nevada	4848
Minnesota	6096	Indiana	4836
Connecticut	6096	Maryland	4776
California	6084	Missouri	4680
Massachusetts	5856	West Virginia	4620
Iowa	5844	Kentucky	4500
New Jersey	5676	New Mexico	4452
Utah	5676	Arizona	4308
North Dakota	5640	North Carolina	4212
Nebraska	5640	Florida	4176
Idaho	5604	Arkansas	4116
Pennsylvania	5556	Louisiana	3972
Rhode Island	5544	Alabama	3780
New Hampshire	5436	Georgia	3780
South Dakota	5388	Tennessee	3780
Illinois	5328	Texas	3708
Montana	5316	South Carolina	3576
Maine	5172	Mississippi	3540
District of Columbia	5172		

Source: Department of Health, Education, and Welfare.

bill showed only 197 Democrats likely to vote aye—clearly not enough if Republican lines held solid. Thus, in the closing hours the main efforts of the speaker, the majority leader, and the whip, as well as of the department [of agriculture] *and the President, were aimed at getting more Democratic votes for the wheat-cotton bill. The appeals were directed especially at urban Democrats and stressed that passage of the food stamp legislation could be assured if they would help to get the wheat-cotton bill through.*

> *At this point almost all of the participants, as well as the press, viewed the struggle in terms of the trade.*[23]

The school lunches provided to these children are supported, in part, by federally funded programs.

President Johnson signed the bill into law on August 31, 1964, and expressed the hope that "as a permanent program, the Food Stamp Plan will be one of our most valuable weapons for the War on Poverty."[24] It must be noted, however, that this weapon only made it to the battlefield after a hectic struggle in the political trenches of Congressional wheeling and dealing. A reasonably similar story can be told about many, if not most, major pieces of legislation.

Education. The federal government provides money to local school systems to help pay for books, lunch programs, and educational materials. This came about through the passage of the Elementary and Secondary Education Act of 1965, which was aimed at those urban and rural schools where economic and educational needs were greatest. In addition, the Higher Education Act of 1965 established programs to provide loans and work-study grants to needy college students.

These Great Society education measures were preceded by earlier federal laws emphasizing the building of land-grant colleges and universities (Morrill Act of 1862) and loans to college students to study science, engineering, mathematics, and foreign languages (National Defense Education Act of 1958). The latter was a response to a growing concern following Russia's 1957 Sputnik launch that this country was not doing enough to further the study of the physical sciences.

Aid to education might not be considered precisely in the category of "social-welfare" policies, but the programs have been influenced by the declining economic capacities of many school districts in recent years. Local public elementary and secondary schools are financed either by local property taxes or by special school taxes levied against local citizens. As the tax base in many cities declines, this shrinks the resource pool on which local school boards rely to support the educational system. Increasingly, the federal government is looked to for additional help. This poses an ideological problem for those persons who feel that education should remain a function of local, not national, authorities. The emerging prominence of the federal government in education was made manifest in 1979, when Congress created a new Department of Education, removing responsibility for education from the Department of Health, Education and Welfare. (The latter department became the Department of Health and Human Services.)

It is unlikely, despite the fears of some people, that the new Department of Education will attempt to "run local school systems." But as we have seen in the chapters on federalism, by using the power of the purse the federal government can exercise considerable influence over local institutions. This is especially true in the case of education, where a local school system will naturally want to take advantage of the funds available to improve the quality of its educational programs.

Housing. We have noted the government's 1937 public-housing effort. In 1949, Congress passed another major housing law. This was the beginning of what has come to be called *urban renewal*. While not really a housing policy *per se*, urban renewal is directly related to the housing needs of low- and middle-income families. It involves cooperation of the federal and local governments and private-sector developers. Through a local public authority, the city can acquire certain tracts of land (through eminent domain, etc.), clear the land,

A government-built housing project, Chicago, Illinois.

relocate persons already living there, and sell the property to a private developer, who is then obligated to build housing and other facilities. The federal government underwrites two thirds of the cost of the urban renewal clearance effort. This process has been critized because in many cases low-income residents have been displaced without having other adequate housing to occupy, and because the new housing has often been too expensive for the former residents of the area to afford. Many political battles have been fought in local areas over just this issue. The program is seen by many as a means not of providing new housing for the poor but as a way of revitalizing (indeed, renewing) a deteriorating economic community. And that frequently means bringing in high-income families who can afford the rents and who will patronize the new commercial shops that go with the renewal projects.

In 1965, the Department of Housing and Urban Development (HUD) was created to administer programs for subsidizing rents of low-income tenants, to provide low-cost loans for rehabilitation, and to direct other housing-oriented services. In 1966, HUD was given the operation of the newly passed model cities program, which aimed at a comprehensive approach to economic and social problems of poor communities. The program had mixed results.

The federal government in recent years has concentrated its housing efforts for the poor on providing rent subsidies. This is seen as more cost-effective than providing money for new housing or for the rehabilitation of old structures. This emphasis began on a major scale under the Nixon administration.

"Guaranteed Annual Income": Nixon's Plan

Shortly after he came to office in 1969, President Nixon introduced his Family Assistance Plan. Many people looked upon it as a welfare-reform

"How could the government possibly afford a guaranteed annual income? As I see it, the average family needs at least $65,000 per year."

measure (which public opinion polls showed was highly favored), but in reality it was a proposal aimed at providing at least a minimum income for the working poor as well as for welfare recipients. But the term *guaranteed income* has negative connotations in American society; it goes against the ethic of individualism and self-reliance. Thus, recognizing this political reality, the main architect of the proposal, Daniel P. Moynihan, who was then serving as President Nixon's domestic adviser, subsequently observed:

> *American public opinion has shown a persistent tendency to associate political radicalism with the abolition of the wage system, an essentially utopian ideal, or with bohemian disdain for the work ethic. Any president proposing a "guaranteed income" in those terms would press that button, and that would be the end of his proposal. . . . "Guaranteed income" was the one label that said "Poison." Accordingly the president declared that the Family Assistance Plan was not a "guaranteed income."* [25]

The plan called for providing a certain amount of financial support for those whose income was low or who had no income. Everyone, of course, would be encouraged to find jobs and as their income increased, the amount of government support would decrease until no support would be needed or given. Moynihan wrote: "The heart of the proposal was to supplement the income of persons already working, and it sincerely looked to the prospect of finding work for others who were not working."[26]

The proposal was defeated in the Senate by a combination of political forces of conservatives and liberals. Ironically, the former feared that the program would be too radical; the latter complained that it was not radical enough.

Humphrey-Hawkins "Full" Employment Act

In the early 1970s, Congressman Augustus Hawkins (D., California) drafted a bill calling for the federal government to pursue policies designed to achieve a "full-employment" economy. Originally, the bill defined full employment as a decent job for everyone able and willing to work. It made the government the "employer of last resort" (that is, if a person could not find a job in the private sector, the government would provide one); it permitted a person to bring a lawsuit to compel such employment. These were considered quite radical measures, going far beyond the 1946 Employment Act.

Later, Senator Hubert Humphrey (D., Minnesota) joined Hawkins in sponsoring the bill.

In time, after considerable political bargaining, a compromise was reached. Full employment was defined as a three-percent unemployment rate for persons twenty and over, and a four-percent rate for persons sixteen years and older. The right to sue was dropped; government was not made the employer of last resort. Decreased unemployment goals were to be sought consistent with "reasonable price stability" and a decrease in inflation and the achievement of a balanced budget. (This compromise reflected the economic policy arguments we looked at in chapter 15.) There was to be more coordination on employment and economic policies among the executive branch, the Congress, and the Federal Reserve Board.

Basically, the new law, passed in 1978, did not specifically require the appropriation of money to create jobs; it was (like its 1946 predecessor) essentially a statement of policy. As in 1946, the proponents of full employment were disappointed with the compromise, but, recognizing political reality, agreed to accept it.

Congressman Ronald V. Dellums (D., California) summed up some advocates' feelings:

On the whole, I feel gladdened that this bill was finally passed after so many years of heated controversy. Passage itself is an achievement not to be taken lightly, especially given the contrary nature of the 95th Congress. The bill is not what we had hoped for, but at least there is now written a commitment to formulating economic policies on a comprehensive, coordinated, and consistent basis instead of in the current piecemeal fashion.

While the Senate did add amendments dealing with a balanced budget and limitation on spending, the full employment goals remain intact. We won a significant but little-noticed victory by defeating an attempt to include a quantitative ratio of federal spending to the gross national product.

Even more important, the bill included a provision which calls for a reduction in the differential in unemployment rates among youth, women, minorities, older persons, the handicapped, veterans, and the overall rate. We have the promise; we must now make certain that it is not a hollow one.[27]

FIGURE 1.
Social Welfare Expenditures Under Public Programs, 1970–1978.
(billions of dollars)

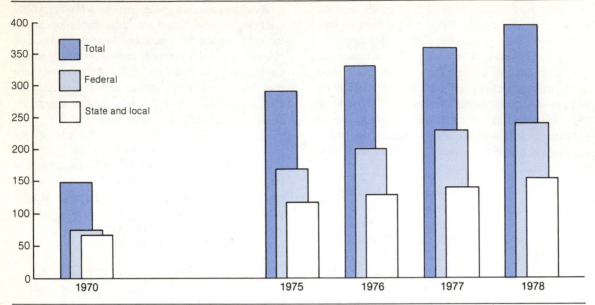

Source: *Statistical Abstract of the United States 1980,*
U.S. Department of Commerce, Bureau of the Census, p. 326.

There are often several laws that deal with various aspects of the same problem. This is especially true in the field of social welfare and aid to urban areas, where one piece of legislation can be related to another to achieve particular policy goals. In 1973, the Comprehensive Employment and Training Act (CETA) was passed, providing federal funds to local, county, and state "sponsors" who were to develop useful ways to train workers and put needy people to work in local communities. The jobs, however, could only be held temporarily (not more than eighteen months), after which time the workers were expected to find employment in the private labor force. Congressman Hawkins made the following connection: "Our recent efforts in improving the Comprehensive Employment and Training Act (CETA), the extension of which was approved on the same day Humphrey-Hawkins passed, is, in my opinion, an encouraging sign because CETA may actually serve as the mechanism for providing last resort

jobs if they are needed."[28] In other words, he was speculating that the Humphrey-Hawkins Act might be linked to CETA to achieve certain full-employment goals.

This is an important lesson to keep in mind about the American political process. The passage of a particular bill should not be seen in isolation and is usually not the end of the matter. It is another stage in a process. After passage comes implementation, efforts at revision, efforts to link it to other existing legislation or even, in some cases, to rescind it. Groups and individuals, as we have seen, might then challenge its constitutionality in court. Governing is an endless, dynamic process.

The Politics of Welfare Reform: The 1980s

For various reasons, the welfare system in this country has been a target of much criticism. Some taxpayers think they are paying people "to do nothing''; some recipients complain that benefits are too meager; conservatives believe that many of those receiving benefits are "cheats and chiselers"; liberals complain that welfare procedures violate the civil liberties of recipients and even encourage husbands to desert their families so the latter can receive benefits; state legislatures are under constant pressure to keep benefit levels at a minimum; welfare administrators complain that they are caught in the middle, trying to administer a welfare bureaucracy that no one appreciates.

As we have seen, the welfare program established in 1935 was intended as a temporary measure to help the "deserving poor"—old people and destitute widows and children. Today, however, the welfare rolls have become identified with the inner city (meaning, in many cases, minority racial groups), and with families whose children are born out-of-wedlock and who seem doomed to live within the cycle of "welfare dependency." Political battles rage over such issues as whether funds should be available to pay for abortions for mothers on AFDC. Gilbert Y. Steiner put his finger on the problem when he wrote: "Public assistance introduces problems of race, of sex, of religion, and of family relationships. It is hard to think of four areas most American politicians would rather avoid."[29]

Periodically, plans are offered to reform the welfare system, as we have seen with the Nixon plan. The Carter administration sought to accomplish the following goals:

- make eligibility requirements uniform from state to state;
- eliminate disparity in benefits between states;
- avoid encouraging the break-up of families;
- provide work incentives to the extent that it would be more profitable to work than to receive public assistance;
- simplify the bureaucratic system to make it easier to avoid fraud and error.

Some reform advocates have strongly urged the complete "federalization" of welfare, whereby the financial burden would not be borne by local or even state governments, but wholly by the federal government. They argue that poverty and welfare dependency are national problems and should be addressed at that level, that no one state should be asked to shoulder the burden for caring for the indigent since no state is able to exclude people from entering its borders. States must take the rich and poor alike, and if poor people choose to locate disproportionately in one state over another, the cost of caring for them should be borne by the taxpayers of the entire country, not just of that state.

Problems are pervasive in attempting to fashion reform that will satisfy the many different parties with specific interests in the structure and goals of the welfare system. As one account noted:

The Carter plan became embroiled in technical questions, such as how much to reduce a person's welfare benefits as his earned income increases, how to account for regional differences in living costs and which government agencies should administer which welfare payments. Finally, exasperated Administration officials and Congressmen gave up. A limited measure that hardly begins to deal with the systemic problems was approved by the House Ways and Means Committee last month. But even this modest legislation may fall victim to disagreement over the details.[30]

In addition, we must be aware of the regional interests involved. Members of the Northeast-Midwest Congressional Coalition (one of the Congressional caucuses discussed in chapter 11) were mindful that a reform bill setting national minimum standards for receiving welfare would help their states. This would tend to stem the migration of potential welfare recipients to those states paying higher benefits, a practice referred to as "wel-

fare shopping.'' There are no certain data on the extent to which this economic incentive has been a factor in the increased welfare rolls of the higher-benefit states, but clearly a number of state legislators and citizens believe welfare-shopping to be a fact.

President Reagan's new administration promised to address the welfare problem. Essentially, he favored reform measures that tied receipt of welfare benefits to some form of employment. This has been called ''work-fare.''

Thus, the politics of welfare reform is intimately involved with issues of race, economics, religion, and region, and all these against the backdrop of a strong ethic that favors individualism and self-reliance. There is no escaping the reality that to receive welfare in this country usually brings with it a stigma—of dependency and, indeed, of being ''less than worthy.'' As long as this stigma persists, social-welfare policy will continue to reflect a concern only grudgingly manifested, notwithstanding the arguments justifying more humane, just, and compassionate social-welfare policies.

Summary

1. Social-welfare policies in the United States are heavily influenced by a strong ethic of individualism and self-reliance. This ethic stresses one's responsibility for one's own well-being and eschews reliance on others, especially the government. A distinction is made between persons who are poor and those who are dependent. A stigma of ''undeserving'' is associated with dependency.

2. The devastating and widespread effects of the Depression of the 1930s caused some reevaluation of the ethic, and the New Deal rapidly developed a series of governmental programs to deal with the economic crises. These programs, however, were mainly seen as temporary and were aimed at a poor constituency that was by and large ''deserving'' of help.

3. The most politically defensible social-welfare measures are those in which the recipients have contributed to the benefits, thus ''entitling'' them to the benefits. Examples are social security (insurance) and unemployment compensation. Such contributions (like private insurance premiums) indicate that the recipient is not receiving "something for nothing." There is no stigma attached to such benefit programs.

4. The Great Society ("War on Poverty") programs of the 1960s were generally aimed at providing welfare services to particular groups that had not been able, for a variety of reasons, to take advantage of the economic prosperity following World War II.

5. Various policy approaches have been suggested for dealing with welfare reform and full employment. Some have failed to pass in Congress; others have been enacted. The politics of welfare reform will continue to be an issue in the 1980s. Efforts will be made to establish national eligibility requirements and benefits; other moves will be made toward having the states assume greater responsibility for welfare. There will also be increased efforts to have welfare benefits tied to some form of public- and private-sector employment.

Notes

1. William Lee Miller, *Welfare and Values in America: A Review of Attitudes Toward Welfare and Welfare Policies in the Light of American History and Culture* (Welfare Policy Project, The Institute of Policy Sciences and Public Affairs of Duke University, The Ford Foundation, Spring 1977), pp. 3–6.
2. Daniel P. Moynihan, *The Politics of a Guaranteed Income* (New York: Random House, 1973), pp. 17, 18.
3. Basil Rauch, *The History of the New Deal* (New York: Capricorn Books, 1963), p. 7.
4. William E. Leuchtenburg, *Franklin D. Roosevelt and the New Deal* (New York: Harper & Row, 1963), p. 27.
5. Ibid., p. 28.
6. Arthur M. Schlesinger, Jr., *The Coming of the New Deal* (Boston: Houghton Mifflin, 1959), p. 268.
7. Quoted in Ibid., pp. 308–09.
8. Moynihan, *The Politics of a Guaranteed Income*, p. 44.
9. Russell A. Nixon, "The Historical Development of the Conception and Implementation of Full Employment as Economic Policy," in Alan Gartner, Russell A. Nixon, Frank Riessman, eds., *Public Service Employment* (New York: Praeger Publishers, 1973) p. 19.
10. Leuchtenburg, pp. 133–34.
11. Ibid., p. 136.
12. Ibid., p. 141.
13. David B. Truman, *The Governmental Process*, 2nd ed. (New York: Alfred A. Knopf, 1971), p. xlvii.
14. Stephen K. Bailey, *Congress Makes a Law* (New York: Vintage Books, 1964), pp. 130–31.
15. Ibid., p. 148.
16. Michael Harrington, *The Other America* (Baltimore: Penguin Books, 1963).
17. Arthur M. Schlesinger, Jr., *A Thousand Days* (Boston: Houghton Mifflin, 1965), p. 166.
18. Quoted in Doris Kearns, *Lyndon Johnson and the American Dream* (New York: Harper & Row, 1976), p. 188.
19. Quoted in Sar A. Levitan and Robert Taggart, "The Great Society Did Succeed," *Political Science Quarterly*, Vol. 91, No. 4 (Winter 1976–77), 601.
20. John C. Donovan, *The Politics of Poverty* (New York: Pegasus, 1967), pp. 37–38.
21. Randall B. Ripley, "Legislative Bargaining and the Food Stamp Act, 1964," in Frederic N. Cleveland, ed., *Congress and Urban Problems* (Washington, D.C.: The Brookings Institution, 1969), p. 293.
22. Ibid., p. 298.
23. Ibid., p. 301.
24. Ibid., p. 308.
25. Moynihan, *The Politics of a Guaranteed Income*, pp. 10–11.
26. Ibid.
27. Ronald V. Dellums, "Humphrey-Hawkins Act: What It Means," *First World*, Vol. 2, No. 2 (1979), 3.
28. Ibid., 2.
29. Gilbert Y. Steiner, *Social Insecurity: The Politics of Welfare* (Chicago: Rand McNally, 1966), p. 4.
30. *New York Times*, October 21, 1979, p. E5.

Foreign Policy and National Security

Chapter
17

GERMANY
ALLEMAGNE

UNITED STATES
ÉTATS-UNIS

All nations seek to achieve and maintain certain goals in the international arena. The first goal for most nations is **sovereignty**, that is, supreme power over their own territories. Societies ruled by countries other than their own are not sovereign; they are politically, economically, or militarily dependent on others. Particular conditions help to maximize the possibility of maintaining sovereignty and independence, conditions which change from time to time, requiring adjustment in the particular policies a country pursues.

Of course, nations have other goals as well, many of them tied to the concept of sovereignty in various ways. For instance, it is common for a nation to wish to increase commercial trade with other nations, and, if possible, to achieve a favorable balance of trade—meaning to export more than one imports. It is equally common for nations to prefer to have friendly neighbors on their borders. This minimizes their vulnerability to military attack or boundary disputes.

In pursuing these and other goals, several strategies may be adopted. At times, nations will enter into alliances for their mutual benefit. They will build up their military defense forces. They will seek to develop their own internal economic capacity to produce goods and services for sale and trade on world markets. They will extend aid (economic, military, and humanitarian) to countries in need. They will enter negotiations and seek agreements of various kinds to achieve specific goals, such as arms limitation, the easing of tensions among nations, and the achievement of stable relations with potentially hostile countries. Negotiations may also result in exchanges of information, cultural groups, and diplomatic representatives, as well as in agreements involving such matters as postal rates, customs duties, patents and copyrights, or shipping lanes. In pursuit of long-term international interests, nations may form and participate in international organizations, such as the United Nations, or in regional bodies, such as the Organization of American States. In other words, the conduct of foreign policy may involve a nation in **bilateral** (between two) as well as **multilateral** (among several) relations.

The larger and more powerful a nation, the greater the likelihood that it will have several foreign-policy goals and diverse relations with the nations of the world. Such a nation will also be very influential in international affairs. Other nations will wish to earn its favor as well as curtail its power. The more powerful a nation, the more likely it is to find itself intervening in world affairs to protect its own interests. This intervention might be interpreted by some as legitimate and quite within the bounds of international relations; by others, it may be seen as nothing less than an act of *imperialism*—that is, an expansion of influence and control to foreign lands by political, economic, or military means.

An important aspect of foreign-policy formulation and implementation involves assessing the goals, capabilities, actions, and motives of other nations. In recent decades, especially since World War II, differences over just such areas have become a major point of dispute between the two most powerful nations in the world—the United States and the Soviet Union. President Ronald Reagan, at his first press conference, made the following statement in response to a question about his perception of "the long-range intentions of the Soviet Union." He said:

> I don't have to think of an answer as to what I think their intentions are. They have repeated it. I know of no leader of the Soviet Union since the revolution and including the present leadership that has not more than once repeated in the various communist Congresses they hold their determination that their goal must be the promotion of world revolution and a one-world socialist or communist state—whichever word you want to use.
>
> Now, as long as they do that and as long as they, at the same time, have openly and publicly declared that the only morality they recognize is what will further their cause, meaning they reserve unto themselves the right to commit any crime, to lie, to cheat, in order to obtain that and that is moral, not immoral, and we operate on a different set of standards, I think when you do business with them—even at a detente—you keep that in mind.[1]

Whether a particular American President takes the view of President Reagan or not, it is safe to say that Russia has been the major concern of the makers of American foreign policy since World War II. A substantial amount of American policy is predicated on responding to what many perceive as the ideological, economic, and military threat posed by Russian competition around the globe. This perceived threat may take the form of military and economic aid to Cuba and other Latin Ameri-

can countries, competition over Middle Eastern oil, or the encouragement of rebellion in southern Africa, Asia, and other trouble spots throughout the world.

Foreign Policy and Public Opinion

Though Russia is seen by many in this country as an important actor on the world stage, there is no general consensus on how best to respond to the Russian challenge. Some believe America's interests can be best served by encouraging newer, less developed countries to achieve their political and economic goals. This, the argument goes, would make them less vulnerable to the appeal of communist ideology and more receptive to American capitalist democracy. Others emphasize the necessity for the world powers to cooperate in an effort to avoid action that would lead to mutual destruction. Thus policies aimed at **detente** (the relaxation of tensions through common efforts) are advocated. Proponents of detente believe that there are always areas of constant competition as well as opportunities for cooperation. Still others believe that the best way to counter potential Soviet aggression is by building and maintaining a superior military force to "deter" the U.S.S.R. from engaging in actions that might upset the power balance.

In some instances, American foreign policy has been hotly debated. As American international involvement has increased, especially since World War II, such debates have become more and more a part of our national life. Some have argued that U.S. involvement in Vietnam was a moral and military mistake; others have seen it as a noble cause. Some have suggested that American interests require involvement in human-rights causes around the world, even to the point of using political and economic resources against countries —such as South Africa and the Soviet Union—that deny basic human rights to their own citizens;

others have said that such involvement only impedes international cooperation. Some have argued that this country should spend more money on highly developed defense weapons to guard against "falling behind" Russia in missiles and other military capabilities; others have countered that we already have the necessary military capacity to defend ourselves and our friends from attack.

The debates continue. For the most part, these positions are based on broad, general views about the state of the world and on preconceived opinions about the intentions and interests of certain nations. They are supported at times by specific ideological commitments, which are frequently reflected in the formulation of broad policy. It would be helpful to know about specific troop levels and deployment of submarine missiles, but lack of such knowledge is no barrier to forming general judgments about foreign policy.

Normally, it is important to point out, debates on the fine points of foreign policy are not engaged in by the majority of the public. Most people really do not know, *and cannot know*, the basic difference between one highly technical weapons system and another. Much of the information concerning such subjects is "classified"—that is, top secret, and available only to a select few who have been given security clearance at the highest levels. For example, some members of the President's own cabinet and many members of Congress are not privy to certain kinds of information, which is available only, perhaps, to the President, the National Security Council, and very few others. Policymakers therefore often have to take the word of experts and those who have access to confidential information. This makes intelligent foreign-policy and national-security discussions difficult.

The result is that most people tend to leave detailed debate to more "attentive" and informed groups. There is just so far the public can go, for instance, in deciding whether a strategic arms limitation treaty should be ratified by the Senate. One could be in favor of general moves toward easing tensions between Russia and the United States, but it would be difficult to know just *how* the United States could monitor the agreement without having to rely on the good-faith assertions of the Soviet Union. Similarly, most people might feel that the seizure of American hostages and the takeover of the American embassy in Iran in November 1979 were intolerable violations of international law. But exactly what tactics should have been used to gain the release of the hostages could hardly have been a matter of public debate. Woodrow Wilson's phrase, "open agreements openly arrived at," is not a likely prescription for international relations. The secrecy that surrounds most foreign policy creates a serious problem in democratic societies that desire to hold decision-makers accountable to those they govern.

In January 1979, when the United States and Russia were concluding an agreement to limit strategic arms (SALT II), one opinion poll (Figure 1 on next page) indicated that over half the respondents had no knowledge of what countries were involved in the negotiations, and did not know the general terms of the agreement. Such a lack of knowledge does not mean that people do not have opinions, however. This is especially true on matters of high visibility and on matters that tend to directly affect the lives of people. Generally, when there is a foreign crisis involving American military commitment, the public tends to register high support for the President. There seems to be a feeling of closing ranks, of presenting a united front to the rest of the world. This reaction does not necessarily depend on the success of presidential action, and it does not apply in all cases. Certainly, President Lyndon Johnson lost support in 1968 as a result of his conduct of the Vietnam War. But from Truman to Carter, public support in times of crisis seems generally to have been the case, as the charts shown in Figure 2

FIGURE 1.
Public Understanding of SALT II.

Question: Can you tell me which countries
are involved in the SALT negotiations—
the negotiations for a treaty that would
limit strategic military weapons?

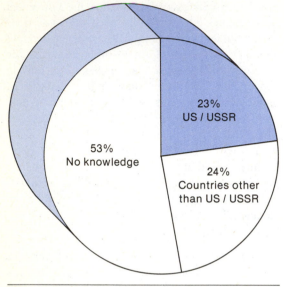

53%
No knowledge

23%
US / USSR

24%
Countries other
than US / USSR

Source: Survey by CBS News/*New York Times,*
January 23–26, 1979.

(pages 588–89) clearly indicate. In each instance
shown in the charts, people were asked to give
their views on how the President was handling his
job, not about any particular policy or action. But
after each international event or crisis, the President's approval rating increased dramatically.

One observer has suggested, however, that the
days of "automatic support" for foreign-policy
decisions might be over. Daniel Yankelovich has
noted: "A President . . . was presumed to possess
vital information unavailable to others, and therefore to be in the best position to judge what actions
were in the nation's interest. . . . Under the conditions that now prevail, not only has automatic
support for presidential policymaking dwindled,
but public opinion data have indicated that the

American people are eager to have more say—both
directly and through their surrogates in Congress
—in the formation of foreign policy."[2] He attributed this, in large part, to Vietnam and Watergate
—two events that led to skepticism about presidential leadership.

From Isolation to "Manifest Destiny" to Permanent Involvement

In his farewell address to the nation in 1796,
President George Washington advised the country
to avoid foreign entanglements. This was perceived as the best course of action for a new, still
developing nation. The United States was looking
for ways to gain time—and geographical space—
to develop and grow. Taking advantage of
France's battles with England in the early 1800s,
the United States, under President Jefferson, negotiated the Louisiana purchase, an acquisition of
vast territory from the mouth of the Mississippi
River up to what is now Montana. In this one act,
the United States acquired over 800,000 square
miles of land, twice the size of the then existing
country. The new nation did not want European
interference as it pursued what came to be called
its "manifest destiny" to explore and settle the
West.

To emphasize this view, President James Monroe issued the Monroe Doctrine in 1823. This
statement proclaimed that Europe should not establish any new colonies in the Western Hemisphere; in return, this country would not intervene
in European affairs.

Ultimately, only Mexico stood in the way of
western expansion. The Mexican War (1846–47)
took care of that obstacle. By the terms of the
Treaty of Guadalupe Hidalgo, Texas, New Mexico, Arizona, Colorado, and California were ceded
to the United States, with the Rio Grande River
established as the borderline.

These western lands were not uninhabited; people—they were called Indian tribes—had been living there for centuries. But they finally proved no match for the new American settlers and the American cavalry, intent on expanding their dominion to the Pacific Ocean. Through a series of wars and treaties (as frequently broken as honored), the only obstacles remaining to consolidation of what is now the continental United States were the natural elements and the Americans' own internal political struggles over such issues as slavery and states' rights.

Therefore, though the early part of American history is often characterized as a period of "isolationism," the isolation the U.S. sought was really an effort to eliminate European influence in the Western Hemisphere while American hegemony was being established on this continent. For the better part of the nineteenth century, the United States was largely free from interference by European nations. To be sure, efforts were made by England, France, and Spain to take advantage of the American Civil War by moving into the Western Hemisphere. During this time, Spain invaded Santo Domingo, and France, under Napoleon III, invaded Mexico. England supported the southern states in the war, and even supplied loans and arms to the Confederacy. But after victory by America's Union forces in the Civil War, France was forced to withdraw from Mexico, and Spain—having failed in Santo Domingo and having turned toward Peru—was successfully rebuked.

Thereafter, the United States was permitted to develop without the nagging international entanglements other countries faced. The Monroe Doctrine was sufficiently respected, and Americans could adopt a policy of peace-through-distance. The oceans served as natural barriers. Canada to the north and Mexico to the south were not threats to American security. They were neighbors who, if not always friendly, were at least not militarily or economically powerful.

Thus, the United States had ideal circumstances in the first hundred years of its existence: an open frontier with room to expand; vast valuable natural resources; a growing economy; and nonthreatening, relatively powerless neighbors.

The end of the century brought the brief, four-month Spanish-American War (1898), which led to American acquisition of colonies: Hawaii, Guam, Puerto Rico, and the Philippine Islands. In accord with the Monroe Doctrine, the United States intervened in Latin America, expelling Spain as a political force in the Western Hemisphere, and exerting influence in the internal affairs of Venezuela, British Guiana, Colombia, Mexico, and Chile. The Panama Canal was completed in 1914, after payment of $25 million to Colombia. Needless to say, the United States became the major power in the Western Hemisphere. Presidents occasionally announced policies of good will and cooperation—the Good Neighbor Policy of President Franklin D. Roosevelt, the Alliance for Progress of President John F. Kennedy—but the overall relationship between this country and its neighbors to the south was highly paternalistic. This has led to, at times, intense feelings of resentment on the part of many Latin Americans, who see American corporations and the U.S. government not in the role of formal colonial rulers, but rather as economic "imperialists" practicing "dollar diplomacy," extending control over other countries through economic power with military forces sent in from time to time to protect American business interests.

There was furthermore a limit to how long the United States could remain uninvolved with contentious European powers. World War I (1914–18) saw this country steadily identifying its interests with England and the Allies. The United States went along with the British blockade of Germany; German submarines sank American ships, and eventually (in April 1917), President Woodrow Wilson requested and received from Congress a

FIGURE 2.
Public Support for Recent American Presidents.

FOR TRUMAN, BERLIN AND KOREA

Question: Do you approve or disapprove of the way Truman is handling his job as President?

Percent approve

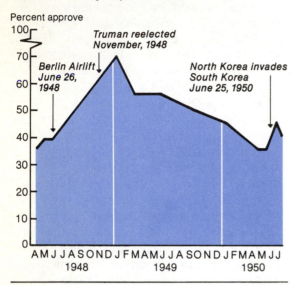

Note: Interview dates in June 1948 were June 19–24, 39%; in 1950, June 4–9, 37%; July 9–14, 46%.
Source: Surveys by the Gallup Organization, latest that of August 1950.

FOR JFK, THE BAY OF PIGS AND THE CUBAN MISSILE CRISIS

Question: Do you approve or disapprove of the way Kennedy is handling his job as President?

Percent approve

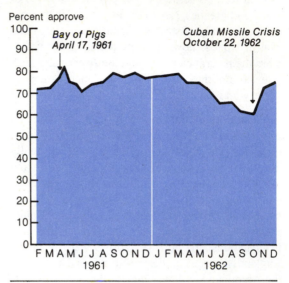

Note: Interview dates in April 1961 were April 6–11, 78%; April 4–May 3, 83%. Interview dates in October 1962 were October 19–24, 61%; November 16–21, 73%.

---

declaration of war against Germany. The United States had moved beyond its own hemisphere onto the European continent, and the relative neutrality and isolationism of the nineteenth century was ended.

While World War I was heralded as a "war to make the world safe for democracy," President Wilson could not get the U.S. Senate to ratify the Treaty of Versailles. And this country never became a member of the League of Nations, an organization designed to serve as a world forum

for discussion and negotiation in hopes of ending the necessity for wars. Perhaps the League was a naive notion, but it was one of Wilson's major goals. Many Americans, still clinging to their nineteenth-century heritage of nonentangling alliances, wanted no part of such a permanent international involvement. They preferred instead a "return to normalcy."

The decades of the 1920s and 1930s were years of economic boom and bust. They were also years when Germany and Japan were intent on gaining

FOR FORD, THE MAYAGUEZ

Question: Do you approve or disapprove of the way Ford is handling his job as President?

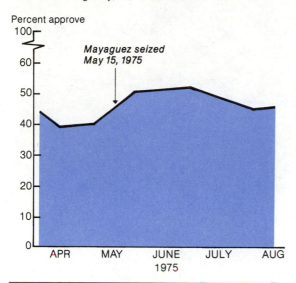

Note: Interview dates in May 1975 were May 2–5, 40%; May 30–June 2, 51%.
Source: Surveys by the Gallup Organization, latest that of August 1975.

FOR CARTER, THE HOSTAGES IN IRAN

Question: Do you approve or disapprove of the way Carter is handling his job as President?

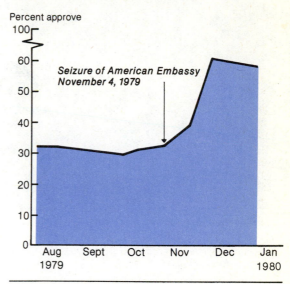

Note: Interview dates in November 1979 were November 2–5, 32%; November 16–19, 38%; December 1–5, 61%.
Source: Surveys by the Gallup Organization, latest that of January 1980.

economic and political benefits at the expense of those who they felt were taking advantage of them. The Germans, especially, felt resentful of the settlement forced upon them at the end of World War I. Disarmament negotiations failed. Italy invaded Ethiopia; Japan marched into Manchuria; the League of Nations was impotent. Hitler began to make aggressive moves in Europe: first Austria, then part of Czechoslovakia. On September 1, 1939, Germany invaded Poland, and World War II began.

It was difficult for the United States to maintain a posture of neutrality. The country was clearly aware that its economic problems were intimately tied to world economic conditions. This thinking was part of the motivation behind the United States' recognition of the Soviet Union in 1933. In 1934, the Reciprocal Trade Agreements Act was passed, giving the President power to raise or lower tariff rates as a means of increasing American exports. The Export-Import Bank was established in 1934 to loan money to countries in order

The sinking of the U.S.S. Arizona after the Japanese attack on Pearl Harbor. The incident marked the beginning of formal U.S. involvement in World War II and ushered in a new era in U.S. foreign relations.

to stabilize their currencies, and to permit them to buy American products.

As war clouds gathered over Europe and Asia, many groups in the United States still wanted to keep this country out of the conflict. The America First committee argued for noninvolvement. But American lend-lease aid to Britain (military supplies to be paid for at a later date) effectively ended American noninvolvement or any pretense at such. The United States was now inevitably involved in international political, economic, and military affairs.

After the attack by the Japanese on Pearl Harbor on December 7, 1941, the United States formally entered World War II. From that point on, the United States was a permanent and, as it developed, powerful actor on the world scene.

New Allies, New Arms, New Agreements

The end of World War II found the nations of the world involved in an interdependent set of relationships far different from any previously known. The victorious alliance soon broke up, and America's enemies (Germany—the western section—and Japan) soon became her allies. Relations between the United States and Russia rapidly deteriorated, and many new nations in Asia and Africa were born, usually with virtually no economic resources to sustain themselves and with geographical boundaries carved out by previous

A devastated Hiroshima, Japan, after the United States dropped the first atomic bomb. Ground zero, or the spot where the bomb actually hit, is one hundred feet to the left of the building.

colonial powers. Two competing ideologies—communism and capitalism—vied for the loyalties of these new fledgling nations.

The dropping of two atomic bombs on Japan in 1945 had drastically and irrevocably changed the nature of modern warfare. Nuclear weapons, including a hydrogen bomb, were soon developed; sophisticated delivery systems (missiles) were built and deployed. Mutual suspicion grew between Moscow and Washington, especially after Russia developed atomic and nuclear capacity. We began to experience what came to be called the **Cold War**. Immediately after World War II, under the leadership of the United States, Russia, England, and France, the United Nations was estab-

lished. This organization was originally composed of the victors of World War II (then allies) and fifty-one other nations; it now consists of 153 member nations.

The central body of the United Nations is the General Assembly, where debates are conducted, where discussions are held and votes taken, but where no action is binding on the member nations. The General Assembly serves as a kind of town-hall meeting of the world.

Only the United Nations Security Council has the authority to make decisions and commit the U.N. to action, which in some cases means sending troops into an area in order to establish or maintain peace. The Security Council has fifteen members, ten of whom rotate every two years, and five of whom (United States, Russia, England, France, China) are permanent members. Nine of the rotating ten, and all five of the permanent members, must agree before action is taken. (Any nation might abstain from voting; this is not counted as a vote against a motion.) Thus, each permanent member has a veto, which is a practical recognition of the fact that if one of the major powers does not agree, the decision is not likely to lead to world peace and security. (In 1971, Nationalist China [Taiwan] was replaced on the Security Council by the People's Republic of China.)

The other principal components of the United Nations are the International Court of Justice, the Economic and Social Council, the Trusteeship Council, and the Secretariat. The secretary-general is appointed by the General Assembly upon the recommendation of the Security Council for a five-year term. United Nations headquarters are in New York City, with various agencies located around the world. Financial support is provided by contributions from the member nations; the amounts of the contributions are based on four criteria: total national income, per-capita income, war-caused economic dislocation, and ability to acquire foreign currency.

Economic alliances.   In 1947, President Harry S Truman announced that it would be U.S. policy "to support free people who are resisting attempted subjugation by armed minorities or by outside pressures."[3] This became known as the Truman Doctrine, and it allowed for aid to be both economic and military (as was the case when Truman came to the aid of Greece and Turkey).

In the same year, the Marshall Plan (named after Secretary of State George C. Marshall) was instituted. The plan provided massive economic assistance to European countries to permit postwar recovery and development. Eighteen countries formed the Organization for European Economic Cooperation (OEEC) in 1948 to administer the Marshall Plan. The United States and Canada became associate members in 1950. As initial recovery goals were reached, the United States proposed a revised structure dealing with broader international economic problems, bringing in other nations and focusing on the less-developed countries of other continents. Hence, in 1961 the Organization for Economic Cooperation and Development (OECD) was established, with the United States and Canada as full members. Member nations of the OECD have permanent representatives serving at the headquarters in Paris. The members represent countries with a total population of about 685 million. The OECD countries represent "60 percent of world industrial production, conduct 70 percent of world trade, and provide 90 percent of the development aid granted to the less-developed countries of the world."[4] The OECD members are

Austria	The Netherlands
Belgium	Norway
Canada	Portugal
Denmark	Spain
Federal Republic	Sweden
of Germany	Switzerland
Finland	Turkey
France	United Kingdom
Greece	United States
Iceland	Yugoslavia
Ireland	(special limited status)
Italy	Australia (member of
Japan	Development Assistance
Luxembourg	Committee only)

Military alliances.   During the decade following World War II, the United States entered a number of military-political alliances: North Atlantic Treaty Organization (NATO, in 1949); Southeast Asia

FIGURE 3.
The United Nations System.

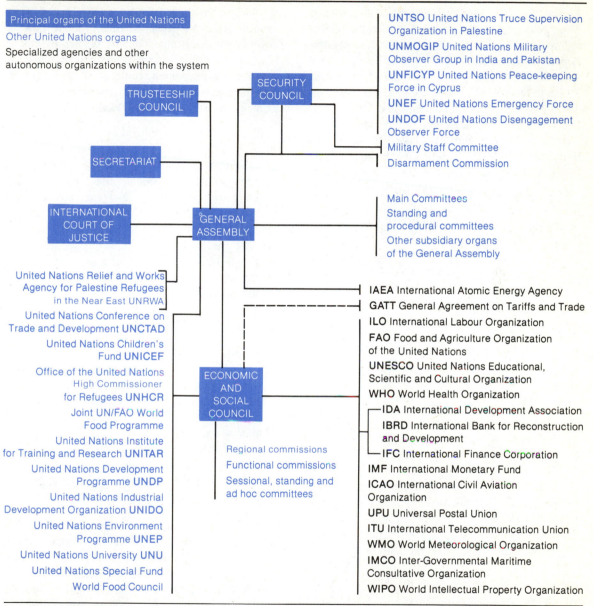

Principal organs of the United Nations

Other United Nations organs

Specialized agencies and other
autonomous organizations within the system

TRUSTEESHIP
COUNCIL

SECURITY
COUNCIL

SECRETARIAT

INTERNATIONAL
COURT OF
JUSTICE

GENERAL
ASSEMBLY

United Nations Relief and Works
Agency for Palestine Refugees
in the Near East UNRWA

United Nations Conference on
Trade and Development UNCTAD

United Nations Children's
Fund UNICEF

Office of the United Nations
High Commissioner
for Refugees UNHCR

Joint UN/FAO World
Food Programme

United Nations Institute
for Training and Research UNITAR

United Nations Development
Programme UNDP

United Nations Industrial
Development Organization UNIDO

United Nations Environment
Programme UNEP

United Nations University UNU

United Nations Special Fund

World Food Council

ECONOMIC
AND
SOCIAL
COUNCIL

Regional commissions

Functional commissions

Sessional, standing and
ad hoc committees

UNTSO United Nations Truce Supervision
Organization in Palestine

UNMOGIP United Nations Military
Observer Group in India and Pakistan

UNFICYP United Nations Peace-keeping
Force in Cyprus

UNEF United Nations Emergency Force

UNDOF United Nations Disengagement
Observer Force

Military Staff Committee

Disarmament Commission

Main Committees

Standing and
procedural committees

Other subsidiary organs
of the General Assembly

IAEA International Atomic Energy Agency

GATT General Agreement on Tariffs and Trade

ILO International Labour Organization

FAO Food and Agriculture Organization
of the United Nations

UNESCO United Nations Educational,
Scientific and Cultural Organization

WHO World Health Organization

IDA International Development Association

IBRD International Bank for Reconstruction
and Development

IFC International Finance Corporation

IMF International Monetary Fund

ICAO International Civil Aviation
Organization

UPU Universal Postal Union

ITU International Telecommunication Union

WMO World Meteorological Organization

IMCO Inter-Governmental Maritime
Consultative Organization

WIPO World Intellectual Property Organization

Source: United Nations

Treaty Organization (SEATO, in 1954); Mutual Defense Treaty (1953) with South Korea; Tri-Partite Security Pact (1952) with Australia and New Zealand, and Inter-American Treaty of Reciprocal Assistance (1947) with twenty-one Latin American countries. The language of the treaty with South Korea proclaimed that "an armed attack in the Pacific area on either of the Parties in territories now under their respective administrative control, or hereafter recognized by one of the Parties as lawfully brought under the administrative control of the other, would be dangerous to its own peace and safety and declares that it would act to meet the common danger in accordance with its constitutional processes."[5] The United States was launched on a major foreign-policy course aimed at containing communism. The view was that communist Russia sought to spread its ideology and influence, if not outright control, to any weak and vulnerable country, and thus it had to be stopped or "contained" through comparable strength. George Kennan called this "a policy of firm containment, designed to confront the Russians with unalterable counterforce at every point where they show signs of encroaching upon the interests of a peaceful and stable world."[6]

Russia countered with the creation of the Warsaw Pact, an alliance of several Eastern European nations designed to provide a defensive bloc to oppose Western nations and NATO.

These structures provided the organizational underpinnings of the Cold War between the East and the West, between competing social-political-economic systems. Two blocs stood facing each other, mutually suspicious and distrusting.

In 1950, the North Koreans attacked South Korea with conventional weapons—infantry, armored divisions, non-nuclear bombs—and the United States (providing the main military component of a United Nations force) responded only in kind. In 1954 (the Korean War ended in 1953), Eisenhower's secretary of state, John Foster Dulles, stated that in the future the United States would make its own judgment about how to respond, unconstrained by the wishes of others. The implication was that if this country chose to use nuclear weapons it would do so notwithstanding the nature of the opponent's attack. Dulles's strategy was called *massive retaliation*.[7]

This policy was criticized by some at home and abroad, who feared that it was not sufficiently flexible and that it unnecessarily limited policy choices. What was needed, the argument went, was a policy of *selective deterrence* which would permit varied responses to different kinds of threats. And this would mean that this country's defense mechanisms should not be confined primarily to the development of a sophisticated air-strike capacity. In some cases, argued some, it would be wise to use conventional ground forces to fight "limited wars." In 1957 Professor Robert E. Osgood wrote:

> The real strategic question facing the nation has never been whether or not to adhere to containment, for we have consistently rejected every alternative, but rather by what methods to implement containment so as to be able to avoid total wars, to keep wars limited, and to fight limited wars successfully. Unfortunately, this problem has always been obscured by our profound distaste for the very notion of containment and limited war.[8]

This view was based on an evolving notion that world politics was not to be understood only in terms of a monolithic force called "Russian communism," but rather that the international situation was extremely complicated, and required a flexible set of strategies, policies, and tactics.

Intense debates took place within this country over general and specific policy options. Should the United States attempt to sign an agreement with Russia limiting the development of nuclear weapons? Could the Russians be trusted? Should there be a nuclear test ban treaty? Should the United States send troops to Southeast Asia to repel a communist attack in Vietnam? If one nation were to fall to communist pressure, would this create a "domino" effect, causing other vulnerable nations to fall? Should the United States act if Russia proceeded to install missile bases in Cuba? Should the United States send a note of protest or troops or neither if Russian tanks moved into Hungary or Czechoslavakia or Poland?

Questions such as these continue to dominate American foreign-policy debates to this day. Obviously, not all of these questions are of equal importance, nor do they all require the same level of attention at the highest sources. Some are more important in terms of America's military security than others. Some affect this country's economic and defense interests more directly than others. Always, however, final decisions are made on the basis of national interests—immediate, intermediate, or long-term. Many individuals and agencies are involved full-time in this critical process.

The Makers of Foreign Policy

As far back as 1936, the Supreme Court recognized a basic difference between the requirements for foreign-policy making and domestic-policy making. The two policy areas, the Court said, are so different that constitutional limitations on the domestic front should not apply to foreign policy. If Congress wanted to pass a joint resolution (as it did in 1934) empowering the President to prohibit the sale of arms and munitions to warring nations, this resolution would be viewed as a constitutional delegation of legislative power to the President. In U.S. v. Curtiss-Wright Export Corporation, the Supreme Court said: "The whole aim of the resolution is to effect a situation entirely external

to the United States, and falling within the category of foreign affairs. . . . In this vast external realm, with its important, complicated, delicate and manifold problems, the President alone has the power to speak or listen as a representative of the nation."[9]

This power, the Court concluded, would exist even if the Constitution were silent on the subject, because the President alone has the capacity to know the facts and negotiate on behalf of the entire nation. Thus, what might be considered an invalid exercise of power in domestic affairs would not necessarily be considered inappropriate in foreign matters. Political scientist Aaron Wildavsky has concluded that in this sense the United States has "two presidencies," one foreign, one domestic. Presidential powers in the foreign-policy arena are clearly more extensive than those on the domestic scene.[10] Professor Richard M. Pious sees the extensive powers of the President in international affairs as "prerogatives" (powers gained through particular interpretations of the Constitution) rather than as formal grants of constitutional power. "Presidents have always relied on prerogative government to make foreign policy. They have successfully advanced their interpretation of their constitutional powers to justify their actions. Rarely has Congress dominated foreign policymaking although it has at times checked presidential initiatives."[11]

The Constitution does give Congress some functions to perform in foreign affairs, functions which cannot be delegated to the President. Treaties must be approved by the Senate; ambassadors must be confirmed by the Senate. Likewise, as we saw in chapter 8, Congress may put limits on the President's power to commit troops to battle (as it did in the War Powers Act of 1973) under its constitutional authority as the one agency that can "declare war."

Yet the President remains the major initiator of

American foreign policy, and the executive branch has developed rather elaborate mechanisms for exercising this authority. The principal agencies in the cabinet are the Departments of State and Defense, with the Central Intelligence Agency playing an important role. The Department of Commerce has a vital role to play in the matter of foreign trade and international economic assistance. Within the Executive Office of the President, the National Security Council is the main vehicle for directly advising the President and coordinating the development of a foreign-policy agenda. The Joint Chiefs of Staff also report directly to the President and Congress. These various agencies and their subunits have grown over the years as the country's involvement in international affairs has grown and become permanent. It is important to point out that relations among the agencies have not always been harmonious.

The Department of State.   This department, the oldest in the cabinet, has approximately 24,000 employees. It is divided into several bureaus based on geographic and functional areas, and there is a "country desk" in each bureau. Foreign-service officers staff these positions, and they provide detailed information to the secretary of state. The department's Policy Planning Staff is responsible for general formulation of foreign-policy strategy. Information is received from each American embassy overseas as well as from a wide range of other intelligence sources. The diplomatic corps is directly responsible to the secretary of state. Periodic reviews of policy are conducted; in times of crisis, the reviews and meetings may occur daily. The officials in this department are expected to have continuing expert knowledge of every conceivable aspect of foreign policy. Theoretically, they analyze and recommend policy but do not make it. Their intimate knowledge makes them important actors in the policy process. Most of the

officers—all but the very top assistant secretaries and above—are permanent employees. They serve no matter which political party occupies the White House, and therefore they are expected not to be partisan. Their job is to provide the most objective analysis possible within the broad policy framework laid down by the elected (executive and legislative) officials and to implement those policies in the most efficient manner.

Of course, it would be naive to assume that these officers do not have policy preferences. They do, and more than a few Presidents have complained about the intransigence or noncooperation of "those people over at State." Usually this is a complaint aimed at bureaucratic resistance to an order or policy. The foreign-service bureaucrats see elected officials come and go, and they are aware that the many layers of State Department decision-making present innumerable ways of frustrating a policy—either by procrastination or by simply failing to act.

Generally, the State Department is seen as an agency that puts considerable stock in quiet diplomacy and negotiation. Career officers are said to prefer the process of protracted discussion with their counterparts from other nations through various multi-lateral, international bodies. At times, such an approach runs contrary to that of officials in the Department of Defense or in the National Security Council or, especially, in the Joint Chiefs of Staff. Overall, the style of the State Department is based on a belief that the conduct of foreign relations requires careful attention to detail, a willingness to maximize patience, and a desire to avoid verbal or military confrontation. It is in the State Department where emphasis is placed on diplomatic *tact*, even to the point sometimes of using language that sounds like "double talk." How often have we seen cartoons of diplomats in pinstriped suits speaking long sentences in order to keep from committing themselves on delicate matters of international concern.

FIGURE 4.
Organizational Chart, Department of State.

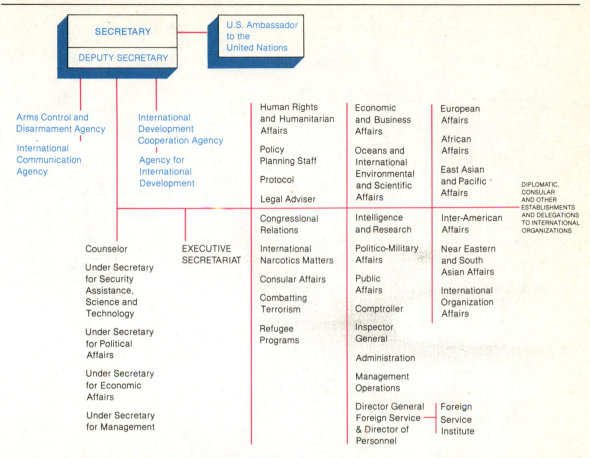

Source: *United States Government Manual 1980–81,* p. 429.

The Department of Defense. This department, housed in the Pentagon, includes the three military departments—army, navy, air force—and is charged with maintaining the country's military defense. A civilian presidential appointee, the secretary of defense, is the top official who supervises approximately three million military and civilian employees. The present structure of the department is a result of the Unification Act of 1947, wherein effort was made to create a cohesive arrangement of the three military branches. This was partially successful, but there remains, understandably, some tension among those who push for supremacy of one form of military posture over the others. And, of course, each branch has its supporters in Congress. There are those who feel that the country is best served by building up conventional ground forces. Others favor strengthening the nation's air power through supersonic bombers and various types of short- and long-range attack missiles. Still others favor a dominant naval capacity. These preferences get articulated in various ways: through budget decisions, strategic policy, discussions of tactics. The

FIGURE 5.
Organizational Chart, Department of Defense.

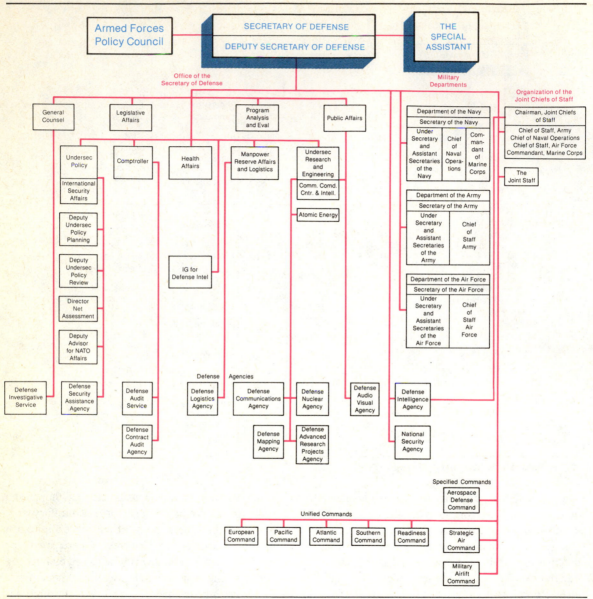

Source: *United States Government Manual 1980–81, p. 186.*

Defense Department conducts "war games" aimed at predicting as accurately as possible what United States' responses should be in the case of attack.

The Joint Chiefs of Staff. This body is composed of the military leaders of the army, navy, air force, and marines. The joint chiefs are nominated by the President and confirmed by the Senate for two-year terms. During peacetime, they can be reappointed for only one term. Their responsibility is to make sure that the country has the military capacity to defend itself at all times. They tend to be less trustful of the diplomatic process of negotiation and more apt to support a policy of peace through power. Their job is to have the country ready to fight wars in whatever form is necessary to protect the country's interests. Thus, they are concerned about such things as *first-strike* capability (the ability to launch an attack and do sufficient military damage to render the enemy unable to retaliate) and *second-strike* capability (the ability to respond to an attack in a manner that would inflict unacceptable damage on the one who struck first). In the lexicon of foreign policy, these people tend to be seen as *hawks* rather than *doves*.

The American political system operates on the principle of civilian supremacy over the military. The President, as commander-in-chief of the armed forces, is an elected civilian. But the military leaders are aware that they have enormous political power. Many people are wary of going against their advice on matters of national security where technical, classified knowledge is involved. Thus in times of crisis the tendency is to defer to the advice of the military. This situation is complicated when the military forces disagree among themselves, as they frequently do.

The National Security Council. In 1947, Congress established the National Security Council (NSC) as an agency to coordinate the vast process of formulating foreign policy in the executive branch, with particular emphasis on military security matters. Coordination takes the form of receiving reports from various agencies—civilian and military—and presenting them (usually in condensed form) to the President in such a manner that the President may consider all the arguments for and against certain proposed policies. Presumably, this will permit the President to make the best decisions. Frequently, the NSC and the national security adviser will be asked to offer evaluative opinions on the matters under consideration.

The council is composed of the President, vice-president, secretary of state, secretary of defense, and any others the President might appoint or ask to attend the meetings. The head of the Joint Chiefs of Staff and the director of the CIA normally attend NSC meetings. The executive secretary of the NSC is the assistant to the President for national security affairs, or national security adviser. Depending on the style and preference of the President, this person can be a most powerful official. In recent times, Henry Kissinger occupied such a role under President Nixon, Dr. Zbigniew Brzezinski under President Carter. Where the role has been given great visibility, there has been constant tension between the national security adviser and the secretary of state. This is especially the case where the President wants to play a very active role in foreign-policy making. As noted in chapter 8, the President meets daily with the security adviser, providing the latter with the invaluable advantage of continuous access. The adviser is supposed to present to the President the various policy options on a particular matter. Certainly, the adviser will have his own views, and these will be solicited by the President. Invariably, however, Presidents claim that the main foreign policy and security advisers are the secretaries of state and defense, (and this will often, in fact, be the case where the President does not feel a particular competence or interest in foreign policy). This was the case with President Ford, and it might turn out to be so with President Reagan. But for the most part Presidents have wanted to keep a large part of foreign-policy making within the White House, and thus have relied heavily on their own staffs, not cabinet members.

Henry Kissinger made the following observation: "For reasons that must be left to students of psychology, every President since Kennedy seems to have trusted his White House aides more than his Cabinet. It may be because they are even more dependent on him; it may be that unencumbered by the pressures of managing a large bureaucracy the Presidential Assistants can cater more fully to Presidential whims; it may be as simple as the psychological reassurance conferred by proximity just down the hall."[12]

A former director of the State Department's Bureau of Politico-Military Affairs, Leslie H. Gelb, drew the following conclusions:

The reasons have to do with domestic and bureaucratic politics. This is not to say that Presidents always make foreign policy for political advantage. Contrary to endemic Washington cynicism about such matters, my own experience, working in the United States Senate and the Pentagon, as well as in the State Department, has been that Presidents are usually quite highminded about the national interest and are often quite prepared to take political lumps for doing what they believe is right. But what is right has to win support, and Presidents often find that the State Department, with occasional exceptions, does a poor job of framing its proposals in terms that will elicit domestic support, and of thinking about potential political costs to the President.[13]

The National Security Council, likewise, provides a useful framework for cutting across departmental boundaries. Various committees and task forces can be formed which include a number of different departmental and military interests. Their reports are less likely to be resisted by agencies that might otherwise view policy options as power plays by a rival cabinet department.

The Central Intelligence Agency. The CIA, created in 1947, has the function of gathering and analyzing information, from all parts of the world, that may contribute to effective foreign-policy decision-making. Structurally, it is part of the National Security Council. Its duties include research, espionage, and a range of functions covering overt and covert activities. At times, the latter have included questionable acts, such as helping to overthrow governments unfriendly to the United States. No one outside of the most "classified" circles knows exactly how many people are actually employed by this agency, because some of its agents must, in the nature of the work, remain unknown. They are, indeed, spies, albeit not in the Hollywood cloak-and-dagger sense. Occasionally, it is revealed that "front groups" have been established as CIA "covers." Such groups receive financial support from the CIA in return for intelligence information. All major powers (and undoubtedly some minor ones) have some kind of intelligence-gathering network, and at times these operations can be an embarrassment to their governments. No country cares to admit that it operates in such a fashion. But neither would any country run the risk of presuming that it is the only one to do so.

Other executive agencies of foreign policy. The United States also functions in the international arena through special operating agencies. The

TABLE 1.
The Nuclear Club's Potential Members, 1981.*

Who has it	Within 3 years	4 to 6 years	7 to 10 years
United States(1945)	Australia	Argentina	Finland
Soviet Union(1949)	Canada	Austria	Iraq
Britain(1952)	West Germany	Belgium	Libya
France(1960)	Israel	Brazil	Rumania
China(1964)	Italy	Czechoslovakia	Yugoslavia
India(1974)	Japan	Denmark	
	Pakistan	East Germany	
	South Africa	Netherlands	
	Spain	Norway	
	Sweden	Poland	
	Switzerland	South Korea	
	Taiwan		

*Countries which appear technically capable of detonating a nuclear bomb within the next decade.
Source: U.S. government estimates cited in the *New York Times,* April 26, 1981, p. E3.

Agency for International Development (AID), housed in the State Department, deals with foreign aid of an economic and military nature.

The Arms Control and Disarmament Agency (ACDA) of the State Department conducts negotiations with other countries on such issues as SALT and the nonproliferation of nuclear weapons. In 1978, Congress passed the Nuclear Nonproliferation Act, which was aimed at preventing the spread of the wartime use of nuclear weapons. The U.S. and the other member nations agreed to cooperate in developing peaceful uses of nuclear fuel. As of 1981, 111 nations had agreed. Despite the efforts of the ACDA and others, most observers predicted that the number of nations with nuclear capability would continue to increase in the coming years (see Table 1).

The United States maintains a permanent mission at the United Nations, headed by an ambassador who has cabinet status, although the position is accountable to the secretary of state. In addition, the U.S. participates in multilateral economic agencies such as the International Bank for Reconstruction and Development (World Bank), which loans money to developing nations. Similar agencies with American involvement are the Inter-American Development Bank, the African Development Bank, and the Asian Development Bank. The United States contributes a certain amount of funds in return for a seat on the board of directors of the agencies.

The International Communication Agency is the official foreign public-relations agency of the government. It broadcasts the Voice of America overseas and maintains libraries in foreign countries where people may obtain materials on virtually any topic relating to the United States. Aware that the "hard sell" is not always the best approach, the ICA attempts at times to present what it believes to be a balanced view of this country. Thus, its libraries include pictures of race riots in the United States and other internal disturbances. But basically it attempts to present the country in a favorable light, emphasizing democratic processes and the exercise of individual rights.

The Peace Corps is now over twenty years old. A popular creation of President Kennedy's administration, this operation sends thousands of volunteers to developing countries to help in a variety of areas, including education, health care, community development, and agricultural development. The Peace Corps volunteers are not government officials, and, in fact, some have been openly critical of certain aspects of American foreign policy. The State Department, however, generally views this agency as a useful instrument of American foreign policy. The Peace Corps presents the positive image of Americans working in other countries—by invitation—and doing so for very little financial remuneration. Since its inception in 1961, the Peace Corps has sent approximately 80,000 people to eighty countries.

The Role of Congress in Foreign Policy

Congress plays an important constitutional and political role in foreign policy and national security. Although most programs are initiated by the executive branch, Congress, operating through its major committees, certainly does get involved. The principal committees in the House of Representatives are International Relations, Armed Services, Interstate and Foreign Commerce, Appropriations, and Ways and Means; in the Senate, Armed Services, Foreign Relations, Appropriations, and Finance. In addition, the budget committees of each chamber are important.

The President must present all treaties and certain agreements (such as Salt II) with foreign governments to the Senate for ratification or approval. Congress is centrally important in finally determining how much money will be appropriated for military defense and foreign aid. This role is not taken casually by the legislators. In addition, Congress can impose international tariffs and restrictions of various kinds on products. Congress can decide what, if any, military weapons can be sold to other countries. And, of course, the Senate can decide who will serve as ambassadors from this country.

All the executive agencies involved in foreign policy pay particular attention to Congress for budget purposes. Members of these agencies testify before Congressional committees and lobby for their projects.

Congress is also involved in foreign policy through its role in considering and enacting domestic legislation. American domestic matters and international affairs are closely connected, demonstrating again the extent to which the United States has shed its isolationist role. This relationship is clearly seen in the field of foreign trade, where domestic policy can affect the ability of American business to compete in world markets. For example, in 1980, Representative Richard L. Ottinger (D., New York) introduced legislation to create a National Industrial Innovation Corporation. This corporation, he said, would stimulate private investment in high-risk economic ventures in advanced-technology industries. It would provide loans, loan guarantees, and equity financing for those companies seeking to develop new products competitive on the world market. Ottinger stated:

Industrial innovation is vital to our national interest. In recent years, we have seen the United States lose its innovative edge in automobiles, steel, electronics, and textiles to Japan and Germany. The German and Japanese governments do far more than our own to foster innovation. Now the United States must commit itself to fostering industrial innovation.[14]

This indicates how far this country has come from the days of emphasizing noninvolvement by government in the economy and from adopting a posture of noninvolvement in international affairs. Both developments were inevitable for a major industrial trading nation. The growing trend of international economic interdependence surely required that the domestic economy be capable of competing with other nations throughout the world. The overlap of domestic and foreign policies under such circumstances was destined to involve Congress in foreign policy.

The War Powers Act of 1973 gave Congress the power to oversee under certain circumstances presidential action involving the deployment of armed forces. There are timetables and reporting deadlines the President must meet to keep Congress informed of any military action short of a formal Congressional declaration of war. In chapter 8, we noted that some observers believe that this law in fact gives the President *more* power to commit troops on his own, but Professor Richard Pious concludes:

The War Powers Resolution may not have transformed the way in which America goes to war, but that is not to say that it has had no impact at all. It forces Congress on record about the wisdom and legality of hostilities at an early stage. Every six months it sparks a debate when the president issues his required report. The new process might induce a president to redefine his war aims or make new diplomatic initiatives in order to retain support within his party.[15]

Yet the War Powers Act is unclear in several areas.

While it calls for the President to "consult" with Congress, it is not clear what form such consultation should take. And, of course, there is always the problem of national security, namely, precisely how much information should be given so as not to jeopardize the safety of American forces or to reveal important classified matters.

Influential Participants in Foreign Policy

Any discussion of foreign policy (as of domestic policy) that overlooked the roles of private, unofficial, but nonetheless influential participants would be incomplete. Although these individuals and groups are not as intimately involved as the government officials discussed earlier, they can be intensely involved and may have considerable influence. We will include in this group the media, special-interest groups, reference authorities, and what can be called "an aroused public."

The media. Throughout this book, there has been mention of the importance of both the print and electronic media. Public officials, we noted in chapters 4 and 8, are always sensitive to the influence of this industry. Television brought the Vietnam War immediately into the homes of millions of Americans every evening and contributed to (if not caused) increased public attention to that war. Columnists constantly comment on and analyze foreign affairs. Reporters are assigned to the Departments of State and Defense, and they become almost as knowledgeable about technical details as legislators. They monitor the words and actions of the official policymakers. They are in a position to check and cross-check, to remind officials of previous statements, of areas of apparent inconsistency. They are recipients of "leaks" of information from "unnamed sources"—although at times the nature of the information is such that it could only have come from a very few

A television cameraman films a demonstration in Soweto, South Africa, through a gas mask. The media play a crucial role in shaping public perceptions of foreign affairs.

(albeit, unnamed) places. In some instances, therefore, when some media people speak, they do so with a stamp of authority and credibility. Of course, it is not known exactly how influential such people are, but officials do not discount the impact such observers might have on an attentive —and in some cases even a casual—public.

Special-interest groups. Most groups, when they focus on international issues, concentrate on a limited number of issues or perhaps only one issue. Farm groups are keenly interested in grain-embargo policy toward Russia. The automobile industry wants the government to impose import quotas on cars from Japan. Greek Americans are vitally concerned about America's policies toward Greece and Turkey. Jewish groups want the government to protest the treatment of Jews in the Soviet Union. Longshoremen may threaten to not unload ships from Iran until that country releases American hostages seized in the American Embassy in Iran. Such groups might not be able to initiate or change particular policies, but, as we pointed out in the chapter on interest groups, they do serve to remind decision-makers of the potential political consequences at election time. Later in this chapter we will see what Theodore Sorensen had to say about the influence of some groups on foreign aid after World War II.

Reference authorities. Interest in foreign policy has led to the creation of a number of specialized institutions devoted to analyzing international political developments and suggesting policies. Some of these are private, independent agencies such as the Council on Foreign Relations, the Tri-Lateral Commission, and the Carnegie Endowment for International Peace. Others are located in study centers at universities. They employ people who have made careers of studying and writing on various aspects of foreign policy: nuclear weap-

ons, geographical studies, international economic relations, and so forth. In a sense, through a few select journals such as *Foreign Affairs* and *Foreign Policy*, this category of actors constitutes an elite corps of foreign-policy *reference authorities*. They are consulted frequently by government officials, attend national and international seminars, write books and articles citing, attacking, praising, and responding to each other, and move in and out of government, where they serve at high and important levels. (The policy of containment described earlier was first suggested in an article in *Foreign Affairs* written by a Mr. *X*. The author turned out to be a high State Department official and later American ambassador to the Soviet Union, George F. Kennan. When he left the government, Kennan joined the faculty of the Woodrow Wilson School at Princeton University.)

These people come to have influence in part because their command of technical facts is much greater than that of most people. And this is especially important in areas where detailed technical knowledge is a precondition to useful policy analyses. These people are generally partisan: they have definite policy preferences, and they usually end up associating with one of the two major political parties.

An aroused public. As was stated earlier, the general public does not involve itself in foreign-policy issues on a continuing basis. But even given this situation and the difficulty posed by secrecy and lack of access to information, the public *does* influence foreign policy. Perhaps the most vivid example in recent times has been the public's attitude on the Vietnam War. Changing from a stance of relative complacency and indifference in the early 1960s to one of intense opposition in the late 1960s and early 1970s, this "aroused public" was instrumental, many believe, in President Johnson's decision not to run for reelection in

1968, and it contributed to growing pressure on President Nixon in the early 1970s to withdraw the United States from that conflict. The aroused feelings were manifested in different forms: mass marches and protests held not only by radical groups, but by middle-class, normally uninvolved Americans; and slow but steady erosion of Congressional support for the war, which was probably a response to pressure from constituents. It is important to point out that such displays did not need to have unanimous support or even majority support (although poll data were beginning to reflect these sentiments) to be effective. Often, in fact, there were prowar demonstrations that were at times as vehement and as large as their counterparts. It was sufficient for significant numbers and segments of the public to become aroused against the war, including people who were normally not disposed to act in such a manner and whose patriotism could not be questioned. Such a mood could not be ignored by policymakers for long.

Foreign-Policy Spending: Ideology and Interests

The costs of defense. How much the government decides to spend on the various programs—foreign and domestic—reflects the twin influences of priorities and politics. It is difficult in the American political system to separate the two. Table 2 indicates the growth of defense expenditures since 1950 in current dollars and constant dollars (meaning, those dollars when adjusted for inflation). Figure 6 on page 608 shows how the United States compared with NATO countries, Russia, and Warsaw Pact countries during the 1970s.

Each year there are major debates between those who want to cut the defense budget and those who want to increase it. The former argue that certain costly items, such as the MX Missile (which is projected to cost $50 billion over a ten-year peri-

od), are not necessary, that the benefits of such weapons do not outweigh the costs. The argument against increased spending is usually based on the view that some weapons constitute defensive overkill, and that the country is spending vast sums of money on weapons that likely will never be used and, given the pace of technological advance, will be outdated almost before they are completed. Furthermore, this camp argues that the country already has the military arsenal to defend itself and destroy a potential enemy. The counter-argument is that the country cannot afford to weaken its defenses by failing to invest in weapons that either give the United States a competitive edge in the arms race or simply keep it abreast of its major adversary, the Soviet Union. This argument states that the weapons may not be used precisely because they exist as effective deterrents to attack.

Whether the defense budget is increased or decreased usually depends on decisions to develop or not to develop particular weapons systems. The debate involves determining who—the United States or Russia—has "nuclear superiority" and what types of weapons will be needed to fight the various kinds of wars. Some believe that the possession of weapons capable of totally destroying an enemy's major cities is sufficient to deter potential attack—if a country has the willingness to use such weapons. This is referred to as a policy of *assured destruction*.[16] Professor Robert Jervis, arguing for a policy of assured destruction, contends: "Deterrence comes from having enough weapons to destroy the other's cities; this capability is an absolute, not a relative, one."[17] The important thing, Jervis says, is to convince the enemy that such ultimate destruction will be launched if necessary. Therefore, all one needs is a second-strike capability. Others maintain that a policy of *flexible response* is required, which permits the United States to respond in a variety of ways to different sorts of military challenges.

TABLE 2.
Federal Budget Outlays for National Defense, 1950–1981.

(through **1976,** for years ending **June 30,** except as noted; beginning **1977,** ending **Sept. 30**)

Year	National Defense Outlays			
	Current dollars			Constant (1972) dollars (in billions)
	Total (in billions)	Percent of federal outlay	Percent of GNP	
1950	12.4	29.1	4.7	29.4
1955	39.8	58.1	10.5	75.8
1960	45.2	49.0	9.1	73.8
1962	49.0	45.9	9.0	77.2
1963	50.1	45.0	8.7	76.8
1964	51.5	43.4	8.4	77.0
1965	47.5	40.1	7.2	69.3
1966	54.9	40.8	7.6	76.3
1967	68.2	43.1	8.8	92.0
1968	78.8	44.1	9.5	101.4
1969	79.4	43.0	8.8	97.9
1970	78.6	40.0	8.2	90.3
1971	75.8	35.9	7.4	81.2
1972	76.6	33.0	6.9	76.6
1973	74.5	30.1	6.0	70.0
1974	77.8	28.9	5.7	67.9
1975	85.6	26.2	5.9	67.2
1976	89.4	24.4	5.5	65.6
1976, TQ	22.3	23.5	(NA)	15.9
1977	97.5	24.2	5.3	66.5
1978	105.2	23.3	4.8	66.6
1979	117.7	23.8	5.1	69.3
1980, est	130.4	23.1	5.2	70.7
1981, est	146.2	23.7	5.3	73.2

NA Not available. TQ Transitional quarter, July–Sept.
Source: U.S. Office of Management and Budget, *The Budget of the United States Government,* annual, and unpublished data. Cited in *Statistical Abstract of the United States 1980,* p. 366.

According to this view, conventional wars or limited nuclear wars are possible, and, therefore, a weaponry system must be built to engage in such encounters. The United States, they argue, must be prepared to fight limited nuclear wars, not just total nuclear wars.

Nuclear weapons may be classified according to their range. **Tactical weapons** are intended to be fired in or near the battlefield, and their use is confined to that area. Others, known as **theater weapons**, are longer range and are aimed at targets behind the enemy's lines, such as communications systems, airfields, and supply facilities. A third type is intended to hit targets such as large cities in the enemy's country itself. These longer-range missiles, or **strategic weapons**, are capable of inflicting widespread damage.[18] All such weapons, of course, are immensely destructive.

FIGURE 6.
Worldwide Military Expenditures, 1970–1978.

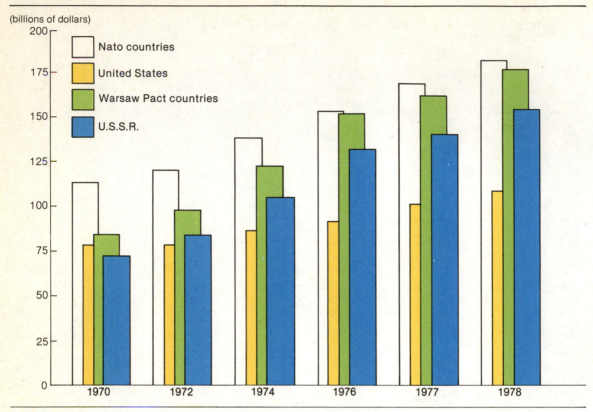

(billions of dollars)

Legend:
- Nato countries
- United States
- Warsaw Pact countries
- U.S.S.R.

Source: Chart prepared by U.S. Bureau of the Census. Cited in *Statistical Abstract of the United States 1980*, p. 367.

Ironically, President Dwight D. Eisenhower, a lifelong military man, provided one of the strongest arguments for cutting the defense budget when, in 1961, on the eve of his leaving office, he warned the country against "the acquisition of unwarranted influence, whether sought or unsought, by the military-industrial complex."[19] This "complex" he referred to consisted of an "immense military establishment and a large arms industry." Coming from such a source, the warning had particular poignancy. Here was an army general, a President, and one who could hardly be identified with liberal, "soft-on-communism" views.

Eisenhower's warning reinforced the idea among some that the defense budget was controlled by overzealous military people intent on spending huge sums for new weapons of war and by big-business arms manufacturers interested in maximizing profits for themselves. Furthermore, many felt that if less money were spent on unnecessary defense items more could be spent on needed social-welfare and human-services programs. (During the Vietnam War, this debate was often described as one over "guns or butter.") One observer, Ruth Leger Sivard, who was once chief of the Economics Division in the U.S. Arms

Control and Disarmament Agency, wrote that the arms race was inflationary, and that it contributed to unemployment and slow economic growth:

> One result has been the spiraling inflation that bedevils every nation. Heavy military spending generates buying power without producing an equivalent supply of economically useful goods for the market. The excess of disposable income adds to pressure on prices and in time becomes a prescription for intractable inflation. . . . Unemployment is another side effect of the arms race. As military purchases restrict investment and growth in the civilian economy, they limit the civilian job opportunities that are essential for an expanding labor force. . . . Government spending on weapons yields only half as many jobs as would equivalent funds if spent on houses, schools, transit systems and health services. Weapons production is capital intensive, and the relatively few jobs that it does provide tend to be concentrated in the higher-skill categories.[20]

In addition to the economic considerations, one side believes that the development and procurement of military weapons of sufficient strength to destroy the world would effectively deter potential enemies from making war. The other side believes that constant expenditures for research, development, and procurement of various weapons are necessary to guard against an adversary achieving a "technological breakthrough." If the latter were to happen, the argument goes, the country could be rendered defenseless, and it would be too late to respond effectively.

Politics and foreign aid. Although there has not been substantial political support in this country for large expenditures for foreign economic (or even military) aid since the Marshall Plan after World War II, all Presidents since then have recognized the importance of such programs. Cer-

Top: American F-16's in flight. Bottom: A Minuteman missile stands in its silo, ready for launching at a moment's notice.

Figure 7.
U.S. Foreign Economic and Military Aid, 1970–1979.

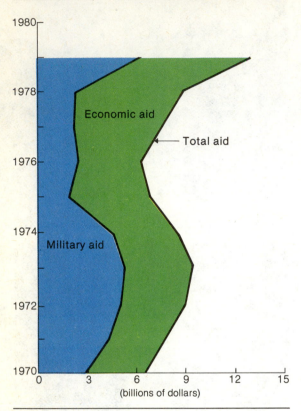

Source: Chart prepared by U.S. Bureau of the Census. Cited in
Statistical Abstract of the United States 1980, p. 856.

tainly, political interests have played a part. One motivation has been to provide economic assistance in order to counter potential communist intrusion into certain countries. This has not always been successful, however. At times, the aid has gone to dictators who have used it to maintain undemocratic regimes. This has caused some difficult choices for American foreign-policy makers.

There are also clear humanitarian reasons for extending American economic assistance to less developed countries. But lack of political enthusiasm here and questionable impact abroad have

been serious obstacles. Theodore Sorensen, writing about President Kennedy's problems in 1961–62, said:

> *Appropriations Subcommittee Chairman Otto Passman of Louisiana felt his annual responsibility was to cut back foreign aid as sharply as possible. . . . Passman had no difficulty in finding examples of waste and error in a program rendered incapable of consistently maintaining efficiency and attracting quality. . . . No powerful constituencies or interest groups backed foreign aid. The Marshall Plan at least had appealed to Americans who traced their roots to the Western European nations aided. But there were few voters who identified with India, Colombia or Tanganyika.*[21]

And yet, other countries continue to look to the United States for economic assistance, and this country continues to have such programs. To be sure, these programs are easier to support in times of economic prosperity, which is not the case in the early 1980s.

An effective foreign-aid policy must serve both political and humanitarian goals. This country should not attempt to buy the friendship of other nations with medical supplies, food, and the like, but it should also not give its adversaries undue political advantage in areas where American interests exist. Economic aid does not necessarily gain friendship, but it would be naive to believe that it does not provide some political leverage. Likewise, American policy is at times predicated on the idea that the more politically stable and economically viable countries are less vulnerable to communist subversion and overthrow.

The humanitarian basis for foreign aid speaks for itself, but it has not had a particularly loud voice in recent decades. On a few occasions, there have been exceptions. The aid to the Cambodian (but not the Cuban) refugees, relief to nations stricken by natural disasters, such as earthquakes,

TABLE 3.
U.S. Foreign Aid—Commitments for Economic Assistance, by Regions and Countries; 1970–1979.
(in millions of dollars)

Region and Country	Gross Cumulative Total 1970-1979[1]	1977, total	1978, total	1979, total	Region and Country	Gross Cumulative Total 1970-1979[1]	1977, total	1978, total	1979, total
Economic assistance	**26,910**	**3,181**	**4,086**	**3,848**	**East Asia**	**4,401**	**105**	**150**	**173**
Near East and South Asia[2]	**10,888**	**1,838**	**1,997**	**2,170**	Kampuchea	322	—	—	—
Afghanistan	118	20	5	3	Indonesia	772	42	74	95
Bangladesh	676	62	95	90	Korea	207	(z)	—	1
Cyprus	103	18	15	15	Laos	256	—	—	—
Egypt	3,344	699	751	835	Philippines	430	35	53	44
Greece	65	—	—	—	Thailand	157	13	8	22
India	639	—	60	91	Vietnam	2,032	—	1	—
Israel	3,575	735	785	785	East Asia Regional	229	15	15	12
Jordan	655	70	93	93	**Africa**[2]	**2,094**	**232**	**363**	**339**
Nepal	57	7	10	12	Cameroon	24	3	12	8
Pakistan	680	71	20	9	Chad	27	7	11	3
Sri Lanka	92	21	23	29	Ethiopia	129	1	5	3
Syria	439	80	90	90	Ghana	102	5	7	8
Turkey	247	—	1	70	Guinea	7	1	2	3
Yemen Arab Rep	53	16	7	17	Kenya	132	30	30	17
Regional	115	20	21	33	Liberia	97	19	5	15
Latin America	**2,871**	**190**	**228**	**255**	Mali	54	10	10	17
Bolivia	262	36	34	29	Morocco	77	2	10	4
Brazil	230	1	—	—	Niger	37	7	11	11
Chile	81	1	(z)	(z)	Nigeria	120	—	—	—
Colombia	406	1	—	(z)	Senegal	41	9	9	15
Costa Rica	75	6	7	16	Sierra Leone	9	1	3	4
Dominican Rep	90	1	1	26	Somali Rep	17	—	3	11
Ecuador	55	—	1	1	Tanzania	90	7	17	21
El Salvador	50	3	8	7	Tunisia	101	11	20	15
Guatemala	147	14	5	17	Upper Volta	36	3	11	16
Guyana	59	6	25	6	Zaire	93	20	10	12
Haiti	86	21	9	9	Regional:				
Honduras	131	8	13	22	Central and West Africa	190	9	10	8
Jamaica	77	18	12	6	East Africa	12	1	1	—
Nicaragua	135	1	13	10	South Africa	164	43	39	16
Panama	154	14	21	20	Africa	279	35	39	37
Paraguay	50	2	2	7	**Europe**[2]	**618**	**88**	**352**	**21**
Peru	162	17	22	34	Italy	50	3	23	4
Uruguay	40	1	—	—	Malta	79	10	10	—
ROCAP[3]	137	3	2	3	Portugal	435	65	300	—
East Caribbean Regional	117	7	24	27	Spain	33	10	7	7
Regional	327	30	31	14	**Nonregional**	**6,038**	**728**	**997**	**890**

Z = Less than $500,000. [1]From 1970 to 1976, years ended June 30. Includes transition quarter, July 1 to Sept. 30, 1976. [2]Includes countries not shown separately. [3]Regional programs covering Costa Rica, El Salvador, Guatemala, Honduras, Nicaragua, and Panama.

Source: U.S. Agency for International Development, *U.S. Overseas Loans and Grants and Assistance from International Organizations*, annual; and unpublished data. Cited in *Statistical Abstract of the United States 1980*, p. 871.

American aid to foreign nations is determined by humanitarian, as well as political and military, concerns.

and American response to the mass starvation caused by drought in several West Africa countries are all examples of foreign aid for humanitarian purposes. Some believe that such limited aid for immediate, relatively short-term purposes is better spent than general aid to politically unstable countries that have inadequately developed economic and social structures to use the assistance most effectively.

American foreign aid will continue to be determined by considerations of Cold War politics, American strategic interests (as in the Middle East), a country's willingness to support the United States in such international bodies as the United Nations, domestic economic and political conditions, and humanitarian motives. It is difficult to say which factors will be more important at any given time. In the calculation of policy, several variables are considered simultaneously and they have varying consequences depending on the circumstances.

Foreign Policy at Work: Two Cases

The grain embargo and food as a weapon. In December 1979, the Soviet Union sent troops into neighboring Afghanistan, where an internal rebellion threatened to topple a government sympathetic to Russia. A few weeks later, on January 4, 1980, President Jimmy Carter announced that the United States would suspend sales of grain to Russia in excess of the eight million tons guaranteed by a 1975 agreement. The purpose of the suspension was to punish Russia for its military invasion of Afghanistan.

At first, there was widespread support for President Carter's decision. One observer noted: "Farm lobby groups, mindful of a rising patriotic tide in support of the President, gave their tentative endorsement."[22] In one extreme case, the members of the International Longshoremen's Association (ILA) threatened to refuse to load cargo ships carrying *any* grain to Russia, including the eight million tons covered by the 1975 agreement. In March 1980, however, through private negotiations, the administration persuaded the ILA not to implement its plans.

To ease the immediate burden on United States grain producers and exporters, the government (through the Department of Agriculture) agreed to assume the contractual obligations of exporters for undelivered embargoed grain. In all, the Soviet Union was slated to buy approximately 25 million tons of U.S. grain (worth about $2.6 billion) in 1980—17 million above the 8 million guarantee. The American government took ownership of this excess and held some of it in an emergency food reserve. For the moment, this action averted a panic sale of future grain, which could have wreaked havoc on farm prices.

In addition, other measures were taken to protect farmers from immediate damage: government "loan prices," or the price the government pays for the farm products it buys, for wheat and corn were increased; market prices were permitted to rise before farmers were required to sell surplus grain from their reserves; and farmers were paid more for the grain stored on their farms.

After a few months, however, it became clear that this policy of using food as a foreign-policy weapon in this particular case was a questionable one. The stipulated objective of the action was not to get Russia to withdraw its troops from Afghanistan, but simply, as President Carter said, to "punish" Russia. This might have been possible if the loss of grain seriously affected the Soviet livestock industry. However, notwithstanding the fact that the United States was the major world supplier of grain, the impact of the embargo on Russia was minimal. In addition to relying on their own reserves and their own production (helped by

a season of good weather in 1980), the Soviets were able to make up some of the loss by purchasing additional grain from other countries. Admittedly, they had to pay higher prices, but Canada, Australia, France, Argentina, South Africa, and Thailand were willing sellers.[23] Australia's sales to Russia increased substantially; Canada's increased by fifty percent in 1980. Argentina, the world's second largest grain exporter, also helped fill the gap left by the American embargo. "The incentive to do so was an attractive price, as much as 25 percent above the American selling price, paid willingly by eager Soviet purchasing agents."[24]

Thus, one problem with the embargo was that several of the United States' friends did not support it. The United States made several attempts to get these other nations to join in, but the reception was lukewarm. They were understandably less than enthusiastic about supporting a decision made without consulting them. In addition, these countries were pressured by their own internal economic interests to take advantage of the economic opportunities. Argentina entered into a new five-year grain agreement with Russia. "The Soviet Vice Minister for Foreign Trade visited Argentina in April, and predicted a tripling of total trade volume between the two countries, to include increased cooperation in the nuclear energy field."[25]

The grain embargo came at the beginning of the 1980 presidential primary elections. Just two weeks later, President Carter scored an impressive victory over Senator Ted Kennedy in the Iowa Democratic party caucuses. Meanwhile, Governor Ronald Reagan, making his way through the Republican primaries toward nomination, condemned the grain embargo as inflicting harm on American farmers. In the summer of 1980, Senator Robert Dole (R., Kansas) issued a statement saying that "Jimmy Carter's grain embargo should be ended . . . now."[26]

Once Ronald Reagan became President, he repeated his campaign promise to "fully assess our national security, foreign policy and agricultural needs to determine how best to terminate"[27] the grain embargo. It was important, he said, not to give the Russians the idea that the United States no longer opposed the move into Afghanistan. Therefore, to the chagrin of farmers, he did not act immediately. However, on April 24, 1981, President Reagan lifted the grain embargo, saying: "In the first few weeks of my presidency, I decided that an immediate lifting of the sales limitation could be misinterpreted by the Soviet Union. I therefore felt that my decision should be made only when it was clear that the Soviets and other nations would not mistakenly think it indicated a weakening of our position. I have determined that our position now cannot be mistaken."[28]

This brief episode in foreign policy thus ended. Starting with relatively high political support for his unilateral action, the President subsequently was unable to convince other nations to effectively join the effort. This, coupled with restive economic interests at home, made the decision to use food as a foreign-policy weapon a risky one. Furthermore, it was difficult to show that Russia had been effectively "punished." If the embargo had a more precise objective (such as the removal of troops from Afghanistan), it might have been easier to determine how long to impose the embargo. A policy that relies on the cooperation of many other nations for its effective implementation must not overlook those nations in its formulation. In the final analysis, the grain embargo did not appear to be an effective policy for achieving one of America's foreign-policy objectives.

The United States and South African apartheid: decisions to be made.   A considerable amount of foreign policy involves deciding what positions to take in relation to conditions existing in another country. These positions do not always reflect an absolute decision to continue or to terminate political and economic relations. Frequently, the situation is too complicated for such all-or-nothing behavior. For example, the Soviet Union is seen by many Americans as a powerful adversary. In a 1981 commencement address to the graduates of the United States Military Academy at West Point, President Reagan, referring to Russia, stated: "The citizens of that society have little more to say about their government than a prison inmate has to say about the prison administration."[29] And yet, the United States still has formal diplomatic and trade relations with that country.

South Africa presents another important case for American foreign-policy makers. South Africa has a legalized system of racial apartheid (segregation) wherein 19.8 million blacks, 2.6 million "coloreds" (persons of mixed racial heritage), and 800,000 Asians are denied political rights. Only the 4.5 million whites are permitted to vote and to engage in various other forms of political activity. The system extends apartheid to the economic and social spheres. Certain jobs are restricted to whites; residential areas are designated for each racial group; education, health, and other areas of social concern are subject to the laws of apartheid. Civil liberties are severely restricted by laws such as *preventive detention* (imprisonment for an indefinite period of time without formal charges or trial) and *banning* (official restriction of individual movement outside certain areas or one's home and limitations on contact with other persons); freedoms of association, press, and assembly are subject to strict curtailment.

The ruling white minority defends its policies as the basis of guarding against a takeover by communist forces and on the grounds that white rule is ordained by God. Keeping the races separate is part of the natural order, the justification goes. At the same time, the South African government sees itself as a part of the Western, capitalist bloc of nations, and it seeks closer ties with the United States and Western Europe, especially England, France, and West Germany. South Africa is aware that its policy of apartheid has been officially condemned by every nation in the modern, civilized world—capitalist and communist. The United Nations Security Council and the United Nations General Assembly have repeatedly passed resolutions condemning apartheid.

Within South Africa, sporadic protests and violence have erupted, resulting at times in mass bloodshed and deaths. Occasional worker strikes, boycotts, mass rallies, sabotage of energy plants, and attacks on police stations have occurred, and the level of tension and animosity in that country continues to rise.

South Africa is an industrially and minerally rich nation. (Gold is one of its main export items.) There are approximately 350 American corporations doing business in that country, employing approximately 70,000 blacks. South Africa sells some important strategic minerals to the United States, specifically chromium, manganese, vanadium, and platinum.

At the same time, American corporations have been pressured at home to divest their South African holdings and pull out of South Africa. Some Americans have urged the U.S. government to impose economic sanctions on that country. On several college campuses, students have demanded that their schools sell any stock they may have in companies doing business in South Africa. There are two basic arguments for such proposals: one based on humanitarian considerations, and the other on self-interest. The humanitarian position insists that the United States should identify with and support human-rights causes wherever those rights are violated in the world, including South Africa. The self-interest argument holds that ex-

In South Africa, the ruling white minority and the black majority are separated by the policy of apartheid, or legal segregation.

tending political recognition to South Africa and by doing business there, the United States lends legitimacy to charges that it supports oppressive regimes. This tends to weaken American influence with other black African countries, which constitute a larger trading market for the United States than does South Africa. (The United States has $4.5 billion in direct investment and $13.7 billion worth of annual trade in African countries other than South Africa. The United States has $2 billion of direct investment and trade totaling $3.4 billion a year in South Africa.)

In 1981, a commission of eleven private American citizens issued a report based on a two-year study of the South African situation. It stated:

The African continent is the only major area in the world where the United States does not have a history of close involvement. But things are changing. Three African countries—Nigeria, Libya, and Algeria—supply the United States with almost 40 percent of its imported oil. . . . South Africa itself has resources that are valued by the West. . . . We cannot ignore South Africa. What happens in that country affects the United States. The uniqueness of apartheid attracts world attention.[30]

A full-scale racial war in South Africa would most likely have serious political implications in the United States. Therefore, while South Africa, in 1981, was not a matter for immediate foreign-policy decisions, it nonetheless posed major foreign-policy problems.

There are at least five important American interests to consider in formulating policy toward South Africa:

- protecting U.S. military and strategic interests and minimizing Soviet influence;
- ensuring adequate supplies of key minerals from South Africa;
- advancing political freedom and civil liberties in South Africa;
- maintaining satisfactory diplomatic and commercial relations with other African countries;
- maintaining commercial relations with South Africa.[31]

The need to balance such a range of interests is typical in foreign-policy making. Seldom will only one interest exist or even be dominant. Thus, in calculating how best to proceed, the foreign-policy maker must examine a range of possibilities under varying circumstances. The policies should be pursued with specific objectives in mind: for example, in the case of South Africa, ultimately ending apartheid; promoting genuine political power for non-whites with a minimum of violence; supporting other black African countries; assisting the internal economy; development of the black South Africans; and reducing United States dependence on South African minerals.

The study commission proposed a series of steps, involving both the U.S. government and American corporations, calculated to achieve these objectives, mindful that internal South African events could alter the picture at any time. Corporations with South African interests, for example, were urged to devote a certain percentage of their profits to social and economic development projects for black South Africans. The government was urged to reconsider the extent to which it should aid South Africa in drilling and exploring for oil. South Africa, which is not an oil-rich nation, relies heavily on American technology for this enterprise.

There are decisions to be made in determining American policy toward South Africa. Several interests must be kept in mind, and at all times, as with the grain-embargo case, the various possible courses of action of other nations must be fully considered.

Foreign Policies in the 1980s

Foreign policies and defense strategies in the 1980s will continue to be determined largely, but not exclusively, by considerations of America's position in relation to the Soviet Union. Decisions will be based on assessments of Russia's short- and long-term goals and military capabilities. Efforts will be made not only to counter Russian strength with American military preparedness, but to convey to other adversaries the consequences of attacking this country or its allies. This latter point is vitally important. In a real sense, a country's military might is ultimately effective if it never has to be used. This is the rationale for the deterrence theory. Thus, the strength of a country must not only be a fact; it must be accompanied by a belief on the part of others that it will be used if necessary.

Credibility is as important with allies as it is with adversaries. Convincing others of one's willingness to act in certain ways under certain circumstances is a function of both what a nation does and what it says, publicly and privately. Therefore, the United States (like any major power) cannot appear to be inconsistent or uncertain. This is not always easy to achieve, especially in situations where it is unwise to adopt positions that prohibit flexibility or even reversal of previous policies.

For political, economic, and strategic reasons, certain regions of the world will continue to be of utmost importance to American national interests. The Middle East and its oil resources are perhaps the most prominent concerns in the early 1980s. Western Europe remains a perennial ally and the United States will strive to maintain viable relationships there. But the Far East (especially, the People's Republic of China, Japan, India, and Pakistan) cannot be neglected. What develops between Moscow and Peking—now two hostile

President Reagan and Mexican President Portillo take time out from political discussions for a ride around the western White House, 1981.

communist nations—will be of utmost importance to Washington, and yet there is probably very little that the United States can do or should try to do to influence that relationship in one direction or another.

In addition, new nations are coming into their political, if not economic, own in Africa south of the Sahara, and the potentially explosive situation in South Africa poses serious problems for foreign-policy planning.

As always, what happens in the Western Hemisphere, especially in Latin America, will be of vital concern to the United States. All nations want friendly neighbors, or at least ones that are not hostile. But the days of American intervention in the affairs of politically volatile Latin American countries are essentially over. New governments will come and go in those countries, as often violently as otherwise, and some are likely to be receptive to socialist or communist ideologies. This will require the United States to adapt to a new relationship of cooperative partnership rather than the co-optive paternalism that has characterized much of American behavior in the last eighty years. America's concern in this hemisphere has not lessened since the Monroe Doctrine; that has been a constant. What has drastically changed have been the conditions in which this concern are to be pursued.

There are many more actors on the world scene today than even twenty years ago. There are two military superpowers with the capacity to destroy each other and the world. But until—if ever—they reach the point of total nuclear destruction, they must be prepared to compete on other terms, including political negotiation and bargaining. We have discussed this aspect of the political process on the domestic scene in several chapters in this book. It is no less a requirement on the international scene, where, in many ways, it is more difficult to pursue. Sovereign nations are not comparable to domestic interest groups; the United Nations Charter does not have the binding force of the United States Constitution; the United Nations General Assembly or Security Council is not Congress; the International Court of Justice is not the Supreme Court. In other words, while the stakes—life and death—in negotiated settlements are higher in foreign politics than in domestic politics, the political structures to achieve negotiated results are weaker or nonexistent.

Foreign policies in the 1980s must be clear enough to convey credibility, and at the same time flexible enough to permit compromise. In the final analysis, the hope is that competitive political systems will be able to perceive enough common interests whereby their own self-interests will be best served by negotiating rather than by fighting.

Summary

1. Political, economic, and military developments over the last two centuries have caused the United States to become permanently involved in world affairs. This evolving situation, accompanied by major arms developments as well as the rise of a powerful adversary in Russia, has caused the United States constantly to rethink its goals, strategies, and tactics.

2. While the President is the principal initiator of foreign policy, there is an elaborate network of influential participants in the making and implementing of America's foreign policies.

3. The budget for defense and foreign aid reflects the decisions made on several foreign-policy issues: what types of weapons will be needed to fight what types of wars; the costs and benefits of certain defense policies; the extent to which other nations support American positions. National self-interest, however, is the paramount consideration, and this motivates all nations in the international system.

Notes

1. *New York Times*, January 30, 1981, p. A10.
2. Daniel Yankelovich, "Farewell to 'President Knows Best,'" *Foreign Affairs*, Vol. 57, No. 3 (1979), 670–71.
3. Robert Endicott Osgood, *Limited War* (Chicago: University of Chicago Press, 1957), p. 148.
4. *Countries of the World and Their Leaders Yearbook 1980* (Detroit: Gale Research Company, 1980), p. 1197.
5. Quoted in Frederick H. Hartmann, *The Relations of Nations* (New York: Macmillan Publishing Co., Inc., 1978), p. 340.
6. George Kennan, *American Diplomacy, 1900–1950* (Chicago: University of Chicago Press, 1951), pp. 120, 126.
7. Osgood, pp. 205–14.
8. Ibid., p. 146.
9. *United States* v. *Curtiss-Wright*, 299 U.S. 304 (1936).
10. Aaron Wildavsky, "The Two Presidencies," in Wildavsky, ed., *The Presidency* (Boston: Little, Brown and Company, 1969), p. 231.
11. Richard M. Pious, *The American Presidency* (New York: Basic Books, Inc., 1979), p. 332.
12. Henry Kissinger, *The White House Years* (Boston: Little, Brown and Company, 1979), p. 47.
13. Leslie H. Gelb, "The Struggle over Foreign Policy," *The New York Times Magazine*, July 20, 1980, p. 34.
14. News release from the office of Representative Richard L. Ottinger (D., New York), September 15, 1980.
15. Pious, p. 415.
16. Robert Jervis, "Why Nuclear Superiority Doesn't Matter," *Political Science Quarterly*, Vol. 94, No. 4 (Winter 1979–80), pp. 617–33.
17. Ibid., p. 618.
18. These weapons are discussed in "Reagan Facing Tough Defense Choices," *CQ Weekly Report*, February 7, 1981, pp. 251–56; and Jeffrey Record, *U.S. Nuclear Weapons in Europe* (Washington, D.C.: The Brookings Institution, 1974).
19. *New York Times*, January 18, 1961, p. A22.
20. Ruth Leger Sivard, "Social Costs and the Arms Race," *The Nation*, June 17, 1978, pp. 731–32.
21. Theodore Sorensen, *Kennedy*, (New York: Harper & Row, 1965), p. 351.
22. Robert L. Paarlberg, "Lessons of the Grain Embargo," *Foreign Affairs*, Vol. 59, No. 1 (Fall 1980), p. 144.
23. Ibid., p. 152.
24. Ibid., p. 153.
25. Ibid., p. 153.
26. *CQ Weekly Report*, March 28, 1981, p. 562.
27. *CQ Weekly Report*, May 9, 1981, p. 827.
28. Ibid., p. 827.
29. *New York Times*, May 28, 1981, p. D20.
30. Foreign Policy Study Foundation, *South Africa: Time Running Out* (Berkeley: University of California Press, 1981), p. xvii.
31. Ibid., p. xxviii.

Overview

Policies and Processes

The chapters in this section have examined how the American political system has dealt (and continues to deal) with some basic substantive issues. Civil-liberties issues require a constant balancing of the values of individual rights and societal interests. Many of these issues are resolved by the Supreme Court, which tries to develop clear guidelines to indicate how far people and governments can go in exercising certain constitutional rights.

The protection of the rights of minority groups has been a perennial issue, demonstrating the tension between theory and practice. Many rights have been established in the Constitution long before they have been realized in practice. Policy-making in this field has been incremental, but steadily in the direction of reconciling policy and practice. An important issue is to what extent the government can and should protect the rights of members of minority groups without infringing on the rights of members of other groups.

The role of the government in the economy and in social welfare has been a particularly important one since the 1930s and the New Deal. The policies developed have been the subject of ideological debates as well as the basis for competition among interest groups.

Since World War II, the United States has been a major power in the international arena. Because of this status, it has been necessary to make policy choices about the size and nature of the country's military defenses, as well as about the various means the country should employ to compete with its major international adversary—the Soviet Union.

Each of these areas requires setting many policy agendas and developing and modifying many different policies. There are many more participants in domestic-policy making than in foreign-policy making, but the political struggle is by no means absent in the latter.

Policy agendas are built in various ways. Individuals or groups go to court over alleged violations of their individual rights. Some groups engage in mass protests to bring their cause to the forefront. An economic depression or inflation might be the catalyst that initiates social-welfare and economic policy agendas.

In each case, the preferred approach to formulating policy is for decision makers to consider a range of policy options. But politics is always a factor to be considered, and the political process does not guarantee the most equitable results in every instance. It does provide a framework for continued struggle, however.

American foreign-policy making will continue to be heavily influenced by our relationship with the Soviet Union. But the United States cannot overlook other nations and regions. The same policymaking process (setting policy agendas, deciding among options, implementing decisions, evaluating programs, reacting to policy feedback) will operate in foreign policy as in domestic policy, but there will be important differences. The President will have greater leeway in developing and implementing policies in foreign affairs than in domestic affairs. Public and Congressional access to relevant data will be more difficult in foreign policy, where national security is a factor. Working with other nations through alliances and through regional and international bodies will be a necessity. Even so, international agreements will be difficult to enforce, precisely because nations are sovereign entities.

Ultimately, however, policymakers in both foreign and domestic matters will have to focus on the same basic concern: obtaining and maintaining maximum political support for their decisions. This support will have to be drawn from all segments of the American social and political structure: the legislative and executive branches of government, the public at large, the various groups and organizations with special interests in specific policy areas, and even (to some extent) the judiciary. The process of gathering support from all these sources while at the same time formulating forward-looking and coherent policies is an extraordinarily challenging task, and one which

will make severe demands on the intellectual and physical resources of our future leaders.

Epilog
American Government
—Retrospect and Prospect

This book has been concerned with how Americans govern themselves. We have described a number of crucial elements in the political system: values and ideals, participants, institutions, and policies. We have seen that the American governing process has been a continuing story of competing interests, of bargaining and compromise. Americans have jealously guarded the individual freedoms won in their war of independence from Great Britain, and at the same time they have struggled to build a government strong enough to guard against internal disintegration and external conquest. In this sense, their goals have been little different from those of people of other sovereign nations. But the American experience has been unique if only because it has involved enormous social and economic growth, along with the attainment, after two hundred years, of a place of preeminent power in the world. No other political system has accomplished quite so much over such an extended period of time.

The Three Themes

In examining the story of American government, we continually returned to the three themes outlined in the Introduction.

Constancy and change. To be sure, one important measure of the success of any political system is the extent to which it has achieved and maintained stability. But stability is not a matter simply of maintaining the status quo. It involves maintaining some established goals and institutions, while at the same time retaining the capacity to adapt to changing situations.

The most constant aspect of American government has been a written Constitution. This document, which remains the central authority that defines the boundaries of permissible action, has been formally amended only twenty-six times in its nearly 200 years of existence. In the process of adapting to new times and circumstances, Americans have interpreted their Constitution in various, sometimes contradictory, ways.

Essentially, the formal institutions have remained constant. Though there has been some modification in the way officials are elected, the three national branches of government have remained intact. The powers exercised by those branches, however, have changed from time to time. The presidency has developed into a powerful institution, especially as the country has become more involved in international affairs. Congress has become' more active in relation to both the executive branch and the states as the country's economy has grown more complex. The Supreme Court has changed from time to time in its approaches to interpreting the Constitution.

The rise and the apparent decline of political parties have been notable events in American political life. Parties are not even mentioned in the Constitution, yet American politics cannot be understood without a knowledge of the role of the two-party system as a distinctively American innovation.

The system of federalism has remained constant, but the relationship between the national government and the states has changed substantially—partly, again, through constitutional interpretation. Changes in the federal system have often resulted from a recognition of the need, at a particular time, to have one level of government as opposed to another perform certain functions. In order to meet the needs of some citizens and local units of government, *fiscal federalism* has been developed to provide a new means of transferring economic resources within the federal system. Adaptive changes have been made to deal with civil-rights problems in response to the feeling that those problems were not being handled adequately at the state and local levels.

Many of these changes have been debated and resisted, and have come about as a result of compromise. Some people believed that some of the changes were unwarranted (as well as unconstitutional). But for the most part (the Civil War being the major exception), disagreements have been confined to the political arena and have been resolved peacefully. Institutions have not always performed in the manner most people would have preferred (as when the Supreme Court overruled several New Deal laws), but the ultimate legitimacy of those institutions as proper governing bodies has persisted.

Theory and practice. American government has always had to grapple with the problem of trying to reconcile what is theoretically desirable with what is practically possible. The theoretical defines ideals, values, goals, and what "ought to be." The practical describes realities, interests, compromises, and what "can be." The theoretical outlines a government equally responsive to all its citizens. The practical tells us that some individuals and groups are more resourceful than others, and thus have more access to (and consequently more influence with) decision-makers. The theoretical stipulates no discrimination based on race or sex; the practical reminds us that this ideal has not been fully achieved. Theoretically, the people select their leaders, and they do so through periodic elections in which the voters may hold officials accountable for their actions. Practically, however, we know that the connection between elections and what finally is enacted into law and implemented is at best a tenuous one: the media intervene to filter issues and create images, incumbents maintain a distinct advantage over challengers, decisions are made and carried out quietly—out of the public view. The theoretical preference for peaceful politics sometimes gives way to more forceful means of bringing a group's policy agenda to the attention of the powers that be. For a number of practical reasons, decision-makers might not take notice of an issue until disruption is threatened or actually occurs. At that point a new reality takes shape and the political system reacts.

In theory, the two major political parties offer the electorate reasonably varied choices. But in practice the parties do not want to stray too far from the middle of a wide spectrum of public opinion. The nature of the electoral system puts a premium on forming a broad base of support before the election; therefore, it is not advisable to be found too far to the left or right on the ideological scale. Differences that might, in fact, exist tend to get muted, and some voters are frequently not able (or at least they say they are not) to discern much difference between the two major political parties.

The gulf between theory and practice can present some problems in the political system. If some groups find that the gap is too wide and too persistent, they might become alienated and refuse to participate in the political process. This is a danger of democracy, because the life of the system depends as much on participation as it does on particular results. If the theory of elections is too often unrealized in the practice of the electoral process, increasing numbers of people may decide not to vote. This has been happening in the American system over the last two decades. A healthy democracy cannot exist without a basic confidence on the part of its citizens in the processes of government. Thus, there must always be care that promises are not too much at variance with performance.

At times, this might call for a reexamination of the theories and ideals on which the system is based. If they are too unrealistic, then more realistic goals might be in order. At the same time, a society should not abandon ideals which, even if unattainable in the near future, can be articulated as the highest and best goals for which the society stands. Constantly striving to bridge the gap between theory and practice ought to be one of the central concerns of political leadership.

Power and consensus. This brings us to the third theme of this book. In the American political system, considerable emphasis is placed on reaching *consensus*. It is one thing to have certain legal powers, it is another to know when and how to exercise those powers. Throughout this book, we have seen instances where a branch of government has the authority and power to act, but we have also seen that without a broad base of support, any action will likely be ineffective. Power must be tempered by sensitivity to the context in which it is exercised. Continued refusal to heed this imperative might lead to formal restrictions on power and substantial alterations in the system.

Knowing when and how to balance power and consensus is what is meant by being politically astute. A President should carefully maintain good relations with Congress, and Congress should work *with* the executive branch, not against it. Interest groups should be mindful of the needs of others. If regulatory agencies do not take this aspect of the process into account, they will ultimately find their rules and regulations resisted in many quarters. The Supreme Court has the power to declare laws unconstitutional, but in the final analysis that power is only as effective as the Court's prestige in the public's view. There must be a consensus that the Court as an institution deserves respect, even if particular decisions are unpopular.

Ultimately, consensus depends on the ability of the political system itself to command respect and loyalty. This is not a function of coercion. It stems from the belief that existing institutions are *legitimate*. Consensus cannot be manufactured.

Even in a formal sense, the American political system puts heavy emphasis on consensus. Much of what ultimately can happen in American government can only occur after several official sources have reached agreement. Even the most popular Presidents have had to face this reality.

This tension between power and consensus is also present when we consider action that involves the interests of other countries. In one instance noted in the text, an American President had the power to restrict grain exports to Russia, but he did not have sufficient consensus, at home or abroad, to make that act effective. Americans tend to unite behind their President in international crises, but this support should never be taken for granted.

The Three Assumptions

The three basic assumptions we discussed in the Introduction have played a vital role in determining the form of American political institutions and the policies that have been adopted by our political leaders. They have not gone unchallenged, however, and much of this book has dealt with the validity and usefulness of these assumptions.

"Fragmented institutions guard against tyrannical government." One of the first and most striking features of the structure of American government is its intricate system of checks and balances. Governmental institutions are fragmented, and the Constitution makes clear in a number of places the necessity for cooperative action. Official power is deliberately dispersed so that no one source will be able to gain ascendancy and rule absolutely. Such rule would inevitably lead, as the constitutional framers believed, to abuse of power, and thus to tyrannical government. Therefore, the American system is a republican (not parliamentary) form of government; the executive, legislative, and judicial powers reside in separate branches. The American system is a federal (not unitary) form of government; the several states have constitutionally guaranteed powers similar to those of the national government.

Because of this dispersal of the formal instruments of power, the accumulation of power by a single entity is very difficult. Many people felt (and still feel) that human beings naturally seek to dominate each other. This tendency, it is argued, must be controlled, and the best means to do this is to ensure that "ambition [is] made to counteract ambition." The governmental structures reflect this deep-seated assumption about human nature and public affairs.

As a consequence, governmental action, more frequently than not, requires the consent of many different bodies. The case study on energy is a good example. This need for consent, of course, has slowed down the final decision-making and policy-implementing processes. It has also meant that change for the most part has occurred in small steps, not in great leaps.

The exceptions to this rule have come in times of crisis. In fact, a rather significant number of major political decisions have involved rapid responses to crisis. In these instances, the underlying problems were initially approached by the normal processes of incrementalism before they reached crisis proportions. Formally dispersed power centers then had to adjust rapidly and gear up for quick action. One could chart this experience throughout the country's history: the crises generated by Shays' Rebellion and the economic problems of the 1780s leading to the constitutional convention; the problems of slavery leading to the Civil War; the Great Depression of the 1930s leading to the New Deal; the racial upheavals of the 1950s and 1960s leading to landmark judicial decrees and civil-rights legislation; the Vietnam War and Watergate leading to major Congressional responses to the exercise of presidential power. One could also point to the more recent problems of inflation and unemployment in the 1970s—followed by the current emphasis of the Reagan administration on "supply-side" economics and budget reductions.

"Free enterprise thrives best on freedom from government." As a capitalist economy, the American system is based on the assumption that governmental control of economic affairs should be kept at a minimum. Reliance on the incentive of private profits and the free market has been a key element in determining the direction of American policymaking.

Generally, government intervention has been seen as potentially discouraging to individual motivation. It has been seen as impeding real economic growth, and, certainly, as having the effect of controlling private economic development to the detriment of an economically competitive market. We have seen this assumption manifested in several instances in the material throughout this book. The case studies on energy, Proposition 13, and labor-law reform dealt with this issue in different contexts. The discussions of government aid to the Chrysler Corporation and of social-welfare policies in chapters 15 and 16 were relevant to this issue. The structure and role of the Federal Reserve System (chapter 15) in determining monetary policy was another case in point.

But just as the concept of fragmented government has changed over the years, so too with this second assumption. For most of America's political history, the government has not been an active participant in the nation's economy. Intense government involvement was not deemed necessary for economic progress or development. But since the New Deal of the 1930s, this has changed considerably. We have seen an increase in public

regulation of business, as well as the development of a set of social-welfare policies touching many aspects of individual lives. These developments, many would argue, were created out of necessity. Government action was needed to help stabilize the economy and to provide assistance to people who simply were unable to provide for themselves and their families. A new industrial economy had made the virtues of an earlier time somewhat anachronistic. Many of these programs have now become so embedded in the system that they can fairly be considered permanent. Even in 1981, the new administration of President Ronald Reagan spoke of maintaining social-welfare programs that helped the "truly needy." Thus even the staunchest advocates of the free-enterprise system have come to recognize the political necessity of softening their position.

"Pluralist politics maximizes participatory effectiveness." The third assumption has its roots in early American political history. James Madison and others clearly understood that factions would arise, reflecting a wide range of social and economic interests. These groups would inevitably attempt to influence government. There is not one segment of this book that does not deal in some way with this process. The initial formation of the government, citizen participation in various organizations (interest groups, political parties), the influence of institutions (family, school, media) in socializing people and forming public opinion, the operation of various governmental agencies—all these phenomena are examples of what can be called *pluralist politics*.

It is widely felt that with more groups forming and making demands, the likelihood that political participation will be effective for all will be the greater. As various groups articulate their grievances, they serve in the broad political arena to check and balance each other, much as (theoretically) fragmented institutions do. In order to achieve its goals, a group must bargain, form coalitions, and compromise. Thus, while no one group gets all it wants, neither does any particular group prevail over the others. The vast number of groups means that no one group will be large enough and powerful enough to dominate continuously. This is the ideal on which the pluralist assumption is based. The labor-law case study describes the political ups and downs of organized labor. We saw the interplay of interest groups in the Proposition 13 study. Success at one time on one issue was not necessarily transferable to another time and another issue. In both cases, of course, the stories are still unfolding.

We are also aware, however, that the pluralist assumption must be approached with caution. We may tend to assume that all groups are equally resourceful and have relatively comparable access to decision-makers. This simply is not the case. Some groups, though not permanent power centers, certainly have long-standing advantages over others. They may have more money, more prestige, larger numbers—all of which unbalances the pluralist scale. Some groups or potential groups find that their policy agendas receive a cooler welcome in many centers of official policymaking than more established and accepted groups. At times, this will make finding allies and forming coalitions exceedingly difficult. Thus, such groups might have to resort to less accepted means of gaining attention, which, in turn, might reinforce resistance to their goals.

In addition, pluralist politics might well invite increased participation, but this should not be confused with maximizing participatory effectiveness. In chapter 5 we noted that the truckers felt they had to resort to disrupting traffic in order to attract attention to their plight, while virtually no member of the Business Roundtable had any trouble contacting a legislator.

Without question, we have seen a proliferation of interest groups over the last two decades, and their participation has taken many forms. In fact, more than a few people have begun to question whether "special interests" are becoming too powerful. This matter was discussed specifically in the chapter on Congress, where some legislators expressed a feeling that pluralist politics had gone awry. The proliferation of interest groups has made it increasingly difficult to achieve discipline and coherence in the policymaking process. This could present serious problems for those policymakers who wish to develop systematic planning mechanisms and more rational approaches to policy. Increased group activity could cause more stagnation and more incrementalism with fewer definitive results. This could lead to some issues not being dealt with properly—until a crisis arises.

In a sense these many groups can be seen as new vehicles for political participation. Perhaps people are no longer satisfied with the traditional institutions and processes, and their dissatisfaction is being expressed in new ways, through new agencies. If so, this could be taken as a hopeful sign.

In the final analysis, the material in this book should have provided substantial evidence for at least one definitive conclusion. Where the *process* (voting, suing, petitioning, marching) is perceived as related to the *product* (jobs, lower inflation, good schools, decent housing), *participation* in that process will probably increase. Without that perceived relationship, participation is likely to fall. People will participate when they think their efforts matter and in ways that they think are likely to be effective.

If democratic government is concerned about anything, it ought to be concerned about making sure that enough people continually believe their participation matters. This remains both as a challenge to the American system of government, and as an opportunity for a people who would be free to govern themselves.

The Constitution

We the People of the United States, in Order to form a more perfect Union, establish Justice, insure domestic Tranquility, provide for the common defence, promote the general Welfare, and secure the Blessings of Liberty to ourselves and our Posterity, do ordain and establish this Constitution for the United States of America.

Article I

Bicameral legislature

Section 1. All legislative Powers herein granted shall be vested in a Congress of the United States, which shall consist of a Senate and House of Representatives.

House of Representatives

Section 2. The House of Representatives shall be composed of Members chosen every second Year by the People of the several States, and the Electors in each State shall have the Qualifications requisite for Electors of the most numerous Branch of the State Legislature.

No Person shall be a Representative who shall not have attained to the age of twenty five Years, and been seven Years a Citizen of the United States, and who shall not, when elected, be an Inhabitant of that State in which he shall be chosen.

Representatives and direct Taxes shall be apportioned among the several States which may be included within this Union, according to their respective Numbers, which shall be determined by adding to the whole Number of free Persons, including those bound to Service for a Term of Years, and excluding Indians not taxed, three fifths of all other Persons.[1] The actual Enumeration shall be made within three Years after the first Meeting of the Congress of the United States, and within every subsequent Term of ten Years, in such Manner as they shall by Law direct. The Number of Representatives shall not exceed one for every thirty Thousand, but each State shall have at Least one Representative; and until such enumeration shall be made, the State of New Hampshire shall be entitled to chuse three, Massachusetts eight, Rhode-Island and Providence Plantations one, Connecticut five, New-York six, New Jersey four, Pennsylvania eight, Delaware one, Maryland six, Virginia ten, North Carolina five, South Carolina five, and Georgia three.

When vacancies happen in the Representation from any State, the Executive Authority thereof shall issue Writs of Election to fill such Vacancies.

[1]Changed by the Fourteenth Amendment.

The House of Representatives shall chuse their Speaker and other Officers; and shall have the sole Power of Impeachment.

Senate

Section 3. The Senate of the United States shall be composed of two Senators from each State, chosen by the Legislature thereof,[2] for six Years; and each Senator shall have one Vote.

Immediately after they shall be assembled in Consequence of the first Election, they shall be divided as equally as may be into three Classes. The Seats of the Senators of the first Class shall be vacated at the Expiration of the second Year, of the second Class at the Expiration of the fourth Year, and of the third Class at the Expiration of the sixth Year, so that one third may be chosen every second Year; and if Vacancies happen by Resignation, or otherwise, during the Recess of the Legislature of any State, the Executive thereof may make temporary Appointments until the next Meeting of the Legislature, which shall then fill such Vacancies.[3]

No Person shall be a Senator who shall not have attained to the Age of thirty Years, and been nine Years a Citizen of the United States, and who shall not, when elected, be an Inhabitant of that State for which he shall be chosen.

The Vice President of the United States shall be President of the Senate, but shall have no Vote, unless they be equally divided.

The Senate shall chuse their other Officers, and also a President pro tempore, in the Absence of the Vice President, or when he shall exercise the Office of President of the United States.

The Senate shall have the sole Power to try all Impeachments. When sitting for that Purpose, they shall be on Oath or Affirmation. When the President of the United States is tried the Chief Justice shall preside: And no Person shall be convicted without the Concurrence of two thirds of the Members present.

Judgment in Cases of Impeachment shall not extend further than to removal from Office, and disqualification to hold and enjoy any Office of honor, Trust or Profit under the United States: but the Party convicted shall nevertheless be liable and subject to Indictment, Trial, Judgment and Punishment, according to Law.

Congressional elections

Section 4. The Times, Places and Manner of holding Elections for Senators and Representatives, shall be prescribed in each State by the Legislature thereof; but the Congress may at any time by Law make or alter such Regulations, except as to the Places of chusing Senators.

The Congress shall assemble at least once in every Year, and such Meeting shall be on the first Monday in December, unless they shall by Law appoint a different Day.[4]

Powers and duties of Congress

Section 5. Each House shall be the Judge of the Elections, Returns and Qualifications of its own Members, and a Majority of each shall constitute a Quorum to do Business; but a

---

[2]Changed by the Seventeenth Amendment.

[3]Changed by the Seventeenth Amendment.

[4]Changed by the Twentieth Amendment.

smaller Number may adjourn from day to day, and may be authorized to compel the Attendance of absent Members, in such Manner, and under such Penalties as each House may provide.

Each House may determine the Rules of its Proceedings, punish its Members for disorderly Behaviour, and, with the Concurrence of two thirds, expel a Member.

Each House shall keep a Journal of its Proceedings, and from time to time publish the same, excepting such Parts as may in their Judgment require Secrecy; and the Yeas and Nays of the Members of either House on any question shall, at the Desire of one fifth of those Present, be entered on the Journal.

Neither House, during the Session of Congress, shall, without the Consent of the other, adjourn for more than three days, nor to any other Place than that in which the two Houses shall be sitting.

Compensation, immunities, restrictions— Members of Congress

Section 6. The Senators and Representatives shall receive a Compensation for their Services, to be ascertained by Law, and paid out of the Treasury of the United States. They shall in all Cases, except Treason, Felony and Breach of the Peace, be privileged from Arrest during their Attendance at the Session of their respective Houses, and in going to and returning from the same; and for any Speech or Debate in either House, they shall not be questioned in any other Place.

No Senator or Representative shall, during the Time for which he was elected, be appointed to any civil Office under the Authority of the United States, which shall have been created, or the Emoluments whereof shall have been encreased during such time; and no Person holding any Office under the United States, shall be a Member of either House during his Continuance in Office.

Legislative procedures

Section 7. All Bills for raising Revenue shall originate in the House of Representatives; but the Senate may propose or concur with Amendments as on other Bills.

Every Bill which shall have passed the House of Representatives and the Senate, shall, before it become a Law, be presented to the President of the United States; If he approve he shall sign it, but if not he shall return it, with his Objections to that House in which it shall have originated, who shall enter the Objections at large on their Journal, and proceed to reconsider it. If after such Reconsideration two thirds of that House shall agree to pass the Bill, it shall be sent, together with the Objections, to the other House, by which it shall likewise be reconsidered, and if approved by two thirds of that House, it shall become a Law. But in all such Cases the Votes of both Houses shall be determined by yeas and Nays, and the Names of the Persons voting for and against the Bill shall be entered on the Journal of each House respectively. If any Bill shall not be returned by the President within ten Days (Sundays excepted) after it shall have been presented to him, the Same shall be a Law, in like Manner as if he had signed it, unless the Congress by their Adjournment prevent its Return, in which Case it shall not be a Law.

Every Order, Resolution, or Vote to which the Concurrence of the Senate and House of Representatives may be necessary (except on a question of Adjournment) shall be presented to the President of the United States; and before the Same shall take Effect, shall be approved by him, or being disapproved by him, shall be repassed by two thirds of the Senate and House of Representatives, according to the Rules and Limitations prescribed in the Case of a Bill.

Powers of Congress

Section 8. The Congress shall have Power To lay and collect Taxes, Duties, Imposts and Excises, to pay the Debts and provide for the common Defence and general Welfare of the United States; but all Duties, Imposts and Excises shall be uniform throughout the United States;

To borrow Money on the credit of the United States;

To regulate Commerce with foreign Nations, and among the several States, and with the Indian Tribes;

To establish an uniform Rule of Naturalization, and uniform Laws on the subject of Bankruptcies throughout the United States;

To coin Money, regulate the Value thereof, and of foreign Coin, and fix the Standard of Weights and Measures;

To provide for the Punishment of counterfeiting the Securities and current Coin of the United States;

To establish Post Offices and post Roads;

To promote the Progress of Science and useful Arts, by securing for limited Times to Authors and Inventors the exclusive Right to their respective Writings and Discoveries;

To constitute Tribunals inferior to the supreme Court;

To define and punish Piracies and Felonies committed on the high Seas, and Offences against the Law of Nations;

To declare War, grant Letters of Marque and Reprisal, and make Rules concerning Captures on Land and Water;

To raise and support Armies, but no Appropriation of Money to that Use shall be for a longer Term than two Years;

To provide and maintain a Navy;

To make Rules for the Government and Regulation of the land and naval Forces;

To provide for calling forth the Militia to execute the Laws of the Union, suppress Insurrections and repel Invasions;

To provide for organizing, arming, and disciplining, the Militia, and for governing such Part of them as may be employed in the Service of the United States, reserving to the States respectively, the Appointment of the Officers, and the Authority of training the Militia according to the discipline prescribed by Congress;

To exercise exclusive Legislation in all Cases whatsoever, over such District (not exceeding ten Miles square) as may, by Cession of Particular States, and the Acceptance of Congress, become the Seat of the Government of the United States, and to exercise like Authority over all Places purchased by the Consent of the Legislature of the State in which the Same shall be, for the Erection of Forts, Magazines, Arsenals, dock-Yards, and other needful Buildings;—And

To make all Laws which shall be necessary and proper for carrying into Execution the foregoing Powers, and all other Powers vested by this Constitution in the Government of the United States, or in any Department or Officer thereof.

Limits on Congressional powers

Section 9. The Migration or Importation of such Persons as any of the States now existing shall think proper to admit, shall not be prohibited by the Congress prior to the Year one thousand eight hundred and eight, but a Tax or duty may be imposed on such Importation, not exceeding ten dollars for each Person.

The Privilege of the Writ of Habeas Corpus shall not be suspended, unless when in Cases of Rebellion or Invasion the public Safety may require it.

No Bill of Attainder or ex post facto Law shall be passed.

No Capitation, or other direct, Tax shall be laid, unless in Proportion to the Census or Enumeration herein before directed to be taken.[5]

No Tax or Duty shall be laid on Articles exported from any State.

No Preference shall be given by any Regulation of Commerce or Revenue to the Ports of one State over those of another; nor shall Vessels bound to, or from, one State, be obliged to enter, clear or pay Duties in another.

No Money shall be drawn from the Treasury, but on Consequence of Appropriations made by Law; and a regular Statement and Account of the Receipts and Expenditures of all public Money shall be published from time to time.

No Title of Nobility shall be granted by the United States: And no Person holding any Office of Profit or Trust under them, shall, without the Consent of the Congress, accept of any present, Emolument, Office, or Title, of any kind whatever, from any King, Prince, or foreign State.

Limits on powers of states

Section 10.   No State shall enter into any Treaty, Alliance, or Confederation; grant Letters of Marque and Reprisal; coin Money; emit Bills of Credit; make any Thing but gold and silver Coin a Tender in Payment of Debts; pass any Bill of Attainder, ex post facto Law, or Law impairing the Obligation of Contracts, or grant any Title of Nobility.

No State shall, without the Consent of the Congress, lay any Imposts or Duties on Imports or Exports, except what may be absolutely necessary for executing its inspection Laws: and the net Produce of all Duties and Imposts, laid by any State on Imports or Exports, shall be for the Use of the Treasury of the United States; and all such Laws shall be subject to the Revision and Control of the Congress.

No State shall, without the Consent of Congress, lay any Duty of Tonnage, keep Troops, or Ships of War in time of Peace, enter into any Agreement or Compact with another State, or with a foreign Power, or engage in War, unless actually invaded, or in such imminent Danger as will not admit of delay.

Article II

Presidency

Section 1.   The executive Power shall be vested in a President of the United States of America. He shall hold his Office during the Term of four Years, and, together with the Vice President, chosen for the same Term, be elected, as follows

Each State shall appoint, in such Manner as the Legislature thereof may direct, a Number of Electors, equal to the whole Number of Senators and Representatives to which the State may be entitled in Congress: but no Senator or Representative, or Person holding an Office of Trust or Profit under the United States, shall be appointed an Elector.

The Electors shall meet in their respective States, and vote by Ballot for two Persons, of whom one at least shall not be an Inhabitant of the same State with themselves. And they shall make a List of all the Persons voted for, and of the Number of Votes for each; which List

[5]Changed by the Sixteenth Amendment.

they shall sign and certify, and transmit sealed to the Seat of the Government of the United States, directed to the President of the Senate. The President of the Senate shall, in the Presence of the Senate and House of Representatives, open all the Certificates, and the Votes shall then be counted. The Person having the greatest Number of Votes shall be the President, if such Number be a Majority of the whole Number of Electors appointed; and if there be more than one who have such Majority, and have an equal Number of Votes, then the House of Representatives shall immediately chuse by Ballot one of them for President; and if no Person have a Majority, then from the five highest on the List the said House shall in like Manner chuse the President. But in chusing the President, the Votes shall be taken by States, the Representation from each State having one Vote; a quorum for this Purpose shall consist of a Member or Members from two thirds of the States, and a Majority of all the States shall be necessary to a Choice. In every Case, after the Choice of the President, the Person having the greatest Number of Votes of the Electors shall be the Vice President. But if there should remain two or more who have equal Votes, the Senate shall chuse from them by Ballot the Vice President.[6]

The Congress may determine the Time of chusing the Electors, and the Day on which they shall be given their Votes; which Day shall be the same throughout the United States.

No Person except a natural born Citizen, or a Citizen of the United States, at the time of the Adoption of this Constitution, shall be eligible to the Office of President; neither shall any person be eligible to that Office who shall not have attained to the Age of thirty five Years, and been fourteen Years a Resident within the United States.

In Case of the Removal of the President from Office, or of his Death, Resignation, or Inability to discharge the Powers and Duties of the said Office, the Same shall devolve on the Vice President, and the Congress may by Law provide for the Case of Removal, Death, Resignation or Inability, both of the President and Vice President, declaring what Officer shall then act as President, and such Officer shall act accordingly, until the Disability be removed, or a President shall be elected.[7]

The President shall, at stated Times, receive for his Services, a Compensation, which shall neither be increased nor diminished during the Period for which he shall have been elected, and he shall not receive within that Period any other Emolument from the United States, or any of them.

Before he enter on the Execution of his Office, he shall take the following Oath or Affirmation:—"I do solemnly swear (or affirm) that I will faithfully execute the Office of President of the United States, and will to the best of my Ability, preserve, protect and defend the Constitution of the United States."

Presidential powers

Section 2. The President shall be Commander in Chief of the Army and Navy of the United States, and of the Militia of the several States, when called into the actual Service of the United States; he may require the Opinion, in writing, of the principal Officer in each of the executive Departments, upon any Subject relating to the Duties of their respective Offices, and he shall have Power to grant Reprieves and Pardons for Offences against the United States, except in Cases of Impeachment.

He shall have Power, by and with the Advice and Consent of the Senate, to make Treaties, provided two thirds of the Senators present concur; and he shall nominate, and by and with the Advice and Consent of the Senate, shall appoint Ambassadors, other public

[6]Changed by the Twelfth Amendment.
[7]Changed by the Twenty-fifth Amendment.

Ministers and Consuls, Judges of the supreme Court, and all other Officers of the United States, whose Appointments are not herein otherwise provided for, and which shall be established by Law: but the Congress may by Law vest the Appointment of such inferior Officers, as they think proper, in the President alone, in the Courts of Law, or in the Heads of Departments.

The President shall have Power to fill up all Vacancies that may happen during the Recess of the Senate, by granting Commissions which shall expire at the End of their next Session.

Section 3.   He shall from time to time give to the Congress Information of the State of the Union, and recommend to their Consideration such Measures as he shall judge necessary and expedient; he may, on extraordinary Occasions, convene both Houses, or either of them, and in Case of Disagreement between them, with Respect to the Time of Adjournment, he may adjourn them to such Time as he shall think proper; he shall receive Ambassadors and other public Ministers; he shall take Care that the Laws be faithfully executed, and shall Commission all the Officers of the United States.

Impeachment

Section 4.   The President, Vice President and all civil Officers of the United States, shall be removed from Office on Impeachment for, and Conviction of, Treason, Bribery, or other high Crimes and Misdemeanors.

Article III

Judiciary

Section 1.   The judicial Power of the United States, shall be vested in one supreme Court, and in such inferior Courts as the Congress may from time to time ordain and establish. The Judges, both of the supreme and inferior Courts, shall hold their Offices during good Behaviour, and shall, at stated Times, receive for their Services, a Compensation, which shall not be diminished during their Continuance in Office.

Jurisdiction

Section 2.   The judicial Power shall extend to all Cases, in Law and Equity, arising under this Constitution, the Laws of the United States, and Treaties made, or which shall be made, under their Authority;—to all Cases affecting Ambassadors, other public Ministers and Consuls;—to all Cases of admiralty and maritime Jurisdiction;—to Controversies to which the United States shall be a Party;—to Controversies between two or more States;—between a State and Citizens of another State,[8]—between Citizens of different States;—between Citizens of the same State claiming Lands under Grants of different States, and between a State, or the Citizens thereof, and foreign States, Citizens or Subjects.

In all Cases affecting Ambassadors, other public Ministers and Consuls, and those in which a State shall be Part, the supreme Court shall have original Jurisdiction. In all the other Cases before mentioned, the supreme Court shall have appellate Jurisdiction, both as to Law and Fact, with such Exceptions, and under such Regulations as the Congress shall make.

The Trial of all Crimes, except in Cases of Impeachment, shall be by Jury; and such Trial shall be held in the State where the said Crimes shall have been committed; but when not committed within any State, the Trial shall be at such Place or Places as the Congress may by Law have directed.

[8]Changed by the Eleventh Amendment.

Treason

Section 3. Treason against the United States, shall consist only in levying War against them, or in adhering to their Enemies, giving them Aid and Comfort. No Person shall be convicted of Treason unless on the Testimony of two Witnesses to the same overt Act, or on Confession in open Court.

The Congress shall have Power to declare the Punishment of Treason, but no Attainder of Treason shall work Corruption of Blood, or Forfeiture except during the Life of the Person attainted.

Article IV

"Full faith and credit"

Section 1. Full Faith and Credit shall be given in each State to the public Acts, Records, and judicial Proceedings of every other State. And the Congress may by general Laws prescribe the Manner in which such Acts, Records and Proceedings shall be proved, and the Effect thereof.

Privileges and immunities, extradition

Section 2. The Citizens of each State shall be entitled to all Privileges and Immunities of Citizens in the several States.

A person charged in any State with Treason, Felony, or other Crime, who shall flee from Justice, and be found in another State, shall on Demand of the executive Authority of the State from which he fled, be delivered up, to be removed to the State having Jurisdiction of the Crime.

No Person held to Service or Labour in one State, under the Laws thereof, escaping into another, shall, in Consequence of any Law or Regulation therein, be discharged from such Service or Labour, but shall be delivered up on Claim of the Party to whom such Service or Labour may be due.[9]

New states

Section 3. New States may be admitted by the Congress into this Union; but no new State shall be formed or erected within the Jurisdiction of any other State; nor any State be formed by the Junction of two or more States, or Parts of States, without the Consent of the Legislatures of the States concerned as well as of the Congress.

The Congress shall have Power to dispose of and make all needful Rules and Regulations respecting the Territory or other Property belonging to the United States; and nothing in this Constitution shall be so construed as to Prejudice any Claims of the United States, or of any particular State.

Protection of states

Section 4. The United States shall guarantee to every State in this Union a Republican Form of Government, and shall protect each of them against Invasion; and on Application of the Legislature, or of the Executive (when the Legislature cannot be convened) against domestic Violence.

Article V

Amendment procedures

The Congress, whenever two thirds of both Houses shall deem it necessary, shall propose Amendments to this Constitution, or, on the Application of the Legislatures of two thirds of

---

[9]Changed by the Thirteenth Amendment.

the several States, shall call a Convention for proposing Amendments, which, in either Case, shall be valid to all Intents and Purposes, as Part of this Constitution, when ratified by the Legislatures of three fourths of the several States, or by Conventions in three fourths thereof, as the one or the other Mode of Ratification may be proposed by the Congress; Provided that no Amendment which may be made prior to the Year One thousand eight hundred and eight shall in any Manner affect the first and fourth Clauses in the Ninth Section of the first Article; and that no State, without its Consent, shall be deprived of its equal Suffrage in the Senate.

Article VI

Supremacy of federal laws

All Debts contracted and Engagements entered into, before the Adoption of this Constitution, shall be as valid against the United States under this Constitution, as under the Confederation.

This Constitution, and the Laws of the United States which shall be made in Pursuance thereof; and all Treaties made, or which shall be made, under the Authority of the United States, shall be the supreme Law of the Land; and the Judges in every State shall be bound thereby, any Thing in the Constitution or Laws of any State to the Contrary notwithstanding.

The Senators and Representatives before mentioned, and the Members of the several State Legislatures, and all executive and judicial Officers, both of the United States and of the several States, shall be bound by Oath or Affirmation, to support this Constitution; but no religious Test shall ever be required as a Qualification to any Office or public Trust under the United States.

Article VII

Ratification

The Ratification of the Conventions of nine States, shall be sufficient for the Establishment of this Constitution between the States so ratifying the Same.

Done in Convention by the Unanimous Consent of the States present the Seventeenth Day of September in the Year of our Lord one thousand seven hundred and Eighty seven and of the Independence of the United States of America the Twelfth In witness whereof We have hereunto subscribed our Names.

[The first ten amendments, the "Bill of Rights," were ratified in 1791]

Amendment 1

Freedom of religion, speech, press, assembly

Congress shall make no law respecting an establishment of religion, or prohibiting the free exercise thereof; or abridging the freedom of speech, or of the press; or the right of the people peaceably to assemble, and to petition the Government for a redress of grievances.

Amendment 2

Right to bear arms

A well regulated Militia, being necessary to the security of a free State, the right of the people to keep and bear Arms, shall not be infringed.

Amendment 3

Quartering soldiers

No Soldier shall, in time of peace be quartered in any house, without the consent of the Owner, nor in time of war, but in a manner to be prescribed by law.

Amendment 4

Searches and seizures

The right of the people to be secure in their persons, houses, papers, and effects, against unreasonable searches and seizures, shall not be violated, and no Warrants shall issue, but upon probable cause, supported by Oath or affirmation, and particularly describing the place to be searched, and the persons or things to be seized.

Amendment 5

Rights of accused, "due process"

No person shall be held to answer for a capital, or otherwise infamous crime, unless on a presentment or indictment of a Grand Jury, except in cases arising in the land or naval forces, or in the Militia, when in actual service in time of War or public danger; nor shall any person be subject for the same offence to be twice put in jeopardy of life or limb; nor shall be compelled in any criminal case to be a witness against himself, nor be deprived of life, liberty, or property, without due process of law; nor shall private property be taken for public use, without just compensation.

Amendment 6

Criminal prosecutions

In all criminal prosecutions, the accused shall enjoy the right to a speedy and public trial, by an impartial jury of the State and district wherein the crime shall have been committed, which district shall have been previously ascertained by law, and to be informed of the nature and cause of the accusation; to be confronted with the witnesses against him; to have compulsory process for obtaining witnesses in his favor, and to have Assistance of Counsel for his defence.

Amendment 7

Common-law suits

In Suits at common law, where the value in controversy shall exceed twenty dollars, the right of trial by jury shall be preserved, and no fact tried by a jury, shall be otherwise reexamined in any Court of the United States, than according to the rules of the common law.

Amendment 8

Bail, cruel and unusual punishment

Excessive bail shall not be required, nor excessive fines imposed, nor cruel and unusual punishments inflicted.

Amendment 9

Unenumerated rights

The enumeration in the Constitution, of certain rights, shall not be construed to deny or disparage others retained by the people.

Amendment 10

Powers reserved to states

The powers not delegated to the United States by the Constitution, nor prohibited by it to the States, are reserved to the States respectively, or to the people.

Amendment 11   [*Ratified 1795.*]

Suits against states

The Judicial power of the United States shall not be construed to extend to any suit in law or equity, commenced or prosecuted against one of the United States by Citizens of another State, or by Citizens or Subjects of any Foreign State.

Amendment 12   [*Ratified 1804.*]

Presidential elections

The Electors shall meet in their respective states and vote by ballot for President and Vice President, one of whom, at least, shall not be an inhabitant of the same state with themselves; they shall name in their ballots the person voted for as President, and in distinct ballots the person voted for as Vice President, and they shall make distinct lists of all persons voted for as President, and of all persons voted for as Vice President, and of the number of votes for each, which lists they shall sign and certify, and transmit sealed to the seat of the government of the United States, directed to the President of the Senate;—The President of the Senate shall, in the presence of the Senate and House of Representatives, open all the certificates and the votes shall then be counted;—The person having the greatest number of votes for President, shall be the President, if such number be a majority of the whole number of Electors appointed; and if no person have such majority, then from the persons having the highest numbers not exceeding three on the list of those voted for as President, the House of Representatives shall choose immediately, by ballot, the President. But in choosing the President, the votes shall be taken by states, the representation from each state having one vote; a quorum for this purpose shall consist of a member or members from two-thirds of the states, and a majority of all the states shall be necessary to a choice. And if the House of Representatives shall not choose a President whenever the right of choice shall devolve upon them, before the fourth day of March next following, then the Vice President shall act as President, as in the case of the death or other constitutional disability of the President.—[10] The person having the greatest number of votes as Vice President, shall be the Vice President, if such number be a majority of the whole number of Electors appointed, and if no person have a majority, then from the two highest numbers on the list, the Senate shall choose the Vice President; a quorum for the purpose shall consist of two-thirds of the whole number of Senators, and a majority of the whole number shall be necessary to a choice. But no person constitutionally ineligible to the office of President shall be eligible to that of Vice President of the United States.

Amendment 13   [*Ratified 1865.*]

Prohibition of slavery

Section 1.   Neither slavery nor involuntary servitude, except as a punishment for crime whereof the party shall have been duly convicted, shall exist within the United States, or any place subject to their jurisdiction.

[10]Changed by the Twentieth Amendment.

Section 2. Congress shall have power to enforce this article by appropriate legislation.

Amendment 14   [*Ratified 1868.*]

Citizenship,
"due process"
applied to the
states, equal
protection of the
laws

Section 1. All persons born or naturalized in the United States and subject to the jurisdiction thereof, are citizens of the United States and of the State wherein they reside. No State shall make or enforce any law which shall abridge the privileges or immunities of citizens of the United States; nor shall any State deprive any person of life, liberty, or property, without due process of law; nor deny to any person within its jurisdiction the equal protection of the laws.

Section 2. Representatives shall be apportioned among the several States according to their respective numbers, counting the whole number of persons in each State, excluding Indians not taxed. But when the right to vote at any election for the choice of electors for President and Vice President of the United States, Representatives in Congress, the Executive and Judicial officers of a State, or the members of the Legislature thereof, is denied to any of the male inhabitants of such State, being twenty-one[11] years of age, and citizens of the United States, or in any way abridged, except for participation in rebellion, or other crime, the basis of representation therein shall be reduced in the proportion which the number of such male citizens shall bear to the whole number of male citizens twenty-one years of age in such State.

Section 3. No person shall be a Senator or Representative in Congress, or elector of President and Vice President, or hold any office, civil or military, under the United States, or under any State, who, having previously taken an oath, as a member of Congress, or as an officer of the United States, or as a member of any State legislature, or as an executive or judicial officer of any State, to support the Constitution of the United States, shall have engaged in insurrection or rebellion against the same, or given aid or comfort to the enemies thereof. But Congress may by a vote of two-thirds of each House, remove such disability.

Section 4. The validity of the public debt of the United States, authorized by law, including debts incurred for payment of pensions and bounties for services in suppressing insurrection or rebellion, shall not be questioned. But neither the United States nor any State shall assume or pay any debt or obligation incurred in aid of insurrection or rebellion against the United States, or any claim for the loss or emancipation of any slave; but all such debts, obligations and claims shall be held illegal and void.

Section 5. The Congress shall have power to enforce, by appropriate legislation, the provisions of this article.

Amendment 15   [*Ratified 1870.*]

Right to vote

Section 1. The right of citizens of the United States to vote shall not be denied or abridged by the United States or by any State on account of race, color, or previous condition of servitude.

[11]Changed by the Twenty-sixth Amendment.

Section 2. The Congress shall have power to enforce this article by appropriate legislation.

Amendment 16   [*Ratified 1913.*]

Income taxes

The Congress shall have power to lay and collect taxes on incomes, from whatever source derived, without apportionment among the several States, and without regard to any census or enumeration.

Amendment 17   [*Ratified 1913.*]

Direct election of senators

The Senate of the United States shall be composed of two Senators from each State, elected by the people thereof, for six years; and each Senator shall have one vote. The electors in each State shall have the qualifications requisite for electors of the most numerous branch of the State legislatures.

When vacancies happen in the representation of any State in the Senate, the executive authority of such State shall issue writs of election to fill such vacancies: *Provided,* That the legislature of any State may empower the executive thereof to make temporary appointments until the people fill the vacancies by election as the legislature may direct.

This amendment shall not be so construed as to affect the election or term of any Senator chosen before it becomes valid as part of the Constitution.

Amendment 18   [*Ratified 1919.*]

Prohibition

Section 1. After one year from the ratification of this article the manufacture, sale, or transportation of intoxicating liquors within, the importation thereof into, or the exportation thereof from the United States and all territory subject to the jurisdiction thereof for beverage purposes is hereby prohibited.

Section 2. The Congress and the several States shall have concurrent power to enforce this article by appropriate legislation.

Section 3. This article shall be inoperative unless it shall have been ratified as an amendment to the Constitution by the legislatures of the several States, as provided in the Constitution, within seven years from the date of the submission hereof to the States by the Congress.[12]

Amendment 19   [*Ratified 1920.*]

Right to vote for women

The right of citizens of the United States to vote shall not be denied or abridged by the United States or by any State on account of sex.

Congress shall have power to enforce this article by appropriate legislation.

Amendment 20   [*Ratified 1933.*]

Terms of office

Section 1. The terms of the President and Vice President shall end at noon on the 20th day of January, and the terms of Senators and Representatives at noon on the 3d day of January,

---

[12]Repealed by the Twenty-first Amendment.

of the years in which such terms would have ended if this article had not been ratified; and the terms of their successors shall then begin.

Section 2.   The Congress shall assemble at least once in every year, and such meeting shall begin at noon on the 3d day of January, unless they shall by law appoint a different day.

Emergency presidential succession

Section 3.   If, at the time fixed for the beginning of the term of the President, the President elect shall have died, the Vice President elect shall become President. If a President shall not have been chosen before the time fixed for the beginning of his term, or if the President elect shall have failed to qualify, then the Vice President elect shall act as President until a President shall have qualified; and the Congress may by law provide for the case wherein neither a President elect nor a Vice President elect shall have qualified, declaring who shall then act as President, or the manner in which one who is to act shall be selected, and such person shall act accordingly until a President or Vice President shall have qualified.

Section 4.   The Congress may by law provide for the case of the death of any of the persons from whom the House of Representatives may choose a President whenever the right of choice shall have devolved upon them, and for the case of the death of any of the persons from whom the Senate may choose a Vice President whenever the right of choice shall have devolved upon them.

Section 5.   Sections 1 and 2 shall take effect on the 15th day of October following the ratification of this article.

Section 6.   This article shall be inoperative unless it shall have been ratified as an amendment to the Constitution by the legislatures of three-fourths of the several States within seven years from the date of its submission.

Amendment 21   [*Ratified 1933.*]

Repeal of prohibition

Section 1.   The eighteenth article of amendment to the Constitution of the United States is hereby repealed.

Section 2.   The transportation or importation into any State, Territory, or possession of the United States for delivery or use therein of intoxicating liquors, in violation of the laws thereof, is hereby prohibited.

Section 3.   This article shall be inoperative unless it shall have been ratified as an amendment to the Constitution by conventions in the several States, as provided in the Constitution, within seven years from the date of the submission hereof to the States by the Congress.

Amendment 22   [*Ratified 1951.*]

Number of terms for President

Section 1.   No person shall be elected to the office of the President more than twice, and no person who has held the office of President, or acted as President, for more than two years of a term to which some other person was elected President shall be elected to the office of the

President more than once. But this Article shall not apply to any person holding the office of President when this Article was proposed by the Congress, and shall not prevent any person who may be holding the office of President, or acting as President, during the term within which this Article becomes operative from holding the office of President or acting as President during the remainder of such term.

Section 2. This Article shall be inoperative unless it shall have been ratified as an amendment to the Constitution by the legislatures of three-fourths of the several States within seven years from the date of its submission to the States by the Congress.

Amendment 23   [*Ratified 1961.*]

Presidential elections, District of Columbia

Section 1. The District constituting the seat of Government of the United States shall appoint in such manner as the Congress may direct:
    A number of electors of President and Vice President equal to the whole number of Senators and Representatives in Congress to which the District would be entitled if it were a State, but in no event more than the least populous State; they shall be in addition to those appointed by the States, but they shall be considered, for the purposes of the election of President and Vice President, to be electors appointed by a State; and they shall meet in the District and perform such duties as provided by the twelfth article of amendment.

Section 2. The Congress shall have power to enforce this article by appropriate legislation.

Amendment 24   [*Ratified 1964.*]

Prohibition of poll taxes

Section 1. The right of citizens of the United States to vote in any primary or other election for President or Vice President, for electors for President or Vice President, or for Senator or Representative in Congress, shall not be denied or abridged by the United States or any State by reason of failure to pay any poll tax or other tax.

Section 2. The Congress shall have power to enforce this article by appropriate legislation.

Amendment 25   [*Ratified 1967.*]

Presidential disability and succession

Section 1. In case of the removal of the President from office or of his death or resignation, the Vice President shall become President.

Section 2. Whenever there is a vacancy in the office of the Vice President, the President shall nominate a Vice President who shall take office upon confirmation by a majority vote of both Houses of Congress.

Section 3. Whenever the President transmits to the President pro tempore of the Senate and the Speaker of the House of Representatives his written declaration that he is unable to discharge the powers and duties of his office, and until he transmits to them a written declaration to the contrary, such powers and duties shall be discharged by the Vice President as Acting President.

Section 4. Whenever the Vice President and a majority of either the principal officers of the executive departments or of such other body as Congress may by law provide, transmit to the President pro tempore of the Senate and the Speaker of the House of Representatives their written declaration that the President is unable to discharge the powers and duties of his office, the Vice President shall immediately assume the powers and duties of the office as Acting President.

Thereafter, when the President transmits to the President pro tempore of the Senate and the Speaker of the House of Representatives his written declaration that no inability exists, he shall resume the powers and duties of his office unless the Vice President and a majority of either the principal officers of the executive department or of such other body as Congress may by law provide, transmit within four days to the President pro tempore of the Senate and the Speaker of the House of Representatives their written declaration that the President is unable to discharge the powers and duties of his office. Thereupon Congress shall decide the issue, assembling within forty-eight hours for that purpose if not in session. If the Congress, within twenty-one days after receipt of the latter written declaration, or, if Congress is not in session, within twenty-one days after Congress is required to assemble, determines by two-thirds vote of both Houses that the President is unable to discharge the powers and duties of his office, the Vice President shall continue to discharge the same as Acting President; otherwise, the President shall resume the powers and duties of his office.

Amendment 26   *[Ratified 1971.]*

Eighteen-year-old voting age

Section 1. The right of citizens of the United States, who are eighteen years of age or older, to vote shall not be denied or abridged by the United States or by any State on account of age.

Section 2. The Congress shall have power to enforce this article by appropriate legislation.

Glossary

Administrative law That branch of public law which deals with the rules and regulations issued by independent regulatory agencies (p. 449).

Advice and consent The power of the Senate, granted in the Constitution, to approve treaties made by the President and to approve certain presidential appointments (p. 333).

Affirmative action The policy of actively seeking to recruit minorities and females to overcome the effects of previous discrimination (p. 533).

Agenda-building The process of establishing a list of specific policy goals, called the *agenda* (p. 484).

Amendment An alteration or addition to a motion, bill, or constitution (p. 45).

Amicus curiae Latin phrase meaning "friend of the court": a person or group not a party to a case permitted to file a brief (written argument) in the court supporting a particular view of the case (p. 455).

Appeal A legal proceeding by which a case is brought from a lower court to a higher court for a rehearing (p. 446).

Appellate court A court which reviews cases originally decided by a lower court. The appellate court acts without a jury and is concerned with reviewing procedural matters and issues of interpretation of the law by the lower court (p. 446).

Articles of Confederation The document, ratified March 1, 1781, that formed the first constitution of the United States (pp. 42–3).

Australian vote The secret ballot (p. 225).

Authority Power recognized by those over whom the power is exercised (p. 27).

Bicameral system A legislature consisting of two houses or chambers (p. 391).

Bilateral Between two nations (p. 583).

Bill A proposal for law to be considered by a legislative body (p. 402).

Bill of Rights The first ten amendments to the Constitution (p. 489).

Block grant A grant-in-aid made by one level of government (usually the national) to another (usually state or local) which combines use of funds for several general programs and permits wide discretion by the grantee as to how the funds may be allocated and used (p. 89).

Brief A written argument presented to a court (p. 446).

Bureaucracy An organization of offices or positions arranged hierarchically and operating (in theory) according to rules rather than according to personal relations (p. 340).

Cabinet An advisory body made up of the heads of government departments (p. 345).

Capitalism An economic system in which the means of production are owned by individuals and operated by them and their assistants for a profit (p. 3).

Cartel A voluntary union of independent enterprises or nations that supply like commodities in a way that limits competition (p. 15). *See also OPEC*.

Categorical grant A grant-in-aid made by one level of government (usually the national) to another (usually state or local) which stipulates the particular purpose for which the funds are to be used (p. 88).

Caucus A meeting of a group of legislators (usually members of the same party) to decide a position on electing leadership, voting on a bill, etc. (p. 197).

Checks and balances A system by which government institutions or branches exercise checks on, and balance the activities of, other government institutions or branches (p. 334).

Civil liberties A series of prohibitions against government interference in the lives of citizens, such as freedom of speech, press, assembly, etc. (p. 490).

Civil rights Regulations permitting government intervention to guarantee the rights of full political participation to groups unfairly excluded from participation (p. 515).

Civil servant A person who works for a government as a member of the civil service (p. 354).

Class-action suit A lawsuit filed on behalf of the specific plaintiff and all other members of an identifiable group similarly situated, that is, who share the same legal interests in the case as the plaintiff (p. 180).

Clear and present danger test A test sometimes used by the courts to determine if certain acts or language are likely to lead to serious harm and are therefore to be prohibited by the courts (p. 496).

Closed primary A primary in which only party members are allowed to vote for a candidate for their party's nomination (p. 238).

Cloture A provision by which the Senate may cut off debate on a particular bill. Once cloture is voted, each member may speak only for one hour on the measure (p. 406).

Cold War Post-World War II conflict between communist countries and western countries, not involving the use of arms (p. 591).

Common law Customary law or precedent applied to court cases (p. 448).

Concurrent powers Powers exercised concurrently by both national and state governments (p. 72).

Concurrent resolution A Congressional action which sets tentative revenue and spending targets for the coming fiscal year (p. 545).

Confederation An organization of governmental units in which the units retain essential powers (p. 59).

Conference committee A committee composed of members of both houses of Congress whose task it is to agree on a compromise version of a bill after each house has produced a different version of the bill (p. 405).

Conflict of interest A situation in which an official's public actions may benefit, or be thought to benefit, his or her private interests (p. 354).

Constituency A body of citizens entitled to elect a representative to a legislative or other public body (p. 430).

Constitutional law Law derived from a constitution, that is, a written document embodying the rules of a political organization (p. 448).

Consumer price index (CPI) The statistical index devised by the government to measure increases in the cost of living (p. 553).

Dangerous tendency test A test sometimes used by the courts to determine if certain laws restricting free-dom of speech should be allowed. The test maintains that legislatures may pass laws prohibiting speech that would lead to "substantive evil" (p. 495–96).

De facto segregation Racial segregation that actually exists even if it has not come about as a result of laws or acts officially performed or legally permitted (p. 516).

Deferral process One form of legislative veto which permits Congress to stop an executive act (performed under statute) within a designated period of time. If Congress does not take such action, the executive act takes effect (p. 332).

Deficit spending The governmental policy of spending more than is received in revenues (p. 543).

De jure segregation Racial segregation brought about by official acts and specific laws. Such acts and laws are now unconstitutional (p. 516).

Democracy Rule by the people (p. 47).

Deregulation The act or process of removing regulations or restrictions to free an industry from government regulation (p. 380).

Detente The relaxation of tensions among nations (p. 584).

Double jeopardy The judicial principle which holds that a person cannot be prosecuted twice for the same crime by the same authorities (p. 507).

Due process A course of legal proceedings carried out in accordance with established principles and rules (p. 508).

Elastic clause The clause in the Constitution giving Congress power "to make all laws which shall be necessary and proper" for executing its enumerated powers (p. 61).

Elector A member of the electoral college (p. 259).

Electoral college system The system by which presidential electors from all states meet state by state in December after a presidential election to cast the official votes for the President (p. 45).

Elite theory The theory that power is held and shared by a small group of people who dominate the major institutions (p. 162).

Equity law Law developed by judges and designed to prevent harm where common law does not apply (p. 448).

Establishment clause A provision in the First Amendment prohibiting Congress from passing a law designating any religion as the official religion of the nation (p. 493).

Exclusionary rule A rule that prevents the use of evidence obtained unconstitutionally in a criminal trial of the person from whom the evidence was obtained (p. 503).

Executive agreement An agreement made between the President and a leader of a foreign country that does not require Senate approval, although it has the force of a treaty (p. 314).

Executive branch The branch of government headed by the President and charged with executing the country's laws (p. 310).

Executive privilege The principle by which the President can withhold sensitive papers from Congress in the interest of national security (p. 308).

Express powers Powers specifically granted to one of the branches of government by the Constitution (p. 60).

Extradition The legal process by which a person is delivered from one state to another in order to face criminal prosecution in the latter state (p. 74).

Federalism A form of government in which power and sovereignty are divided between central and regional authorities (p. 57).

Federalist papers A series of essays written by Alexander Hamilton, James Madison, and John Jay in 1787–1788 stressing the need for a strong government and conformity of the Constitution to the principles of republican government (p. 391).

Federalists Those who, in the early years of the Republic, favored a strong central government (p. 194).

Filibuster A term for the process by which a small group of senators can "talk a bill to death," eventually forcing the bill's withdrawal so that other business can be dealt with (p. 406).

Fiscal federalism The relationship involving transfer of economic resources among the national, state, and local governments, usually referring to grants-in-aid (p. 91).

Fiscal policy Policy relating to taxation, public revenues, and public debt (p. 543).

Franchise The right to vote (p. 221).

Free elections Processes by which decisions can be made and leaders chosen by means of free exercise of the right to vote (p. 3).

Free-enterprise The idea that private business should be allowed to freely operate in a competitive economy with a minimum of government interference (p. 4). *See also Capitalism.*

General revenue sharing The allocation of federal funds to states and localities with minimal restrictions on use (p. 90).

Grandfather clause A provision that only those who could demonstrate that their fathers or grandfathers had voted were exempt from the strict literacy tests and property requirements limiting the franchise (p. 516).

Grand jury A group of citizens convened to decide whether or not there exists in a given case enough evidence to merit a trial (p. 446).

Grants-in-aid Financial aid from the federal government to the states, usually for specific purposes (p. 86).

Grass roots At the local level, i.e., at a distance from the centers of social and political power (p. 176).

Great Society A set of large-scale programs for dealing with social, economic, and political problems that was initiated by President Johnson in the 1960s and that was meant to wipe out poverty (p. 569).

Guaranteed annual income A proposed welfare reform that would provide a minimum income to poor families in need of assistance (p. 576).

Habeas corpus A writ requiring that a prisoner be brought before a court to determine the legality of his or her imprisonment (p. 45).

Hegemony Special influence or power exercised by one nation over another (p. 587).

Horizontal federalism The relations among the various states of the union (p. 74).

Impeachment The formal charging of a public official with misconduct in office by a competent tribunal; for the President, the charge is brought by the House of Representatives (p. 45).

Implied powers Those powers derived from interpretation of powers expressly mentioned in the Constitution (p. 61).

Impoundment A presidential refusal to allow an agency to spend funds appropriated by Congress (p. 327).

Incumbent The current holder of an office (p. 233).

Inflation Continual rise in prices, generally attributed to an increase in the volume of money and credit relative to the amount of available goods (p. 553).

Inherent powers Those powers that belong to the federal government because it is a state or nation (p. 69).

Initiative A law voted on by the general public after it is proposed by petition (p. 212).

Injunction A writ granted by a court whereby a person or group is required to do or to refrain from doing a specified act (p. 449).

Interest groups Organized groups whose members have common views about certain policies or actions and so undertake activities to influence government officials and policies (p. 162).

Interposition The theory that each state in the union may determine the constitutionality of national laws (p. 70).

Item veto The power of the executive to reject certain parts of a bill passed by the legislature while consenting to the remainder of the bill (p. 327).

Judicial branch The branch of government consisting of the Supreme Court and other courts (p. 444).

Judicial review The power of the courts to assess the actions of individuals and agencies or to interpret the laws of Congress, states, and localities to determine whether or not such persons, agencies, or laws are in accord with the Constitution (p. 459).

Jurisdiction The authority granted courts to hear and decide cases brought before them (p. 446).

Legislative branch The branch of government consisting of members of Congress and Congressional agencies and organizations (p. 397).

Legislative oversight The process whereby Congress monitors the work of executive agencies to see if laws are being properly and efficiently carried out (p. 363).

Legislative veto The provision in a bill reserving to Congress ("two-house veto") or to a Congressional committee ("committe veto") or to the entire House or Senate ("one-house veto") the power to nullify by majority vote an act by an agency (p. 332).

Legitimacy Authority accepted as legal and proper (p. 27).

Lobbies Groups formed for the purpose of influencing the votes of public officials (p. 162).

Lobbyist A representative of a group or organization seeking the passage or the defeat of certain legislative measures (p. 92).

Majority leader The leader of the majority party in a legislative body (p. 397).

Majority opinion Written explanation of the views of court justices voting in the majority on a case (p. 457).

Majority whip The whip of the majority party (p. 397). *See also Whip.*

Means test Criterion used to determine if an individual qualifies to receive public assistance due to lack of sufficient resources to care for himself or herself and family (p. 564).

Middle voter A member of the group of citizens (usually middle-class) most likely to vote (p. 229).

Military-industrial complex President Eisenhower's term for the alleged alliance between the military and material goods suppliers to influence defense spending for mutual gain (p. 608).

Minority leader The leader of the minority party in a legislative body (p. 396).

Minority whip The whip of the minority party (p. 397). *See also Whip.*

Miranda rights Rights that stem from a Supreme Court decision requiring law enforcement officers to advise persons being arrested of their right to counsel prior to questioning (p. 504).

Monetary policy Primarily, decisions about currency supply and about credit levels extended to banks for use in making loans to businesses or individuals (p. 550).

Multilateral Among three or more nations (p. 583).

New Deal A series of programs calling for greater government intervention in the economy that was initiated by President Franklin D. Roosevelt during the Great Depression of the 1930s (p. 563).

Nullification The theory that each state in the union has the right to decide whether particular national laws should apply to that state (p. 70).

OPEC (Organization of Petroleum Exporting Countries) A cartel organized in the 1960s by the Arab oil-producing countries in order to gain favorable pricing on the world market (pp. 15–16). *See also Cartel.*

Open primary A primary in which persons can vote for candidates of any party regardless of their own party membership (p. 238).

Original court The court where a lawsuit is first filed and the case is heard and tried (p. 446).

Party *See Political party.*

Patronage Government jobs given to political supporters (p. 195).

Petit jury A jury that is selected to decide on the facts at issue in a single case (p. 446).

Platform A declaration of the principles and positions held by a political party or by a candidate for office (p. 243).

Plebescite A vote by which the citizens of a state or region voice an opinion concerning a government proposal (p. 264).

Pluralist system A system in which power is shared among a number of different groups, none strong enough to dominate but each able to protect its own interests with help from others (p. 4).

Plurality The margin of votes by which one candidate leads the next candidate—not necessarily a majority (p. 189).

Pocket veto An indirect veto of a legislative act by an executive who refuses to sign the act or formally veto it and who instead simply holds it until after the adjournment of the legislature (p. 318).

Policy evaluation The assessment of a policy's effectiveness (p. 486).

Policy formulation The systematic process of defining and developing policy (p. 485).

Policy implementation The process of putting into action policy goals and agendas (p. 486).

Policymaking The process whereby goals are set and alternative approaches to solving identified problems are outlined, adopted, and pursued (p. 483).

Political action committees The political agencies of organized interest groups established primarily to participate in lobbying activities and to support or challenge the candidacies of selected individuals (p. 245).

Political machine A well-entrenched organization of leaders and followers with considerable power in determining nominations and elections (p. 199).

Political party An organization that supports particular candidates in elections (p. 189).

Political socialization The process by which people acquire certain political values, beliefs, and orientations toward the political system (p. 135).

Poll, opinion A survey of a few people designated or intended to represent the thinking of a larger group on a given topic (p. 152).

Poll tax A fee paid when an individual registers to vote. The poll tax was declared illegal by the Twenty-fourth Amendment (p. 222).

Power The capacity to perform certain acts and achieve certain goals (p. 27).

Preferred position test A test sometimes used by the courts to determine if certain restrictions on First Amendment freedoms should be allowed. The test adopts a strong presumption that the freedoms are inviolate and that very strong evidence must be presented to allow restrictions (p. 496).

President pro tempore The presiding officer of the Senate when the vice-president is not present—always a senator of the majority party (p. 397).

Pressure groups Organized special-interest groups that put pressure on government institutions in order to get what they want (p. 162).

Prior restraint Restrictions imposed on certain First Amendment rights—such as speech, press, and assembly—prior to the exercise of those rights (p. 497).

Probable cause The view that there are reasonable grounds to conclude that an accused person is guilty of an offense (p. 503).

Procedural due process The requirement that the acts and laws of public officials be implemented correctly and fairly (p. 508).

Progressive tax A tax that takes a larger percentage from those with larger resources (p. 549). A **regressive** tax places a heavier burden on low-income households.

Proportional representation The allocation of seats in the legislature so that each political party receives a percentage of the seats which accurately reflect the percentage of the vote received in the election (p. 200).

Proposition 13 A referendum provision passed by California voters in the spring of 1978 to set strict limits on possible increases in local property taxes (p. 104).

Public opinion The set of ideas and opinions concerning candidates, policies, parties, and political ideologies held collectively by the people (p. 150).

Public policy The general goals and actions outlined by government officials in their efforts to resolve problems of public concern (p. 483).

Random sampling In polls, a group of people randomly selected to represent the population being surveyed (p. 152).

Recall The system by which people seek a referendum to decide whether or not an elected official should be removed from office (p. 212).

Referendum A law or resolution voted on by the general public after it is proposed by the legislature or by petition (p. 212).

Regulatory agency A government agency or advisory panel that regulates some commercial activity or sector of the economy and that is independent of any regular executive department (p. 369).

Republican government A government in which supreme power resides in the people but in which power is exercised by elected officers and representatives who are responsible to the people and who govern according to law (p. 47).

Rescission process A form of legislative veto requiring Congress to agree to an executive act before that act can take effect (p. 332).

Reserve powers Those powers reserved by the Constitution to the states (p. 47).

Residual clause That clause in the Constitution (Article 1, Section 8, Paragraph 18) which stipulates that Congress shall have all powers necessary for carrying out those powers specifically delegated to it (p. 61).

Revenue sharing A program by which the federal government gives funds to state and local governments without specifying the use to which the funds must be put (p. 90).

Reverse discrimination Preferential treatment given to those previously discriminated against in order to overcome the effects of previous discrimination (p. 533).

SALT (Strategic Arms Limitations Talks) Negotiations between the United States and the Soviet Union to prevent unchecked growth in the development of sophisticated weapons systems (p. 313).

Segregation The separation or isolation of a racial or other group by setting up barriers to regular interaction; *de jure* segregation is grounded in law, whereas *de facto* segregation is grounded in custom or practice (p. 516).

Semiclosed primary A primary election in which a voter is allowed to declare his or her political party affiliation on the day of the election at the polling place. After such declaration, the voter is permitted to vote only in that party's primary (p. 238).

Senatorial courtesy The unwritten rule that the President should consult with senators of a state before appointing a federal judge in that state and should allow a senator of his own party an absolute veto over the nomination (p. 334).

Seniority system The informal system in Congress whereby first choice of committee positions, etc., goes to the longest serving members (p. 416).

Separation of powers Allocation of powers among branches of government at the same level (p. 48).

Shield laws Laws permitting reporters to refuse to disclose their sources of information gathered in the course of performance of their journalistic functions (p. 498).

Socio-economic status The various factors—such as occupation, income, and social class—that determine status in society (p. 133).

Sovereignty Supreme power over a body politic (p. 583).

Speaker of the House The member of the majority party in the House of Representatives selected by the party to preside over sessions of the House (p. 396).

Spoils system Civil-service system by which a political victor replaces present officeholders with his or her own supporters (p. 197).

Stagflation An economic condition in which high inflation and high unemployment occur simultaneously (p. 556).

Standing committees The permanent committees in the Senate and the House (p. 399).

Standing to sue The state of being legally entitled to go to court to bring suit (p. 458).

Stare decisis Latin phrase meaning "let the decision stand": a rule of law derived from English common law whereby courts follow the decisions of previous cases in deciding current cases with similar facts (p. 449).

States' rights All rights not granted to the federal government by the Constitution nor forbidden by it to the separate states (p. 47).

Statutory law   Legislation; law made by statutes (p. 448).

Strategic weapons   Those nuclear weapons, delivered by missiles or bombers, which can inflict widespread damage over large areas and at long range (p. 607).

Strict construction   Literal interpretation of the meaning of the Constitution (p. 333).

Subpoena   A court order declaring that something must be done under penalty of punishment (p. 409).

Subsequent punishment   A situation in which the publication of libelous materials leads to compensation for the victim and penalty against the offender (p. 497).

Substantive due process   The requirement that the acts and laws of public officials be reasonable and constitutional (p. 509).

Sunbelt   General term for the southern states (p. 276).

Sunday Blue Laws   Laws requiring businesses to close on Sunday in observance of the Christian Sabbath (p. 140).

Sunshine laws   Laws requiring that meetings of agencies or government units be open to the public (p. 417).

Supremacy clause   A constitutional clause (Article VI) stipulating that the Constitution, laws of the national government, and treaties are "the supreme law of the land," and these shall take precedence over state laws (p. 70).

Tactical weapons   Nuclear weapons deployed in local battle situations and, generally, for short distances. Tactical nuclear weapons in Europe are not included in the SALT negotiations (p. 607).

Tariff   A tax on an imported good that is a percentage of the good's value. Same as "duty" (p. 540).

Tax subsidy   A special tax break granted to businesses or individuals in efforts to affect their behavior; e.g., interest deductions and investment tax credits (p. 247).

Theater weapons   Long-range nuclear weapons aimed at specific targets behind enemy lines (p. 607).

Theory of Incorporation   The process of interpretation whereby certain protections of the Bill of Rights concerning national government action are included within the meaning of the Fourteenth Amendment to apply to action by the states (p. 507).

Truman Doctrine   A policy announced by President Truman in March 1947 declaring that the United States would use its vast resources to support nations in fighting communism (p. 592).

Unitary system   A political system wherein ultimate power is concentrated in the central government. All other governmental units exist at the sufferance of the central government (p. 59).

Vertical federalism   The relations between the national, state, and local governments (p. 73).

Veto   The power of the President to refuse to sign a bill passed by Congress; the bill may then become law only if two thirds of each house vote in favor of overriding the veto (p. 327).

Watergate   A 1973 scandal involving agents of the Nixon campaign who were arrested while illegally entering the Democratic campaign headquarters in the Watergate Hotel in Washington, D.C. Investigation led to disclosure of widespread abuse of presidential powers (p. 141).

Whip   The person in a legislative body who, with deputy whips, is responsible for rounding up, or "whipping into line," party members when a vote is coming up (p. 397).

Writ of certiorari   An order from an appeals court to a lower court to send up the record of a case so that it can be studied on appeal (pp. 446–47).

Writ of mandamus   A court order directing an official to perform a nondiscretionary act (p. 460).

Zero-based budgeting   A system that requires each governmental program or agency to justify itself and each aspect of its budget every year (p. 545).

Acknowledgments

PHOTOGRAPHS AND CARTOONS

Cover and title page: Robert C. Shafer/Lensman

FM: vi, detail from "Signing of the Constitution" by Howard Chandler Christy. National Geographic photographer George F. Mobley. Courtesy of U.S. Capitol Historical Society; vii, Fred Ward/Black Star; viii, Dennis Brack/Black Star; x, Bill Fitz-Patrick/The White House; **I:** xii, Bohdan Hrynewych/Stock Boston; 3, Michael Sullivan; 4, Copyright © 1935 (renewed 1963) by The Conde Nast Publications, Inc.; 6(l), Bonnie Stutski/Photri, (r) Paul Conklin; **P1:** 10(t), Paul Conklin, (b) Dennis Brack/Black Star; 11, Courtesy of U.S. Capitol Historical Society; **1:** 13, Dennis Brack/Black Star; 14(l), Nick Nichols/Black Star, (r) Bert Miller/Black Star; 17, Ira Wyman/Sygma; 19(t), Diana Walker/Liaison/Gamma, (bl), Wide World, (br), D. B. Owen/Black Star; 24, Arthur Grace/Sygma; 28, Dennis Brack/Black Star; 29, Dennis Brack/Black Star; 30, Scott, Foresman; 32(t), Library of Congress, (b) The Metropolitan Museum of Art, bequest of Charles Allen Munn, 1924; 33(both), Library of Congress; 34, Library of Congress; 35, "Second and High Street" by Thomas Birch, Historical Society of Pennsylvania; 36, Library of Congress; 37, Library of Congress; 38, Historical Society of Pennsylvania; 41, Bettmann Archive; 43, Library of Congress; 44, Library of Congress; 46, New York Public Library, Astor, Lenox & Tilden Foundation; 49, Courtesy of U.S. Capitol Historical Society; **2:** 56, Larry Downing/Woodfin Camp; 59, House of Commons, 1833, By courtesy of the National Portrait Gallery, London; 61(t), Paul Conklin, (b) Daniel Brody/Stock Boston; 62, Library of Congress; 63(tl), Library of Congress, (tr) H. Armstrong Roberts; 64, Erich Hartmann/Magnum; 64/5, "Integration, Supreme Court" by Ben Shahn. Des Moines Art Center, James D. Edmundson Fund, 1964; 65(t), Scott, Foresman, (b) Tom Kane/Black Star; 66(t), Owen Franken/Sygma, (c) Arthur Grace/Sygma, (b) Courtesy Franklin Delano Roosevelt Library; 67, "The Old House of Representatives, 1821," Samuel F. B. Morse. In the collection of The Corcoran Gallery of Art, Washington, D.C.; 69, Historical Society of Pennsylvania; 70, Bettman Archive; 72, Bob Llewellyn/Picture Cube; 73, Dave Johnson/Picture Cube; 75, Rick Friedman/Black Star; 76, 77, 78, UPI; **3:** 80, Jim Markham; 82, Roger Werth, Longview Daily News/Woodfin Camp; 83(t), Michelle Bogre/Sygma, (b) Michael J. Philippot/Sygma; 86, Library of Congress; 87, National Archives; 88, Photograph Archives, Division of Library Resources, Oklahoma Historical Society; 89(t), Scott, Foresman, (b) Scott, Foresman; 93, Steve Liss/Liaison; 94, Sygma; 96, S. Greenwood/Gamma; **P2:** 102–3, "Election Day at the State House," John Krimmel. Historical Society of Pennsylvania; 102, Ebony Magazine, Johnson Publishing; **C2:** 105, Lester Sloan/Woodfin Camp; 107, Chris Springman/Black Star; 108, Jeff Lowenthal/Woodfin Camp; 110(l,r), Tony Korody/Sygma; 111, Chris Springman/Black Star; 113, Tony Korody/Sygma; 116, Tony Korody/Sygma; 123, Bob Englehart; 124, CONRAD © 1978, Los Angeles Times. Reprinted with permission Los Angeles Times Syndicate; 125, Chris Springman/Black Star; **4:** 128, UPI; 136(l), Michael Sullivan, (r) Scott, Foresman; 137, Stephanie Maze/Woodfin Camp; 138, Courtesy William Cohen; 140, UPI; 142, UPI; 144, Jim Wells/Pictorial Parade; 145, Copyright 1963. The Dallas Times Herald. Photographer Bob Jackson/UPI; 146, Tiziou/Sygma; 147, Sygma; 151, Sidney Harris; 152, Scott, Foresman; **5:** 160, UPI; 162, Paul Conklin; 163, Michael Sullivan; 166(l), Martha Adler Levick/Black Star, (r) Bert Miller/Black Star; 167, Michael Sullivan; 168, © 1978 by the New York Times Company. Reprinted by permission; 170(l),(r) and 171, UPI; 174, 175(t), Michael Sullivan; 175(b), Paul Conklin; 177, Tom Flannery, Courtesy Baltimore Sun; 180, George Tames; 182, The Granger Collection, New York; 183, UPI; 184, Charles Moore/Black Star; 185, Peter Simon/Stock Boston; **6:** 188, Owen Franken/Stock Boston; 190, Ken Love; 192(t), John Chao/Woodfin Camp, (b) Wide World; 195, The Granger Collection, New York; 196, Bettman Archive; 197, Courtesy Franklin Delano Roosevelt Library; 198, UPI; 199, Paul Sequeira/Photo Researchers; 201, UPI; 202, Ken Love; 203, UPI; 205, Copyrighted *Chicago Tribune*. Used by permission; 206, UPI; 210, 211, Cameramann International; **7:** 220, Howard Simmons; 222, Historical Pictures Service, Chicago; 223, Library of Congress; 225, Owen Franken/Stock Boston; 226, Jim Anderson/Woodfin Camp; 234, Bettman Archive; 236(t), Chie Nichio/Nancy Palmer, (b) Peter Southwick/Stock Boston; 238, Pamela Price/Picture Cube; 240, Cornell Capa/Magnum; 241, Richard Stromberg; 242, Peter Southwick/Stock Boston; 244, UPI; 246, Ray Hillstrom; 248, "Union Skirmish," Gilbert Gaul. West Point Museum Collections. U.S. Military Academy; 249(bl), Mark Godfrey/Magnum, (br) Frank Johnston/Black Star; 250(c), Courtesy Smithsonian Institution. Photo No. 76-4475; 250–1, Fred Ward/Black Star; 251, "County

Election,'' George Caleb Bingham. Courtesy The Boatmen's National Bank of St. Louis; 251, Dennis Brack/Black Star; 252, ''Trail of Tears'' by Robert Lindneux. Courtesy Woolaroc Museum, Bartlesville, Oklahoma; 253(tl), Photo by Dorothea Lange. War Relocation Authority in National Archives; 253(cr), Merritt/Black Star, (bl) Stephanie Maze/Woodfin Camp; 254, Dennis Brack/Black Star; 257, By permission of Bill Mauldin and Wil-Jo Associates, Inc.; 258, UPI; 263, UPI; 264, Ray Osrin. Courtesy Cleveland Plain Dealer; **P3:** 270(tr), Historical Pictures Service, Chicago, (b) United States Capitol Historical Society; 271, Ollie Atkins; **C3:** 273, Owen Franken/Stock Boston; 274, 275, 276, 277, 279, Courtesy Wayne State University, Labor History Archives; 280, UPI; 281, Chicago Tribune photo by William Yates. Used with permission; 284, UPI; 286(t), Robert Gumpert, (b) Courtesy Amalgamated Clothing & Textile Workers Union; 288, UPI; 290, Illinois Labor History Society; 291, Courtesy Wayne State University, Labor History Archives; 293, Robert Gumpert; 295(l,r), UPI; 301, Courtesy Amalgamated Clothing & Textile Workers Union; **8:** 302, Fred Ward/Black Star; 304, Courtesy Chicago Historical Society; 306, Bettman Archive; 307, Wide World; 308, UPI; 311(t, bl), UPI, 311(br), Wide World; 314, Courtesy The White House; 317, Don Casper/Chicago Tribune; 320, Arthur Grace/Stock Boston; 325, Wide World; 329, Alex Webb/Magnum; 330, Bill Fitz-Patrick/White House; 334, Wide World; **9:** 338, Elliot Erwitt/Magnum; 340–1, John Fischetti © 1978 Chicago Sun-Times; 342, Leo deWys; 343, Brian Basset. Courtesy Seattle Times; 346, Sygma; 353, Michael Sullivan; 354(t), Dennis Brack/Black Star; 354(b), UPI; 355(t), The Granger Collection, New York; 357(t), DUNAGIN'S PEOPLE by Ralph Dunagin © 1978 Field Enterprises, Inc. Courtesy of Field Newspaper Syndicate; 357, Baldy. Courtesy Atlanta Constitution; 360(t), Michael Alexander, (b) U.S. Postal Service; 362, Pavlousky/Melloul/Sygma; 364, U.S. Navy photo; **10:** 368, Courtesy U.S. Steel; 370, Reprinted by permission of the Chicago Tribune-New York News Syndicate, Inc.; 371, Courtesy Great Northern Railway; 372, Courtesy U.S. Steel; 373, Scott, Foresman; 378, Courtesy Caterpillar; 380, Courtesy Boeing Company; 385(tr), Jean-Claude Lejeune, (b) Scott, Foresman; 387, Courtesy U.S. Steel; **11:** 390, United States Capitol Historical Society; 392, UPI; 394, Dennis Brack/Black Star; 395, Chicago Tribune photograph by Charles Osgood. Used with permission; 396, Dennis Brack/Black Star; 398, United States Capitol Historical Society; 399, Paul Fusco/Magnum; 401, United States Capitol Historical Society; 404, UPI; 406, © 1958 The New York Times/Carl Rose; 408, United States Capitol Historical Society; 409, UPI; 410, Historical Society of Pennsylvania; 411(tc), Courtesy of the Newberry Library, Chicago (bc) ''The Strike'' by Robert Koehler, one of the earliest American paintings (1886) depicting industrial conflict. Courtesy of District 1199, National Union of Hopsital and Health Care Employees, RWDSW/AFL-CIO and Lee Baxandall; 412(tc,c), Tom Stack and Associates, (br) Roland Freeman/Magnum; 413(tc), Art Rickerby/Black Star, (bc) Wide World; 414(tl), Diane Gentry/Black Star, (br) Brett/Liaison; 415(tl), Tom Lesley/Black Star,

(tr) Jim Nachtwey/Black Star; 419, Dennis Brack/Black Star; 421, Penelope Breese/Liaison; 422, Dennis Brack/Black Star; 431, Courtesy office of Congressman Jack Kemp; 435, CONRAD, Denver Post, 1963. Historical Pictures Service, Chicago; 439, Scott, Foresman; **12:** 442, Wide World; 444, Historical Society of York County; 446, Wide World; 448, 450, UPI; 452, Wide World; 456, Reprinted by permission of the Supreme Court Historical Society from *Equal Justice Under Law: The Supreme Court in American Life,* published in cooperation with the National Geographic Society; 461, Courtesy Maryland Historical Society; 463, Frank Leslie's Illustrated Newspaper, June 27, 1857; 464, Historical Pictures Service, Chicago; 465, Wide World; 466(t), Larry Nighwander, (b) Reprinted by permission of the Supreme Court Historical Society from *Equal Justice Under Law: The Supreme Court in American Life,* published in cooperation with the National Geographic Society; 467, Bill Fitz-Patrick/The White House; **P4:** 474(t), Hiroji Kubota/Magnum, (b) U.S. Army photo; 475, Paul Conklin; **C4:** 485, Salhani/SIPA Press/Black Star; 487, Bill Fitz-Patrick/The White House; **13:** 488, David Burnett; 490, Peter Whitney/Pictorial Parade; 493(t), John Launois/Black Star, (b) Burk Uzzle/Magnum; 494, J. Clarke/Shostal; 498, Gilles Peress/Magnum; 499, Bart Bartholomew/Black Star; 500, UPI; 501, Owen Franken/Sygma; 502, Thomas Simon/Liaison/Gamma; 504, UPI; 505, Tony Korody/Sygma; 506, Joe Marquette/UPI; 507, Bill Levin; 511, Holland © 1968 by Chicago Tribune; **14:** 514, James H. Karales photo © 1965 Cowles Communication, LOOK Magazine, Library of Congress; 517, New York Public Library, From *W. E. B. DuBois* by Virginia Hamilton; 518(l), Danny Lyon/Magnum, (r) UPI; 521, Bruce Davidson/Magnum; 524, UPI; 526(t), Paul Conklin, (b) UPI; 529, Clay Templin/Jeroboam; 530, Bettmann Archive; 532(t), Rose Skytta/Jeroboam, (b) The First Women's Bank, 111 East 57th Street, New York City; 534, Martin A. Levick/Black Star; **15:** 538, Scott, Foresman; 540, Suzanne Engelman/Shostal; 542, UPI; 543, Reprinted by permission of the Chicago Tribune-New York News Syndicate, Inc.; 547, UPI; 550, Diana Walker/Liaison; 551, Courtesy of Federal Reserve; **16:** 560, Courtesy Detroit News; 565, Social Security Administration; 568, Library of Congress; 570, Wide World; 571, Paul Conklin; 572, Thomas England; 574, Rick Freedman/Picture Cube; 575, Chicago Housing Authority; 576, Sidney Harris; 580, Dan Wasserman © 1981 by the New York Times Company. Reprinted by permission; **17:** 582, Diego Goldberg/Sygma; 590, U.S. Navy; 591, Department of Defense; 602, T. Zimberoff/Sygma; 604, Campbell/Sygma; 609(t), Sygma, (b) Herman Kokojan/Black Star; 612, Nogues/Sygma; 615, Peter Jordan/Liaison; 617, Michael Evans/The White House.

FIGURES AND TABLES

4: Figures 1, 2, 3, 4, 5, pp. 130, 131, 132: From ''Opinion Roundup,'' PUBLIC OPINION, Vol. 1, No. 3, pp. 26–28, July/August 1978. Copyright 1978 American Enterprise Institute. Figure 6, p. 133: Adapt Table titled, "Views of Americans on Social Issues by Educational Attainment." Source: 1972–1977 "General Social Surveys," National Opinion Research Center. Table 1, p. 134: From "Opinion Roundup," PUBLIC OPINION, Vol. 1, No. 3, p. 32, July/August 1978. Copyright 1978 American Enterprise Institute. Figure 7, p. 148: Surveys by National Opinion Research Center, "General Social Survey," 1975 and 1977. Survey by American Institute of Public Opinion (Gallup) December 9–12, 1977. Figure 8, p. 149: From PUBLIC OPINION, May/June 1978. Copyright American Enterprise Institute, and The Gallup Poll, Princeton, New Jersey. **5:** Table 2, p. 178: From *The Almanac of American Politics 1978* by Michael Barone, Grant Ujifusa, and Douglas Matthews. Copyright © 1972, 1973, 1975, 1977 by Michael Barone, Grant Ujifusa, and Douglas Matthews. Reprinted by permission of the publisher, E. P. Dutton. **6:** Figure 2, p. 213: From Everett Carll Ladd, Jr., WHERE HAVE ALL THE VOTERS GONE? Copyright © 1978, 1977 by W. W. Norton & Company, Inc. Table 2, p. 214: From Everett Carll Ladd, Jr., WHERE HAVE ALL THE VOTERS GONE? Copyright © 1978, 1977, by W. W. Norton & Company, Inc. Source: Gallup Organization Inc. Figure 3, p. 215: From Everett Carll Ladd, Jr., WHERE HAVE ALL THE VOTERS GONE? p. 6. Copyright © 1978, 1977 by W. W. Norton & Company, Inc. Figure 4, p. 216: "© 1980 by The New York Times Company. Reprinted by permission." Table 3, p. 217: From Everett Carll Ladd, Jr., WHERE HAVE ALL THE VOTERS GONE? pp. 40–41. Copyright © 1978, 1977 by W. W. Norton & Company, Inc. Source: National Opinion Research Center. **7:** Figure 3, p. 229: From Norman H. Nie, Sidney Verba, John R. Petrocik, THE CHANGING AMERICAN VOTER, p. 167. Reprinted by permission of the publishers, Harvard University Press, © 1976, 1979 by the Twentieth Century Fund. Figure 4, p. 229: From Norman H. Nie, Sidney Verba, John R. Petrocik, THE CHANGING AMERICAN VOTER, p. 86. Reprinted by permission of the publishers, Harvard University Press, © 1976, 1979 by the Twentieth Century Fund. Table 3, p. 237: From CONGRESSIONAL QUARTERLY-Weekly Report, Vol. 38, No. 27, July 5, 1980, p. 1869, and GUIDE TO CURRENT AMERICAN GOVERNMENT, Spring 1978, p. 126. Copyright 1977 and 1980 by Congressional Quarterly Inc. Table 4, p. 239: From "Guide to Current American Government," CONGRESSIONAL QUARTERLY WEEKLY REPORT, Fall 1980, p. 55. Copyright 1980 by Congressional Quarterly Inc. Table 5, p. 255: From "Senate Races," CONGRESSIONAL QUARTERLY WEEKLY REPORT, Vol. 35, No. 12, p. 488, 1977. Copyright 1977 by Congressional Quarterly Inc. Table 6, p. 256: From CONGRESSIONAL QUARTERLY WEEKLY REPORT, Vol. 35, No. 44, October 28, 1977, p. 2303. Copyright 1977 by Congressional Quarterly Inc. Figure 7, p. 245: "© 1980 by The New York Times Company. Reprinted by permission." **9:** Table 1, p. 344: From TODAY: Journal of Political News and Analysis, January 30, 1981, p. 9. Copyright King's Court Communications, Inc. **11:** Figure 1, p. 403: From GUIDE TO CURRENT AMERICAN GOVERNMENT, Spring 1981, p. 145. Copyright 1980 by Congressional Quarterly Inc. Table 1, p. 424: From GUIDE TO CURRENT AMERICAN GOVERNMENT, Spring 1981, p. 53. Copyright 1980 by Congressional Quarterly Inc. Table 2, p. 425: From GUIDE TO CURRENT AMERICAN GOVERNMENT, Spring 1981, p. 54. Copyright 1980 by Congressional Quarterly Inc. Table 3, p. 426: From GUIDE TO CURRENT AMERICAN GOVERNMENT, Spring 1981, p. 52. Copyright 1980 by Congressional Quarterly Inc. Table 5, p. 433: From GUIDE TO CURRENT AMERICAN GOVERNMENT, Fall 1980, p. 41. Copyright 1980 by Congressional Quarterly Inc. **14:** Table 2, pp. 522–523: From Milton D. Morris, "Black Electoral Participation and the Distribution of Public Benefits," 1980 ROSTER OF BLACK ELECTED OFFICIALS, Vol. 10. Copyright 1981 by the Joint Center for Political Studies. **15:** Figure 1, p. 545: "Reprinted by permission of THE WALL STREET JOURNAL, © Dow Jones & Company, Inc. 1979. All Rights Reserved." Table 2, p. 546: From CONGRESSIONAL QUARTERLY ALMANAC, Vol. XXXI, 1975, p. 918. Copyright 1976 by Congressional Quarterly Inc. **17:** Figure 1, p. 586: From PUBLIC OPINION, March/May 1979, p. 27. Copyright 1979 American Enterprise Institute. Figure 2, pp. 588–589: From PUBLIC OPINION, February/March 1980, pp. 28–29. Copyright 1980 American Enterprise Institute.

LITERARY SELECTIONS

Part 1

p. 98: Samuel H. Beer, "Federalism, Nationalism, and Democracy in America." THE AMERICAN POLITICAL SCIENCE REVIEW, vol. 72, no. 1, March 1978.

Part 2

p. 133: From "The New Lines Are Drawn: Class and Ideology in America" by Everett Ladd, Jr., from PUBLIC OPINION, July/August 1978, vol. 1, no. 3. Copyright 1978 American Enterprise Institute. Reprinted by permission of the American Enterprise Institute for Public Policy Research.

p. 167: Excerpts from AMERICANS FOR DEMOCRATIC ACTION circular by John Kenneth Galbraith. Reprinted by permission.

p. 173: From "Lobbies Act to Shape Key Panels in Next Congress" by Steven V. Roberts, NEW YORK TIMES, December 7, 1978. Copyright © 1978 by The New York Times Company. Reprinted by permission.

p. 176: From "Firearms Rule Draws a Fusillade" by Charles Babcock, WASHINGTON POST, May 17, 1978. Copyright © 1978, The Washington Post Company. Reprinted by permission.

p. 179: From "Will Lobbying Kill the Proposed Lobbying Bill?" by David Rosenbaum, NEW YORK TIMES, September 12, 1976. Copyright © 1976 by The New York Times Company. Reprinted by permission.

p. 238: From ''Democratic Primary: Flirting with Disaster'' from DALLAS MORNING NEWS, July 31, 1979. Reprinted by permission.

pp. 256–57: Joe McGinniss, THE SELLING OF THE PRESIDENT 1968. New York: Trident Press, 1969.

Part 3

p. 370: From ''Mobile Home Industry Likes U.S. Regulation'' by Larry Kramer, WASHINGTON POST, April 19, 1979. Copyright © 1979, The Washington Post Company. Reprinted by permission.

p. 418: From WHAT CAN JIMMY CARTER LEARN ABOUT CONGRESS FROM PREVIOUS PRESIDENTS? by Eric L. Davis, delivered at the Annual Meeting of the American Political Science Association, August 31–September 3, 1978. Reprinted by permission of the American Political Science Association.

p. 418: Excerpt from WASHINGTON POST editorial, October 12, 1978. Copyright © 1978, The Washington Post Company. Reprinted by permission.

p. 418: Reply to editorial by Frank Annunzio from WASHINGTON POST, October 23, 1978. Reprinted by permission of the author.

p. 437: From ''Proposed Cuts in School Impact Aid,'' THE NEW YORK TIMES, February 20, 1981. Copyright © 1981 by The New York Times Company. Reprinted by permission.

Part 4

pp. 482–83: From NEW YORK TIMES editorial, December 28, 1980. Copyright © 1980 by The New York Times Company. Reprinted by permission.

p. 524: From ''New Voters and New Policy Priorities in the Deep South'' by M. Elizabeth Sanders. Reprinted by permission of the American Political Science Association.

p. 546: Excerpt from CONGRESSIONAL INSIGHT, October 12, 1979, vol. 3, no. 41. Copyright © 1979 by Congressional Quarterly Inc. Reprinted by permission.

p. 561: William Lee Miller, WELFARE AND VALUES IN AMERICA: A REVIEW OF ATTITUDES TOWARD WELFARE AND WELFARE POLICIES IN THE LIGHT OF AMERICAN HISTORY AND CULTURE. WELFARE POLICY PROJECT: The Institute of Policy Sciences and Public Affairs of Duke University and The Ford Foundation, Spring 1977.

pp. 572–74: Excerpts from ''Legislative Bargaining and the Food Stamp Act, 1964'' by Randall B. Ripley from CONGRESS AND URBAN PROBLEMS. Copyright © 1969 by The Brookings Institution. Reprinted by permission.

p. 609: From ''Social Costs and the Arms Race'' by Ruth L. Sivard from THE NATION, June 17, 1978. Copyright © 1978 The Nation Associates. Reprinted by permission.

Index

Abortion, 129
  funding of, 456
  Supreme Court rulings on, 467
Adams, John, 35, 324
  midnight judicial appointments
    by, 460
Adams, John Quincy, 197, 260
  1824 election, 195–196
ADC. *See* AFDC
Adrian, Charles R., 75
Advisers
  on labor-law reform, 282–283
  military, 313, 322
  presidential, 319–322
Advisory Commission on Intergov-
    ernmental Relations, 97
AFDC
  change in recipients, 565–566,
    table, 566
  establishment of, 565
Affirmative action, 467, 533–536
AFL-CIO, 164
  in California, and Proposition
    13, 112, 161
  Committee on Political Educa-
    tion, 246
  government employees in, 359
  image and membership decline,
    277–278
  as lobbyist, 279, 280–281, 282,
    285, 292–293, 298–299. *See
    also* Labor; Unions
African Development Bank, 601
Agency for International Develop-
    ment (AID), 601
Agenda
  building and changing, 484–485
Agnew, Spiro T., 244, 324
  resignation and conviction of,
    325

Agriculture
  effect of Depression on, 564,
    565, 567
  effect of grain embargo on, 612–613
  House Committee on, and legis-
    lative bargaining, 572
Agriculture, Department of, 87,
    164, 612–613
Aid to families of dependent children.
  See AFDC
Alaska pipeline
  as energy solution, 555
Albany Plan, 31
Alcohol, Tobacco and Firearms,
    Bureau of (BATF), 176
Allen, Clifford, 275
Alliances, U.S.
  economic, 592
  military, 592, 594–595
Ambassadors
  appointment, 304, 313–314
Amendment(s), 45, 50, 325
  filibuster by, 294
  First, 179, 183, 245, 491, 493–
    502
  Second, 508
  Third, 508
  Fourth, 502–503
  Fifth, 503–504, 506, 508, 527
  Sixth, 505–506
  Seventh, 505–506, 508
  Eighth, 505–506
  Tenth (states' rights), 47, 70–71,
    508
  Eleventh, 468
  Thirteenth, 51, 516
  Fourteenth, 51–52, 468, 507,
    508, 516, 530
  Fifteenth, 51, 222, 463, 516, 530
  Sixteenth, 468, 549

  Seventeenth, 45, 221
  Eighteenth, 55 n14
  Nineteenth, 222, 530
  Twenty-first, 55 n14
  Twenty-fourth, 222
  Twenty-fifth, 326
  Twenty-sixth, 223, 468
  formulation, 50
  lobbying, 179, 183
  on rights of criminally accused,
    504–506
  Supreme Court and, 468
  v. black Americans, 516–517
  and women's rights, 530–532.
    See also Bill of Rights; Constitu-
    tion, U.S.
American Bar Association (ABA)
  on judicial appointments, 450
  on judicial retirement, 468
American Federation of State,
    County, and Municipal Em-
    ployees, 282
American Federation of Workers
    and Congress of Industrial Or-
    ganizations. *See* AFL-CIO
American Medical Association
    (AMA), 246
  as antihealth care lobby group, 566
American Political Science Associ-
    ation, 97
Americans for Constitutional Ac-
    tion (ACA)
  rating by, table, 178, 189
Americans for Democratic Action
    (ADA), 167
  rating by, table, 178, 189
American Tax Reduction Act of
    1979, 165, 167
Amicus curiae briefs, 454–456
Anderson, John B., 257

Eagleton, Thomas F., 339, 369
Easton, David, 142
Economic Cooperation Develop-
    ment, Organization for,
    (OECD)
    members and function of, 592
Economic Opportunity Act
    legislation under, 570–571
Economic system
    and constitutional interpretation, 53
    in early government, 40–42.
    See also Economy
Economy
    capitalistic, 539
    and CEA, 321–322
    consumer price index and,
        1967–1980, fig., 552
    and cost of deregulation, 386–387
    and decreased dollar value,
        1940–1980, fig., 553
    Depression effect on, 563
    employment and, 555–556, 577–
        578
    energy and, 14, 15, 17, 554–555
    growth of, 85–86
    and Federal Reserve System, 549–551
    food stamps and, 573
    income tax and, 85
    national bank and, 61, 68
    and political labels, 129, 131
    political opinion, 129–131, 194–195
    regulatory effect on, 369, 371–
        372, 381
    solutions to, 556–558
    v. inflation, 553–554
    wages, rates of, and, 1970–
        1980, table, 553.
    See also Budget, Free enterprise
Edelman, Murray, 262
Education
    bilingual, 351
    and class, 133, table, 134, 135
    federal aid to, 91, 574–575
    and impact aid, 435–436, table, 437
    and political socialization, 137–
        138, 154
    religious, and federal aid, 493–495
    and school prayer, 468
    segregation *v.* integration in,
        51–52, 70–71

and social liberalism, 131, 133,
    fig., 133
and voting factor, 226–227, 265,
    fig., 227
War on Poverty legislation and,
    574–575
Education, Department of, 84, 339
    creation of, 575
Edwards, James B., 482–483
EEOC. *See* Equal Employment
    Opportunity Commission
    (EEOC)
Eisenhower, Dwight D., 231, 324,
    326, 328, 345, 393
    on defense spending, 608
    as diplomat, 313–314
    and nuclear test ban treaty, 404–405
    vetoed bills by, 327
Eizenstat, Stuart E., 282
    on energy crisis, 12–13, 16, 476–477
Elections
    1800, 195
    1816, 195
    1824, 195–196, 260
    1828, 196–197
    1876, 260
    1888, 260
    1912, 205–206
    1932, 199
    1936, 464
    1948, 205, 224, 235
    1952, 231
    1952–1974, GOP support with-
        drawal, fig., 215
    1956, 231
    1960, 232, 261
    1968, 231, 261
    1972, 216, 231, 261
    1976, 191, 193, 217, 261
    1980, 194, 201, 214, 217, 224,
        232–233, table, 207, fig.,
        216, 218
    1980, voting pattern, 229, table,
        230–231
    in caucuses, 197
    certification, 276
    Congressional patterns of, 233–
        234, fig., 233
    deviating, 231
    expenditures, 244–245, fig.,
        245, table, 255–256

initiative, 263–264, 266
maintaining, 232
and minority voting rights, 516–
    517, 520–521
minor parties in, 205–206, table,
    207
popular *v.* electoral vote and, 260
process, presidential, 45–46
purpose and practice of, 261–263
realigning, 231–232
recall, 263–264, 266
referendum, 263–264, 266
reinstating, 232–233
short-term forces, 228, 231,
    fig., 229
types of, 231–233
voter turnout, by year and type,
    fig., 224.
See also Electoral College sys-
    tem; Electorate; Political par-
    ty(ies); Voting
Electoral College system
    elitist theory within, 221
    and national bonus plan, 261
    and 1980 election, 201, 202–203
    and presidential elections, 259–261
    proposed reforms of, 260–261
Electoral process
    and political opinion, 149–150,
        151–152
    single-member districts in, 200–
        201
Electorate, 190
    categories of, 226–228
    eligibility, 222–223, 225
    party appeal to, 191, 193
    turnout, by election, 224–226,
        265, figs., 224, 227, table, 228.
    See also Political party(ies);
        Voting
Electors
    selection and duties of, 259
Elementary and Secondary Educa-
    tion Act of 1965, purpose of,
    574
Elisburg, Donald, 288
Elitism
    interest groups and, 162, 164,
        171–172, 186
    and voting franchise, 221–222,
        265

Employment
and Economic Opportunity Act, 570–571
equal, authorities of, table, 520. *See also* Employment Opportunity Commission (EEOC)
in government. *See* Bureaucracy, federal
Humphrey-Hawkins bill and, 577–578
legislation, 272–273
v. arms race, 608–609
War on Poverty through, 570–571
Employment Act of 1946
passage and effect of, 568–569
Energy
alternate sources of, 556–557
crisis, growth of, 12–13, 14–17. *See also* Camp David summit
effect on economy, 554–555
policies defeated, post-Camp David, 480–481
Policy Task Force, and Reagan, 482
solutions, 477–479, 554–555
and windfall profits tax, 477, 479
Energy, Department of (DOE), 84
and energy crisis, 12–13, 18. *See also* Energy; Oil
Energy Information Administration (EIA)
budget for, 547
Energy Mobilization Board, 26–27
defeat of, 479
Energy Policy Task Force
recommendations of, 482
Engel v. *Vitale*
and school prayer, 493
Environment
energy sources from, 556–557
legislation on, 180–181
Environmental Protection Agency (EPA) 181, 369, 372, 379
Equal Employment Opportunity Commission (EEOC), 355–356
and employment discrimination, 519
function, 375
and quotas, 533–535
Equal Pay Act, 530

Equal Rights Amendment (ERA), 50, 182
influence, 235, 237
purpose and history of, 530–532
Era of Good Feelings, 195, 196
Erlenborn, John, 285
Ervin, Samuel
and Watergate, 408, 416
Establishment clause
and separation of church and state, 493–495
European Economic Cooperation, Organization for (EEOC), 592
Exclusionary rule
and illegal search and seizure, 502–503
Executive branch. *See* Bureaucracy, federal
Executive bureaucracy, 310. *See also* Bureaucracy, federal
Executive Office of the President
agencies and functions of, 321–322, 323–324
flow chart of agencies, fig., 323
Export-Import Bank
purpose of, 589–590

FAA. *See* Federal Aviation Agency
Family
Assistance Plan, 576–577
and political socialization, 135–136, 154
Fair Labor Standards Act, 272–273
Farming. *See* Agriculture
Farm Security Administration (FSA)
purpose and politics of, 567
FCC. *See* Federal Communications Commission (FCC)
FDA. *See* Food and Drug Administration (FDA)
Fed, the. *See* Federal Reserve System
Federal aid
decentralized authority, 95–97
distribution by region, selected years, table, 91
to education, 574–575
foreign, 609–610, 612, fig., 610, table, 611

for housing, 575–576
impact aid, 435–436
usage, by year and recipient, 86–92, 98, table, 90. *See also* Public assistance; Social welfare
Federal Aviation Agency (FAA), 373
criticisms toward, 379
Federal Communications Commission (FCC), 379
on obscenity, 500
television regulation by, 384, 386
Federal Election Campaign Act
purpose and results of, 247
Federal Election Commission, 224, 245
and campaign financing, 254
Federal Emergency Relief Administration (FERA)
establishment and function of, 564
and unemployment, 566
Federal government. *See* Government, federal
Federalism, 81–82, 84
cooperative *v.* representative, 94–98
fiscal, 86–92, 98, 101
Supreme Court on, 463
Federalist Papers, 7–8, 46, 222
No. 78, and judicial review, 459
Federalists, 68
platform, 194–195
Federal Labor Relations Authority (FLRA), 359
Federal Open Market Committee (FOMC)
function and organization of, 551
Federal Power Commission, 371
Federal Regulatory Commission (FERC), 347, 349
Federal Reserve System, 371
organization of, 550–551
responsibility of, 550
Federal Trade Commission (FTC), 371
Fenno, Richard, 432, 438
FERA. *See* Federal Emergency Relief Administration (FERA)
Ferris, Charles D., 384
Filibuster
by amendment, 294, 407
cloture on, 406–407

function and process of, 406–407
  on NLRB reform bill, 294–298
Flanigan, William H., 231
Food and Drug Administration
    (FDA), 379
  function of, 373
Food for Peace Program
  tobacco in, 407
Food stamps
  legislative bargaining for, 573
Ford, Gerald, 89, 113, 234, 257,
    280, 321, 324, 359, 465, 599
  1976 election, 261
  vetoed bills by, 327
Foreign Military Sales Act
  amendment to, 393
Foreign policy
  as classified information, 585
  as communist adversary, 591,
    593–594
  constitutional powers in, 69–70
  economic agencies and, 601
  economic and military aid in,
    609–610, 612, fig., 610,
    table, 611
  executive agreement and, 314–315
  and federalism, 85
  formulation and implementation,
    583–584
  and grain embargo, 612–614
  Hamilton v. Jefferson viewpoint,
    194–195
  isolationism period of, 586–587
  makers of, 595–602
  massive retaliation v. selective
    deterrence, 594–595
  pre-World War II, 589–590
  public relations in, 601–602
  reference authorities and, 605
  and SALT II, 313, 585–586, fig., 586
  and South African apartheid,
    614–615
  and Spanish-American War, 587
  treaties, 45, 71, 591, 593
  trends in, 586–590, 617–618
France
  as economic ally, 592
  multi-parties in, 59, 200–201
  v. Britain, 37
Frankfurter, Felix, 458
Franklin, Benjamin, 31, 33, 34,
    35, 42, 44–45

Freedom of Information Act, 365
Free enterprise
  v. government regulation, 539–542.
    See also Economy
Free Soil party, 198.
    See also Political party(ies)
French and Indian Wars, 31
Frost, David, 308
Fulton, Robert, 52

Gag order, 497
Galbraith, John Kenneth, 167
  on government intervention, 541
Galloway, Joseph, 34
Gann, Paul, 165
  and Proposition 13, 107–108.
    See also Proposition 13
Gans, Curtis B., 229
Gelb, Leslie H., 600
General Accounting Office (GAO)
  and Federal Reserve Board, 551
  function of, 430
  on NRC, 377
George III, 31, 35, 46
  and Bill of Rights, 489
Germany
  v. U.S. and allies, World War I,
    587–588
  and World War II, 588–589
Gideon v. Wainwright, 505–506
  and council for indigents, 455–456
Gitlow v. New York, 507
Glazer, Nathan, 534–536
Glenn, John, 177, 426
Gold, Lawrence, 276
GOP. See Republican party
Government, federal
  agencies, civil-rights activities
    in, 519, fig., 519
  and Articles of Confederation,
    40–42
  assistance, emergency v. disas-
    ter, 81
  authority, 94–95. See also Power
  concurrent powers within, 71–72
  control, 129
  economic intervention by, 539–
    542. See also Budget
  employees, and Hatch Act, 273
  employees of, 339

expenditures, increase, 544, fig.,
    544
  federalism growth, 85–86
  grants-in-aid from, 86–92, 98
  lobby groups within, 92–94, 98
  OMB in, 321
  powers under Constitution,
    60–61, 68–70
  public land from, 86–88
  supremacy, 70–71
  systems, 57, 59–60
  welfare debate, poor v. indepen-
    dent, 561–562.
    See also Budget; Bureaucracy,
    federal; Foreign policy; Inter-
    est groups; Tax(es)
Government, local, 77–79
  black leadership in, 521–525
  electoral system of, 467
  federal aid to, 90–91, 95–97
  lobby groups within, 92–93, 98
  problems of cities, 523
  unitary system of, 59–60.
    See also Federalism
Government, state
  amendments by, 50
  authority, 94–95
  banks, 68
  bill of rights in, 39
  constitutions, 70–73, 74, 85–86
  court systems, 76
  formation, 37, 38, 39–40
  grants-in-aid to, 86–92, 98
  horizontal federalism within, 73–74
  interstate relations within, 73–74
  legislation by Supreme Court,
    463
  legislature, 75–77
  lobby group within, 92–93, 98
  and presidential nominations,
    234–235
  regulation by, 371
  and Shays' Rebellion, 41
  sovereignty of, 70–71, 74
  structure, 75–77
  and Tenth Amendment, 47,
    70–71, 508
  and theory of incorporation, 507–508.
    See also Constitution, U.S.;
    Federalism
Governmental Process, The
  excerpt, 8 n3

Morrill, Justin S., 87
Morrill Act of 1862, 87, 574
Morris, Gouverneur, 45
Morse, Wayne, 406
Mott, Lucretia, 529
Mount St. Helens, 81–82
Moynihan, Daniel Patrick, 451
    on guaranteed income, 576–577
    as Nixon's adviser, 322–323
    on poor *v.* dependent, 562
Muckrakers, 212
Munn v. *Illinois*, 371
Murphy, Peter J., 428
Muskie, Edward, 244
Mutual Defense Treaty, 594

NAACP, 171, 522
    and civil rights, 180, 516
    grass-roots lobbying by, 176–177
    and judicial appointments, 450–451
    v. school segregation, 518.
    See also Civil rights
Nader, Ralph
    consumer protection under, 169, table, 168
Nader's Raiders, 169, 179, table, 168
Nathan, Richard P., 95–96
National Action Committee
    as lobbyist, 281, 285, 289, 291–292
National Association for the Advancement of Colored People.
    See NAACP
National Association of Black School Superintendents, 522
National Association of Black State Elected Officials, 522
National Association of Black United Front, 522
National Association of Counties, 24, 93, 98, 554
National Association of Realtors, 246
National Automobile Dealers Associations, 246
National Bank, 61, 68–69, 72, 194
    and Supreme Court, 463
National bonus plan, 261
National Chamber Litigation Center, 181

National Council of Negro Women, 522
National Defense Education Act, 574
National Emergencies Act
    function and effect of, 393
National Endowment for the Humanities and Arts
    organization of, 349, fig., 351
National Environmental Policy Act of 1969, 181
National government. *See* Government, federal
National Governors' Conference (NGC), 18
    as lobby group, 92–93, 97
National Labor Relations Board. *See* NLRB
National League of Cities, 92
National Legal Center for the Public Interest, 181
National Recovery Act, 406
National Rifle Association (NRA), 171, 176
    v. BATF, 176
National Right to Life Committee
    political power of, 176
National Security Council (NSC)
    purpose and members of, 322, 324, 599–600
National Urban League, 522
National Youth Administration, 567
Native Americans
    analysis of progress, 527
    v. Western expansion, 587
NATO, 592
Neustadt, Richard E., 18
New Deal
    building, public and private under, 567
    coalition, 233
    FDR's economic recovery program in, 564
    and government intervention, 542
    growth of regulatory agencies with, 371–372
    and labor, 273
    and political opinions, 133
    and political reform, 212
    social programs under, 85–86, 563–568
    as social revolution, 567–568
    and Social Security Act, 564–566

    social welfare means test under, 564
    and Supreme Court, 463–465
    v. unemployment, 566–567.
    See also Depression
New Federalism
    block grants and, 89–90, 95, 98
New Jersey Plan, 44, 48. *See also* Constitution, U.S.
New York
    as 1976 site, convention, 237
Nie, Norman, 228
Nixon, Richard M., 89, 90, 95, 193, 231, 244, 257, 599, 606
    on adviser appointments, 322–323
    on bureaucratic control, 363
    as diplomat, 313–314
    elections, 261
    Family Assistance Plan by, 576–577
    impoundment and, 327
    media image, 256–257
    on presidential role, 307–308
    resignation, 141–142, 143
    resignation letter, 307
    on Supreme Court appointments, 333, 453, 465
    vetoed bills by, 327
    as vice-president, 324
NLRB, 371, 375
    criticisms of, 379–380
    proposed reforms, 1976, 278, 283, 288, 298
    purpose and revisions, 273–274
    reform bill, in House of Representatives, 284–287
    as statutory law, 448.
    See also Lobbying
North, geographic region
    political ideology, 196
North Atlantic Treaty Organization (NATO), 592
NSC. *See* National Security Council (NSC)
Nuclear arms
    proliferation of, 601, fig., 601
Nuclear Nonproliferation Act
    function of, 601
Nuclear Regulatory Commission (NRC), 375
    structure and function of, 375, 377, 379, table, 376
Nunn, Samuel, 189, 521

and labor, 273
as party leader, 316
prerogative theory of presidency, 306–307
social-welfare programs under, 564–568
v. Hatch Act, 359
v. Supreme Court, 463–465.
See also New Deal
Roosevelt, Theodore, 324
legislative role of, 318
on presidential role, 305–306, 307
Rosenthal, Benjamin S., 178, 379
Rossiter, Clinton, 196
Rostenkowski, Daniel
on Ways and Means Committee, 391, 395, 397
Rudder, Catherine, 417
Russia. *See* Soviet Union

Sadat, Anwar el, 18, 299
Safire, William, 95
Saliency, 226
Salinger, Pierre, 319, 322
SALT II
defined, 313
public opinion on, 585, 586, fig., 586
Reagan on, 313
Sanford, Terry, 85
Schattschneider, E. E., 225
Schlesinger, Arthur M., Jr., 307, 570
on work relief, 564
Schlesinger, James R.
on gasoline allocation, 18
Schneider, William, 388
Schultz, George, 361
Schultze, Charles L., 282
Sears, Roebuck & Company
and NLRB reform bill, 289
SEATO, 594
Secretary of state, 75
Securities and Exchange Act, 416
Securities and Exchange Commission, 371
Segregation, 532–533
de jure v. *de facto*, 516, 518
sanctioning of, by Supreme Court, 463, 516–517
and *The Southern Manifesto*, 70–71.

See also Civil rights
Seidman, Harold, 97, 361
Senate, 44
cabinet confirmation by, 352–354
cloture on filibuster, 294–298
committee memberships within, 398–401
election, 48–49
ethics committee, 428
on executive agreements, 314
filibuster, 294–298, 406–407
filibuster on NLRB reform bill, 294–298
and judicial appointments, 444–445, 449–453
judiciary committee, function of, 451
leadership roles within, 397–398, 400–401, 439–440
legislative and committee staffs in, 424–426, 428–429, 440, table, 427
NLRB reform bill in, 287–298
number of delegates, 394
and OMB, 321
and presidential appointments, 304, 333–334
term, 45.
See also Congress; Electoral college system; House of Representatives; Presidency
Senate Finance Committee
and tax laws, 549
Senators
election saliency, 233–234.
See also Senate
Senior citizens
and Proposition 13, tables, 134, 135
Shabecoff, Philip
on labor-law reform, case study, 272–301
Shah of Iran, 16
Shalala, Donna E., 84
Shays, Daniel, 41, 46
Sherman, Roger, 35
Shipley, George, 423
Shriver, Sargent, 244
Sieberling, John, 409
Silk, Leonard, 542
Simon, William E.
in *A Time for Truth*, 8 n2
Sirica, John, 180

Sivard, Ruth Leger
on arms race, 608–609
Skolnick, Jerome, 181
Slavery
as political issue, 198–199
political socialization and, 139
trade, 36.
See also Black Americans; Constitution, U.S.
Social liberalism
issues, 131, 133, 135, figs., 130, 131, 132, 133, table, 135
Social Security Act
public-assistance programs under, 565–566
types of protection through, 564–565
Social welfare
and AFDC, 565
and education, 574–575
and employment, 564, 565–567, 568–569, 570–571
expenditures, 1970–1978, fig., 578
and food stamps, 572–574
and health benefits, 571–572
and housing, 567, 575–576
public-assistance expenditures, by year, 81–82, 98, tables, 90, 573
reform of, 212, 579, 580
and Social Security Act, 564–566.
See also Public assistance
Socio-economic status. *See* Class
Solicitor general
function of, 452, 455
Sons of Liberty, 32
Sorensen, Theodore, 334
South, geographic region
antiunion movement in, 276–277
Democratic influence from, 235
and NLRB reform bill, 299
political ideology, 196
v. black American voting rights, 516–517
Southeast Asia Treaty Organization (SEATO), 594
Southern Christian Leadership Conference, 522
Southern Manifesto: Declaration of Constitutional Principles, The, 70–71

Watergate
  effect on children, 141–144
  effect on presidency, 393
  and inherent president powers, 307–308
  investigations, 408, 416
  and public campaign financing, 247
Wayne, Stephen, 318
Webster, Daniel, 197
Weidenbaum, Murrey L., 386
Weiss, Theodore, 393
Welfare. *See* Social welfare
Wertheimer, Frederick, 254
Whig party
  foundation, 197–198.
  See also Political party(ies)
White House staff
  growth and function of, 319–321, 322–324
  OCR within, function of, 331
  press secretary of, 329
Wickard v. *Filburn*, 53
Williams, Harrison A., 284, 288
Wills, Garry, 36
Wilson, James, 305
Wilson, Woodrow, 205, 307, 392
  legislative role of, 318

and World War I involvement, 587–588
Winner, Charles
  No on 13 manager, 110–111, 114, 117, 119, 120
  and public opinion polls, 150–152.
  See also Proposition 13
Women
  analysis of liberation movement, 529–532
  in Congress, 420–421
  on Congressional staffs, 426, 428
  as delegates, 241–243
  employment and earnings of, 529, 530–531, table, 531
  and ERA, 530–532
  franchise and, 222
  historical protests by, 182
  on national party committee, 208
  in state party structure, 208
  voting pattern of, by race and region, table, 228
Woodward, Robert, 447
Works Progress Administration (WPA)

v. unemployment, 565–566
World Bank, 601
World War I
  and U.S. involvement, 587–588
World War II, 85, 588–589
Wright, Esmond, 42
Wright, James, 476
Writ of mandamus, 460
Writs of assistance, 31
Wurf, Jerry, 282

Yankelovich, Daniel, 586
Yes on 13 Committee
  as interest group, 161
Young, Andrew, 438
  and Carter's election, 193
Younger, Evelle J., 204

Zeidenstein, Harold G., 393
Zingale, Nancy H., 231
Zoning, 78